IMPROVING INQUIRY
IN SOCIAL SCIENCE
A Volume in Honor of

Lee J. Cronbach

IMPROVING INQUIRY IN SOCIAL SCIENCE
A Volume in Honor of
Lee J. Cronbach

Edited by
RICHARD E. SNOW
Stanford University
DAVID E. WILEY
Northwestern University

LEA LAWRENCE ERLBAUM ASSOCIATES, PUBLISHERS
1991   Hillsdale, New Jersey   Hove and London

Lawrence Erlbaum Associates, Inc., Publishers
365 Broadway
Hillsdale, New Jersey 07642

Library of Congress Cataloging in Publication Data

Improving inquiry in social science : a volume in honor of Lee J.
  Cronbach/edited by Richard E. Snow, David E. Wiley.
        p.   cm.
    Includes bibliographical references and indexes.
    ISBN 0-8058-0542-7 (hard).—ISBN 0-8058-0748-9 (pbk.)
    1. Psychology—Research.   2. Educational psychology—Research.
  3. Social sciences—.   4. Psychometrics.   I. Cronbach, Lee
  J. (Lee Joseph), 1916⁻   .   II. Snow, Richard E.   III. Wiley, David E.
  BF76.5.I56   1990
  150′.72—dc20   90-13950
                                                                     CIP
Printed in the United States of America
10 9 8 7 6 5 4 3 2 1

Contents

Contributors

Hiroshi Azuma, Professor of Education, University of Tokyo

Leigh Burstein, Professor of Education, University of California, Los Angeles

Donald T. Campbell, Professor of Psychology and Social Relations, Lehigh University

John B. Carroll, Professor of Psychology, University of North Carolina

Lee J. Cronbach, Vida Jacks Professor of Education, Stanford University

Linda Crespo Da Silva, University of Cincinnati

Donald W. Fiske, Professor of Behavioral Science, University of Chicago

Robert Glaser, Professor of Education and Psychology, University of Pittsburgh

Goldine Gleser, Professor of Psychology, University of Cincinnati

J. Thomas Hastings, Professor of Education, University of Illinois

E.S. Johnson, Associate Professor of Psychology, University of North Carolina

Ann C. Meade, Department of Public Instruction, University of North Carolina

Paul E. Meehl, Professor of Psychology, University of Minnesota

Samuel Messick, Vice President for Research, Educational Testing Service

Michael Ravitch, Director, Office of Medical Eduction, Northwestern University

Charles S. Reichardt, Professor of Psychology, University of Denver

David Rogosa, Associate Professor of Education, Stanford University

Richard Shavelson, Dean and Professor of Education, University of California, Santa Barbara

Valerie Shute, Research Scientist, Air Force Human Resources Laboratory

Richard E. Snow, Professor of Education and Psychology, Stanford University

Robert L. Thorndike, Professor of Education, Teachers College, Columbia University

Ralph W. Tyler, System Development Foundation

Noreen Webb, Associate Professor of Education, University of California, Los Angeles

David E. Wiley, Dean and Professor of Education and Social Policy, Northwestern University

Preface

This volume celebrates Lee J. Cronbach's career as a scholar, as a teacher, and as a scientific and professional leader. It cannot fully recount that career. Rather, it seeks to advance thinking and research in some of the central fields of inquiry that Cronbach's work has helped establish, shape, develop, and revise.

The chapter authors are collaborators and contemporaries of Cronbach's. Some have been coauthors. Some have debated competing views with him. Some are former students. In the generic sense, however, all of us have been his students. All of us have benefitted immeasurably from his public contributions, but also from his personal friendship and his informal professional interactions and communications over the years. All of us have learned and continue to learn much from him. But he has not only taught us when we did not know; he has caused us to unlearn and relearn many things we thought we knew. Therein is a lesson all social science needs to incorporate. Improving inquiry in social science means questioning conventional wisdom, criticizing conventional method, unlearning these conventions, and learning radically new ones. Cronbach is the acknowledged master of this process. We think all social science today badly needs to follow his example.

Chapter 1, our introduction, picks up this theme and provides a framework for the chapters to follow.

Each chapter is written expressly for this book. Each picks up on an aspect of Cronbach's work and makes a further contribution to it. The book thus provides a range of ideas, perspectives, and new approaches to improving inquiry in social science that should be useful to students and young researchers, as well as to mature investigators concerned with the present state and future of social science research.

We wish to thank the many students and friends of Lee J. Cronbach who encouraged us in developing the idea for this volume and in persisting to its completion. We especially thank Donald W. Fiske for many helpful suggestions along the way.

Richard E. Snow
David E. Wiley

Lee J. Cronbach

1 Straight Thinking

Richard E. Snow
David E. Wiley

This volume honors Lee J. Cronbach—the man, the career, and the contributions. We have chosen to use the phrase "improving inquiry" in the book's title because it captures, for us, the goal to which Cronbach's life and work has been consistently and systematically dedicated. But there is also a distinct and coherent style to Cronbach's pursuit of this goal. In summary he would call it (and has called it) "straight thinking." Hence our title for this introduction. Cronbach has improved all of our inquiries by straightening our thinking.

The Cronbach style is first to find the root problems, the hidden difficulties, the tacit assumptions, and the theoretical and methodological conventions that blind the investigator to limits and alternatives and thus impede progress in socially important fields of inquiry. He then learns how to think straight about the core issues by cutting away this excess and malconceived conceptual and methodological baggage to criticize the basic questions being pursued. Often this is accomplished by recasting existing data from some important study, reaching a new synthesis and pursuing implications that go well beyond those of the original investigator. His revision then emerges as a carefully tutored central example for a field. He thus raises the level of conceptualization with which diverse investigators work by sharpening the questions that guide them and by reconfiguring the line of investigation, to clarify the meaning of evidence and to improve the opportunities for earlier solid payoff, both theoretical and practical.

Over and over again, in many fields of social science, Cronbach has shown his uncanny ability to do this. In each case, he rethinks the root and seeks the change that will have the most multiplicative effect, in the target field but in related fields as well—he is, in short, the quintessential methodologist.

To understand the Cronbach style as methodology, as that term is typically used however, is to underestimate it—one must also appreciate the central role of his substantive thinking. New methodology can be, and too often is, invented in the abstract, based only on an understanding of the limits of present methods for structuring some class of data; the inventor then goes in search of applications that will demonstrate the new beauties. Too often in such work the focus is on method, and it is then the method that drives the research questions. By contrast, Cronbach devises new methodology based on a deep understanding of and respect for the substantive phenomenon, as well as the limits of current methods and current substantive thinking as they intertwine to impede the advance of inquiry; the starting point is the scientific or practical question which ought to be answered, not the method. It is commonly said that methodological developments have multiplicative effects because they improve inquiry across the range of substantive fields to which they apply. They often do, though often without changing the substantive questions being asked in those fields. Cronbach changes these questions, sometimes in revolutionary ways. His methods forge new concepts and issues while at the same time casting the old ones in critical light.

There is also a personal-social dimension to the style. As an individual scholar and faculty member, Cronbach understands how best to use himself for the common good, and wastes no time or talent in diversions. He understands how to bring out the best in people he has chosen to work with, as advisor, collaborator, or mentor. He applies critical thinking to his own ideas and to those of others as a surgeon would a scalpel, and expects and encourages others to do the same in return. He understands furthermore that science is a social enterprise. To improve it one must improve its human resources—find promising young researchers, help form relationships among them, re-educate them beyond their normal science, mentor their continuing scholarship. The postdoctoral research conferences he has organized or taught, both in the U.S. and abroad, stand as one major public example of this aspect of Cronbach style. But another is his textbooks. They each exhibit a social responsibility for reorganizing the conceptualization of a field and prompting deeper thought with rich examples and discussion questions from within it, and at its boundaries, for younger readers—they never merely recite the state of an art. His books as well as his research invariably engage the fundamental questions of a field, revise them, and place them in a new synthesis.

Cronbach's contributions to the improvement of inquiry now span half a century. They range over many disciplinary boundaries in basic and applied social science—across psychology, both individual and social, educational research, and evaluation research, particularly. One might try to classify the many pieces of his work into convenient categories; his contributions to several substantive fields of psychology and education, to measurement theory and instrument development, to the methodology of research and evaluation studies, and to the philosophy of educational and social inquiry. But to do so superficially risks missing a central integrating theme in Cronbach's scholarship, as well as its style. Substantive conception, measurement, methodology, and philosophy are underlying interacting dimensions of the work, not separate categories, even though any one study or report might be seen as emphasizing more of one than another. At a deeper level, the core theme makes the work a coordinated whole. This theme, as best we can capture it, runs as follows: *Nature is always more complex and continuous than we imagine, so particular methods and many concepts must necessarily be cut to fit only pieces. These must at least be cut to fit particular pieces well. Beyond this, however, conceptual unification of disparate understandings—both substantive and methodological—is the best way to synthesize those concepts which can connect the pieces. We, therefore, reach better ways of asking questions, and better questions. Concepts and questions, not generalized theories, are thus the primary products of social science.* We can consider here only some brief examples to bring this theme out.

In the 1940s and early 1950s, Cronbach was investigating problems of personality assessment, particularly as these limited research in psychotherapy (Cronbach, 1948, 1953; Edwards & Cronbach, 1952). He recognized that conventional psychometric analysis of projective tests distorted the substance of what clinicians were trying to do with them, so he devised improved validation designs consistent with that substance. He also saw that personality assessment could be advanced with methods of profile analysis that might reach unified interpretations from lists of separate scores (Cronbach 1949, 1950; Cronbach & Gleser, 1953), and further that the problems faced by social psychologists studying interpersonal similarity, perception of others, and the like, had much the same structure (Cronbach, 1955). The methods he developed were sensitive to the substantive research goals of both fields. Furthermore, his continuing consideration of the most important of those goals, and his ever-present style of self criticism, are evident in later clarifications, revisions, and specializations in his methodological advice (Cronbach, 1958).

In a related development, he also considered the kinds of practical decisions for which clinicians, as well as educators and personnel managers, often used psychological measures and this suggested a common underlying problem. Many of these decisions involved placements of individuals in alternative settings, i.e., classification decisions; they were not simple selection-rejection decisions. A decision theoretic view of such situations, as opposed to a traditional psychometric view, meant that test validation required a demonstration of interaction between the measure used for classification and the alternative placements available for persons (Cronbach & Gleser, 1957, see 1965). The routine method of criterion-related validation was insufficient. It was also clear that experimental contrasts between alternative placements or treatments that produced interactions with the predictor-criterion relation provided important sources of evidence for construct validation of seemingly different—experimental and correlational— constructs. Experimental psychologists had generally ignored person differences in their work, both basic and applied, whereas differential psychologists had routinely ignored situation differences. To capitalize on this view, however, a radical revision in conventional experimental and correlational methodology was required. The limits of each approach could be overcome only by their unification; the problem was general for psychology wherever joint person-situation effects had to be understood (Cronbach, 1957). Person-situation interaction, or aptitude-treatment interaction, was thus the form for research that needed to become common to much of educational, clinical, and personnel psychology (Cronbach & Snow, 1977). But scientific generalizations had to be qualified or bounded by such interactions as well. Indeed, the complexity of these interactions muddles the conventional scientific search for *laws* and the old philosophy of science supporting it (Cronbach, 1975a). This leads to new methodological considerations and new concepts to undergird the substance of inquiry (Cronbach 1982b, 1986). Thus, the nature of a phenomenon, its measurement, and the methodology and philosophy for reaching an understanding of it, are clearly bound together in the stream of Cronbach's work.

Unification has also been an underlying theme in Cronbach's many contributions to the development of measurement theory, and there are substantive and philosophical sides here too. Coefficient Alpha is a unification of the various psychometric concepts and methods of reliability estimation as they then existed (Cronbach, 1951). The expansion of these concepts into generalizability theory is based on the overarching recognition that errors of measurement are not random but have real substantive causes, the causes are multiple, and they can be investigated for any given situation by appropriate choices from a general system of experimental design (Cronbach, Rajaratnam, & Gleser, 1963; Cronbach, Gleser, Nanda, & Rajaratnam, 1972). Again, the wedding of experimental and psychometric methods clarifies and multiplies the purview of each, removes ambiguities concealed in narrower views of each, and strikes closer to a fundamental issue in all social science—improving our understanding of the phenomena we study and the measures we use to do so.

Still another view of these and other contributions distinguishes Cronbach from most of his colleagues, both historical and contemporary. This view can be illustrated by the way in which Cronbach treats psychological constructs. Constructs are conceptual interpretations that order observations and so improve scientific understanding and communication. But they are to be judged by their usefulness for some local purpose, not by their truthfulness. No one structure for understanding human personality or human ability should be regarded as more fixed or more "true" than another; different uses call for different conceptual structures, and social scientists ought to be as tolerant of alternative constructs as they are of alternative works of art (Cronbach, 1982b, 1986).

Thus, for example, while he would accept, in his own way, the common notion that human abilities are hierarchically structured, the structure is—for him—fluid and adaptable, not fixed. This "fluidity" is required by the social life of the individuals displaying the abilities. Their social interactions, their work, their learning histories, cluster and group abilities as they are required for the tasks at hand, not in the arbitrary, particular fashions of the experimental laboratory or the testing room. Thus, the specific narrow-gauge abilities or skills that individuals possess may be seen as arranged as cities and towns on a map, but each individual may have a somewhat different map. Higher level constructs are groupings of narrower ones which are in some sense proximal to one another. The particular groupings chosen are more or less useful according to whether they bear on the processes—the work, learning, human interactions—which make use of these abilities for human action. It is the tasks of personal life which group and regroup human abilities into alternate psychological constructs. For particular persons or particular test uses, different constructs may be appropriate. For screening persons or making broad predictions, a higher level ability construct may serve best. For counseling or career decision-making, a range of alternative narrow constructs may be more appropriate (Cronbach, 1990). Validity of measurement is then defined, assessed, and confirmed or revised according to the pattern of expected relations among constructs. These relations are tested against a network of expectations constructed, in part, from understandings of the life processes to which the abilities contribute.

The view that the uses of tests, testing and human abilities are central to their conceptualization and their analysis is not unique to Cronbach. But the full integration of this view with the broad range of technical and analytical issues of testing is unique to his contribution. The perspective is seen in many of Cronbach's works, especially including his view of the concept of intelligence and his social history of controversies about testing (Cronbach, 1975b, 1990).

The continuing development of Cronbach's work in recent years has recast the very character of social inquiry. His conclusion that social science has been misled by emulating an inaccurate and oversimplified model of inquiry in the natural sciences is now shared widely. That conclusion, however, is a subtle one. It is founded on a Darwinian sense of the large number of paths in which complex systems can evolve. Whether one studies individuals, or groups, or social movements—or one of these in relation to another—the path of changes that can occur over the time line of an inquiry is only one of a very large number. These paths are strongly segmented; that is, future states of a system are strongly conditioned by past transitions and states. And the evolutions always take place in a context. These properties make it impossible to *isolate* the effects of interventions because, at the time intervention occurs, the several systems in which the intervention is tried are dissimilar. This evolutionary character of system state and context prior to intervention results in subsequent dissimilarities in the consequences of the interventions across systems, and also within systems across time. Effects are difficult to explain because the initial system states themselves are such a small selection of possible states and because the relevant aspects of these states are difficult to characterize. Without knowing how to characterize the state of a system—which requires both a conceptual analysis of how it might evolve and a historical analysis of its past evolution—one cannot know what kinds of generalizations about intervention effects one ought to seek, much less adopt.

Cronbach's recommendation is to pursue the richest possible description of each intervention and each site. Every study in social science, including laboratory experiments, is a case study bounded by the persons, systems and contexts it includes. It is important to note that these complexities are not unique to social science. As the analysis of *natural* systems has shifted from smaller complexes to larger and more *artificial* ones—in physics and chemistry as well as biology and the engineering sciences—the role of experimentation has changed. In many disciplines, controlled experiments are now used in partnership with simulations, naturalistic observations, and explicit studies of a system's evolutionary dynamics. A symptom of this is the recent popularity of chaos and chaotic models for these phenomena; a sign of Cronbach's view is his early interest in their relevance (see Cronbach, 1988).

The traditional model of inquiry has had a depressive effect on social program evaluation. As this field has changed over the past 10 years, the combined effects of paradigm decay and funding decay have led to a variety of narrow-perspective evaluation models emphasizing the political, value, and contextual issues. Thus, the question of generalization of evaluation results is no longer seen as focal. This is not bad, as the old paradigm had run its course for too long any way. The problem, as we see it, is that there has been too much of a retreat to narrow-perspective studies. If the key concept in all of this, as Cronbach concluded, is the diversity of evolutionary histories, the main work to be done is developmental and descriptive. Effort must be invested primarily in the detailed characterization of states and changes in states of these complex systems. These descriptions are themselves historical records of events in some place and time, because the systems they describe inevitably move on—they evolve beyond the point of each description. There is no unified method for designing evaluations of these systems. But there is a general practical form for thinking about the very different particulars of each descriptive study (Cronbach, 1982a). And eventually, these descriptions provide the experiential base that is a prerequisite for understanding system evolution in general.

Improving inquiry, then, means getting better, richer, thicker descriptions from which to generate deeper conceptions and, most importantly, better questions. This is not a pessimistic view. It is rather, as one of Cronbach's (1982b) titles suggests: "a prudent aspiration for social science." Scientific inquiry is goal oriented. It is a search but a directed, not a random one. The directions come not only from individual scientists who are the first to point to them, but also from the conceptual systems formed and sustained by the social networks and organizational supports of the scientific field as a whole. It is these conceptual frameworks and this social infrastructure which constitutes the essential core of a scientific enterprise.

Most scientists, the very best as well as the mediocre, go about their work without giving much thought to the social infrastructure which makes their work possible. They experience the communal as well as the individual activities, they participate in the committees, hold the organizational offices, referee the journal articles. But their "true" vocation is "real science,": collecting and analyzing data, thinking, and writing. That is, they inquire.

Lee Cronbach has also inquired, but in a more general sense his real contribution has been to improve inquiry. In so doing, he has multiplied his own effect manyfold. Not only are the results of his inquiries useful in themselves, his contributions enable others to contribute more and thus he has enhanced the scientific enterprise as a whole. Most of those who would improve inquiry seek to do so by producing better answers. Lee Cronbach's central contributions involve asking better questions. "Improving inquiry" thus captures, for us, the essence of the communal activity of the contributors to this volume and a central goal in the scientific life of Lee Cronbach.

We have said that the interwoven character of Cronbach's contributions makes the grouping of particular pieces of his work into categories an unsatisfactory representation. Therefore this volume is not subdivided into sections. Rather, the ordering of the chapters attempts to move more smoothly among the dimensions of Cronbach's work than categories would allow, while still touching each piece of that work.

Meehl's Chapter 2 begins the process, as would Cronbach, with a general rejection of the hypothesis testing tradition that has dominated so much of psychology and social science. On both philosophical and methodological grounds, he argues that most of our research literatures are rendered uninterpretable because of a series of obfuscating factors the effects of which are often sizable, variable, operating in opposite directions, and left unmeasured. As a starting point, he urges that we come to full appreciation of how little we really know, and how little can ever be learned through null hypothesis testing; only with this recognition as a bottom line can we hope to improve inquiry and thus its results.

In Chapter 3, Fiske confronts another part of the problem—the level at which psychological constructs are typically defined and analyzed. He contrasts the macropsychology of research using ability and personality measures, and the broad, loosely specified constructs on which they are based, with the micropsychology of behavioral event protocols obtained within explicit contexts. He sees in the latter the possibility of obtaining more precise linkages among low-level constructs with clear if highly restricted boundaries. This micropsychological knowledge can remain valid over time, especially as it can be linked with psychophysiological and neuro-psychological functioning. Attempts at macropsychological generalizations, as Cronbach argued, are doomed by the inconstancy of persons and situations.

The difficulty of construct validation is further addressed by Wiley, in Chapter 4. He distinguishes between the *intent* and the *use* of measurement, arguing that the validation of test intent is a narrower, more feasible goal for research than the iterative long-range enterprise of construct validation of measures within their nomological networks and uses that was envisioned by Cronbach and Meehl. Using the example of ability tests, Wiley would restrict test validation (as distinguished from construct validation) to specifying the skill pattern or profile intended for measurement and comparing that with an empirical decomposition to determine the constituents and dimensions of skill actually involved in test performance. Validity is then depicted in the match between the dimensions of skill intended and actually measured; invalidity is undesired dimensionality. Test validation is then a proximal and profitable goal for research that need not assume the burden of validating the whole interpretive theoretical network in which the test resides. Construct validation assumes that more distal goal.

In Chapter 5, Carroll, Meade, and Johnson propose a method of test analysis based on the person characteristic function that seems to provide much of what Wiley's proximal validation goal requires. The method, which applies mainly to ability tests, can be used to determine whether the same linear combination of skills underlies all items or tasks in a series, and to establish meanings for the resulting ability scale in terms of the task features that are the principal sources of difficulty in performance.

Gleser and Crespo da Silva then take up the multivariate profile case, in Chapter 6, concentrating mainly on generalizability in personality measures. They also bring back into focus the importance of considering in test analysis how the measures are used in practice. A comparison of different methods suggests that the preferred procedures base interpretations on estimated universe score profiles that reflect the original scales, rather than observed score profiles or on composites that maximize discrimination among persons but do not preserve the original dimensions that the interpreter actually uses.

In Chapter 7, Messick also comes back to the larger construct validation questions that need to be addressed in relation to response style variations prompted by the format and context of measurement. He revisits Cronbach's early contributions on response sets, traces the controversial history of the issues, and predicts a return to research on the score-invalidating and relationship-obscuring effects of response styles in many kinds of psychological and social measures today.

In Chapter 8, Campbell and Reichardt begin with the response set issue and then give much further evidence of Cronbach's collaborative and critical style, drawn from many interactions between Cronbach, Campbell, and Reichardt, and their colleagues over the years. They then provide a searching discussion of the pretest–posttest comparability problem as it appears in many kinds of repeated measures analyses, longitudinal designs, and growth models. They see strengths of analysis in assuming comparability where it is plausible to do so, but agree with Cronbach's assessment that it may often not be.

Rogosa follows in Chapter 9 by recasting the problems of repeated measures, and of individual differences in response to intervening treatments, in the form of growth model analysis. "Natural" maturation, response to intervention, and aptitude-treatment interaction are seen as special cases of this more general form. It is shown that studies using standard analyses often appear discordant because results can depend crucially on such factors as the choice of pretest measures, the form of individual maturation, the times at which measures are taken, the duration of intervention, and the kinds of incremental changes that can occur. These factors often attenuate the regression slope differences usually used to identify ATI effects, and even limit their relevance for many traditional purposes. The results suggest how a reconstruction of the methodology of ATI research might now proceed.

Snow's Chapter 10 continues toward a reconstruction of aptitude research, emphasizing more the substantive side of construct interpretation. Misinterpretations of the aptitude concept are reviewed to show that only Cronbach's long-standing view maintained the multivariate person-situation interactional character of the original construct. Some old and new forms for conceptualization and conduct of research on aptitude theories are reviewed, in the light of Cronbach's recommendations for social science generally. Examples of new kinds of aptitude constructs useful in educational, industrial-organizational, and clinical psychology are given. These often combine cognitive, conative, and affective aspect of behavior in local situations.

In Chapter 11, Thorndike examines intelligence as one such aptitude construct. He reviews research ranging from the micropsychology of physiological correlates, through the information processing components of current cognitive theory, to the macropsychological intelligence construct used in educational and personnel research. Thorndike concludes that the molar intelligence construct and measures remain more useful than differentiated ability profiles for most purposes.

Beyond the theoretical and methodological problems of social science, Cronbach has also always been concerned with the practical problems of educational evaluation and the development and uses of tests and other kinds of assessments for different purposes therein. His work in this direction has shown the influence of his mentor at Chicago, Ralph Tyler, and his associate under Tyler and then at Illinois, Tom Hastings. In Chapter 12, Hastings reviews the history of Tyler's approach to evaluation and contrasts Tylerian behavioral objectives with the sorts of behavioral objectives emphasized in some other contemporary approaches. He demonstrates the clear and consistent connection between Tyler's and Cronbach's thinking in this field, but also notes some other aspects of Tyler's style that emerge in Cronbach's: the two obviously share a focus on higher mental processes and transfer, on fitting evaluations to the particularity of individual school programs, persons, and sites, and on the need for comprehensive description in each case.

Then, in Chapter 13, Tyler follows with his own forward-looking discussion of the varieties of new kinds of tests, assessments, and related procedures that might actually help teachers and school administrators do the job of improving education. This means focussing test development on actual teacher and principal needs and fitting it to local conditions. Tyler's wise counsel in the face of current criticisms of conventional educational tests strikes us as very close to what Cronbach would also recommend.

Chapter 14 rounds out our representation of Cronbach's interests in educational research and evaluation with an excellent example of current work on instructional systems that help diagnose and improve student inquiry and understanding in particular subject-matter domains. Shute and Glaser describe their research using a computerized discovery microworld in economics to study how students develop problem solving and induction skills and exploratory strategies, as well as specific knowledge. The system yields just the sort of deep analysis and rich description of active student functioning during complex learning that Cronbach long ago saw as a central need for both instructional research and assessment.

Chapters 15 and 16 offer personal statements depicting Cronbach as mentor. First, Azuma describes his Illinois years with Cronbach but also provides some sense of Cronbach's substantial influence in the international sphere. Then, Burstein, Ravitch, Shavelson, and Webb review their collective years with Cronbach at Stanford. Taken together, a rich picture of the Cronbach style with students emerges.

Finally, Chapter 17 gives Lee Cronbach's own retrospective, focused mainly on the technical, measurement side of his career. The origins of many of the theoretical developments for which he is famous are traced, and some of the twists and turns along the way are noted. There is important advice for the young investigator and some suggested directions for further work. The reader can combine this chapter with the one Cronbach (1989) has written for Lindzey's *History of Psychology in Autobiography* to gain a more complete autobiographical picture.

REFERENCES

Cronbach, L. J. (1948). A validation design for qualitative studies of personality. *Journal of Consulting Pyschology, 12,* 365–374.

Cronbach, L. J. (1949). "Pattern tabulation:" A statistical method for analysis of limited patterns of scores, with particular reference to the Rorschach test. *Educational and Psychological Measurement, 9,* 149–171.

Cronbach, L. J. (1950). Statistical methods for multi-score tests. *Journal of Clinical Psychology, 6,* 21–26.

Cronbach, L. J. (1951). Coefficient alpha and the internal structure of tests. *Psychometrika, 16,* 297–334.

Cronbach, L. J. (1953). Correlation between persons as a research tool. In O. H. Mowrer (Ed.), *Psychotherapy: Theory and research* (pp. 376–388). New York: Ronald.

Cronbach, L. J. (1955). Processes affecting scores on "understanding of others" and "assumed similarity." *Psychological Bulletin, 52,* 177–194.

Cronbach, L. J. (1957). The two disciplines of scientific psychology. *American Psychologist, 12,* 671–684.

Cronbach, L. J. (1958). Proposals leading to analytic treatment of social perception scores. In R. Tagiuri & L. Petrullo (Eds.), *Person perception and interpersonal behavior* (pp. 351–379). Stanford: Stanford University Press, 1958.

Cronbach, L. J. (1975a). Beyond the two disciplines of scientific psychology. *American Psychologist, 30,* 116–127.

Cronbach, L. J. (1975b). Five decades of public controversy over mental testing. *American Psychologist, 30,* 1–14.

Cronbach, L. J. (1982a). *Designing evaluations of educational and social programs.* San Francisco: Jossey-Bass.

Cronbach, L. J. (1982b). Prudent aspirations for social science. In W. W. Kruskal (Ed.), *The social sciences: Their nature and uses* (pp. 61–81). Chicago: University of Chicago Press.

Cronbach, L. J. (1986). Social inquiry by and for Earthlings. In D. W. Fiske & R. A. Shweder (Eds.), *Metatheory in social science: Pluralities and subjectivities* (pp. 83–107). Chicago: University of Chicago Press.

Cronbach, L. J. (1988). Playing with chaos. *Educational Researcher, 17* (6), 46–49.

Cronbach, L. J. (1989). In G. Lindzey (Ed.), *A history of psychology in autobiography* (Vol. VIII) (pp. 63–93). Stanford, CA: Stanford University Press.

Cronbach, L. J. (1990). *Essentials of psychological testing.* New York: Harper and Row. Fifth edition.

Cronbach, L. J. & Gleser, G. C. (1953). Assessing similarity between profiles. *Psychological Bulletin, 50,* 456–473.

Cronbach, L. J. & Gleser, G. C. (1957, sec ed 1965). *Psychological tests and personnel decisions.* Urbana: University of Illinois Press. Second edition 1965.

Cronbach, L. J., Gleser, G. C., Nanda, H., & Rajaratnam, N. (1972). *The dependability of bahavioral measurements: Theory of generalizability for scores and profiles.* New York: Wiley.

Cronbach, L. J., Rajaratnam, N., & Gleser, G. C. (1963). Theory of generalizability: A liberalization of reliability theory. *British Journal of Statistical Psychology, 16,* 137–163.

Cronbach, L. J. & Snow, R. E. (1977). *Aptitudes and Instructional Methods: A Handbook for Research on Interactions.* New York: Irvington.

Edwards, A. L. & Cronbach, L. J. (1952). Experimental design for research in psychotherapy. *Journal of Clinical Psychology, 8,* 51–59.

2 Why Summaries of Research on Psychological Theories Are Often Uninterpretable*

Paul E. Meehl
University of Minnesota

Recently, I read an article in the *Psychological Bulletin* summarizing the research literature on a theory in personology. I had some interest in it both for its intrinsic importance and because the theorist is an old friend and former academic colleague. The reviewer seemed scrupulously fair in dealing with the evidence and arguments, and I do not believe any reader could discern even faint evidence of bias pro or con. The empirical evidence on this theory has now accumulated to a considerable mass of factual reports and associated theoretical inferences, so we are not dealing with a recently advanced conjecture on which the evidence is sparse in amount or confined to too narrow a fact domain. Despite this large mass of data and the scholarly attributes of the reviewer, upon completing the reading I found myself puzzled as to what a rational mind ought to conclude about the state of the evidence. Given all these facts and arguments based upon them, pulled together by a reviewer of competence and objectivity, am I prepared to say that my friend X's theory has been refuted, or strongly corroborated, or is in some vague epistemic region in between? If, taken as it stands, the theory seems to have been refuted, is it nevertheless doing well enough, considering the whole fact domain and the plausible explanations of some seeming predictive failures, so that we should continue to investigate it and try to patch it up (i.e., does it seem to have enough verisimilitude to warrant occupying psychologists with amending it so its verisimilitude may increase)? Or, is the state of the evidence

*This paper is based upon materials used by the author in teaching a philosophical psychology seminar and upon earlier theoretical and empirical work (see *Psychological Reports*, 1990, 66, 195–244).

such a mess conceptually and interpretatively that perhaps the thing to do is to give it up as a bad job and start working on something else?

Inquiry among my colleagues suggests that this befuddled state following the reading of a research literature review is not peculiar to me, or even a minority of faculty in a first-class psychology department, but is so frequent as to be almost the norm. Why is this? This personal phenomenon of cognitive bafflement writ large is, of course, the well known deficiency of most branches of the social sciences to have the kind of cumulative growth and theoretical integration that characterizes the history of the more successful scientific disciplines. I do not here address the question whether psychology and sociology are really in poorer shape as regards replication of findings than chemistry or astronomy, although I am aware that there is a minority report on that score. In what follows I shall presuppose that, by and large, with certain striking exceptions (which I think are rather easy to account for as exceptions), theories in the "soft areas" of psychology have a tendency to go through periods of initial enthusiasm leading to large amounts of empirical investigation with ambiguous overall results. This period of infatuation is followed by various kinds of amendment and the proliferation of ad hoc hypotheses. Finally, in the long run, experimenters lose interest rather than deliberately discard a theory as clearly falsified. As I put it in a previous paper on this subject (1978), theories in the "soft areas" of psychology have a fate like Douglas MacArthur said of what happens to old generals, "They never die, they just slowly fade away." The optimistic reader who does not agree with this assessment may still find the material that follows of interest because much of it bears upon the improvement of research and interpretation.

The discussion that follows, except as specifically noted otherwise, is confined to surveys of research evidence sharing three properties, to wit, (a) theories in so called "soft areas," (b) data correlational, and (c) positive findings consisting of refutation of the null hypothesis. I do not offer a precise specification of "soft area," which is not necessary for what I am doing here, but I am sure the reader knows approximately what branches of psychology are normally so classified. I will content myself with listing the chief ones, namely, clinical, counseling, personality theory, and social psychology. Let me emphasize that I am concerned here wholly with the testing of *explanatory theories* in these areas, and that most of what I say does not apply to purely technological generalizations such as the question whether a certain Rorschach sign is statistically predictive of suicide risk, or that tall mesomorphic males make better military leaders on the average. By (b) *correlational* I mean simply that the lawful relationship obtained in the observations is based on calculating a statistic on cross-sectional data, taking the organisms as they come, rather than experimentally manipulating certain factors while other factors are held constant or subjected to a randomizing process. By property (c) I mean that the theory under scrutiny is not powerful enough to generate a numerical point value, from which an experimental finding may or may not deviate significantly, but is so weak that it merely implies that one group will score higher than another, or that there is some nonzero cross-sectional correlation between two measured variables.

It is important to take explicit notice of the methodological point involved in property (c). Strong theories leading to numerical predictions are subjected to danger of falsification by a positive significance test, which is the way the equivalent of "statistical significance" is commonly used in chemistry, physics, astronomy, and genetics. Whereas weak theories only predict a directional difference or an association between two things without specifying its size within a narrow range of values, so the way in which a significance test is employed by psychologists and sociologists is precisely the reverse from its use in hard science. This leads to the paradox that an enhancement of statistical power, say by improvement of the logical design, increased reliability of the measures, or increased sample size has precisely the opposite effect in soft psychology from the one that it has in physics (Meehl, 1967).

An important extension of condition (b) is experimental research in which, while causal factors are manipulated by the experimenter and subjects assigned to treatments on the basis of some mixture of equated factors and randomization, a crucial feature of the statistical analysis is an interaction effect between the manipulated factor and an attribute (trait, demographic, life-history, psychometric, or whatever) of the individuals. When experimental interpretation hinges upon the presence of such an interaction, so that the main effect induced by the manipulated variable, taken by itself, does not suffice to test the substantive theory, such an experimental study is classified as "correlational" in sense (b) above, and the criticisms below apply with the full force that they have in a purely correlational (nonmanipulative) investigation.

With these rough stipulations, I propound and defend a radical and disturbing methodological thesis. *Thesis: Null hypothesis testing of correlational predictions from weak substantive theories in soft psychology is subject to the influence of ten obfuscating factors whose effects are usually (1) sizeable, (2) opposed, (3) variable, and (4) unknown. The net epistemic effect of these ten obfuscating influences is that the usual research literature review is well-nigh uninterpretable.*

I want to emphasize that I am not about to offer a list of nit-picking criticisms of the sort that we used to hear from some statisticians when I was a graduate student as, for example, that somebody used a significance test that presupposes normality when the data were not exactly normal, or the old hassle about one-tail versus two-tail significance testing, or, in the case of experiments having higher order interactions, the argument about whether some of these sums of squares are of such marginal significance (and so uninterpretable theoretically) that they should really be pooled as part of the error term in the denominator. I am making a claim much stronger than that, which is I suppose the main reason that students and colleagues have trouble hearing it, since they might not know what to do next if they took it seriously! The italicized thesis above is stated strongly, but I do not exaggerate for emphasis, I mean it quite literally. I mean that my befuddled response upon reading that literature review of my friend's theory is not due to Meehl being obsessional, senile, or statistically inept, but is precisely the right response of a rational mind, given the combined operation of the ten obfuscating factors that I am about to explain. These obfuscating factors are not typically of negligible size, although in a particular case one or two of them may not be very large, *but we do not know which ones.* They vary from one domain and from one experiment and from one measuring instrument to another, but we do not typically know how big a given one is in a given setting. About half of them operate to make good theories look bad, and the other half tend to make poor theories look good, and at least one of the factors can work either way. Because of these circumstances, I take my thesis above to be literally true. The combined operation of ten factors—powerful, variable, unmeasured and working in opposition to each other, counterbalancing one another's influence with an indeterminate net result—makes it impossible to tell what a "box score" of statistical significance tests in the research literature proves about the theory's verisimilitude. If the reader is impelled to object at this point "Well, but for heaven's sake, you are practically saying that the whole tradition of testing substantive theories in soft psychology by null hypothesis refutation is a mistake, despite R. A. Fisher and Co. in agronomy," that complaint does not disturb me because that is exactly what I am arguing.

This *Festschrift* not being devoted to philosophy of science, I will confine my remarks here to a brief statement of the usual situation in testing a substantive theory by predicting some observational relationship, which is good enough for present purposes and is not, I think, controversial in the relevant aspects. All logicians and historians of science agree upon the essentials. Theories do not entail particulars, that is, single observations; but theories taken with a statement of conditions entail relations between particulars. The derivation of a prediction about observational facts (for present purposes I take "observational" to be unproblematic although in strict epistemology it remains a knotty question) involves, when spelled out in detail, a conjunction of several premises, and this will I think always be true in the testing of theories in soft psychology. At least I am not aware of any exceptions. Let the substantive theory of interest be T. We have one or more auxiliary theories (some of which may be about instrumentation and others about the psyche) which are not the main focus of the investigator's interest, $A_1, A_2, \ldots$. Then we need a negative statement which is not formulated with concrete content like an auxiliary but which says "other things being equal." Following Lakatos (1970, 1974), I shall refer to this simply as the *ceteris paribus* clause, designated C_p. Finally, we have statements about the experimental conditions designated C_n for "conditions," achieved either by manipulation or, in the case of individual differences variables (traits, test scores, demographics, life history facts), by selection of subjects. In other words, for the derivation we require to trust that the investigator did what he said he did in getting the subjects and in doing whatever he did to the subjects. Then, if (O_1,

O_2) are observational statements, the structural model for testing a substantive theory looks like this:

Derivation of observational conditional: $T \cdot A_1 \cdot A_2 \cdot C_p \cdot C_n \rightarrow (O_1 \supset O_2)$

Theoretical risk: Prior probability $p(O_2 \mid O_1)$, absent theory, should be small (Cf. Popper, 1959, 1962, 1983; Schilpp, 1974).

   I now present and briefly discuss, without rigorous "hammer blow" proofs in all cases but hopefully with sufficient persuasiveness, the ten obfuscating factors that make H_0-refutation in the soft areas largely uninterpretable:

   1.   Loose Derivation Chain.   Very few derivation chains running from the theoretical premises to the predicted observational relation are deductively tight. Logicians and historians of science have pointed out that this is even true in the "exact" mathematicized sciences such as theoretical physics. *A fortiori* there are few tight, rigorous deductions in most areas of psychology, and almost none in soft psychology. While the theorist or the experimenter may present a tight derivation for certain portions of the prediction (e.g., those that involve a mathematical model), he often relies upon one or more "obvious" inferential steps which, if spelled out, would require some additional unstated premises. These unstated premises are of an intuitive, commonsensical, or clinical experiential nature, and sometimes involve nothing more complicated than reliance upon the ordinary semantics of trait names. I do not wish to be understood as criticizing this, but we are listing sources of logical slippage, and this is obviously one of them. To the extent that the derivation chain from the theory and its auxiliaries to the predicted factual relation is thus loose, a falsified prediction cannot constitute a strict, strong, definitive falsifier of the substantive theory. The extent to which a successful prediction mediated by such a loose derivation chain with unstated premises *supports* the theory is somewhat more difficult to assess, and I will pass this for now.

   2.   Problematic Auxiliary Theories.   Here the auxiliary theories, whether of instrumentation or about the subject matter proper, are not suppressed as unstated premises but explicitly stated. Now in soft psychology it sometimes happens— arguably as often as not—that each auxiliary theory is itself nearly as problematic as the main theory we are testing. When there are several such problematic auxiliary theories, the joint probability that they all obtain may be considerably lower than the prior probability of the substantive theory of interest. Here again, since the valid form of the syllogism involved in a refutation reads:

$$T \bullet A_1 \bullet A_2 \bullet C_p \bullet C_n \longrightarrow (O_1 \supset O_2)$$
$$O_1 \bullet \sim O_2 \qquad \text{Observational result}$$
$$\therefore \sim (T \bullet A_1 \bullet A_2 \bullet C_p \bullet C_n), \quad \text{formally equivalent to}$$
$$\sim T \, V \sim A_1 \, V \sim A_2 \, V \sim C_p \, V \sim C_n$$

so that what we intended to refute if the observations didn't pan out was T, but the logical structure leaves us not knowing whether the prediction failed because T was false or because one or more of the conjoined statements A_1, A_2, C_p, or C_n were false. This reasoning applies to sections 3 and 4 following as well.

   3.   *Problematic Ceteris Paribus Clause.*   The *ceteris paribus* clause does not, of course, mean by "everything else being equal . . . " that the individual subjects are all equated; in a typical study in soft psychology they are definitely not, and the individual differences among them appear in the denominator of the significance test. What *is* meant here by *ceteris paribus* when we test a theory by showing a statistical relationship to be nonzero (significant t, F, r, chi-square) is that while the individuals vary in respect to those factors that we have not controlled but allowed to vary (and which we hope are, therefore, "taken care of" in the statistics by randomization), the alleged causal influence does not in some significant subset of subjects have an additional effect operating systematically in a direction opposed to the one that our theory and the auxiliaries intend. *Example:* Suppose I am trying to test a theory about the difference between introverts and extraverts in their need for social objects in relationship to experienced stress. I am manipulating a factor experimentally by an operation intended to induce anxiety. But this "experimental study" falls under the present thesis because I am examining the substantive theory via the interaction between the experimental factor and an individual differences variable that the subjects bring with them, to wit, their scores on a social introversion questionnaire. To make the subjects anxious without physical pain I give the experimental group misinformation that they got a grade of "F" on the midquarter exam. I administer a projective test, say the TAT, scored for current regnant *n Affiliation*. The critical (statistical) analysis bearing on the theory is the interaction between social introversion as measured by the questionnaire and the effect of the experimental stress on the output variable, TAT affiliative score. Every psychologist realizes immediately that there is a problematic auxiliary theory involved here, namely, the psychometric validity of the TAT as a projective measure of currently regnant affiliative motives. Further, there is the auxiliary theory that telling people that they failed a midquarter will make them anxious. Surely nobody will deny that these are both highly problematic, arguably as problematic as the initial theory itself.

   As regards the *ceteris paribus* clause, it may be that telling an "A" student that he failed the midquarter will result either in his disbelief or in some cases in a response of resentment, since he knows he did better and therefore somebody must have done a bum job of scoring or made a clerical mistake. What will such induced anger do to the kinds of TAT stories he tells about human subjects? On the other hand a poor student may not have his anxiety mobilized very much by the reported "F," since for him that's par for the course.

   It is clear that we have a couple of highly problematic auxiliaries, one on the input and one on the output side, together with a problematic *ceteris paribus* clause. If the impact of the grade misinformation is a strong correlate of an individual differences variable that's *not explicitly part of the design,* there may be a subset of individuals for whom the scored TAT behavior is suppressed by the induced state of rage, even if the misinformation has also produced in most or all of those subjects an increase in anxiety.

I don't think any psychologist would consider these unpleasant possibilities the least bit farfetched. The main point is that the joint problematicity of (1) the auxiliary theories about the psychometric validity of the TAT, (2) the adequacy of the grade misinformation as an eliciter of strong anxiety in all of the subjects, and (3) the *ceteris paribus* that there are no significant correlations between individual differences variables of the subjects (including perhaps their social introversion as well as their usual scholastic performance) and the affective or cognitive states induced, could to some extent countervail the induced state on which we have our eye.

4.   Experimenter Error.   Here I refer on the input side to an imperfect realization of the particulars, experimenter mistakes in manipulation. Perhaps the investigator's research assistant is enthusiastic about her theory and without consciously intending—I am completely omitting conscious faking of data— slants the way the grade information is given or picks up cues about anxiety while administering the TAT and consequently shuts off the stories a little quicker or whatever. Exactly how much experimenter error occurs either in experimental manipulation or experimenter bias in recording observations is still in dispute, but again no knowledgeable psychologist would say that it is so rare as to be of zero importance (Rosenthal, 1966; see also Mahoney, 1976).

5.   Inadequate Statistical Power.   It is remarkable, and says something discouraging about the sociology of science, that more than a quarter century after Jacob Cohen's (1962) classic paper on the power function in abnormal- social psychology research, only a minority—I have not done a formal count, but leafing through a few issues of any journal in the soft areas will convince the reader that it is a *very small* minority—of investigators mention the statistical power function in discussing experimental design or interpreting data, although naturally there is some temptation to allude to it when explaining away those failures to reach statistical significance whenever facing a mixed bag of results. Because of its special role in the social sciences and the fact that like some of the other obfuscators it does lend itself to some degree of quantitative treatment, I have listed inadequate statistical power separately. A philosopher of science might justifiably argue that the statistical power should be included in the guise of an auxiliary.

Because I believe that one of the commonest confusions in thinking about statistical significance testing lies in the conflation of substantive and statistical hypotheses, I throughout use the word "theory" or the phrase "substantive theory" to designate the conjectured processes or entities being studied, and "hypothesis" to refer to the statistical hypothesis that allegedly flows from this substantive picture. I do not know quite how to go about formulating the statistical power function as an auxiliary, and for that reason and its special role in social science I list it separately. Despite Cohen's empirical summary and his tentative recommendations, one has the impression that many psychologists and sociologists view this whole line of concern as a kind of nit-picking statistician's refinement, or perhaps a "piece of friendly advice to researchers," which they may or may not elect to act upon. A moment's reflection tells us that this last view is a grave methodological mistake. Suppose that the substantive theory has perfect verisimilitude, ditto the auxiliaries and the *ceteris paribus* clause; but, as is usual in soft psychology, the substantive theory does not make a numerical point prediction as to the *size* of, say, a correlation coefficient between two observational measures. However, suppose that, if pressed, the theorist will tell us that if his theory has high verisimilitude, a correlation of at least .35 is expectable, and that he would consider a value lower as hardly consistent with his causal model. Then any correlation larger than .35 will count as a corroborator of the theory, and, to play the scientific game fairly (whether we are Popperians or not, we have given Popper this much about *modus tollens!*), a failure to find a correlation $r > .35$ constitutes a refutation. That is, the theorist says that, while he doesn't know just how big the correlation is, if it isn't at least that big he would admit that the facts, if not totally slaying the theory immediately, speak strongly against it. At the lower end of this region of allowable true values, suppose our sample size is such that we would have only a 60% statistical power at the conventional .05 significance level. Surely this is not some minor piddling defect in the study, it is a gross abuse of the theory taken as it stands.

Imagine a chemist who, relying on the old fashioned litmus test for whether something is an acid, told us that the test papers he uses are unfortunately only about 60% blue litmus (that one expects to turn red) and the other 40% are phenolphthalein papers (which, if I recall my undergraduate chemistry, turn red in the presence of a base). If it were important for us to know whether something was acidic or basic, or simply whether it was an acid or not an acid, how dependable would we think the work of a chemist who drew test slips from a jar, 40% of which he can foresee will give the wrong answer, so that of 100 batches of substances studied (even if they were all acid as predicted by some theory) we would get a box score of only 60 to 40? In chemistry it would be considered scandalous.

It will not do to say that such an approach is excusable in psychology because chemistry is easier to do than psychology. Unlike some of the other obfuscators in my list, the establishment of sufficient statistical power can easily be achieved, as Cohen pointed out, so that deficient power is not a plausible explanation of a falsifying result. I am really at a loss to understand the sociology of this matter in my profession. Of course if people never claimed that they had proven the null hypothesis by failing to refute it (taking some of Fisher's injunctions quite literally), this would not be so serious. As we know, Fisher himself was not very tractable on the subject of power, although he got at it in his discussion of precision. But despite the mathematical truth of Fisher's point (which we can sidestep by changing from a point to a range hypothesis and formulating the directional null hypothesis that way), a null result, a failure to reach significance, is regularly counted against a theory. Despite Fisher, it is hard to see how psychologists could do otherwise: if we only count the pluses and ignore the minuses, it is a foregone conclusion that all theories will be corroborated, including those that have no verisimilitude at all.

6.   *Crud Factor.*   In the social sciences and arguably in the biological sciences, "everything correlates to some extent with everything." This truism, which I have found no competent psychologist disputes given 5 minutes reflection, does not apply to pure experimental studies in which attributes that the subjects bring with them are not the subject of study except in so far as they appear as a source of error and hence in the denominator of a significance test. (My colleague, David Lykken, and several high-caliber graduate students who have heard me lecture on this topic, hold that I am too conservative in confining my obfuscator thesis to correlational research, and they make a strong if not to me persuasive case, but I set that aside with this mere mention of it in the present context.) There is nothing mysterious about the fact that in psychology and sociology everything correlates with everything. Any measured trait or attribute is some function of a list of partly known and mostly unknown causal factors in the genes and life history of the individual, and both genetic and environmental factors are known from tons of empirical research to be themselves correlated. To take an extreme case, suppose we construe the null hypothesis literally (objecting that we mean by it "almost null" gets ahead of the story, and destroys the rigor of the Fisherian mathematics!) and ask whether we expect males and females in Minnesota to be precisely equal in some arbitrary trait that has individual differences, say, color naming. In the case of color naming we could think of some obvious differences right off, but even if we didn't know about them, what is the causal situation? If we write a causal equation (which is not the same as a regression equation for pure predictive purposes but which, if we had it, would serve better than the latter) so that the score of an individual male is some function (presumably nonlinear if we knew enough about it but here supposed linear for simplicity) of a rather long set of causal variables of genetic and environmental type $X_1, X_2, \ldots X_m$. These values are operated upon by regression coefficients $b_1, b_2, \ldots b_m$.

Now we write a similar equation for the class of females. Can anyone suppose that the beta coefficients for the two sexes will be exactly the same? Can anyone imagine that the mean values of all of the X's will be exactly the same for males and females, even if the culture were not still considerably sexist in child-rearing practices and the like? If the betas are not exactly the same for the two sexes, and the mean values of the X's are not exactly the same, what kind of Leibnitzian preestablished harmony would we have to imagine in order for the mean color naming score to come out exactly equal between males and females? It boggles the mind; it simply would never happen. As Einstein said, "the Lord God is subtle, but He is not malicious." We cannot imagine that nature is out to fool us by this kind of delicate balancing. So, anybody familiar with large-scale research data takes it as a matter of course that when the N gets big enough she will not be looking for the statistically significant correlations but rather looking at their patterns, since almost all of them will be significant. In saying this, I am not going counter to what is stated by mathematical statisticians or psychologists with statistical expertise. For example, the standard psychologist's textbook, the excellent treatment by Hays (1973, p. 415), explicitly states that, taken literally, the null hypothesis is always false.

Twenty years ago David Lykken and I conducted an exploratory study of the crud factor which we never published but I shall summarize it briefly here. (I offer it not as "empirical proof"—that H_0 taken literally is quasi-always false hardly needs proof and is generally admitted—but as a punchy and somewhat amusing example of an insufficiently appreciated truth about soft correlational psychology.) In 1966 the University of Minnesota Student Counseling Bureau's Statewide Testing Program administered a questionnaire to 57,000 high school seniors, the items dealing with family facts, attitudes toward school, vocational and educational plans, leisure time activities, school organizations, etc. We cross-tabulated a total of 15 (and then 45) variables including the following (the number of categories for each variable given in parentheses): father's occupation (7), father's education (9), mother's education (9), number of siblings (10), birth order (only, oldest, youngest, neither), educational plans after high school (3), family attitudes towards college (3), do you like school (3), sex (2), college choice (7), occupational plan in 10 years (20), and religious preference (20). In addition, there were 22 "leisure time activities" such as "acting," "model building," "cooking," etc., which could be treated either as a single 22-category variable or as 22 dichotomous variables. There were also 10 "high school organizations" such as "school subject clubs," "farm youth groups," "political clubs," etc., which also could be treated either as a single 10-category variable or as 10 dichotomous variables. Considering the latter two variables as multichotomies gives a total of 15 variables producing 105 different cross-tabulations. All values of chi-square for these 105 cross-tabulations were statistically significant, and 101 (96%) of them were significant with a probability of less than 10^{-6}.

If "leisure activity" and "high school organizations" are considered as separate dichotomies, this gives a total of 45 variables and 990 different cross-tabulations. Of these, 92% were statistically significant and more than 78% were significant with a probability less than 10^{-6}. Looked at in another way, the median number of significant relationships between a given variable and all the others was 41 out of a possible 44!

We also computed MCAT scores by category for the following variables: number of siblings, birth order, sex, occupational plan, and religious preference. Highly significant deviations from chance allocation over categories was found for each of these variables. For example, the females score higher than the males; MCAT score steadily and markedly decreases with increasing numbers of siblings; eldest or only children are significantly brighter than youngest children; there are marked differences in MCAT scores between those who hope to become nurses and those who hope to become nurses aides, or between those planning to be farmers, engineers, teachers, or physicians; and there are substantial MCAT differences among the various religious groups.

We also tabulated the five principal Protestant religious denominations (Baptist, Episcopal, Lutheran, Methodist, and Presbyterian) against all the other variables, finding highly significant relationships in most instances. For example, *only* children are nearly twice as likely to be Presbyterian than Baptist in Minnesota, more than half of the Episcopalians "usually like school" but only 45% of Lutherans do, 55% of Presbyterians feel that their grades reflect their abilities as compared to only 47% of Episcopalians, and Episcopalians are more likely to be male whereas Baptists are more likely to be female. Eighty-three percent of Baptist children said that they enjoyed dancing as compared to 68% of Lutheran children. More than twice the proportion of Episcopalians plan to attend an out of state college than is true for Baptists, Lutherans, or Methodists. The proportion of Methodists who plan to become conservationists is nearly twice that for Baptists, whereas the proportion of Baptists who plan to become receptionists is nearly twice that for Episcopalians.

In addition, we tabulated the four principle Lutheran Synods (Missouri, ALC, LCA, and Wisconsin) against the other variables, again finding highly significant relationships in most cases. Thus, 5.9% of Wisconsin Synod children have no siblings as compared to only 3.4% of Missouri Synod children. Fifty-eight percent of ALC Lutherans are involved in playing a musical instrument or singing as compared to 67% of Missouri Synod Lutherans. Eighty percent of Missouri Synod Lutherans belong to school or political clubs as compared to only 71% of LCA Lutherans. Forty-nine percent of ALC Lutherans belong to debate, dramatics, or musical organizations in high school as compared to only 40% of Missouri Synod Lutherans. Thirty-six percent of LCA Lutherans belong to organized nonschool youth groups as compared to only 21% of Wisconsin Synod Lutherans. [Preceding text courtesy of D. T. Lykken.]

These relationships are not, I repeat, Type I errors. They are facts about the world, and with $N = 57,000$ they are pretty stable. Some are theoretically easy to explain, others more difficult, others completely baffling. The "easy" ones have multiple explanations, sometimes competing, usually not. Drawing theories from a pot and associating them whimsically with variable pairs would yield an impressive batch of H_0-refuting "confirmations."

Another amusing example is the behavior of the items in the 550 items of the MMPI pool with respect to sex. Only 60 items appear on the *Mf* scale, about the same number that were put into the pool with the hope that they would discriminate femininity. It turned out that over half the items in the scale were not put in the pool for that purpose, and of those that were, a bare majority did the job. Scale derivation was based on item analysis of a small group of criterion cases of male homosexual invert syndrome, a significant difference on a rather small N of Dr. Starke Hathaway's private patients being then conjoined with the requirement of discriminating between male normals and female normals. When the N becomes very large as in the data published by Swenson, Pearson, and Osborne (1973), approximately 25,000 of each sex tested at the Mayo Clinic over a period of years, it turns out that 507 of the 550 items discriminate the sexes. Thus in a heterogeneous item pool we find only 8% of items failing to show a significant difference on the sex dichotomy. The following are sex-discriminators, the male/female differences ranging from a few percentage points to over 30%:

Sometimes when I am not feeling well I am cross.

I believe there is a Devil and a Hell in afterlife.

I think nearly anyone would tell a lie to keep out of trouble.

Most people make friends because friends are likely to be useful to them.

I like poetry.

I like to cook.

Policemen are usually honest.

I sometimes tease animals.

My hands and feet are usually warm enough.

I think Lincoln was greater than Washington.

I am certainly lacking in self-confidence.

Any man who is able and willing to work hard has a good chance of succeeding.

I invite the reader to guess which direction scores "feminine." Given this information, I find some items easy to "explain" by one obvious theory, others have competing plausible explanations, still others are baffling.

Note that we are not dealing here with some source of statistical error (the occurrence of random sampling fluctuations). That source of error is limited by the significance level we choose, just as the probability of Type II error is set by initial choice of the statistical power, based on a pilot study or other antecedent data concerning an expected average difference. Since in social science everything correlates with everything to some extent, due to complex and obscure causal influences, in considering the crud factor we are talking about *real* differences, *real* correlations, *real* trends and patterns for which there is, of course, some true but complicated multivariate causal theory. I am not suggesting that these correlations are fundamentally unexplainable. They would be completely explained if we had the knowledge of Omniscient Jones, which we don't. The point is that we are in the weak situation of corroborating our *particular* substantive theory by showing that X and Y are "related in a nonchance manner," when our theory is too weak to make a numerical prediction or even (usually) to set up a range of admissible values that would be counted as corroborative.

Some psychologists play down the influence of the ubiquitous crud factor, what David Lykken (1968) calls the "ambient correlational noise" in social science, by saying that we are not in danger of being misled by small differences that show up as significant in gigantic samples. How much that softens the blow of the crud factor's influence depends on the crud factor's average size in a given research domain, about which neither I nor anybody else has accurate information. But *the notion that the correlation between arbitrarily paired trait variables will be, while not literally zero, of such minuscule size as to be of no importance is surely wrong.* Everybody knows that there is a set of demographic factors, some understood and others quite mysterious, that correlate quite respectably with a variety of traits. (SES is the one usually considered, and frequently assumed to be only in the "input" causal role.) The clinical scales of the MMPI were developed by empirical keying against a set of disjunct nosological categories, some of which are phenomenologically and psychodynamically opposite to others. Yet the 45 pairwise correlations of these scales are almost always positive (scale *Ma* provides most of the negatives) and a representative size is in the neighborhood of .35 to .40. The same is true of the scores on the Strong Vocational Interest Blank, where I find an average absolute value correlation close to .40. The malignant influence of so called "methods covariance" in psychological research that relies upon tasks or tests having certain kinds of behavioral similarities such as questionnaires or ink blots is commonplace and a regular source of concern to clinical and personality psychologists. For further discussion and examples of crud factor size, see Meehl (1990).

In order to further convince the reader that this crud factor problem is nontrivial, let us consider the following hypothetical situation with some plausible numerical values I shall assign. Imagine a huge pot of substantive theories about all sorts of domains in the area of personality. Then imagine a huge pot of variables (test scores, ratings, demographic variables, and so forth) of the kind that soft psychologists have to deal with in nonexperimental work. I remind the reader that I include experimental studies in which these subject-variables, attributes that they bring with them rather than factors we impose by manipulation and randomization, play a critical role in the experimental design as interaction terms. Now suppose we imagine a society of psychologists doing research in this soft area, and each investigator sets his experiments up in a whimsical, irrational manner as follows: First he picks a theory at random out of the theory pot. Then he picks a pair of variables randomly out of the observable variable pot. He then arbitrarily assigns a direction (you understand there is no intrinsic connection of content between the substantive theory and the variables, except once in a while there would be such by coincidence) and says that he is going to test the randomly chosen substantive theory by pretending that it predicts—although in fact it does not, having no intrinsic contentual relation—a positive correlation between randomly chosen observational variables X and Y.

Now suppose that the crud factor operative in the broad domain were .30, that is, the average correlation between all of the variables pairwise in this domain is .30. I repeat, this is not sampling error but the true correlation produced by some complex unknown network of genetic and environmental factors. Suppose he divides a normal distribution of subjects at the median and uses all of his cases (which frequently is not what is done, although if properly treated statistically that is not methodologically sinful). Let us take variable X as the "input" variable (never mind its causal role). The mean score of the cases in the top half of the distribution will then be at one mean deviation, that is, in standard score terms they will have an average score of .80. Similarly, the subjects in the bottom half of the X distribution will have a mean standard score of $-.80$. So the mean difference in standard score terms between the high and low X's, the one "experimental" and the other "control" group, is 1.6. If the regression of output variable Y on X is approximately linear this yields an expected difference in standard score terms of .48, so the difference on the arbitrarily defined "output" variable Y is in the neighborhood of half a standard deviation.

When the investigator runs a t test on these data, what is the probability of achieving a statistically significant result? This depends on the statistical power function and hence upon the sample size, which varies widely, more in soft psychology because of the nature of the data collection problems than in experimental work. I do not have exact figures, but an informal scanning of several issues of journals in the soft areas of clinical, abnormal, and social gave me a representative value of the number of cases in each of two groups being compared at around $N_1 = N_2 = 37$ (that's a median because of the skewness, sample sizes ranging from a low of 17 in one clinical study to a high of 1000 in a social survey study). Assuming equal variances, this gives us a standard error of the mean difference $= .2357$ in sigma-units so that our t is a little over 2.0. The substantive theory in a real life case being almost invariably predictive of a direction (it is hard to know what sort of significance testing we would be doing otherwise), the 5% level of confidence can be legitimately taken as one-tailed and in fact could be criticized if it were not (assuming that the 5% level of confidence is given the usual special magical significance afforded it by social scientists!). The directional 5% level being at 1.65, the expected value of our t test in this situation is approximately .40 t units from the required significance level. Things being essentially normal for 72 *df,* this gives us a power of detecting a difference of around .64.

However, since in our imagined "experiment" the assignment of direction was random, the probability of detecting a difference in the *predicted direction* (even though in reality this prediction was not mediated by any rational relation of content) is only half of that. Even this conservative power based on the assumption of a completely random association between the theoretical substance and the pseudopredicted direction should give one pause. We find that the probability of getting a positive result from a theory with no verisimilitude whatsoever, associated in a totally whimsical fashion with a pair of variables picked randomly out of the observational pot, *is one chance in three!* This is quite different from the .05 level that people usually think about. Of course, the reason for this is that the .05 level is based on a strict holding of H_0 if the theory were false. Whereas, because in the social sciences everything is correlated with everything, for epistemic purposes (despite the rigor of the mathematician's tables) the true baseline if the theory has nothing to do with reality and only a chance relationship to it—so to speak, "any connection between the theory and the facts is purely coincidental"—is 6 or 7 times as great as the reassuring .05 which the psychologist focuses his mind upon. If the crud factor in a domain were running around .40, the power function is .86 and the "directional power" for random theory/prediction pairings would be .43.

The division of the statistical power by two on the grounds that the direction of the difference has been whimsically assigned is a distinct overcorrection, because the variables found in soft psychology (whether psychometric, demographic, rated, or life history) are by no means as likely to be negatively as positively correlated. The investigator's initial assignment of what might be called the "up" direction, based on the christening of the factors or observable test scores by the psychological quality thought characteristic of their high end, means that although the theory may have negligible verisimilitude and hence any relationship between it and the facts is coincidental, the investigator's background knowledge, common sense, and intuition—what my friend and former colleague Festinger calls the "bubba factor"—will cause the predicted direction to be not random. If we consider, for example, the achievement and ability test area, we have something close to positive manifold, and a knowledgeable investigator might be using a theory that had negligible verisimilitude but nevertheless his choice of *direction* for the correlation between two such tests would almost never be inverse. A similar situation holds for psychopathology, and for many variables in personality measurement that refer to aspects of social competence on the one hand or impairment of interpersonal function (as in mental illness) on the other. Thorndike had a dictum "All good things tend to go together." I rather imagine that the only domain in which we might expect anything like an even-handed distribution of positive and negative correlations would be in the measurement of certain political, religious, and social beliefs or sentiments, although even there one has the impression that the labeling of scales has been nonrandom, especially because of the social scientist's interest in syndromes like authoritarianism and the radical right. There is no point in guesstimating the extent to which the division by two in the text supra is an overcorrection, but it is certainly fair to say that it is excessive when the influence of common sense and the bubba factor is taken into account as a real life departure from the imagined totally random assignment. *The statistical power of significance tests for theories having negligible verisimilitude but receiving a spurious confirmation via the crud factor is underestimated by some unknown amount, but hardly negligible, when we divide the directional power function by two on the random assignment model.*

An epistemological objection to this reasoning holds that it is illegitimate to conceptualize this crazy setup of a pot of theories whose elements are randomly assigned to a pot of variable pairs, since such a hypothetical "population" cannot be precisely defined by the statistician. I cheerfully agree with the premise but not the conclusion. The notion of a random assignment of direction taken as a lower bound to the power, given a certain representative value of the crud factor in a domain, is just as defensible as the way we proceed in computing the probability of poker hands or roulette winnings in games of chance. The point is that *if* we conceive such a class of substantive theories, and *if* we assign the theories to the finite but indefinitely large and extendable collection of variables measured in soft psychology (which runs into millions of pairs with existing measures), there is nothing objectionable about employing a mathematical model for generating the probabilities provided one can make a defensible statement about whether they are lower bounds on the truth, as they are in this case.

If it is objected that the class of experiments, or the class of theories, cannot be enumerated or listed and consequently it is a misuse of the probability calculus to assign numbers to such a vague open-ended class, my answer would be that if that argument is taken strictly as an epistemic point against the application of mathematics to the process of testing theories, it applies with equal force to the application of mathematical methods to the testing of statistical hypotheses, and hence the whole significance testing procedure goes down the drain. When we contemplate the $p = .05$ level in traditional Fisherian statistics, everyone knows (if he paid attention in his undergraduate statistics class) that this does not refer to the actual physical state of affairs in the event that the drug turns out to be effective or that the rats manifest latent learning, but rather to the expected frequency of finding a difference of a certain size if in reality there is no difference. Assume with the objector that a hypothetical collection of all experiments that all investigators do (on drugs, or rats, or schizophrenics) is not meaningful empirically because of the vagueness of the class and its openness or extensibility. It is *not* defined precisely, the way we can say that the population from which we sampled our twins is all of the twins in the State of Minnesota, or all pupils in the Minneapolis school system who are in school on a given day. It follows that there is no basis for the application of Fisherian statistics in scientific research to begin with. As is well known, if some mischievous statistician or philosopher says "Well, five times in a hundred you would get this much of a difference even if the rats had learned nothing, so why shouldn't it happen to you?" the only answer is "It could happen to me, but I am not going to assume that I am one of the unlucky scientists in 20 to whom such a thing happens. I am aware, however, that over my research career, if I should perform a thousand significance tests on various kinds of data, and nothing that I researched had any validity to it, I would be able to write around 50 publishable papers based upon that false positive rate."

There are admittedly some deep and fascinating epistemological (and perhaps even ontological?) questions involved here that go beyond the scope of the present paper. All I am concerned to argue is that I will not hear an objection to the whimsical model of random assignment from a psychologist who routinely employs statistical significance tests in an effort to prove substantive theories, since the objection holds equally against that whole procedure. The class of all experiments that will ever be conducted with a choice of a set of variables assigned to a set of theories is no vaguer or more open-ended—and there is certainly nothing self-contradictory about it—than the class of all experiments that people will ever do on the efficacy of penicillin or latent learning in rats, or all of the experiments that all of the scientists in the world will ever conduct, on any subject matter, relying upon statistical significance tests. That fuzzy class is the reference class for the alpha level in Fisherian statistics, so that if the vagueness of such a class of "all experiments using t tests" makes it inadmissible, we have to stop doing significance tests anyway.

7. *Pilot Studies.* Low awareness of Cohen's point about inadequate statistical power has been disappointing, but I must now raise a question that Cohen did not discuss (quite properly, as he was not concerned with the crud factor in his paper): there is a subtle biasing effect in favor of low verisimilitude theories on the part of investigators who take the power function seriously. I have no hard data as to how many psychologists perform pilot studies. A show of hands in professional audiences to whom I have lectured on this subject shows that the practice is well-nigh universal. I do not here refer loosely to a "pilot study" as being one that is mainly oriented to seeing how the apparatus works or whether your subjects are bothered by the instructions or whatever. I mean a study that essentially duplicates the main study insofar as the variables were manipulated or controlled, the subjects randomized or matched, and the apparatus or instruments employed were those that are going to be subsequently employed. *A true pilot study is, except perhaps for a few minor improvements, a main study in the small.* Such pilot studies are conducted with two aims in mind. First, most often, to "see whether an appreciable effect seems to exist or not," (the point being

that, if in the pilot study one does not detect even a faint trend, let alone a statistically significant difference in the direction the theory predicts, one will not pursue it further). Secondly, for those who take the power function seriously, one attempts to gain a rough notion of the relationship between a mean difference and the approximate variability as the basis for inferring the number of cases that would be necessary, with that difference, to achieve statistical significance at, say, the .05 level. What is the effect of carrying out these two aims via the conducting of pilot studies? A proper pilot study (not merely one to see whether an apparatus works but which, in effect, is a small scale adumbration of the large study that one may subsequently conduct) *is itself a study*. If the investigator drops this line of work as "unpromising" on the grounds that one detects no marginal evidence of an effect, this means that one has conducted a study—perhaps one fairly adequate in design although with small statistical power—and a *real finding* has happened in the world which, under the policy described, never surfaces in the research literature.

Thus, in a given soft area of psychology, or in a subdomain, say, researching a particular variable or instrument, there are hundreds (if you count masters and doctoral dissertation projects, more like thousands) of pilot studies being conducted every year that will never be published, and many of which will not even be written up as an unpublished MA or PhD thesis for the simple reason that they "did not come out right." We do not ordinarily think of this as somehow reprehensible or as showing a bias on anybody's part, and I am not condemning people for this approach, as I have done it myself both in animal and human research. I am merely pointing out that a properly conducted pilot study is itself a research study, and if it "doesn't show an effect" when that effect was allegedly predicted from a certain substantive theory, it is a piece of evidence against the theory. The practice of doing pilot studies not to publish them but to decide whether to pursue a certain line means that there is a massive collection of data, some unknown fraction of which come out adverse to theories, which never see the light of day. *A fact that occurs in the laboratory or exists in the clinic files is just as much a fact whether Jones elects to write it up for a refereed journal or to forget it*. A class of potential falsifiers of substantive theories is subject to systematic suppression in perfectly good scientific conscience. We do not know how big it is, but nobody knowledgeable about academia could conceivably say that it was insignificant in size.

As to the second function of pilot studies, if, as above, we conceptualize the subset of substantive theories that have negligible verisimilitude linked randomly to observed variable pairs so that the "relationship" between the theory and the facts is coincidental, such investigations are dependent upon the crud factor for obtaining positive results. Now what will be the effect of the almost universal practice of doing pilot studies in such a situation? If the crud factor in a subdomain is large, investigators doing pilot studies on it will get positive results and proceed to do the main study and get positive results there as well, although they will not have to expend as much energy collecting as many cases as they would if the crud factor in the subdomain were small. But given that the crud factor, even if small, is not zero in any domain, investigators operating in that area will discover (on the average) that an effect exists, the crud factor being ubiquitous. Depending upon their motivation and the kind of data involved (e.g., questionnaires are easier to collect than tachistoscope runs), they will see to it that the main investigation uses a large enough sample that statistical significance will be achieved by differences roughly of the size that they found in the pilot study. Hence, investigators eager to research a certain theory in a loosely specified fact domain *are not wholly at the mercy of the crud factor size.* They are not stuck willy nilly with a fixed power on its average value in the domain, since the second (and legitimate!) use of pilot studies is precisely to see to it that a trend of roughly so-and-so size, if found in the pilot study, will be able to squeak through with statistical significance in the main study subsequently conducted. The limiting case of this, which fortunately does not exist because money and time are finite, would be that of investigators doggedly pursuing the testing of a particular theory by regularly doing pilot studies that give them a fairly accurate estimate of the size of the trend and if a trend seems to exist, invariably conducting the large scale experiment with a sample size having nearly perfect statistical power. This nightmare case is therapeutic for psychologists to contemplate, if as I believe, *it is the present real situation writ large and horrible.* It means that in the extreme instance of a pot of theories none of which have any verisimilitude, they would all come out as well corroborated if the investigators consistently (a) didn't pursue those lines where the pilot studies suggest a trend in the opposite direction and hence "not a profitable line to follow up" and, on the other hand, for those that are in the theoretically expected direction, (b) invariably did the main experiment using huge N's generating super power. I do not know, and neither does anybody else, how far different the present situation in the social sciences is from that nightmare situation, especially given the terrible publish or perish pressure upon young academics.

    8.   Selective Bias in Submitting Reports.   Some years ago, when the Minnesota Psychology Department moved to a new building, I went through my old files of research studies and discarded those that it was obvious I was for one reason or another never going to submit for publication or pursue further. Due to my Minnesota training by Hathaway, Paterson, and Skinner, all of whom (for quite different reasons) disparaged the publication of piddling average results with large overlap merely because they achieved statistical significance, I found a number of studies that were statistically significant that I had not submitted. This was mainly in the clinical area, and what it meant was that a particular MMPI scale or a currently popular test for detecting minimal brain damage was only "statistically significant" but not of practical value because of large overlap. But, I did find quite a few studies of adequate sample size so that one could trust the results from the power function standpoint that were not submitted simply because they did not show a trend. Now for technological purposes this may be legitimate, although I am inclined to think not. For purposes of testing substantive theories, it is an example of bias. Several rat latent learning studies that I had done with MacCorquodale were not submitted because they were in the grey region, showing probabilities hovering around .10, so that we were hardly in a position to say much as to whether the rats had learned anything or not.

I began inquiring among colleagues and students as to whether they thought they were completely evenhanded in submitting to journals results that achieved statistical significance and those that did not, and I haven't found a single person who claims to have been. Some people say rather shamefacedly that they are not evenhanded in the matter, and others point out—sometimes quoting R. A. Fisher on the point—that a statistically significant finding "proves something" whereas a failure to refute H_0 does not prove anything. This of course involves a serious disarticulation between Fisherian statistics and Popperian ideas of theory testing, since if a null result does not disprove anything it is at least arguable that one ought not to have done the experiment in the first place, because he is only going to count it if it comes out "positive," a major Popperian sin! I do not want to go into the very difficult and technical philosophical issues of that problem, but the point is that everyone acknowledges, some more freely than others and some by offering justificatory arguments, that they are considerably more likely to submit an article to a journal if they got significant results than if they failed to reach significance. This stems partly from thinking that a null result "doesn't prove much," partly from a recognition of the role of inadequate power, and partly because of the next factor to be discussed, to wit, that editors, also recognizing an epistemic asymmetry here, are more likely to reject a paper that fails to reach statistical significance, especially if it is plausible to attribute it to inadequate power.

9.   Selective Editorial Bias.   I find no hard data in the literature on the practice of editors and referees, but people who have served in either of these capacities report the same thing as investigators do: they are somewhat more favorably disposed to a clear finding of refuted H_0 than one that simply fails to show a trend. And here, as in the case of investigators, this behavior can be defended on the ground of what R. A. Fisher said about the asymmetry.

10.   Detached Validation Claim for Psychometric Instruments.   It is typical of research articles in soft psychology that a certain instrument, say, the MMPI social introversion scale, is going to be employed to test a substantive theory in which a concept claimed to be measured by that instrument is one of the embedded constructs. The investigator accepts an obligation to persuade the reader that the scale is valid for the trait (attribute, construct) that it names. Whether one can simultaneously validate a psychometric instrument and corroborate a substantive theory in which the construct labeled by the instrument's title finds a postulated place is a deep matter which was discussed over 30 years ago by Cronbach and myself (Cronbach & Meehl, 1955) and I shall say no more about it here. But it would seem that if I am going to confirm or refute a theory about the relation of social introversion to anxiety-based affiliative drives, I ought to have grounds for thinking that the test is sufficiently valid for use in the way I am using it, since the internal network of most experiments is not sufficiently rich to make a strong argument of the kind that Cronbach and I offered in 1955 about simultaneous testing.

How do investigators typically go about buttressing this initial validation claim for an instrument so that they can get on with doing the main study? We all know how it looks in the journals. What the writer does is to list a series of authors who have either "validated" or "failed to validate" the introversion test and perhaps summarizes by counting noses as to how many found it had validity and how many did not and then, if we are lucky, gives us a representative validity coefficient. What happens next? The author writes some such sentence as, "Since the majority of studies showed respectable validity for Fisbee's Test, and in the more favorable studies the validity coefficients were in the range .40 to .50, it was felt that Fisbee's Test was perhaps the best available test of introversion and it was therefore used in the present investigation." Following this summary remark, a *qualitative* claim of "respectable validity" and a *quantitative* claim based upon a representative value, the rest of the article typically presupposes that X is valid for introversion, without any further reference to the actual numbers. Typically, negligible attention is given the unreliable component as pushing correlations down and the reliable but invalid component of the test score as pushing them sometimes up but possibly down (since we cannot be completely confident about the *ceteris paribus* clause). Except for persons strongly interested in methodology and concerned with the problem presented in Campbell and Fiske's classic paper (1959) and its relationship to factor analysis, I find few psychologists who are sensitive to this obfuscating factor in the qualitative sense, let alone appreciative of its likely quantitative influence. This blindness comes, I think, from the yes-or-no use of the word "valid" (or "validated") which is a bad semantic habit acquired in beginning psychology courses due to the somewhat crude and inaccurate way the concepts of reliability and validity are typically presented. Every sophisticated psychologist, and certainly anybody concerned with psychometric theory, knows that tests have multiple validities or, putting it another way, they have a validity and multiple invalidities, depending upon which component you have your eye. But the verbal habit of saying that a test "has been validated," and hence, for purposes of the current research we are engaged in, "can be taken as substantially valid," prevents an adequate appreciation of the danger of a detached validity claim.

Having shown by a survey of studies that validity coefficients are in some range we have agreed to consider respectable (and I cannot resist pointing out that validities of .40, accounting for one-sixth of the variance, would hardly be considered "respectable" by a chemist or geneticist), the nonquantitative blanket category word "valid" is now picked up and employed in the subsequent discussion in a research paper. Obviously this can present a very misleading picture if the reader does not keep harking back to that distribution of validity coefficients that are not subsequently mentioned.

In deductive logic one speaks of the Rule of Detachment, which says that if we have written $p \rightarrow q$ and we have also written p then we are entitled in the rest of our discourse to assert q without having continually to repeat the syllogism or allude to the process of deductive inference. In that context all is well, and I have spoken of *detached validation claim* to highlight the point that *in the inductive logic of a pattern of correlations of various sizes, nothing comparable to a rule of detachment can properly operate with respect to the qualitative designation "valid."* This is so obvious a point that its statement would seem to suffice, and I do not expect any reader to disagree with me about it. But, is it a point of any quantitative impact on interpretation? It most certainly is, as is shown by the following numerical example employing values not the least outlandish as data go in soft psychology.

Suppose I am going to investigate some theory about introversion and intend to rely on the *Si* scale of the MMPI for measurement of an individual differences component that's going to interact with some experimental factor in my design. I offer a representative validity coefficient of say .40 (not unlike what we find, and one can find examples in the literature of soft psychology where people invoke validities less than .40 as "at least substantial validity for trait X" in an instrument they wish to use in their experiment). Suppose I properly report that I have a reliability coefficient of, say, .80 for my introversion test. (It is interesting how happy psychologists are with high reliabilities and low validities, since it should occur to one that this combination might have unfortunate consequences due to the possible falsity of the *ceteris paribus* clause.) Sixty-four percent of the variance of the observed test scores is reliable variance and 16% is valid variance, i.e., valid for my purposes. Hence about three-fourths of the reliable variance is invalid variance, that is, it is measuring something nonchance but not what we have our eye on, not what the scale is named for. Absent further data which may or may not be known and which in any case is likely not to be reported by the investigator and hence not available for the reviewer of research in a domain, one does not know whether that three-fourths of invalid reliable variance is a collection of other smaller factors or possibly even one or more factors that may be larger than the reliable component named by the test! Now when I find out that such a test correlates significantly with something else in my design, with what confidence am I entitled to attribute that to introversion, when three-fourths of the reliable variance of the test is something other than introversion as I have conceptualized it? Or putting it the other way around, what about the possibility that the three-fourths of reliable but invalid variance counteracts the influence of the component of the validly-measured introversion component in my particular design; consequently the falsity of the *ceteris paribus* clause with respect to components of the invalid variance prevents me from achieving a significant result even if my theory about introversion and its interaction with a manipulated variable has verisimilitude? It may be objected that it would be too onerous to require that investigators plug in a whole bunch of things that they ought to be worried about with the Campbell-Fiske discriminant validation in mind. All I can say to that is that, absent a tradition of so doing, I do not know how much confidence to have in detached validity claims for testing substantive theories.

This concludes my list of obfuscating factors. I hope I have convinced the reader that they are almost always if not invariably present in a soft psychology study, and that their quantitative impact, while varying from one project to another and on the average from one domain to another, will rarely be of negligible size. The worst part of it is that obfuscating factors (1) to (5) will tend to make good theories look bad; obfuscators (6) to (9) will tend to make poor theories look good; and I suppose obfuscator (10) can work either way and we frequently would not know in a given research design which way it might be working. As I said in my introductory thesis, we have ten factors, sizeable, variable, and typically unassessed in a given setting, working in opposite directions to produce a net "box score" of successful or unsuccessful attempts to refute the null hypothesis.

It might be objected that, in assessing the state of the empirical literature on a theory, we take it for granted that "all theories are lies," that it is not a question of a theory being absolutely true or totally false but that some theories are in better shape than others, and what the reviewer does is evaluate the evidence in some over-all sense. It is true that reviewers sometimes focus on particular assumptions of a research study or of a subset of studies all employing the same basic design or instrument, but this focusing is not very helpful in adjudicating the merits of the theory at the end of the review article unless it leads to some sort of *refined* "box score" from which highly doubtful studies, excessively problematic because of their auxiliary assumptions or because of low statistical power, are excluded. Ideally, this would be what happens, but since the ten obfuscators vary in size and in most cases we do not have a rational basis for assigning a numerical value to an obfuscator's influence one way or the other (e.g., can the reviewer assign a numerical value to the probability of a specific auxiliary?), the box score is going to be slanted one way or the other very much depending upon the reviewer's crude sifting on the basis of commonsensical or theoretically-based assignment of these unknown numerical values.

I do not believe psychologists in the soft areas can take much consolation from what is admittedly a correct statement in rough qualitative form, "We don't allow a single experiment, however replicable, to kill a theory that is otherwise good, and we aren't impressed with a collection of truly feeble statistical significances, rather we look at the over-all shape of the factual terrain and make a reasoned judgment." I do not suggest that there ought to be an inductive algorithm which avoids the necessity for making reasoned judgments, although because of some of my writings on clinical decision making people have attributed that idea to me. My point is rather that I don't see how cogently "reasoned" a so called "reasoned judgment" can be, when you have ten obfuscators none of which is likely to be of negligible influence in a given research domain, and some of which may be of very strong influence in one subdomain or another, varying a lot from one subdomain to the other, most of them not accurately assessable even in a subdomain let alone in a particular research study reported on, and operating in opposite directions.

Consider a domain in which only two auxiliaries are needed to make the derivation to the predicted empirical result and both are stated explicitly, say, an "input" auxiliary which postulates that a certain experimental manipulation will induce such and such an inferred psychic state in subjects, as in our introversion example above, and only a single "output" auxiliary, such as a piece of psychometric theory about the Rorschach or MMPI. Surely this is a conservative case since, if spelled out in the way we don't because of obfuscator (1), there are likely to be several input and output auxiliaries in most empirical tests of a theory that possesses sufficient conceptual richness to be causally interesting.

Hull and Co.'s famous *Mathematico-deductive theory of rote learning* (1940) is seldom read today even for historical interest because the theory, a kind of tour de force, is pretty well dead. Some poked fun at Hull and his collaborators for going through all of that symbolic logic (one of the collaborators was a mathematical logician brought into the crew specifically for that purpose) as not really necessary. Some critics even called the use of logic "mere window dressing" because Hull was infatuated with philosophy of science. But one thing that book made very clear, which was *not* clear to everybody before, was the fact that when one really requires one's derivation chain to be deductive and rigorous, it turns out one has to put in an awful lot of statements which a nonlogician psychologist would either take for granted or would not even be aware were required to make the derivation. And if such a thing is true in the case of a theory about memorizing nonsense syllables, *a fortiori* it is true in theories about emotion, motivation, social perception, achievement, and the like.

Consider a domain in which the true theory involves a quantitatively moderate effect that would amount to a Pearson correlation of .50 between the observables. Suppose both the input and output auxiliaries have a probability of .85, the *ceteris paribus* clause is moderately dangerous, say its probability is .80, and the experimenter's faithful fulfillment of the conditions as described is .90. The expected value of the mean difference on the output variable cutting the input variable at its median as described above is .80 standard score units, which is 1.74 t units from the value required for a 5% directional significance test, so we have a power of .96. Multiplying the power by the product of the two auxiliaries and of the *ceteris paribus* and experimental conditions gives us a net probability of a "successful" outcome of .59. So of 100 studies conducted in such a domain, we might expect around 59 to come out "positive," meaning a statistically significant result in the predicted direction, and the other 41 to come out negative, that is, adverse to the theory. Suppose that there is a strong bias in submission and editorial acceptance in that all positive studies are submitted and accepted (absent a gross defect in design or analysis which I will for the moment assume is not happening) but only a bare majority of negative studies are submitted. Of those submitted a bare majority are accepted by the editor. So all 59 positive studies are submitted, and all those submitted are accepted, whereas of the 41 negative studies 11 are submitted and accepted. Hence the box score for true theories is $59/(59 + 11) = 84\%$ "successes" in the literature.

Compare that with the case of a wholly false theory, that is, one having zero verisimilitude. While the crud factor in this domain is only .30 or even .25, the use of pilot studies to decide whether to pursue it further results in an effective crud factor in the domain somewhat higher, say, of .40 in those variable pairs that are further pursued by investigators who do not report the pilot studies on the pairs they drop. Then the expected value of the mean standard score difference on the output variable will be $(.40)(1.60) = .64$ which is $1.07\ t$ units from the critical t, yielding a power at the 5% level of .86. If now we assume (neglecting bubba factor, common sense, and the tendency for correlations of variables in the randomly chosen variable pot to be positive) a "pure chance" situation as to directionality, we must divide that power by two, getting a power of .43 on a wholly random pairing. Since this theory has no verisimilitude, the auxiliaries and derivation chain are irrelevant. What we are dealing with is a crud factor probability of a positive result. So of 100 studies conducted 43 come out positive and 57 come out negative. Again, all 43 positive ones are submitted and if their design is otherwise adequate are accepted, whereas of the 57 negative studies $(.51)(.51)(57) = 15$ are accepted. So the box score for this totally false theory is $43/(43 + 15) = 74\%$ "successful" outcomes. On these perhaps somewhat pessimistic but not farfetched assumptions about the domain, *true theories and false theories show box scores in the literature that are only about 10% different from each other*. Surely we cannot suppose that a sympathetic but skeptical reader can interpret *Bulletin* articles meaningfully, realizing that such a domain situation is possible and not wildly improbable? If the reader will plug in some other values he will, I think, be impressed with how wildly the box score percentages can bounce around as a function of trustworthiness of auxiliaries and the extent to which the use of pilot studies has led to an exclusion of those variables whose crud factor is low. Without making outlandish assumptions, one can show that in one domain the box score for theories with zero verisimilitude could run higher than for a perfectly true theory in some other domain.

One of the biggest contributions to this frightening possibility is in the economics and sociology of science. Differences in availability of money for currently popular fads being studied by highly visible psychologists, and the pronounced differences among theories and domains with respect to the ease of increasing statistical power by boosting N, will mean that a prestigious investigator, who has an easy time getting a grant and whose method of study is questionnaires, is going to get a lot of mileage out of the crud factor compared with a graduate student, little known investigator, or someone working in a currently not popular domain and whose data are of an experimental nature or involve extensive testing of individuals, so that the purely logistic and temporal difficulties of accumulating a large df mean that the researcher will have a lot more trouble eking out statistical significance on the basis of the crud factor. The investigator may have so much trouble reaching statistical significance even for a high verisimilitude theory that the expected value of the box score is actually lower than for a false theory in a domain of the other sort.

These are not far-out, nightmare, implausible occurrences. I am not relying on the fact that the statistician tells us in advance that once in a while we will be committing a Type I error, which is not the point at all. Type I errors in the mathematical sense have not been adduced at any point in this paper and will not be. We could add insult to injury by including considerations about the prior probability of substantive theories in soft psychology, which if one goes by the track record of history must be considerably less than one half and, as I read the record, would be running down around 10%, if that high. For example, in my youth there were a half dozen major theories of animal learning (Hull, Guthrie, Tolman, Skinner, etc.) and a few minor ones, all of which I think it fair to say have been refuted, although some are capable of covering more of the fact domain than others. If the track record for theories of rat learning suggests a prior probability of truth (or of verisimilitude high enough to remain in the running after a generation of research) as low as .16, I cannot get myself to believe that the corresponding prior probability for theories in personology, psychodynamics, or social psychology is higher than that. If the likelihood ratio of a theory on its evidence at a given time were as high as 2 to 1 (based on the conditional probabilities given my obfuscating factors), but we take into account that the prior on any given theory for either truth or very high verisimilitude is, say, only one in 10, then the Bayes Formula posterior probability on the theory having high verisimilitude is still only .20, so that the odds are still running 4 to 1 against! But since many psychologists seem to think that the prior on theories in soft psychology is pretty good—I cannot for the life of me understand why they think this, either from armchair grounds or from the track record of our field—I will forego further discussion of that aspect of the problem. One does not have to be a Bayesian in one's view of statistical inference to accept the statistical reasoning on which this paper relies.

Students and colleagues sometimes respond to these pessimistic notions by saying, in effect, "Well, I don't know *exactly* what's wrong with the reasoning of

Bakan, Lykken, Meehl, Rozeboom, and Co. (Bakan, 1966; Lykken 1968; Meehl, 1967, 1978; Rozeboom, 1960) but it's obvious that there must be something wrong with it, because significance testing has worked fine in agronomy, which is where R. A. Fisher developed most of it." I do not know whether Sir Ronald was impressed by the progress of theories in psychology and sociology. I have been told that he looked upon them with considerable disdain, but I am unaware of any published statements to this effect. The reader should not reassure himself by *ad verecundiam* in the name of the great R. A. Fisher, with whom I am not in any kind of technical mathematical combat (a combat I would be certain to lose). Assuming it true that significance testing enabled great strides to be made in agronomy (I am acquainted with a biometrician who has doubts on that score which I am not competent to assess), this cannot provide reassurance with regard to my ten obfuscators in testing theories in soft psychology because there are several differences between the two domains. These differences are intimately connected, but they do represent different ways of looking at the problem, so I will distinguish them without pressing the possibility that they can be reduced to one core difference. That might not be persuasive to some readers, and there is no harm in separating them even if they do have a deep common root.

The first difference is that investigating whether manure is better than potash for fertilizing corn is essentially a technological question rather than the testing of a substantive theory, unless the term *theory* is used in a broader sense than that which this chapter is about. The efficacy of a fertilizer on plant growth is a question similar to a comparison of two sulfonamides in the treatment of strep throat, or the question asked a quality control statistician requested to determine at a fixed confidence level whether more than 2% of the cartridges manufactured by an ammunition factory are defective.

Second, experimenters in agronomy develop a somewhat implicit lore about the subject matter which includes a rough range of economically and logistically feasible values of the manipulated variable, as well as plausible empirical bounds on the output increments. Thus, no one proposes to apply potassium nitrate in a density of a pound per square yard, and no one expects to quintuple the yield of wheat from any economically feasible amount of fertilizer. Even a statistician who, due to strong Fisherian identifications, has a distaste for the decision theoretical term *power,* has a pretty good idea of the number of plots in a design of a certain logical complexity that is likely to be needed to detect a difference of the size that the agronomist cares about as worthwhile. If we get a 2% increase in wheat yield using fertilizer F_1 over fertilizer F_2 when the more effective one is 20% more expensive to the farmer, we are not going to fool around with such a thing. A comparable "reasonable range" of either input or output usually does not exist, or at least is not as narrowly demarcated, in the case of testing theories in soft psychology. This problem of the selection of appropriate levels of experimental factors remains an unsolved problem of psychological methodology despite the important methodological contribution of Brunswik (1947) concerned with representative design. The great majority of investigators in theoretical psychology pay very little attention to Brunswik's powerful arguments, so that after all these years most investigators will focus all of their planning concerning representativeness on that of the sample of organisms, negligible attention being paid to representativeness or stratification of the experimental factors. whether manipulated or differential.

Third, my thesis concerns nonmanipulated factors either as main influences or as potentiators of a manipulated factor in an interaction effect. Agronomy deals with *experiments,* not correlational studies of purely cross-sectional data. Even the corresponding variable, the "individual differences" variable, which belongs one might say to the micro-regions of soil or to the grains of wheat seed, is in agronomy not quite like psychology because wheat strains can and will be chosen for *appropriate economic inference* after the experiment is done, which need not involve any problem of representativeness of design.

Fourth, and this is the most interesting methodologically, as I have pointed out elsewhere (Meehl, 1978), *there is a negligible difference between the substantive theory of interest and the counter null hypothesis in agronomy, whereas in theoretical soft psychology they are distinctly different and frequently separated by what one could call a large "logical distance."* If I am testing Festinger's theory of dissonance or Meehl's theory of schizoidia or Freud's theory of dreams by a correlational study in soft psychology, the propositions of the substantive theory, even taken jointly with their implications, are not the logical equivalent of the statistical hypothesis of a directional difference which I attempt to prove by refuting a directional null hypothesis. The unfortunate conflation of these two things in statistics courses, in which the word 'hypothesis' is used throughout as if one did not have to worry about this critical distinction, leads the psychologist who does not reflect upon the epistemology of the situation to think of them as nearly the same, although very few would maintain that error on reflection. The psychologist often does something he has been taught not to do in the statistics course, namely, he thinks of the "opposite" or "alternative" to the null hypothesis as somehow constituting the hypothesis he is testing, and as a result he is tempted to think (despite the undergraduate statistics class warnings) that if the t test, F test, chi-square, or whatever has a probability only .05 of arising on the null hypothesis, then it's "sort of true" that he can be 95% confident that the alternative—which he then translates as the directional difference—is true. Then, because he does not distinguish theory and hypothesis clearly, it seems (vaguely) as if he can be 95% confident that his substantive theory is true. Nobody who got an "A" in a statistics course is likely to make the first of these mistakes, although one frequently runs across persons who can be seduced into saying something close to that on a PhD oral. But even if he avoids making the first of those mistakes, or tries to legitimate it on some Bayesian ground that Fisher would not approve of, he still may attach the confidence level to the substantive theory. The point is that one does not have to make an explicit mistake in undergraduate statistical formulation to make a more subtle mistake of thinking (roughly and inexplicitly) that somehow if the probability of getting what we got is very small if there were no difference, then we can be quite confident that there is a difference, and then we equate the existence of a difference with the theory that suggested the difference to us. Consequently, without exactly taking the complement to the significance level as our theory-confidence, we nevertheless think it must be "quite large," as long as the significance level we have achieved is "quite small."

I am convinced that both among students and faculty this inexplicit, surreptitious carry-over of a confidence, of a strength of belief in the substantive theory because it is vaguely associated in one's mind with the statistical hypothesis that is considered the alternative to the directional H_0, is quite common. I suggest this is only partly because of the fact that statistics books and lectures in elementary statistics use the word 'hypothesis' in a somewhat indiscriminate way, not highlighting the difference between a substantive (causal, structural, or compositional) theory and a statistical hypothesis about numerical values of observables. It is also because only a minority of social scientists ever take a course in either philosophy of science or freshman logic, so they don't get exposed to the logician's business about inductive inference being an invalid syllogistic figure. As everyone learns in beginning logic, while *modus ponens* and *modus tollens* are valid syllogistic figures, what used to be called the ordinary "confirmation" hypothetical syllogism $p \rightarrow q, q, \therefore p$ is, alas, deductively invalid and at first blush appears to be the form of inference in empirical science. As one of the logic texts I studied as an undergraduate neatly put it, "Elementary logic books are divided into two parts. In the first part, on deductive inference, the formal fallacies are explained; in the second half, on inductive inference, they are committed." To go into the current state of confirmation theory is beyond the scope of this paper and my competence. However, when social scientists are not sufficiently alerted to the elementary logic that the inductive inference is a formally invalid figure, they sometimes talk as if they thought there was some kind of solid gold *proof* possible using an inductive inference, of a kind which philosophers agree cannot exist. That this is not an imaginary danger is shown by the frequency with which criticisms of research studies that conclude for a certain theory contain sentences like "But merely because X correlates with Y does not prove that . . . ." which, given the nature of inductive logic, is a trivial remark unless expanded in a form that explains why such and such an observational result does not tend strongly to *confirm* or *corroborate* a substantive theory, which is presumably what the writer wanted to say and would have said had he been more sophisticated in the logician's terminology.

But, it may be objected, we were supposed to be explaining why theory testing by null hypothesis refutation in soft psychology may be a rather weak and misleading strategy despite the success of that approach in agronomy. Don't these troubles about formal logic and the inherent fallibility of all inductive inference apply equally strongly there? The rebuttal to this objection takes us to the heart of my doctrine in this paper. While all ten of the obfuscators play important roles in causing trouble for the investigator of a psychological theory, and while the fact that they are so numerous, variable, and countervailing makes the task of unscrambling well-nigh hopeless in some domains, this point about the logical distance between statistical hypothesis and substantive theory, *when combined with the crud factor,* introduces a difference between correlational theory testing in soft psychology and experimental manipulation in agronomy that amounts to a difference of kind and not of degree. If I don't manage to convince readers of anything else in this chapter, I will have succeeded in large part if I convince them of this radical qualitative difference. It is precisely the logical distance between the statistical hypothesis and the substantive theory, when combined with the ubiquity of nonzero correlations, that makes the strategy radically defective and probably not improvable, even if the other obfuscators could be eliminated or greatly reduced in their size and influence.

When one has distinguished clearly a substantive theory from a statistical hypothesis (*which in agronomy is a "hypothesis" subject to problematic induction only because of sampling error—not* because the subject matter is about hypothetical constructs or unobserved events in the past, as in psychology) both in his concepts and his semantic habits, one sees the following point immediately: Suppose our null hypothesis in agronomy (or medical testing or quality control or any of those minimally theoretical, mainly technological domains to which statistics is applied) is that "potash makes no difference to wheat yield," or "tetracycline makes no difference to strep throat," or "there are not more than $\frac{1}{10}$th of 1% defective cartridges in this batch." We neglect the possibility that potash or tetracycline has an adverse effect. (If preferred, reformulate the null hypothesis as a directional null hypothesis to the effect that "potash either has no effect on the growth of corn or affects it adversely.") Despite the vagueness of the directional null, including not merely H_0: d = 0 but everything on the wrong side of it (which led Fisher not to like this form), it is a matter of logic, independent of one's statistical orientation or the power function or anything else, that the directional null and its counter null exhaust the possibilities. If the directional null "potash has no effect or an adverse effect" is false, it follows as the night the day that the counter null "potash has a positive effect" must be true.

But, you may say, I have surreptitiously shifted from a statistical to a causal statement. Yes, so I have, because it is so easy *and harmless* in this instance. Between the statement "plots of corn fertilized with potash differ from plots of corn not fertilized with potash" stated in purely statistical terms without reference to causation, and the substantive "theory" of interest, that "putting potash on plots of corn seeds increases the yield of corn," is not a difference that anybody but a philosopher cares about. It's not a difference that makes a difference. Even a philosopher, if he is a philosopher of science talking about methodology, would allow himself to move freely back and forth between the statistical counter null and the causal substantive "theory" that potash helps you to grow more corn. *Except in a seminar on Hume, nobody bothers to distinguish between the counter null hypothesis and the causal conjecture in agronomy.* Not a farmer, a professor of agricultural economics, the sales director of a fertilizer manufacturing company, or a politician in India cares one whit about the fine-line distinction between "fertilized plots have a bigger yield" and "fertilizer produces a bigger yield." The nature of the problem and our general background knowledge guarantee that there will be no difference between these two that's worth talking about unless you were discussing Hume and the metaphysics of causality in a philosophy seminar. For example, nobody in his right mind thinks that the harvesting of the corn in the late summer exerts backward causality upon what we did in the spring about fertilizing plots, let alone the fact that the process was based upon a table of random numbers! Plants take the substance they use in growing from the air and soil; for heaven's sake where else would they get it from? Long before modern biochemistry every farmer, going back to thousands of years B.C., became unavoidably aware of the fact that some soil was "better soil" than others for growing purposes. Whether we start with the background knowledge of horticulturists, botanists, and biochemists, or the background knowledge of my sainted grandmother who never finished the third grade, we *know* that plants get their nutriment from the soil. Today we also know scientifically about the fixation of nitrogen, etc. If we put chemical compounds or animal products that contain nitrate radicals that can go into solution into the ground, it does not take a PhD in physical chemistry to figure out that this might be a plausible way for plants to grow better.

But I don't want to engage in overkill. The simple and obvious point is that there is no appreciable difference between the semantic content of the counter null hypothesis (proven with the same confidence with which we have refuted the directional null) and the "substantive theory" that there is a causal connection between fertilizer and yield. If a certain fertilizer has no effect on a certain type of plant, or if two different fertilizers have an equal effect, the null hypothesis will be literally true, and we will correctly fail to refute it except for Type I errors in 5% of the cases if that is our alpha level. Neither of these two things obtains in soft psychology. There is a vast difference, involving numerous intervening steps and auxiliary assumptions, between "Meehl's theory of schizotaxia is substantially correct" and "Many schizophrenics show a ± dysdiadochokinesia." Second, the improbability of statistically refuting H_0 set at some high significance level is equal to that significance level when H_0 is literally true, but the improbability of successfully refuting it at that same level is much different in a domain where everything is correlated and where the crud factor is not of negligible size.

Another way of looking at the problem is in terms of the existing competitor theories, some formulated, some easily formulable with a little imagination. For most statistical findings in soft psychology studies, I daresay a group of faculty or graduate students could come up with a dozen plausible alternatives to the theory of interest if allowed a morning's conversation over coffee and Danish, whereas in the agronomy case there are no such plausible alternatives. If somebody in agronomy were to say, "Well, since you have refuted the null hypothesis at such a small alpha level, and several other people have replicated your result, I grant that fertilized plots in England, India, and Iowa yield more corn. But that doesn't conclusively *prove* (= *demonstrate,* deductively) that the fertilizer had anything to do with it," the obvious reply would be an incredulous, "Oh, strictly speaking we haven't a deduction, but what in the devil else would you have in mind?" and to this counter question no sane option would be forthcoming in the agronomy case. If that same counter question were put in discussing Meehl's theory of schizotaxia, Festinger's theory of cognitive dissonance, Freud's theory of dreams, Schachter's theory of affiliation, or other theories in soft psychology, it would not be difficult for the questioner to come up with alternatives. Even if one did not have enough imagination or smarts to come up with plausible looking alternatives, he could always say simply, "Well, there are always alternative explanations of anything complicated, we take that for granted in science and in philosophy, do we not?" Meehl, Festinger, Schachter or whoever would have to say "yes" to that, whether or not the questioner was motivated and ingenious about inventing specific competing theories.

Despite the current technical problems in confirmation theory among philosophers of science, there is nothing obscure or recondite about the point I am making here. It is not commonly seen because of the way null hypothesis testing is taught in statistics courses, but it is not difficult to see. If I refute a directional null hypothesis in agronomy or in a biochemical medical treatment, I thereby prove (in a strong although not strictly deductive sense of that term) the counter null; and the counter null is essentially equivalent to the substantive theory of interest, namely, that fertilizer makes a difference to corn, or tetracycline to strep throats. If you have "almost conclusively proved" the one, you have "almost conclusively proved" the other. But a complex substantive theory involving hypothetical psychological entities, states, and processes, conjectured residues of past learnings in the life history, latent contents underlying dreams or parapraxes, "factors" influencing the correlations of psychometric instruments— here it is not strong "proof" of anything to refute either the point or the directional H_0, because of the crud factor. So that whatever theory we happen to be talking about, we know that the correlations will *not* be zero, and that we will *show* them not to be zero given sufficient statistical power. Hence, (nearly) definitive falsification of the directional null hypothesis, while it (nearly) conclusively proves the directional counter null (taken literally, a trivial result given the crud factor, except for the directionality), does *not* thereby prove with high confidence the truth of the substantive theory. *The substantive theory has a host of alternatives,* some of which are interesting theoretically, some of which are not, and *most of which nobody has thought of* but could in a morning's free-wheeling speculation. That is simply not the case in agronomy, or the testing of the therapeutic efficacy of a drug, or sampling from a batch of rifle cartridges.

I believe that the foregoing line of argument, although it may be subject to some degree of quantitative correction here and there, is unanswerable. I have been teaching it to classes of doctoral candidates for 20 years, aided and abetted by a couple of Bayesian statisticians who come in as guest lecturers, and I have not heard a strong objection, reply, or "effective softening of the blow" yet. Nor have I heard such from colleagues with whom I have conversed or corresponded. I am inclined to think that if 300 doctoral candidates at a first-rate psychology department, not to mention several PhD candidates in statistics, psychometrics and philosophy of science who have taken the course, and perhaps two dozen eminent psychologists who have been exposed to these ideas in similar form, have not come up with an answer to this line of thought, then if it is not substantially correct it must contain a mistake of great depth and subtlety. In what follows I shall therefore allow myself the assumption that, pending better instruction and until further notice, I am correct in viewing these ten obfuscators as strong, variable, countervailing, and from case to case not accurately estimated, supporting my thesis that: Null hypothesis testing of correlational predictions from weak substantive theories in soft psychology is subject to the influence of ten obfuscating factors whose effects are usually (1) sizeable, (2) opposed, (3) variable, and (4) unknown. The net epistemic effect of these ten obfuscating influences is that the usual research literature review is well-nigh uninterpretable.

I do not subscribe to the pollyanna doctrine that one should not engage in "purely destructive criticism" if he doesn't have anything to offer instead. There is such a thing as killing a theory even though one is not prepared to advocate another one, although admittedly the ideal Popperian case is two theories in competition which are sufficiently strong so that the corroboration of one theory by a risky point prediction involves observing a numerical value that slays the other theory *modus tollens.* I am prepared to argue that a tremendous amount of taxpayer money goes down the drain in research that pseudotests theories in soft psychology, and that it would be a material social advance as well as a reduction in what Lakatos has called "intellectual pollution" (Lakatos, 1970, fn. 1, p. 176) if we would quit engaging in this feckless enterprise. I think that if psychologists would face up to the full impact of the above criticisms, something worthwhile would have been achieved in convincing them of it. Besides, before one can motivate many competent persons to improve an unsatisfactory cognitive situation by some judicious mixture of more powerful testing strategies and criteria for setting aside a complex substantive theory as "not presently testable," it is necessary to face the fact that the present state of affairs is unsatisfactory.

My experience has been that most graduate students, and many professors, engage in a mix of defense mechanisms (most predominantly, denial), so that they can proceed as they have in the past with a good scientific conscience. The usual response is to say, in effect, "Well, that Meehl is a clever fellow and he likes to philosophize, fine for him, it's a free country. But since we are doing all right with the good old tried and true methods of Fisherian statistics and null hypothesis testing, and since journal editors do not seem to have panicked over such thoughts, I will stick to the accepted practices of my trade union and leave Meehl's worries to the statisticians and philosophers." I cannot strongly fault a 45 year old professor for adopting this mode of defense, even though I believe it to be intellectually dishonest, because I think that for most faculty in soft psychology the full acceptance of my line of thought would involve a painful realization that one has achieved some notoriety, tenure, economic security and the like by engaging, to speak bluntly, in a bunch of nothing. It is a bit much to expect that of anybody, even a psychology professor. In the case of graduate students, I find to my surprise a little more open mindedness on the point, although it can mean that a student has to change his doctoral dissertation topic from something that is more theoretically interesting to something less so but testable. It is my belief, after 45 years on the faculty at Minnesota, that well over half of the doctoral dissertations in soft psychology that are set up with the intention of testing an interesting causal theory are incapable of doing so. I don't see how any fair-minded person could dispute this who has sat on PhD final orals, even without having read my list of obfuscators!

However, despite my firm insistence that purely negative criticism of an intellectual boondoggle leading to Lakatos's "intellectual pollution" in the journals is an important form of academic husbandry, I do have some tentative suggestions for improving the situation. I am afraid that the best and clearest of them are still of a "negative" sort (e.g., critical editorial policies), but some of them offer a possibility of positive advance.

For Investigators.   Psychologists attempting to test a substantive theory in soft psychology should strive for a rationale by which an expected *amount* of effect could be predicted from the theory. Point values are ideal, but even in physics and astronomy they are surrounded by a tolerance based on an estimate of the experimental error. One hopes that when enough persons become sufficiently skeptical about the weak corroboration provided by merely showing that the X's get higher scores than the Y's, that cheap and easy derivation might be replaced by one that says something about the range of non-null differences that would be consistent with the theory. At the very least, one might say that a theory accounting for less than such and such percent of the reliable variance is an uninteresting theory and does not deserve high priority for investigation, except for special consideration (e.g., a weak correlate of psychopathology that could serve as a genetic marker). I don't deny that there are cases in which small effects play a critical role in theory testing. But those are special cases in science. Because of the crud factor's ubiquity, merely saying that "there ought to be a difference between A and B" is such a feeble test of anything, and we ought to work harder than we usually do to come up with some statement about points and ranges.

We should pay attention to Jacob Cohen's advice; given the bad effect of multiplying doubtful auxiliaries and *ceteris paribus* by the power function, I would push for higher statistical power than he did, perhaps saying that if you want to have a test of a theory you ought to set your sample size at a power of .9 or better. If there are two or more measures of a trait, the experimental or correlational design should include a discrepancy analysis in relation to interaction. I do not know whether a "standard" statistical method for doing this exists. Pilot studies ought to be fully reported and it should be emphasized in methodology courses that there is an ethical obligation, if one has done one or more pilot studies, *particularly pilot studies that were used to reject a possible line of investigation,* to publish all pilot studies that led the investigator to perform a large-scale investigation. Even now, tradition requires that an unsuccessful attempt to replicate the main study should be reported, yet people do not always publish.

For Editors, Referees, Journals.   It would be helpful if journal editors regularly imposed the requirement of a successful replication, with certain exceptions such as studies that are terribly costly, or diseases that are very rare, or procedures that are dangerous. All statistical tables should be required to include means and standard deviations, rather than merely a *t, F,* or chi-square, or even worse only statistical significance. A table, offered for theoretical interpretation or for proposed clinical application of some device or procedure, that is confined to stating the significance level achieved and does not allow the reader to look at overlap, is as misleading and incomplete scientific reporting as failing to say from where you got your subjects, or how they were chosen, or what their instructions were. I don't look upon this as a minor refinement that is merely pleasing to a perfectionist statistician. I look upon it as correcting a fundamental defect in our present habits (not true 30 or 40 years ago in psychology) resulting from overemphasis of null hypothesis refutation. Confidence intervals for parameters ought regularly to be provided. If they cannot be, it should be said why not. In many circumstances it is possible to make a reasonable estimate of the percentage of variance accounted for by a given factor.

If the theory bears on some clinical problem such as a correlate or possible indirect indicator of a conjectured causal source for schizophrenia or whatever, appropriate alternative overlap statistics should be presented. A clinician who submits a paper advocating the use of a structured or projective test or some behavioral sample method for a given discrimination in psychopathology and does not offer an appropriate overlap measure is unscholarly. For some purposes Tilton's (1937) overlap measure is all right, but as a clinician I would also impose the requirement—not a mere preference or suggestion by the editor but an absolute requirement as part of complete scientific reporting—that the percent of one group reaching or exceeding the 10th, 50th, and 90th percentile of the other group should routinely be reported.

I think that it would be helpful to have a section of almost every journal reserved for publication of negative pilot studies. The shortest possible statement of the design compatible with scientific adequacy and an absolute minimum of theoretical discussion other than a brief statement of what motivated the pilot study being done, would add to people's yardage in a painless way and greatly increase the presently feeble and sometimes even negative motivation to publish negative pilot studies. This would also indirectly save a great deal of scientific time and taxpayer money. We must surely assume that many pilot studies that come out negative and hence might lead to abandonment of a a once-promising line, probably have been done over and over again, especially at the graduate student level, because students do not know that some other investigator has already tried this and dropped it because he "failed to get an effect." One would have to make these papers short, easy, painless without too rigid criteria on quality, interest, or statistical power function.

For Reviewers.   Mention of statistical power should be obligatory in the review of every negative result. If it is objected that this is too much work for reviewers, then editors ought to adopt a policy of requiring that authors always state the statistical power. The present status of meta-analysis as a formalized method being still in dispute, I would not impose a requirement for it. But I think it fair to suggest that meta-analysis related to the auxiliaries ought to be helpful, even for readers who don't like the approach of Glass and Co. (Glass, McGaw, & Smith, 1981; see also Hunter, Schmidt, & Jackson, 1982). It helps us focus on the culprits, the auxiliaries that might be responsible for giving a good theory a black eye. Reviewers ought to be sophisticated enough to know, and say explicitly in summary, that a mildly positive "box score" of tallies on reaching or failing to reach significance is *not* a strong sign of a theory's verisimilitude. The present reviewing practice is to do such a tally, after explaining away some of the positive and negative findings. Faced with the need to do some sort of integrated summary, the idea seems to be that, if a theory pans out with successful predictions appreciably more often than it fails, the box score speaks strongly in its favor. I cannot imagine any logician agreeing with this practice, as it fails to take into account the basic logical asymmetry between confirmation and falsification, and pays no attention to the above list of obfuscators. Testing a theory in soft psychology in the light of those obfuscators and finding that its batting average is seven to three or six to four in the literature, while not totally worthless, is about as close to worthless as one can get for evaluating the theory's verisimilitude.

For Theoreticians.   I think we should be more optimistic about the possibility of making predictions other than merely non-null difference predictions from rather weak theories. There are examples in the physical sciences in which at a given state of knowledge the theory was too weak or incomplete to permit derivation of numerical values, but was still capable of predicting rough function forms (see e.g., Eisberg, 1961 pp. 49–51 on Wien's law). Sometimes what appear to be extremely weak general qualitative statements, incapable of generating anything numerical, turn out to generate quite interesting quantitative predictions when the applied mathematician goes to work on them, such as the relation of the sizes of certain second derivatives or regions in which there is a turn around or a flex point, or statements of that sort. Catastrophe theory is a recent example of astonishing quantitative richness. We should try harder for intermediate strength theories that, while they might not be capable of yielding point predictions, nevertheless yield statements about signs of derivatives, about inequalities without the parameters being known, about curve shapes, and so forth. It is, for example, sometimes possible to construct latent structural models of situations, as in my own current work in taxometrics, where the theory is far too weak to yield numerical values at the observational level but is still strong enough to yield a statement of numerical *equality* between two computed values based on observation (Meehl, 1973, Meehl & Golden, 1982).

One has the uneasy feeling that if this had been possible in soft psychology, it would have happened more than it has by now. While I cannot definitely refute that argument, I would emphasize that we do not work hard at doing something that is difficult, and different from our accustomed modes of thought, if we think that the way we are now doing it is working just fine! We are familiar with it, the other members of our troop of gregarious primates are busy doing it the same way, people get elected to high professional offices, and others receive various kinds of prizes for doing it this way. It is not surprising that clinical, social, and personality psychologists spend little time trying to figure out whether they could perhaps derive theorems about stronger consequences from semi-qualitative causal, compositional, or structural theories of the mind.

For Teachers and Doctoral Programs. I think that PhDs in psychology should be required to learn a little undergraduate mathematics, which is different from learning cookbook statistics. Inability to think mathematically among psychologists except in certain special areas is sometimes so gross as to be embarrassing to one familiar with the quantitative sophistication in the other sciences. The Minnesota Department has been recommending mathematics courses to its undergraduate majors since I became chairman in 1951, with negligible results. Mathematics is hard, sociology is easy; we will never persuade the majority of psychology majors to take any mathematics unless we combine (a) a little mathematical content *used* and *on the final exams* in the courses they take with (b) explicit math requirements for our majors. Most arts colleges today offer undergraduate mathematics through calculus in a variety of forms, including some that are small in total hours required, and not so heavily geared to traditional problems of the physical sciences (like the volume of footballs) as when I was a student. There is an unfortunate circular feedback here at work. Since psychologists in the soft areas rarely know undergraduate mathematics, they do not think or talk mathematically as teachers, advisors, or research directors. As a result it is only natural that even a competent student forms the notion that for the kind of psychology he wants to do, knowing elementary mathematics is irrelevant. Busy people can hardly be expected to learn something that is a little difficult and quite time-consuming unless they can see its relation to what they intend to do; and they can't see any such relation if their mentors can't do it because they never studied any mathematics either. I entertain the dismal conjecture that this is incurable, since my efforts to cure it (off and on over 45 years) have had negligible local impact.

The question of what kind of mathematics, in connection with which research procedures, psychology students should be thoroughly familiar with (as contrasted with having only a nodding acquaintance or being totally ignorant) is not easy to answer. But the common rationalization of mathematically ignorant psychologists ("Well, I understand the logic of factor analysis even though I don't understand the math") should not be tolerated in intellectually polite circles! The "logic" of a procedure like factor analysis is, of course, mathematical. There simply isn't any way you can "understand the logic" of the varimax solution to the rotation problem if you don't understand why there is a rotation problem. This is nothing but a rationalization by people who don't want to take the trouble to learn a little probability theory, vector algebra, or elementary calculus.

I am not merely being a purist about this. I have sat on PhD orals and read scientific articles by professors of renown that are fallacious in what they do with their quantitative results, because the theorist or investigator was so mathematically naive that it didn't occur to him to ask, for instance, whether a certain function might be decelerated in a region and hence give rise to the appearance of an interaction effect, or whether his abitrary choice of metric might determine the character of his results, or whatever. I would draw the line at requiring a psychologist who wants to use chi-square, for instance, to have fought his way through the proof of the theorems used in constructing the chi-square tables. I don't think that fighting your way through all those gamma and beta functions (though one should know what a gamma function is!) sheds much of any light upon the properties of chi-square. Whereas if a student doesn't know that one of the more general ways of conceiving chi-square is as a composite based upon summing the squares of variables that are themselves Gaussian, or if he doesn't know where that rule of thumb in statistics about "cells should have an expected frequency of 10 or more" comes from in terms of the underlying binomial construct, then he doesn't know what he ought to know as a scientist about his research methods.

I give you an extreme example which I think suffices to show that there is something the matter with psychology in this regard: Can anyone imagine a PhD in physics putting the Schroedinger equation on the blackboard, explaining how he was going to do his experiment in quantum mechanics, and then when asked what that funny little backward curlicue (like sort of a deformed lower case Greek delta) was, saying glibly, "Oh, that's a partial derivative," and when asked what a partial derivative is, saying he didn't know? We don't even have to ask whether he would flunk the exam, because it is simply inconceivable to any informed person that a physics student would not know what a partial derivative is and does. You couldn't get a bachelor's degree in physics at West Overshoe Teacher's College if you didn't know that. Yet I have seen instances where a psychologist's doctoral dissertation consisted of factor analyzing somebody else's data, so that the student did not construct the test items, did not validate the test, did not test the subjects but found them in somebody's file, so that his sole intellectual contribution is that he did a factor analysis. He did it by using the varimax rotation, but when asked what the varimax rotation is can't even tell you who developed it, let alone what it does. You ask him whether he knows the relationship between John B. Carroll's breakthrough and Thurstone's simple structure criterion, and he hasn't a clue. You ask him how the use of fourth powers in this context is analogous to something Karl Pearson did about measuring leptokurtosis, and he hasn't the faintest idea what you're talking about. Now I think to get a PhD by factor analyzing somebody else's test, administered by somebody else, so that your sole contribution is the factor analysis (via canned computer program) and providing a possible conceptual interpretation (usually very weak), when you do not understand the factor analysis, can best be described as scandalous.

It might help to require some reading of classic experiments and theoretical derivations in the other sciences, both biological and physical. I find that many psychologists literally do not know what a good theoretical derivation in a developed cumulative science looks like! While the mediocre students might not be grabbed much by this, I think that superior students will get the point and will become restive about the way in which soft psychology research goes about its business. It doesn't take many examples from chemistry, physics, genetics, physiology, and astronomy for a bright and intellectually alive student to come to the realization that these other scientists really have something in the way they get from the theory to the facts and back that is a lot more impressive—and, importantly for bright people, more intellectually satisfying—than the usual dismal prediction that the null hypothesis is false.

It would help if we could reduce the pathological emphasis on publication rate in regard to salary, tenure, and promotion. One reason for the uncritical reliance on mere null hypothesis refutation as if it constituted a respectable test of the substantive theory is that it is a pretty safe way to spend one's time enroute to a publication. The change in the expectations of how much a student will have published already before his PhD between now and when I was in graduate school 45 years ago is frightening. The pressure is so great that I know students who are not intellectually dull or morally careless, who have sat in my office and said explicitly that while it was subject X that really interested them, they were putting in for a grant to study subject Y "because that's safer, and I'm sure to get grant support." I think this is pitiable. It is not only bad for the student's mental hygiene but in the long run it has a cancerous impact upon the discipline. But speaking either as a clinician or as an observer of the social scene, I am at a loss to suggest any remedy for it given the insane requirement today that nobody can be promoted or tenured in the academy unless he continues to grind out many papers (cf. the provocative and insightful book by Mahoney, 1976). In evaluating faculty for raises, promotion, and tenure, perhaps there should be more emphasis on *Science Citation Index* counts, *Annual Review* mentions, and evaluation by top experts elsewhere rather than on mere publication yardage. The distressing thing about this is that while academics regularly condemn "mere publication count," a week later in a faculty meeting or a Dean's advisory meeting they are *actually counting pages* in comparing Smith with Jones. This is a disease of the professional intellectual, resting upon a vast group delusional system concerning scholarly products, and I know my recommendations in this respect have a negligible chance of being taken or even listened to seriously. Since the null hypothesis refutation racket is "steady work" and has the merits of an automated research grinding device, scholars who are pardonably devoted to making more money and keeping their jobs so that they can pay off the mortgage and buy hamburgers for the wife and kids are unlikely to contemplate with equanimity a criticism that says that their whole procedure is scientifically feckless and that they should quit doing it and do something else. In the soft areas of psychology that might, in some cases, mean that they should quit the academy and make an honest living selling shoes, which people of bookish temperament naturally do not want to do.

Finally, I raise the delicate question—without pressing an answer, which I do not pretend to have—whether we should invest time and dollars in wide-ranging, large scale studies of the crud factor. Colleagues and students who have heard me lecture on the "ten malignant obfuscators" tend to focus on the crud factor magnitude as the weakest component of my argument. "The null hypothesis, taken literally, is always false in correlational (nonexperimental) studies" does not, of course, immediately imply "Pairwise correlations of arbitrarily (= atheoretically) chosen variables in most soft domains tend to run large enough to yield frequent pseudoconfirmations of unrelated substantive theories, given conventional levels of the statistical power function based on pilot studies." I daresay mathematical statisticians would look askance at the question "How big is the crud factor in Domain D?" given the unavoidable vagueness in specifying the variable set. What, one asks, is *the parameter* being estimated? "Estimating the crud factor" sounds too much like trying to find the tonic chord of the Universe.

However, given the sorry state of the art and the gravity of the problem, this attitude may be puristic. After all, we *do* commonly make similar rough-value statements in soft psychology. We allow ourselves to say such things as "SES usually correlates low to moderate with psychometric measures of ability and school achievement"; "Tests of so-called 'mechanical ability' correlate low to moderate and positive"; "Assortative mating coefficients vary from negligible to a high of around .50 and are almost never negative"; "Prediction of college grades (pre-inflation!) seems to have an upper limit, with a half-dozen predictors in the regression equations, of around .70." Such summary statements do not purport to be precise, but they are surely not empty of empirical content, nor are they useless. Since the proper baseline in testing substantive theories is not H_0 but the crud factor in a domain, so that a theory's "doing better than chance" is closer to "beating out the crud factor" than it is to "correlating nonzero," it is arguable that even a crude range estimate of the crud factor in a domain would be worth having. It requires very large N's, sizeable variable sets qualitatively heterogeneous and chosen with minimal theory in mind. Such data are hard to come by. How narrowly to specify "a domain" is a tough problem, and methods covariance within a domain (structured tests, projectives, interviews, ratings, ward behavior samples, work products, critical incidents, demographics, life-history facts) would surely not be equal. We might want to "bootstrap" the domain specification partly *post hoc,* in light of the mean and dispersion of pairwise correlations. It would be a lot of work and infected with much arbitrariness. Whether the resulting collection of crud factor values classified by domains and methods would be worth the trouble I am not prepared to say, although I lean slightly to "Yes" and will leave it at that.

All of these possible methods of improvement should be tried. In addition there is a more fundamental philosophical point to be raised, which I have moral conflict about raising in my seminar every year and require reassurance about "tough love" from my colleague Lykken to get me to do it. *We should accustom ourselves and our students to the idea that there are some interesting causal theories in the soft areas that cannot presently be researched,* and it is arguably wrong to waste the taxpayer's money in state supported institutions to pretend to do it. I may mention briefly here, without strong proofs, a methodological issue in social science that deserves an article as long as this chapter in its own right. There exists an implicit misconception, ubiquitous among students and professors studying soft areas, which could be cured or at least ameliorated by more extensive reading in the histories of the physical and biological sciences, together with a small dose of up-to-date philosophy of science. This misconception is that, if a theoretical conjecture is "scientifically meaningful" (not theological or metaphysical or so vague as to cover anything), then it must be possible to test it at the present time. Even a slight familiarity with the history of astronomy, physics, chemistry, medicine, and genetics shows that such a metatheoretical notion is plainly false. These other sciences are replete with examples of perfectly good "empirical" questions, askable by sophisticated scientists at a given point in time, it being realized that they could not be answered either because of deficiencies in the required auxiliary theories, or the lack of an adequate instrumentation, whether for control of variables on the one side or, more commonly, measurement of variables on the other. A classical example of this for historians of science is August Comte's (originator of "positivism" and usually considered the founder of sociology) description of the transition of human knowledge through the three phases of the theological or fictitious, the metaphysical or abstract, and the scientific or positive. Comte said that in the scientific or positive intellectual mode, it was obvious that there were certain things that human beings could never learn, such as the chemical constitution of the stars. For Comte, writing in the first part of the 19th century, the only way to find out the chemical constitution of any material body was to perform certain testing operations upon it in the laboratory such as exposure to reagents, litmus tests, and direct determination of precise weights and measures. Since one cannot put Alpha Centauri in a beam balance, or drop a chunk of it into a chemical retort, it seemed blindingly obvious to Comte that one could not ever find out its chemical constitution. It never occurred to him that the stars being hot gases that give off light, and the spectrum of light from an incandescent source indicating its chemical elements (spectroscopy had not been discovered in 1835), there could be an indirect way of determining their chemical compositions. He would have been stupefied to learn that this method is so precise that we know the percentage of various elements in the sun with a higher precision than we do for our own earth. A contemporary example from astronomy would be Feyerabend's suggestion about possible nonrelativistic departures from the Newtonian predictions of planetary motions, some of which might be explainable by a slightly altered estimate of the sun's oblateness, the measurement problem being that as the sun is not a smooth cue ball from a billiard table, we cannot by any instruments or methods available to us, or likely ever to become available, determine the oblateness of the sun to the accuracy that would be required. The most dramatic example from biological science in recent times, and one of the two or three greatest scientific discoveries ever made, is Crick and Watson's theory of the DNA. No amount of theoretical ingenuity would have enabled them to do this, let alone test it, until chemical methods were sufficiently precise to be able to show that in any organism the adenine and thymine are always precisely equal in the number of molecules present, as are the guanine and cytosine. It would not suffice to show that they are "correlated" or more or less equal. The important thing was demonstrating that the associated base pair were always precisely matched in number of molecules, to within a minuscule error of measurement. Nor would it have been possible to formulate such a theory in the first place until there was sufficient knowledge about the structure of these four organic bases, including exact details of the angles and distances between their component atoms, so that one could do the right kind of theoretical fiddling that Crick and Watson did for hours on end with their model pieces of cardboard and tin to see how they could fit together and have the right amount of stability. Finally, it was necessary that the technology of X-ray observation of extremely small physical systems should be so advanced that Wilkins could get pictures sufficiently detailed and clear to corroborate the conjectured helical structure. Even if somebody had by divine inspiration concocted the correct theory of DNA immediately after Thomas Hunt Morgan and collaborators presented the theory of the gene (40 years earlier), *there would have been no possibility of empirically testing it.* In physicists' current discussion of quarks and gluons, or astronomers' discussions about the Big Bang and about black holes, there are questions constantly being raised to which the answer is, "Yes, that's an interesting conjecture, but unfortunately we have no way of testing it at the present time, and perhaps we never will."

How do psychologists and sociologists come to be blind to this familiar fact about the more developed sciences, concerning the limitations on testing theories imposed by incompletely developed auxiliary theories and absence of measurement technologies? Some of my behaviorist friends consider it a fatal defect of Freud's theories of dreams or parapraxes that they cannot be presently tested in a rigorous quantitative manner, a claim with which I largely and cheerfully agree. I think that in order to test Freud's theories regarding the guiding of free associations during a psychoanalytic hour following the patient's presentation of the manifest content of a dream (see Meehl, 1970, 1983) we would probably require a more suitable type of statistical analysis than we presently have available, plus a well worked out and highly corroborated auxiliary theory of psycholinguistics, which we also do not have today. I think there are two reasons for mistakenly supposing that any "scientifically meaningful" or "truly empirical" theory must, if one is determined and ingenious, be strongly testable at the present time, over and above the optimism required to stay in the publishing business. First, there is the residue (or even the unmodified form) of 1929 operationism and logical positivism, which made the strange mistake of tying the very meaning or content of a scientific theory with the method of its verification. If one combines this notion of translation with insistence upon an available verification method, and then further ignores the distinction that even the Vienna Positivists made between logical unverifiability, empirical unverifiability, and technical unverifiability at a given point in time, it seems to follow that if a theory is "meaningful" (i.e., not metaphysical or theological or tautological) by positivist standards, then it is *ipso facto* testable.

Suppose one abandons the notion of complete conceptual reducibility of all concepts to observable predicates or functors, hence sentence verifiability as a meaning criterion, and hence operationism as a requirement for theoretical definitions. A proper subset of theoretical concepts may be operationally defined, but the great majority of them are not so, being defined only contextually by the mathematical network, if such exists, along with the interpretative text, that text *not* being confined to ostensive linkages. Even if one accepts the last ditch positivist effort at defining an empirical meaning criterion (Carnap, 1956), it says that a theoretical term is meaningful because it appears in at least one derivation chain somewhere. This gives rise to a *concept empiricism* upon which a *statement empiricism* is erected. Roughly, this says that, if a theoretical statement is well formed syntactically from such meaningful concepts (and perhaps certain further metaconstraints semantically?), then the statement is scientifically meaningful, even if it does not itself appear in a derivation chain terminating in a pure observational statement and, hence, is neither confirmable or falsifiable. If cross-eyedness is recessive in the Siamese cat (I have not looked this one up but its correctness doesn't matter in our example), and a neutered stray cat of unknown lineage comes to live with us the question "Does he carry the recessive gene for cross-eyes?" is a perfectly legitimate scientifically meaningful query, although we have no means of answering it.

Now if a pre-1956 statement empiricism is subscribed to uncritically, as it is by many psychologists raised in an outdated philosophy of science, a person so mal-instructed can then start with the old notion that if a sentence is scientifically meaningful it must be completely reducible to observational statements. He then connects these observational statements with some counter null statistical hypothesis, so that he thinks that proving the one proves the other. It follows that any meaningful theoretical statement you can make must be testable by H_0-refutation on appropriate data. Whereas the truth of the matter is that many meaningful theories, including theories that most of us would consider quite interesting intellectually and of great theoretical importance to find out about, simply cannot be tested at the present time, either because they are embedded in a vast net of highly problematic auxiliaries and *ceteris paribus* clauses or because we have no adequate technology of measurement. Sometimes a theory is untestable because the technology is too loose (as in the obfuscator about detached validation claim above), or sometimes it's because there is literally no measure available.

I frequently have the experience where a student asks me to serve on a doctoral examining committee, tells me about a design aimed at testing a theory in soft psychology, and my heart sinks as I listen. A great cloud of cognitive gloom descends upon me, because the thought that keeps coming into my mind is "You can't test it like that, you'll just never manage to test it like that." But if I try to explain to the student why it can't be tested, he takes me to mean that it somehow is an illegitimate theory, or a theory that is "metaphysical" or permanently beyond our ken, which is not my claim at all. The problem is that the majority of theories in soft psychology are related to the data in somewhat the same way as the constitution of the stars was to the data extant before anybody discovered spectroscopy in the terrestrial lab. *Point: We should maturely and sophisticatedly accept the fact that some perfectly legitimate "empirical" scientific theories may not be strongly testable at a given time, and that it is neither good scientific strategy nor a legitimate use of the taxpayer's dollar to pretend otherwise.*

ADDENDUM

Local readers of this manuscript have asked why I do not discuss meta-analysis (Glass, McGaw, & Smith, 1981; Hunter, Schmidt, & Jackson, 1982), and I would not want to leave the impression that I am unaware of it or view it unfavorably. On the contrary, I think meta-analysis is one of the most important methodological contributions of this generation of psychologists, arguably *the* most important, and have so stated to Professor Glass in our correspondence. This paper could be viewed as helping make the meta-analysts' case against the conventional narrative, impressionistic, "box-score" approach to reviewing research. However, the chief reasons for my not discussing meta-analysis were these:

1. Meta-analysis has become a highly technical ramified system of conceptual and mathematical issues, many articles and several whole books being devoted to it. To discuss these matters briefly and superficially would be inappropriate. To do it in depth is precluded by space limits on an already longish chapter, as well as being beyond my statistical competence.

2. Meta-analysis was developed to study outcomes of interventions (e.g., influence of class size, efficacy of psychotherapy or psychotropic drugs) rather than as a method of appraising the verisimilitude of substantive theories. We do not normally assume *theoretical corroboration* to be a monotone function, even stochastically, of *effect size;* and in developed sciences an observed value can, of course, be "too large" as often as "too small."

3. A representative ("typical") effect size, whether of aggregated or disaggregated studies, is interpreted or qualified in meta-analysis via estimates of its standard error, emphasizing its trustworthiness as a numerical value. This statistical stability (under the laws of chance) is a very different question from how closely the effect approximates to a theoretically predicted value. More importantly, it does not ask how "risky" the latter was in terms of the theoretically tolerated interval, in relation to the *a priori* range of possibilities. These two questions, taken jointly as the basis of theoretical appraisal, require a different approach from that of evaluating technological outcomes in a pragmatic context.

Whether a quantitative index of the "corroborative increment" given a theory by a particular experiment is constructable is doubtful, but I am currently exploring that notion (Meehl, 1990). Briefly: A theory predicts an interval, I (= intrinsic tolerance) for a numerical value observable in a specified experimental setup. (The intrinsic tolerance could be widened by the standard error, or by 2 SE [based on the data], to yield an adjusted tolerance, but I do not favor that adjustment.) The ratio of this to the *a priori* range of values S (= *Spielraum*) is termed the relative tolerance, I/S; and the latter's complement $(1 - I/S)$ is the theory's intolerance, In (i.e., the Popperian experimental prediction risk). The deviation D of the observed value x_o from the edge of the tolerated interval is also divided by S to give the relative accuracy, D/S. Then the corroborative increment associated with this experiment is defined as $C_i = (1 - D/S)(1 - I/S)$. Over m studies, the statistics (m, M_C, σ_C) jointly provide a basis for appraising the theory, and disaggregating with respect to fact domains should provide leads for modifying the theory, auxiliaries, or *ceteris paribus* clauses.

REFERENCES

Bakan, D. (1966). The test of significance in psychological research. *Psychological Bulletin, 66,* 423–437.

Brunswik, E. (1947). *Systematic and representative design of psychological experiments.* (University of California Syllabus Series, No. 304) Berkeley, CA: University of California Press.

Campbell, D. T., & Fiske, D. W. (1959). Convergent and discriminant validation by the multitrait-multimethod matrix. *Psychological Bulletin, 56,* 81–105.

Carnap, R. (1956). The methodological character of theoretical concepts. In H. Feigl & M. Scriven (Eds.), *Minnesota studies in the philosophy of science, I: The foundations of science and the concepts of psychology and psychoanalysis* (pp. 38–76). Minneapolis: University of Minnesota Press.

Cohen, J. (1962). The statistical power of abnormal-social psychological research: A review. *Journal of Abnormal and Social Psychology, 65,* 145–153.

Cronbach, L. J., & Meehl, P. E. (1955). Construct validity in psychological tests. *Psychological Bulletin, 52,* 281–302.

Eisberg, R. M. (1961). *Fundamentals of modern physics.* New York: Wiley.

Glass, G. V., McGaw, B., & Smith, M. L. (1981). *Meta-analysis in social research.* Beverly Hills/London: Sage.

Hays, W. L. (1973). *Statistics for the social sciences* (2nd ed.). New York: Holt, Rinehart and Winston.

Hull, C. L., Hovland, C. I., Ross, R. T., Hall, M., Perkins, D. T., & Fitch, F. G. (1940). *Mathematico-deductive theory of rote learning.* New Haven, CT: Yale University Press.

Hunter, J. E., Schmidt, F. L., & Jackson, G. B. (1982). Meta-analysis: cumulating research findings across studies. (*Studying organizations: innovations in methodology,* V. 4). Beverly Hills, CA: Sage.

Lakatos, I. (1970). Falsification and the methodology of scientific research programmes. In I. Lakatos & A. Musgrave (Eds.), *Criticism and the growth of knowledge* (pp. 91–195). Cambridge, England: Cambridge University Press.

Lakatos, I. (1974). The role of crucial experiments in science. *Studies in History and Philosophy of Science, 4,* 309–325.

Lykken, D. T. (1968). Statistical significance in psychological research. *Psychological Bulletin, 70,* 151–159. Reprinted in D. E. Morrison & R. E. Henkel (Eds.), *The significance test controversy* (pp. 267–279), 1970, Chicago: Aldine.

Mahoney, M. J. (1976). *Scientist as subject: The psychological imperative.* Cambridge, MA: Bollinger.

Meehl, P. E. (1967). Theory-testing in psychology and physics: A methodological paradox. *Philosophy of Science, 34,* 103–115. Reprinted in D. E. Morrison & R. E. Henkel (Eds.), *The significance test controversy* (pp. 252–266), 1970, Chicago: Aldine.

Meehl, P. E. (1970). Some methodological reflections on the difficulties of psychoanalytic research. In M. Radner & S. Winokur (Eds.), *Minnesota studies in the philosophy of science, IV: Analyses of theories and methods of physics and psychology* (pp. 403–416). Minneapolis: University of Minnesota Press. Reprinted *Psychological Issues,* 1973, *8,* 104–115.

Meehl, P. E. (1973). MAXCOV-HITMAX: A taxonomic search method for loose genetic syndromes. In P. E. Meehl, *Psychodiagnosis: Selected papers* (pp. 200–224). Minneapolis: University of Minnesota Press.

Meehl, P. E. (1978). Theoretical risks and tabular asterisks: Sir Karl, Sir Ronald, and the slow progress of soft psychology. *Journal of Consulting and Clinical Psychology, 46,* 806–834.

Meehl, P. E. (1983). Subjectivity in psychoanalytic inference: The nagging persistence of Wilhelm Fliess's Achensee question. In J. Earman (Ed.), *Minnesota studies in the philosophy of science, X: Testing scientific theories* (pp. 349–411). Minneapolis: University of Minnesota Press.

Meehl, P. E. (1990). Appraising and amending theories: The strategy of Lakatosian defense & two principles that warrant using it. *Psychological Inquiry, 1,* 108–141.

Meehl, P. E., & Golden, R. R. (1982). Taxometric methods. In P. Kendall & J. Butcher (Eds.), *Handbook of research methods in clinical psychology* (pp. 127–181). New York: Wiley.

Popper, K. R. (1959). *The logic of scientific discovery.* New York: Basic Books.

Popper, K. R. (1962). *Conjectures and refutations.* New York: Basic Books.

Popper, K. R. (1983). *Realism and the aim of science.* Totowa, NJ: Rowman and Littlefield.

Rosenthal, R. (1966). *Experimenter effects in behavioral research.* New York: Appleton-Century-Crofts.

Rozeboom, W. W. (1960). The fallacy of the null hypothesis significance test. *Psychological Bulletin, 57,* 416–428. Reprinted in D. E. Morrison & R. E. Henkel (Eds.), *The significance test controversy* (pp. 216–230), 1970, Chicago: Aldine.

Schilpp, P. A. (Ed.). (1974). *The philosophy of Karl Popper.* LaSalle, IL: Open Court.

Swenson, W. M., Pearson, J. S., & Osborne, D. (1973). *An MMPI source book: Basic item, scale, and pattern data on 50,000 medical patients.* Minneapolis, MN: University of Minnesota Press.

Tilton, J. W. (1937). The measurement of overlapping. *Journal of Educational Psychology, 28,* 656–662.

3 Macropsychology and Micropsychology: Natural Categories and Natural Kinds

Donald W. Fiske
University of Chicago

Lee Cronbach has pointed out a number of critical problems in psychological methodology, especially in measurement and in the conceptualization of research investigation. He showed us that subjects taking tests often choose their response to an item on bases unrelated to the concept we are trying to measure; response sets (Cronbach, 1946, 1950) are systematic components in the measuring process producing a datum. They are intrusive components that vary over subjects, even among several giving the same overt response. So the actual measuring process is often not what the investigator wants it to be, or interprets it as being. A few years later, Cronbach and Meehl (1955) explicated the basic scientific process by which both measuring instruments and constructs are validated in work on rather global constructs such as those used in personality. Then Cronbach (1957) differentiated two contrasting disciplines in scientific psychology, the study of persons and the study of treatments. More recently (Cronbach, 1982a), he developed an analytic framework for program evaluation, specifying the inferences from units (such as persons), from treatments, and from particular measuring operations—a framework that can, I have found, be adapted fruitfully to inferential decisions in other areas of research. He has also cautioned us against being naively optimistic about the future of the course we have been following in psychology and other social sciences (Cronbach, 1975, 1982b, 1986).

These are but a few of his publications that have contributed to this paper on the state of psychology today, with particular attention to the measurement of individuals as contrasted to the measurement of brief behavioral processes. The following section of this chapter examines how macropsychology, the measurement of gross variables, is severely handicapped by the vagueness and complexity of our natural categories, the person attributes that we seek to measure. Next, we examine construct validity and process validity in this context. The final section contrasts macropsychology and micropsychology, the study of brief behavioral processes, the investigation of natural kinds. Although macroscopic generalizations may decay over the years, microscopic knowledge seems more stable.

MACROPSYCHOLOGY

Joe Smith marks alternative b on item 13 of a test labeled Aptitude A. There is nothing wrong with that datum per se: we can all agree that at a particular time, under certain conditions, Joe did that. But what can we do with that datum? It covaries only very weakly with any other available datum, such as the response to another item. So we lump it together with Joe's responses to other items to obtain a total test score on Aptitude A that is more useful, more dependable, and does covary with other scores and measurements. But what does that score indicate? What is Aptitude A? In the terms of Cronbach, Gleser, Nanda, and Rajaratnam (1972), the score estimates a universe score for Aptitude A. But has anyone explicated a full description of Aptitude A? How many such explications of universe scores have been published?

This is an instance of macropsychology, of inferring from a piece of information to an attribute of a person. The inferential route is long and full of assumptions, and we don't really know what we have when we get to the end. We state loosely but confidently that, under some conditions, Joe will have a tendency to produce actions that have a certain quality. To be sure, we find Joe's score on the test of some limited practical value in making decisions about Joe: What training can he master? What jobs is he likely to perform adequately? But such measurement and such concepts have little general scientific utility.

In macropsychology, we make inferences from fairly complex events—multistep behavioral processes—to other events only somewhat similar to those processes. In part, the difficulty lies in the complex behavioral process, the protocol from which the datum is derived. That protocol is too long. Also, in going through the entire procedure culminating in a test response, the subject may take any of several routes. (See Newell [1973] and Simon [1980] on the importance of knowing the method the subject uses for a task in cognitive psychology and the importance of not lumping together subjects using different methods.) In test taking, the process may involve sets such as the general one of speed vs. accuracy; in the exercise of mental ability, there are the various components identified by Sternberg (1983).

Test scores exemplify the aggregated measurements used in macropsychology. Such composite measurements allow us to determine only approximate relationships between variables. And if we want to claim from a correlation between X and Y that X determines Y, we may fall back on the argument that the measurement of X preceded the measurement of Y by days, months, or years. With gross variables, we establish relationships and determination only rough-ly—we have made little progress toward definitive statements about the strengths of such relationships. In addition, we are handicapped by the fact that one aggregated score designed to assess Aptitude A has itself only a moderate correlation with another such score aimed also at Aptitude A. But the matter of instrument or method specificity cannot be examined here (see Fiske, "Specifici-ty of Method and Knowledge in Social Science," 1986).

Natural Categories.   The variables used in macropsychology come from attributional psychology, from the way everyone describes everyone else. They originate in natural categories (Rosch, 1978). As Rosch uses that phrase, these categories reflect the attributes perceived in the world and coded into the lan-guage of the culture. Category boundaries are not well defined; furthermore, the members of a category are not equivalent, are not equally representative (Mervis & Rosch, 1981); some are much more prototypic than others.

The attributes we assign to persons are clear instances of natural categories. They evolve from descriptions of actions. As Carr and Kingsbury (1938) so aptly describe the process, statements like "She acted intelligently" lead to the attribu-tion that "She is intelligent" and the assertion that "She has intelligence." Psychologists quickly recognized that intelligence has many forms and began differentiating among the kinds of content in test items. Further removed from lay descriptions are such technical conceptualizations as the distinctions among types of content, types of operations performed on that content, and types of products (Guilford, 1967). Many alternative analyses of intelligence have been proposed. Which is superior? Which seems likely to be most fruitful scien-tifically? After many decades of research, we have no consensus. The analysis of personality is in the same or worse state. To be sure, we have found that, for a given applied problem, some lists of dimensions are of greater practical value than others: E.g., some predict academic success better but others predict job performance better. In sum, if we want to make attributions to people, we can do it quite systematically by using tests chosen from the multitude available. And aggregated scores work pretty well, pragmatically. Frequently, we use tests or combinations of tests that are not factorially pure because they are better predic-tors of the complex criterion measures encountered in the world of social deci-sions about persons. Of course, we also have purer tests, assessing some re-stricted factors, tests that are psychometrically elegant but that measure narrow concepts with little practical utility. Although such tests are available, we do not have bodies of scientific conceptualization to make the tests useful in basic research.

The study of the attributions that people make to each other and to themselves is an important research topic in its own right. In contrast, attributions made by formal testing have limited scientific utility. Given the nature of natural categories and of technical categories derived from them, we can at best only estimate roughly the value to be assigned to a person: How much of each category does a person have? For any given category label, the estimate varies with the specific measuring procedure or procedures used (cf. Campbell & Fiske, 1959; Fiske, 1982). Even more critical is the fact that the estimate applies to a property of a person's behavior over some vague extended period of time. Hence it is difficult to conceptualize a mechanism by which that property can determine some other variable, or be determined by something else. When and how does Attribute A affect Attribute B? In the typical instance, all we can say is that a person with a high level of A is more likely to develop a high level of B. Our speculations about the mechanism or mechanisms can rarely be subjected to convincing experimental testing.

Attributions obviously convey information. We all know that a description of a person tells us something. For example, such a prior description may affect the way we first interact with someone to whom we are introduced. Decades ago, Asch (1946) demonstrated the effect of a single adjective in a list of descriptors. Yet it is very difficult to pinpoint any overt effects of such attributions on actual behavior. Attributions made by others or by ourselves probably generate sets or tendencies. How these dispositions contribute to the complex cognitive processing that eventuates in manifest behaviors is indeed an elusive matter.

CONSTRUCT VALIDITY

As Cronbach and Meehl (1955) observed, construct validity is inherent in all scientific work. Their classic paper was formulated in terms of constructs for attributes of persons, as in individual differences. In a sense, our applied work with tests has been a crude but incomplete form of construct validation: We reason that intelligence is required for good academic performance; we propose that Test A measures intelligence, and we therefore hypothesize that it should correlate with subsequent academic performance. If our data show such a correlation, we conclude that Test A is a valid measure of intelligence and also that our conceptualization of intelligence as related to academic performance is valid. For applied purposes, then, we may demonstrate predictive validity as contributory evidence for construct validity.

In such work, we are looking for relationships between two behavioral protocols—a set of actions while taking a test (each action lasting several seconds) and an extended protocol involving many large segments of behavior occurring over weeks or years, but all summarized in some aggregate measure (grade point average or a single judgmental rating taking a few seconds to make). The relationship between two such separated samplings of behavior is necessarily low, the value decreasing with the duration of the temporal gap (see Roberts, Hulin, & Rousseau, 1978, pp. 112–113).

In all individual difference work, the big problem is the gap between measurements, taken from several response processes on one occasion, and the target, an inferential predictive judgment about a person. The target may be concrete, as in some applied work, or vaguely conceived, as manifested in the label and the brief verbal definition of our construct. In most cases, neither the label nor the definition give us much help in identifying the relevant conditions under which the attribution of the construct to a person holds: Where and when will the person's behavior demonstrate the attribute?

The construct validity approach provides a norm, an ideal that we would like to reach. But how many complete applications of the approach have we seen in print over the last quarter of a century? The usual paper with the phrase "construct validity" in the title reports a few empirical relationships, much less than the full set required to validate an instrument and a construct.

The core of the difficulty lies in the constructs we employ in making attributions about people: they are typically broad and poorly specified. It is sobering to reread in Cronbach and Meehl (1955, p. 294) a comment about "a vagueness in our constructs" and to recognize that such vagueness still persists. Those authors argue that the vagueness stems from "our incomplete knowledge of the laws of nature" (p. 294) but that incompleteness comes in part from our fuzzy constructs. Improvements in our constructs should lead to improvements in our knowledge about those laws and vice versa. Improvements on both sides have, however, been very modest.

Process Validity.   An alternative strategy is to look backward from the product, the test responses, to the processes that generated them. We do that now by inference. We recognize that subjects may resort to guessing in aptitude testing, and so introduce a correction in our aggregate scores. Or we may look for the systematic but construct-irrelevant patterns of answers suggesting the operation of response sets. But these procedures are applied to the array of responses provided by each subject. We need to make sure that, in answering our test items, our subject is going through appropriate processes. But what processes are appropriate? We should not just speculate a priori; we have to find out by empirical research. Newell and Simon (1972) have demonstrated that the process in problem solving can be examined in great detail. Sternberg (1983) has analyzed conceptually and empirically the processes in responding to an item in a test of mental ability. Various investigators (e.g., Kuncel, 1981; Kuncel & Fiske, 1974) have studied the processes in responding to a personality item. If we want to maximize the construct validity in our tests, we should insure that the tests have process validity, that subjects are engaging in the right processes (cf. Fiske, 1971). Once we have determined what are the right processes, we can design instructions and select items that make more likely the occurrence of those processes.

To be more specific, we have to distinguish between the behavioral protocol to which the measurement applies and the measuring process generating the product, the datum. A full conceptualization of a variable should indicate the kind of behavioral protocol that is to be measured and the appropriate measuring procedure. The behavioral protocol underlies the usual references to behavior in verbal definitions of constructs. For example, the protocol may be a designated period of behavior under particular conditions, as in observational ratings. In an aptitude test, it is the problem solving in which the subject engages. But that protocol is, of course, taken as representing the problem-solving processes of the subject in activity outside the testing situation.

The measuring process is the process leading to the datum. It is most clearly seen when an observer produces the datum: How does he or she go from perceptions of a person's behavior through impressions and inferences to the final judgment that is recorded? In the testing situation where the subject produces the datum, it could be construed as the entire operation but it can better be restricted to the final step: After the subject has arrived at an answer to the question or problem, how does he or she select the response alternative to be marked?

Process validity is a part of construct validity. It involves assessing the behavioral theory for the measurement of the construct. The delineation of a construct includes not only relationships to other constructs but also the conditions under which one can observe behavior with the target attribute. In the nomological net described by Cronbach and Meehl (1955), there are "laws" relating "observable properties or quantities to each other" (p. 290) and to theoretical constructs. So the full specification of a construct should indicate how to design procedures for measuring it. All too often, we pay little or no attention to this step: we all know how to create a test or other assessment device because we have countless examples in front of us. But rarely do we make explicit the rationale underlying measurement (cf. Fiske, 1988). Part of our difficulties in optimizing psychological measurement lie in the gap between our actual measuring operations and the unstated ideal procedures implied by our conceptualizations. Our conceptualization of a construct may tell us what the aspects of behavior indicative of the construct look like but do not tell us how to distill a datum from them.

In some work on individual differences, we seek to measure an inferred property of a person, a property that may never be manifested in pure form in actual everyday behavior. An aptitude test may be aimed at a potential capacity that individuals never exercise, or that they display only under conditions that limit its full utilization. The rules of thumb for the testing of intelligence constitute an informal theory for the manifestation of maximum capacity: motivating the subject but reassuring him or her so as to avoid disruptive affective reactions, controlling the situation to avoid distractions, etc.

Other work on individual differences has a more difficult task: It seeks to determine typical performance, typical behavior. The difficulty is that we do not have any good way of determining what is typical. Of course, for a given construct, we can sketch the conditions under which it is observable. But, even under ideal circumstances, how can we establish when these conditions are met and how do we go from observing a large number of relevant behavioral protocols to an estimate of "typical" behavior for that person? A complicating factor is the matter of deciding what behaviors are truly indicative of the construct. Our individual difference variables are fuzzy concepts, fuzzy around the edges. Especially in the personality domain, there may be relatively pure prototypical instances of a given concept along with many fringe instances, as Buss and Craik (1983) have demonstrated for dominance.

For economy and dependability, we assess our individual difference constructs in a testing room, rather than in the field. To measure aptitude, we ask the subject to carry out a particular cognitive task on each of a set of items. The stimuli embedded in those items typically do not correspond exactly to those the subject encounters in everyday functioning. Instead, they can be said to be *simulated stimuli*—they resemble the stimuli embodied in the conceptualization of the construct. The cognitive processing of those simulated stimuli, however, is assumed to be representative of the processing required in the conceptualization.

For other constructs, we use an *a priori related process* (Fiske, 1971, pp. 113–116). We may ask subjects to tell us about themselves. If they say they would rather be an entertainer than a clerk, we interpret that process as indicating exhibitionistic tendencies. If subjects report that they have been successful in getting others to do as they wish, we assume a priori that they are dominating people (or are they persuasive, or charismatic?). For such constructs, then, subjects process our items and produce data that we assume are indicants of the construct in which we are interested. But is the process in the subjects just what we want it to be? When subjects reflect on their success in getting others to do as they wish, do they tend to remember just the times they were successful? Do they perceive such success as desirable, and if somewhat uncertain about their response, give themselves the benefit of the doubt and mark the positive response alternative? In other words, the process of responding may well involve response sets, cognitive aspects other than those we want in our measuring process.

It is significant that, in both these types of tests, the behavioral protocol is not manifest and gets confounded with the measuring process. For aptitude tests, the cognitive processing constituting the protocol occurs internally and is not observable. In tests using a priori related processes, the protocol is also an internal process in which the subject reacts to the test item. During that process, the subject may create or retrieve impressions of self or, alternatively, may retrieve one or more memories of earlier behavior and experience. (As Kuncel [1973] has shown, the same subject may use one process on some items and the other on other items in a test and the same item may elicit one process in some subjects but the other in other subjects.) Thus, only very indirectly does the subject's actual earlier behavior come into the process.

A third kind of test design uses an *empirically related process*. Given a criterion, the test constructor simply determines what response choices are empirically related to it, with no concern for the process that leads subjects to pick each choice. In fact, different subjects may use different processes—that fact is considered immaterial as long as the overt responses differentiate subjects on the criterion variable.

MICROPSYCHOLOGY

When our measurements are based on tests, the unit of behavior is the entire process culminating in a recorded response to an item. Each response provides us with a bit of information, but a bit in which we place little trust, a bit to which we attach little value when taken by itself. To obtain measurements in which we have some confidence, we aggregate such bits to obtain chunks of information, scores at a level of conceptual abstraction comparable to that for our everyday descriptive attributions about persons. But, as described earlier, even the bit of information in a response to an item is chunky—it integrates over several discriminable stages in the responding process. The typical time required to read and respond to an item in a test of personality or interests is about 7 seconds, and the time required to respond to an aptitude item may be about the same or somewhat longer. Much cognitive processing can occur in a few seconds, and some of that processing takes only milliseconds.

Our test scores can be viewed as based on large units of behavior, on the total period required for completing a test. These large units yield chunks of information that are useful for their purpose of ascribing a construct or a level on a construct to a person, but they are much too large for basic research studying and understanding behavior. For that kind of work, we need to operate at the level of micropsychology. In everyday adapting, in real-life interaction, reactions occur with very short latencies. For example, in a conversation, one person typically starts talking less than a second after the other person stops (Jaffe & Feldstein, 1970) and yet the frequency of simultaneous talking or interruptions is low. Cognitive psychology offers many indications of person-environment reactions requiring less than half a second. The initiation of an act (the onset) and the termination (offset) each provide a bit of information that can have an effect. Although we ordinarily think about the effect upon another person, an act can also have an effect upon the actor, as in a sequence of acts such as starting a car. In responding to an ability item, the subject goes through a process that, although not directly observable, appears to involve several steps, one internal act leading to the next (Sternberg, 1983). The duration of each step can be as short as a fraction of a second. Each step seems to have an effect on the subsequent one.

Tests are fine, then, for measurements useful in studying long segments of behavior, general impressions about people, and how people are construed in everyday life. They provide us with scores on broad, loosely specified constructs. Our efforts to measure such natural categories are handicapped in many ways, including the intrusion of effects associated with the particular observer producing the data—the subject. (For example, see Fiske, 1986.) But to understand behavior for the purposes of basic research, we need to go far beyond natural categories, or to put them aside completely. We have to seek data that are dependable, data on which observers agree, data that minimize the unwanted contributions of the observer, especially those found when the object of measurement, the subject, produces the data.

Natural Kinds.   Scientific data in the social sciences are most valuable when they pertain to fruitful natural kinds. Originally used by J. S. Mill, the term natural kind has been invoked by Rosenberg (1980, 1983) in his critical analyses of the obstacles confronting social science. In this phrase, "natural" means present in nature, as in "natural history" or the "natural sciences." Thus, the meaning is more general than when used in "natural categories," where the reference is to categories generated by lay persons in describing and construing their world of experience. Natural kinds, in Rosenberg's sense, are causally homogeneous classes of events (1980, p. 6). For him, desire and hope are not natural kinds like oxygen; synaptic transmissions would seem to qualify. In the present paper, a natural kind is a class of units of behavior, as illustrated shortly. Each unit in a class is interpreted as having a given effect on subsequent units falling into other classes and as being affected by antecedent units of one or more kinds.

Our emphasis will be on units that make a difference in a person-environment interaction, that provide bits of information to other people. An illustration at the verbal level is a greeting:

"Hi!"
"Hi!"
"How are you?"
"Fine!"

Fairly simultaneous are the nonverbal units: A looks at B, B looks at A, one person smiles, the other smiles back. That entire sequence may be preceded by a very quick eyebrow flick, a crosscultural unit described by Eibl-Eibesfeldt (1972). (For a close analysis of greeting behavior, see Ferber and Kendon, 1973.) We have yet to identify definitively the most fruitful levels of analyses into natural kinds. Clearly, we need one lower internal level for the neuropsychological sequence corresponding to each unit at the overt, observable level: for instance, the second person processes "Hi!" aurally, central neural processes culminating in the production of the reply, "Hi!".

At both of these levels, the units are contiguous in time. One unit occurs and within a fraction of a second another unit is initiated. As Kurt Lewin (1931) observed several decades ago, a bit of behavior must be seen as determined only by factors present in some form at the moment it is initiated. The explanation of a behavioral event or unit is most convincing when it refers to units of behavior or physical events directly discernable just before it. It seems also to be true that empirical relationships involving a unit of behavior are strongest with temporally contiguous units, rather than with events occurring much earlier or later. Curiously, the relationships of an overt bit of behavior are typically stronger to antecedent events than to subsequent: if Y is observed, we can predict with high confidence that X preceded it, but we cannot be as confident that some other event, Z, will follow it (see Duncan, Brunner, & Fiske, 1979).

Recall for a moment the strengths of typical relationships in macropsychology. The correlations in work with tests are usually quite modest, reflecting small amounts of common variance. Correlations between items are always low. Correlations between aggregate scores are very high only for reliability estimates. Correlations between two tests tend to be higher when the purported target constructs are semantically similar. And regardless of content, test scores tend to correlate more highly when the two instruments are more similar in format or other aspects of method (Fiske, 1982). When we are studying natural categories or constructs refined from them and when we look at relationships between test scores obtained at different times, we have to be content with demonstrating weak empirical associations that leave large portions of the variance unexplained.

The simplest form of a natural kind is an event or, more strictly speaking, a change of behavior: e.g., a change in the direction of gaze; beginning to speak or stopping. The event as observed is the initiation of an action or its termination. It is an on/off, present/absent matter. (Note that the absence of an event or action can itself convey information: If you greet an approaching friend and the friend looks directly toward you but does not reply, you receive information from the absence of the expected response.) Thus, the unit is an instance of a class or type. As such, it is easier to observe dependably than a degree of some property. This is one major advantage of micropsychological work.

Micropsychological work has another major advantage over macropsychology: Its classes have clearer boundaries. Such categories as gaze direction, smile, and eyebrow flick have less fuzzy boundaries than attention, positive affect, and recognition. This feature also contributes to the high levels of agreement on the coding of such events in a behavioral protocol. Associated with this advantage is the restricted generalization: The observed behavior is interpreted as containing instances of the specified classes, such as smiles, and inferences are made only to smiles in similar contexts. The clearer identification of the object of study is associated with clearer delineation of the conditions under which it is observed; both features contribute to uncovering strong and regular relationships. As Cronbach (1982b) has aptly phrased it, ". . . data never speak for themselves . . . without a carefully framed statement of boundary conditions generalizations are misleading or trivially vague . . ." (p. 71).

Note also the ease with which the behavioral protocol can be kept distinct analytically and operationally from the measuring process. Especially when the protocol is recorded, as with a videotape of an interpersonal interaction, the same protocol can be examined and measured for a variety of purposes. Some investigators may measure chronological aspects (e.g., Denny, 1985; Jaffe & Feldstein, 1970), others may code the nonverbal acts (e.g., Duncan & Fiske, 1977), while still others consider the semantic or phonetic aspects of the protocol. (A local set of videotapes has been used for several such varied purposes, and even for a study of relationships between nonverbal acts and natural categories for personal attributions: see Shrout and Fiske [1981].)

Construct Validity in Micropsychology.   Most of micropsychology deals with low level constructs, with labels referring to simple, brief behavioral events that typically can be defined ostensively: "This is an instance of X, but that is not." Its few broad concepts refer to research topics, to domains to be explored. Hence, in micropsychology, the linkages between constructs and observables can be stated with greater precision. It is only a short step from the laws in its nomological networks to experimental hypotheses that can be subjected to empirical testing.

Although developed in the context of tests, our psychometric concepts of reliability and validity are applicable to all measurements. But validity is less problematic in micropsychology because the behavioral protocol of interest is directly observed, rather than approached indirectly with a paper-and-pencil test. High observer reliability can be obtained and strong regularities, corresponding to reliability over items or trials, can be identified and examined. The data of micropsychology are simply more adequate for the theoretical goals of the investigator.

Time Identifies Conditions.   Many of the preceding sections have emphasized the concept of time. It has been used to refer to the duration of a behavioral protocol and to the interval between making two measurements. While such usages are convenient for descriptive purposes, they are oversimplifications that may mislead us. Designating a point in time is useful primarily as a way of referring to a set of conditions. At a moment in time, each person is in a particular state and each person is in a setting, interpersonal and physical, that can be described on a multitude of dimensions. The values on the dimensions describing the person's state and the state of the setting change more or less rapidly as time passes. When a behavioral protocol extends over hours, minutes, or even seconds, many background conditions change to some significant degree. Hence measurements applied to an extended protocol integrate not only over changes in the behaviors but also over changes in some conditions.

Similarly, the comparison of measurements made at different times involves effects from different sets of conditions. The decline of predictive validity coefficients, mentioned earlier, is presumably the consequence of more and larger changes in both personal state variables and environmental characteristics. The curse of macropsychology is inconstancy of conditions. In contrast, micropsychology approaches the ideal research paradigm. When one observation succeeds another very closely in time, then it is easy to identify any important element, such as a short behavioral unit, that is different at the two moments, and to feel confident that other conditions have remained constant, or nearly so, from one moment to the next. Writing within the context of social history, Cronbach (1975) has offered us the maxim that "generalizations decay" (p. 122) as the general situation changes. For the much shorter perspective taken in this chapter, conditions in macropsychological work change between the times two variables are measured, and even during the briefer periods required to make each measurement. Effects decay. In micropsychological work, the changes in conditions between two measurements are minimal and effects are observed when they are strongest.

Cronbach took a pessimistic stance in his 1975 paper, stating that "enduring systematic theories about man in society are not likely to be achieved" (p. 126) because the times change. He argues persuasively that our research is plagued with both simple and complex interactions: relationships vary with individuals and with time or conditions. His position is difficult or impossible to refute in the domain of macropsychology. It is realistic for us to adopt his "Prudent Aspirations for Social Inquiry" (Cronbach, 1982b). In contrast, the future for micropsychology appears more promising. We are making progress in understanding behavior within explicit contexts. To be sure, we will find our knowledge holds only within restricted boundary conditions, cultural or psychological. And human beings a hundred years from now may function differently from our subjects today. But it does seem reasonable to believe that much micropsychological knowledge will remain valid through the decades, especially that part which is linked to psychophysiological or neuropsychological functioning.

ACKNOWLEDGMENT

I am indebted to Steven Shevell for his helpful comments on an earlier version of this paper.

REFERENCES

Asch, S. E. (1946). Forming impressions of personality. *Journal of Abnormal and Social Psychology, 41*, 258–290.
Buss, D. M., & Craik, K. H. (1983). The act frequency approach to personality. *Psychological Review, 90*, 105–126.

Campbell, D. T., & Fiske, D. W. (1959). Convergent and discriminant validation by the multitrait-multimethod matrix. *Psychological Bulletin, 56,* 81–105.

Carr, H. A., & Kingsbury, F. A. (1938). The concept of traits. *Psychological Review, 45,* 497–524.

Cronbach, L. J. (1946). Response sets and test validity. *Educational and Psychological Measurement, 6,* 475–494.

Cronbach, L. J. (1950). Further evidence on response sets and test design. *Educational and Psychological Measurement, 10,* 3–31.

Cronbach, L. J. (1957). The two disciplines of scientific psychology. *American Psychologist, 12,* 671–684.

Cronbach, L. J. (1975). Beyond the two disciplines of scientific psychology. *American Psychologist, 30,* 116–127.

Cronbach, L. J. (1982a). *Designing evaluations of educational and social programs.* San Francisco: Jossey-Bass.

Cronbach, L. J. (1982b). Prudent aspirations for social inquiry. In W. H. Kruskal (Ed.), *The social sciences: Their nature and uses.* Chicago: University of Chicago Press.

Cronbach, L. J. (1986). Social inquiry by and for earthlings. In D. W. Fiske & R. A. Shweder (Eds.), *Metatheory in social science: Pluralisms and subjectivities.* Chicago: University of Chicago Press.

Cronbach, L. J., Gleser, G. C., Nanda, H., & Rajaratnam, H. (1972). *The dependability of behavioral measurements: Theory of generalizability for scores and profiles.* New York: Wiley.

Cronbach, L. J., & Meehl, P. E. (1955). Construct validity in psychological tests. *Psychological Bulletin, 52,* 281–302.

Denny, R. M. T. (1985). Pragmatically marked and unmarked forms of speaking-turn exchange. In S. Duncan, Jr. & D. W. Fiske, *Interaction structure and strategy.* Cambridge, England: Cambridge University Press.

Duncan, S., Jr., Brunner, L. J., & Fiske, D. W. (1979). Strategy signals in face-to-face interaction. *Journal of Personality and Social Psychology, 37,* 301–313.

Duncan, S., Jr., & Fiske, D. W. (1977). *Face-to-face interaction: Research, methods, and theory.* Hillsdale, NJ: Lawrence Erlbaum Associates.

Eibl-Eibesfeldt, I. (1972). Similarities and differences between cultures in expressive movements. In R. A. Hinde (Ed.), *Non-verbal communication.* Cambridge, England: Cambridge University Press.

Ferber, A. A., & Kendon, A. (1973). A description of some human greetings. In R. P. Michael & J. H. Crook (Eds.), *Comparative ecology and behavior of primates.* New York: Academic Press.

Fiske, D. W. (1971). *Measuring the concepts of personality.* Chicago: Aldine.

Fiske, D. W. (1982). Convergent and discriminant validation in measurements and research strategies. In D. Brinberg & L. Kidder (Eds.), *New directions in methodology of social and behavioral science: Forms of validity in research,* No. 12. San Francisco: Jossey-Bass.

Fiske, D. W. (1986). Specificity of method and knowledge in social science. In D. Fiske & R. Shweder (Eds.), *Metatheory in social science: Pluralisms and subjectivities.* Chicago: University of Chicago Press.

Fiske, D. W. (1988). Measuring to understand and understanding measuring. In S. G. Cole & R. G. Demaree (Eds.), *Applications of interactionist psychology: Essays in honor of S. B. Sells.* Hillsdale, NJ: Lawrence Erlbaum Associates.

Guilford, J. P. (1967). *The nature of human intelligence.* New York: McGraw-Hill.

Jaffe, J., & Feldstein, S. (1970). *Rhythms of dialogue.* New York: Academic Press.

Kuncel, R. B. (1973). Response processes and relative location of subject and item. *Educational and Psychological Measurement, 33,* 545–563.

Kuncel, R. B. (1981). Reducing diversity in subject interpretations of items. In D. W. Fiske (Ed.), *New directions for methodology of social and behavioral science: Problems with language imprecision,* No. 9. San Francisco: Jossey-Bass.

Kuncel, R. B., & Fiske, D. W. (1974). Stability of response process and response. *Educational and Psychological Measurement, 34,* 743–755.

Lewin, K. (1931). The conflict between Aristotelian and Galilean modes of thought in contemporary psychology. *Journal of General Psychology, 5,* 141–177.

Mervis, C. B., & Rosch, E. (1981). Categorization of natural objects. *Annual Review of Psychology, 32,* 89–115.

Newell, A. (1973). You can't play 20 questions with nature and win: Projective comments on the papers of this symposium. In W. G. Chase (Ed.), *Visual information processing.* New York: Academic Press.

Newell, A., & Simon, H. A. (1972). *Human problem solving.* Englewood Cliffs, NJ: Prentice-Hall.

Roberts, K. H., Hulin, C. L., & Rousseau, D. (1978). *Toward an interdisciplinary science of organizations.* San Francisco: Jossey-Bass.

Rosenberg, A. (1980). *Sociobiology and the preemption of social science.* Baltimore, MD: Johns Hopkins University Press.

Rosenberg, A. (1983). Human science and biological science: Defects and opportunities. In N. Rescher (Ed.), *Scientific explanation and understanding* (pp. 37–52). Lanham, MD: University Press of America.

Rosch, E. (1978). Principles of categorization. In E. Rosch & D. B. Lloyd (Eds.), *Cognition and categorization.* Hillsdale, NJ: Lawrence Erlbaum Associates.

Shrout, P. E., & Fiske, D. W. (1981). Impressions and nonverbal behaviors: Effects of target and observer sex. *Journal of Personality, 49,* 115–128.

Simon, H. A. (1980). How to win at Twenty Questions with nature. In R. A. Cole (Ed.), *Perception and production of fluent speech* (pp. 535–548). Hillsdale, NJ: Lawrence Erlbaum Associates.

Sternberg, R. J. (1983). Components of human intelligence. *Cognition, 15,* 1–48.

4 Test Validity and Invalidity Reconsidered

David E. Wiley
Northwestern University

Over the past 3 decades considerable progress has been made in the formulation and development of theories and models for social and psychological measurement. In the context of educational and psychological research, conceptions relating to the adequacy of measurement have historically been categorized in one of two areas: validity and reliability.

Reliability is the rubric under which problems associated with instability of measurements have been classified. *Instability,* in this sense, means unpredictable, unsystematic, or "random" differences among alternate measurements of the same characteristics. In practice, these differences are really any which manifest themselves among measurements that are considered equivalent.[1]

It is in the *reliability* area that tremendous strides have been made since the end of World War II. Comprehensively formalized with the publication of Lord's (1952) monograph, which publicized and eventually popularized an integrated theory of latent traits, a whole new class of models emerged which refined and redefined the concept of *stability* and, by implication, narrowed the boundaries of the reliability concept.

The other major thread of work in the area: generalizability theory (Cronbach,

---

[1]We note at this point that there is rarely any formal definition of equivalence classes for such measurements. As in many scientific areas, "equivalence" is more of a normative than a formal concept, being "adjusted" over time because of theoretical and empirical developments. It applies more to the absence of a framework for making distinctions than to a positive definition of equivalence. In practice, measurements may be considered equivalent if they occur at different times, under different circumstances, or if they involve distinct tasks to be performed by the individual who is measured. And with the elaborated statistical models now available for measurements, equivalence classes may even be implicit because "instability" is indicated by deviations from model constraints.

75

Gleser, Nanda, & Rajarathum, 1972)—broadened this domain. It did so by integrating and elaborating the structure and specification of the hitherto ill-defined equivalence classes. But in doing so it also allowed them to expand without substantive boundary. This expansion has thoroughly blurred many of the traditional distinctions between reliability and validity.

In contrast to the area of *reliability*, systematic conceptual progress concerning the validity of educational or psychological measurements have progressed slowly since the publication of Cronbach and Meehl's seminal (1955) article on construct validity. That paper identified the validity of psychological measures with the validity of total theoretical substructures which (presumably) underlay them. By doing so it made the validation of new measurement procedures and instruments extremely complex. That is, it implied that an adequate validation required a full-blown specification of a network of theoretical relations and a thorough empirical verification of these relations.

I believe that this task, if possible at all in the current state of inquiry, can only be the burden of an entire field rather than that of each deviser of a new procedure or instrument. This conceptual restructuring of validity has advanced thinking, but has also left the area of applied measurement without clear, practicable standards for validation. And consequently it has, in effect, obscured the boundaries between scientific advance, testing practice, and political debate.

One area of extensive recent debate has concerned selection processes for employment and educational participation. Much research on this topic has been viewed as bearing on the ("criterion-related") *validity* of the educational or psychological test(s) used in the selection procedure (see Cronbach & Gleser, 1965, for the foundations of this work). However, for an extended period, most theoretical psychometric work on validity-related matters has focused directly on the *use* of tests for such selection decisions. This work was strongly stimulated by legal concerns about the fairness of selection procedures; primarily those used in the employment process.

The focus of this research has not been on the nature of the tests themselves or the measurements deriving from them, but on the social selection procedures that incorporate these measurements. Thus, the implications of the work for changes in the process of validation relate only to the ways in which the scores of individuals with different nontest characteristics are incorporated into the criteria for selection, not to such issues as item content, item format, method of scoring, etc.

As an organizing perspective, this use-orientation fragments the concept of test validity—in that specific tests are used in different ways—and it forecloses whole classes of questions that relate to item and test format, content selection, scoring, and scaling. In my view, the new work does not focus on *test* validity at all. It primarily is a conceptual framework and a set of standards for assessing the social worth of selection procedures incorporating any criteria that are (a) quantitative, and (b) measured with error. Problematically, it focuses primary attention on external criteria and allows those who should be forced to attend to important concerns about the validity of their devices to ignore them.

Most other psychometric research, until recently, has been focused on issues of error and reliability rather than on bias and validity. Theoretical frameworks for the analysis of measurement errors has become conceptually sophisticated, elaborate, and full of concrete detail. They have progressed to the point that primitive correlational indices are no longer scientifically respectable as having clear meaning and where the conceptual and analytic frameworks for test items and responses to them are fully integrated with those for test scores.

In contrast, I believe the conceptual orientations to validity of tests have become diffuse, fragmented, and fundamentally incomplete. The frameworks for *item* and test task assessment have never been fundamentally integrated with those for tests. Thus, *item bias* has no bearing on *test bias*. Content validity, at the operational level, seems to mean the sampling or selection processes for the *items* or test tasks which make up the test. And it has no relation to test validity, which at the operational level, seems to mean a relation to a single external criterion in the (implicit or explicit) context of a selection decision. The fact that these nonoverlapping processes can be tenuously linked via the vagaries of construct validity does not imply that they could actually be integrated.

This paper is to reconsider the concept of validity—specifically test validity—from the perspective of what is intended to be measured rather than the uses to which the measurements might be put. Admittedly, uses and intents are (or ought to be) closely related. But an exclusive focus on use embeds one in the analysis of the social and political processes which determine and influence those uses. And such a perspective inhibits analysis of social and psychological processes which the test performances are supposed to reflect. Thus, we begin with these processes and try to extract from them some insights about the concept of test validity.

THE STRUCTURE OF SKILLS AND THE DETERMINANTS OF TEST PERFORMANCE

Measurements of the characteristics of individuals vary in the degree to which the conditions of measurement are designed and carried out by intervening in the life course of the individual measured. An example of one extreme, is the use of administrative records. Such records are created routinely in the course of life activity and *measurers* who come to these records after the fact have no influence on the character of the record or on the specific activities which contributed to that record. The fact that such records or the measurements based on them may affect the subsequent life course of the individual has no relevance for either the definition or the content of the specific record.

At the other extreme is a test. In this mode of measurement the individual's participation is required and his or her cooperation is solicited and desired. The circumstances under which the measurement is to take place are—to some degree—specified. One or more specially created tasks are to be undertaken, goals are specified, instructions are given, testing is begun, individuals undertake the task(s), performances are recorded, testing is ended.

This distinction is, to some degree, a matter of perspective. The administrative records may reflect performance on one or more life tasks of the individual in question. But if so, these tasks were not given to the individual by the measurer. They formed a part of that individual's life course whether or not a measurement was created. Other individuals who were measured did not undertake the same tasks under specified conditions. Similar distinctions obtain for measurements based on the unstructured behavioral observations.

In this chapter I address the issue of test validity and by using the term *test* I imply that the measurement is carried out by means of *tasks* and that these tasks have been organized, administered, and carried out in the planned fashion described earlier.

The Task Basis for Skill Definition

Skills, from the perspective taken here, are abilities to perform tasks. Most such abilities are acquired, i.e., learned. Tasks are goal-oriented activities that begin and end and on which performances can, in principal, be judged with respect to the accomplishment of relevant goals.

Tasks can, for some purposes, be roughly grouped into three categories: life, learning, and test. These groups are overlapping as the categories refer more to context, setting, or use than to the nature of the tasks, in and of themselves. Thus, writing an essay could be a normal life activity of a newspaper columnist, a school assignment intended to teach writing, and/or a part of a college entrance examination.

Life tasks, for our purposes, are the commonplace segments of goal-oriented life activities of individuals, where the formal learning and formal evaluation aspects of these tasks are secondary to other facets of their goals. Learning tasks are those whose primary goal is to acquire an ability to perform similar or related tasks, i.e., to learn a skill. Test tasks are those whose purpose is to establish whether or not an individual possesses such an ability.

In educational work all three kinds of tasks are central. Abilities to perform life tasks constitute the primary goals of the educational system. The specification and performance of learning tasks fulfills the process of education in terms of curricular design and instructional implementation. And test tasks channel the delivery of instruction by diagnosing and confirming the abilities of students.

Both tasks and abilities may be structured. Structure, for our purposes here, consists of subdivisions of a group of entities such that those entities within the same subdivision are considered more similar than those in different subdivisions. Structures can be complex in that subdivisions may be partial, may be further divided, may be overlapping, or may be recombined. That is, structures need not be hierarchical. Structure is conceptually essential because once tasks are successfully performed it seldom makes sense for them to be done again. We desire learning to enable learners to successfully perform new tasks which are structurally linked to the tasks undertaken in the learning process. As a consequence, we group similar tasks into equivalence classes within which tasks are considered to be structurally identical.

Much current educational work, especially that linked to testing, is premised on the direct correspondence of abilities and tasks. Thus, tasks often are hierarchically organized into "content domains" and skills.[2] These are usually defined by identifying them with a class of task-ability pairs without explicitly distinguishing whether the skill category system applies to the tasks or to the abilities. However, it need not be the case that there is a one-to-one correspondence between abilities and tasks. For example, Thurstone's (1947) concept of "multiple" factor analysis explicitly incorporated the notion of more than one skill (ability) contributing to performance on a single task.

The issue here is not whether ability distinctions can be unlinked from task distinctions. They clearly cannot as skills are *abilities to perform tasks*, i.e., they are linked by definition. The main point is that skill structures are (potentially complex) joint structures of abilities and tasks and need not derive from simple presumptions of one-to-one correspondence of task and ability.

Individual task implementations themselves, as well as the structures that classify tasks as tasks, may be joined and subdivided. Thus a task episode such as mowing the law may be temporally divided into preparatory, operational, and clean-up subtasks—i.e., by subgoal. Such subtask analysis is one way that subskill definitions evolve.

Alternatively, several individual mowing tasks can be merged conceptually, into a whole summer's mowing activities. Task episode *poolings* and *dividings* are conceptually distinct from aspects of a structural system of classification which might, for example, abstractly group hedge-trimming with lawn mowing into a gardening category.

Note, however, that our first episodic example—preparation, operation, clean-up—requires an abstractive structural conception of task subdivision—based on timing as well as task goal—to accomplish the temporal segmentation. On the other hand, the second episodic example—a summer's mowing—requires only the (temporal) pooling of distinct episodes in the same structural category and thus does not involve new aspects of a structural classification.

Category structures for life tasks, and thus skill structures for task-based

---

[2]Cognitive psychologists use the terms "declarative knowledge" and "procedural knowledge" to distinguish what is in ordinary parlance termed "knowledge" and "skill." In what follows I use "skill" to denote knowledge of both kinds.

conceptions, are inevitably founded on the social organization of life activities. Thus, we have work tasks, leisure tasks, school tasks, family tasks, and so on. These broad task categories are hierarchically subdivided so that, for example, "work" has an extensive occupational structure associated with it; thus the 1977 *Dictionary of Occupational Titles* (U.S. Department of Labor) includes 12,099 occupations, each with an extensive skill profile based on the work tasks common in the specific occupation.[3]

Structures imposed on ability conceptions are *based* on distinctions among tasks and, therefore, on task structures. But historically, as psychologically based inquiry has proceeded, these structural ability distinctions have departed from the holistic life task categories which form the traditional base for task structures.

There is still a fundamental linkage, however, especially in educational settings. Test tasks assess the skills that learning tasks are supposed to produce and these skills, in turn, constitute the abilities to perform the life tasks which are the goals of schooling.

As was discussed earlier, these linkages are not necessarily one-to-one. For example, the development of skill concepts has often proceeded by analyzing holistic task performance into components (e.g., see Sternberg, 1977). Thus, many learning tasks are focused on component skills required for a variety of life tasks. And test tasks frequently diagnose subcomponents of abilities which are the intended outcomes of learning tasks.

Learning Tasks and Goal Tasks

Whereas in life tasks, the task goals are instrumental only in the sense that such tasks and task episodes are linked into larger structural frameworks, for example, a sequence of task episodes such as the preparation, operation, and clean-up cited earlier—learning tasks are *primarily* instrumental. That is, learning tasks have as a central goal skill learning which extends beyond the particular task episode that is intended to produce the learning. That is, the concept of *ability* is one that bears on a group of tasks and a class of potential task episodes, not merely a single episode. Thus, skills are enabling, in the sense that they contribute to future task performances. If these future performances are to be on learning tasks, we term the skills *aptitudes* (see Snow, this volume).

Conceptually then, a skill cannot be defined solely in terms of the learning tasks which are intended to bring about its realization. It must instead also be defined in terms of the classes of tasks for which it is enabling. This is the essence of the broadened notion embedded in the concept of construct validity. I.e., "constructs"—in this discussion I have restricted myself to "skills"—are defined only by specifying a network of interrelationships relating the focal construct to a collection of other constructs. Only when this network is suffi-

---

[3]See Cain and Treiman (1981) for an extended discussion.

ciently *dense* with constraints on the relational specifications is the construct well-defined.[4]

In the context of skills, the critical component of this network is the class of tasks for which the learner is enabled, i.e., the goals of the learning. Because we have no way of measuring skills without giving individuals tasks and assessing their performances, the required *density* can only be attained by imposing constraints on patterns of task performance using a predicated skill structure jointly representing abilities and tasks. Thus, these goal tasks also constitute criterion tasks, which form the pool from which the most obvious test tasks may be selected.

These "goal" or "criterion" tasks are not the same as the holistic "life" tasks which were discussed above. There it was noted that the "life, learning, and test" categories are informal, not structural distinctions. The notion of a "goal" task is structural in that it embodies a set of task-capacity relations which together with other such relations *define* one or more skills.

If learning tasks led to the acquisition of single skills and if goal tasks represented those skills singly, these issues would be straightforward. However, this is not and cannot be the case. Learning tasks contribute to the development of multiple skills. And even when scientific knowledge of skills and skill structures accumulate, it is difficult or impossible to construct goal tasks which are specifically enough targeted on the specific skill to make a unifocal approach to test tasks unambiguous.

An example, to which I will return below, is reading. Most analyses of reading processes distinguish between familiarity with the words in a passage to be read and the comprehension of the other information contained in the passage. But it is not possible to measure comprehension skills without using words and therefore test tasks focused on reading comprehension inevitably will also reflect differences in vocabulary knowledge.

Thus, traditional tests of reading embody two subtests. One is labeled "Reading Comprehension" and reflects both vocabulary knowledge and reading comprehension abilities. The second is labeled "Vocabulary Knowledge" and presumably reflects abilities for recalling or recognizing the meaning of words, but not abilities to understand longer and more complex blocks of text.

The Experience of Learning and the Development of Skills and Abilities

If tests or test tasks are to be validated, they must be analyzed in relation to the skills which they reflect. These developed skills are a consequence of learning

---

[4]The construct validation process, which we discuss below, is essentially a specification of procedures for establishing the reality of a potentially well-defined construct by empirically testing these constraints.

tasks, either formally or informally experienced. Thus, when test validation takes place, the learning experiences of those to be tested should be understood in relation to the skills acquired and the test tasks used to assess these skills. Under these circumstances, an extensive network of relationships is available to facilitate validation.

Learning tasks, of course, are undertaken outside of school as well as in school, although the extent to which out-of-school experiences are relevant to school-learning goals varies with curricular area. Thus, listening and speaking tasks outside of and prior to schooling strongly overlap in terms of required and acquired abilities with school-oriented reading and writing tasks. And the basic requirements for actual learning, whether in or out of school, are exposure to and practice on learning tasks.

> All influences on pupil achievement must be mediated through a pupil's pursuits. No one can gain knowledge or take up new ways of thinking, believing, acting, or feeling except through seeing, looking, and watching, hearing and listening, feeling and touching. These control what and how one learns. Less proximal influences, whether as general as the district curriculum and policy and the school organization or as idiosyncratic as a given teacher's education, personality, planning, and activities, directly control and condition these pursuits and not the student's ultimate achievement. The focus on this particular causal linkage is the central uniqueness of the model; most earlier studies, by contrast, have regarded teacher behaviors as directly, if mysteriously, influencing achievement.
>
> Harnischfeger and Wiley (1975)

This statement summarizes the central tenet of Harnischfeger's and my conceptual framework for the teaching/learning process. Later in our model development, we summarized the commonality of our perspective with those of Bloom and Carroll.

> The consensus of the three models is simply stated: Pupils' experiences, adequately plumbed by the amount of time spent actively learning, and pupils' characteristics including their cognitive capabilities, are the sole proximal and distinctive determinants of achievement. Instruction influences active learning directly via the allocation and use of instructional time (opportunity) and indirectly via pupil motivation.
>
> Harnischfeger and Wiley (1977)

This formalized notion that the *active* learning time expended on learning tasks is solely responsible for learnings and that the amount of it needed to accomplish this learning is dependent on an individual's cognitive capabilities is due to Carroll (1963).

From the general perspective of our own model, the quantity of schooling to be experienced by a particular pupil is a collection of potential pupil participations in educative experiences, i.e., in the pursuit of learning tasks. An actual teaching activity transforms a segment of the pupil's school attendance into an actual pupil pursuit. This pursuit, from our perspective, can be characterized by

1. the active learning it contains, with its
2. specific content or subject matter, occurring within
3. a particular learning context, i.e., the implementation of a pupil grouping and a supervisory mode, use a set of instructional materials, and the consumption of other learning resources.

This conception thus combines learning tasks, pupil participation, and learning resources into actual and educative experiences. These pupil pursuits thus exhaust both (a) pupil time and (b) the resources that were required to mount the teaching activity which occupied and transformed this time (for a fuller elaboration of this conception, see Harnischfeger and Wiley, 1981, 1985.)

Thus, in the context of our model for the teaching-learning process, exposure to (time allocated to) and practice on (active learning or learning activity within) learning tasks is prerequisite to the acquisition of abilities for future task performance, i.e., to skill acquisition.

The Sources of Variation in Test Performance

As the social organization of life activities—both in school and out of school—directly controls exposure to and practice on learning tasks, features of that social organization create and form the sequences and co-incidences of that exposure and practice as well as the time durations allocated and actively experienced by individuals. In the context of intended and actively created school experiences, we usually term this social organization: the curriculum, and the experiences themselves: the teaching-learning process. Outside of school we tend to lump these issues under the rubric of *socialization.*

Figure 4.1 summarizes this conception of learning processes and skill acquisition and extends it to the testing process. Just as acquired abilities are the result of learning experiences *and* the prior cognitive characteristics of the learners, test-task responses are the outcome of both skills *and* test-task characteristics.

Thus *three* structures can be imposed which contribute to the interdependen-

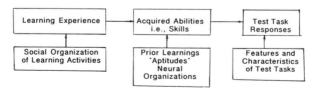

FIG. 4.1. A conception of learning, skill, and testing.

cies and interrelations among the test item responses that we generally use to infer structure, including issues of homogeneity and multidimensionality,

1. Features of the test tasks themselves. These contribute directly to the response structure via (a) the tasks selected vs. those not selected, which control the set of skills which are actually represented in the total collection of tasks used, and (b) the "weighting" of particular skills in each specific task.

2. Structural constraints on the actual abilities or skills possessed by individuals—e.g., logical relations among skills, neurological prerequisites to learning, or earlier learnings—obviously also directly contribute to the responses and their interrelations, and finally

3. The learning experiences of individuals and their social organization indirectly contribute via the skills acquired. These experiences are structurally central, however, in that sequences and coincidences of learning experiences (tasks) strongly condition the coincidence of acquired skills.

The last two of these have their impact on the skills themselves and their development. Thus, they control the levels and the structure of covariations among skills (or constructs). The first, on the other hand, determines the set of skills actually reflected in the tests. Both covariations of skills and their representations in tests influence the covariations among test performances.

Of these three structures underlying test-task responses, only two have been assessable independently of these responses. These are (a) the learning activities and their social organization—via assessments of curriculum and instruction in school settings or assessments of out-of-school socialization distantly via social class or other backgrounds of pupils—and (b) the (stimulus) characteristics and structural organization of test tasks. It is this dual conception that underlies the discussion.

A CONCEPTION OF VALIDITY

Inherently, the notion of test validity must rest on two conceptions: (a) that which a test *ought* to measure and (b) that which a test *does* measure. It is the discrepancies between the two, somehow defined, that bear on validity. Central theoretical and practical problems for psychometrics are (1) the mode of specification of the *ought* and (2) the form or expression of the discrepancy. Recent discussions of the validity concept in the psychometric literature (Cronbach, 1971, 1980) have focused on the *interpretation* as the entity which is validated. However, a central interpretation of "interpretation" has, at least since Cronbach and Meehl (1955), centered on the idea of a definition or theoretical conception of what is intended to be measured (i.e., a "construct" or combination of "constructs")—our *ought*.

The problem with the specification of the *ought* is that, if it occurs at all in the actual world of test construction—beyond an undefined label—it is formulated in ways that make it difficult to separate valid from invalid components of the measurements.

Cronbach (1971) gives a salient example of a specification of an intent of measurement that highlights this issue of separation:

> Consider further reading comprehension as a trait construct. Suppose that the test presents paragraphs each followed by multiple-choice questions. The paragraphs obviously call for reading and presumably contain the information needed to answer the questions. Can a question about what the test measures arise? It can, if any counterinterpretation may reasonably be advanced. Here are a few counterhypotheses (Vernon, 1962):
>
> 1. The test is given with a time limit. *Speed* of reading may contribute appreciably to the score. The publisher claims that the time limit is generous. But is it?
> 2. These paragraphs seem abstract and full. Perhaps able readers who have little *motivation* for academic work make little effort and therefore earn low scores.
> 3. The questions seem to call only for recall of facts presented in simple sentences. One wants to measure ability to comprehend at a higher level than word *recognition and recall*.
> 4. Uncommon words appear in the paragraphs. Is the score more a measure of *vocabulary* than of reading comprehension?
> 5. Do the students who earn good scores really demonstrate superior reading or only a superior *test-taking strategy?* Perhaps the way to earn a good score is to read the questions first and look up the answers in the paragraph.
> 6. Perhaps this is a test of *information* in which a well-informed student can give good responses without reading the paragraphs at all.
>
> These miscellaneous challenges express fragments of a definition or theoretical conception of reading comprehension that, if stated explicitly, might begin: "The student considered superior in reading comprehension is one who, if acquainted with the words in a paragraph, will be able to derive from the paragraph the same conclusions that other educated readers, previously uninformed on the subject of the paragraph, derive." Just this one sentence separates superior vocabulary, reading speed, information, and other counterhypotheses from the construct, reading comprehension. The construct is not identified with the whole complex practical task of reading, where information and vocabulary surely contribute to success. A distinctive, separate skill is hypothesized. (pp. 463–464)

Cronbach's example implies several things in this context. First, it makes clear that *reading comprehension* as an intent of measurement is not all things to all persons; it is not speed, vocabulary, test-wiseness, or prior information, regardless of whether these "constructs" contribute to success on the test task itself, other tasks given contemporaneously, or future tasks.

If we take this further and realize that such sources of invalidity in the assessment of *reading comprehension* are (a) themselves valid intents of measurement with other instruments and are (b) irremovable sources of variation in test performance for many "constructs,"[5] then two further implications flow

— the problem of test validation, whether focused on the notion of "interpretation" or not, cannot be shifted entirely to an analysis of test use, and that

— the labeling of the test by the description of what it is intended to measure must be sufficiently precise to allow the separation of components of invalidity from valid variations in performance.

Also, these sources of invalidity are often co-related to the characteristic that is the intent of measurement. Thus, in the Cronbach example, those who have the skills necessary for "comprehension" of passage content or derivation of correct conclusions, given adequate vocabulary, will also be more likely to have previously acquired that vocabulary knowledge.

As I indicated on p. 84, covariation among test tasks has two distinct sources: (i) covariation among the skills or constructs that are measured, and (ii) similarities in the compositional profiles of the measures, in terms of these constructs. Thus, two measurements will relate highly to one another if they reflect similar compositions regardless of the magnitudes of the interrelations among the constructs they reflect. Alternatively, two measures will also relate highly—even when the constructs they reflect are distinct—if those constructs themselves are highly co-related. This latter circumstance might occur, for example, when the learning tasks which give rise to different skills are always given to pupils in conjunction.

For example, a reading comprehension test might produce scores that strongly correlate with a (valid) test of vocabulary knowledge for several distinguishable reasons. [Valid in this sense means a test which primarily reflects the vocabulary knowledge construct.] These reasons can be logically categorized in terms of differences in relations (A) between test tasks and constructs or (B) among constructs.

(A) *Test-Construct relations*
  1. The "reading comprehension" test primarily measures Vocabulary Knowledge (VK);
  2. The "reading comprehension" test primarily measures Reading Comprehension (RC).

---

[5]E.g., vocabulary knowledge is a *logical* prerequisite for appropriate performance on comprehension test tasks. Although variation in performance due to differences in vocabulary can be suppressed by experimental training or selection of words, it cannot be removed as a source of extraneous (invalid) variation in practical test situations.

(B) *Construct-Construct relations*
1. Reading Comprehension (RC) is strongly related to Vocabulary Knowledge (VK);
2. Reading Comprehension (RC) is only weakly related to Vocabulary Knowledge (VK).

These particular (extreme) alternative relations may be arranged in a four-fold table with the entries reflecting the strength of the implied relation between the test scores (Table 4.1). Thus—given the constrained alternatives I proposed—the two tests may be strongly related for three quite distinctive reasons:

(a) the "reading comprehension" test is invalid—i.e., measures VK and not RC—and the constructs (VK and RC) are strongly related;
(b) the "reading comprehension" test is valid and the constructs (VK and RC) are strongly related;
(c) the "reading comprehension" test is invalid—i.e., it measures VK and not RC—and the constructs (VK and RC) are *not* strongly related.

If someone were to use the test for a predictive purpose where, at least on the surface, the test label was not considered of basic importance, that person might be unconcerned about which of these were actually the case. However, if one were engaged in placement of individuals in remediation programs in reading one might not be concerned about (a) or (b) but (c) would be troublesome. But if the test were used for diagnosis as well as placement or if one were evaluating a curriculum or engaging in a national assessment of reading comprehension abilities then only (b) would constitute a satisfactory state of affairs.

Note that this analysis implies that criteria for discriminant validity—i.e., measures of different constructs should relate less highly than measures of the same construct—can be difficult to implement unless a clear distinction is made between construct-construct relations and test-construct relations. The first relation derives from learning histories and the second from test characteristics.

TABLE 4.1
Strength of Empirical Relations Between Test Scores Under Different Test-Construct and Construct-Construct Relations

A. Test-Construct Relation	B. Construct (RC)-Construct (VK) Relation	
	Strong (1)	Weak (2)
"Reading Comprehension" Test relates		
(1) Strongly to VK (invalid)	Strong (a)	Strong (c)
(2) Strongly to RC (valid)	Strong (b)	Weak (d)

MEASUREMENT INTENT, MULTIDIMENSIONALITY, AND THE IDENTIFICATION OF INVALIDITY

As I discussed on p. 82 pupils are differentially exposed to educative tasks and they devote or are able to devote different amounts of practice to these tasks. In the extreme, one pupil will learn some skills and not others, while another pupil may learn the latter but not the former ones. For many combinations of skills (or ways of defining them) the possible patterns of learning opportunity are more constrained, however. If skills are of fundamental importance to the daily lives of children, e.g., speaking and understanding speech, the exposure and practice of a group with the same native tongue will be strongly homogeneous in comparison to those in other language groups. For different sets of skills, some may be logical or psychological prerequisites of others.

For these kinds of skills, there will be strong co-relations, regardless of the group of individuals. For other kinds of skills, the co-incidences of learning opportunities and experiences will vary from one individual or learning setting to another. Thus, co-relations among skills will differ from one group to another. Depending on the ways in which task domains are broken up and test tasks are constructed, collections and subcollections of items may or may not allow scorings which are sensitive to differences in the sequences and types of experiences.

From the ground of our theoretical framework, we distinguish between the *intent* of measurement and the *ancillary* skills required to actually respond correctly to the items. In statistical terms, both the intent of measurement and the ancillary skills are dimensions of measurement.[6] Such ancillary skills, their distribution over test items and their relations—among themselves and with the characteristic intended to be measured—are the key to an adequate conception of test validity and to the meaningful assessment of multidimensionality. Thus, invalidity in measurements is, in reality, undesired or malconfigured dimensionality.

In this framework, a test is not simply valid or invalid. Instead a score or measurement resulting from the test is made up of components (variations along specific dimensions), some combination of which constitutes the intent of the measurement; the remaining parts being sources of invalidity. Because these undesired components are—in general—co-related to the intended component, simple correlational indices do not accurately reflect the validity of the measurement.

---

[6]The statistical setting within which this discussion takes place is traditional and relatively straightforward: Individuals differ from one another in their states and functionings. Some aspects of these differences can be profitably represented by means of a multidimensional space with individual states or functionings corresponding to points in the space. This does not prohibit the differences from being conceived as qualitative, quantitative, or a mixture of qualitative and quantitative variation as all of these kinds of variation can be represented in these terms. It does, however, allow us to consider more than one aspect or "dimension" of variation at a time.

Thus, the key to the distinction between invalidity and valid multidimensionality is *intent*. Clearly, if one were to accept Cronbach's (or Vernon's) sidesteps toward a definition of reading comprehension, vocabulary knowledge *is not* part of the intent and therefore *is* a source of invalidity. However, if on the other hand, the intent is to measure some mixture of comprehension and vocabulary knowledge—called *reading,* then this is clearly multidimensionality of the intents of measurement, not invalidity. Obviously, a sharp specification of the *intent* is required before validity can be assessed.[7]

In order to further clarify these issues I shall return here to the concept of task and use it to refine what I mean by *intent* and to clarify the structural relations between ability and task. In the earlier discussion I focused on the logical relations between tasks and abilities, but I did not fully develop the features of test tasks in relation to the concept of intent.

As I indicated on p. 78, tasks are—by definition—goal oriented. One must distinguish, however, (a) the goal pursued in a particular task from the perspective of the person undertaking it—i.e., the performance goal—and (b) the goal(s) pursued by the person giving the task—i.e., the measurement goal. In the context of measurement—and in particular—tests, it is the latter set of goals for which I use the word intent.

I would here also distinguish between *intent* and *use*. Intent is a specification of the combination(s) of abilities which the test constructor/user desires to be reflected in the measurement(s) resulting from the application of a collection of tasks. The use to which these measurements will be put may (should) influence the intent but it is not identical to it. A valid set of measurements—defined in terms of realized intent—may be badly used. E.g., a test of computation skill might be used to select individuals into a program requiring problem solving abilities. The understanding of these *use errors* is conceptually and socially important, but involves social and moral analyses beyond the scope of test validation as defined here and would needlessly complicate the conception and definition of test validity.

The measurement intent—however vaguely it may be specified—has several important consequences for the measurement process: It provides the criteria for

1. *task creation or selection,* which involves
   (a) specifying the specific performance goal of that task,
   (b) specifying the circumstances of measurement,
   (c) specifying the "charge"—i.e., communicating the task requirements to the person undertaking the task;
and for
2. *performance assessment and scoring.*

---

[7]A pointed example of the relevance of intent to validity may be found in Cronbach (1980) where he discusses the validity of a physics knowledge item for qualifying firemen.

The setting of these criteria provides the basis for defining an equivalence class of tasks and resulting measurements. Members of an equivalence class will meet identical criteria for task selection, performance, and scoring.

As I indicated above, tasks cannot generally be conceived as unifocal. Tasks, and the performances they stimulate, form a part of a structure which links (hypothetical) abilities for task performance with the (potential) performances of particular tasks. This structure involves multiple abilities and multiple categories of tasks. And the relationship between these abilities for task performance and the task categories is not one-to-one. That is, task performances deriving from a given task category reflect multiple abilities.

This complexity occurs because (a) tasks and performance goals cannot be found which precisely match the measurement intent, (b) the circumstances of measurement bring into play additional abilities which are not explicitly part of the goals, and (c) the communication of the task requirements may be inaccurate or misunderstood. Thus, some of the abilities that were intended may not be present or may not be *weighted* appropriately in the performance and its assessment and other abilities not part of the intent may form a part of the performance or its assessment. All of these will result in multidimensionality and, as this will most often be unintended, in invalidity.

In the previous discussion, I termed this latter group of abilities: ancillary skills. Thus in the Cronbach discussion quoted earlier, the "counter interpretations" he cites are ancillary in relation to the reading comprehension intent of measurement.

I have also noted that tasks do not exist by themselves. The very nature of ability or skill definition requires that tasks be categorized or classified into equivalence classes. Abilities must apply to more than one task or they would not be *abilities*. These equivalence classes are homogeneous with respect to the intent of measurement, that is each of the tasks within them are presumed to have the same profile of skills—both intended and ancillary. The definition of these equivalence classes is based on the criteria—as described earlier—derived from the specified intent. In test validation, these criteria are based upon the current understanding of the relationships between task characteristics and the abilities the tasks reflect.

I do not mean to imply by this statement that actual measuring devices— tests—are constituted of collections of tasks which represent each of the specified equivalence classes by more than one task. It may be that some classes of tasks implied by the intent of measurement are not represented at all and that others are represented by only one task. The completeness of this representation will, of course, affect the validity of the test.

Another example of this distinction between intended and ancillary skills is the Campbell–Fiske notion of the multimethod, multitrait matrix (Campbell & Fiske, 1959). From my perspective, each cell in this matrix represents an equivalence class of measures. The method dimensions represent differences in ancillary skills or abilities and the trait dimensions represent either (a) different profiles of skills which are aspects of the intent of measurement or (b) wholly different intents.

Viewed from this perspective, the Cronbach example implicitly relates to equivalence classes of test tasks. Perhaps the test items contained in his hypothetical reading comprehension test form a single equivalence class. In this case these items would all be conceived as homogeneous in the mixture of speed, motivation, recognition and recall, vocabulary, test-taking skills, and information as well as reading comprehension. In order to fully validate such a test, one would have to have to create or find measurements representing sufficient additional equivalence classes so that each of these "counter interpretations" could be discarded, credited, or assessed as an invalid component or a "threat to validity." If, on the other hand, the items could be categorized into distinct equivalence classes, each representing a different mixture of intended and ancillary skills, then some or all of these counter interpretations might be addressed with information derived internally from the test itself.

Using these concepts, it is possible to expand and clarify some of the basic ideas of construct validity in the context of skill measurement. The "nomological net" of Cronbach and Meehl is a specification of the underlying skill components—both those intended in the measurement process and those which are ancillary to the intent—connected to a set of equivalence classes of test tasks. Each equivalence class is thus represented by a mixture of the skill components.

The intent of measurement—as a skill or combination of skills—is external to the net. I mean by this that the net may be specified without having defined an intent. The specification of intent involves the selection of a skill or set of skills with an accompanying set of "weightings." This intent is *attached* to an equivalence class—or collection of classes—of test tasks. This collection constitutes the formal specification of the measuring instrument—"the test."

Validation of an instrument consists of assessing the actual composition of the instrument—i.e., decomposing it—in terms of its intended and unintended components. Two different test constructors/users may have different intents for the same instrument, in which case the instrument will have two different compositions into intended and ancillary skills and, thus, two different validity assessments. As the composition of a new instrument becomes better understood, the intent may change in order to make the instrument more valid. This "wisdom" may accumulate: e.g., "Use test x to measure skill y [$= z + w$], but don't use it to measure skill z unless skill w is not well developed in your group."

The "net" is consistent in defining the collection of skills if the relationship between the hypothetical or latent part of the net—i.e., the skills, on the one side, and the potentially observable part—the collection of equivalence classes of test tasks, on the other, is *reversible,* i.e., if the collection of test tasks is sufficiently informative about the skills. This issue of consistency is tied to what is known in econometrics and statistics as the "identification problem." If a statistical model or other relational specification linking a set of *latent* characteristics to another set of *manifest* ones can be reversed—i.e., if the equations linking the one set of values to the other are mathematically invertible—then the system is "identified."

This consistency check on a hypothetical system is not empirical. That is, it has nothing to do with data. It only addresses the issue of whether the hypothesized system is internally consistent in that (a) the latent components are not defined in a contradictory or redundant manner, and (b) whether the density and character of the hypothesized latent-manifest relationships are, under any circumstances, sufficient to assess the latent structure. This latter part addresses the issue of whether empirical information can, even hypothetically, provide evidence about the network.

However, this identification issue for the entire network bears only on the specification tested; it does not imply that simple modifications in the network are not sufficient to correct a problem, or that component subsystems of "underidentified" systems are not identified. It is surely true that in most stages of scientific work, our conceptions are not only partially wrong, they are ultimately inconsistent. This inconsistency may be both necessary and useful at many stages of investigation.

Empirical data seldom bear on a whole network at once. As suggested earlier, in relation to the Cronbach example, a particular collection of test tasks will represent a subset of the inevitably potential equivalence classes of test tasks. Each of the classes represented reflects a particular mixture of skills and thus the realized classes in the data together with their model specifications represent a subnetwork. This subnetwork itself may be underidentified, just identified, or overidentified. In the first case the available empirical evidence is not sufficient to inform us about the subsystem. In the second, the evidence can only tell us about the magnitude of system components and then only if we assume that the hypothesized structure is correct. In the third, the evidence can inform us about whether the hypothesized structure is correct. However, depending on the structure of the relationships, it will only be diagnostic of specific inadequacies in the system.

REQUIREMENTS AND METHODS
FOR TEST VALIDATION

The conceptual framework outlined above has four features:

1. It segments the concept of a nomological network by separating (a) the skill constructs and their interrelations from (b) their manifestations in the test tasks. This distinguishes the *latent* part of the network from the potentially *manifest* portions and allows the consistency and testability of the network to be

assessed. This distinction is not new. It was explicit in Cronbach and Meehl and has been implicit in much of the subsequent discussion of construct validity. I emphasize it here because of the centrality of the distinctions to the rest of my argument.

2. This conceptual distinction allows us to see that the empirical interrelations among test task performances can be explained in two ways: (a) by means of the interrelations of the skill constructs which are represented in the tasks, and (b) by means of the pattern or profile of representation of those constructs in these tasks.

3. The distributions (including interrelations) of the constructs themselves are a consequence of the history of learning experiences of the individuals performing the test tasks, together with the logical, psychological, and neural constraints on the learning tasks and processes. The pattern or profile of skill representation in a test task is a consequence of task design and implementation, i.e., the goal of the task, the conditions under which the task is administered, and the understanding of the task requirements by the person undertaking the task.

4. The intent of measurement is a concept which applies to a test task or to a collection of tasks. As such, it is a specification for a particular task of the skill pattern or profile desired or expected. Thus, once it is possible to identify the actual skill pattern or profile represented in the task performance, the validity of the task for this intent can be assessed by analyzing the discrepancies between the two patterns.

If we are to understand validation in the spirit of Cronbach and Meehl, the above framework is to be used in the iterative fashion typical of scientific work. At the point that a particular empirical study is undertaken, there is a (partial) understanding of the structure of the network. The constraints imposed by this understanding allow one to test specific hypotheses about additional constraints—e.g., threats to the validity of a new measure. The testing of those hypotheses cast light on the structure of the new measure, but this new understanding is conditional on the prior structure of the network. To the extent that the study can also reform the original understanding, it may also result in the formulation of a new structure for the whole network. Thus, the scientific research process iterates between empirical investigation and modification of theory.

To quote Cronbach (1971):

> To explain a test score, one must bring to bear some sort of theory about the causes of the test performance and about its implications. Validation of test interpretations is similar, therefore, to the evaluation of any scientific theory. . . . Since each experiment checking upon a theory is an opportunity to modify or extend the theory, validation is more than corroboration; it is a process for developing sounder interpretations of observations. Construction of a test itself starts from a theory about behavior or mental organization, derived from prior research, that suggests

the ground plan for the test. Studies of the new test show how to improve it and sometimes lead to a change in the very conception of the variable to be measured. (p. 443)

For practical purposes of test validation, however, the process need not be iterative. The usual results of a well-conducted test validation study will be, in these cases, conditional on the understanding of the network at the time the study is undertaken and the design of such studies is focused on the new measure and not on a larger part of the network.

By emphasizing the conditional nature of test validation, I am departing from the emphasis given by Cronbach in the foregoing quotation. I thus formally distinguish *test* validation from *construct* validation. The latter—"scientific"—task involves taking the "opportunity to modify or extend the theory," while the former—"engineering"—task can be restricted to checking the ability composition reflected in the test and contrasting this to the measurement intent. From my perspective, this lifts an excessive burden from the shoulders of the test validator and makes it possible for excellent validations to occur without incurring the responsibility to refine a whole network of constructs.

Measurement Models

In order to make this framework concrete enough to actually use for purposes of test validation, some further specifications must be imposed. Over the period since Lord's monograph (Lord, 1952), many such specifications have taken the form of measurement models for test task performance scores, usually termed "test item responses."

These "response models" assume that the responses reflect (a) the state of skill or ability of the individual who responds to the item and (b) the item or test task, including the specific types of skills and knowledges required and the difficulty or complexity of the task. Thus, these models "explain" the responses of an individual with two classes of "parameters": (a) those characterizing the individual and (b) those characterizing the item. One of the intents of these models is, therefore, to define the skill of the individual independently of the particular (classes of) items or tasks used to test it and thus explain differences in correct rates of response over tasks with similar skill profiles via differences in the values of the "item parameters."

Implicitly, the models also assume that the same *abilities* are reflected in more than one test task and that it is possible, independently of the models themselves and their application to response data, to designate groups of items which reflect these abilities.

Currently existing models also have several distinguishable parts:

(a) Ability parameters representing the skills of an individual symbolically. These parameters can be conceived as numerical values on continua of such values or something more "qualitative," e.g., numerical values representing one of two dichotomous states, say "possess" and "not possess" a particular skill;

(b) Item parameters representing characteristics which translate the influence of the individual's abilities on his or her probability of correct response, together with a specific form of that translation. This aspect of the currently used models has several distinguishable parts:

  1. the ability parameters themselves,
  2. the first stage translation, i.e., the formula which translates one or more "abilities" into a single "ability to respond correctly to this particular item,"
  3. a second state translation or transformation which changes "ability to respond correctly to this particular item" into "probability that a person with this ability will be able to correctly respond to this item under 'ideal' circumstances," and
  4. distorting parameters which change the "ideal probability" to an hypothetical actual one, and, finally

(c) a statistical part which defines how a specified probability of correct response is linked to a potential distribution of correct and incorrect responses.

The structure of these models parallels the segmentation of the nomological network discussed earlier. However, in the context of that discussion, only the skills themselves [(a) and (b)(1) in the model segmentation] and their representation in the test task [(b)(2) in the model segmentation] were explicit. In what follows, we ignore those aspects of the models which explicitly represent the response structure [(b)(3), (b)(4), and (c)] in order to eliminate unneeded complexity in the argument. By doing this, we substitute item "constructs" for item responses, but still maintain a functional equivalence to the "nomological network."

If we further restrict the form of the model to continuous skills and linear additive representations, the resulting model is formally equivalent to a covariance structure or factor analysis model with factors representing skills and variables representing test task constructs. By making this restriction, I do not imply that skills and test tasks often or always should be represented in this way. Indeed, much of the model creation in which I have been involved (Haertel, 1980; Wiley, Haertel, & Harnischfeger, 1981) has argued that this specification is often inappropriate. My intent in using this restriction is to simplify the argument and to make it more readily interpretable to the reader. Other model specifications merely change the technique of implementation, not the logic of the procedures.

In the discussion of the nomological network, I introduced an analogy to the problem of identification for statistical models as a definition of consistency and testability of the network. Once the restriction to a factor or covariance structure analysis model is made, this analogy becomes a precise representation for this class of models. In fact, in the history of model and methodological development in this area, it has been enhanced model specification with increasingly explicit substantive rationales for constraints that have clarified previously obscure issues such as factor "rotation" as problems of model specification and identification. It is now clear (e.g., Bock & Bargmann, 1966; Bock, Dicken, & Van Pelt, 1969; Jöreskog, 1970; Wiley, Schmidt, & Bramble, 1973) how constraints on test task skill compositions relate to the identification of parameters representing interrelations among skill constructs.

Formal Assessment of Validity and Invalidity

Application of a statistical estimation procedure to data conforming to an identified measurement model will result in three distinct categories of information (see p. 95):

(a) *The response component* [(b)(3), (b)(4), and (c), above]: Parameter estimates delineating the transformation of the task-specific abilities to the scored response for the item. There will be a different set of these parameter estimates for each test task.

(b) *The ability composition reflected by the item* [(b)(2) above]: Parameter estimates exhibiting the particular combination or function of the abilities or skills measured by the test task. Again, there will be a different set of estimates for each task. In the context of the linear-additive model which characterizes covariance structure analysis and its extensions to item response models, this takes the form of $y = \Sigma_i b_i q_i$. Here the q_i represent distinct skills and the b_i their weights which constitute the skill profile of the task. Thus, the skill, y, that is measured by a specific test task is the particular composition of the skill components created by these weights.

(c) *The ability distribution of the group tested* [(b)(1) or (a) above]: The ability of every individual is specified in terms of a set of q_i, one corresponding to each skill component. The collection of these components for the tested group constitutes a multidimensional distribution. Estimation procedures produce either (a) estimates of the elements of this collection, i.e., estimates of the component abilities for each person tested, or (b) summary statistics for their multivariate distribution, usually a mean vector and covariance matrix for the group.

It is assumed in this type of model—via the linear-additive composition rule—that the skill mixture measured by a test task is the same regardless of the individual or group tested. This assumption divides the model parameters *cleanly* between item characteristics and person characteristics. It implies that individuals with very different ability profiles will combine these abilities in the same way when they perform the task.

The simplicity of this assumption is viewed by some cognitive psychologists as contradicted by their process findings (see e.g., Snow & Lohman, 1989). In fact, existing models can be conceptually extended to make the task-specific skill, y, a more general function of the component abilities—thus avoiding the linear-additive assumption. Thus, skills might be combined in nonlinear and nonadditive fashions which would allow for the fact that different ability profiles might produce "qualitatively" distinct performances. Current estimation technologies (e.g., Bock & Aitkin, 1981; Mislevy, 1984; and Bock, Gibbons, & Muraki, 1985) allow the estimation of a much wider class of models than previously. With these extensions, it is the *function* itself which is the same for each person because it incorporates all of the distinctive response processes, whether or not they are actually engaged by an individual with a particular profile of skills.

The approximation made by the linear-additive models should not be discarded too readily, however. If, say, an *expert* and a *novice* process task information differently by making use of distinct abilities, then a conception of ability which incorporates a true zero—representing the complete lack of a specific skill—can partially treat this issue within a linear-additive framework. In this case, the expert abilities could be characterized for novices by zero levels. However, the nonuse of novice skills by experts could only be treated by departing from the linear-additive composition rule if the experts are conceived as still maintaining their novice skills. In the following, I continue to use the linear-additive functional form for the sake of simplicity. The main points, however, carry over to more complex functional forms. I also indicate how the linear-additive framework can produce indices sensitive to differences in validity for distinct ability levels.

Within this framework, the specification of intent becomes the specification of a target profile of abilities for a test task [or equivalence class thereof]. Thus, intent becomes

$$y^* = \Sigma_i b_i{}^* q_i$$

and a well-specified intent will completely define the profile or combination of skills desired to be measured. [In the more general case, the intended *function* might be specified in a non-linear, non-additive form.]

Thus, from this perspective, the *in*validity of the test task would be

$$y - y^* = \Sigma_i (b_i - b_i{}^*) q_i$$

and the set of differences, $b_i - b_i{}^*$, would constitute the *invalidity profile* of the test task.

This specification decomposes the measured test-task-specific skill, y, into two parts:

$$y = y^* + (y - y^*).$$

The first—the intent (y^*)—being the *valid* part and the second—the invalidity ($y - y^*$)—being the *invalid* part. Consequently, the measured skill profile $\{b_i\}$, is also decomposed into the intended skill profile $\{b_i^*\}$, and the invalidity profile $\{b_i - b_i^*\}$.

In general, the valid and invalid parts will covary and the variance of the measured skill, y, will be

$$\sigma_y^2 = \text{Var}(y) = \text{Var}(y^*) + \text{Var}(y - y^*) + 2\text{Cov}(y^*, y - y^*).$$

Note that

$$\mu_y = \Sigma_i b_i \mu_i; \ \mu_y = \Sigma_i b_i \mu_i; \ \mu_{y-y^*} = \Sigma_i (b_i - b_i^*)\mu_i$$

$$\sigma_y^2 = \Sigma_i \Sigma_j b_i b_j \text{Cov}(q_i, q_j);$$

$$\sigma_{y^*}^2 = \Sigma_i \Sigma_j b_i^* b_j^* \text{Cov}(q_i, q_j);$$

$$\sigma_{yy^*} = \Sigma_i \Sigma_j b_i b_j^* \text{Cov}(q_i, q_j);$$

$$\sigma_{y-y^*}^2 = \Sigma_i \Sigma_j (b_i - b_i^*)(b_j - b_j^*)\text{Cov}(q_i, q_j); \text{ and}$$

$$\text{Cov}(y^*, \ y-y^*) = \Sigma_i \Sigma_j b_i^*(b_j - b_j^*)\text{Cov}(q_i, q_j);$$

All of these means and variance or covariance components combine task-specific parameters (b_i and b_i^*) with distributional parameters for the tested group [the m_i and the $\text{Cov}(q_i, q_j)$]. Thus, they are not functions solely of the task characteristics, but also of the group tested. Within the framework of the linear-additive specification, only the skill and invalidity profiles—e.g., the set $b_i - b_i^*$—are not dependent on the group tested. To the extent that the *actual* functional form conforms—within boundary conditions—to a specification with a similar invariant decomposition, the validity of the test task can be characterized independently of the group tested.

Validity indices based on the variance-covariance decomposition given above will be specific to the group tested and the indices' properties will depend on the invalidity profile and on group's skill means and covariance structure. Formulation of indices is also complicated by the fact that the valid and invalid parts of the measurement covary. Thus, a correlational index such as

$$\sigma_{y^*}^2/(\sigma_{y^*}^2 + \sigma_{y-y^*}^2)$$

is not appropriate because the denominator is not equal to σ_y^2. And

$$\sigma_{y^*}^2/\sigma_y^2 \quad \text{or} \quad \sigma_{y-y^*}^2/\sigma_y^2$$

do not conform to usual expectations because they can be greater than one. One correlational index which may have better integrative value is

$$\rho_{yy^*} = \sigma_{yy^*}/\sigma_y \sigma_{y^*}$$

which measures the correspondence between the actual and intended skills.

From my perspective, better group-specific indices are based upon the overall distributions of y, y^*, and $y - y^*$ or on the conditional expectations or conditional variances relating them. The expected value of the invalid part, $E[y - y^*] = m_y - m_{y^*}$ gives the average bias—in a statistical sense—resulting from the use of y in place of y^* and $\sigma_{y-y^*}^2$ is the bias variance around this mean. It should be recalled that since the invalidity values are combinations of undesired component skill constructs, all of these variance components index reliable but undesired variations.

If the invalid and the valid parts of the measurement were orthogonal to one another, the conditional expectation of y given y^* would merely be y^*. However, since, in general, y^* and $y - y^*$ covary, this expectational or regression function is

$$E[y|y^*] = \alpha_0 + \alpha_1 y^*, \quad \text{where}$$

$$\alpha_1 = \sigma_{yy^*}/\sigma_{y^*}^2, \quad \text{and}$$

$$\alpha_0 = \mu_y - \alpha_1\mu_{y^*} = \Sigma_i(b_i - \alpha_1 b_i^*)\mu_i$$

The residual from this regression, $y - \alpha_0 - \alpha_1 y^*$ is therefore orthogonal to y^*. Note that correlation ρ_{yy^*} is a standardized regression coefficient corresponding to the unstandardized α_1.

If the values of the additional (e.g., marker) variables for an identified covariance structure model were available, the intended construct values could be estimated directly by using the parameter estimates. This would constitute a multiple "regression adjustment" accomplished by subtracting the undesired skill components using appropriate coefficients. The validity of this adjustment would depend upon whether the model used to describe the skill composition was correct.

However, since the values of such variables are not available for general uses of y as a measure of y^*, improvements can be made by transforming y into the "metric" of y^*. This can be done by means of the other conditional expectation

$$E[y^*|y] = \gamma_0 + \gamma_1 y, \quad \text{where}$$

$$\gamma_i = \sigma_{yy^*}/\sigma_y^2, \quad \text{and}$$

$$\gamma_0 = \mu_{y^*} - \gamma_1\mu_y = \Sigma_i(b_i^* - \gamma_1 b_i)\mu_i$$

This transformation is similar to a linear "equating" of y and y^*. It should be noted that $E[y - y^* \mid y^*]$ gives the invalidity of y at each intended skill level. When more general functional forms than the linear additive are appropriate, this relation together with its variance version, $\sigma^2_{y-y^*|y^*}$, would be especially useful in assessing differential validity of the measure for individuals of varying ability. For example, a test task might be valid for low skilled persons, but not for high.

Similar conditional expectations could be based on vectors of component skills for more refined analyses.

A Further Elaboration of an Example

I continue with a brief analysis of the Cronbach (-Vernon) reading comprehension example. In his discussion, Cronbach listed six "counterhypotheses" which were threats to the validity of a measure of reading comprehension. Within the conceptual framework I have outlined, these potential components of "invalidity" (speed, motivation, recognition and recall, vocabulary, test-taking strategy, and information) are skill constructs within an implicit nomological network of which the test (construct) is also a part. [I note here that since the Cronbach contribution in 1971, considerable effort has been devoted to cognitive analyses of reading comprehension tasks (e.g., Kintsch & van Dijk, 1978; Perfetti, 1985; see also Snow & Lohman, 1989). These imply the subdivision of the reading comprehension constructs into finer components, but this refinement is omitted here.]

Thus, within the context of a restricted covariance structure model, there would be seven distinct skills (the six *threats* plus the reading comprehension construct) and a test task (collection) which is intended to measure reading comprehension. In terms of actual expectations, this *intent* could mean that none of the other skills contribute to task performance on this task or merely that *most* of the test task construct—i.e., the magnitude of the weight for the reading comprehension construct is large relative to the weights for the other skills.

To fully validate the reading comprehension test task in this example, one would have to invent or select a series of test tasks in which the patterns of skill representation were (a) distinct from the pattern(s) of the test tasks to be validated, and (b) composed in sufficiently known and distinct ways so that the implied constraints *identify* the network. That is, allow estimation of both the variances and covariances of the seven skills and the weights with which they are represented in the test tasks to be validated.

In practice, this would require a collection of additional test tasks. The most likely constraints would be "marker" tasks, which pin down the location of the "ancillary" skills in the network. For example, if an independent, focused measure of vocabulary knowledge were available—as discussed on p. 91, one constraint would be the *nonrepresentation* of the reading comprehension skill construct in this measure. Thus, the requirement would be an existing, consistent network of constructs and tasks which are identifiable in terms of their structure. To this would be added new tasks to be validated. The total, augmented network would allow estimation of the following parameters:

1. The mean values of the skills in the new sample;
2. The covariance structure of the skills in a new sample; and
3. The weights of the skills in the new tasks.

TABLE 4.2
Hypothetical Parameter Values for Validation of a Reading Comprehension Test

Skill Construct	Weights from Actual Skill Profile	Means	Covariance Structure						
			1	2	3	4	5	6	7
1. Speech	0.05	50	100						
2. Motivation	0.20	50	0	100					
3. Recognition & Recall	0.05	50	0	5	100				
4. Vocabulary	0.50	50	0	10	50	100			
5. Test Taking Strategy	0.10	50	10	5	15	15	100		
6. Information	0.05	50	5	5	70	60	15	100	
7. Reading Comprehension	0.90	50	10	10	35	50	10	20	100

Given this information, together with the intended weights, one could assess the validity of the new test tasks using the framework elaborated earlier. For purposes of concreteness, I give some hypothetical values for these parameters in Table 4.2. In devising these values, I have assumed that the data used to estimate them included marker variables for each of the six validity threats [sources of invalidity] and that these markers identified the location (mean) and scale (standard deviation) values for these constructs. Because of this assumption, the means and variances of these constructs (set here at 50 and 100 respectively) are meaningfully distinct from their weights in the test's skill profile.

Without an independent measure of reading comprehension, however, the mean and standard deviation of this construct are fixed by that of test (tasks) to be validated and its (their) relations to the markers. Therefore, the value of the weight for the reading comprehension construct is not identifiably distinct from its standard deviation—only the product is identified. In an actual analysis, the last row of the table would be calculated from the mean and variance of the test being validated together with its covariances with the markers and their means. I have constructed the table in a manner that corresponds to a restandardization of the reading comprehension construct (also) to a mean of 50 and a standard deviation of 10. This implies that the weight for this construct is, in principle, empirically determined, given the standardization.

Table 4.3 repeats the weights from the actual skill profile together with three possible intended profiles for the reading comprehension test. Note that the first intended profile for the test solely involves reading comprehension. This profile may be impossible to achieve, if—as I stated earlier—vocabulary knowledge is necessary for comprehension of text. The second and third profiles represent intentions which combine the reading comprehension construct with the vocabulary construct in varying amounts.

Using this information, one can calculate various structural parameters bearing on the validity of the instrument for the tested group. These include the regression relations between the intended and actual skills as well as the vari-

TABLE 4.3
"Actual" and Intended Skill Profiles for a Hypothetical Reading Comprehension
Test

Construct	Profile			
	"Actual"	Intended #1	Intended #2	Intended #3
1. Speech	0.05	0.00	0.00	0.00
2. Motivation	0.20	0.00	0.00	0.00
3. Recognition and Recall	0.05	0.00	0.00	0.00
4. Vocabulary	0.50	0.00	0.50	0.75
5. Test Taking Strategy	0.10	0.00	0.00	0.00
6. Information	0.05	0.00	0.00	0.00
7. Reading Comp.	0.90	1.00	1.00	0.75
Sum	1.85	1.00	1.50	1.50

ances and covariance of the valid and invalid parts, as already discussed. These are given in Table 4.4. Note that the first intended skill has the smallest variance—because the sum of squares of its weights is smallest—but it also has the smallest covariance with the actual skill. This is because vocabulary has relatively strong representation in the actual skill but is not represented in the intent. In correlational terms, the validity of the test with respect to this intent is only 0.674. However, once vocabulary is made part of the intent, as in numbers one and two, the covariance increases and the correlation rises into the nineties. The variances of the valid and invalid parts decrease correspondingly, but the covariances—which are negative because the other sources of invalidity are positively related to the reading comprehension and vocabulary constructs—do not vary much. This results in larger negative correlations between the valid and invalid parts. Also note that the metric transformation, $\gamma_0 + \gamma_1 y$, is most extreme

TABLE 4.4
Validity Analysis of a Hypothetical Reading Comprehension Test

Parameter	Actual Skill	Intended Skill		
		#1	#2	#3
Mean (μ)	92.5	50.0	75.0	75.0
Variance (σ^2)	178.1	100.0	175.0	168.8
Cov (y, y^*)		90.0	162.5	157.5
Cov ($y^*, y - y^*$)		-10.0	-12.5	-11.3
a_0		47.5	22.8	22.4
a_1		0.900	0.929	0.933
γ_0		3.3	-9.4	-6.8
γ_1		0.505	0.912	0.884
ρ_{yy^*}		0.647	0.920	0.908

for the first construct because the large "invalid" weight for vocabulary knowledge and the high covariance of this skill with reading comprehension.

The foregoing numerical example begins with the values given in Table 4.2. However, these values characterize tests rather than test tasks. It is therefore necessary to discuss the relations between the skill profiles for test tasks and those for tests. The perspective from which this paper is written is based on the notion that each test task will measure more than one skill. That is, in general, that skill structures are multidimensional. Once multidimensionality is admitted, however, certain simplifications which are built upon the assumption of unidimensionality vanish. In particular, unidimensionality implies that any two items measure exactly the same item construct. Once more than one construct is measured by a collection of test tasks, it cannot be assumed that the construct mixture reflected in each task is identical. That is, it cannot be assumed that assumptions of strict item equivalence for all members of nominally specified equivalence classes are met.

At the item level, each item corresponds to a particular construct mixture. Because the mixtures (slightly?) vary, even in a nominally "homogeneous" test, a question of skill definition arises for test as a whole. When unidimensional item response models are used in conjunction with a real (multidimensional) test, an "averaging" occurs with the resulting "latent trait" test score corresponding to an aggregate of the item constructs similar to the principal component of a set of variables.

If the test were strictly unidimensional—in this context this would mean that the skill profile weights were the same for each item—ordinary methods of scoring are readily interpretable and correspond to the same skill definition as "latent trait" scoring. The reason for this is that a total test score is the sum of the dichotomous (zero or one) item scores. The expected value of the total score (i.e., the "true" score) is, therefore, the sum of the expected values of the item scores and since these item scores measure the same mixture of constructs, the total will also do so. Thus, the number correct "true score" will be an exact (nonlinear) function of the "latent trait score." (For a brief discussion of this and the implications of multidimensionality for the correspondence, see Lord & Novick, 1968, p. 386.)

Even with models incorporating the linear-additive composition rule, multidimensionality eliminates the precise correspondence between a "latent trait score" and a (number correct) total score. There are a number of different ways to specify the definition of the skill being measured by the collection of test tasks as a whole. Each corresponds to a different scoring method. One way is to use the "principal component," i.e., to apply a unidimensional model as well as a multidimensional one and establish the "location" of the particular (one-dimensional) "average" skill created by this method in the larger multidimensional space. Another is to define the "average" skill as the actual average of the individual linear compositions of the items. A third is to use a linearization of the expected value of the (number correct) total score in terms of the overall multidimensional space. All three of these potential definitions will be similar to the extent that the test is (approximately) homogeneous, i.e., to the extent that the skill profile weights are similar from item to item.

Once an "actual skill" definition is specified, each item construct can be partitioned into the sum of the defined (composite) skill and a residual. This decomposition is similar to the intended-unintended decomposition discussed above. If the second definition above—i.e., the "average"—is used, then the mean of the residuals will be zero. This is so even though these residuals will (individually) covary with one another, with the "average" skill itself, and with the "intended" skill. This particular specification thus simplifies the computation of weights such as those given in the second and the subsequent tables. However, any particular specification of an "actual skill" makes it possible to calculate appropriate weights.

Information Relevant for Test Validation

Any conception of the validity of a measure must, within this framework, be specific to the network as well as the intent of the measure. That is, the weights which represent the relative contributions of the ancillary skills are dependent on the total set of skills specified in the network. Omission or inclusion of specific skills will change the task-skill specifications in the network and lead, in both theory and practice, to different weights. My thesis is that a specification of intent and this set of weights alone are sufficient to define the validity of the task with respect to the network.

This thesis is based on the notion that, within specifiable boundary conditions, the interrelations among the skills have no bearing on the validity of a task. The interskill relations are based on the learning histories of individuals in the sample used to validate the task. If the structure of the network is to apply to different individuals with different learning histories and if tasks are to occupy the same structural position in the network for different individuals and groups, then the network cannot completely specify the learning histories of the individuals to whom it applies. If it were to specify these, the network would be "static" and not apply to new individuals with different learning histories. I am not asserting here that some boundary conditions do not apply, only that the interrelations of skills will vary over groups because the network must apply beyond a single individual or a single group of individuals if it is to be scientifically meaningful.

Thus, the set of weights or—in the more general framework—the task-specific skill function, which estimates the extent to which a test task reflects each of the skills in the network, contains all of the relevant information about the validity of the task. This implies that simple correlational evidence, whether relating the manifest scores to external criteria or relating the internal skill components to such criteria, is fundamentally flawed as a primary criterion for validity. This is true because it confuses information which is specific to the validation sample, i.e., the variabilities and the interrelations of the skills, with information appropriate for validity assessment, i.e., the representation of the skills in the task.

This paper has reconsidered the problem of test validation. It has done so from a perspective that incorporates several concerns:

a. The considerable advances that have been made in extending and improving conceptions of measurement precision—i.e., reliability—have not been paralleled in the arena of validity.

b. The preoccupation with test use in recent discussions of validity has diverted attention from the fundamental roles of skills and task characteristics.

c. The most important conceptual advance in the understanding of validity—construct validity—has not led to significant improvements in test validation; in fact, it has tended to obscure the responsibilities of the validator by imposing the seemingly impossible task of scientifically validating the constructs themselves.

Motivated by these concerns, I have attempted to elaborate a conceptual framework for test validation. Much of this framework is not new; it is drawn from the construct validity perspective—but it is specialized to notions about skills and tasks and it alters some of the emphases given by others using the framework.

The framework builds on and develops a series of concepts and issues:

1. what tests measure—"skill" in the language of this paper—is fundamentally delimited by the concept of task: *a goal-oriented activity of determinable duration on which performance can be evaluated.*

2. skills are *abilities to perform tasks* and, as such, are structurally linked to other skills and to collections of tasks.

3. tests are *deliberately administered collections of tasks which have measurement intents.*

4. measurement intents are *specifications of skills or skill mixtures intended to be measured by a collection of tasks*—i.e., a test.

5. skill patterns in individuals are primarily *determined by learning histories and logical, neurological, and psychological constraints.*

6. skill profiles of test tasks are *determined by the particular characteristics of the task.*

7. task performance is *determined by an individual's skill pattern and the task's skill profile.*

8. the networks formed by skills and tasks are the *theories of learnings*—as

opposed to learning—which construct validation—as a scientific activity—*develops and tests;* this process proceeds *iteratively by* alternately *reforming network structures and empirically testing them.*

9. test validation—as opposed to construct validation—presumes a network structure and an intent of measurement and collects sufficient information to *decompose the skills measured into intended and unintended* and consequently assesses the validity of the test using this decomposition.

My hope is that this framework, which in my view makes test validation both feasible and profitable, will encourage the validation of existing and new instruments via

(a) specification of an assumptive network of skills and (potential) test tasks without the burden of validating the network itself,

(b) specification of the intended skill composition to be measured by the collection of tasks, and

(c) data collection allowing identification of skill components, conditional on the assumed network.

REFERENCES

Bock, R. D., & Aitkin, M. (1981). Marginal maximum likelihood estimation of item parameters: Application of an EM algorithm. *Psychometrika, 45,* 443–459.

Bock, R. D., & Bargmann, R. E. (1966). Analysis of covariance structures. *Psychometrika, 31,* 507–534.

Bock, R. D., Dicken, D., & VanPelt, J. (1960). Methodological implications of content-acquiescence correlation in the MMPI. *Psychological Bulletin, 71,* 127–139.

Bock, R. D., Gibbons, R. D., & Muraki, E. (1985). *Full-information item factor analysis* (MRC Report No. 85-1). Chicago: National Opinion Research Center.

Cain, P. S., & Treiman, D. J. (1981). The "Dictionary of Occupational Titles" as a source of occupational data. *American Sociological Review, 46,* 253–278.

Campbell, D. T., & Fiske, D. W. (1959). Convergent and discriminant validation by the multitrait-multimethod matrix. *Psychological Bulletin, 56,* 81–105.

Carroll, J. B. (1963). A model for school learning. *Teachers College Record, 64,* 723–733.

Cronbach, L. J. (1971). Test validation. In R. L. Thorndike *Educational measurement, second edition.* Washington, D.C.: American Council on Education.

Cronbach, L. J. (1980). Validity on parole: How can we go straight? *New Directions for Testing and Measurement, 5,* 99–108.

Cronbach, L. J., & Gleser, G. C. (1965). *Psychological tests and personnel decisions.* Urbana: University of Illinois Press.

Cronbach, L. J., Gleser, G. C., Nanda, H., & Rajaratnum, N. (1972). *The dependability of behavioral measurements: Theory of generalizability for scores and profiles.* New York: Wiley.

Cronbach, L. J., & Meehl, P. E. (1955). Construct validity in psychological tests. *Psychological Bulletin, 52,* 281–302.

Haertel, E. (1980). *A study of domain heterogeneity and content acquisition.* Evanston: CEMREL, Inc.

Harnischfeger, A., & Wiley, D. E. (1975). Teaching-learning processes in elementary school: A synoptic view. *Studies of Educative Processes, 9,* University of Chicago. (Also in *Curriculum Inquiry, 6,* 1976, 5-43. And in, D. A. Erickson (Ed.), *Readings in Educational Research: Educational Organization and Administration.* American Educational Research Association. San Francisco: McCutchan, 1976, 195–236.)

Harnischfeger, A., & Wiley, D. E. (1977). Conceptual issues in models of school learning. *Studies of Educative Processes, 10,* CEMREL, Inc. Also in *Journal of Curriculum Studies, 10,* 1978, 215–231. Also as Kernkonzepte des Schullernens. *Zeitschrift für Entwicklungspsychologie und Pädagogische Psychologie, IX,* 1977, 207–228.

Harnischfeger, A., & Wiley, D. E. (1981). Origins of active learning time. *Studies of Educative Processes, 18,* Northwestern University, 1981. An updated version is reprinted in C. Fisher & D. Berliner (Eds.), *Perspectives on instructional time.* New York: Longman, 1985.

Jöreskog, K. G. (1970). A general method for analysis of covariance structures. *Biometrika, 57,* 239–251.

Kintsch, W., & van Dijk, T. A. (1978). Toward a model of text comprehension and production. *Psychological Review, 85,* 1978, 363–394.

Lord, F. M. (1952). A theory of test scores. *Psychometric Monographs, 7.*

Mislevy, R. J. (1984). Estimating latent distributions. *Psychometrika, 49,* 359–381.

Perfetti, C. A. (1985). *Reading Ability.* New York: Oxford University Press.

Snow, R. E., & Lohman, D. F. (1989). Implications of cognitive psychology for educational measurement. In R. L. Linn (Ed.), *Educational measurement* (Third edition). New York: Macmillan.

Sternberg, R. J. (1977). *Intelligence, information processing and analogical reasoning: The componential analysis of human abilities.* Hillsdale, NJ: Lawrence Erlbaum Associates.

Thurstone, L. L. (1947). *Multiple factor analysis.* Chicago: University of Chicago Press.

U.S. Department of Labor (1977). *Dictionary of occupational titles.* Washington, D.C.: U.S. Government Printing Office.

Vernon, P. E. (1962). The determinants of reading comprehension. *Educational and Psychological Measurement, 22,* 269–286.

Wiley, D. E., Haertel, E., & Harnischfeger, A. (1981). Test validity and educational assessment: A conception, a method, and an example. *Studies of Educative Processes. 17,* ML-GROUP for Policy Studies in Education, Northwestern University.

Wiley, D. E., Schmidt, W. H., & Bramble, W. J. (1973). Studies of a class of covariance structure models. *Journal of the American Statistical Association, 68,* 317–323.

5

Test Analysis with the Person Characteristic Function: Implications for Defining Abilities

John B. Carroll
Ann Meade
Edward S. Johnson
University of North Carolina at Chapel Hill

INTRODUCTION

Some of Lee Cronbach's contributions to educational measurement have taken the form of elegant disquisitions on appraising the construct validity of psychological and educational tests (for example, see Cronbach, 1971). Most of these have concerned the use of external criteria. This chapter shows how analysis of certain internal characteristics of test data may promote improved definition and understanding of abilities.

The analysis uses the person characteristic function (PCF), which describes the relation, over individuals and tasks, between an individual's probability of performing a task correctly and the difficulty of the task. By *correct* performance we mean performance that meets or surpasses some set standard; in most cases, the task is a test item, and correct performance is taken to be indicated when the individual gives a keyed answer, even if that answer is a result of guessing or other extraneous effects. Task difficulty is usually indexed in terms of the proportion of individuals in some sample or population who perform the task correctly. Task difficulty can also be indexed in terms of attributes of the task, and indeed, doing so can aid in the definition of the ability underlying the task.

The formulation of PCF theory that follows is based, for the sake of simplicity, on the assumption that all tasks assembled in a test under consideration measure the same ability or cluster of abilities. The theory could be extended to the case of multiple abilities underlying tasks in a differential way, but such an extension is beyond the scope of this chapter. We show, in any case, that the assumption of a single ability not only is convenient, but also can often be confirmed in test analysis.

109

The idea underlying the PCF is not new. Although Mosier (1940, 1941) did not use the term, it is implicit in his work on a psychophysical treatment of test data. In a test development project done for the Navy some years ago (Carroll & Schohan, 1953), it was termed the "operating characteristic function." The idea is more explicit in work of Trabin and Weiss (1983), who speak of the "person response curve" and discuss the degree to which data for an individual fit the IRT (item response theory) model. It appears, however, that no systematic investigation of the person characteristic function is available in the literature.

The plan is first to present PCF theory, with a Monte Carlo investigation of certain sampling statistics, and then to illustrate its application to several sets of data. As in IRT, the problem of estimating the parameters underlying a set of data has to be addressed. With the PCF model, parameters can be estimated with reasonable accuracy even for small data sets.

THEORY AND METHOD

The person characteristic function employs the same mathematical model as that customarily used in item response theory (Lord, 1980; Lord & Novick, 1968). That is, the probability that a person will correctly perform a task is given as

$$p = c + \frac{1 - c}{1 + \exp[-1.7a(\theta - b)]}, \qquad [1]$$

where θ is a parameter specifying the ability of an individual, a is a parameter characterizing the slope of the function, b is a parameter characterizing the difficulty of the task, and c is a parameter specifying the probability of correct performance for an individual of infinitely low ability θ, or loosely, the probability of chance success by guessing. The parameters θ and b are in normal deviate metric. The logistic model specified in equation (1) yields approximately the same values as the normal ogive model (Lord, 1980, equation 2–2), and is used in place of the normal ogive for ease in computation.

The person characteristic function differs from the item response model only in that the probabilities yielded by the equation are to be studied for a single individual (or group of individuals with similar values of θ) as a function of different values of b, for different tasks. For the purposes of the following exposition, it is assumed that the values of the parameters a and c are the same for all items or tasks in a test, and, of course, for all individuals. Indeed, it is proposed that the value of the parameter a is not only constant for all items, but also is *characteristic of the ability being measured* rather than being specific to particular items or tasks, as is usually assumed in IRT.

While a may take any nonzero positive value, plots of the PCF function with respect to b give negative slopes, as may be seen in Fig. 5.1, which plots the

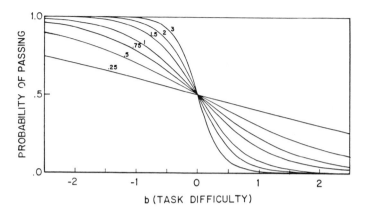

FIG. 5.1.   Person characteristic functions (PCFs) for an individual with $\theta = 0$, $c = 0$, for several values of a.

function, for an individual with $\theta = 0$, for several values of a. Fig. 5.2 shows plots of the function for $a = 1$ for individuals with selected values of θ.

Given a set of test data for which it can be assumed that all items measure the same ability, with constant a and c, the problem arises of estimating the value of a. Pilot work using Monte Carlo and other procedures has led to the suggestion that a useful estimate of a may be obtained by computing a certain regression slope, here designated ζ_1, of liminal values of PCF functions, for individuals or groups of individuals at different levels of the raw score distribution, on normal deviate values for those individuals (or groups) with respect to the raw score distribution. This idea can be illustrated with actual data on the Seashore

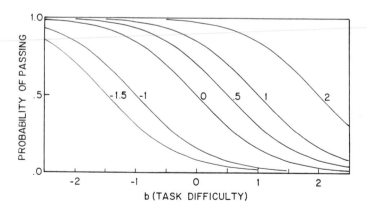

FIG. 5.2.   Person characteristic functions (PCFs) for individuals with several values of θ, $a = 1.00$, $c = 0$.

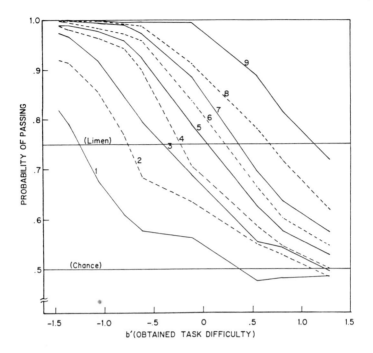

FIG. 5.3.   Person characteristic functions (PCFs) for noniles of the raw score distribution, Seashore Sense of Pitch Test (1919 edition), N = 1080.

Sense of Pitch test (previously discussed by Carroll, 1983). Figure 5.3 shows PCF functions for each jth nonile (ninth) of the raw score distribution; average probabilities, p_{jk}, of passing item sets (k) of different difficulties are plotted against normal deviate transforms, b'_k, of the obtained item set difficulties, p_k, as corrected for chance, p'_k. (For these data it is reasonable to assume, at least initially, that $c = .5$. In subsequent analysis a better fit to the model was obtained by assuming $c = .52$.)

In Fig. 5.4, these PCFs are shown in normal deviate form. That is, the average probabilities p_{jk} have been corrected for chance by the formula $p'_{jk} = (p_{jk} - c)/(1 - c)$ and are then transformed to normal deviate values ξ_{jk}. For convenience these values are denoted ξ_p. Using only the central portion of the data (where ξ_p lies between -1.64 and $+1.64$), it is possible, using linear regression slopes, to estimate the values of b' at which these functions cross the limen, i.e., where $\xi_p = 0$. These values are designated ϕ_j, for nonile j.

In Fig. 5.5, these crossing points, ϕ_j, are plotted against the mean normal deviate values, ψ_j, for the noniles. The slope of this function is computed as

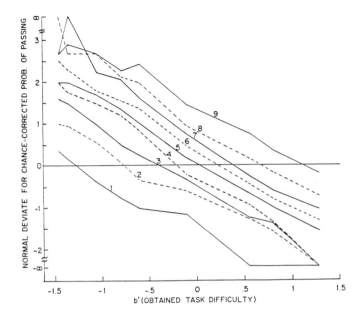

FIG. 5.4.   PCFs of Figure 3 shown in normal deviate form after correction of $p_{j,k}$ for $c = .5$.

.6895 using only points for noniles 2 through 8. The points for the noniles at the tails of the distribution are in general too unreliable to be used in estimating the slope.

It appears, now, that the value of a for these data can be computed from this slope by the equation

$$a = \zeta_1/\sqrt{1 - \zeta_1^2} \qquad [2]$$

Note further that the inverse of this relation is

$$\zeta_1 = a/\sqrt{1 + a^2} \qquad [2a]$$

No attempt is made here to derive this function. However, it is the same as the function relating values of b_k, true item difficulty values, to what Lord and Novick designate γ_g, the normal deviate transform of empirical item difficulties, but which we will designate b'_k. That is, by Lord and Novick's (1968) equation [16.9.4], with a slight change in notation,

$$b'_k = b_k a_k/\sqrt{1 + a_k^2} \qquad [3]$$

or

$$b'_k = b_k \zeta_2 \qquad (3a)$$

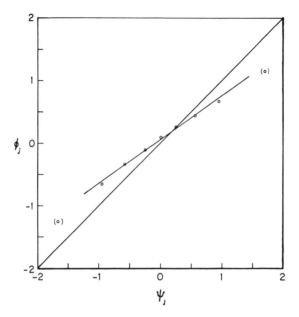

FIG. 5.5.   Plot of ϕ_j against ψ_j and the resulting linear slope, .6895, for data shown in Fig. 5.4. The parenthesized points are not used in computing the slope. For comparison, the diagonal line is the line of equivalence.

Here ζ_2 is used to denote the parameter in equation (3a) because, although it is usually close to ζ_1, it is in general not identical to it, being estimated in a different way. Further, since a is assumed constant for all items and item sets, the subscript k may be dropped from a_k.

Solving equation (3a) for b_k,

$$b_k = b'_k/\zeta_2 \tag{4}$$

Thus, from empirical data one can first estimate ζ_1 from "crossings" (measured in the metric of b') of PCF functions with the limen and then use ζ_1 as an estimate of ζ_2 to obtain "true" values of b_k for item sets k. Generally data on sets of items with closely similar values of b' are averaged in order to obtain more reliable data on p values. The averaging of data for individuals grouped in terms of noniles of the raw score distribution also tends to produce smoother and more stable PCF's.

To investigate the properties of PCF parameters and their estimation, an extensive series of Monte Carlo runs was conducted for selected values of a, c, and N. Ten samples were generated for each combination of the values $a = .25$, .5, .75, 1, 1.5, 2, and 3, $c = 0$, .25, and .5, and $N = 49$, 99, and 199 (thus, 630 samples in all). It was assumed that the test consisted of 50 items, with 10 items at each value of $b = -2, -1, 0, 1$, and 2. Individuals were assumed to be normally distributed with respect to θ; for any given value of N, values of θ were assigned as the mean normal deviate values of the successive N portions, each with area $1/N$, of the normal density function. (Values of N were odd numbers in order to include an individual with $\theta = 0$ and to increase the likelihood of a true middle nonile.) Item responses were generated by random number procedures; that is, a score of 1 was assigned when a random number from a uniform distribution extending from 0 to 1 equaled or exceeded the probability given by the PCF, a score of 0 otherwise. (Over all samples, 3,643,500 item responses were generated.)

For each sample, a number of statistics were derived, as follows, together with appropriate score distributions:

1. The raw score mean.

2. The raw score S.D.

3. The raw score reliability, computed as the square of the Pearsonian correlation between raw scores and the assigned values of θ.

4. The raw score reliability corrected for c, computed by Carroll's (1945) equation (34).

5. ζ_1: The linear regression slope of estimated limen values of b', ϕ_j, for noniles of the raw score distribution on mean normal deviate values, ψ_j, for those noniles. (See further details below.)

6. ζ_2: The linear regression slope of normal deviate values of empirical item set difficulties corrected for chance, b'_k, on the true item difficulties, b_k. (See further details below.)

7. Means and S.D.s of scores on item sets.

Computation of the ζ_1 and ζ_2 statistics can best be explained with reference to a representative PCF table for a generated sample as shown in Table 5.1, for $a = 1.5$, $c = .25$, $N = 49$. Boundaries of noniles of the raw score distribution are established by an algorithm that puts as close as possible to $N/9$ cases in each nonile, maintaining separation between different raw scores (these frequencies are shown as $N_j = 6, 5, 5, \ldots, 5$ in the table).

Estimation of the ζ_1 statistic requires computation of two values, ψ_j and ϕ_j, for each nonile j of the raw score distribution (in the table, the computed values are shown as the second and third values in the last column for each nonile). The value of ψ_j is the mean normal deviate for the cases in the nonile, assuming an underlying normal distribution of ability, computed as $(z_1 - z_2)/A$, where $A =$ the proportional area N_j/N, and z_1 and z_2 are the ordinates of the normal distribution function at the lower and upper boundaries of the nonile. The value of ϕ_j depends on computations that start from the probabilities of passing the items in the designated item sets. For example, for persons with raw scores up to 22,

TABLE 5.1
PCF Table for a = 1.5; c = .25; N = 49
Generated Sample 1, Monte Carlo Runs

Nonile	b (Theoretical Task Difficulty)					p	N_j ψ_j ϕ_j
	-2.00	-1.00	.00	1.00	2.00		
No. Items	10	10	10	10	10		
To 22:	.733	.433	.317	.233	.233	.390	6
* ξp:	.37	-.69	-1.35	-2.32	-2.32	-.89	-1.66
$r_{b',\zeta}$	*	*	*			-.9941	-1.36
To 24:	.980	.640	.260	.300	.160	.468	5
* ξp	1.93	.05	-2.22	-1.50	-2.32	-.55	-.95
$r_{b',\zeta}$		*				-1.0000	-.82
To 28	1.000	.780	.340	.240	.300	.532	5
* ξp:	2.32	.54	-1.17	-2.32	-1.50	-.32	-.60
$r_{b',\zeta}$		*	*			-.9865	-.52
To 30:	.975	.950	.675	.150	.225	.595	4
* ξp	1.83	1.50	.17	-2.32	-2.32	-.10	-.34
$r_{b',\zeta}$		*	*			-.9669	-.25
To 32:	1.000	.933	.678	.233	.311	.631	9
* ξp:	2.32	1.35	.18	-2.32	-1.40	.02	.00
$r_{b',\zeta}$		*	*			-.9603	-.27
To 35:	1.000	.925	.800	.425	.250	.680	4
* ξp	2.32	1.28	.62	-.73	-2.32	.18	.34
$r_{b',\zeta}$		*	*	*		-.9864	.26
To 38:	1.000	.983	.917	.550	.300	.750	6
* ξp:	2.32	2.01	1.22	-.25	-1.50	.43	.63
$r_{b',\zeta}$			*	*	*	-1.0000	.62
To 42:	1.000	1.000	.900	.740	.400	.808	5
* ξp:	2.32	2.32	1.11	.39	-.84	.66	1.03
$r_{b',\zeta}$					*	-.9786	.89
To 48	1.000	1.000	.960	.980	.540	.896	5
* ξp	2.32	2.32	1.61	1.93	-.29	1.09	1.75
$r_{b',\xi}$					*	-1.0000	1.41
Mean p:	.963	.847	.647	.416	.304		
*b'_j	-1.65	-.83	-.07	.77	1.46		

$r_{\phi\psi} = .9754$ $\zeta_1 = .8782$ Est. $a_1 = 1.836$
$r_{b,b'} = .9996$ $\zeta_2 = .7824$ Est. $a_2 = 1.256$

* ξp and b' values are corrected for chance; starred values are used in regular ϕ_j computations.

these probabilities are shown in the table as .733, .433, .317, .233, and .233. The probabilities are first corrected for chance by the formula $p' = (p - c)/(1 - c)$ and then converted to normal deviate equivalents, ξ_p. They are then appraised for their usefulness in computing ϕ_j, which is the estimated value of b' at which the true, smoothed PCF for nonile j has a value of 0, i.e., the value of b' (on the empirical task difficulty scale) at which the PCF for a particular nonile crosses the threshold. Experience suggests that values of ξ_p outside the range -1.6449 to 1.6449, corresponding to p' values of .05 and .95 respectively, are too unreliable to be used; values within this range are therefore indicated by asterisks in the next line of the table. Let the number of "usable" data points be denoted NC. Next, a series of rules dictates how the data points are to be used, for any given nonile, in computing the linear slope of the ξ_p values against the values of b', shown towards the bottom of the table—a slope that is used in finding the intercept with $\xi_p = 0$ by the equation

$$\phi_j = b^r - \frac{r_{\phi b'}\bar{\xi}\sigma_{b'}}{\sigma_\xi} \qquad [5]$$

The rules that have been developed are complex and are difficult to state verbally. Possibly further improvements could be made in them. The computer subroutines that implement them, written in Applesoft BASIC, are given in Table 5.2, with definitions of variables. The overall effect of these rules is to use normally at least 3 data points in estimating the intercept, in the metric of b', of the average PCF with $\xi = 0$. If NC is less than 3, one or more data points are added to the left or right of the usable points. Also, if there is no variance in the usable data points, or if the slope is positive rather than negative (as will occasionally happen), data points are added. When NC = 0 (a rare event that occurs only for high values of a or widely separated values of b'), the value of ϕ_j is taken to be the average of adjacent values of b' straddling the point at which the function turns negative.

Finally, the correlation, $r_{\phi\psi}$, between the middle 7 values of ϕ_j and ψ_j, weighted by the frequencies (N_j) of these values, is computed. Experience has indicated that the data points in the end noniles ($j = 1, 9$) tend to introduce undue error in estimation, being based largely on probabilities near 1 or 0. The value of ζ_1 is then computed as the slope

$$\zeta_1 = r_{\phi\psi} \sigma_\phi/\sigma_\psi. \qquad (6)$$

Occasionally, by chance, this slope exceeds .9999, or even 1, giving extremely high or impossible estimates of a, in which case ζ_1 is arbitrarily set exactly equal to .9999.

The value of ζ_2 is computed as the linear slope of the empirical item set difficulties, b'_k, on the true item difficulties, b_k. Generally, estimates of a based on ζ_2 are closer to the true value of a than those based on ζ_1, presumably because they are based directly on the obtained values of b' (as shown toward the bottom of Table 5.1), whereas ζ_1 is based on somewhat imperfect estimates of ϕ_j. The correlation between b_k and b'_k is invariably very high, and on the average slightly higher than $r_{\phi\psi}$.

Tables 5.3 and 5.4 present the means and S.D.'s of ζ_1 and ζ_2, respectively, over the ten samples for each combination of values of a, c, and N. (The S.D.'s

TABLE 5.2
Computer Routines for Computing $\phi(j)$ for a Single Nonile

Lines from Main Executive Program:

```
11762 FOR IB = 1 TO NB: X = SB (IB) / (NI (IB) *N):
              GOSUB 900:
              EB(IB) = -IT:
          NEXT IB:
          PT=1/(2*N): GOSUB 830:EB(0)=IT:
          EB(NB+1) =-IT
....
13184 REM LINE 13185 INITIALIZES VARIABLES
              IN PREPARATION FOR SUBS 930 & 950
13185 XC=0:SC=0:XG=0:SG=0:CG=0:FG=1:NC=0:NT=0:BO=0
13190 FOR IB=1 to NB:
              X=DA(IK,IB) / (NI (IB) * NJ (IK)):
              GOSUB 900
13220   GOSUB 930:
              NEXT IB
13240     GOSUB 950
```

Subroutines Called from the Above:

```
900 REM CORRECTS X FOR CHANCE & CONVERTS TO NORMAL DEVIATE
902 X=(X-C(IC)) / ((1-C(IC)):
          IF X<=0 THEN PT=1 / (2*N): GOSUB 830: RETURN: REM RETURNS IT
910   IF X>=1 THEN PT=1 / (2*N): GOSUB 830: IT=-IT: RETURN
920   PT=X:
          GOSUB 830: REM SUB 830 (NOT SHOWN HERE)
              RETURNS NORMAL DEVIATE=IT FOR PT
925   RETURN

930   REM COMPUTE DATA FOR PH(IK)=CROSSING, FROM SINGLE CELL
932   IF IT<0 AND NT=0  THEN NT=IB: REM NT=IB FOR 1ST NEGATIVE CELL
934   IF FG=0 THEN RETURN
936   IF IT>1.6449 THEN XC=0: SC=0: XG=0: CG=0: NC=0: RETURN
938   IF IT<-1.6449 THEN FG=0: RETURN
942   XC=XC+IT:
          SC=SC+IT*IT:
          XG=XG+EB(IB):
          SG=SG+EB(IB)^2
944   CG=CG+IT*EB(IB):
          NC=NC+1:
          BO=IB:
          RETURN

950   REM COMPUTE CROSSING=PH(IK)
952   IF NC =0 THEN CG=0:
          IF NT=1 THEN PH(IK)=(EB(1)+EB(0)) / 2: RETURN
954   IF NC=0 AND NT=0 THEN PH(IK)=(EB(NB)+EB(NB+1)) /2: RETURN
956   IF NC=0 THEN PH(IK,=(EB(NT)+EB(NT-1)) / 2: RETURN
958   IF NC<3 THEN 993
960   XC=XC/NC:
          IF(SC/NC-XC*XC)<1E-9 THEN 992
962   SC=SQR(SC/NC-XC*XC)
964   XG=XG/NC:
          SG=SQR(SG/NC-XG*XG):
          CG=(CG/NC-XC*XG) / (SC*SG):
          IF CG>=0 THEN 987:REM POS. OR ZERO SLOPE
```

```
966   PH(IK)=XG-CG*SG*XC/SC: RETURN: REM NORMAL RETURN
987   REM RECOVER ANY SUM X,Y,X2,Y2,XY NECESSARY
988   CG=NC*(CG*SG + XC*XG)
989   SG=NC*(SG^2 + XG^2)
990   XG=XG*NC
991   SC=NC*(SC^2 + XC^2)
992   XC=XC*NC:  REM CALLED 960
933   REM USE RULES IN ADDING DATA POINTS
944   IF BO=0 AND NC=NB THEN AX=EB(NB+1): AE=EB(0): GOTO 998
995   IF BO=0 THEN AX=EB(NB+1): AE=EB(NB-NC): GOTO998
996   IF BO-NC+1=1 OR XC/NC>=0 THEN AX=EB(0): AE=EB(BO+1: GOTO 998
997   AX=EB(NB+1): AE=EB(BO-NC)
998   NC=NC+1
      XC=XC+AX
      SC=SC+AX^2
999   XG=XG+AE:
      SG=SG+AE^2:
      CG=CG+AX*AE:
      GOTO 960
```

Definitions of Variables:

AE	An added data point, assumed value of b'
AX	An added data point, assumed value of ξ_p
BO	Index: value of IB for last "usable" initial data point
CG	Sum of crossproducts of ξ_p and b' values, also the correlation
C(IC)	The currently applicable value of c.
DA(IK,IB)	Sum of scores for nonile IK and item set IB
EB(IB)	Value of b' for item set IB = 0, 1, ..., NB+1
FG	A flag used in finding usable data points
IB	Index for item set, IB =0, 1, ..., NB+1
IC	Index for current value of c
IK	Index for current nonile
IT	A normal deviate value
N	No. of cases
NB	No. of item sets
NC	No. of points used in computing r_ϕ, b' and intercept PH(IK)
NI(IB)	No. of items in set IB
NJ(IK)	No. of cases in nonile IK
NT	First value of IB where ξ_p is negative
PH(IK)	Intercept of slope with ξ =0 for nonile IK
PT	A probability of passing items in an item set, for persons in nonile IK
SB(IB)	Total sum of scores for item set IB, over N persons
SC	Sum of squares of ξ_p values, and S.D.
SG	Sum of squares of b' values, and S.D.
X	A value used in subroutines
XC	Sum of ξ_p values, and mean
XG	Sum of b' values, and mean

are sample statistics based on $n = 10$ rather than population estimates based on $n = 9$; they are designated s.e. (standard error) in the tables.) These data yield information on the degree of bias and variability inherent in the statistics generated, and thus on the degree of confidence that can be placed on estimates of a developed from actual empirical data.

Table 5.3 suggests that ζ_1 can be estimated with considerable reliability,

TABLE 5.3
Obtained Mean ζ_1 and s.e. Over Ten Samples in Monte Carlo Runs Given
a, c, and N*

a	True ζ	N	$c = 0$		$c = .25$		$c = .5$	
			ζ_1	s.e.	ζ_1	s.e	ζ_1	s.e.
.25	.242	49	.297	.020	.296	.037	.313	.057
		99	.302	.040	.331	.026	.332	.033
		199	.300	.014	.331	.023	.360	.034
.50	.447	49	..472	.022	.496	.056	.533	.069
		99	.465	.019	.486	.042	.509	.044
		199	.475	.012	.485	.029	.533	.037
.75	.600	49	.594	.023	.590	.051	.643	.061
		99	.598	.026	.630	.040	.612	.055
		199	.593	.014	.630	.025	.644	.035
1.00	.707	49	.714	.040	.730	.081	.756	.099
		99	.701	.034	.714	.024	.765	.066
		199	.704	.017	.714	.031	.769	.029
1.50	.832	49	.830	.063	.865	.085	.924	.181
		99	.863	.074	.869	.091	.819	.082
		199	.839	.068	.843	.075	.889	.083
2.00	.894	49	.914	.058	.904	.070	1.089	.160
		99	.867	.090	.974	.084	.936	.073
		199	.878	.042	.924	.087	.939	.142
3.00	.949	49	.974	.024	.982	.109	.949	.215
		99	.986	.019	1.002	.057	1.053	.109
		199	.998	.020	.988	.062	1.031	.073

*For each sample, a normal distribution of θ was assumed, mean $\theta = 0$; S. D. = 1. There were 10 items at each value of $b = $ -2, -1, 0, 1, and 2.

especially for lower values of a. Standard errors tend to increase with a and with c and to decrease with N. For reasons that are not clear at this time, there tends to be a slight upward bias in estimations, but for practical purposes this can be ignored.

Somewhat similar phenomena are revealed in Table 5.4, but because the standard errors are generally much smaller than those in Table 5.3, the data lend confidence to the idea of using the value of ζ_1 derived from empirical data as an estimate of ζ_2, useful in estimating theoretical values of b_k by equation (4).

Not shown here in tabular form, because of space limitations, are other results from the Monte Carlo runs. Of interest are the following points:

1. Raw score means are essentially constant through all runs for different values of a; for any given value of c, they vary only by small chance fluctuations. They are, however, a function of the average value of b_k, which was

TABLE 5.4
Obtained Mean ζ_2 and s.e. Over Ten Samples in Monte Carlo Runs Given a, c, and N*

a	True ζ	N	c = 0		c = .25		c = .5	
			ζ_2	s.e.	ζ_2	s.e.	ζ_2	s.e.
.25	.242	49	.257	.013	.256	.021	.260	.043
		99	.258	.010	.252	.020	.250	.022
		199	.251	.009	.251	.012	.262	.011
.50	.447	49	.458	.018	.439	.019	.471	.020
		99	.444	.008	.462	.016	.443	.023
		199	.45˙	.014	.450	.014	.456	.017
.75	.600	49	.593	.013	.574	.031	.587	.049
		99	.598	.006	.596	.014	.583	.024
		199	.601	.008	.579	.014	.610	.020
1.00	.707	49	.690	.009	.703	.022	.671	.040
		99	.690	.013	.677	.027	.697	.034
		199	.695	.008	.696	.013	.703	.028
1.50	.832	49	.819	.031	.831	.060	.804	.075
		99	.818	.019	.809	.030	.786	.030
		199	.818	.010	.815	.030	.818	.041
2.00	.894	49	.887	.020	.899	.052	.879	.081
		99	.884	.015	.893	.051	.821	.042
		199	.883	.009	.874	.021	.879	.095
3.00	.949	49	.947	.025	.928	.089	.928	.057
		99	.942	.012	.934	.030	.931	.064
		199	.939	.009	.924	.035	.929	.060

*For each sample, a normal distribution of θ was assumed, mean $\theta = 0$, S. D. = 1. There were 10 items at each value of $b = -2, -1, 0, 1$, and 2.

constant at zero for our runs. Raw score means vary with c as predicted by Carroll's (1945) equation (25).

2. Raw score standard deviations increase with a, more so for $c = 0$ than for $c > 0$. Given the expected standard deviation for $c = 0$, the standard deviations expected for other values of c can be predicted by Carroll's (1945) equation (26). Standard errors of standard deviations tend to decrease with a and with N.

3. Uncorrected raw score reliabilities increase with a but decrease with c. Their standard errors decrease with a and with N. Obtained reliabilities are also a function of the distribution of the values of b_k, but this distribution was constant for our Monte Carlo runs.

4. When obtained reliabilities are corrected for chance by Carroll's (1945) equation (34), they are not significantly different over values of c.

Estimation of Parameters from Empirical Data.   The goal is to estimate parameters a and c such that data generated from those parameters will fit the empirical data as closely as possible in terms of distributions of total scores and scores on individual item sets, fits being assessed by chi-square tests. The estimation procedures that have been developed are described below. It has been found that they depend critically upon appropriate estimation of the parameter c, a matter that can be discussed most readily after the procedures for estimating a, as a function of an estimated value of ζ_1 and associated values of b_k, are presented:

1. Biserial correlations of items with total score are computed. Items with correlations less than a certain critical value, which may be chosen somewhat arbitrarily and which may differ from test to test depending on the distribution of r_{bis}, are eliminated from further analysis. In particular, items with very low or negative r_{bis} are to be discarded. The items remaining in the analysis are therefore to be relatively homogeneous with respect to r_{bis}.

2. These remaining items are ordered in terms of p values and grouped into item sets with similar p values. Scores on these item sets, as well as the total scores on all selected items, are then computed. Each item set should contain at least 3 items.

3. The total score distribution on the selected items is divided into noniles (or sometimes lesser portions, say quintiles) and PCF data are compiled, i.e., data on the mean probabilities, p_{jk}, of passing each item set k for each nonile group j.

4. These PCF data, with a specified value of c (as estimated by procedures to be described below), are input to a computer program that applies the same rules as described above to estimate the value of ζ_1 and a corresponding value of a, by equation (2).

5. To confirm that an appropriate value of a has been estimated, at least 5

samples are generated for the given estimate of a, using values of b estimated from values of b' by equation (4). To accept a value of a, the mean values of the mean, S.D., and reliability yielded by the generation process must fit within 2 standard errors of the empirical values. Also, chi-square tests of the fits of yielded total and item set score distributions to the empirical distributions must be acceptable. If these tests do not produce acceptable fits of data to the model, different values of a, possibly obtained by interpolation on different values of ζ_1, can be tried until an acceptable fit is obtained, if any. Occasionally it is found that an acceptable fit can be found by changing the S.D. of the θ distribution from 1.00 to some other value, generally smaller. Data sets for which acceptable fits cannot be found probably violate one or more assumptions of the model.

Estimation of the Parameter c.   Although it may sometimes be acceptable to estimate c on apriori grounds as the reciprocal of the number of alternatives in a multiple-choice test format, use of PCF theory makes it possible to estimate this parameter on a more objective and empirical basis. In step (4), above, it was stated that a computer program estimates ζ_1 and a corresponding value of a for a specified value of c. By varying c, this same program can be used for observing the effect of c on various other functions, in particular, $r_{\phi\psi}$ and the weighted average value of $r_{b'\xi}$ over noniles 2–8. The value of $r_{b'\xi}$ for nonile 1 is also a useful indicator of an appropriate value of c, especially when it is based on at least 3 data points, because it reflects the responses of the lowest-scoring examinees, who are most prone to guessing. In general, it may be inferred that an appropriate value of c is selected when these functions are together maximized. Using various sets of empirical data where c could be tentatively selected on apriori grounds, the rule was adopted that c would be selected at that value where $r_{\phi\psi}$ was a maximum while the average negative value of $r_{b'\xi}$ over noniles 2–8 and the negative value of $r_{b'\xi}$ for nonile 1 were high or still increasing. It seemed reasonable to assume that these functions would be at or near their maxima when c was properly selected, in the sense that a correct value of c would produce the best fit of the model in terms of the $r_{\phi\psi}$ and $r_{b'\xi}$ functions. It was realized that the assumption of a constant value of c for all item sets might be questionable, but the goal was to obtain the best estimate of an *average* value for this parameter. This was found to be important because the value estimated for ζ_1 was found to be strongly dependent on the value of c selected. Further problems in the estimation of c are discussed below in connection with analysis of various data sets.

APPLICATION TO DATA SETS

This section describes application of the PCF model to several data sets, including one that has already been presented briefly for illustrative purposes, and others from a series of spatial ability tests. The object here is to show that the PCF model does indeed fit most of these data sets quite well. The resulting values of a, which differ from one data set to another, are also of interest. In a later section, an effort is made to relate item difficulty data to attributes of items.

The Seashore Sense of Pitch Test.   In a previous analysis of data from this test (Carroll, 1983), a value of $c = .5$ was assumed on apriori grounds. In the present analysis, however, it was found that a value of $c = .52$ produced the best fit of the data for the total scores in terms of $r_{\phi\psi}$ and $r_{b'\xi}$ functions as described earlier. For this value of c, ζ_1 was estimated as .7591, corresponding to $a = 1.17$. Samples generated with these values produced an acceptable fit to the total score distribution, but not for most of the subtests. Because in the previous analysis it had been found that the first 5 subtests and the last 4 subtests had different response bias characteristics, it was decided to analyze total scores on these sets of subtests separately. The different response biases, it was thought, would be reflected in different values of c, and this indeed appeared to be the case. For the total score on subtests A–E, c was estimated as .59, with $\zeta_1 = .8861$ and $a = 1.91$. (In this case, because of the highly skewed score distribution, ζ_1 was estimated on the basis of the slope of ϕ_j on ψ_j for noniles 2–6 only.) Samples generated from these parameters produced acceptable fits for the total score distribution and most of the subtests. For the total score on subtests G–J, c was estimated as .43, but several values of a had to be tried before generally acceptable fits for total and subtest distributions were achieved. The finally accepted value of a was .58. The present analysis appears to confirm the findings of the previous analysis that values of a differ substantially over the various subtests. It is believed that only a test freed of the defects of the 1919 edition of the Seashore Sense of Pitch Test, as used for these data, would give more satisfactory fits to the PCF model. Nevertheless, the present results are not totally unsatisfactory.

The Block Counting test.   This test was one of a series of paper-and-pencil spatial ability and other tests administered to 119 10th-grade boys and girls. Data on five of the spatial ability tests are analyzed here. The tests were given in such a manner that all examinees had time to attempt every item.

The Block Counting test, taken with minor adaptations from one published by J. E. King (1947–50), contains a total of 32 items, each presenting a perspective drawing of a pile of blocks. The respondent is told that in any given pile, all the blocks are of the same shape; some piles have cubes, others have rectangular parallelopipeds of various dimensions. Sample items are seen in Fig. 5.6, which illustrates that items vary in "symmetry" and in the proportion of visible blocks. The respondent is required to state the number of blocks represented in each item. For each item, a score of 1 is assigned only if the respondent states exactly the correct number of blocks; otherwise the score is 0. Because of the free response nature of this test, the apriori assumption would be that $c = 0$, and this assumption was confirmed by the analysis of $r_{\phi\psi}$ and $r_{b'\xi}$ functions as c was

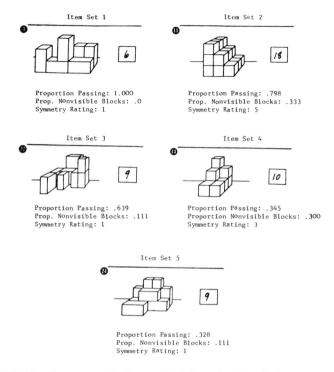

FIG. 5.6. Representative items, Block Counting Test, by item set. Test items copyright 1986 by Industrial Psychology Inc., 515 Madison Avenue, New York NY 10022. All rights reserved. Permission granted for limited reproduction in this instance only.

varied. Notice also that the PCF curves (shown in Fig. 5.7) tend to descend to a lower limit of 0.

In the PCF analysis, 6 items with $r_{bis} < .3$ were eliminated. From data with the remaining 26 items (divided into 5 item sets, with b'_k values ranging from -1.58 to .61), ζ_1 was found to be .6093, corresponding to $a = .768$. Mean values from 5 generated samples using $a = .77$ produced acceptable fits in all cases. Empirical raw score mean, standard deviation, and reliability were 15.08, 5.10, .848, with corresponding values from the model of 15.15, 5.27, and .848, respectively. Chi-square tests of total and item set score distributions had p values that ranged from .10 to .96.

As mentioned previously, items varied in the degree of *symmetry* they exhibited, that is, the degree to which a subject might use simple arithmetical processes to arrive at the number of blocks, as opposed to items in which the blocks had to be counted more or less one by one. (In a later section, it is shown that the symmetry characteristic is a significant predictor of item difficulty, along with the proportion of nonvisible blocks.) Separate analyses were therefore made for

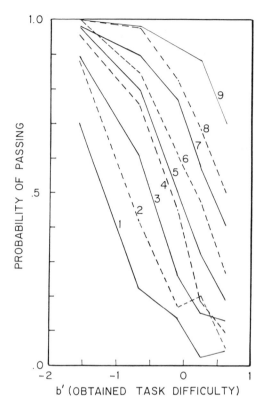

FIG. 5.7.   PCF curves for noniles of the raw score distribution, Block Counting Test, $N = 119$.

18 low symmetry and 9 high symmetry items (including one item not used in the previous analysis for 26 items). Analysis of low symmetry items produced estimated $a = .589$, while the value was .760 for high symmetry items. In both cases all fits of data to model were highly satisfactory, except that for high symmetry items the K-R(20) reliability was .715 as contrasted with .648 yielded by the model as the square of the correlation between raw score and θ.

The Cubes Test.   This test was adapted from one by L. L. Thurstone (1938), and contained 32 items. After elimination of 6 items with $r_{bis} < .35$, PCF analysis used 26 items whose r_{bis} ranged from .355 to .828, divided into 6 item sets whose b'_k values ranged from -1.23 to .29. Figure 5.8 depicts 6 items, one from each set. Subjects are required to indicate whether the two cubes in each item can be the same (S) or must be different (D), assuming the same design is never used twice on the faces of a cube. Because items are two-choice, the apriori value of c would be taken to equal .5. However, analysis of $r_{\phi\psi}$ and $r_{b'\xi}$

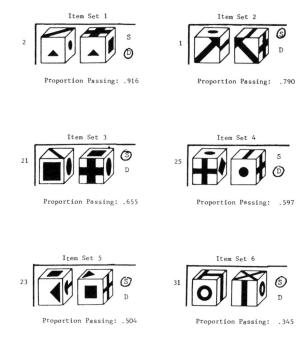

FIG. 5.8.   Representative items, Cubes Test, by item set.

functions as c was varied indicated a best-fit value of .10. It seems that subjects saw the pairs of cubes as either same or different (whether correctly or incorrectly); they rarely *guessed* at answers.

Using $c = .10$, PCF analysis yielded $\zeta_1 = .6313$, corresponding to $a = .814$. Generated samples using this value produced excellent fits to both total and item set distributions.

The Flags Test.   This also was a test from Thurstone's series. It contained 48 items, of which 45 with $r_{bis} > .35$ were used, divided into 6 item sets with b'_k values ranging (after correction for chance) from $-.93$ to $-.02$. The value of c was determined to be .49 on the basis of analysis of $r_{\phi\psi}$ and $r_{b'\xi}$ functions; this is close to the value that would be assumed on apriori grounds. The items in this test are relatively easy for the sample tested. Figure 5.9 depicts one item from each set. The subject has to state whether the flags in each pair are same or different after rotation of one or the other.

Considerable difficulty was encountered in estimating parameters for this test. The program used for the PCF analysis yielded $\zeta_1 = .8506$, corresponding to $a = 1.618$. Fitting the model with this value to the data was unsuccessful. Trial of several values led to the tentative acceptance of a value of $a = 1.64$, but with $\sigma_\theta = .87$ (as opposed to generally assumed 1.00). Even these values did not uni-

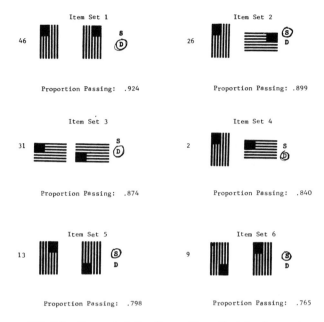

FIG. 5.9.   Representative items, Flags Test, by item set.

formly produce acceptable fits. Fit was poor for the total distribution, but acceptable for 5 out of the 6 item sets. The difficulty appears to be due to a few cases at the lower end of the score distribution—individuals who possibly did not properly understand the task and therefore had scores considerably less than chance (with a consequent inflation of the standard deviation and reliability).

The Hands Test.   Data from this test, another from Thurstone's series, presented problems of analysis similar to those just mentioned for the Flags test. It contains 49 items, of which 10 with $r_{bis} < .5$ were eliminated for our analysis. (The high rate of item rejection here was based on the effort to select only items with high values, in view of the fact that a relatively large number of items were available.) Typical items from the test are shown in Fig. 5.10. By procedures described previously, c was estimated as .19. By trial of several values, a was finally estimated as 1.18, with $\sigma_\theta = .83$. These values produced an excellent fit for the total score distribution, and excellent fits for 6 out of the 7 item set distributions. There remained an unexplained discrepancy between the average generated reliability, .772, and the empirical reliability, .899.

The Spatial Rotations Test.   This test was adapted from the Mental Rotations test prepared and studied by Lansman, Donaldson, Hunt, and Yantis (1982). It contains 42 items presenting pairs of block figures depicted in 3 dimensions. The

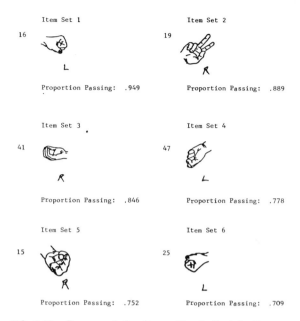

FIG. 5.10.   Representative items, Hands Test, by item set.

subject has to decide whether the block figures in each pair are same or different, considering a rotation in the plane of the picture. (No item involved rotation in a third dimension.) Figure 5.11 shows typical items, one from each of the item sets used in our PCF analysis.

For our purposes, 4 items with $r_{bis} < .225$ were eliminated. The parameter c was estimated as .40. Using this value, it became possible to estimate $a = .83$, and $\sigma_\theta = .70$. Chi-square tests of fit of samples generated with these parameters to the empirical distributions were uniformly good to excellent.

Summary of Parameter Estimations.   For the Seashore Sense of Pitch Test, the c parameters estimated for total scores and for subtests of the test appeared to vary as a function of differential response biases over item sets. The a parameters also varied. It is to be noted that the a and c parameters estimated for the total score distribution were rough averages of those estimated for the first five (easier) subtests and the last four (harder) subtests. These findings tend to go contrary to the hypothesis that the parameter a is constant for pitch discrimination ability, but it is possible that data from an improved test would disclose a more constant value.

For the spatial ability tests, the c parameter varied as a function of test format and also, apparently, as a function of differences in subjects' propensity to guess. For three of the tests (Block Counting, Cubes, and Spatial Rotation) in which the fit of the PCF model was best, the estimated values of a ranged only from .77 to

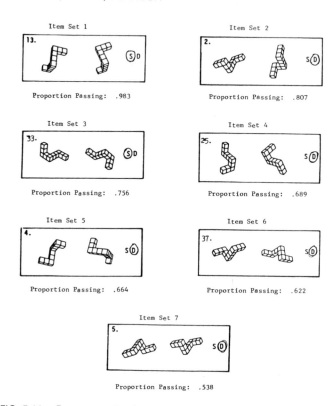

FIG. 5.11.   Representative items, Spatial Rotations Test, by item set.

.83, lending credence to the hypothesis that this parameter is constant and characteristic of spatial ability. The values estimated for the other two tests (1.64 for Flags and 1.18 for Hands), where the fit of the model was less satisfactory, may have been incorrectly estimated due to anomalies in the data. It is possible that the difficulties in estimating them could be traced to inequalities among item sets in the true values of c, which were assumed to be equal over item sets in the PCF analysis employed here.

TASK DIFFICULTY AND TASK ATTRIBUTES

PCF theory and the procedures described in the previous section should make it possible to attach meanings to the task difficulty scale (measured either by b' or b) by associating item difficulty values with various attributes of those tasks. A further extension is to associate raw score values with the meanings assigned to the task difficulty scale, since by PCF theory raw score values are associated with liminal values on the task difficulty scale. In this way it should be possible to specify levels of ability in terms of task attributes. This idea is illustrated with each of the data sets whose analysis has been reported earlier.

The technique employed in each case is to identify task attributes that make a significant contribution, either singly or in a linear multiple regression system, to the prediction of task difficulty as measured by ξ_p or $\xi_{p'}$. In some instances multiplicative variables have been found useful. The average values of these predictors for the items in each set are computed, along with the predicted values of b' for the item set. Further, given the value of ϕ_j for each nonile, the raw score at which performance of each item set is liminal (i.e., with p or $p' = .5$) is determined. The percentile value of this raw score in the group studied is also determined. These data are exhibited in a table which also presents the multiple regression system used in predicting ξ_p or $\xi_{p'}$.

In some cases, certain item attributes were found to be correlated with r_{bis}.

Data from the Seashore Sense of Pitch Test.   In all computations for this data set, c was assumed to be equal to .52, as determined previously. It was also assumed that all items in an item set were equivalent due to the presumably constant pitch difference in the stimuli for each subtest. Data on individual items had not been preserved; the data available consisted only of item set scores and the total raw scores. Thus, only the values of b'_k for the 9 item sets were available as the dependent variable for predictions from item set characteristics. Two independent variables were used, the chief one being the logarithm of the difference in pitch, in Hertz, between the 2 tones in an item. This variable had a correlation of $-.995$ with b'_k (as contrasted with $-.896$ for the raw pitch difference). The second predictor was a code for a response bias that was found to be present in the test (Carroll, 1983). The response bias was coded -1 for item sets 1–5 (subtests A–E), and $+1$ for sets 6–9 (subtests J, I, H, G respectively). Although the value of t for this predictor was not significant (at $\alpha = .05$) in the multiple regression, this predictor was nevertheless used because it was considered that it would have been significant if it had been possible to use data for all 90 items individually. Parameters and results of the analysis are shown in Table 5.5. The table shows approximate values of raw scores for which performance on each of the item sets is liminal, as well as the percentile values of these raw scores in the college population that was tested ($N = 1080$). It is possible to say, for example, that a person with a raw score of 70 has a pitch difference limen of 5 Hz. The median score of 73.5 corresponds to a limen of 4.6 Hz. Since the test presents a wide span of pitch differences, the percentiles corresponding to each pitch difference span the range from 3.6 to 99.8.

Data from the Block Counting Test.   The items of the test were scanned for properties that could be either objectively coded or rated subjectively with reasonable reliability, and that appeared to show some relation with item difficulty

TABLE 5.5
Data for Item Sets, Seashore Sense of Pitch Test
(Assumed c = .52)

Set (k)	Number of Items	b'_k	Hz	Aver. Val. Predictors 1	2	Predicted b'_k	Liminal Score	Percentile
1	10	-1.43	30	1.48	-1	-1.55	52.5	3.6
2	10	-1.33	23	1.36	-1	-1.32	54	4.4
3	10	-1.03	17	1.23	-1	-1.06	58	8
4	10	-.77	12	1.08	-1	-.77	61.5	13
5	10	-.57	8	.90	-1	-.42	63.5	17
6	10	-.08	5	.70	+1	.11	70	36
7	10	.63	3	.48	+1	.54	79	79
8	10	.93	2	.30	+1	.89	82	91
9	10	1.53	1	.00	+1	1.47	88	99.8

		r	weight	t
Predictors: 1. log (Hz)		-.9945	-1.946	-12.79***
2. Response Bias		.8886	.072	.99
Regression constant			1.401	
R			.9951	
$F(2,6) =$		302.7,	p = .00005	

as indexed by a normal deviate transform of the total probability of passing. Some overlap among these properties was permitted. Five such properties were investigated:

1. the correct answer (i.e., correct number of blocks),

2. the number of blocks that were not directly visible (i.e., whose existence has to be inferred from visible blocks that they support),

3. the *proportion* of such nonvisible blocks to the total number,

4. a rating of symmetry, i.e., the degree to which actual or imaginable sets of blocks formed symmetrical groups such that simple arithmetical processes could be used in arriving at answers, and

5. a variable created by assigning the mean difficulty for all items with blocks of a given shape.

These 5 variables, along with item number, were evaluated in linear multiple regressions for their use in predicting item difficulty and the item's r_{bis}. Against item difficulty, three variables had significant regression weights: item number, proportion of nonvisible blocks, and symmetry rating. Item number was significant, however, only because presumably various task attributes had been employed (either deliberately or intuitively) by the test constructor in arranging the items of the test. Item difficulty significantly increased with the proportion of nonvisible blocks, and decreased with symmetry. From these two variables

TABLE 5.6
Data for Item Sets, Block Counting Test
(Assumed c = 0)

Set (k)	Number Items	b'_k	Average Value Predictors		Predicted b'_k	Liminal Score	Percentile
			1	2			
1	5	-1.58	.087	3.8	-1.49	2	1
2	5	-.68	.163	3.4	-.78	9.5	20
3	6	-.11	.179	2.3	-.20	14.5	48
4	5	.24	.298	2.6	.53	17.5	66
5	5	.61	.284	2.8	.35	20.5	87

	r	Weight	t
Predictors: 1. Prop. nonvisible blocks	.625	7.22	7.98***
2. Symmetry rating (1-5)	-.193	-.42	-5.38***
Regression Constant		-.53	
R		.828	
$F(2, 29) =$		31.6, $p = .000003$	

alone, item difficulty was predicted with multiple $R = .828$. Results of the analysis are shown in Table 5.6.

Note that average values of predictors, and of predicted b', do not change perfectly monotonically with increasing difficulty of item sets. Presumably, item characteristics that were not analyzed or that could not be readily coded account for the discrepancies. Nevertheless, the results suggest an important interpretation for what is measured by the Block Counting test. It measures chiefly the ability to visualize *nonvisible* blocks that support visible blocks; it also measures the ability to use symmetry characteristics of block piles to arrive at the number of blocks. But because symmetry is negatively correlated with item difficulty, items with low symmetry are more challenging and are presumably better measures of the underlying ability than items with high symmetry. It is possible that a better test of the ability could be constructed by restricting it to items of low symmetry.

The symmetry rating was significantly correlated ($r = .669$) with r_{bis}. That is, the more discriminating items tend to have higher symmetry ratings. This finding should not, however, discourage the construction of a purer test with items of low symmetry. Performance on high symmetry items may be unduly influenced by arithmetical ability.

Data from the Cubes Test.   As in the previous analysis, the value of c was taken to be .10. In all, 8 variables were investigated as possible predictors of item difficulty:

1. item number;
2. the item's answer (same or different);

3. the number of similar faces presented in the pair of cubes;

4. the total amount of "symmetry" in these similar faces (i.e., a credit of 1 was scored for each face that would remain the same with rotation);

5. the number of 90° rotations on the front-back axis that would be necessary in a process of bringing the first cube into the same perspective as the second;

6. similarly, the number of 90° rotations on the horizontal axis;

7. similarly, the number of 90° rotations on the vertical axis; and

8. the total of variables 5–7.

In the full regression model for variables 1–7, variables 1, 2, 5, 6, and 7 were significant at the 5% level or better. Variable 1 (item number) was excluded from further consideration for logical reasons. In a regression for variables 2, 5, 6, 7, the t-value of variable 2 (item answer) was nonsignificant. Variable 8 (total number of rotations) alone had $r = .759$ with item difficulty, but the multiple correlation for the component variables 5–7 was slightly higher, .776. It was decided to use these variables as the final predictors since, interestingly enough, the zero-order r of variable 5 was only $-.052$, while the t-value was significant. It appeared that the interaction among variables 5–7 made some contribution to item difficulty. It should be pointed out, incidentally, that the codings of the items for variables 5–7 were the first author's judgments of how high ability subjects would tend to rotate the cubes, and are not the only possible codings, since some items present alternative possibilities.

Results are shown in Table 5.7. As in Table 5.6, average values of predictors for item sets, and of predicted item set difficulties, are not perfectly ranked like the actual item set difficulties. Nevertheless it is clear that the ability measured by the Cubes test is that of being able to visualize possible rotations of cubes to bring them into comparable perspective so that similarity of faces can be checked. The more difficult items are those in which more rotations, particularly those on the horizontal axis (involving rotation through a third dimension), are necessary. The items of this particular test are generally easy; only item sets 5 and 6 have $b'_k > 0$. The percentile value of the raw score (20.5) at which performance on item set 6 is liminal is only 70; an improved test would have to include a larger number of difficult items, in order to characterize the performance of high ability subjects in terms of item set difficulties.

Even in a full regression model for variables 1–7 against r_{bis}, the multiple R of .601 was not significant, and no individual variables had significant t-values.

Data from the Flags Test.   The value of $c = .49$ was assumed in all computations involving item difficulties. Five variables were investigated as possible predictors of item difficulty:

1. item number;

2. item answer, "same" being coded 1, "different" being coded 2;

TABLE 5.7
Data on Item Sets, Cube Test
(Assumed c = .10)

Set (k)	Number of Items	b'_k	Average Value of Predictors			Predicted b'_k	Liminal Score	Percentile
			1	2	3			
1	6	-1.17	.67	0	0	-.86	5	0
2	4	-.61	.75	.25	.25	-.59	10.5	10
3	5	-.31	.60	.80	.20	-.33	13.5	32
4	5	-.13	.60	.80	.80	-.12	15	39
5	3	.13	.67	.67	.67	-.22	17.5	53
6	3	.47	.67	1.33	.67	.18	20.5	70

Predictors	r	Weight	t
1. No. 90 Rotations, Front-Back Axis	-.052	.359	2.42*
2. No. 90 Rotations, Horizontal Axis	.701	.612	4.43***
3. No. 90 Rotations, Vertical Axis	.432	.349	2.22*

Regression constant -1.104
R .776
$F(3,22) =$ 11.13, $p = .0002$

3. whether the horizontal or vertical position of the two flags was the same (1) or different (2);

4. whether the first flag was horizontal (1) or vertical (2) (there being no oblique presentations); and

5. whether the "star" block of the flag is at the same end (1) or a different end (2), for flags in the same position (both being horizontal or vertical), or would be at the same or different end if the first flag is rotated 90° to the right.

In a full regression model for all variables against $\xi_{p'}$, multiple R was .718, with variables 3 and 5 having significant t-values. These two variables alone produced multiple $R = .661$, variable 3 having a negative weight. It was found, however, that prediction could be improved significantly, with $R = .715$, by using multiplicative variables reflecting presumed interactions. The final regression system used is shown in Table 5.8.

This test is quite easy for the group tested. Whether it would be possible to make a more difficult test, perhaps by including flags in oblique positions, could be determined only by trial. In any case, it seems clear that an ability tapped by this test is one of being able to visualize possible rotations or overturnings of flag figures in order to match their characteristics. On the other hand, it should be recognized that visualizing rotations of flag figures may not be the only strategy possible for good performance on this test. It seems that another possible strategy is to compare each flag with the image of a standard flag (as usually shown with

TABLE 5.8
Data on Item Sets, Flags Test
(Assumed c = .49)

			Average value of Predictors					
Set k	Number of Items	b'_k	5	6	7	Predicted b'_k	Liminal Score	Percentile
1	7	-.97	1.00	1.57	1.00	-.64	29.5	11
2	8	-.80	1.12	1.88	2.12	-.73	31	13
3	10	-.63	1.88	2.10	2.50	-.46	33	16
4	9	-.52	1.67	2.56	2.78	-.35	35	23
5	6	-.32	1.67	2.33	1.83	-.43	37.5	32
6	5	-.09	1.80	3.20	2.20	-.36	40.5	50

Predictors:	r	weight	t
2. Answer: Same (1), Diff. (2)	.068	--	--
3. Position: Same (1), Diff (2)	-.422	--	--
5. Position of End: Same (1), Diff. (2)	.563	.393	4.47***
6. Var. 2 X Var. 5	.506	.088	2.27*
7. Var. 3 X Var. 5	.100	-.142	-3.72***
Regression Constant		-1.032	
R		.715	
$F(3,41) =$		14.32, p= .00002	

the star block in the upper left corner). But even this strategy may involve some visualized rotation. Considering all the spatial ability tests studied here, prediction of item difficulty was least successful for this one.

The only significant predictor of item r_{bis} was variable 5, with $r = -.573$. That is, more discriminating items are those in which the *ends* of the flags are the same, either in their original positions or after a 90° rotation of the first flag. This variable apparently interacts with item construction in some complex way.

Data from the Hands Test.   As determined previously, a value of $c = .19$ was assumed for this test, even though items are two-choice in format. Inspection of items in relation to their difficulties suggested several variables as possible predictors of item difficulty. Item number was used as the first variable, on the assumption that the test constructer had arranged the items in some order of empirical or intuited difficulty. The other variables, and their codes, were as follows:

2. the item answer—left (1), right (2);

3. whether the hand presented could easily (1) or with great difficulty (3) be seen as a position of the viewer's own hand, as opposed to the hand of another person facing the viewer;

4. whether the wrist of the hand was shown consistent with (1) or opposite to (3) the answer (for example, the item would be coded (1) if the wrist of a *left* hand was shown at the *left*, as in item 16 of Figure 10, but (3) if the wrist of a *left* hand was shown at the *right*, as in item 47);

5. whether the hand pointed up (1) or down (5) or in some intermediate position; and

6. whether the hand was completely or mostly open (1), completely closed or clenched (5), or in some intermediate position.

In the full regression model for variables 1–6 against ξ_p, the multiple R was .872 but only variables (3) and (4) had significant t-values. The multiple regression for these variables alone was .846, and these variables were used in preparing Table 5.9. Predictor (3), which may be called a "proximal/distal" variable, seems to indicate that one aspect of the ability measured by this test is the ability to detect or visualize whether the hand shown is one that could be seen easily as one's own, and if not, to determine its rightness or leftness when seen as a hand of a person facing the viewer. Predictor (4) indicates that another aspect of the underlying ability is the ability to overcome the confusion when the hand is presented as appearing to extend from an arm that is not the arm of the answer. That is, a right hand that appears to extend from the left is more difficult to perceive as a right hand than a right hand that appears to extend from the right. Actually, perhaps this variable captures the difficulty only indirectly; the perceiver must also take account of the position of the thumb.

TABLE 5.9
Data for Item Sets, Hands Test
(Assumed c = .19)

Set k	Number of Items	b'_k	1	2	Predicted b'_k	Liminal Score	Percentile
			Average value of Predictors				
1	3	-1.42	2.00	1.00	-1.07	7	0
2	8	-1.06	1.25	2.12	-1.07	14	1
3	8	-.87	2.50	1.25	-.89	17	4
4	5	-.70	2.80	2.20	-.63	20	8
5	4	-.53	3.00	2.25	-.57	22.5	17
6	5	-.42	3.00	2.80	-.47	24.5	20
7	6	-.27	3.00	3.00	-.43	27	29

Predictors:

	r	weight	t
1.Proximal (1); Distal (3)	.692	.270	7.31***
2.Wrist w/Ans (1); Opposite (3)	.563	.187	5.63***
Regression Constant		-1.801	
R		.896	
	$F(2,36) =$	45.4, $p < .00001$	

All the items of this test are quite easy for the group tested. Whether it would be possible to construct items that would be more difficult is unclear. In any event, the percentile of the raw score at which performance on the most difficult item set is liminal is only 29.

Variables (4) and (5), alone, predicted r_{bis} with a multiple R of .418, significant with $p = .03$, both variables having significant t-values. Items with higher r_{bis} tended to be those showing the wrist opposite to the answer, and those with the hand pointing down rather than up. In a sense, variable (5) reflects a proximal vs. distal characteristic of an item; it is difficult to perceive one's own hand as pointing down in one's own field of vision. Nevertheless, this variable did not have a significant t-value against item difficulty when teamed with variables (3) and (4); indeed, the corresponding regression coefficient was negative.

Data from the Spatial Rotations Test. As determined previously, a value of $c = .40$ was assumed for this test in all computations involving item difficulties. The following variables were investigated as possible predictors of item difficulty:

1. item number;

2. item answer—same (coded 1) or different (coded 2);

3. the number of 30°-angle units by which the first figure had to be rotated to match the second at least partially;

4. whether the number of blocks at the ends of the figure was the same (coded 2) or different (coded 1); and

5. whether the arrays of blocks at the ends of the figure are parallel to each other.

Variable 3, of course, is the variable that a number of investigators (e.g., Just & Carpenter, 1976; Shepard & Metzler, 1971) have shown is related to the speed of arriving at an answer; here, however, it is studied as related to answer accuracy. It should be noted that all items in the Spatial Rotations test used in this study presented rotations only in the picture plane; there were no rotations in a third dimension. Variables 4 and 5 suggested themselves in the course of the writers' attempts to find aspects of the items contributing to their difficulty.

In multiple regression analyses, it became evident that multiplicative variables, reflecting interactions, could be used to improve predictions beyond those afforded by non-multiplicative variables. The model finally used involved variables 2, 3, and 5, with two multiplicative variables formed from them; results are shown in Table 5.10 along with data on liminal values of raw scores and their percentiles. The results suggest that there are several critical aspects of this task. The significant operation of variable 2 (in interaction with variable 5) indicates that the test contains a comparison task; it is harder for subjects to conclude that two figures are different than that they are the same. The influence of variable 3

TABLE 5.10
Data on Item Sets, Spatial RotationsTest
(Assumed c = .40)

			Average value of Predictors					
Set k	*Number of Items*	b'_k	*5*	*6*	*7*	*Predicted* b'_k	*Liminal Score*	*Percentile*
1	5	-1.28	1.80	1.80	4.00	-1.42	17	2
2	6	-.42	1.50	2.16	5.84	-.35	24.5	33
3	6	-.23	1.16	1.50	5.33	-.23	26	42
4	5	-.12	1.00	1.40	4.40	-.16	27.5	53
5	6	.11	1.33	2.00	6.00	-.11	29.5	73
6	5	.35	1.80	3.60	8.80	.50	31.5	82
7	5	.82	1.80	3.60	9.40	.61	36.5	98

Predictors:		r	weight	t
2. Answer: Same (1), Diff. (2)		.529	–	--
3. No. 30° Rotations		. 561	--	--
5. Ends Parallel: No (1), Yes (2)		-.066	-1.776	-9.77***
6. Var. 2 X Var. 5		.398	.602	8.13***
7. Var. 3 X Var. 5		.496	.174	8.41***
	Regression Constant		.008	
	R		.896	
	$F(3,34) =$		46.3, p < .00001	

indicates, as expected from previous studies, that the task involves visualized rotation of figures. Finally, the effect of variable 5, in interaction with both variables 2 and 3, suggests that comparisons of figures become more difficult to make when the terminal segments of the block figures are parallel.

No significant relations of the variables with r_{bis} were observed. The mean r_{bis}, .398, was relatively low, and the S.D. was only .094.

CORRELATIONS OF THE SPATIAL ABILITY TESTS

Although it is not of immediate concern in the present context, the question of the factorial structure of the spatial ability tests is of interest. Because of the limited number and variety of tests studied, this question cannot be adequately answered with the present data. However, factor analysis of their correlations, which are shown in Table 5.11, yields useful information. A maximum likelihood analysis, performed with the LISREL VI program (Jöreskog & Sörbom, 1984), produced an acceptable fit when it was hypothesized that the data reflected one factor with correlated error between the two scorings of the Block Counting test. Results are shown in Table 5.12. The correlated error term is justified by the fact that the two scorings of the Block Counting test are not experimentally dependent.

These results suggest that all the tests measure a general spatial ability factor, perhaps conforming to the Gv (general visual perception) factor postulated by Horn (1978). Surely our analyses have suggested that all the tests involve processes of visualization and imagery. Because the tests in this study were administered under unspeeded conditions, the abilities measured are associated with level (accuracy) of performance, regardless of how much they may also be associated with speed of performance.

TABLE 5.11
Correlation Matrix, Spatial Ability Test Scores*
N = 119

Variable	1	2	3	4	5	6
1.Block Counting - Low Symm.	(.670)	.916	.749	.582	.582	.580
2. Block Counting - High Symm.	.633	(.715)	.639	.598	.474	.603
3. Cubes	.555	.530	(.819)	.636	.479	.753
4. Flags	.452	.479	.546	(.899)	.609	.628
5. Hands	.452	.380	.411	.547	(.898)	.596
6. Spatial Rotations	.398	.427	.571	.499	.473	(.701)

*K-R(20) reliability coefficients on the diagonal; zero-order correlations below diagonal; correlations corrected for attenuation above diagonal.

TABLE 5.12
Maximum Likelihood Factor Analysis
Spatial Ability Tests*

Variable	Factor 1	h^2
1. Block Counting, Low Symmetry Items	.656	.430
2. Block Counting, High Symmetry Items	.646	.417
3. Cubes	.767	.589
4. Flags	.737	.543
5. Hands	.642	.412
6. Spatial Rotations	.698	.487

Chi Square (8) = 12.63, p = .125

* The analysis also confirmed a hypothesized correlated error of .210 between variables 1 and 2, t = 3.045.

DISCUSSION AND SUMMARY

A method of test analysis, based largely on PCF (person characteristic function) theory, has been presented that is believed to have several virtues and advantages. First, it is relatively simple and can yield useful information even for small data sets. Second, it can establish the unidimensionality of a test—if unidimensionality is taken to mean that all items of a test measure the same ability or linear combination of abilities. Third, it can establish meanings for an ability scale that take into account the attributes of tasks that make for task difficulty, and it can construct a meaningful relation between such a scale and person characteristics as indicated by a test raw score scale. Finally, the person characteristic functions indicated by this analysis go far towards establishing the existence of an ability and supporting its construct validity.

The method appears to be most immediately applicable in the analysis of cognitive ability tests that involve tasks of different difficulties that are scored or evaluated in terms of correctness of performance. With some adaptations, the method might also be applied to tasks involving speed. This would require the administration of individually timed tasks, and item-passing would be defined in terms of whether the task is performed within a given time limit. For example, a series of reaction time tasks, with different stimuli and conditions of performance, might be given and analyzed by the PCF method.

In any event, it is suggested that the PCF method illustrated here should be applied to a wide variety of cognitive tests in order to promote the better understanding of the abilities measured by the tests, to investigate the proposal that the value of a is characteristic of a particular ability, and to provide more meaningful scaling of test scores.

"Stop press" addendum. Since submission of this chapter for publication, two further articles (Carroll, in press *a*, in press *b*) have been prepared. The first presents further refinements in methodology; the second illustrates application to three subtests of a widely-used cognitive abilities battery.

ACKNOWLEDGMENTS

This material is based in part upon work supported by the National Science Foundation under Grant No. BNS-8212486 to the first author. An earlier version of this paper was presented at the ONR Contractors' Meeting on Model-Based Measurement, University of Illinois, Champaign, IL, October 1983, and thanks are due to L. R. Tucker for suggestions he offered at that meeting. The first author is responsible for developing and presenting material on the person characteristic function, and for all data analyses. The second and third authors are responsible for designing the study of spatial abilities and for collecting the data on spatial abilities that were used and analyzed here. They also contributed a number of suggestions regarding the analysis of the spatial ability data based on their own analyses. Their study was designed to explore the origin of the sex difference in spatial ability and is reported more fully elsewhere (Johnson & Meade, 1987). Their research was supported in part by grants from the Virginia Department of Education and The University Research Council of the University of North Carolina.

REFERENCES

Carroll, J. B. (1945). The effect of difficulty and chance success on correlations between items or between tests. *Psychometrika, 10,* 1–19.

Carroll, J. B. (1983). The difficulty of a test and its factor composition revisited. In H. Wainer & S. Messick (Eds.), *Principals of modern psychological measurement: A Festschrift in honor of Frederic M. Lord* (pp. 257–283). Hillsdale, NJ: Lawrence Erlbaum Associates.

Carroll, J. B. (in press *a*). Some statistics of homogeneous tests: Estimating ability and item difficulty parameters with the person characteristic function. *Applied Psychological Measurement.*

Carroll, J. B. (in press *b*). Test theory and the behavioral scaling of test performance. In N. Frederiksen, R. J. Mislevy, & I. Bejar (Eds.), *Test theory for a new generation of tests.* Hillsdale, NJ: Lawrence Erlbaum Associates.

Carroll, J. B., & Schohan, B. (1953). *Construction of comprehensive achievement examinations for Navy officer candidate programs.* Pittsburgh, PA: American Institute for Research.

Cronbach, L. J. (1971). Test validation. In R. L. Thorndike (Ed.), *Educational measurement,* Second edition (pp. 443–507). Washington, DC: American Council on Education.

Horn, J. L. (1978). Human ability systems. In P. B. Baltes (Ed.), *Life-span development and behavior,* Vol. 1 (pp. 211–256). New York: Academic Press.

Johnson, E. S., & Meade, A. (1987). *Developmental patterns of spatial ability: An early sex difference. Child Development, 58,* 725–740.

Jöreskog, K., & Sörbom, D. (1984). *LISREL VI: Analysis of linear structural relationships. User's guide.* Mooresville, IN: Scientific Software.

Just, M. A., & Carpenter, P. A. (1976). Eye fixations and cognitive processes. *Cognitive Psychology, 8,* 441–480.

King, J. E. (1947–1950). *Factored aptitude series.* Chicago, IL: Industrial Psychology, Inc.

Lansman, M., Donaldson, G., Hunt, E., & Yantis, S. (1982). Ability factors and cognitive processes. *Intelligence, 6,* 347–386.

Lord, F. M. (1980). *Applications of item response theory to practical testing problems.* Hillsdale, NJ: Lawrence Erlbaum Associates.

Lord, F. M., & Novick, M. R. (1968). *Statistical theories of mental test scores.* Reading, MA: Addison-Wesley.

Mosier, C. I. (1940). Psychophysics and mental test theory: Fundamental postulates and elementary theorems. *Psychological Review, 47,* 355–366.,

Mosier, C. I. (1941). Psychophysics and mental test theory, II. The constant process. *Psychological Review, 48,* 235–249.

Shepard, R. N., & Metzler, J. (1971). Mental rotation of three-dimensional objects. *Science, 171,* 701–703.

Thurstone, L. L. (1938). Primary mental abilities. *Psychometric Monographs,* No. 1.

Trabin, T. E., & Weiss, D. J. (1983). The person response curve: Fit of individuals to item response theory models. In D. J. Weiss (Ed.), *New horizons in testing: Latent trait test theory and computerized adaptive testing* (pp. 83–108). New York: Academic Press.

An Approach to Multivariate Generalizability of MMPI Profiles

Goldine C. Gleser
Linda Crespo da Silva
University of Cincinnati

INTRODUCTION

One of the topics dealt with under generalizability theory (Cronbach, Gleser, Nanda, & Rajaratnam, 1972) has aroused relatively little attention among test developers and test users despite its importance to educational and psychological measurement. This topic pertains to the reliability or generalizability of a set of multiple scores used conjointly to assess certain attributes or traits of individuals. Such scores are usually obtained by one administration of a multiply-scored instrument such as the Wechsler Adult Intelligence Scale or the Minnesota Multiphasic Personality Inventory. They are interpreted by consideration of certain patterns or configurations or by the formation of weighted composites.

Recently, Shavelson and Webb (1981) have written a review of the developments in generalizability theory from 1973 to 1980 which covered multivariate generalizability as one of the topics. They point out that most generalizability studies involving multiple scores have failed to consider the total set simultaneously but rather have treated each variable separately. According to them, the reason for this is twofold: (1) the paucity of theory and procedures for examining multiple outcomes, and (2) the difficulties involved in understanding the multivariate literature. Several other problems can be noted. Foremost among them is the difficulty of determining which if any of the available techniques is appropriate for the investigator's intended decision making purpose. Also there is the problem of finding the appropriate computer program to handle the analysis. For the most part multivariate generalizability programs are available only to the most sophisticated computer users who can supplement them with programs of their own.

The Shavelson and Webb review has attempted to remedy some of these deficits by their discussion of the multivariate generalizability coefficients of Bock (1966) and Conger and Lipshitz (1973) for one-facet designs, and that of Joe and Woodward (1976) for multifaceted designs with crossed and nested facets. In their review and also in their article on "Multivariate Generalizability of General Development Ratings" (Webb & Shavelson, 1981) they have presented examples of the application of the Joe and Woodward multivariate reliability approach. They point out, however, that these approaches do not address the generalizability of the profile of scores, per se, but rather are intended to determine the most reliable composites under various assumptions regarding the decision data.

Unfortunately, from the standpoint of the user of a multivariate test, the most reliable composites do not usually involve the most meaningful contrasts. This is particularly true for the clinician who is interested in the personality attributes measured by the test scores, per se, and in their salience as indicated by the patterning of scores in particular individuals. What the clinician would like to know is how generalizable is the information being used to make these interpretations and whether it is possible to improve on the information provided by the observed scores to yield more generalizable interpretations.

Two possible answers to the first question have been proposed. Bock (1966) defines a multivariate analogue of reliability, P, utilizing the Type II multivariate analysis of variance of the scores of N individuals each administered r different forms (or administrations) of a test battery consisting of K tests. Starting with the mean products between persons (M_b) and the mean products for error (M_e) he transforms the original scores into canonical variates by solving the homogeneous equations.

$$(M_b - \lambda_j M_e)\, a_j = 0 \tag{1}$$

where the λ_j are the characteristic roots, and the vectors a_j are the coefficients used to compute the canonical variates from the original scores. Since the lengths of these vectors are arbitrary, Bock chooses them such that the error variance is always unity. Then the multivariate analogue of reliability (P_K) is defined as

$$P_k = \frac{\sum_{j=1}^{k} W_b^{(j)}}{\sum_{j=1}^{k} W_b^{(j)} + k} \tag{2}$$

where W_b is the component of variation between individuals for the jth canonical variate. In other words, P is the proportion of total variance in an uncorrelated vector space that is "true" or universe score variance. In terms of the characteristic roots (2) becomes

$$p_k = \frac{\sum\limits_{j} \lambda_j - K}{\sum\limits_{j} \lambda_j + (r-1)K} \tag{3}$$

Conger and Lipshitz (1973) have also defined a multivariate analogue of profile reliability, very similar to that of Bock. They start out, however, by considering that the interpretation of the total profile of K test scores involves a consideration of the distances among individual score vectors in a K dimensional space. Reliability is the ratio of average squared distances among true score vectors to the average squared distances among observed score vectors. Distances can be defined in terms of any distance function, but in particular Conger and Lipshitz deal with the Mahalonobis distance and the D^2 measure used by Cronbach and Gleser (1953) in their work on profile similarity. The Mahalonobis distance treats the space as oblique to the extent that the original test scores are correlated whereas the D^2 measure treats the space as orthogonal.

In line with assumptions of classical test theory, the covariance matrix of the observations ΣXX can be expressed as

$$\Sigma XX = \Sigma TT + \Sigma EE \tag{4}$$

where ΣTT is the covariance matrix of true scores and ΣEE is a diagonal matrix of error variances. Then for standard Mahalonobis distances, the profile reliability is shown to be equivalent to

$$\rho_p = \frac{1}{k} \mathrm{Tr}(\Sigma_{TT} \Sigma_{xx}^{-1}) \tag{5}$$

Since the trace of $\Sigma_{TT} \Sigma_{xx}^{-1}$ is equal to the sum of the eigenvalues of the matrix, equation 5 can be evaluated as

$$\rho_p = \frac{1}{k} \Sigma v_k^2 \tag{6}$$

where the v_k^2 are roots of the equation $|\Sigma_{TT} - v^2 \Sigma_{xx}| = 0$.

Conger and Lipshitz show that equation (5) or (6) is precisely what would be obtained if profile reliability were defined as the average squared canonical correlation between the set of observed scores and the set of true scores. It is also equal to the canonical correlation between two sets of strictly parallel forms.

Application of the Conger-Lipshitz definition of profile reliability to the D^2 measure yields the simple result

$$P_D = \frac{\sum_{.k} \sigma^2_{T(k)}}{\sum_k \sigma^2_{X(k)}} \qquad (7)$$

or the ratio of the average univariate true score variance to the average univariate observed score variance. If the variables are standardized the index reduces to the average of the univariate reliabilities. This index is of interest as the upper limit to canonical reliability for correlated variables.

In a subsequent article, Conger (1974) shows that the eigenvalues, v_k^2, obtained by his approach are equal to the reliabilities of the canonical variates obtained using the Bock approach. Thus the Conger-Lipshitz reliability can be obtained via a Bock analysis by simply averaging the reliabilities of the canonical vectors. This value is lower than that obtained using Bock's index of reliability because the two definitions utilize different lengths of the canonical vectors. Conger and Lipshitz equate the canonical composite score variances to one, whereas Bock equates the error variances to one. As a result, Bock's reliability index is higher than that of Conger and Lipshitz except in the trivial case when all of the canonical roots are equal. Neither is incorrect, but the Conger-Lipshitz index has the advantage that it is invariant under any orthogonal rotation. Therefore, it would apply to any set of K orthogonal weighted composites that one might want to make from the information provided by the profile, whereas the Bock index would not apply.

To date, the only method available for improving on the reliability of the profile of observed scores is that suggested by Cronbach et al. (1972). This approach consists of estimating the universe score profile by multiple regression from the observed scores obtained from two or more administrations of the test battery. Classical reliability assumptions are also employed for this approach. The method will be described below in some detail using scores on the Minnesota Multiphasic Personality Inventory (MMPI) as illustration. Results obtained by this method will be compared to those obtained using Bock's canonical analysis. The earlier described multivariate indices of reliability will also be computed for the example and results discussed.

ESTIMATING UNIVERSE PROFILES: AN EXAMPLE

The MMPI

The MMPI is a widely used personality inventory composed of 550 items that yield scores on ten clinical and three validity scales. The raw scores on the clinical scales are converted to T scores by reference to a normative sample of midwestern American adults tested before World War II (Hathaway & Mckinley, 1967). The test has been used in many psychiatric and non-psychiatric situations ranging from selection of personnel to assignment to differential psychiatric treatments (Butcher, 1969; Tiffin & McCormick, 1965; Welsh & Dahlstrom, 1956).

Interpretation of the MMPI usually starts with ordering the clinical scales[1] from highest to lowest according to their T scores. Interpretation may then proceed by consideration of one scale at a time, starting with the highest, or by only dealing with combinations of the two or three highest scores. Elevation of the scores as well as their ordering is taken into account. Following these approaches, several code systems and atlases have been developed to facilitate the interpretation of the MMPI profiles in terms of personality descriptions (Dahlstrom & Welsh, 1960; Drake & Oetting, 1959; Hathaway & Meehl, 1951; Marks, Seeman, & Haller, 1974; Welsh & Dahlstrom, 1956). Such descriptions imply a generalization of the information obtained in the test situation to a broader set of conditions. As a consequence, a component of error is involved in these inferences such that any conclusion drawn from the test is always a probabilistic statement.

The usual approach to the reliability of the MMPI has consisted of computations of test-retest coefficients and internal consistency analyses for separate scales (Dahlstrom & Welsh, 1960). Intervals between test and retest have varied from a few hours to several years. The samples have ranged from high school students to hospitalized psychotics, and both the individual card and the group booklet forms have been used. Reliability coefficients are usually higher for internal consistency analyses than for test-retest, but both types of coefficients vary substantially across studies. Reported stability coefficients computed from test scores separated by short periods of time are also higher than the ones separated by longer intervals, implying that temporary factors are probably contributing to inflate shortterm stability coefficients.

A few sporadic attempts have been made to determine the consistency of some code types. Furthermore, for the purpose of interpretation Marks, Seeman and Heller treat as equivalent profiles whose two highest T scores are in reverse order; i.e., 4–6 and 6–4.

Subjects

The subjects for this study were 60 male inmates who took the MMPI routinely upon admission to the Mansfield State Reformatory in Ohio and were transferred

---

[1]The ten clinical scales are (1) Hypochondriasis; (2) Depression; (3) Conversion Hysteria; (4) Psychopathic Deviate; (5) Masculinity–Femininity; (6) Paranoia; (7) Psychasthenia; (8) Schizophrenia; (9) Mania; (10) Social Introversion. In coding, they are referred to by their code scale numbers.

to the Lebanon Correctional Institute within 6 weeks after admission. They ranged in age from 18 to 30, had at least a 7th-grade education, I.Q. above 94, and MMPI profiles mainly of the types 4–8, 9–4, and 4–9–8. These subjects made up three control groups[2] that were retested twice under standard instructions in a research study carried out by Lanier (1972) at the Lebanon Correctional Institute. These retests were obtained no later than 26 weeks after the original testing and were usually obtained on the same day, morning and afternoon. T-scores equal or above 70 on the clinical scales constituted the criterion for code type assignments; the highest two constituting the code. The stratified sampling of groups resulted in data that were considerably restricted in range on certain of the clinical scales. Furthermore, the short interval between the second and third testing suggested that they would be more highly correlated with each other than with the first testing by virtue of shared temporary factors.

Procedure for Obtaining Universe Score Estimates

The first step in the procedure consisted of intercorrelating all the MMPI scales within and across the testing sessions. For this example only the clinical scales were used, although inclusion of the validity scales L, F, and K would likely increase the reliability of the estimates. This step yielded a 30 by 30 matrix R of intercorrelations composed of nine submatrices: three symmetric submatrices (R11, R22, and R33) of intercorrelations among test scores within each test setting: three asymmetric submatrices (R12, R13, and R23) of intercorrelations among test scores obtained on different occasions: and the transposes of R12, R13, R23 (i.e., R21, R31, R32).

$$[R] = \begin{bmatrix} R11 & R12 & R13 \\ R21 & R22 & R23 \\ R31 & R32 & R33 \end{bmatrix}$$

In order to use the observed scores to estimate universe scores on the MMPI scales, it is necessary to compress the intercorrelations in matrix R into two correlation matrices: a matrix P of average intercorrelations among observed scores on any one occasion (linked correlations) and a matrix PC_1 of average correlations between observed scores obtained on different occasions (unlinked correlations). The classical assumptions of equivalence of means, variances, and correlations across testings are implicit in these procedures.

---

[2]One of Lanier's control groups was allegedly composed of 20 4–9 subjects and another one of 20 4–8 subjects. The third group of 20 consisted of miscellaneous profiles.

Matrix P is simply the 10 by 10 matrix obtained by averaging the three within-occasions submatrices R11, R22, and R33, i.e.,

$$[P] = \frac{R11 + R22 + R33}{3}$$

If the three occasions had been chosen at random intervals, matrix PC_1 would be obtained by averaging the six submatrices of independent correlation R12, R13, R23, R21, R31, R32. For our data, however, this PC_1 matrix was not considered appropriate because the variables from which the correlations in R23 (and its transpose) were obtained were not completely independent. The scores on the two experimental sessions were obtained on the same day and shared the contribution of temporary factors. To obtain an unbiased estimate of PC_1 we omitted R23 and R32 from the computations averaging only the remaining submatrices; i.e.,

$$[PC_1] = \frac{R12 + R13 + R21 + R31}{4}$$

The matrices P and PC_1 for the MMPI data are shown in Table 6.1. The diagonals of PC_1 are the univariate generalizability coefficients; i.e., estimates of the squared correlations between observed and universe scores for each separate scale. It may be noted that these values are for the most part rather low, particularly that for scale 4 for which the range of scores was severely restricted. The pattern of correlations among scales is very similar in the two matrices, but tends to be lower in the PC_1 matrix as compared to the P matrix. This would normally be true for any multiply-scored test given on two or more occasions.

In order to obtain multiple regression estimates of universe scores it is necessary to obtain estimates of the correlations between observed and universe scores. This is achieved by dividing the entries in each column of PC_1 by the square root of the generalizability coefficients in the column diagonal, thus correcting for attenuation in the second variable of each pair. The resulting matrix is PC shown in Table 6.2. Estimates of the correlations among universe scores were also computed, by dividing entries in PC_1 by both the row and the column diagonal to correct for attenuation in both variables in the pair. The resulting matrix C is also shown in Table 6.2. As may be expected, correlations in these matrices are substantially higher than those in the P and PC_1 matrices. The correlations in PC are quite low indicating relatively little redundancy of information. Therefore, it can be expected that only small gains will be obtainable via multiple regression (Cronbach et al., 1972).

Matrices, P, PC, C and the transpose of PC were then assembled into a supermatrix S of intercorrelations among observed and universe scores and analyzed by a stepwise regression program to obtain the multiple regression coeffi-

TABLE 6.1
Average Intercorrelations Among Observed Scores
The P Matrix

Scale	1	2	3	4	5	6	7	8	9	0
1	1.00	.40	.34	.12	.03	.14	.20	.04	.05	.23
2	.40	1.00	.26	.15	.13	.26	.17	.13	-.16	.34
3	.34	.26	1.00	.02	-.08	.20	.00	-.01	-.06	.12
4	.12	.15	.02	1.00	-.03	.01	.07	.04	.14	-.06
5	.03	.13	-.08	-.03	1.00	-.06	.13	.07	.19	-.16
6	.14	.26	.20	.01	-.06	1.00	.08	-.19	.02	.21
7	.20	.17	.00	.07	.13	.08	1.00	.19	.22	.34
8	.04	.13	-.01	.04	.07	-.19	.19	1.00	-.21	.10
9	.05	-.16	-.06	.14	.19	.02	.22	-.21	1.00	-.21
0	.23	.34	.12	-.06	-.16	.21	.34	.10	-.21	1.00

Average Correlations of Observed Scores Over Occasions
The PC_1 Matrix

Scale	1	2	3	4	5	6	7	8	9	0
1	.68	.33	.33	-.03	.01	.18	.12	.00	-.01	.21
2	.33	.53	.22	.03	.12	.21	.07	.04	-.17	.18
3	.33	.22	.50	-.07	-.02	.11	.01	-.07	.03	.08
4	-.03	.03	-.07	.30	-.01	-.01	.04	-.05	.16	-.07
5	.01	.12	-.02	-.01	.53	.00	.18	.08	.16	-.11
6	.18	.21	.11	-.01	.00	.67	.06	-.26	.01	.20
7	.12	.07	.01	.04	.18	.06	.65	.12	.20	.23
8	.00	.04	-.07	-.05	.08	-.26	.12	.56	-.18	.09
9	-.01	-.17	.03	.16	.16	.01	.20	-.18	.53	-.16
0	.21	.18	.08	-.07	-.11	.20	.23	.09	-.16	.68

cients for the equations to be used to estimate universe scores for each separate MMPI scale.

$$[S] = \left[\begin{array}{cc} P & PC \\ \hline CP & C \end{array} \right]$$

Actually, matrices CP and C were not used in the computations. Their only role was to make [S] a square matrix in order to enter the SPSS multiple regression program.

Each observed score entered the corresponding regression equation in the first step and the other observed scores were included in whatever order maximized the multiple correlation between the composite and the universe score for the scale under consideration.

The square of the multiple correlation coefficient indicates the proportion of universe score variance predictable from the weighted composite. An increase of .01 or greater in this proportion was the criterion used to determine the number of predictors to keep in estimating universe scores for each MMPI scale. B coeffi-

TABLE 6:2
Estimated Correlations Between Observed and Universe Scores

The PC Matrix

Scale	1	2	3	4	5	6	7	8	9	0
1	.83	.45	.47	-.06	.01	.22	.15	.01	-.02	.25
2	.40	.73	.32	.05	.17	.26	.09	.05	-.23	.22
3	40	.31	.71	-.12	-.03	.13	.01	-.09	.04	.09
4	-.04	.04	-.09	.55	-.01	-.01	.04	-.06	.21	-.08
5	.01	.17	-.03	-.01	.73	.00	.22	.10	.22	-.13
6	.22	.29	.16	-.01	.00	.82	.08	-.35	.01	.24
7	.15	.10	.01	.06	.24	.07	.81	.16	.27	.28
8	01	.05	-.09	-.08	.10	-.32	.14	.75	-.25	.11
9	-.01	-.23	.04	.28	.22	.01	.25	-.25	.73	-.19
0	.25	.25	.11	-.12	-.15	.25	.28	.13	-.21	.83

Estimated Correlations Among Universe Scores

The C Matrix

Scale	1	2	3	4	5	6	7	8	9	0
1	1.00	55	.57	-.07	.02	.26	.18	.01	-.02	.31
2	.55	1.00	.43	.07	.23	.36	.12	.07	-.32	.30
3	.57	.43	1.00	-.17	-.04	.19	.01	-.13	.05	.13
4	-.07	.07	-.17	1.00	-.02	-.01	.08	-.11	.39	-.15
5	.02	.23	-.04	-.02	1.00	.00	.30	.14	.31	-.18
6	.26	.36	.19	-.01	.00	1.00	.09	-.43	.01	.30
7	.18	.12	.01	.08	.30	.09	1.00	.19	.34	.34
8	.01	.07	-.13	-.11	.14	-.43	.19	1.00	-.34	.15
9	-.02	-.32	.05	.39	.31	.01	.34	-.34	1.00	-.26
0	.31	.30	.13	-.15	-.18	.30	.34	.15	-.26	1.00

cients for the T-score regression equations were then computed and used to generate universe score profiles for each of the observed score profiles.

The means and standard deviations for the three occasions were averaged, yielding the values shown in Table 6.3. These were the values used to obtain the B weights and constant terms for the regression equations. The average mean scores were also taken as the means of the universe scores, while the universe standard deviations were the mean standard deviations multiplied by the square root of the univariate reliability. The univariate reliability coefficients are shown in the third column of Table 6.3.

Looking at the first column of Table 6.3 it is evident that on the average the sample had a 9-4-8 profile. This was true for the three occasions as well as for the overall means. Thus the sample as a whole showed considerable profile stability. The average standard deviations tend to be low, particularly so for scales 3 and 4. This again indicates the homogeneity of the sample and accounts to some extent for the fact that the reliability of individual differences among the subjects is rather low, averaging .56 over the 10 scales.

TABLE 6.3
Combined Means and Standard Deviation and Generalizability Coefficients for
MMPI Clinical Scales

Scale	Combined Mean	Combined S.D.	Univariate Coefficient	Multivariate Coefficient	Percentage Decrease in Error
1	55.73	8.22	.68	.72	12.8
2	61.26	8.21	.53	.61	17.0
3	58.27	6.68	.50	.58	16.0
4	72.49	6.19	.30	.36	8.6
5	56.96	7.70	.53	.55	4.2
6	60.99	7.74	.67	.71	12.1
7	61.05	7.52	.65	.67	5.7
8	69.53	8.86	.56	.61	11.4
9	73.08	8.09	.53	.63	21.3
0	50.31	8.49	.68	.68	0.0

The multivariate generalizability coefficients, obtained by squaring the multiple correlations between the universe scores and their estimates, are shown in the fourth column of Table 6.3. These average 0.61, an increase in overall reliability of .05. The last column of Table 6.3 indicates the percentage decrease in error variance obtainable using the multiple regression equations. These decreases ranged from zero for scale 0 for which no additional predictors was found, to 21.3% for scale 9 with six additional predictors. The B weights and constant term used to obtain the estimated universe scores are shown in Table 6.4.

Some indication of the improved consistency in profile interpretation obtainable from the multiple regression estimates of universe scores as compared to observed scores is indicated by the comparisons in Table 6.5. Two comparisons are used: (1) changes in the set of scores at or above 70 on the clinical scales as indicated by comparing observed scores and estimated universe scores from the

TABLE 6.4
B Weights for Estimating Universe Scores

Observed Score	1	2	3	4	5	6	7	8	9	0
1	.66	.15	.15	-.06		.09			-.16	
2		.41								.12
3	.14		.40							
4	-.16		-.10	.29					.15	
5		.10			.51		.09		.11	
6		.10				.62		-.21		
7					.11	-.13	.64	.51	.14	
8									-.10	
9		-.13		.09					.42	
0								.08		.68
Bo	22.08	25.44	33.60	47.77	20.91	26.93	16.83	42.42	26.22	15.97

TABLE 6.5
Comparison of Stability of Observed and Estimated Universe Score Profiles

	Frequency of Changes in Set of Scores at or above 70			
	Observed Scores		Est. Universe Scores	
Comparison	T(1) - T(2)	T(1) - T(3)	T(1) - T(2)	T(1) - T(3)
No Change	13	6	30	25
Minor Change *	28	38	26	32
Radical Change **	19	16	4	3

		Frequency of Changes in Set of Highest Scores in Profile			
		Observed Scores		Est. Universe Scores	
Comparison		2 Highest	3 Highest	2 Highest	3 Highest
No Change	T(1) - T(2)	25	24	45	35
	T(1) - T(3)	26	18	45	40
One Change	T(1) - T(2)	33	32	15	24
	T(1) - T(3)	33	39	15	19
Two or More Changes	T(1) -T(2)	2	4	0	1
	T(1) - T(3)	1	3	0	1

Permutations in order were not considered to be changes.
* Minor changes: addition. deletion or replacement of one scale
** Radical Changes: anything beyond a minor change

first to the second and from the first to the third occasion; (2) changes in the highest two or highest three scores on the clinical scales, without regard to their elevation.

These comparisons are striking. Only 13 of the 60 subjects (21.7%) had high observed scores (70 or greater) on the identical scales from the first to the second occasion and only 6 (10%) from the first to the third occasion. These agreements increased to 30 (50%) and 25 (41.7%) respectively when multiple regression universe estimates were used. Furthermore radical changes (two or more changes of scales having scores above 70) decreased from 19 to 4 from the first to the second occasion and from 16 to 3 from the first to the third occasion of testing.

Looking now at the two peak scores, these were on identical scales for 25 of the 60 cases (41.7%) from time one to time two and in 26 cases (43.3%) from time one to time three when observed scores were compared. Using universe score estimates, the two peak scales were identical in 45 of the 60 cases (75%) for both comparisons. Furthermore, 35 estimated universe score profiles had the same three highest scales on occasions one and two and 40 had the same three peak scores on occasions one and three.

As might be expected in this homogeneous sample, most of which had high scores on scales 4, 8, and 9, the increased consistency arises from the fact that regression to the mean had the effect of sharpening these peaks while flattening the occasionally occuring high scores on other scales. Thus stability over time was increased, but actually somewhat less individual or group differences in interpretation appear warranted than was implied by the original selection of the three subgroups as identified by their initial profiles. More reliable differentiation among individuals in this sample could be made, not on the peak scores which are characteristic of the group as a whole but on scales 1, 6, 7, and 0 which are the most reliable. Unfortunately these scales would not be used to any extent in most interpretations of these profiles.

The importance of the more reliable scales for maximizing individual differences became even clearer when we obtained the sucessively most reliable canonical variates using Bock's method of analysis. (Correlations between occasions two and three were again omitted.) These results are shown in Table 6.6. The first and most reliable composite appears to be merely a weighted sum of scales 1 and 6, two of the most reliable scales in the sample. It has a reliability of .82. The second composite, with a reliability of .74 is mainly a contrast of scales 6 and 7 with scales 8 and 0: The third variate, with a reliability of .73, is a contrast between scales 2 and 0. While these three variates are all more reliable

TABLE 6.6
Variance Components, Reliabilities, and Coefficients for the Canonical Variates

Canonical Variate	Variance Component for Subjects	Reliability Coefficient
I	4.46	.82
II	2.87	.74
III	2.69	.73
IV	2.16	.68
V	1.41	.58
VI	.82	.45
VII	.59	.37
VIII	.52	.34
IX	.37	.27
X	.17	.15
Average Reliability		.51
Bock's Multivariate Analogue of Reliability		.62

Canonical Variate

Scale	I	II	III	IV	V	VI	VII
1	.66	.12	-.19	-.37	.19	-.33	-.34
2	.13	-.15	-.42		-.37	.23	.54
3	.11	-.14	-.22	-.41	.45	.34	.16
4	-.26	-.11	.20	.27		.10	.29
5		-.24	.18	-.28	-.40	.46	-.38
6	.52	-.35	.33	.42	-.31	-.19	-.31
7	-.25	-.52	.27	-.50	-.20	-.50	.42
8	-22	.38		-.30	-.23		-.23
9	-.15	-.18	.20	-.14	.16	.30	
10	.22	.55	.67		.49	.35	

than any of the universe score estimates obtained via the method of Cronbach et al. their interpretability in terms of the original variables is somewhat more difficult, and the fact that scales 4 and 9 are the salient scales is completely lost.

Our example indicates that improvement in reliability can be obtained by making use of the redundant information in the score set to estimate universe score profiles. It should be noted that the particular results obtained apply only to a highly selective sample of prisoners and cannot be generalized. If a sample of MMPI scores from normal adults had been used, no doubt reliabilities would have been somewhat more evenly distributed, the average sample profile would have been much flatter, and individuals' peak scores would be moderated, but more differentiated one from the other. Unfortunately, we were unable to obtain such a sample for this study. We hope, however, that this example will encourage further research in this area, using the MMPI or other multivariate personality instruments.

Estimating Observed and Universe Profile Reliability

As shown in Table 6.6 the canonical variates ranged in reliability from .15 to .82 with an average reliability of .51. From our earlier discussion, recall that this average value corresponds to the Conger-Lipshitz generalized reliability coefficient. The average univariate reliability, from Table 6.3, was .56. This average is approximately the profile reliability that would be obtained using the Conger–Lipshitz coefficient for individual differences measured by D^2 as discussed earlier. (The more precise estimate from equation (7) is .58.)

The Bock multivariate analogue of reliability, on the other hand, is .62, which is considerably higher than the Conger-Lipshitz reliability and even higher than the average univariate reliability of .56. It is also slightly higher than the average multiple correlation, .61 which can be taken as the universe profile reliability. While the Bock coefficient is appropriately used in conjunction with his total method, as a general coefficient by which to evaluate test profiles it seems rather too optimistic and its meaning in a practical sense is unclear. The Conger-Lipshitz approach which defines multivariate reliability in terms of the distances among score profiles in an appropriately chosen multidimensional space seems much more useful for the purpose of differentiating profile types. Furthermore, the average reliability gives a reasonable approximation to the reliability of Mahalanobis distances when observed scores are only moderately correlated, as well as an accurate index of the reliability if D^2 distances are used.

SUMMARY AND CONCLUSION

This chapter has illustrated approaches to two practical questions regarding the generalizability of multiply-scored tests. The first of these questions has to do with the reliability or generalizability of a set of scores taken together rather than one at a time. While both Bock (1966) and Conger and Lipshitz (1973) have provided coefficients for this purpose, that of Conger and Lipshitz, which defines multivariate reliability as the ratio of the average squared distances among true score vectors to the average squared distances among observed score vectors, appears more analogous to the univariate generalizability coefficient. This coefficient has the advantage of applying to any set of orthogonal contrasts rather than to just the successively most reliable composites. Thus it is more applicable to what the clinician is likely to do in practice. Furthermore, this approach enables the clinician to quickly obtain an estimate of the upper limit of reliability simply by averaging the reliabilities over occasions of the separate scales that make up the profile. This result may come as a shock to clinicians who have always believed that interpretation of the profile yields more reliable information than do the scales taken separately. However, our example using the MMPI illustrates clearly that whether one interprets only scores above 70 in the profile or the two or three highest scores, there is low consistency from one occasion to another when the reliability of individual scales is low.

The second question addressed in this chapter is how one can use the information in the matrix of intercorrelations among sets of scores on two or more occasions to improve observed score profiles. The usual treatment of this problem in the multivariate literature consists of obtaining the successively most reliable composites under various assumptions, leaving it up to the user to determine what clinical interpretations can be placed on these new scores. However, Cronbach et al. (1972) have suggested a different approach, one which enables the investigator to deal with variables defined in terms of the original scales. As has been shown here, this method also involves obtaining composites of the observed scores, but these composites yield approximations to the set of "true" or universe scores for each person as estimated from all the information available in the observed scores. The MMPI data demonstrated that this approach yields somewhat less differentiated and more conservative profiles for which reliability is increased. The analysis is easily made with current computer facilities, and the resulting composites are interpretable in the same manner as the original scores. Therefore, clinicians who analyse profiles would do well to employ this approach in future studies.

REFERENCES

Blanton, R., & Landsman, T. (1952). "The retest reliability of the group Rorschach and some relationships to the MMPI." *Journal of Consulting Psychology, 16,* 265–267.

Bock, R. D. (1966). Contributions of multivariate experimental designs to educational research. In R. B. Cattell (Ed), *Handbook of Multivariate Experimental Psychology* (pp. 820–840). Chicago: Rand McNally.

Butcher, J. N. (1969). *MMPI–Research development and clinical applications.* New York: McGraw Hill.

Conger, A. J. (1974). Estimating profile reliability and maximally reliable composites. *Multivariate Behavioral Research, 9*, 85–104.

Conger, A. J., & Lipshitz, R. (1973). Measures of reliability for profiles and test batteries. *Psychometrika, 38*, 411–427.

Cronbach, L. J., & Gleser, G. C. (1953). Assessing similarity between profiles. *Psychological Bulletin, 50*, 456–473.

Cronbach, L. J., Gleser, G. C., Nanda, H., & Rajaratnam, N. (1972). The Dependability of Behavioral Measurements. New York: Wiley.

Dahlstrom, W. G., & Welsh, G. C. (1960). *An MMPI Handbook*. Minneapolis: University of Minnesota Press.

Drake, L. E., & Oetting, G. R. (1959). *An MMPI codebook for counselors*. Minneapolis: University of Minnesota Press.

Hathaway, S. R., & McKinley, J. C. (1967). *The MMPI Manual. Revised*. New York: The Psychological Corporation.

Hathaway, S. R., & Meehl, P. E. (1951). *An atlas for the clinical use of the MMPI*. Minneapolis: University of Minnesota Press.

Joe, G. N., & Woodward, J. A. (1976). Some developments in multivariate generalizability. *Psychometrika, 41*, 205–217.

Lanier, N. S. (1972). *MMPI role taking by sociopathic and non-sociopathic prison inmates*. Unpublished doctoral dissertation, University of Cincinnati.

Marks, P. A., Seeman, W., and Haller, D. L. (1974). The actuarial use of the MMPI with adolescents and adults. Baltimore: Williams and Wilkins.

Shavelson, R. J., & Webb, N. M. (1981). Generalizability theory: 1973–1980. *British Journal of Mathematical and Statistical Psychology, 34*, 133–166.

Tiffin, J., & McCormick, E. J. (1965). *Industrial Psychology*. Englewood Cliffs, NJ: Prentice Hall.

Webb, N. M., & Shavelson, R. J. (1981). Multivariate generalizability of general educational development ratings. *Journal of Educational Measurement, 18*, 13–22.

Welsh, G. C., & Dahlstrom, W. G. (1956). Basic readings on the MMPI in psychology and medicine. Minneapolis: University of Minnesota Press.

7 Psychology and Methodology of Response Styles

Samuel Messick
Educational Testing Service

Although some earlier notice had already been taken of acquiescent response set (Fritz, 1927; Lentz, 1938; Lorge, 1937), it was a series of research inquiries by Cronbach (1941, 1942, 1946, 1950) in the 1940s, especially two extensive reviews published in 1946 and 1950, that conceptualized and popularized the problem of response sets in educational and psychological measurement. It had long been presumed that the score a person attains on an educational or psychological test is determined by relevant responses to the specific content of the stimulus items. Moreover, it was usually taken for granted that this score reflected the respondent's knowledge on achievement tests, abilities on aptitude tests, interests on interest inventories, traits on personality measures, and opinions on attitude scales. Evidence in support of these presumptions is critical in establishing the meaning or construct validity of the scores. However, the responses a person makes to a test are a function not only of item content but of item form, as well as of other aspects of the assessment context.

For example, item form or test directions or instructions for guessing may induce response preferences that systematically influence scores, such as an emphasis on speed as opposed to accuracy or a tendency to gamble. In addition, the respondent may characteristically bring to tests of certain formats (such as true–false or agree–disagree) various test-taking attitudes and habits (such as a tendency to agree when in doubt) that produce a cumulative effect on his or her scores. Aspects of item and test form, then, may differentially influence an individual's mode of item response and permit or even facilitate the operation of preferred or habitual styles of response. These stylistic consistencies in response to formal properties apart from specific item content were called response sets, which Cronbach (1946) defined as any tendency causing a person consistently to give different responses to test items than would be the case if the same content were presented in a different form.

A test presumed to measure one characteristic may thus also be inadvertently measuring another characteristic (response set) that might not have contaminated the score if some other form of test had been administered. For example, if the same content is tapped in true-keyed and false-keyed forms and consistently higher trait scores are obtained with one form than with the other, then an agreement response set may be a contaminating influence. In contrast, if one uses a forced-choice or multiple-choice format, which precludes the operation of a tendency to agree when in doubt, and the results are the same as with a true-false format—that is, trait levels and trait relationships are similarly estimated with the two forms—then an agreement response set may be effectively discounted.

The term *form* is used broadly here to embrace all aspects of the test situation (apart from specific item content) to which the respondent may react. This includes the form of the item, the direction and tone of its phrasing, the degree of desirability in its connotation, the number and nature of response alternatives provided, the test directions, instructions for guessing, and the presumed use to which the scores will be put. By virtue of stylistic consistencies in the manner of response to such formal aspects, a number of response sets have been identified empirically. These include reliable tendencies to acquiesce when in doubt on true-false or agree-disagree formats; to be inclusive in self-attribution; to respond desirably; to fake or manage the impression presented; to respond deviantly; to be critical; to be confident; to be evasive, indecisive, or indifferent; to respond extremely as opposed to moderately on rating scales or Likert-type formats of strongly agree to strongly disagree; to gamble or guess; to emphasize speed versus accuracy; and, to interpret judgment categories differentially (Cronbach, 1946; Messick, 1968).

Response sets become more and more influential to the degree that the respondent is at a loss to answer in terms of specific content—for example, when he or she lacks pertinent knowledge or self-knowledge, is unsure or inaccurate in self-perception, or finds the item ambiguous. Given comparable kinds and levels of ambiguity or lack of structure, response sets appear to be relatively stable and general in their operation (Cronbach, 1946, 1950; Messick, 1968). Although these stable response consistencies may reflect durable but relatively trivial individual differences (perhaps in language usage or expressive habits), Cronbach (1946) also suggested that they may reflect significant aspects of personality. To emphasize this latter point and to underscore that response sets are not just annoying contaminants in trait measurement but potentially useful indicants of stylistic consistencies in personality, Jackson and Messick (1958) proposed that they be renamed *response styles*.

Once Cronbach had opened the response-set floodgates, hundreds of empirical studies and dozens of research reviews inundated the measurement literature (e.g., Berg, 1967; Christie & Lindauer, 1963; Dahlstrom & Welsh, 1960; Dahlstrom, Welsh, & Dahlstrom, 1975; Edwards, 1970; Edwards & Abbott, 1973; Hamilton, 1968; Holtzman, 1965; Klein, Barr, & Wolitzky, 1967; McGee, 1962, 1967; Messick, 1961; Moscovici, 1963; Rorer, 1965; Wiggins, 1968). A first wave of studies examined the impact of acquiescence on the California F scale of authoritarianism, all items of which are keyed "true." This was quickly followed by a torrent of research on the roles of acquiescence and social desirability in self-descriptive personality questionnaires, especially the Minnesota Multiphasic Personality Inventory (MMPI).

Before long, however, a vigorous backwash swelled up disputing the importance of acquiescence and desirability on personality inventories. In this crosscurrent, attempts were launched not only to downplay the challenge of response sets (Block, 1965) but to dismiss response styles themselves—or more precisely, acquiescence—as a great myth (Rorer, 1965; Rorer & Goldberg, 1965a, 1965b). Efforts to stem this backwash were equally vigorous and led to whirlpools of controversy but little consensus between contending parties (e.g., Bentler, 1966; Bentler, Jackson, & Messick, 1971, 1972; Block, 1971, 1972; Jackson, 1967a, 1967b; Jackson & Messick, 1965; Messick, 1967; Morf & Jackson, 1972).

Although the waters were relatively calm for the next decade, there is still sufficient roiling to indicate that response styles are far from mythical and that they forbode serious consequences for psychological measurement. Specifically, response styles, when they are operative, serve to invalidate content-based interpretations of scores and to confound group comparisons (e.g., Bachman & O'Malley, 1984). Worse still, response styles serve to obscure trait relationships and to distort the dimensional structure of psychological domains. Some examples here include the effects of response styles in obscuring bipolar relationships in the mapping of semantic space (Bentler, 1969); in the measurement and conceptualization of affects and mood states (Lorr & Shea, 1979; Lorr & Wunderlich, 1980; Russell, 1978, 1979); and, in the appraisal of masculinity, femininity, and androgyny (Jackson & Paunonen, 1980).

The topic of response sets is old work in the Cronbach oeuvre. And the major counterclaims by Block (1965), by Rorer (1965), and by Rorer and Goldberg (1965a, 1965b) are old criticisms. On the grounds that these critiques may have been more influential over the years than their substance warrants, this chapter examines one of them in detail—namely, Block's (1965) monograph on *The Challenge of Response Sets*—and will also comment briefly on Rorer's (1965) attempt to mythologize response styles. The work of Rorer and Goldberg (1965a, 1965b) based on item reversals for the MMPI is not addressed here as the issues have been confronted at length elsewhere (Bentler et al., 1971; Jackson & Messick, 1965; Messick, 1967; Morf & Jackson, 1972). Furthermore, this old critique by Block will be countered by old analyses and arguments that were presented at the 1965 meetings of the Western Psychological Association, but have not been previously published. The main purpose is to commemorate Cronbach's seminal work on response sets and to affirm its relevance and importance, not only for its own time but for the present as well.

THE RESPONSE STYLE CONTROVERSY

First let us summarize the gist of the running controversy about the roles of content and style in personality assessment. One side claims that some of the major common factors in personality inventories of the true–false or agree–disagree type, particularly those derived from the empirical discrimination of criterion groups, are interpretable primarily in terms of stylistic consistencies in response to some aspect of item form or item connotation, such as desirability, rather than in terms of specific item content. Furthermore, it is thought that these stylistic consistencies, or response styles, reflect significant personality characteristics, that they are relatively enduring over time and display some degree of generality across both test and nontest behaviors (Edwards, 1957, 1970; Jackson & Messick, 1958, 1962a). This side of the argument admits the operation of content factors, and even considers that response styles may interact with aspects of content, but it also maintains that content dimensions would be better defined if specific efforts were made both to reduce the influence of response styles and to increase content saturation in the measurement process (Jackson, 1971, 1980).

The other side of the controversy questions whether response styles have any real personality correlates at all, thereby casting doubt upon their presumptive status as personality variables (McGee, 1962; Rorer, 1965). Furthermore, the very operation of these response styles on personality inventories is thought to have been greatly exaggerated, particularly in the case of acquiescence, and attempts have been made to reinstate the major dimensions of inventory response as factors of specific content consistency (Block, 1965; Lichtenstein & Bryan, 1965; Rorer & Goldberg, 1965a, 1965b).

One of these latter efforts is the study by Block (1965) that is the central concern of this chapter. Briefly, Block attempted to demonstrate that MMPI scales can be revised to eliminate the influence of response styles and still measure the same dimensions and reveal the same factor structure as the original unrevised scales. The implication is that response styles were not operating very powerfully on the original scales after all. In a later section, we attempt to evaluate the logic and empirical evidence underlying Block's position in contrast to the logic and empirical evidence afforded in other factor analytic studies that interpreted MMPI factors in terms of response styles (Edwards, Diers, & Walker, 1962; Edwards & Walsh, 1964; Jackson & Messick, 1961, 1962b).

RESPONSE STYLES AS PERSONALITY VARIABLES

Before embarking on a detailed analysis of these factor studies of the MMPI, we need to consider the purported nature of response styles and some of their behavioral correlates. Because of their prominence in discussions of the MMPI, attention is restricted here to the response styles of acquiescence and desirability. Traditionally, *acquiescence* refers to individual consistencies in the tendency to agree (or disagree) with personality or attitude statements. Also pertinent, however, are tendencies to accept (or reject) many heterogeneous characteristics as descriptive of the personality or belief system. Both agreement and acceptance tendencies, which are often confounded in measures of acquiescence, operate primarily on items that respondents are at a loss to answer—for example, because they lack self-knowledge about the characteristic in question, because they are uncertain about the specific meaning of the item, or because perceived neutrality of value connotation renders item desirability ambiguous to them as well. The *desirability* response style refers to individual consistencies in the tendency to give answers that are considered desirable by social consensus, a tendency that has been taken by some to mean that the respondent is consciously or unconsciously attempting to place himself or herself in a favorable light. As we shall see, agreement tendencies and acceptance tendencies form distinct dimensions relevant to the expression of acquiescence response style, while deliberate impression management and the nondeliberate expression of a (distorted) self-image form distinct dimensions in connection with desirable responding.

Rorer (1965) has suggested that the term "style" not be used to refer to both acquiescence and desirability, but that instead desirability be characterized by the term "set." In his words, a " 'set' connotes a conscious or unconscious desire on the part of a respondent to answer in such a way as to produce a certain picture of himself. . . . To say that a respondent has a set in this sense is akin to saying that he is motivated" (p. 133). However, to say that particular response consistencies are motivated at some level is saying very little, in the sense that such a position could be defended for almost any behavioral consistency, including acquiescence. On the other hand, to say that a response consistency stems from the direct expression, whether conscious or unconscious, of a present motive state is saying very much, very likely too much in the case of desirability consistencies.

As is maintained subsequently, the psychological basis of desirable responding is quite complicated and may involve, for example, autistic biases in self-perception and self-regard. Although these biases were likely motivated at some stage of development, the recurrence of these motivational states may have come to mold and crystallize the cognitive structure of the self-picture in a distorted form, thereby allowing the possibility of a cognitive and not a direct motivational basis for subsequent desirable responding in self-description (Damarin & Messick, 1965; Murphy, 1947). Thus, a person who consistently responds extremely desirably and receives a high score on, say, the Edwards SD scale may not actually be so desirable, but may think he or she is—and may not be directly motivated to produce a certain self-picture deliberately in a particular instance. To characterize desirable responding, then, as a "set" in Rorer's sense would be to prejudge the psychological basis of the observed response consistency in a way that is far from warranted by current data and conceptualizations.

Rorer (1965) also distinguished between "styles" and "sets" in terms of their differential dependence on item content: Style, in his words, "refers to a tendency to select some response category a disproportionate amount of the time independently of item content" (p. 134), whereas "a set requires at least some content" (p. 134). However, since acquiescence appears to be related both to item ambiguity and to the degree of desirability or neutrality of the item, it would seem that both acquiescence and desirable responding depend in part on some general aspects of item content other than *specific* item meaning. Thus, this attempt to separate styles and sets as content-independent versus content-dependent, respectively, would be a blurred distinction at best (Damarin & Messick, 1965; Jackson & Messick, 1962a). There is a further danger that one might be led by an extension of the internal logic of this proposed distinction to seek "pure" criterion measures of acquiescence in so-called "content-free" formats, such as the pseudo-ESP experiment (Bass, 1957) or the phony language examination (Nunnally & Husek, 1958). However, it is likely that these procedures elicit response tendencies that are markedly different from the test-taking attitudes displayed in voluntary self-description (Damarin & Messick, 1965).

For these reasons, the specific bases offered for Rorer's (1965) distinctions between set and style seem counterproductive. In general, such attempts to characterize these observed stylistic consistencies in terms of their presumed psychological underpinnings or their hypothetical stimulus-response properties are not only premature but possibly misleading. Unfortunately, this may already have been the case for some individual response styles such as acquiescence, where presumed associations with conformity and submission led to years of unproductive research (Messick, 1967). It seems preferable at this stage of development, therefore, to encompass both acquiescence and desirable responding with the term "style," defined in a relatively noncommittal way as a reliable consistency in the *manner* of response to some aspect of item form or item connotation other than specific item meaning (Jackson & Messick, 1962a).

By reclassifying desirability as a "set," the response styles that Rorer (1965) attempts to mythologize refer only to consistent disproportionate uses of particular response categories. Even then, the target is limited mainly to acquiescence. For example, extremity response style—that is, consistent use of extreme as opposed to intermediate response categories on rating scales or Likert formats—is ignored by Rorer, along with its documented reliability and extensive behavioral correlates (Damarin & Messick, 1965; Hamilton, 1968).

It is impossible to summarize here all of the many reviews, both positive and negative, that bear on the properties of response styles, on the extensiveness of their effects, or on their status as personality variables. However, because of its pertinence to Block's (1965) psychological interpretations of MMPI factors that are discussed later, a brief summary is provided of a survey by Damarin and Messick (1965) of multivariate research that includes both response style scores and objective behavioral measures of personality. Damarin and Messick (1965) reviewed 14 factor analytic studies of response styles and questionnaire measures, as well as eight factor studies from the laboratory of Raymond B. Cattell (Hundleby, Pawlik, & Cattell, 1965) that investigated intercorrelations among objective performance tests of personality (including measures of response styles) in widely different samples of college students, psychotics, air force cadets, and young children. These factor studies provided evidence for at least two distinct dimensions underlying acquiescence scores, each with its own pattern of behavioral correlates; similarly, two distinct dimensions also emerged in connection with desirable responding.

Dimensions of Acquiescence

On one of the factors in Cattell's work, measures of acquiescence were found to be associated with low verbal ability, poor performance in interpreting riddles correctly, low social taste, and little logical consistency of attitudes. (In the measure of social taste, respondents chose among three alternatives rationally keyed for high-brow, middle-brow, and low-brow taste. In the measure of logical consistency of attitudes, attitude statements were presented in random order for endorsement, but the statements were originally written in triads that formed syllogisms and the respondent was scored for the logical consistency of his or her endorsements.) On this dimension, acquiescence scores are negatively associated with verbal comprehension skills, suggesting that this type of acquiescer may have difficulty in interpreting statements unambiguously. For convenience, this intellectually based stylistic dimension can be referred to as "uncritical agreement" (Messick, 1967). Several other studies have reported negative correlations between measures of intellectual ability and acquiescence, usually as measured on some such scale as the Bass (1956) social acquiescence scale or the California F scale where the items comprise sweepingly worded, unqualified statements of general attitude or belief.

Another of Cattell's factors, the rudiments of which appeared in several studies, associated measures of acquiescence with high speed of judgment and reaction in perceptual and perceptual-motor tasks as well as with ideational fluency and rapid tempo in preferred rates of movement. This dimension is reminiscent of the Couch and Keniston (1960) clinical formulation of yeasaying versus naysaying, in that it appears to relate acquiescence to a temperament characteristic of unreflective impulsiveness. According to Couch and Keniston

(1960), extreme yeasayers are impulsive, undercontrolled, stimulus accepting extraverts; whereas extreme naysayers are cautious, overcontrolled, stimulus rejecting introverts. Similarly, high scorers on this Cattell factor react quickly and impulsively with little reflection and probably little monitoring of performance, both on judgmental and perceptual-motor tasks and on questionnaires. Low scorers, in contrast, are more reflective, but in the extreme may also be handicapped in effectiveness because of an obsessively cautious and overly controlled stance. For convenience, this temperamentally based stylistic dimension was referred to as "impulsive acceptance" (Messick, 1967).

Attitude items—especially items written in the sweeping style of the California F scale—tend to elicit agreement propensities more strongly than acceptance propensities, while personality items tend to elicit both agreement and acceptance propensities to about the same degree (Morf & Jackson, 1972). In some previous writings (Bentler et al., 1971), these two propensities were called "agreement acquiescence" and "acceptance acquiescence," respectively. The stress here is on the terms "agreement" and "acceptance," rather than on "acquiescence," to signal the distinct personality roots of the two tendencies, the former being intellectually based in difficulties with resolving verbal ambiguity and the latter being temperamentally based in difficulties with impulse control.

Dimensions of Desirable Responding

The factor studies reviewed by Damarin and Messick (1965) also afforded evidence for two relatively uncorrelated dimensions of desirable responding. The first factor was marked at one pole by purported desirability measures such as Edwards' SD scale and at the other pole by measures of maladjustment, neuroticism, and anxiety (Bendig, 1960; Cattell & Scheier, 1961; Edwards et al., 1962; Edwards & Walsh, 1964; Jackson & Messick, 1961, 1962b). The second desirability dimension was marked primarily by empirically derived role-playing measures of dissimulation, such as the Wiggins (1959) Sd scale and the Cofer, Chance, and Judson (1949) positive malingering scale, and to a considerable extent also by the MMPI Lie scale and the Marlowe-Crowne scale of need for social approval (Edwards et al., 1962; Edwards & Walsh, 1964; Jackson & Messick, 1962b).

The Marlowe–Crowne scale not only correlates highly with this second desirability factor but also substantially with the first, so that the extensive behavioral correlates that Crowne and Marlowe (1964) report for their scale might be due sometimes to one, sometimes to the other, and sometimes to both of these factors. If these behavioral correlates are attributed primarily to the second desirability factor that apparently reflects dissimulation, then for the considerably larger factor that Edwards calls social desirability we are left with a paucity of behavioral correlates that consistently replicate across population groups (Damarin & Messick, 1965).

The second or smaller factor of desirable responding appears to represent a dimension of bias in self-report, an at least partially deliberate attempt to produce a desired picture. But it may be too strong to label this factor "lying" or "deliberate misrepresentation." It might be better to describe it in terms of what Goffman (1959) has called "impression management," which includes partly stylistic tendencies to emphasize and even overplay social roles and personal characteristics to achieve dramatic effects. But if this second desirability factor represents a partially deliberate attempt on the part of the respondent to place himself or herself in a desired light, what does the first, large factor of desirable responding represent—the one that Edwards found to be so pervasive in self-description, even under conditions of anonymity?

Milholland (1964) suggested that this large desirability factor is primarily a reflection of accuracy in self-description—that people give desirable responses, "if for no other reason, simply because most people who are allowed to roam at large are in fact socially desirable" (p. 315). Block (1965) also considers the association of this large factor with desirability to be an epiphenomenon of accurate self-report—it is not surprising, for example, "that the behaviors and feelings acknowledged by a schizophrenic are evaluated in a societal context as undesirable" (p. 71). But it *is* surprising that accurate self-descriptions should produce a primary pervasive dimension intimately associated with desirability that on many questionnaires overshadows the various content dimensions of personality. Should not accurate self-description yield an array of distinguishable personality dimensions similar to those revealed by behavior ratings and performance tests? Or is personality structure revealed through self-description organized around a monolithic dimension on which desirable traits covary and oppose undesirable traits?

Damarin and Messick (1965) proposed a heuristic model for this large desirability factor that acknowledges the contribution of accurate self-description, as Block (1965) and Milholland (1964) would desire, but that also permits the operation of distorting biases. A person who responds in extremely desirable terms, for example, may not actually be so desirable; he or she may be defensively maintaining a biased self-image. In another context, Block pointed out that extreme self-satisfaction, as reflected in the correlation between self and ideal-self ratings, may be based on repressive mechanisms and that self-satisfaction might therefore be curvilinearly and not directly related to adjustment (Block & Thomas, 1955). Similar mechanisms may be operating in the tendency to respond in desirable terms, whether based on personal or social criteria of desirability, and the possibility of such mechanisms should be considered in formulating a psychological rationale for this factor.

The heuristic conception offered by Damarin and Messick (1965) incorporates three basic elements: a set of self-descriptive item responses or self-ratings by each individual (represented by s in equations 1 and 2); the average judged social desirability scale values for these same items (represented by d in the equations);

and, a set of accurate (unbiased) descriptions of each person obtained from an external assessment, say from a team of assessment specialists or perhaps from behavioral tests (represented by a in the equations). The correlation, r_{sd}, between each person's self-descriptive responses and the social desirability scale values represents a desirability score for the person that reflects the tendency to describe oneself in a socially desirable manner. The correlation, r_{sa}, between the person's self-description and the external assessment represents the accuracy of the self-report. The correlation, r_{ad}, between the external assessment and the desirability scale values represents the assessed or *true* desirability of the person's characteristics.

Given these three correlational scores, a fourth score can be computed to represent the net bias from all other sources in the person's self-description. This fourth score, the correlation between self-description and desirability for a given level of accuracy, is presented in equation 1:

$$r_{sd.a} = \frac{r_{sd} - r_{sa}\, r_{ad}}{\sqrt{1 - r_{sa}^2}\,\sqrt{1 - r_{ad}^2}}. \tag{1}$$

This equation may be rearranged to express r_{sd} as a function of the other three scores, as in equation 2:

$$r_{sd} = r_{sa}\, r_{ad} + r_{sd.a}\,\sqrt{1 - r_{sa}^2}\,\sqrt{1 - r_{ad}^2}. \tag{2}$$

Thus, in this formulation each person's tendency to respond in a socially desirable way (r_{sd}) is seen to be a function of his or her accuracy of self-perception (r_{sa}), true desirability of personal characteristics (r_{ad}), and biases ($r_{sd.a}\,\sqrt{1 - r_{sa}^2}\,\sqrt{1 - r_{ad}^2}$). It can be seen from this equation that a person's score for desirable responding (r_{sd}) will indeed reflect his or her actual desirability (r_{ad}) when the self-descriptions are perfectly accurate (when $r_{sa} = 1$). However, to the extent that the person is less than perfectly accurate in describing his or her personal characteristics, this score may include the influence of bias factors, which could be either positive or negative.

Since desirable responding is partly a function of accuracy in self-perception, then, it might well have different meanings—and very likely different correlates—for different types of people, such as normal college students, young children, or psychotics (Damarin & Messick, 1965). Since partially deliberate *biases in self-report* appear to operate on the second (smaller) factor of desirable responding, the biases operating on this larger desirability factor might better be conceptualized as nondeliberate or autistic *biases in self-regard*. Whereas the smaller factor is characterized by impression management, the larger factor (for relatively inaccurate respondents) is characterized by image maintenance, where the image is defensively maintained to be consistent with the biased self-picture. To use the labels popularized by Sackeim and Gur (1979; Gur & Sackeim, 1979), the larger desirability factor might be interpreted in terms of degree of *self-*

deception and the smaller factor in terms of *other-deception*. This two-factor theory of desirable responding has been supported and clarified in factor-analytic and experimental studies by Paulhus (1984, 1986), especially with regard to the involvement of processes of self-deception and of other-deception or impression management.

THE FACTORIAL INTERPRETATION OF THE MMPI[1]

When scales from the MMPI are factor analyzed, two large factors and several smaller ones usually appear (see Dahlstrom et al., 1975; Messick & Jackson, 1961a). The controversy that is the main concern of the present chapter arose when it was claimed that the two major factors of the MMPI could be rotated into positions interpretable as response styles of acquiescence and desirability. The smaller "impression management" factor of desirable responding also emerges as one of the minor MMPI factors when appropriate marker scales are included in the analyses, but its role is not in dispute in the present argument (Edwards et al., 1962; Jackson & Messick, 1962b). First let us consider some of the evidence supporting the response style interpretation of the two major MMPI factors, and then let us evaluate the basis of Block's (1965) claim that acquiescence and desirability could not reasonably account for these major dimensions of MMPI responses.

Stylistic Interpretation of MMPI Factors

Jackson and Messick (1961, 1962b) performed three factor analyses of MMPI scales on separate samples of prison inmates, normal college students, and hospitalized mental patients. In these studies, each of several MMPI scales was separated into its true-keyed and false-keyed parts (the sum of which yields the usual MMPI scale score). In addition, five special desirability scales, labeled Dy1 to Dy5, were also constructed as possible markers for response style factors.

---

[1]Factor analyses were based on the following MMPI scales: EC-4, Ego-control 4 (Block); F, Frequency; Hs, Hypochondriasis; D, Depression; Hy, Hysteria; Pd, Psychopathic deviate; Mf, Masculinity-femininity; Pa, Paranoia; Pt, Psychasthenia; Sc, Schizophrenia; Ma, Hypomania; Pn, Psychoneurosis (Block); SD, Social desirability (Edwards); Es, Ego-strength (Barron); Ie, Intellectual efficiency (Gough); Lp, Leadership (Gough); Sp, Social participation (Gough); St, Social status (Gough); Do, Dominance (Gough, McClosky, & Meehl); Si, Social introversion (Drake); and, NUC, Neurotic under-control (Block). In addition, the following scales were projected into the factor space by extension methods: EC-5, Ego-control 5 (Block); ER-O, Ego-resiliency, obvious (Block); K, Test-taking attitudes (Meehl & Hathaway); Dy1–Dy5, Desirability to undesirability (Jackson & Messick); A, Anxiety (Welsh); R, Repression (Welsh); and, Aq, Acquiescence (Fulkerson). Most of these scales and their research underpinnings are described in detail in Dahlstrom and Welsh (1960) and in Dahlstrom et al., (1975).

Construction of these Dy scales was accomplished by dividing all MMPI items into five levels of judged desirability and by selecting items at random within each level to form a scale, with the proviso that item overlap between Dy scales and the MMPI clinical scales be kept to a minimum. All of the items in the Dy scales were keyed true; Dy1 had the highest judged desirability and Dy5 the lowest, while Dy3, which was considered to be a potential measure of acquiescence, contained items judged to be neutral in desirability.

All three factor analyses produced two large factors and several minor ones, and the factor loadings for the first two rotated dimensions, at least, were well replicated across the three samples. One of the rotated factors had its highest loadings for Dy1 and the Edwards SD scale in one direction and for Dy5 in the other. The second rotated factor received its highest loadings for Dy3 and the Fulkerson (1958) acquiescence or Aq scale in one direction and for Welsh's (1956) repression or R scale (all items of which are keyed false) in the other. In view of this pattern of high loadings for these marker scales, the factors were deemed interpretable as the response styles of desirability and acquiescence, respectively. Two large dimensions similarly marked by measures of desirability and acquiescence were also obtained by Edwards et al. (1962) in their factor analysis of 58 MMPI scales.

Block (1965) has objected, however, to stylistic factor interpretations that are based on patterns of loadings for putative response style measures on the grounds that the content of these scales, not their presumed stylistic properties, may be determining the results. Although, in principle, content consistencies were (or at least could have been) avoided in the construction of these response style measures, enough content homogeneity may have crept in inadvertently to render the interpretation of certain response style scales equivocal until further studies are performed. Such studies might involve the construction of content-heterogeneous response style measures that take special care to avoid content consistencies or, perhaps, the demonstration that alternative response style scales can be developed that have the same psychometric properties and reflect the same factor but have markedly different item content.

This latter approach was followed by Edwards (1966, 1970), who selected from a large pool of experimental (nonMMPI) personality items without regard to content a set that would match each item of the MMPI in social desirability scale value and in frequency of endorsement. The MMPI items were then scored for 57 MMPI scales, and the same keys were applied to the experimental items. When all 114 scales were factor analyzed, two large factors were obtained with loadings for both types of scales. The loadings of the MMPI scales on the largest factor correlated .98 with the first-factor loadings of the experimental scales and above .90 with the correlations of the MMPI and experimental scales with two different SD scales (one based on MMPI items and one on experimental items). The factor loadings also correlated above .90 with the proportion of items keyed for social desirability in the scales. Moreover, the loadings of the MMPI scales on the second factor correlated .67 with the second-factor loadings of the corresponding experimental scales. Thus, the two-dimensional factor structure cut across both MMPI and experimental (nonMMPI) scales, with high-loading marker scales containing MMPI content mirrored by marker scales with completely different (experimental) content.

Although the potential importance of content consistencies in presumed response style measures can thus be discounted experimentally, it turns out that the main support for the response style interpretation in the Jackson and Messick studies did not stem from the high factor loadings of any particular marker scale, equivocal or not, but rather from certain structural relations *between* scales. Jackson and Messick (1961, 1962b) reasoned that if the largest factor on the MMPI actually reflected a tendency to respond desirably, then not only should SD scales receive high loadings on this factor but the first-factor loadings of all MMPI scales should be directly related to independent measures of their desirability level. When correlations were computed between these factor loadings and average social desirability scale values for the items of each scale, coefficients above .90 were obtained in all three samples (see also Jackson & Messick, 1969). It was also reasoned that if the second MMPI factor actually reflected acquiescence, then not only should acquiescence marker scales receive high loadings but all of the true-keyed subscales should receive positive loadings on the factor and all of the false-keyed subscales negative loadings. This is precisely what happened in all three samples.

In each case, the first two rotated factors produced a circular array of test vectors, with one factor serving as a diameter that separated true-keyed from false-keyed subscales and the other as a diameter that roughly separated desirable from undesirable responses. This pattern of loadings was generated in part by the tendency for true-keyed subscales to correlate much more highly with other true-keyed scales than they did with their own corresponding false subscales, which in turn tended to correlate more highly with other false scales than with their own corresponding true subscales. This is contrary to the common presumption that true- and false-keyed parts should correlate highly with each other to generate a consistent total score. The circular nature of the factor plot indicates that acquiescence (or naysaying) is highest for scales in the neutral range of desirability and falls off systematically toward zero as scales become either more and more desirable or more and more undesirable. Consistent with this picture, the correlations between true and false parts of MMPI scales—except, of course, for some very desirable or undesirable scales, such as the Edwards SD scale, the Taylor (1953) anxiety scale, Hs, Pt, and Sc—were found to be much smaller than their respective reliabilities would permit and were sometimes even negative.

Block (1965) attempted to account for these low correlations between the true and false parts of several MMPI scales by conjecturing that the corresponding true and false parts actually measure different contents. In addition to posing severe difficulties for the interpretation of the usual total scores on the original

MMPI scales, this conjecture fails to deal with the main burden of the Jackson and Messick evidence: The problem is not only that true and false parts appear to measure different things when considered scale by scale, but one of those different things appears to be the same in all scales—that is, the subscale intercorrelations are accounted for primarily by two factors, one of which separates all of the true subscales from all of the false subscales. If a general content dimension is to serve this purpose, what is its nature and by what process does it separate true-responding from false-responding?

The Problem of Item Overlap

From a different point of attack, Block (1965) attempted to account for this factorial separation of true and false subscales on the MMPI as an artifact of item overlap. He noted that item overlap, which is a general problem on the MMPI, occurs most frequently among true-keyed subscales or among false-keyed subscales, with very little overlap between true- and false-keyed parts. When intercorrelations are computed among true and false subscales as a function of item overlap alone, "a clear clustering is visually apparent" (p. 14) that should generate at least two independent factors, and perhaps a few more. One of these factors should receive loadings for many of the true-keyed subscales, and another orthogonal factor should receive loadings for many of the false-keyed subscales.

Block extracted two factors from the matrix of overlap correlations; these factors are plotted in Fig. 7.1. It can be seen in Fig. 7.1 that all of the true subscales received positive loadings on the second factor and all of the false subscales negative loadings, a finding that Block argues can account for the similar separation in the Jackson and Messick (1961, 1962b) results as an artifact of item overlap. If that is so, what about the first factor in Fig. 7.1? What kind of artifact did it introduce? It cannot be claimed to account for the large factor Jackson and Messick interpret as desirability, since its loadings are not particularly related to desirability scale values. It cannot even be interpreted in simple terms as a dimension of item overlap, since the highest loadings were obtained by Hy_f and Sc_t, which have no items in common at all. Yet both factors were generated by overlap correlations, so something seems amiss in Block's factorial resolution.

The difficulty lies in the fact that the overlap factors discussed by Block are unrotated. The factors underlying the clear visual clusters apparent in the overlap correlation matrix are those represented by dashed lines in Fig. 7.1: two uncorrelated factors, one accounting for overlap correlations among true-keyed subscales and one accounting for overlap among false-keyed subscales. Since Jackson and Messick (1961, 1962b) included several minor MMPI factors in their analytic rotations to simple structure, they succeeded in all three samples in uncovering factors such as these, which they explicitly interpreted in terms of item overlap and which were controlled by virtue of their orthogonal orientation

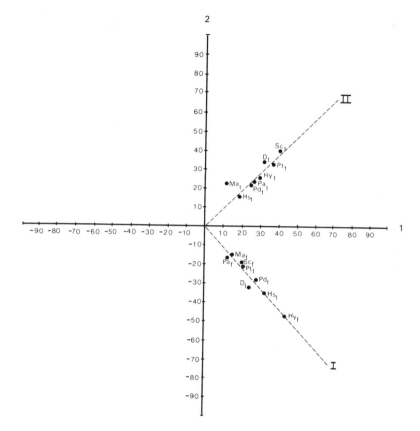

FIG. 7.1. Two factors from overlap-based MMPI correlations.

to the stylistically interpreted MMPI factors. Thus, over and above factors of
item overlap, Jackson and Messick (1961, 1962b) have isolated a large factor on
the MMPI that is not only marked by putative measures of acquiescence but that
clearly separates true subscales from false subscales. Interpretations of this factor
in terms other than acquiescence must therefore provide some rationale to explain this replicated separation.

It is also of importance to note that in a factor analysis of nonMMPI questionnaire scales dealing with nonpsychopathological content and containing no item
overlap whatsoever, Messick (1962) found two large factors, among others, that
produced a circular array of test vectors. One of these factors was marked by two
specially constructed SD scales, and its loadings correlated .78 with the average
item desirability ratings of the content scales. The other factor was marked by
two specially constructed acquiescence scales that were heterogeneous in content
as well as counterbalanced for both content and desirability. Once again, this

factor completely separated true-keyed subscales from false-keyed subscales. Furthermore, the order of the loadings on this factor were predictable from the size of the correlations between true and false parts of each content scale, as evidenced by a rank-order correlation of $-.92$ between the true–false correlations and the average of the absolute loadings of corresponding true and false subscales. Thus, the separation of true and false scales effected by a factor marked by putative measures of acquiescence not only occurs in the complete absence of item overlap contamination, but it is not even unique to the MMPI item pool.

Moreover, Morf and Jackson (1972) similarly identified an agreement factor that completely separated true-keyed and false-keyed subscales having non-pathological content and no item overlap. They also isolated an acceptance factor that separated trait-acceptance from trait-rejection regardless of the direction of keying, a dimension that was subsequently shown to be related to an individual's threshold value on the item desirability scale marking his or her transition from false-responding to true-responding (Jackson, 1986; Voyce & Jackson, 1977). This unconfounding of agreement and acceptance tendencies depends on having both positively and negatively phrased versions of both true- and false-keyed subscales. Since roughly 85% of the items on the MMPI are positively phrased, the two dimensions are confounded on the MMPI as well as in most acquiescence response style scores. They become unconfounded when both original and reversed MMPI items are included in the same factor analysis (Bentler et al., 1971; Jackson & Messick, 1965) and when positive and negative phrasing as well as true- and false-keying are taken into account in constructing distinct response style scores.

The Efficacy of Balanced Scales

To pursue the main thrust of his critique of the acquiescence interpretation, Block (1965) constructed balanced forms of several MMPI scales by eliminating at random enough items from the predominant part, whether true or false, to produce equal numbers of true and false items in each revised scale. Block reasoned that acquiescence could not possibly operate on such balanced scales, since any contaminating effects due to a consistent agreement tendency would cancel out over the equal numbers of true and false items. He then factor analyzed 21 MMPI scales, first in their original unbalanced form and then in their revised balanced form, separately for five different samples. The scales analyzed were F, Hs, D, Hy, Pd, Mf, Pa, Pt, Sc, Ma, and Si, along with the Edwards SD scale, Block's psychoneurosis scale (Pn), Barron's ego strength scale (Es), Gough's intellectual efficiency scale (Ie), Gough's leadership scale (Lp), Gough's social participation scale (Sp), Gough's social status scale (St), the Gough, McClosky, and Meehl dominance scale (Do), Block's ego-control scale (EC-4), and Block's neurotic undercontrol scale (NUC) (see Dahlstrom & Welsh, 1960; Dahlstrom et al.,

1975). This set of scales included several that were not in the Jackson and Messick studies and vice versa, so that differences in factor placement have to be taken into account before making detailed comparisons with their results. In addition, Block chose to interpret unrotated factors; hence, disparities between his factor placement and the Jackson and Messick rotated factor orientation are likely, especially for the disputed "acquiescence" factor at issue in this analysis of balanced scales.

When Block's first two unrotated factors for the unbalanced scales were compared with his first two unrotated factors for the balanced scales, the structures were found to be extremely similar, as indicated by coefficients of factor similarity in the high nineties in all five samples. (Incidentally, however, if the factor structures for both the balanced and unbalanced scales are plotted on the same graph and lines drawn connecting corresponding points, it is clear that many changes in scale position, usually slight but sometimes fairly moderate, do occur in going from the unbalanced to the balanced form and that these changes occur on the first factor as well as the second. This suggests that in eliminating items at random to produce balanced scales the desirability levels of the scales may also have been changed in uncontrolled ways.) In addition to being extremely similar within each sample, the unrotated factor structures for the unbalanced and balanced forms were also found to be impressively parallel from sample to sample, except in one case where a rotation was needed to improve congruity. In view of these findings, Block (1965) concluded that "the factor structure of the MMPI does not change when the possibility of interference from acquiescence response set is removed" (p. 47). The implication seemed clear that acquiescence could not have accounted for the factor structure of the original unbalanced scales after all.

But all of this depends on the extent to which acquiescence has in fact been removed by the simple expedient of balancing the number of true and false items—that is, on the extent to which scales with balanced keys are acquiescence-free. Let us consider briefly the counterarguments and evidence undercutting this assumption. In the final analysis, a simple balancing of the number of true and false items in the scoring key does not control for acquiescence, Block's (1965) protestations to the contrary notwithstanding. This is the case for a number of reasons, not the least of which is that true and false subscales, even with equal numbers of items, might still contribute different amounts of variance to the total score. This circumstance is illustrated in Fig. 7.2, where a yeasaying versus naysaying or acquiescence factor is plotted against a desirability (or content) factor. The test vector for a true-keyed subscale is portrayed as twice as long as the vector for the false-keyed subscale to indicate that the true part in this example manifests twice the variability of the false part. As can be seen, the dashed line representing the total-score vector is offset from the desirability (or content) factor in the direction of the subscale with greater variability.

To investigate the extent to which differential variance occurs on true and false

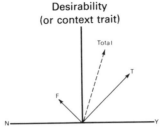

FIG. 7.2.   Total score contaminated by yeasaying (or naysaying) when the true-keyed (or false-keyed) subscale has greater variance.

parts having equal numbers of items, MMPI protocols for Block's 21 balanced scales as well as for EC-5, ER-O, and ER-S (Ego-resiliency, subtle) were scored on two separate samples from the Jackson and Messick research program, one comprising 167 college students (80 males and 87 females, labeled sample D) and the other comprising 162 college students (80 males and 82 females, labeled sample J). The observed variances on the true and false parts of these scales are presented in Table 7.1 for one sample and in Table 7.2 for the other, along with t-values for the significance of differences in correlated variances. It can be seen that 13 significant differences between true and false variances are reported in Table 7.1 and 15 in Table 7.2. Furthermore, it is not sufficient to consider only the observed variances on these true and false subscales, since their reliabilities may also be grossly unequal. One could not expect an unreliable subscale to balance a reliable subscale in determining the total score. Moreover, differences in both observed variances and reliabilities contribute to differences in the true variances of the true and false parts (true variance being the product of observed variance and reliability). It can be seen in Tables 7.1 and 7.2 that the reliabilities and true variances of many of the corresponding subscales are indeed considerably unbalanced.

To relate these results to Block's factor analyses, it should be noted that the two scales that most consistently marked Block's second factor were EC-4 in one direction and Ma in the other. And in Tables 7.1 and 7.2, EC-4 has an imbalance in variance and reliability in favor of the false part while Ma has an imbalance in variance and reliability in favor of the true part. Thus, there is still a distinct possibility that Block's second factor may be interpreted in terms of the response style of acquiescence, the factor being reflected so that EC-4 loads appropriately in the negative or naysaying direction and Ma in the acquiescent or yeasaying direction. However, to pin the acquiescence interpretation down, Block's unrotated second factor needs to be rotated to a position more in line with the usual placement of the second MMPI factor—for example, as marked by Welsh's (1956) R scale in the negative direction. The consequences of this misalignment of Block's second factor for his results and interpretation are described later in this chapter.

TABLE 7.1
Internal Properties of MMPI Scales Balanced for Number of Items .85
Keyed True and False (Using Block's Balanced Keys)
Sample D (N = 167)

Scale	Observed Variance		t^a	KR-20 Reliability		True Variance		r_{TF}	r_{TF} Corrected for Attenuation
	True Scale	False Scale		r_{TT}	r_{FF}	True Scale	False Scale		
EC5	5.16	7.51	2.74**	.46	.64	2.37	4.83	.46	.85
ER-0	39.9	48.21	1.51	.82	.85	32.92	41.12	.61	.72
EC4	3.22	4.73	2.48*	.15	.45	.49	2.14	.07	.25
F	1.75	2.05	1.07	.46	.39	.80	.80	.13	.31
Hs	1.29	2.59	4.78**	.63	.46	.82	1.19	.31	.57
D	8.65	4.49	4.31**	.72	.30	6.19	1.36	.12	.26
Hy	2.45	3.22	1.78	.57	.26	1.39	.85	-.06	-.15
Pd	11.21	5.28	4.96**	.73	.20	8.22	1.04	.06	.16
Mf	18.20	13.0	2.37*	.75	.64	13.65	8.38	.40	.57
Pa	2.24	5.83	6.57**	.54	.53	1.20	3.10	-.24	-.46
Pt	3.18	2.31	2.30*	.53	.47	1.68	1.08	.44	.89
Sc	3.04	2.72	.80	.52	.50	1.58	1.36	.45	.89
Ma	4.12	2.24	4.11**	.58	.00	2.40	.00	-.27	--
Pn	3.79	2.29	1.64	.59	.45	2.22	1.34	.36	.70
SD	1.92	3.11	3.45**	.49	.59	.95	1.82	.43	.80
Es	5.76	7.39	1.62	.32	.55	1.82	4.05	-.12	-.28
Ie	3.71	3.85	.24	.44	.52	1.64	1.99	.13	.27
Lp	5.46	5.22	.29	.57	.63	3.10	3.27	.19	.31
Sp	1.70	1.86	.61	.35	.42	.60	.78	.20	.52
St	4.84	4.37	.68	.39	.45	1.88	1.95	.23	.55
Do	1.65	1.47	.75	.06	.19	.10	.27	-.16	> -.00
Si	32.14	20.88	2.86**	.83	.73	26.73	15.31	.22	.28
NUC	3.03	1.75	3.60**	.49	.25	1.49	.43	.07	.21
ER-S	7.96	10.95	2.16*	.52	.66	4.12	7.26	.30	.51

a t-test for the significance of differences between correlated variances.
* $p < .05$.
** $p < .01$.

It is important not to leave this discussion of the efficacy of balanced scales with an implication that acquiescence can be effectively controlled by balancing the observed variance, reliability, and true variance of true and false subscales. Even if successful, the balance would breakdown and vary from sample to sample since it would depend partly on the number of acquiescers present and partly on the extent of their acquiescence. In any event, attention must additionally be paid to the balance of the subscales in judged desirability level. Because of the predominance of desirability, acquiescence tends to operate less potently on scales that are relatively desirable or undesirable and more potently on scales in the intermediate neutral range (Edwards & Diers, 1963; Jackson & Messick, 1961, 1962b).

Thus, even though the true and false parts of a scale might be perfectly balanced in variance and reliability, if one of the components is relatively neutral in desirability and the other relatively extreme, acquiescence would still be expected to operate differentially on the neutral part. This is illustrated in Fig. 7.3, where test vectors for true-keyed and false-keyed subscales are portrayed as equal in length to signify a balance in variability. But the false-keyed subscale is shown as highly correlated with desirability while the true-keyed subscale is less so, and the total-score vector is once again offset in the acquiescence direction.

In a complete assessment of the potential influence of acquiescence on total scores—even when balanced with respect to variance, reliability, and desirability of true and false parts—one more property of the true and false components should be taken into account, namely, the correlation between them. Although not as informative as a factor analysis of intercorrelations among true and false parts of several scales, an examination of true–false correlations scale by scale permits quick preliminary inferences about certain scale properties. In general, the smaller this correlation between true and false parts when compared with their respective reliabilities, the greater the indication that more than one underlying characteristic is being measured by the scale.

In this regard, it can be seen in Tables 7.1 and 7.2 that the correlations between true and false parts of many of Block's balanced scales are considerably lower than their reliabilities would permit and are sometimes even negative. In such cases, acquiescence is a particularly good candidate for the additional

TABLE 7.2
Internal Properties of MMPI Scales Balanced for Number of Items .85
Keyed True and False (Using Block's Balanced Keys)
Sample J (N = 82)

Scale	Observed Variance		t^a	KR-20 Reliability		True Variance		r_{TF}	r_{TF} Corrected for Attenuation
	True Scale	False Scale		r_{TT}	r_{FF}	True Scale	False Scale		
EC5	4.75	7.41	3.29**	.40	.64	1.90	4.77	.51	1.01
ER-0	39.24	47.77	1.67	.80	.83	31.50	39.71	.67	.81
EC4	3.81	5.11	1.93	.28	.49	1.05	2.50	.25	.67
F	2.17	2.41	.69	.45	.35	.98	.84	.19	.47
Hs	1.19	2.61	5.30**	.55	.44	.65	1.15	.27	.54
D	8.13	5.38	2.70**	.65	.40	5.26	2.15	.23	.45
Hy	2.16	3.48	3.06**	.49	.29	1.06	1.00	-.01	-.02
Pd	12.21	5.19	5.66**	.72	.16	8.77	.82	.16	.49
Mf	17.24	13.85	1.56	.73	.66	12.62	9.14	.45	.65
Pa	2.68	4.61	3.62**	.50	.39	1.35	1.81	-.28	-.62
Pt	3.86	2.56	2.96**	.59	.47	2.28	1.21	.46	.88
Sc	3.72	2.37	3.15**	.54	.30	2.02	.71	.41	1.02
Ma	3.43	3.37	.11	.48	.35	1.64	1.17	-.22	-.54
Pn	3.93	2.82	2.32*	.59	.39	2.31	1.09	.43	.90
SD	2.32	3.71	3.45*	.52	.63	1.21	2.35	.50	.86
Es	4.74	8.48	3.73**	.19	.57	.91	4.83	-.02	-.06
Ie	3.01	3.91	1.73	.26	.47	.79	1.83	.26	.73
Lp	5.28	5.54	.33	.54	.58	2.84	3.22	.35	.63
Sp	1.88	2.78	2.62**	.38	.61	.72	1.68	.32	.67
St	3.76	4.38	.96	.18	.40	.69	1.77	.04	.15
Do	1.87	1.33	2.18*	.19	.10	.36	.14	-.06	-.45
Si	38.58	18.42	4.95**	.85	.67	32.66	12.36	.26	.34
NUC	3.31	1.65	4.54**	.53	.14	1.74	.23	.16	.59
ER-S	7.45	9.70	1.83	.49	.61	3.64	5.90	.39	.72

^{a} t-test for the significance of differences between correlated variances.
* $p < .05$.
** $p < .01$.

Desirability

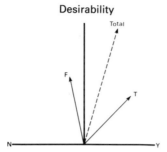

FIG. 7.3.   Total score contaminated by yeasaying (or naysaying) when the false-keyed (or true-keyed) subscale is more highly correlated with desirability, even though the two parts have equal variability.

characteristic measured on each scale, since it accounts in a simple way for differential operation—and hence low correlation—between true and false components: The content being measured (or perhaps the tendency to respond desirably) contributes to high scores on both true and false parts, whereas acquiescence tends to influence scores on the two parts in opposite directions. Thus, even for perfectly balanced scales, if the correlation between true and false parts is low, acquiescence may still operate to influence individual scores and must be taken into account in score interpretation. The low correlation indicates that individual scores may be determined in more than one way, so that identical total scores for two individuals might have been achieved for very different reasons.

Thus, even if perfectly balanced scales could be constructed, it is a peculiar kind of control that would be exercised over acquiescence. The operation of acquiescence on true and false parts would not so much be cancelled out as it would be folded over, thereby attenuating to some degree the correlation of the balanced scales with acquiescence measures but not eliminating the influence of acquiescence in determining individual scores. On a perfectly balanced scale with a score range from 0 to 20, for example, a completely acquiescent respondent would receive a score of 10, but less marked acquiescent tendencies would also act to force scores into the middle range regardless of the true content position of the person (Jackson, 1967a). Worse still, the amount of this distortion would be a function of the desirability level of the scale: Acquiescence tends to produce scores not in the middle of the score distribution but in the middle of the *key*. On a very undesirable scale, for example, where the mean score on a 20-point scale might be near 4, acquiescence could lead to the highest scores obtained, whereas on a very desirable scale it could produce the lowest scores obtained.

If we take all of these effects into account, then, it would seem that Block's chain of reasoning for the development of acquiescence-free scales breaks down at its most critical point—in the establishment of the premise. The hard fact is that—except perhaps for maximizing the content saturation of the scales—there is no sure way to control for acquiescence within a true-false or agree-disagree format (Jackson, 1967a). But the role of acquiescence, if any, can be clarified and taken into account in interpretation by scoring true-keyed and false-keyed subscales separately and examining their intercorrelations or, better still, their alignment within a factor space. That is, having equal numbers of true and false items in a scoring key—or at least some items keyed true and some keyed false on each scale—permits one to appraise the potential impact of acquiescence on score interpretation and to delineate the nature of its distorting influence by means of multivariate analyses of score relationships. Hence, balanced scales are desirable for a number of reasons, but they do *not* eliminate acquiescence.

The Resiliency of Desirability

Block (1965) next proceeded to challenge the desirability interpretation of the largest MMPI factor. Although he would have preferred to make a content or characterological interpretation of this dimension outright, he recognized that an alternative basis in terms of desirability would also be tenable because all of the measures of this factor were intimately, but in his opinion epiphenomenally, associated with social desirability. Block maintained that this confounding could be undone, however, if only a scale could be developed that would measure the factor adequately but not reflect social desirability. This "desirability-free" measure of the first MMPI factor would then represent an "untenable anomaly" for the desirability hypothesis and would indicate that the first factor had only been fortuitously, not intrinsically, linked to desirability all along.

Block constructed such a scale by selecting from a large pool of MMPI items previously shown to discriminate empirically between high and low first-factor scores, a set that fell in the neutral range of the desirability continuum or were even keyed in the opposite direction for the desirability hypothesis. For aesthetic purposes, statements were selected to provide equal numbers of true and false items in the key. This scale, labeled ER–S (ego-resiliency, subtle), was found to correlate in the 60s and 70s with the Edwards SD scale in nine different samples and, when corrected for attenuation, appeared to measure virtually the same dimension as the SD scale (Block, 1965).

Block had apparently succeeded, then, in constructing a subtle social desirability scale, in the sense that all of the items are related to an empirical distinction between high and low scorers on the first MMPI factor, as well as on the SD scale, but at the same time had been rated by judges as not desirable and sometimes even as undesirable. Block's conclusion, however, that the dimension underlying the original empirical distinction could not therefore have been desirability seems peculiar when considered in this context of subtle scales and their rationale (Seeman, 1952; Wiener, 1948). The subtle items on the D scale, for example, are all related to an empirical differentiation between depressives and normals, yet clinicians judge that the content of these items do not reflect the emotional disturbance of depression. Does this indicate that the basis for the original empirical discriminability of the subtle items could not have been depression?

In an attempt to resolve the subtlety of a subtle SD scale, let us consider possible bases for responses to ER–S items that could account for their relation to the SD scale and to the first MMPI factor. To begin with, even though ER–S items were restricted to the intermediate category on the desirability continuum, perhaps they varied somewhat in desirability scale values within this range and happened to be keyed in the desirable direction. It turns out, however, that although 13 out of the 20 true items were keyed in the desirable direction according to the Messick and Jackson (1961b) scale values, only 7 of the 20 false items were, making a total of 20 items keyed desirable and 20 items keyed undesirable.

But because discriminating items were selected for this scale solely on the basis of their neutral or contrary desirability values, it is possible that these items may vary extensively on some other uncontrolled dimension that happens to be highly correlated both with desirability level and with the first MMPI factor. Such a dimension might be what Wiggins (1962) has called hypercommunality versus noncommunality, a dimension reflecting the tendency to endorse items in the direction of the modal response of some normative group. To be scored on this dimension, items would be keyed on the basis of endorsement frequency: Items with endorsement frequencies greater than .5 would be keyed true and items with endorsement frequencies less than .5 would be keyed false.

It might be objected at this point that such a variable is not a reasonable dimension of individual response, since respondents do not know what the endorsement frequencies are. However, Jackson and Messick (1969) asked college students to judge both the frequency of item endorsement and the frequency of occurrence of the characteristic described in each statement for all of the items on the MMPI, and they found that these judgments were made readily and consistently. Over the 566 MMPI items, judged frequency of endorsement correlated .96 with actual endorsement frequencies in an independent sample, and .92 with desirability scale values. So, apparently, respondents are indeed sensitive to differences in the endorsement frequencies of personality items. Furthermore, judged frequency of occurrence correlated .79 with judged frequency of endorsement, .75 with actual endorsement frequencies, and .55 with desirability scale values. Moreover, judged frequency of endorsement correlated .74, while judged frequency of occurrence correlated .26, with first-factor loadings obtained from a different college sample. Along with the previously noted difference in their correlations with desirability scale values (.92 vs .55), this attests to the distinctiveness of the two types of frequency judgments. These various judgments also displayed appropriate differences one from the other in that, for example, the set of items exhibiting a marked discrepancy between desirability scale values and judged frequency of occurrence included 12 of the 15 items from the MMPI Lie scale.

When the ER–S scale was examined for the extent of its keying in the direction of endorsement frequency, it was found that 70% of the items were keyed in the frequent direction according to college norms and that nearly 80% of the items were keyed either for frequency or desirability. The possibility thus exists that the relation of the ER–S scale to the SD scale and to the first MMPI factor is determined in part by their mutual relation to the highly correlated dimension of endorsement frequency. Since the items on the ER–S scale vary widely in endorsement frequency but are intermediate in desirability values, they exhibit a discrepancy between frequency and desirability that is reminiscent of the Lie scale. This is particularly so for the false ER–S items.

If endorsement frequency does influence performance on ER–S, then, one might expect the scores to be related to the "impression management" factor of the MMPI. In support of this conjecture, Edwards and Walsh (1964; Edwards, 1970) found that ER–S loaded .45 (normalized) on a factor marked by SD scales and .52 on a factor marked by the Lie scale. Hence, ER–S cannot be considered to be an exemplary or even a good measure of the first desirability factor and, in any event, is a better measure of the second desirability factor of impression management. It thus appears that Block's attempt to deny a desirability basis for MMPI responses by developing a subtle measure of the first factor that would in *no* way be related to social desirability fails both on logical and empirical grounds.

BEHAVIORAL CORRELATES OF MMPI FACTORS

Block (1965) next investigated some of the salient behavioral correlates of the first two MMPI factors. The participants in five of his samples had been previously observed in various clinical settings by psychologists who recorded their assessments of each individual by Q-sorts of descriptive statements. Within each sample, Q-sort items were then tabulated that discriminated empirically between high and low scorers on his first MMPI factor and, in a separate tabulation, between high and low scorers on his second MMPI factor. These tables of Q-sort items differentially associated with high and low factor scores were then perused to educe common characterological themes that might suggest a basis for the MMPI factors in personality differences. Since, as Block (1965) has indicated, "this kind of data is difficult to come by" (p. 99), it was important to review these Q-sort results as a source of possible behavioral correlates of relevance to the alternative response style interpretations of the MMPI factors, which—in light of the arguments and evidence presented in this chapter—remain plausible or even preferable.

Before reviewing the Q-sort data, however, it seemed prudent to reanalyze Block's balanced scales to ascertain whether the two factors used as criteria in the Q-sort analyses were located in their customary position—that is, in relation, for example, to SD scales and to Welsh's A and R scales. The latter is the factor orientation that has been interpreted in terms of desirability and acquiescence. The possibility of a difference in factor placement arises because Block dealt with *unrotated* factors and did not include in his study any of the usual measures of acquiescence to serve as markers. Therefore, to clarify the situation, factor analyses of intercorrelations among true and false parts of Block's 21 balanced scales were performed separately for the two samples (D and J) described previously.

Delineating Differences in Factor Placement

In these analyses, marker scales for acquiescence and desirability, including the five Jackson and Messick (1961, 1962b) Dy scales and Fulkerson's (1958) acquiescence scale, were projected into the obtained factor space by extension methods (Dwyer, 1937); the MMPI K scale, Welsh's (1956) A and R scales, Block's ER–O and EC–5 scales, and sex (scored in the female direction) were also included in the extension matrix. The extension method of analysis (Cattell, 1978) was utilized to estimate the factor loadings of the marker scales without permitting them to distort or in any way influence the factor space determined by Block's balanced scales. After an examination of the latent roots, ten factors were retained for the sample labeled D in the tables and 11 factors were retained for the sample labeled J. These factors were rotated analytically to the equamax criterion of simple structure with additional patterned rotation of the two largest factors to balance the loadings of the Dy scales, as done previously in the Jackson and Messick (1962b) studies.

Loadings for the five largest rotated factors are presented in Table 7.3 for sample D and in Table 7.4 for sample J. Some of the smaller rotated factors were interpretable in terms of the contaminating effects of item overlap, as was the fifth factor included in each table. It should be noted that factor IV in sample D and factor III in sample J provide good examples of content measurement by an MMPI scale: both true and false parts of the Mf scale load above .6 on these factors, as does the dichotomous extension score for sex.

It can be seen in Tables 7.3 and 7.4 that the first factor is marked in the negative direction by both true and false parts of Block's ER–O scale and both true and false parts of Edwards' SD scale. It is marked in the positive direction by Welsh's A scale and in opposite directions by Dy1 and Dy5. It thus appears to be oriented fairly well in the position interpreted by Edwards and by Jackson and

TABLE 7.3
Rotated Factor Loadings for True- and False-Keyed Parts of MMPI Scales
(Using Block's Balanced Keys)
Sample D (N = 167)

	Scale	Factor				
		I	II	III	IV	V
True Scales	EC5^e	-.29	.-.11	-.50	.20	.09
	ER^e	-.89	.20	.04	-.16	-.02
	EC4	.00	.07	-.54	.13	.02
	F	.56	.28	.19	-.02	-.09
	Hs	.45	.13	.10	.07	.49
	D	.68	.25	-.08	.15	.30
	Hy	.68	.28	.07	-.01	.50
	Pd	.67	.40	.19	.04	.12
	Mf	.10	.19	-.11	.67	.09
	Pa	.66	.24	.02	.12	.23
	Pt	.66	.42	-.04	.18	.22
	Sc	.65	.30	.15	.02	.29
	Ma	.48	.61	.06	-.01	.01
	Pn	.52	.43	-.30	.14	.08
	SD	-.64	.16	.09	-.18	.01
	Es	-.08	.63	.06	-.07	.00
	le	-.39	.27	.09	.06	.05
	Lp	-.63	.43	.22	.00	.17
	Sp	-.32	.47	.09	.07	.16
	St	-.20	.45	.07	.54	-.05
	Do	.01	.40	.06	-.02	.12
	Si	.73	.28	-.36	.09	-.05
	NUC	.53	.55	.08	.01	-.19
False Scales	EC5^e	-.09	-.57	-.31	.16	.00
	ER^e	-.81	-.43	-.10	-.06	-.13
	EC4	.01	-.65	-.21	-.28	.13
	F	.43	-.33	.02	-.07	-.09
	Hs	.61	-.15	-.08	.16	-.08
	D	.22	-.44	.02	.18	.13
	Hy	-.08	-.38	.22	.10	.11
	Pd	.24	-.42	.51	-.02	.00
	Mf	.05	-.55	-.16	.63	.18
	Pa	-.26	-.49	-.04	.08	.28
	Pt	.67	-.12	.12	.08	.08
	Sc	.62	-.12	.05	-.05	.08
	Ma	-.32	-.12	.52	-.02	.10
	Pn	.59	-.00	-.00	.19	-.02
	SD	-.67	-.18	.18	-.14	-.11
	Es	-.53	-.34	.09	-.18	-.29
	le	-.69	-.40	.03	.04	.02
	Lp	-.61	-.48	.05	-.05	-.11
	Sp	-.55	-.08	.56	-.03	.21
	St	-.50	-.24	.38	.21	.01
	Do	-.15	-.43	-.01	.36	-.14
	Si	.35	-.70	-.33	-.09	-.09
	NUC	.34	-.20	.14	.16	-.02
	K^e	-.62	-.58	.11	-.12	.08
	Dyl^e	-.80	.33	-.02	.03	-.00
	Dy2^e	-.61	.57	.07	-.04	.10
	Dy3^e	.24	.81	-.04	-.00	-.01
	Dy4^e	.75	.54	.06	.01	-.06
	Dy5^e	.82	.30	.03	.01	.17
	A^e	.77	.39	-.13	.16	.17
	R^e	-.06	-.77	-.12	.10	-.07
	Aq^e	.39	.73	.05	-.02	-.13
	Sex^e	-.09	-.22	-.00	.67	-.09

^{e} Variable projected into the factor space by extension methods.

TABLE 7.4
Rotated Factor Loadings for True-and False-Keyed Parts of MMPI Scales
(Using Block's Balanced Keys)
Sample J (N = 162)

	Scale	Factor				
		I	II	III	IV	V
True	EC5	-.18	-.17	.20	-.34	-.12
Scales	ER-0	-.90	.16	-.12	.02	-.17
	EC4	.16	-.13	.01	-.67	-.10
	F	.55	.26	-.10	.04	.13
	Hs	.32	.09	-.05	-.03	.09
	D	.72	.09	.19	.01	-.21
	Hy	.65	.15	-.01	.07	-.02
	Pd	.66	.34	.10	.11	.13
	Mf	.26	.24	.79	-.05	-.01
	Pa	.71	.22	.10	.00	.09
	Pt	.69	.31	.14	-.03	-.10
	Sc	.70	.22	.02	.12	-.07
	Ma	.53	.48	-.14	.03	.08
	Pn	.64	.17	.27	-.13	-.18
	SD	-.69	.21	-.21	.03	.03
	Es	-.08	.42	-.02	-.11	-.02
	Ie	-.42	.24	.10	.17	.13
	Lp	-.52	.35	.04	.19	.36
	Sp	-.29	.35	.10	.37	.09
	St	-.03	.32	.60	.04	.06
	Do	.06	.27	.06	.09	.04
	Si	.80	.19	.10	-.16	-.36
	NUC	.47	.55	-.08	.04	.01
False	EC5	-.04	-.52	.20	-.18	-.26
Scales	ER-O	-.82	-.36	-.04	-.04	-.01
	EC4	-.14	-.63	-.22	-.19	-.05
	F	.35	-.27	.01	.00	.01
	Hs	.61	-.13	.13	.04	.34
	D	.33	-.43	.16	.25	.12
	Hy	-.14	-.21	.02	.13	.61
	Pd	.07	-.20	.03	.49	.47
	Mf	.22	-.50	.61	.02	.09
	Pa	-.24	-.41	.13	.01	.03
	Pt	.61	-.09	.13	.19	.04
	Sc	.53	-.07	-.15	.05	.16
	Ma	-.48	.01	-.11	.58	.11
	Pn	.63	-.08	.19	.07	.19
	SD	-.72	-.16	-.22	.08	.22
	Es	-.57	-.33	-.36	-.07	-.01
	Ie	-.72	-.23	.08	.09	-.01
	Lp	-.71	-.30	-.13	-.13	.20
	Sp	-.64	-.00	.06	.45	.33
	St	-.43	-.24	.10	.27	.22
	Do	-.24	-.39	.24	-.01	.31
	Si	.25	-.70	-.09	-.23	-.25
	NUC	.41	-.01	.06	.17	.08
	K	-.65	-.50	-.07	.14	.08
	Dy1	-.80	.24	.02	-.02	-.14
	Dy2	-.63	.46	-.02	.02	.12
	Dy3	.41	.68	.01	-.01	-.02
	Dy4	.76	.47	.01	.03	.04
	Dy5	.81	.30	-.02	-.01	-.01
	A	.84	.25	.24	.05	-.19
	R	.05	-.76	.07	-.14	-.17
	Aq	.34	.62	-.09	-.01	.08
	Sex	.13	-.15	.71	-.06	.04

[e] Variable projected into the factor space by extension methods.

Messick in terms of undesirability. The second factor is marked by Dy3 and Fulkerson's acquiescence scale in the positive direction and by Welsh's R scale and the false parts of EC-4 and EC-5 in the negative direction. It should be noted that with only a few slight transpositions in either sample this second factor separates true-keyed scales from false-keyed scales. This striking separation, even as applied to Block's balanced scales, thereby reinforces the factor's interpretation in terms of the response style of acquiescence. The plots of factor I against factor II for the two samples are presented in Figs. 7.4 and 7.5, so that the separation of true and false scales as well as the circular or reciprocal relation between acquiescence and desirability may be visually appraised.

It is of particular interest to note that only the false parts of Block's EC-4 and EC-5 scales load on this second rotated factor; the true parts of these scales load on an independent factor (factor III in sample D and factor IV in sample J) that also includes the false parts of Ma, Pd, and Sp. Balanced forms of these five scales were salient on Block's second (total-score) factor, but only one half of each scale loads on the second factor when true and false subscales are analyzed. The other half-scales are pulled off onto an unrelated factor. This latter factor is probably partly generated by item overlap contaminations, since the overlap correlations of EC-4_t, with EC-5_t, Ma$_f$, Pd$_f$, and Sp$_f$ are .35, $-.25$, $-.23$, and $-.20$, respectively. (Overlap with EC-5_t could not have generated the factor, of course, since EC-5_t was in the extension matrix, but such overlap could have determined the correlations of EC-5_t with this factor in the extension solution. And remember, even correlations of this modest magnitude yield factor loadings on the order of .5 in generating a single overlap factor.) This discrepancy between the true and false parts of the EC scales is also apparent in their pattern of correlations with other measures: In sample D, for example, EC-4_t and EC-4_f correlated only .07 with each other; EC-4_f correlated $-.52$ with Dy3, whereas EC-4_t correlated only .05.

The plots of the second factor, which contains the false EC items as well as R and Dy3, against the factor containing the true EC items are presented in Figs. 7.6 and 7.7 for samples D and J, respectively. It is apparent from these figures that the dimension marked by Dy3 and Fulkerson's acquiescence scale in one direction and by R and the false EC subscales in the other direction is a much larger factor than the one marked by the true EC subscales. It is also apparent that when the true and false parts of the EC scales are added together to form their respective total scores, these balanced scales will fall part way between these two factors, somewhere near the dashed lines drawn on the figures. Since Block's factor analyses were performed on total scales and since Block's second factor was consistently marked by the EC-4 total scale, it is highly probable that his second factor is located in a position much like the dashed lines in the figures and not in the position of the present factor II, which is the more typical orientation of the second MMPI factor (i.e., anchored by Welsh's R scale).

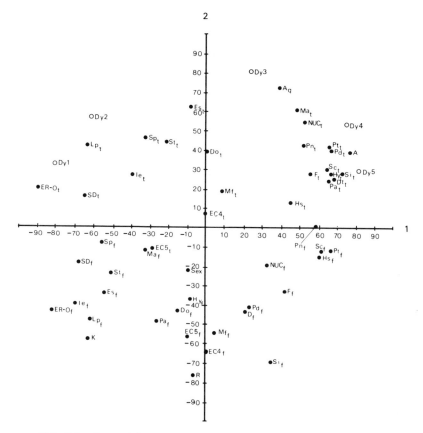

FIG. 7.4. Rotated factors 1 and 2, analysis of MMPI true and false subscales, Sample D.

Thus, one consequence of factor analyzing total scores when true and false subscales measure different dimensions is that the factors determined by the total scales may fall in less than optimal compromise positions between the dimensions underlying subscale responses. Because the true and false parts are locked together in the total score, it may not be possible to recover the underlying dimensions of the subscales even by rotation. Consequently, the factor space derived from the total scales may give a distorted picture of the factors underlying consistent responses to the subscales. In the present case, for example, the total-scale factor that falls along the dashed lines in Figs. 7.6 and 7.7 would have high loadings for EC-4 in one direction and Ma, Pd, and Sp, among others, in the opposite direction, just as the second factor does in Block's studies. In addition, if Dy3 and R were projected into the total-score factor space, they would also

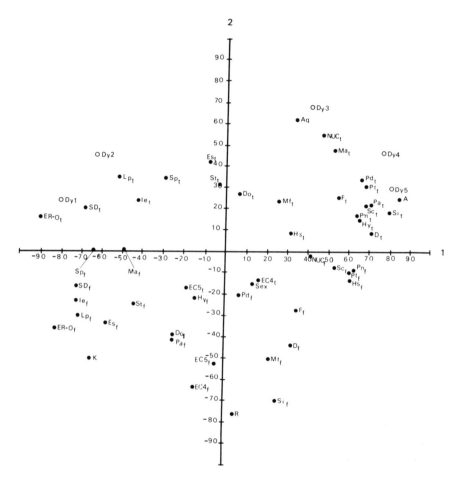

FIG. 7.5. Rotated factors 1 and 2, analysis of MMPI true and false
subscales, Sample J.

receive moderately high loadings in opposite directions. But the normal hyper-
plane to this misaligned factor, if drawn on Figs. 7.6 and 7.7, would not quite
separate true scales from false scales. There would be some exceptions in the
upper left and lower right quadrants.

In order to clarify the nature of the factor space determined by total scales,
intercorrelations among total scores on Block's 21 balanced scales were factor
analyzed separately for samples D and J, with scores for the true and false parts
of these scales projected into the factor space by extension methods along with

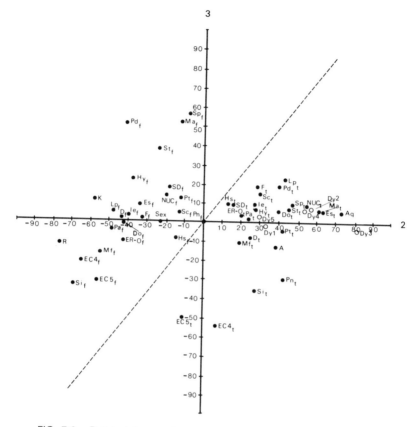

FIG. 7.6. Rotated factors 2 and 3, analysis of MMPI true and false subscales, Sample D.

the Dy scales, K, A, R, EC-5, ER-O, and sex. Five factors were retained in each sample for rotation to the equamax criterion of simple structure, with the same kind of patterned rotation added as was used previously to balance the loadings of the Dy scales on the two largest factors. The largest factor was found to be marked by Dy1, the Edwards SD scale, and ER-O in one direction and by Dy5 and Welsh's A scale in the other. The second factor was defined by EC-4 and Welsh's R scale in one direction and had high loadings for Dy3, Fulkerson's acquiescence scale, and Ma in the other.

As anticipated in the foregoing considerations, the second factor did not perfectly separate the extended true and false subscales, but the division was still

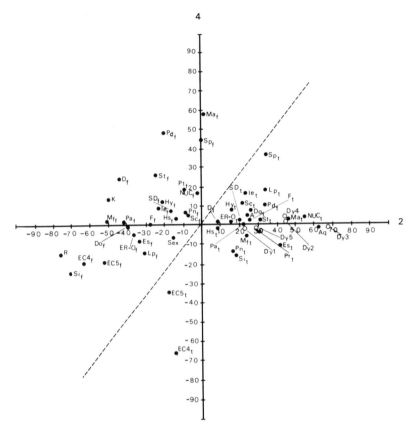

FIG. 7.7. Rotated factors 2 and 4, analysis of MMPI true and false subscales, Sample J.

substantial and about what might be expected in light of Figs. 7.6 and 7.7: Only 12% of the scales receiving positive loadings on the second factor in sample D were false-keyed and only 9% of those receiving negative loadings were true-keyed; in sample J, 22% of the scales with positive loadings were false-keyed and 22% of the scales with negative loadings were true-keyed. These findings suggest that distortions may sometimes occur in factor analyzing total scores and that the strategy of analyzing subscales leads to greater clarity whenever there is some possibility that true and false parts may be measuring different things.

In sum, then, the false-keyed EC scales load quite highly on the present second factor in Tables 7.3 and 7.4, which—being marked by Welsh's R scale as well as by Dy3—is in the customary orientation for the second MMPI factor. In contrast, the true-keyed EC scales load highly on an independent factor that appears to be determined in part by item overlap. Block's second factor, being based on total scores which are an amalgam of the true and false parts, falls somewhere in between. Because of this contamination, Block's second factor does not directly represent the acquiescence dimension but is probably substantially correlated with it. Hence, Block's (1965) argument that his second MMPI factor cannot be due to acquiescence is somewhat beside the point because his second factor does not coincide with the factor at issue but, rather, is an overlap-contaminated distortion of it.

As a consequence, the behavioral correlates of Block's second factor as uncovered in the Q-sort analyses may not all be equally relevant to the acquiescence dimension. Although behavioral correlates of the false EC component might bear directly on the personality basis of acquiescence, behavioral correlates (if any) of the true EC component could be virtually unrelated to acquiescence. With this in mind, let us consider Block's distillation of the Q-sort results and attempt to integrate it with the behavioral correlates of response styles as summarized by Couch and Keniston (1960) and by Damarin and Messick (1965).

Personality Interpretations of Response Styles and MMPI Factors

In Block's (1965) reading of the Q-sort findings, high and low scorers on his second factor (i.e., naysayers and yeasayers, respectively, in terms of the response style interpretation) tended to differ "in diverse yet coherent ways . . . in the extent to which they suppress impulse or are spontaneous with it" (p. 113). He suggested that the dimension underlying this distinction is one of ego-control, which refers to the individual's characteristic mode of monitoring impulse. This dimension extends from "excessive containment of impulse and delay of gratification at one end" to "insufficient modulation of impulse and an inability to delay gratification at the other end" (Block & Turula, 1963, p. 946). This description accords well both with the clinical characterization of acquiescence given by Couch and Keniston (1960) and with the objective performance correlates of acquiescence that Damarin and Messick (1965) gleaned from Cattell's factor studies. It will be recalled that acquiescers were characterized by unreflective impulsiveness, quickness of response, and little monitoring of performance either on judgmental and perceptual-motor tasks or on questionnaires. There thus appears to be a convergence of evidence to support the interpretation of one type of acquiescence (or at least the interpretation of the second MMPI factor) as a correlate, or perhaps a derivative, of a personality dimension of impulse-control.

However, in this convergence we must make clear that simply identifying the second MMPI factor with impulse-control is not sufficient in itself to account for the empirical separation of true-keyed and false-keyed scales. One possibility in this regard is that impulse-control functions as a "source trait" and acquiescence response style as a "surface trait," in Cattell's (1957, 1977) sense of these terms. That is, impulse-control may indeed underlie the set of behavioral consistencies associated with the second MMPI factor. But in questionnaire responding, impulse-control (or the lack thereof) may manifest itself as acquiescence response style, which then serves to channel response choices in systematic directions. Thus, in the guise of acquiescence, impulsivity versus impulse-control becomes linked to the uncritical agreement and acceptance tendencies that lead to a separation of true and false scales as well as to the score relationships that generate the second MMPI factor.

Hence, this second MMPI factor is interpretable at a surface level in terms of acquiescence, which in turn is interpretable at a deeper or source level as a function of impulse- or ego-control. Unfortunately, however, although acquiescence response style may be consistent with this construct interpretation of the second MMPI factor in terms of impulsivity, the operation of acquiescence distorts the measurement of other traits and factors and serves to obscure trait relationships and dimensional structures, whether on the MMPI or other affected instruments. Consequently, the convergent interpretation of both acquiescence response style and the second MMPI factor in terms of impulsivity versus impulse-control does not lessen the need to take acquiescence effects into account in personality assessment.

In his summary integration of the Q-sort results for the first MMPI factor, Block (1965) concluded that the high scorers (i.e., persons who responded desirably in terms of the response style interpretation) were generally "perceived by psychologists as being genuinely psychologically healthy—they are evaluated as integrated and yet open to experience, able to cope resourcefully with their complex worlds" (p. 110). Low scorers, on the other hand, were perceived as "more disturbed and more brittle individuals" (p. 110). Block suggested that this factor be identified as "ego-resiliency," which refers to personality capabilities of resourcefulness and adaptation.

This interpretation is partly consistent with the Damarin and Messick (1965) formulation of desirable responding, in that one might expect ego-resilient individuals to have positive self-regard. As high first-factor scorers on the MMPI, they certainly describe themselves in a positive and desirable way. In Block's view, however, this positive self-regard is an accurate reflection of positive personal qualities, while in the Damarin and Messick framework it is an attitude toward the self, replete with all of the mechanisms that determine social attitudes in general, including not only accurate perception to the degree that it occurs but also autistic biases in self-perception as well as mechanisms of self-deception. The Damarin and Messick formulation thus allows for the possibility that persons who respond in extremely desirable ways, whether in terms of personal or social criteria of desirability, may not represent optimum levels of personality integration or adaptability, but may be defensive—a possibility that has also been emphasized by Block and others in earlier writings (Block & Thomas, 1955; Rogers & Dymond, 1954). Furthermore, for relatively inaccurate respondents at any level of desirability, the first-factor scores may be more reflective of autistic biases in self-regard, whether positive or negative, rather than degree of ego-resiliency.

Clinical versus Psychometric Evidence

At the conclusion of his monograph, Block (1965) chided psychometric researchers for failing to take into account in their interpretations of MMPI factors the voluminous literature on clinical usage and valid case interpretations with the MMPI. Block argued that if clinical validity had been seriously considered, for example, the finding that prison inmates on the average earn a high peak score on the Pd scale would not have permitted an interpretation of the dimension underlying Pd in terms of acquiescence. Yet in the Jackson and Messick (1961) prison study, it is clear that there is no single dimension underlying Pd. There are at least three, and one of them was explicitly interpreted clinically in relation to "alcoholism, impulsivity, chronic trouble with the law, an amoral outlook, rebellion against established authority, a degree of social brashness, and employment instability" (p. 786). However, the credibility of this clinical interpretation associated with part of the Pd variance in a prison sample does not obviate the operation of the other two substantial dimensions underlying Pd responses, which were interpreted in terms of social desirability and acquiescence. Nor does it dispel the problem of validly interpreting individual Pd scores when a combination of three factors, two of them potentially invalidating with respect to the proposed clinical construct interpretation, can influence the individual responses.

Or again, Block (1965) complained that the repeated findings that hospitalized psychiatric patients score higher than normals on the MMPI clinical scales were being blandly assimilated with "belle indifference" to an acquiescence or desirability explanation: "The interpretive rule appears to have been to value relationships existing among MMPI scales and indices more highly than relationships existing between the MMPI and external behavioral criteria" (p. 119). On the contrary, explicit attempts were made in the response style literature to account for both types of data, both similarities in factor structures and differences in mean scores. It was suggested that hospitalized mental patients may engage the same stylistic response dimensions as normals in questionnaire responding but may differ from normals in extensiveness or potency of response styles, particularly in the direction and degree of desirable responding (Barnes, 1956; Jackson & Messick, 1962, 1962b; Wahler, 1961).

In this regard, the subtle and profound influence of desirability on MMPI mean scores may be illustrated experimentally. The two samples D and J, described previously, were two random subsets of a larger group. They differed, however, in experimental treatment: A few days before taking the MMPI under standard self-description instructions, the D sample had rated the items on the MMPI for social desirability. In contrast, the J sample had previously been engaged in a judgment task not involving desirability. It should be emphasized that the D sample then responded to the MMPI a few days later under the same standard conditions as the J sample. That is, individuals in the D sample were not instructed to respond desirably or in any way dissimulate; they merely had occasion to think about the items in terms of desirability a few days before, while individuals in the J sample had not.

It can be seen in Tables 7.1 through 7.4 that consistent individual differences within these two samples produced very similar psychometric properties and factor structures, yet the groups differed markedly in mean scores. On the average, sample D responded more desirably than sample J on the ER-O, F, Pd, Pt, Pn, SD, Ie, Lp, Si, NUC, K, Dy4, Dy5, A, and Aq scales of the MMPI. Thus, the sensitizing of sample D to the desirability characteristics of MMPI items led to significantly more desirable mean scores on many of the scales having high loadings on the first factor, which is what one might expect in connection with a construct theory of the first factor that stresses social desirability of response. It also seems more consistent with a view of the first factor that stresses bias rather than accuracy of self-perception.

RESPONSE STYLES REDUX

The intent of this chapter was to portend a return of response styles as a critical issue in self-report personality assessment. But it is not really a return, because response styles never vanished. Rather, their score-invalidating and relationship-obscuring effects have been largely ignored for a decade or so. And the price that is paid for ignoring response styles is validity—validity of score interpretation and validity in structuring and measuring psychological domains. The warning today is thus the same as the one Cronbach (1946, 1950) issued at midcentury. But it is not enough that warnings are voiced, they must also be heeded. At the very least, response styles pertinent to the particular response format should be routinely discounted as plausible rival hypotheses potentially accounting for the research results, as Campbell (1960) contended in his recommended additions to the APA test standards. Otherwise, evidence of their operation should be systematically taken into account in the research analyses. In other words, one should either show that relevant response styles are not operating in the particular instance or else explicitly cope with their consequences.

ACKNOWLEDGMENTS

The original research reported in this chapter was supported in part by the National Institute of Mental Health, United States Public Health Service, under Research Grant M-2878.

Grateful acknowledgments are due to Henrietta Gallagher for supervising the data preparation and David R. Saunders for performing the computer analyses. Special thanks are also extended to Douglas N. Jackson for his comments on this manuscript, for his suggestions regarding the original analyses, and for his warm collaboration in probing the problems of response styles over the past three decades.

REFERENCES

Bachman, J. G., & O'Malley, P. M. (1984). Yea-saying, nay-saying, and going to extremes: Black-white differences in response styles. *Public Opinion Quarterly, 48,* 491–509.

Barnes, E. H. (1956). Response bias and the MMPI. *Journal of Consulting Psychology, 20,* 371–374.

Bass, B. M. (1956). Development and evaluation of a scale for measuring social acquiescence. *Journal of Abnormal and Social Psychology, 53,* 296–299.

Bass, B. M. (1957). Undiscriminated operant acquiescence. *Educational and Psychological Measurement, 17,* 83–85.

Bendig, A. W. (1960). Factor analyses of "anxiety" and "neuroticism" inventories. *Journal of Consulting Psychology, 24,* 161–168.

Bentler, P. M. (1966). Review of J. Block, *The challenge of response sets. American Scientist, 54,* 495–496.

Bentler, P. M. (1969). Semantic space is (approximately) bipolar. *Journal of Psychology, 71,* 33–40.

Bentler, P. M., Jackson, D. N., & Messick, S. (1971). Identification of content and style: A two-dimensional interpretation of acquiescence. *Psychological Bulletin, 76,* 186–204.

Bentler, P. M., Jackson, D. N., & Messick, S. (1972). A rose by any other name. *Psychological Bulletin, 77,* 109–113.

Berg, I. A. (Ed.). (1967). *Response set in personality assessment.* Chicago: Aldine.

Block, J. (1965). *The challenge of response sets.* New York: Appleton-Century-Crofts.

Block, J. (1971). On further conjectures regarding acquiescence. *Psychological Bulletin, 76,* 205–210.

Block, J. (1972). The shifting definitions of acquiescence. *Psychological Bulletin, 78,* 10–12.

Block, J., & Thomas, H. (1955). Is satisfaction with self a measure of adjustment? *Journal of Abnormal and Social Psychology, 51,* 254–259.

Block, J., & Turula, E. (1963). Identification, ego control, and adjustment. *Child Development, 34,* 945–953.

Campbell, D. T. (1960). Recommendations for APA test standards regarding construct, trait, or discriminant validity. *American Psychologist, 15,* 546–553.

Cattell, R. B. (1957). *Personality and motivation structure and measurement.* New York: World Book.

Cattell, R. B. (1977). A more sophisticated look at structure: Perturbation, sampling, role, and observer trait-view theories. In R. B. Cattell & R. M. Dreger (Eds.), *Handbook of modern personality theory* (pp. 166–220). New York: Wiley.

Cattell, R. B. (1978). *The scientific use of factor analysis in behavioral and life sciences.* New York: Plenum.

Cattell, R. B., & Scheier, I. H. (1961). *The meaning and measurement of neuroticism and anxiety.* New York: Ronald Press.

Christie, R., & Lindauer, F. (1963). Personality structure. *Annual Review of Psychology, 14,* 201–230.

Cofer, C. N., Chance, J., & Judson, A. J. (1949). A study of malingering on the Minnesota Multiphasic Personality Inventory. *Journal of Psychology, 27,* 491–499.

Couch, A., & Keniston, K. (1960). Yeasayers and naysayers: Agreeing response set as a personality variable. *Journal of Abnormal and Social Psychology, 60,* 151–174.

Cronbach, L. J. (1941). An experimental comparison of the multiple true-false and multiple-choice tests. *Journal of Educational Psychology, 32,* 533–543.

Cronbach, L. J. (1942). Studies of acquiescence as a factor in the true-false test. *Journal of Educational Psychology, 33,* 401–415.

Cronbach, L. J. (1946). Response set and test validity. *Educational and Psychological Measurement, 6,* 475–494.

Cronbach, L. J. (1950). Further evidence on response sets and test design. *Educational and Psychological Measurement, 10,* 3–31.

Crowne, D. P., & Marlowe, D. (1964). *The approval motive.* New York: Wiley.

Dahlstrom, W. G., & Welsh, G. S. (1960). *An MMPI handbook: A guide to use in clinical practice and research.* Minneapolis: The University of Minnesota Press.

Dahlstrom, W. G., Welsh, G. S., & Dahlstrom, L. E. (1975). *An MMPI handbook—Vol. II: Research applications.* Minneapolis: The University of Minnesota Press.

Damarin, F., & Messick, S. (1965). *Response styles as personality variables: A theoretical integration of multivariate research* (ETS RB 65-10). Princeton, NJ: Educational Testing Service.

Dwyer, P. S. (1937). The determination of the factor loadings of a given test from the known factor loadings of other tests. *Psychometrika, 2,* 173–178.

Edwards, A. L. (1957). *The social desirability variable in personality assessment and research.* New York: Dryden.

Edwards, A. L. (1966). A comparison of 57 MMPI scales and 57 experimental scales matched with the MMPI scales in terms of item social desirability scale values and probabilities of endorsement. *Educational and Psychological Measurement, 26,* 15–27.

Edwards, A. L. (1970). *The measurement of personality traits by scales and inventories.* New York: Holt, Rinehart and Winston.

Edwards, A. L., & Abbott, R. D. (1973). Measurement of personality traits: Theory and technique. *Annual Review of Psychology, 24,* 241–278.

Edwards, A. L., & Diers, C. J. (1963). Neutral items as a measure of acquiescence. *Educational and Psychological Measurement, 23,* 687–698.

Edwards, A. L., Diers, C. J., & Walker, J. N. (1962). Response sets and factor loadings on sixty-one personality scales. *Journal of Applied Psychology, 46,* 220–225.

Edwards, A. L., & Walsh, J. A. (1964). Response sets in standard and experimental personality scales. *American Educational Research Journal, 1,* 52–61.

Fritz, M. F. (1927). Guessing in a true-false test. *Journal of Educational Psychology, 18,* 558–561.

Fulkerson, S. C. (1958). *An acquiescence key for the MMPI* (Report No. 58–71). Randolf Air Force Base, TX: USAF School of Aviation Medicine.

Goffman, E. (1959). *The presentation of the self in everyday life.* Garden City, NY: Doubleday Anchor Books.

Gur, R. C., & Sackeim, H. A. (1979). Self-deception: A concept in search of a phenomenon. *Journal of Personality and Social Psychology, 37,* 147–169.

Hamilton, D. L. (1968). Personality attributes associated with extreme response. *Psychological Bulletin, 69,* 192–203.

Holtzman, W. H. (1965). Personality structure. *Annual Review of Psychology, 16,* 119–156.

Hundleby, J. D., Pawlik, K., & Cattell, R. B. (1965). *Personality factors in objective devices: A critical integration of a century's research.* San Diego: Knapp.

Jackson, D. N. (1967a). Acquiescence response styles: Problems of identification and control. In I. A. Berg (Ed.), *Response set in personality assessment* (pp. 71–114). Chicago: Aldine.

Jackson, D. N. (1967b). Review of J. Block, *The challenge of response sets. Educational and Psychological Measurement, 27,* 207–219.

Jackson, D. N. (1971). The dynamics of structured personality tests: 1971. *Psychological Review, 78,* 229–248.

Jackson, D. N. (1980). Construct validity and personality assessment. *Construct validity in psychological measurement: Proceedings of a colloquium on theory and application in education and employment* (pp. 79–90). Princeton, NJ: Educational Testing Service.

Jackson, D. N. (1986). The process of responding in personality assessment. In A. Angleitner & J. S. Wiggins (Eds.), *Personality assessment via questionnaires* (pp. 123–142). New York: Springer-Verlag.

Jackson, D. N., & Messick, S. (1958). Content and style in personality assessment. *Psychological Bulletin, 55,* 243–252.

Jackson, D. N., & Messick, S. (1961). Acquiescence and desirability as response determinants on the MMPI. *Educational and Psychological Measurement, 21,* 771–790.

Jackson, D. N., & Messick, S. (1962a). Response styles and the assessment of psychopathology. In S. Messick & J. Ross (Eds.), *Measurement in personality and cognition* (pp. 129–155). New York: Wiley.

Jackson, D. N., & Messick, S. (1962b). Response styles on the MMPI: Comparison of clinical and normal samples. *Journal of Abnormal and Social Psychology, 65,* 285–299.

Jackson, D. N., & Messick, S. (1965). Acquiescence: The nonvanishing variance component. *American Psychologist, 20,* 498.

Jackson, D. N., & Messick, S. (1969). A distinction between judgments of frequency and of desirability as determinants of response. *Educational and Psychological Measurement, 29,* 273–293.

Jackson, D. N., & Paunonen, S. V. (1980). Personality structure and assessment. *Annual Review of Psychology, 31,* 503–551.

Klein, G. S., Barr, H. L., & Wolitzky, D. L. (1967). Personality. *Annual Review of Psychology, 18,* 467–560.

Lentz, T. F. (1938). Acquiescence as a factor in the measurement of personality. *Psychological Bulletin, 35,* 659.

Lichtenstein, E., & Bryan, J. H. (1965). Acquiescence and the MMPI: An item reversal approach. *Journal of Abnormal Psychology, 70,* 290–293.

Lorge, I. (1937). Gen-like: Halo or reality? *Psychological Bulletin, 34,* 545–546.

Lorr, M., & Shea, T. M. (1979). Are mood states bipolar? *Journal of Personality Assessment, 43,* 468–472.

Lorr, M., & Wunderlich, R. A. (1980). Mood states and acquiescence. *Psychological Reports, 46,* 191–195.

McGee, R. K. (1962). Response style as a personality variable: By what criterion? *Psychological Bulletin, 59,* 284–295.

McGee, R. K. (1967). Response set in relation to personality: An orientation. In I. A. Berg (Ed.), *Response set in personality assessment* (pp. 1–31). Chicago: Aldine.

Messick, S. (1961). Personality structure. *Annual Review of Psychology, 12,* 93–128.

Messick, S. (1962). Response style and content measures from personality inventories. *Educational and Psychological Measurement, 22,* 41–56.

Messick, S. (1967). The psychology of acquiescence: An interpretation of research evidence. In I. A. Berg (Ed.), *Response set in personality assessment* (pp. 115–145). Chicago: Aldine.

Messick, S. (1968). Response sets. In D. L. Sills (Ed.), *International encyclopedia of the social sciences* (pp. 492–496). New York: Macmillan.

Messick, S., & Jackson, D. N. (1961a). Acquiescence and the factorial interpretation of the MMPI. *Psychological Bulletin, 58,* 299–304.

Messick, S., & Jackson, D. N. (1961b). Desirability scale values and dispersions for MMPI items. *Psychological Reports, 8,* 409–414.

Milholland, J. E. (1964). Theory and techniques of assessment. *Annual Review of Psychology, 15,* 311–346.

Morf, M. E., & Jackson, D. N. (1972). An analysis of two response styles: True responding and item endorsement. *Educational and Psychological Measurement, 32,* 329–353.

Moscovici, S. (1963). Attitudes and opinions. *Annual Review of Psychology, 14,* 231–260.

Murphy, G. (1947). *Personality: A biosocial approach to origins and structure.* New York: Harper.

Nunnally, J. C., & Husek, T. B. (1958). The phony language examination: An approach to the measurement of response bias. *Educational and Psychological Measurement, 18,* 275–282.

Paulhus, D. L. (1984). Two-component models of socially desirable responding. *Journal of Personality & Social Psychology, 46,* 598–609.

Paulhus, D. L. (1986). Self-deception and impression management in test responses. In A. Angleitner & J. S. Wiggins (Eds.), *Personality assessment via questionnaire* (pp. 143–165). New York: Springer-Verlag.

Rogers, C. R., & Dymond, R. F. (1954). *Psychotherapy and personality change.* Chicago: University of Chicago Press.

Rorer, L. G. (1965). The great response-style myth. *Psychological Bulletin, 63,* 129–156.

Rorer, L. G., & Goldberg, L. R. (1965a). Acquiescence in the MMPI? *Educational and Psychological Measurement, 25,* 801–817.

Rorer, L. G., & Goldberg, L. R. (1965b). Acquiescence and the vanishing variance component. *Journal of Applied Psychology, 49,* 422–430.

Russell, J. A. (1978). Evidence of convergent validity on the dimensions of affect. *Journal of Personality and Social Psychology, 36,* 1152–1168.

Russell, J. A. (1979). Affective space is bipolar. *Journal of Personality and Social Psychology, 37,* 345–356.

Sackeim, H. A., & Gur, R. C. (1979). Self-deception, other-deception, and self-reported psychopathology. *Journal of Consulting and Clinical Psychology, 47,* 213–215.

Seeman, W. (1952). "Subtlety" in structured personality tests. *Journal of Consulting Psychology, 16,* 278–283.

Taylor, J. A. (1953). A personality scale of manifest anxiety. *Journal of Abnormal and Social Psychology, 48,* 285–290.

Voyce, C. D., & Jackson, D. N. (1977). An evaluation of a threshold theory for personality assessment. *Educational and Psychological Measurement, 37,* 383–408.

Wahler, H. J. (1961). Response styles in clinical and nonclinical groups. *Journal of Consulting Psychology, 25,* 533–539.

Welsh, G. S. (1956). Factor dimensions A and R. In G. S. Welsh & W. G. Dahlstrom (Eds.), *Basic readings on the MMPI in psychology and medicine* (pp. 264–281). Minneapolis: University of Minnesota Press.

Wiener, D. N. (1948). Subtle and obvious keys for the MMPI. *Journal of Consulting Psychology, 12,* 164–170.

Wiggins, J. S. (1959). Interrelationships among MMPI measures of dissimulation under standard and social desirability instructions. *Journal of Consulting Psychology, 23,* 419–427.

Wiggins, J. S. (1962). Strategic method and stylistic variance in the MMPI. *Psychological Bulletin, 59,* 224–242.

Wiggins, J. S. (1968). Personality structure. *Annual Review of Psychology, 19,* 293–350.

8

Problems in Assuming the Comparability of Pretest and Posttest in Autoregressive and Growth Models

Donald T. Campbell
Lehigh University

Charles S. Reichardt
University of Denver

BIOGRAPHICAL INTRODUCTION BY CAMPBELL

In my relationship with Lee Cronbach I have never completely gotten over my initial perception, in which I was the young outsider building upon the work of a highly respected and already established scholar. Although the calendar of birth makes me only 7 months his junior, the 7 years between our Ph.D.'s (his 1940, mine 1947) better expresses my perception (the accuracy of which would be supported by citation analysis). Here is a chronology of examples:

My own dissertation (1947) was on social attitude measurement, and, while independent, was done in the Berkeley environment which was producing the "authoritarian personality" studies (Adorno, Frenkel-Brunswik, Levinson, & Sanford, 1950; Frenkel-Brunswik, Levinson, & Sanford, 1947). When I became aware of Cronbach's (1946; see also 1950) work on response sets, I immediately regretted that each of my 25 scales had 5 items (two pro and three anti) and thus were unbalanced for direction-of-wording effects. The implications for the Frenkel-Brunswik, Levinson, and Sanford studies were more serious. Response sets exaggerated the relationship between the F scale of authoritarian personality trends and the Ethnocentrism (E) scale, since all items in both scales were in the anti direction. This artificially raised the correlation between prejudice and personality, and artificially lowered the correlation with political and economic conservativism (the PEC scale) which contained a mixture of both liberal and conservative items (in one widely used form, 9 liberal and 5 conservative).

Soon after arriving for my first job at Ohio State University in 1947, I inspired a graduate student to develop revised F, E, and PEC scales, in a too-grandiose effort on which data collection was never completed. Others published first on

201

this, but eventually I coauthored 6 articles on response sets. When a book by Block (1965) and a conspicuous article by Rorer (1965) strongly denied that response sets were a problem, I was galvanized into a final effort (Campbell, Siegman, & Rees, 1967). In a fine example of scientific cooperation, Block and Rorer reanalyzed their own data to my specifications, showing strong response-set problems in many of the MMPI scales. Peabody and Wrightsman (non-combatants in this debate) each also provided new analyses of their data. My paper coincided with a cessation of publications on the problem, reinstating in the literature the conclusion first enunciated by Cronbach 21 years earlier.

Cronbach and Meehl's, "Construct Validity in Psychological Tests" (1955), was a major event for two separate groups of psychologists. For applied psychologists, it offered a major addition to the concept of validity for tests of individual differences in ability, achievement, and personality. For psychological theorists, it was recognized as a major achievement in employing philosophy of science to improve the scientific status of psychology. Don Fiske's and my "Multitrait-multimethod matrix" (Campbell & Fiske, 1959) was offered as an elaboration of "construct validity." I have a memory, probably authentic, of first presenting the multitrait-multimethod matrix concept at a small session at an APA meeting, with Lee Cronbach present and approving. In our published article we cited not only Cronbach and Meehl (1955), but also Cronbach (1946) for calling attention to the *method* factors that we were stressing (and that had been neglected in the presentation of construct validity). "The assumption is generally made . . . that what the test measures is determined by the *content* of the items. Yet the final score . . . is a composite of effects resulting from the content of the items and effects resulting from the *form* of the items used" (Cronbach, 1946, p. 475). I also remember first presenting the paradoxically multiplicative (rather than additive) character of the method factors actually found in multitrait–multimethod matrices (Campbell & O'Connell, 1967, 1982) to a colloquium Lee hosted at Stanford in the Spring of 1966. It exemplifies Lee's generous behind-the-scenes collaborative style (celebrated throughout this essay) that I have a 14 page letter-memo from him on this subject, dated January 22, 1985.

In my methodological teaching (if not yet in my published research), his great "Proposals Leading to Analytic Treatment of Social Perception Scores" (Cronbach, 1958) plays a central role, and indeed may be his paper that best epitomizes my own perspective on measurement. In my teaching (published and unpublished) on regression artifacts (error-in-variables, stressing the error in the so-called "independent" variables), Cronbach and Furby (1970) is regularly invoked as a legitimating authority. His "Coefficient Alpha" (Cronbach, 1951), in part because of its immediate appropriateness both to "Likert-type" attitude scale scoring and to totals of ratings, has been the orthodoxy in my teaching materials and published articles. While there is evidence that I've never fully assimilated his concept of "generalizability" (Campbell, 1986), at least I remain aware of the deficiency.

These notes set the stage for the biography of the unfinished paper that Chip

Reichardt and I offer as our contribution to this celebration. It was first circulated in a January 1977 draft entitled "One Perspective on Cronbach Day (October 28, 1976) at Northwestern University." After August, 1977, the version I circulated included Lee's comments. Thus, it is an exemplification both of Lee Cronbach's influence and his style of operating. It is also an illustration of an ideal type of productive scientific disagreement, based on friendship and the shared valuation of both problems and goals.

October 28, 1976, was the largest and best organized of three or more "Cronbach Days," instigated in each case by Lee's notifying us that he would be passing through Chicago, would be happy to spend a day in Evanston, and would like to discuss our shared problems and differences. One previous Cronbach Day had been celebrated (as near as I can reconstruct) on October 15, 1970, with Andy Porter also present. It was focused on Campbell and Erlebacher (1970), and had been preceeded by three letters and commentaries from Lee, dated September 4, September 19, and September 23, a total of some 20 pages of algebra and text. After the face-to-face conference, we prepared a two page, single spaced errata which was included with all reprints of Campbell and Erlebacher distributed thereafter. Where it has been reprinted in other collections (e.g., Struening & Brewer, 1983, pp. 321–341) there has been a deletion of the section which we had become convinced was in error.

For the October 28, 1976 occasion, Lee had provided two memoranda. The most central was a 29-page challenge, entitled "A Communication to Campbell, Kenny, and Associates," dated September 21, 1976. The targets included Kenny (1975a) and Campbell and Boruch (1975). There was also a September 23, 1976, letter (5 single-spaced pages of prose and algebra) addressing an earlier version of Magidson (1977). All these materials, plus a June, 1976 version of Reichardt (1979a) and the four 1970 Cronbach letters were distributed in advance. The all day session had a formal agenda, catered coffee, and was held in a meeting room overlooking the lake to the downtown Chicago skyline. Present were not only the Northwestern University contingent (including, if memory serves, Bob Boruch, Tom Cook, Al Erlebacher, Chip Reichardt, Jerry Sacks, David Rindskopf, Jay Magidson, Bill Trochim, Jerry Ross, Joe Cecil, Jim MacMillen, John Burns, and others), but also David Wiley from the University of Chicago and Brad Huitema from Western Michigan. (Andy Porter had planned to come but was ill. David Kenny was not present, but had met with Lee in Cambridge on the September 21st memorandum.)

Also central to that meeting was the brilliant manuscript by Cronbach, Rogosa, Floden, and Price (1976, 1977), well-known to us as "CRFP," or "Temptress." This paper was the single most important authority for Chip Reichardt's (1979a) chapter for Cook and Campbell (1979), a chapter that was already available in a 1976 draft. It also played a similar role in Chip Reichardt's (1979b) dissertation, then in progress. Had we all been on the same campus, Lee should have chaired Reichardt's dissertation committee. Chip, while pinch-hitting for me on a West Coast advisory panel meeting, had met with Lee at Stanford in 1975. (Later, while

Lee was on sabbatical in London, 1977–1978, Lee continued generous correspondence with Chip.)

The degree of collaboration between Lee and me that this testifies to is made still clearer when I add that in those years Chip was my closest advisor and tutor on quasi-experimental statistics, my main translator in collaboration with Jerry Sacks of Northwestern's mathematics department, and his students Cliff Spiegelman and George Knafl who worked with us summers on a range of issues including the regression discontinuity design (in both fuzzy and sharp forms) (see Campbell, 1984, for this history) and the spectral analysis approach to causal inference in lagged time-series. It was also Chip who convinced me that David Rogosa (1978, 1980) had sounded the death knell for my approach to interpreting the Cross Lagged Panel Correlation and who tutored me in what I think of as my "funeral oration" for that beloved child (Cook & Campbell, 1979, pp. 314–317). (It was Tom Cook who insisted on publishing the whole methodological history, including that oration, rather than just dropping the topic entirely. David Kenny's approach [1975b, 1979; Kenny & Harackiewicz, 1979; Kenny & Campbell, 1984] is, in his judgment, not affected by Rogosa's criticism.)

Only one of the challenges of Lee's September 21, 1976 memorandum is dealt with here. For example, this essay does not cover his rejection of my dogmatic insistence that matching, partialing out with partial correlations, or other regression adjustments, always "underadjust" for selection biases. Lee's position has been accepted by Reichardt (1979a, 1979b), and since Reichardt (1979a) appears in Cook and Campbell (1979), I count this as at least a grudging admission of the possibility, if not likelihood, of "overcorrection." Several other points of both agreement and disagreement I will leave undocumented here, but will volunteer to continue to distribute Cronbach's September 21, 1976, and my August, 1977, memos which includes Cronbach's reaction to our January, 1977, memo.

The sole challenge that is at all dealt with here is our overdependence in quasi-experimental analyses upon an assumed comparability of the "pretest" and posttest. This contrasts with Cronbach's preference to disregard any special comparability, and to treat a so-called pretest just as one would treat any other covariate. Even here, this chapter does not constitute an answer to Cronbach, but offers instead a free-association on his challenge, in which we raise additional objections and perplexities beyond those Cronbach has specified, albeit still within an agenda that seeks to give to a pretest a special status over other covariates, due to its potentially much greater comparability to the posttest (dependent variable or outcome measure).

PRETEST-POSTTEST "SIMILARITY": BACKGROUND

Consider a posttraining measure of skill, for a population of trainees starting with no prior task experience. As Cronbach points out, efforts to prepare a "pretest" for use prior to training will be hopeless, if by pretest one assumes a measure of comparable factorial composition, variance, and reliability. Likewise, in tests of reactions to surprise and stress, or tests of creativity, "comparable" pretests will often be unavailable. Just as factor analyses of individual differences at various stages of learning show different factorial composition, so measures taken on children growing rapidly in height, weight, or vocabulary can be expected to have different factorial composition when taken 1 year apart. And if the tests are close together in time, the learning that takes place as a result of pretesting has an impact on the posttest, in a manner apt to make the two measures dissimilar in more than just their means. On the other hand, pretreatment measures *treated as predictors or covariates* rather than pretests, would still be useful. There results a preference for treating all so-called pretests just as any other covariate, giving them no special status, and obviating any need to assume similarity between pretest and posttest. As Cronbach summarizes his position, "I can see no warrant . . . for treating the pretest differently from other initial measures in regression analyses" (Cronbach, 1982, p. 190).

Such an analytic approach stands in sharp contrast with the central modes of quasi-experimental analysis. Following from above, most obviously vulnerable is the nonrandomized control-group design with a single pretest. On the one hand, concerns about pretest–posttest comparability are represented in some of our warnings about specific threats to validity. But on the other hand, we (e.g., Campbell and Boruch, 1975) do assume such comparability in recommending Lord's (1960) or Porter's (1968) reliability corrected covariance approaches, or Director's (1979) covariance on regressed pretest scores, all of which implicitly assume similarity of pretest and posttest in factorial structure at least. And when we (Campbell & Boruch, 1975) substitute test–retest correlations for Porter's recommended pretest reliability, we also assume similar reliabilities for pretest and posttest. Kenny's (1975a) standardized gain scores are another example of this dependence. Even when in growth situations, means, variances, reliabilities, and communalities, are obviously changing, there is dependence upon an assumption of factorial similarity, including constancy for the relative size of the factor loadings (e.g., Kenny's "correction for communality" [Crano, Kenny, & Campbell, 1972; Kenny, 1975a]).

In defense of our practice, it should be noted that there is often substantial evidence supporting the assumption of comparability within the quasi-experimental data collection itself. Particularly valuable are the control group data. Comparable bodies of data from similar but nonexperimental settings are also relevant. In general, the assumption of comparability may usually be found to be plausible for measures of achievement and aptitude for frequently tested populations such as those in educational institutions.

Comparability among repeated waves of measurement is also assumed in the interrupted time-series designs. Here too it may be quite plausible for recent waves if the measurement process has been going on for a long time. So too for the cross-lagged panel correlation: If there are three or more waves of measurement, and if the pattern is stably replicated in each pair of waves, comparability may be regarded as demonstrated.

But to say that our pretest–posttest comparability assumption is often justified, and that we can tell when, does not in itself explain our continuing reluctance to adopt the "just another covariate" approach. Nor is this reluctance developed here. It has its roots in the mischief that results from asymmetrical handling of pretest and posttest as exemplified in "matching" on the pretest, "partialing out" pretest differences, "regression adjustments" for pretest differences, etc. In these, the asymmetrical handling implicitly assumes that the many sources of the less-than-unity correlation between pretest and posttest are all contained in the posttest, and thereby assumes that *all* of the variance of the pretest (including its error, invalidity, irrelevance, and unique variance) is contained within the posttest. This asymmetry results in the so-called "regression artifacts" (e.g., Campbell & Boruch, 1975, pp. 210–248; Cook & Campbell, 1979, pp. 295–309).

Even when LISREL (Jöreskog & Sörbom, 1979, 1988; Magidson, 1977) measurement models are used to remove this asymmetry (thus modeling the pretest as also fallible and otherwise responsible for the less-than-unity correlation), the assumptions involved will most often be less plausible than the assumption that the pretest and posttest are comparable. But, as we have said, such arguments are postponed for another paper. Instead, our musings on the Cronbach Day of October 28, 1976, led us to further soul searching on what "similarity" or "comparability" might mean, given the autoregressive nature of relationships among repeated measures and the "fan-spread" of scores during growth.

FACTORIAL SIMILARITY IN THE FACE OF TEMPORAL EROSION OF RELATIONSHIPS

Evidence supporting the "factorial similarity" of pretest and posttest could come from patterns of intratest correlations among the items constituting pretest and posttest, or if there were several different measures repeated on each occasion, factorial similarity could be shown in the correlation patterns among these variables. These two cases merge into one another if items are considered variables, and if identical test-forms are used on each occasion. Let's consider the case of three variables (A, B, C) measured at two time periods (1, 2) perhaps 1 year apart, generating the multitrait-multitime matrix of Fig. 8.1.

Accepting as a fact that all relationships get smaller as time-lags between measures increase, this example otherwise shows a high degree of "factorial similarity." First, let us look at the "heterotrait-monotime" areas, designated by the free-hand loops numbered 1 and 2. The same pattern of correlation among the

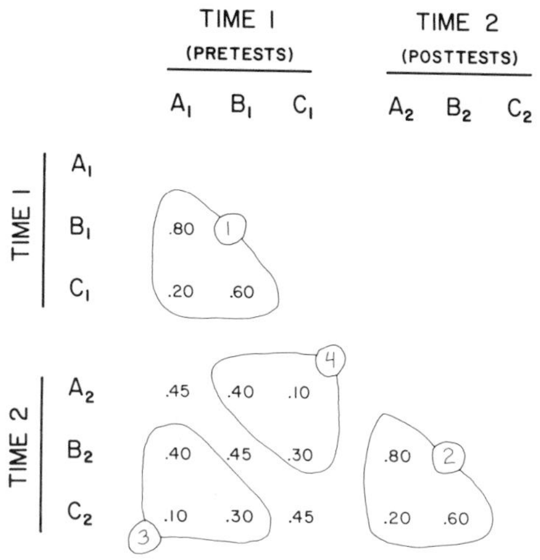

FIG. 8.1. Hypothetical intercorrelations among three measures, each repeated upon two occasions (a "multitrait-multitime matrix").

traits exists at each occasion. This is the kind of evidence employed in asserting factorial similarity when different populations have been measured. It makes the assumption that whereas the character of individuals might differ considerably between occasions, overall there is some justification for giving the measures the same name on both occasions. Further, it assumes that if the character of the traits has changed it would take an incredible coincidence for all of the changes to end up producing the same pattern of interrelationships. This kind of "pattern matching" of course does not constitute proof, but is depended upon in all of science (Campbell, 1966). It becomes more plausible the more widespread the pattern. In our immediate case, for example, the argument for factorial similarity would be furthered if the pattern were extended to include other covariates, background variables, etc., and this we should do in actual situations. (Because experimental treatments will affect traits differentially, and thus create differences in correlation patterns on the posttest when experimental and comparison groups are pooled, these matrices should be run within treatment groups, and with greatest attention to the control group. Pooled analyses are of course useful as null models.)

Next, let us look at the "heterotrait–heterotime" correlations, areas 3 and 4. These are lower, showing in the cross trait correlations the "temporal erosion" that is almost always found in repeated measures of the "same" trait. In Fig. 8.1, except for being lower, the correlations in areas 3 and 4 show the same pattern of intercorrelation found in areas 1 and 2. This is taken as further confirmation of factorial similarity. Note that the relationship between 3 and 4 on the one hand and 1 and 2 on the other is not additive, as though 1 and 2 each had a time-specific factor "subtracted" in 3 and 4, but is rather "multiplicative" (Campbell & O'Connell, 1967) or proportional. (Such a model is permitted as an option in

Jöreskog's [1969] multitest, multioccasion factor model.) The similarity between areas 3 and 4 is also highly confirmatory of factorial similarity.

Multitrait–multitime matrices, involving many more traits, and showing almost as perfect evidence of factorial similarity as shown in Fig. 8.1, have been repeatedly found. At Northwestern, these searches were initially part of shot-gun explorations for cross-lagged panel correlations. These were expected to show up as asymmetries between areas 3 and 4 (Crano et al., 1972; Kenny, 1972; Rozelle, 1965). Such asymmetries as found were minor compared to the overwhelming constancy of pattern. In Campbell and O'Connell (1967, Table 3 and Figure 6), one of the four multitrait–multitime matrices is based on 9 attitude scales administered to 756 Vassar College students as freshmen and as seniors. The similarity of the pattern of intertrait correlations, expressed as a correlation coefficient (after reflecting variables to maximize the number of positive correlations) was .99 between areas 1 and 2, and .95 between areas 3 and 4. (The other comparisons [1 vs. 3, etc.] are inflated by shared arrays, and are all .98 or .99.)

Those of you who have joined us so far in regarding such evidence as supporting factorial similarity for the measures on each occasion (as much factorial similarity as is compatible with the autoregressive situation) should note that *we have substantially modified the traditional factorial concept*, which has always identified "the same" factor as a fixed attribute of the individuals measured. For Fig. 8.1 to have occurred, individuals have had to change in their true underlying factor scores between times 1 and 2, even while the "factorial composition" of the tests has somehow remained the same. This shift is fundamental, but we believe it is required. To accommodate such repeated-measures, "simplex" outcomes, we must come to see the underlying true factor scores as themselves having an autoregressive or moving average pattern over time. While perhaps this should lead us to abandon efforts to speak about "the same" variables at different times, our tentative preference is to retain this notion. We shall, however, try to remind ourselves of this shift by using the phrase "Markov-same" factorial structure.

MOVING AVERAGE VERSUS AUTOREGRESSIVE MODELS

As we have already noted, when measures of "the same" trait are repeated over time, it is uniformly found that the longer the time lapse, the lower the correlation. As general terms for this phenomenon, we use *temporal erosion* or *temporal attenuation*. The specific form best known in the psychometric literature is what Louis Guttman has called the "simplex" correlation matrix (e.g., Humphreys, 1960), so labeled because it has a fundamental simplicity, but one which would not show up as "simple" in usual modes of linear additive factor analysis. Consider Table 8.1 as a hypothetical and idealized example of an

TABLE 8.1
Hypothetical Correlations Among Vocabulary Tests at Successive Grades,
Illustrating the "Temporal Erosion" of Relationships

Grades	1	2	3	4	5	6
1	(.90)	.81	.73	.66	.59	.53
2		(.90)	.81	.73	.66	.59
3			(.90)	.81	.73	.66
4				(.90)	.81	.73
5					(.90)	.81
6						(.90)

annual vocabulary test administered in grades 1 through 6. A traditional factor analysis of this matrix would produce 5 factors, in a messy fashion with grades 3 and 4 showing the highest communalities merely because they are central in this arbitrarily chosen set of years. Adding higher grades (or preschool testings) with the same form will change the factor loadings for grades 1 through 6. An a priori conceptual analysis limited to additive components would have still more factors. Each pair of adjacent years shares a different specific factor, each 3-year set another different specific factor, etc. (Fig. 8.1 and all of the empirical explorations of multitrait–multitime matrices referred to earlier, support the empirical generalization that the temporal attenuation of relationships also holds for the intertrait correlations.)

To accommodate the temporal attenuation of relationships, several mathematical models are possible. In this section, we compare two: a moving average model, and a first order Markov process (first-order autoregressive) model. To anticipate the results of our comparison, while certain crucial aspects of our conceptual model are more easily expressed in the moving average model, both empirical findings and algebraic convenience support the autoregressive.

Figure 8.2 shows a crude moving average model. The lines or bars represent components of variance which persist for a specific number of time periods. To simulate this "moving average true-score," each individual would be given a normal random number, appropriately weighted, corresponding to each horizontal line or bar, and the individual's total "true score" would be the sum of these numbers that were operating at any given time. A measurement process ("pretest" or "posttest") graphed as a vertical slice would also contain a time-specific error (e_1 or e_2). Because of the moving average process, there is a true score component, U_1, that the pretest contains which is not represented in the posttest, the latter containing instead U_2. It is because of the U_1 component that the pretest reliability corrections of Lord and Porter have been regarded as still "undercorrecting" (Campbell & Boruch, 1975, pp. 225–241).

In contrast to this symmetrical imagery for the components of pretest and posttest, the autoregressive model used by Boruch (Campbell & Boruch, 1975) and most others seems profoundly asymmetrical in time. As Fig. 8.3 illustrates,

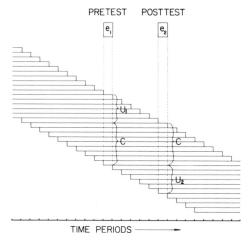

FIG. 8.2. A moving average model of a pretest and a posttest, distinguishing time specific error (e_1 and e_2), unique systematic components in pretest (U_1) and posttest (U_2), and common components (C).

components enter abruptly but never entirely exit. Their weight in the total variance rapidly diminishes, however. (If the Time 1–Time 2 correlation were .9, then the weight of a component entering at Time 1 is .9 at Time 2, $.9^2$ at Time 3, and $.9^9$ at Time 10.) In this model the U_2 component in the posttest is easily identified as the new components which have entered since the pretest. The U_1 component in the pretest is formally missing, even though correlation coefficients decrease in an identical manner whether going forward or backward in time. Figure 8.3 has been graphed for an autoregressive true score that has constant variance, according to some such formula as the following one, where X_t is the observed score, e_t is a time specific error, normally distributed with

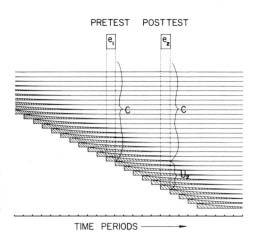

FIG. 8.3. An autoregressive model of a pretest and posttest, with components labeled as in Fig. 8.2. Note the "absence" of U_1.

mean of zero, X^* is the true score, and x^* is the new true score component of X entering at that time, a new normal random number:

$$X_t = X_t^* + e_t$$
$$X_t^* = \rho X_{t-1}^* + x_t^*$$

X_t^* has constant variance only if this simulation has been run for many time periods. (To have a constant variance for X_t^* at once, drawing one normal random number for X_{t-1}^* and another with equal variance for x_t^*, the formula should read

$$X_t^* = \rho X_{t-1}^* + (\sqrt{1 - \rho^2})\, x_t^*.)$$

The discussions in Campbell and Boruch (1975) seem based on the assumption that, hidden within Fig. 8.3 for the pretest, there would be something like the U_1 of Fig. 8.2, comparable in magnitude to the U_2 of Fig. 8.3. But there is not. One tends to be attracted to formulae in which the components "imitate nature" in their relationships with each other, as well as producing a product which does so. On the other hand, all of us are reconciled to using formulae which only *imitate* a product, with no pretense to imitating the process. The so-called Taylor theorem, which asserts that any function can be imitated by a long enough string of additive components, underlies curve fitting with higher order polynomial series, and spectral analysis, if not factor analysis. These are increasingly recognized as presenting serious problems when extrapolating beyond the range of data upon which they were based. What are we to think here? Is the moving average model the more componentially realistic? And the autoregressive model merely a more convenient mathematical notation which successfully imitates its product but not its composition?

There is a major respect in which our simple moving average model fails to imitate nature: in it, the decrement in correlation coefficient units is constant with each longer lag, rather than being a constant proportion of the previous value. A top row for Table 8.1 would read like (.90) .80 .70 .60 .50 .40, eventually hitting zero abruptly, rather than approaching it asymptotically. Empirically, a pattern of diminishing decrements is nearly always found, even if not of the perfect first-order autoregressive form. One moving average model that would avoid this would have a nearly infinite number of components, staying in for varying lengths of time, some of them infinitely long. Such a model would retain the virtue of comparably conceptualized U_1 and U_2, and in this would be more compatible with our implicit conceptualization than is the autoregressive model.

Where we have only two waves of measurement (pretest and posttest), we may perhaps disregard such problems, conceptually lumping U_1 with e_1, and U_2 with e_2. In the long run, however, for longitudinal and panel studies, such models must be developed and refined. When this is done, we feel confident that they will then also inform two-wave and one-wave studies.

MEASURES COMPOSED OF SEVERAL
AUTOREGRESSIVE COMPONENTS

A look at the items in a test makes it seem more likely that tests have multiple components than that they are truly single factored in underlying structure. If single factoredness occurs, it should be as a discovery, not as a by-product of an assumed single factoredness which is thereby precluded from disconfirmation. We conclude from this that to accommodate the fact of temporal erosion of relationships, we need a multiple factor model, with each factor autoregressive in nature. As Kenny has pointed out (Judd & Kenny, 1981, Chapter 6; Kenny, 1975a), this proposed, it becomes immediately obvious that it is arbitrary to assume that all factors have the same ρ or (non) erosion rate. A conceptualization allowing different ρ's immediately escalates the difficulty of applying and testing the model.

Let's make the problem a little more concrete. While the difference between vocabulary tests labeled "intelligence" and ones labeled "achievement" is hard to specify, nonetheless a 1-hour intelligence test will produce as high correlations with other measures 5 years later as will several hours of achievement tests. Let's conceptualize this difference as a difference in ρ's. Let's now consider a test made up of equal parts of an intelligence type component ($\rho = .9$) and an uncorrelated achievement type component ($\rho = .5$). What will the overall erosion rate of the composite look like? In Table 8.2, we offer a primitive illustration of the problem, in an effort to call attention to the need for models that merge autoregressive models with some kind of componential analysis. While each factor is modeled autoregressively (as a first order Markov process), in Table 8.2, we borrow from factor analysis the old custom of conceiving of an observed correlation coefficient as made up of additive components.

The second line from the bottom in Table 8.2, labeled "r for Composite," corresponds to a series of correlation coefficients, akin to the top row of Table 8.1. The value of (1.00) in the column "Sync" is like a reliability. In this example, there is no time-specific error, and that value becomes unity.

In the top two pairs of rows, the contributions to the correlation (r) are presented, plus the ρ's, which are also the ratios of two correlation coefficients of adjacent time periods. In these component sets, the correlation values were in fact generated from the ρ's. But the composite ρ_c's have been computed from the composite correlation coefficients.

Superficial consideration might have led to the expectation that the ρ_c's for the composite would have been constant at some level intermediate between .90 and .50. But instead, for the longer lags the contribution from the more stable component dominates, asymptoting at .90 for extremely long delays. Considering the likelihood of more than two factors, each with a unique ρ, there is little chance of our ever being able to infer the nature of the composite solely from such a series of ρ_c's.

TABLE 8.2
Correlations Over Increasing Lags for Components of Differing

	Sync.	Increasing Lags in Time						
		1	2	3	4	5	6	7
Contributions to r of Component of = .9 $r_{t_n}/r_{t_{n-1}} = \rho_1$	(.50)	.45	.405	.3645	.32805	.2952	.2657	.2391
		[.90]	[.90]	[.90]	[.90]	[.90]	[.90]	[.90]
Contribution to r from Component of = .5 $r_{t_n}/r_{t_{n-1}} = \rho_2$	(.50)	.25	.125	.0625	.03125	.0156	.0078	.0039
		[.50]	[.50]	[.50]	[.50]	[.50]	[.50]	[.50]
r for Composite $r_{t_n}/r_{t_{n-1}} = \rho_C$	(1.00)	.70	.530	.4270	.35925	.3108	.2735	.2430
		[.70]	[.7557]	[.8057]	[.8413]	[.8651]	[.8800]	[.8885]

Very precious for exploring such problems are longitudinal data sets. In work related to his MA thesis (Kenny, 1972), making use of Thomas Hilton's ETS longitudinal study of achievement and ability measures in grades 5, 7, 9, and 11, David Kenny began such an exploration, comparing ρ_c's for lags of 2, 4, and 6 years for some 8 measures. Even though there was a source of inhomogeniety in the wholesale repetition of the same items in grades 7 and 9, but not elsewhere, constancy of ρ_c's was generally found (if memory serves), the few deviations being (as illustrated in Table 8.3) for higher ρ_c's for ratios based on the longer lags. As we write this, we do not have access to these data and, therefore, are unsure about which of the following suggested analyses have already been done, or with what outcome. Probably there were marked differences in the ρ's for different tests, perhaps (as in Crano et al., 1972) with those for tests classified as ability being higher than those classified as achievement. This suggests experiments generating composite scores from two measures with markedly different ρ's, and computing the ρ_c's from the lagged correlations of this composite variable. While there may be other explanations of increasing ρ_c's for longer lags, do constant ρ_c's imply that only first-order Markov processes need be posited? If so, can one also assume that the components of a measure (if multi-factored) all have the same erosion rate? In addition to the decline of test-retest correlations, there is evidence of the ρ's in the heterotrait-heterotime coefficients. Can this be converted into additional estimates of the ρ's of individual tests?

Integrating Time-Specific Errors and Group Differences

However much it complicates statistical analysis, conceiving of all measures as composites of components with different erosion rates (or ρ's) offers a unifying perspective for incorporating two features which have previously seemed ad hoc. First, the time-specific errors (e_1 and e_2 of Figs. 8.2 and 8.3) could be regarded as autoregressive components with a very low ρ.

The second advantage may be still more important. In Campbell and Boruch (1975, pp. 224–241), there is criticism of Porter's (1968) approach to a true-score covariance analysis based upon correction for pretest unreliability, on the grounds that it implies a steady dimunition over time in the size of the difference initially observed between the quasi-experimental comparison groups (for example, when using one school as an experimental group, and another as a comparison group). Porter's approach is interpreted as assuming that in the null case the pretest difference would steadily diminish with the same erosion rate as exemplified by the achievement measures within groups. Campbell and Boruch argue that it is more reasonable to assume that the relative school-to-school difference would remain at the same level in subsequent years and in higher grades (or even increase). In modeling this, they employed an arbitrary, constant (relative) selection difference. However, it undoubtedly would be more realistic to have a selection difference with a "test-retest correlation" of less than 1.00, although higher than that found for the tests. Thus those complex neighborhood and subcultural factors that continually regenerate the school-to-school differences might be best represented as an autoregressive component with a very high ρ, yet less than 1.00. Such a move had been foreshadowed in earlier conceptual explorations (Campbell, 1970, 1971). Vast archives of relevant data are available in school records of achievement test scores. For many reasons, in addition to providing more dependable background assumptions underlying quasi-experimental analysis, these data should be thoroughly examined.

(In their discussion of Porter, Campbell and Boruch give a token acknowledgment, unelaborated, of the possibility that school-to-school differences increase in the higher grades. An unintegrated section of their paper, entitled "Grouping Feedback Effects" [pp. 272–275] makes such a prediction on the grounds that school children both learn test-relevant vocabulary from each other and interfere with each other's learning in ways correlated with achievement level.)

DIFFERENTIAL GROWTH RATES AND THE FAN-SPREAD HYPOTHESIS

Prodded by Cronbach's focus on our assumption that pretests were comparable to posttests, we have escalated his challenge, and in the foregoing sections have convinced ourselves that *our quasi-experimental approaches require a competent modeling of processes in time* which will be very difficult to achieve. In this section, we add to that burden by a brief and preliminary consideration of some problems of realistically modeling growth.

In quasi-experimental analyses under growth conditions using such measures as estimates of vocabulary size, means and standard deviations increase each year. When (as in compensatory education) we have considered comparison groups that start out with a significant difference on a pretest, we have assumed as a null condition for experimental treatment effects that the mean difference between groups would increase proportionately to the increase of the means and standard deviations, i.e., that in terms of standardized scores, the selection difference would be constant. Such an assumption lies behind Kenny's (1975a) standardized gain scores. It has been casually labeled "the fan spread hypothesis" (Campbell & Erlebacher, 1970), or the "limp" or "droopy" fan-spread hypothesis (Campbell & Boruch, 1975, p. 252) to accommodate declines in rate of growth as maturity approaches. It has been used to criticize the expectation that students 1 year behind grade at age 6 in the 1st grade, should still be only 1 year behind in the 6th grade (age 12) unless the schools are failing. Instead, depending on the "droop," the expectation should be for such students to be nearly 2 years behind grade level at grade 6.

What would be conceptually useful would be to have an algebraic model in which growth was expressed naturally. Instead, we are so used to using random standardized normal numbers that the easiest way to simulate growth would be to first simulate the standard scores and then add growth components; e.g.:

$$X_t = a(c + X_t^*) + e_t$$

where c is a constant making X_t^* all positive, and a is an age dependent multiplier (X_t^* would be generated as above). This model naturally shows increasing reliability as a gets larger, holding e's variance constant. Another model, with constant reliability, would be

$$X_t = a(c + X_t^* + e_t)$$

But both of these are uncomfortably artificial. With measured vocabulary in mind, a more natural formula might be

$$X_t = X_t^* + e_t$$
$$X_t^* = X_{t-1}^* + x_t^*$$

with x_t^* being normally distributed but constrained to be positive, and the mean and variance of X^* getting larger and larger. For X_t^* this is technically a "random walk" process, which is a first-order Markov process with a ρ of 1.0, so the process is not stationary. It is an abrupt entry and no exit model, in which old components continue in full magnitude, but because of the increasing total variance, become a decreasing part of the total. However, this model does not allow for the forgetting of words once learned, so some further modification, part-way back to the autoregressive model, but with a steady net increase in mean and variance, may be needed. Moreover, it does not allow for the recency effect so typical of learning and bank accounts, in which X_t^* is much more affected by x_t^* than by a long ago x_{t-5}^*. Similarly, it would predict ever-increasing correlations between X_{t_n} and $X_{t_{n-1}}$ for later time periods, rather than the relational stationarity illustrated in the constant diagonals for lags of a given length in Table 8.1 (which are regularly found in longitudinal studies, even while means and variances are increasing). So this is clearly *not* the natural fan-spread model we want.

WHERE WE PAUSE IN OUR QUEST

Thorough examination of the many assumptions underlying quasi-experimental analyses can often be regarded as arguments for random assignments to treatments (e.g., Campbell & Boruch, 1975). In the exchanges surrounding Cronbach Day, October 28, 1976, Lee shared this position. In a letter of February 9, 1977, he said:

> I would have been inclined to add an area of agreement that you touch on only tangentially. The class of designs in which assignment to treatment is controlled probabilistically on a known covariate, a class of which regression-discontinuity

and random-assignment designs are particular instances, share the same property of being free from bias in principle if properly analyzed.

This comment of his should not be allowed to stand alone without also mentioning his frequent (and frequently valid) criticism of "the Northwestern School" for allowing its enthusiasm for randomized assignment to treatments to lead to an exaggeration of the ease with which they can be implemented and (perhaps most sinfully) the extent to which available exemplars have been able to live up to that model. At best we have been ambivalent and inconsistent on this issue. Embedded within two of our worst excesses of such over advocacy are also arguments that in practice, random assignments drift into quasi-experiments due to systematic and differential loss of cases (Cook & Campbell, 1979, pp. 356–366; Riecken, Boruch, Campbell, et al., 1974, pp. 55–81).

But, there will remain many settings in which we will want to study the impacts of new programs and in which random assignment to treatments is not feasible. In response to such legitimate needs to know, we will want to do the best we can, comparing several approaches including analysis models growing out of Cronbach's CRFP (Cronbach et al., 1977), Jöreskog's (Jöreskog & Sörbom, 1979, 1988) LISREL measurement modeling, and quasi-experimental designs assuming some degree of special comparability between a "pretest" and a "posttest." We remain committed to attempting to make available improved versions in the "comparable pretest" tradition, and (with continued help from Lee Cronbach), scrupulously facing up to the assumptions being made and to their plausibility in specific applications.

REFERENCES

Adorno, T. W., Frenkel-Brunswik, E., Levinson, D. J., Sanford, R. N. (1950). *The authoritarian personality*. New York: Harper & Brothers.

Block, J. (1965). *The challenge of response sets*. New York: Appleton-Century-Crofts.

Campbell, D. T. (1966). Pattern matching as an essential in distal knowing. In K. R. Hammond (Ed.), *The psychology of Egon Brunswik* (pp. 81–106). New York: Holt, Rinehart & Winston.

Campbell, D. T. (1970). *Time-series of annual same-grade testings in the evaluation of compensatory educational experiments*. Unpublished research report to the National Science Foundation, Department of Psychology, Northwestern University.

Campbell, D. T. (1971). Temporal changes in treatment-effect correlations: A quasi-experimental model for institutional records and longitudinal studies. In G. V Glass (Ed.), *Proceedings of the 1970 invitational conference on testing problems* (pp. 93–110). Princeton, NJ: Educational Testing Service.

Campbell, D. T. (1984). Forward [An informal history of the regression-discontinuity design]. In W. M. K. Trochim, *Research design for program evaluation: The regression-discontinuity approach* (pp. 15–43). Beverly Hills, CA: Sage.

Campbell, D. T. (1986). Relabeling internal and external validity for applied social scientists. In W. M. K. Trochim (Ed.), *Advances in quasi-experimental design and analysis* (pp. 67–77). San Francisco, CA: Jossey-Bass.

Campbell, D. T., & Boruch, R. F. (1975). Making the case for randomized assignment to treatments by considering the alternatives: Six ways in which quasi-experimental evaluations in compensatory education tend to underestimate effects. In C. A. Bennett & A. A. Lumsdaine (Eds.), *Evaluation and experiment: Some critical issues in assessing social programs* (pp. 195–296). New York: Academic Press.

Campbell, D. T., & Erlebacher, A. (1970). How regression artifacts in quasi-experimental evaluations can mistakenly make compensatory education look harmful. In J. Hellmuth (Ed.), *Compensatory education: A national debate*. Volume 3, *Disadvantaged child* (pp. 185–210). New York: Brunner/Mazel. Reprinted in E. L. Struening & M. Guttentag (Eds.), *Handbook of evaluation research*. Beverly Hills, CA: Sage Publications, 1975, 597–617.

Campbell, D. T., & Fiske, D. W. (1959). Convergent and discriminant validation by the multitrait–multimethod matrix. *Psychological Bulletin, 56*, 81–105.

Campbell, D. T., & O'Connell, E. J. (1967). Methods factors in multitrait-multimethod matrices: Multiplicative rather than additive. *Multivariate Behavioral Research, 2*, 409–426.

Campbell, D. T., & O'Connell, E. J. (1982). Methods as diluting trait relationships rather than adding irrelevant systematic variance. In D. Brinberg & L. Kidder (Eds.), *Forms of validity in research* (pp. 93–111). San Francisco, CA: Jossey-Bass.

Campbell, D. T., Siegman, C. R., & Rees, M. B. (1967). Direction-of-wording effects in the relationships between scales. *Psychological Bulletin, 68*(5), 293–303.

Cook, T. D., & Campbell, D. T. (1979). *Quasi-experimentation: Design and analysis issues for field settings*. Boston, MA: Houghton Mifflin.

Crano, W. D., Kenny, D. A., & Campbell, D. T. (1972). Does intelligence cause achievement?: A cross-lagged panel analysis. *Journal of Educational Psychology, 63*(3), 258–275.

Cronbach, L. J. (1946). Response sets and test validity. *Educational and Psychological Measurement, 6*, 475–494.

Cronbach, L. J. (1950). Further evidence on response sets and test design. *Educational and Psychological Measurement, 10*, 3–31.

Cronbach, L. J. (1951). Coefficient alpha and the internal structure of tests. *Psychometrika, 16*, 297–334.

Cronbach, L. J. (1958). Proposals leading to analytic treatment of social perception scores. In R. Tagiuri & L. Petrullo (Eds.), *Person perception and interpersonal behavior* (pp. 353–379). Stanford, CA: Stanford University Press.

Cronbach, L. J. (1982). *Designing evaluations of educational and social programs*. San Francisco, CA: Jossey-Bass.

Cronbach, L. J., & Furby, L. (1970). How we should measure "change"—or should we? *Psychological Bulletin, 74*, 68–80.

Cronbach, L. J., & Meehl, P. E. (1955). Construct validity in psychological tests. *Psychological Bulletin, 52*, 281–302.

Cronbach, L. J., Rogosa, D. R., Floden, R. E., & Price, G. G. (1976). Analysis of covariance: Angel of salvation or temptress and deluder. *Occasional Papers, Stanford Evaluation Consortium*. Stanford, CA: Department of Education, Stanford University.

Cronbach, L. J., Rogosa, D. R., Floden, R. E., & Price, G. G. (1977). Analysis of covariance in nonrandomized experiments: Parameters affecting bias. *Occasional Papers, Stanford Evaluation Consortium*. Stanford, CA: Department of Education, Stanford University.

Director, S. M. (1979). Underadjustment bias in the evaluation of manpower training. *Evaluation Quarterly, 3*(2), 190–218.

Frenkel-Brunswik, E., Levinson, D. J., & Sanford, R. N. (1947). The antidemocratic personality. In T. M. Newcomb, E. L. Hartley, et al. (Eds.), *Readings in social psychology* (pp. 531–541). New York: Henry Holt.

Humphreys, L. G. (1960). Investigations of the simplex. *Psychometrika, 25*(4), 313–323.

Jöreskog, K. G. (1969). Factoring the multitest-multioccasion correlation matrix. *Research Bulletin 69-62*. Princeton, NJ: Educational Testing Service.

Jöreskog, K. G., & Sörbom, D.(1979). *Advances in factor analysis and structural equation models.* Edited by J. Magidson. Cambridge, MA: Abt Books.

Jöreskog, K. G., & Sörbom, D. (1988). *LISREL 7: A guide to the program and applications.* Chicago: SPSS, Inc.

Judd, C. M., & Kenny, D. A. (1981). *Estimating the effects of social interventions.* Cambridge, England: Cambridge University Press.

Kenny, D. A. (1972). *A model for temporal erosion and common factor effects in cross-lagged panel correlation.* Master's thesis, Department of Psychology, Northwestern University.

Kenny, D. A. (1975a). A quasi-experimental approach to assessing treatment effects in the nonequivalent control groups design. *Psychological Bulletin, 82,* 345-362.

Kenny, D. A. (1975b). Cross-lagged panel correlation: A test for spuriousness. *Psychological Bulletin, 82,* 887-903.

Kenny, D. A., (1979). *Correlation and causality.* New York: Wiley-Interscience.

Kenny, D. A., & Campbell, D. T. (1984). Methodological considerations in the analysis of temporal data. In K. J. Gergen & M. M. Gergen (Eds.), *Historical social psychology* (pp. 125-138). Hillsdale, NJ: Lawrence Erlbaum Associates.

Kenny, D. A., & Harackiewicz, J. M. (1979). Cross-lagged panel correlation: Practice and promise. *Journal of Applied Psychology, 64,* 372-379.

Lord, F. M. (1960). Large-scale covariance analysis when the control variable is fallible. *Journal of the American Statistical Association, 55,* 307-321.

Magidson, J. (1977). Toward a causal model approach for adjusting for pre-existing differences in the nonequivalent control group situation. *Evaluation Quarterly, 1*(3), 399-420.

Porter, A. C. (1968). *The effects of using fallible variables in the analysis of covariance.* Doctoral dissertation, University of Wisconsin, 1967. Ann Arbor, MI: University Microfilms.

Reichardt, C. S. (1979a). The statistical analysis of data from nonequivalent group designs. In T. D. Cook & D. T. Campbell, *Quasi-experimentation: Design and analysis issues for field settings* (pp. 147-205). Boston, MA: Houghton Mifflin.

Reichardt, C. S. (1979b). *The design and analysis of the nonequivalent group quasi-experiment.* Unpublished doctoral dissertation, Department of Psychology, Northwestern University.

Riecken, H. W., Boruch, R. F., Campbell, D. T., Caplan, N., Glennan, T. K., Pratt, J., Rees, A., & Williams, W. (1974). *Social experimentation: A method for planning and evaluating social intervention.* New York: Academic Press.

Rogosa, D. (1978). Causal models in longitudinal research: Rationale, formulation and interpretation. In J. R. Nesselroade & P. B. Baltes (Eds.), *Longitudinal research in human development: Design and analysis.* New York: Academic Press.

Rogosa, D. (1980). A critique of cross-lagged correlation. *Psychological Bulletin, 88*(2), 245-258.

Rorer, L. G. (1965). The great response-style myth. *Psychological Bulletin, 65,* 129-156.

Rozelle, R. (1965). *Causal relations in attitude change as demonstrated through cross-lagged panel correlations.* Duplicated Research Report, Northwestern University, U.S. Office of Education, Education Media Branch, Project C-998, Contract 3-20-001.

Struening, E. L., & Brewer, M. B. (Eds.). (1983). *Handbook of evaluation research: University edition.* Beverly Hills, CA: Sage.

9

A Longitudinal Approach to ATI Research: Models for Individual Growth and Models for Individual Differences in Response to Intervention

David Rogosa
Stanford University

This chapter provides a fresh look at the traditional statistical analyses in Aptitude-Treatment Interaction (ATI) research. Part I presents (a) statistical models for individual maturation in the outcome variable and (b) statistical models for individual differences in response to an intervention. In Part II simple combinations of these two kinds of models are used to evaluate the usefulness of the regression models commonly used in ATI research.

Typically in ATI research, two experimental groups are formed, measurements on individual characteristic(s) are obtained, the individuals in each group are exposed to an intervention (e.g., one of two different types of instruction), and subsequently, measurements on the outcome variable(s) are obtained. For convenience, the two experimental groups are called the treatment and control groups. Three different specifications for the formation of these two groups are considered: (i) The treatment and control groups are formed by random assignment of individuals to groups; (ii) the assignment of individuals to the treatment and control groups is by non-random (often unknown) mechanisms (selection processes); (iii) individuals are members of intact groups (e.g., classrooms) which are assigned to treatment and control groups. Results are worked out most fully for random assignment of individuals.

The *natural maturation* of an individual is the individual growth in the absence of an intervention. That is, in the absence of any intervention, a functional representation of change over time in an outcome measure Y is specified for each individual. Furthermore, simple models for individual response to the intervention are formulated. These models incorporate both a "main effect" between the treatment and control groups and an "interaction effect" representing systematic individual differences in response to the intervention.

PART I: SIMPLE LONGITUDINAL REPRESENTATIONS FOR ATI RESEARCH

1. Models for Individual Growth

The first component of this approach is a model for the growth (change) of an individual's level or score on the outcome measure Y. (The outcome Y may be, for example, a score on an achievement test.) In the absence of an intervention, the individual growth curve specifies the value of the outcome measure as a function of time, Y(t). For simplicity, consider Y to be measured without error; errors of measurement in the outcome variable would be easy to incorporate but would complicate the exposition of results. Individual differences in growth are represented by differences in the parameter values of the individual growth curves. Two functional forms for individual growth are considered: straight-line growth and asymptotic exponential growth.

Straight-line Growth. A simple representation for natural maturation is a model which specifies that each individual has a constant rate of change in Y. That is, for individual p:

$$dY(t)/dt = \pi_p \tag{1}$$

Different individuals may have different values of π_p; individual differences in the rate of growth (learning) exist whenever the π_p values differ over individuals. Of course, this constant rate of change is equivalent to specifying a straight-line growth curve for each individual:

$$Y_p(t) = Y_p(0) + \pi_p t \tag{2}$$

Although the constant rate of change representation is undoubtedly an over-simplification of natural maturation in most instances, this simple model may be considered a reasonable approximation to actual growth over short time intervals (i.e. an average rate of change) and serves well for illustrating the mathematical framework of the present approach to ATI analyses.

Asymptotic Exponential Growth. An alternative model, which may be a more realistic representation of individual growth, specifies that rate of change depends on the distance to the asymptote:

$$dY(t)/dt = \gamma_p(\lambda_p - Y(t)) \tag{3}$$

In this model, the parameter λ_p represents the ceiling or asymptote on Y for individual p. Thus, if $Y_p(t)$ represents the level of academic achievement for individual p at time t, then $\lambda_p - Y_p(t)$ represents the amount yet to be learned before the asymptote is reached. The parameter γ_p has been referred to as the "learning rate constant" because for this growth curve the time taken to grow from $Y_p(t)$ to $Y_p(t) + 1/2(\lambda_p - Y_p(t))$ is $(1/\gamma_p)\ln2$. Psychological applications of this model are widespread, one of the most familiar being Hull's model for "habit strength" (see Hilgard, 1951). Also, Hicklin (1976) applies variants of this model to the study of mastery learning.

In this chapter γ_p (the learning rate constant) is specified to be identical for all p. The individual growth curve corresponding to this restriction is:

$$Y_p(t) = \lambda_p - [\lambda_p - Y_p(0)]e^{-\gamma t} \qquad (4)$$

Individual differences in growth result from differences in λ_p and in $Y_p(0)$.

2. Models for Response to Intervention

Simple models for the (differential) effects of the intervention in the treatment and control groups complete the formulation. For each individual, the effect of the intervention is represented by an increment δ_p, which may depend upon both the group membership (treatment or control) of individual p and on individual characteristics. In this presentation, such individual characteristics are summarized by the variable A (assumed to be unchanging over time). For convenience, A_p may be termed the *aptitude* of individual p. It is best to interpret A_p broadly; as Cronbach and Snow (1977) advise, "Any aspect of the individual, including some matters untouched by conventional ability and personality measures, can predict response to instruction and hence can be a source of 'aptitude' " (p. 6). A representation for δ_p, which includes a "main effect" of group membership, and also allows for individual differences in response to the intervention is:

$$\delta_p = \begin{matrix} \eta_1 + \kappa_1 A_p = \eta_1 + \kappa_1 \mu_A + \kappa_1(A_p - \mu_A) & \text{for treatment} \\ \eta_0 + \kappa_0 A_p = \eta_0 + \kappa_0 \mu_A + \kappa_0(A_p - \mu_A) & \text{for control} \end{matrix} \qquad (5)$$

A dichotomous group membership variable G is defined such that G_p is 1 if individual p is a member of the treatment group, and G_p is 0 if individual p is a member of the control group. Then, combining the two parts of (5):

$$\delta_p = [\eta_0 + \kappa_0 A_p] + [(\eta_1 - \eta_0) + (\kappa_1 - \kappa_0)A_p]G_p.$$

Equation 5 is a simple mathematical representation of the basic idea underlying ATI research, that there are individual differences in response to treatment. The representation for δ_p in (5) specifies that all individual differences in response to the intervention are governed by values of A_p. For individual p (or any individual having the same value of A_p) the differential in incrementation between membership in the treatment vs. the control group is:

$$\eta_1 - \eta_0 + (\kappa_1 - \kappa_0)A_p \text{ or } [\eta_1 - \eta_0 + (\kappa_1 - \kappa_0)\mu_A] \\ + (\kappa_1 - \kappa_0)(A_p - \mu_A).$$

Consequently, if $\kappa_1 = \kappa_0$, the "treatment effect" (differential incrementation between the two alternative interventions) does not depend on individual characteristics and is therefore the same for all individuals. (Note that only $\kappa_1 = \kappa_0$, not $\kappa_1 = \kappa_0 = 0$, is required.) When $\kappa_1 \neq \kappa_0$ the differential effect between membership in the treatment and control groups depends on the individual characteristic (aptitude) A. The situation $\kappa_1 \neq \kappa_0$ is consistent with the common interpretation of the term "interaction," where the interaction is between group membership and aptitude. (That use of the term interaction would be most familiar in the simple case in which A_p were dichotomous (e.g., presence or absence of a skill; high/low ability split).

The average treatment effect (or differential for a person of *average* aptitude) is:

$$\eta_1 - \eta_0 + (\kappa_1 - \kappa_0)\mu_A = \beta_{\delta G}. \tag{6}$$

If $\kappa_1 \neq \kappa_0$ this average differential will change for populations or subpopulations having different μ_A. The artificial data example in section 5.2 provides additional discussion of these parameters with explicit numerical examples.

The increment δ is specified to be in the same metric as Y; thus, η is also in the same metric as Y, and κ is in units of Y/A. Any scale or translation transformations of A can be absorbed in η and κ. It's convenient to think of A as having mean zero and unit variance; for full generality this restriction will not be used in stating the results of Part II.

To complete this representation of the effect of the intervention, it is necessary to specify the quantity that δ_p increments. That is, given a δ_p, there are alternative answers to the question, What is the effect of the intervention? In this presentation, two types of incrementation will be considered: increment directly to the status on the outcome measure (Y), and increment to parameters of the natural maturation model. Specifically, the following combinations of the individual growth models and incrementation resulting from the intervention are studied:

(i)   Straight-line growth (Equation 2) with increment to status
(ii) Asymptotic exponential growth (Equation 4) with increment to status
(iii) Asymptotic exponential growth (Equation 4) with increment to asymptote ("learning potential" parameter) λ_p.

In Part II these combinations are used to explore what the standard ATI regression analyses can reveal about individual differences in response to the intervention.

3.   Complete Representation of an ATI Study

The chronology of an ATI study, as depicted in Fig. 9.1, provides a convenient scaffolding for the use of the models for maturation and for response to interven-

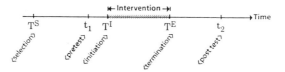

FIG. 9.1.   Temporal representation of an ATI study.

tion. The time of selection T^S marks the division of the full sample into the two groups, treatment and control. The selection may be by random assignment of individuals, or by some systematic (or even haphazard) assignment of individuals, or even by assignment of intact classrooms to the two groups. At t_1 marks the time of initial measurement (often termed the pretest). The time t_1 measurements may be obtained on the outcome Y or on some exogenous individual characteristic X. (For the depiction in Fig. 9.1, T^S is shown to precede t_1; the mathematical results do allow T^S and t_1 to coincide or for t_1 to precede T^S, but for convenience the temporal ordering of Fig. 9.1 is adopted.) T^I marks the time at which the intervention for both treatment and control groups (e.g., two different curricula or types of instruction) is initiated, and T^E marks the time at which the intervention ends. Thus, the effects of the intervention occur between T^I and T^E. Finally, t_2 marks the time of measurement of the outcome following the end of the intervention (often termed posttest). For notational convenience observations on Y for individual p at the discrete times t_1 and t_2 are written as Y_{1p} and Y_{2p}.

The effects of the intervention are usually treated as occurring in a "black box": there being no attempt to model, or to otherwise investigate, exactly how or when the intervention affects the individual. Researchers have not explicitly considered questions such as, Are the effects of the intervention instantaneous (at some time between T^I and T^E)? Or more plausibly, Are the effects gradual (spread out between times T^I and T^E or perhaps beyond)? And, if so, do these effects accrue uniformly, or at rates that vary over the interval? Through the combination of the representation of δ_p in (5) with the models for individual growth, an attempt is made to open this "black box," even if just a smidgen.

This formulation linking maturation and effects of intervention is close in spirit to "value-added analysis" developed by Bryk and Weisberg (for example, see Bryk & Weisberg, 1976). Also, expositions of time-series intervention experiments enumerate of various forms for the effects of an intervention (see Glass, Willson, & Gottman, 1975, Chapter 3, especially Figure 17.)

Straight-line Growth with Increment to Status.   Figure 9.2 shows the representation for straight-line growth with increment to status for a single individual. In the Figure, the incrementation to status is shown to occur instantaneously at a time half way between T^I and T^E. (Without measurements in the interval [T^I, T^E], such an incrementation is indistinguishable from one of the same magnitude

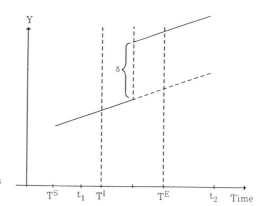

FIG. 9.2. Increment to status
with straight-line growth.

at some other instant or from an equivalent gradual incrementation to status
during the entire interval of the intervention.) For measurements at times t_1 and
t_2, where the value of Y_{1p} is determined by (4) evaluated at $t = t_1$, the combination of the growth model and the effect of intervention can be written:

$$Y_{2p} = Y_{1p} + \pi_p(t_2 - t_1) + \delta_p \qquad \text{(for } t_2 > T^E\text{)}. \qquad (7)$$

and the difference between the mean outcomes in the treatment and control
groups is:

$$\beta_{Y_2G} = \eta_1 - \eta_0 + (\kappa_1 - \kappa_0)\mu_A$$

which equals $\beta_{\delta G}$ in (6).

Incrementing the rate of change π_p is essentially equivalent to incrementing
status and will not be considered separately. That is, consider an instantaneous
increment of δ_p to π_p occuring at some time between T^I and T^E denoted here by
T^*. This incrementation to the rate translates into an increment of $\delta_p(t - T^*)$ to
$Y(t)$, which makes individual differences in the two incrementations equivalent,
as can be easily seen by substitution.

Exponential Growth with Increment to Status.   Figure 9.3 shows a representation of exponential growth towards an asymptote with an increment to status
occurring in the interval $[T^I, T^E]$, but with no effect of the intervention on the
asymptote, λ_p. For each individual, status is incremented instantaneously at a time
between T^I and T^E. The symbol τ is used in Fig. 9.3 to indicate the time interval
between the instantaneous incrementation and t_2, the time of posttest. (A gradual
increment to status throughout the interval $[T^I, T^E]$ would yield just slightly
different results.) This type of incrementation serves to decrease dY/dt after time
$t_2 - \tau$ producing a local change to the level of $Y(t)$ that tends to wear off.

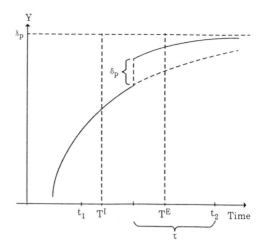

FIG. 9.3. Increment to status
with exponential growth.

For measurements at times t_1 and t_2, where Y_{1p} is determined by (4) evaluated at $t = t_1$, the combination of the individual growth curve with the effect of the intervention yields:

$$Y_{2p} = \lambda_p - (\lambda_p - Y_{1p})\exp[-\gamma(t_2 - t_1)] + \delta_p\exp(-\gamma\tau) \qquad (8)$$

From (8) the difference between the mean outcomes in the treatment and control groups is:

$$\beta_{Y2G} = [\eta_1 - \eta_0 + (\kappa_1 - \kappa_0)\mu_A]\exp(-\gamma\tau),$$

which is always less than $\bar{\beta}_{\delta G}$ in (6). A consequence of the increment to status without any change in the asymptote is that the difference between the group means on Y_2 decreases as τ increases (t_2 more distant from the occurrence of the incrementation to status).

Exponential Growth with Increment to Asymptote. Figure 9.4 shows an alternative representation for the effect of the intervention when natural maturation follows the growth curve in (4). The effect of the intervention is to increment λ_p, the asymptote for individual p. This form of representation serves to increase dY/dt with no local or immediate incrementation to $Y(t)$. In Fig. 9.4 this incrementation is shown to occur instantaneously at a time between T^I and T^E, with τ indicating the interval between the time of incrementation and t_2. For measurements at times t_1 and t_2, where Y_{1p} is determined by (4) evaluated at $t = t_1$, the combination of individual maturation and the incrementation to λ_p yields:

$$Y_{2p} = \lambda_p - (\lambda_p - Y_{1p})[\exp(-\gamma(t_2 - t_1)] + \delta_p[1 - \exp(-\gamma\tau)] \qquad (9)$$

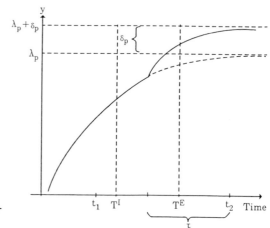

FIG. 9.4. Increment to asymptote with exponential growth.

From (9) the difference between the mean outcomes in the treatment and control groups is:

$$\beta_{Y_2G} = [\eta_1 - \eta_0 + (\kappa_1 - \kappa_0)\mu_A][1 - \exp(-\gamma\tau)],$$

which is less than $\beta_{\delta G}$ in (6). In contrast to (8) the difference between the group means on Y_2 is larger as t_2 is more distant from the occurrence of the incrementation.

PART II: RECONSIDERING TRADITIONAL ATI
REGRESSION ANALYSES

4. Conventional ATI Analyses

The conventional statistical analysis of ATI studies is a comparison of the within-group conditional expectations of outcome on initial status for the treatment and control groups. In studies in which the initial characteristic is a prior measure on the outcome variable Y, the data are Y_2 and Y_1, measures of Y at time 2 (posttest) and time 1 (pretest), respectively, and the within-group regressions are

$$\begin{aligned} Y_2 &= \alpha_1 + \beta_1 Y_1 + \epsilon && \text{(for treatment)} \\ Y_2 &= \alpha_0 + \beta_0 Y_1 + \epsilon && \text{(for control)} \end{aligned} \qquad (10)$$

Using the group membership variable G (G_p is 1 if individual p is a member of the treatment group, and G_p is 0 if individual p is a member of the control group) the within-group regressions in (10) can be written as a single equation:

$$Y_2 = \theta_0 + \theta_1 G + \theta_2 Y_1 + \theta_3 GY_1 + \epsilon \qquad (11)$$

For either version of the regression model, interest centers on (a) the difference between the slopes of the within-group regressions (as a non-zero difference is the common condition for an ATI to exist) and (b) values of initial status for which the within-group regressions differ (i.e., the Johnson-Neyman region of significance). The difference between the within-group regression slopes is $\beta_1 - \beta_0 = \theta_3$, and the difference between the conditional expectations (regression functions) is $\Delta(Y_1) = \theta_1 + \theta_3 Y_1$; $\Delta(Y_1)$ can be thought of as representing the "treatment effect" as a function of initial standing, Y_1 (Rogosa, 1980).

The abscissa of the point of intersection of the within-group regressions in (10) is the Y_1 value for which $\Delta(Y_1) = 0$ which is $-\theta_1/\theta_3$. This value is often thought of as a *cutting score* for determining instructional placement; see Figure 2.3 in Cronbach and Snow (1977). For θ_3 greater than zero, individuals with Y_1 values greater than $-\theta_1/\theta_3$ have greater expected outcome in the treatment group, and individuals with Y_1 values less than $-\theta_1/\theta_3$ have greater expected outcome in the control group. For θ_3 less than zero, these conditions are reversed.

In empirical research, estimation of these model parameters is necessary. Interval estimates of θ_3 indicate the magnitude of the ATI, and interval estimates of $-\theta_1/\theta_3$ define the complement of the Johnson-Neyman region of significance. Cronbach and Snow (1977, Chaps. 2, 3, 4) present the conventional statistical methods for ATI studies. Rogosa (1980) presents similar methods for making inferences about treatment effects as a function of the premeasures (e.g., $\Delta(Y_1)$).

The Y_2 on Y_1 within-group regressions in equation (10) have a natural interpretation in terms of the amount of gain $D = Y_2 - Y_1$ between times 1 and 2. The well-known relation $\beta_{DY_1} = \beta_{Y_2Y_1} - 1$ implies that $\Delta(Y_1)$ is unchanged if the outcome Y_2 is replaced by $Y_2 - Y_1$. Thus, an ATI analysis using Y_2 as outcome and Y_1 as initial status will yield the same results as an ATI analysis using $Y_2 - Y_1$ as the outcome. Another implication is that a difference between the within-group regressions in (10) can be interpreted as indicating that the regression of change on initial status differs in the treatment and control groups.

The measure of initial status (or ability) is not always a prior measure on the outcome variable. In terms of a general (assumed unchanging over time) individual characteristic X, equations (10) and (11) can be rewritten:

$$\begin{aligned} Y_2 &= \alpha_1 + \beta_1 X + \epsilon \qquad \text{(for treatment)} \\ Y_2 &= \alpha_0 + \beta_0 X + \epsilon \qquad \text{(for control)} \end{aligned} \qquad (12)$$

or

$$Y_2 = \theta_0 + \theta_1 G + \theta_2 X + \theta_3 GX + \epsilon \qquad (13)$$

Values of the parameters in equations (12) and (13) will not be the same as those in equations (10) and (11), to the extent that an ATI may exist for Y_1 as premeasure but not for X as premeasure, or vice versa. The difference between the within-group Y_2 on X regressions as a function of X is $\Delta(X) = \theta_1 + \theta_3 X$ (in terms of equation 13). Cronbach and Snow (1977, pp. 73–75) demonstrated that the difference between the within-group regression slopes is not altered if the outcome measure, Y_2, in (12) is replaced by the gain, $Y_2 - Y_1$. Although results here will be limited to a single X or Y_1 as the measure of initial status, in applications the use of multiple X's, or one or more X's in conjunction with Y_1, is common.

5. Random Assignment with the Maturation-Incrementation Models

In this section, the formation of the treatment and control groups is by random assignment of individuals at time T^S. Following sections examine the consequences of each of the three combinations of a model for individual maturation and a model for effects of the intervention (see Equations 7, 8, and 9). Properties of the quantities central to standard ATI analyses are scrutinized within each of these combinations. For each of the measures of initial status (A, X, or Y_1), three quantities are presented:

i. the difference between the within-group regression slopes (as a statistical test that this difference is zero is used to indicate an ATI),

ii. the vertical distance between the within-group conditional expectations (as the confidence band for this indicates the Johnson-Neyman region of significance)

iii. the abscissa of the point of intersection of the within-group regressions (the estimate of which is often used as a cutting score if a disordinal interaction is found).

The key question that these results address is: Do the traditional ATI analyses work (i.e., yield dependable results) under these maturation-incrementation models? More specific questions that follow are: What are the consequences of the choice of the initial status measure (e.g., A, X, or Y_1)? What are the implications of the different models for individual maturation and effects of the intervention for improved ATI analyses?

Straight-line Growth

From the specification of straight-line growth and increment to status, as represented in Equation 7, explicit results are obtained for ATI analyses using A, X, or Y_1 as the measure for initial status.

A as Initial Status.   The aptitude is identified by A (specified by the model in Equation 5 as the "right" measure of aptitude). Results for the use of A as a measure of initial status are a useful benchmark for comparison with the results for ATI analyses in which either Y_1 or X is used as the measure of initial status. The difference between the within-group Y_2 on A regression slopes is:

$$\kappa_1 - \kappa_0, \tag{14}$$

which recovers the interaction built into Equation 5 (the differential between the treatment and control groups in individual differences in response to intervention). The simplicity of this result is pleasing and surprising. For instance, the difference between the within-group regression slopes has no dependence on σ_π^2, the amount of individual differences in growth, or on any other properties of the collection of straight-line growth curves that control the time 1, time 2 correlations.

The vertical distance between the within-group Y_2 on A regression functions is:

$$\Delta(A) = (\eta_1 - \eta_0) + (\kappa_1 - \kappa_0)A \tag{15}$$

And the abscissa of the point of intersection of the Y_2 on A within-group regressions is:

$$\frac{\eta_0 - \eta_1}{\kappa_1 - \kappa_0} \tag{16}$$

Thus, individuals with A_p values greater than (16) have greater expected outcome in the treatment group than in the control group (providing $\kappa_1 > \kappa_0$).

X as Initial Status.   In empirical research, investigators may not be able to identify the trait A precisely, or not be able to obtain accurate measures of A for the individuals in the ATI study. It may be useful to think of the individual characteristic X as a fallible and not completely valid measure of A. The difference between the within-group Y_2 on X regression slopes (the parameter θ_3 in Equation 13) is:

$$(\kappa_1 - \kappa_0)\beta_{AX} \tag{17}$$

Expressions 14 and 17 differ by the factor β_{AX}. If X and A are related by a classical test theory model, then β_{AX} is the reliability of X, and the consequence of using X instead of A is the attenuation of the interaction.

The vertical distance between the within-group regressions as a function of X is:

$$\Delta(X) = [(\eta_1 - \eta_0) + (\kappa_1 - \kappa_0)\mu_A] + (\kappa_1 - \kappa_0)\beta_{AX}(X - \mu_X). \tag{18}$$

Note that $\Delta(\mu_X)$ in (18) equals $\Delta(\mu_A)$ in (15). The abscissa of the point of intersection of the within-group regressions in (12) is:

$$\mu_X - \frac{1}{\beta_{AX}} \left[\mu_A + \frac{\eta_1 - \eta_0}{\kappa_1 - \kappa_0} \right] \tag{19}$$

Certain similarities between (19) and (16) emerge upon closer examination. Denote the value in (16) as A* and the value in (19) as X* to obtain:

$$\frac{X^* - \mu_X}{\sigma_X} = \frac{1}{\rho_{AX}} \frac{[A^* - \mu_A]}{\sigma_A}$$

Thus, except for the factor ρ_{AX}, X* is scale-translation equivalent to A* in the sense that X* would be the same number of standard deviations above or below its mean as A* with respect to its mean. The factor ρ_{AX} will serve to make X* farther (in standard deviation units) from its mean than is A*.

Another implication of (19) is seen by considering X to be a fallible measure of A by a classical test theory model with reliability $\rho(X) = \beta_{AX}$. For this particular case (19) with X as initial status yields an interesting relation with (16) for A as the initial status:

$$A^* = \rho(X)X^* + (1 - \rho(X))\mu_X$$

which implies that X* is always further away from the mean $\mu_X = \mu_A$ than is A*. (That is, A* is between X* and the mean.) Rogosa (1977, Equation 3.19) also finds this result (without consideration of models for maturation or incrementation).

Y₁ as Initial Status. The difference between the within-group Y_2 on Y_1 regression slopes (represented by θ_3 in 11) is

$$(\kappa_1 - \kappa_0)\beta_{AY_1}. \tag{20}$$

The vertical distance between the within-group regressions as a function of the initial status Y_1 is

$$\Delta(Y_1) = [(\eta_1 - \eta_0) + (\kappa_1 - \kappa_0)\mu_A] + (\kappa_1 - \kappa_0)\beta_{AY_1}(Y_1 - \mu_{Y_1}),$$

and $\Delta(\mu_{Y_1}) = \Delta(\mu_A)$. The abscissa of the point of intersection of the within-group regressions is:

$$\mu_{Y_1} - \frac{1}{\beta_{AY_1}} \left[\mu_A + \frac{\eta_1 - \eta_0}{\kappa_1 - \kappa_0} \right] \tag{22}$$

With Y_1 as the measure of initial status, (20, (21), and (22) indicate that the results of an ATI analysis depend on β_{AY_1}. Furthermore, the value of β_{AY_1} depends on both the configuration of the individual straight-line growth curves and, most important, upon the choice of t_1, the time at which initial status on Y is measured. In the Appendix $\beta_{AY(t)}$ is expressed as a function of time, and this result indicates that the difference between the within-group Y_2 on Y_1 regression slopes may, depending upon the time chosen to be t_1, differ in magnitude, and even in sign, from $\kappa_1 - \kappa_0$. Thus, the use of Y_1 as the measure of initial status appears to have more severe consequences for ATI analyses than does the use of an unchanging individual characteristic X.

ATI Analyses of Artificial Data for Straight-line Growth

We use numerical examples and analyses of artificial data to illustrate the consequences of the formulation of models for maturation and response to intervention for conventional ATI data analyses. The description of the analysis of artificial data consists of construction of the individual increments in response to the intervention, construction of the measures of outcome and initial status and results of ATI analyses using A, X, or Y_1 as the measure of initial status.

Parametric Structure of Group Differences. The value of the individual increment in response to intervention δ_p is determined from (5). For the population of individuals let A have mean 40 and variance 123. For the treatment and control groups the parameters in (5) for this example are: $\eta_0 = 16.0$, $\kappa_0 = 0.2$, $\eta_1 = 4.0$, and $\kappa_1 = 0.6$. For the artificial data we use 100 individuals in each group. Individual values of δ_p can be computed once the individual's value on the aptitude A is given. Thus the incrementation is greater in Group 0 (control) for individuals with $A_p < 30$ (about one standard deviation below the mean of A). For an individual with $A_p = \mu_A$, the incrementation in Group 1 is 28 in Group 1 and 24 in Group 0. Or from (6) the average group difference in incrementation is $-12 + .4(40) = 4.0$ (in favor of Group 1).

These parameter values also define the following population quantities for an ATI analysis using A as the aptitude measure. According to (14) the difference between the within-group Y_2 on A regression slopes is $0.6 - 0.2 = 0.4$. Also, from (15) the vertical distance between the within-group regressions is $\Delta(A) = -12 + .4A$. From (16) the abscissa of the point of intersection of the within-group regressions is $12/.4 = 30.0$.

Outcome measures. The outcome measure Y_2 is the value of $Y(t)$ at $t = t_2$ from (2) plus the increment δ from the intervention (see Equation 7). In these examples $Y(t)$ contains no error of measurement; individual differences result from individual differences in the parameters of the growth model. For these examples the parameters of the growth curves have the values, $t^0 = 3$, $\mu_\pi = 5$, $\sigma_\pi^2 = 4.87$, $\mu_{Y(3)}$ and $\sigma_{Y(3)}^2 = 43.8$. Furthermore, values of A were constrained to have specific correlations with the parameters of the maturation model and thus with $Y(t)$; in particular, $\rho_{A\pi} = .7$ and $\rho_{AY(3)} = .6$. The difference between the mean outcomes in the treatment and control groups is 4.0, regardless of the value of t_2. (This identity between group differences in Y and in δ is a consequence of straight-line growth and would not hold for exponential growth.)

Measures of initial status. Values of X are obtained by adding "measurement error" to A; that is, the individual characteristic $X_p = A_p + u_p$, where u is Gaussian with mean 0 and variance 30.75. These values indicate the reliability of X to be .80. For this construction of X, the difference between the regression slopes has the population value given in (17); .80(.4) = .32. The intersection point given in (19) has the value .40 − (10/.80) = 27.5. Values of Y_1 for each individual are determined by the parameters (π and Y(0)) of the individual growth curve (2) and the choice of t_1.

Theoretical results. Table 9.1 displays the population values of quantities relevant to ATI analyses for choice of initial status A, X, or $Y(t_1)$. Note that for straight-line maturation the difference between the within-group regression slopes and the intersection point are independent of the choice of t_2. The results for the use of $Y(t_1)$ as the initial status diverge strongly from the use of A. The best way to interpret the results for $Y(t_1)$ is by reference to the mean of that $Y(t_1)$ distribution.

Analyses of Artificial Data. Given the choices of t_1 and t_2 the ATI regression analyses can be carried out with $Y(t_2)$ as outcome and either A, X, or $Y(t_1)$ as the measure of initial status. Table 9.2 reports the estimated difference between the within-group regression slopes and the associated standard error, the estimate of the abscissa of the point of intersection, and the Johnson-Neyman simultaneous region of significance for the indicated $[t_1,t_2]$ pairings. The analyses using A or X as initial status are reported for $t_2 = 2$; similar results are obtained for the other t_2 values. The sample quantities are close to the values specified by the model parameters from Table 9.1. The results for $Y(t_1)$ as initial status show pronounced departures from the results obtained from use of A. The difference

TABLE 9.1
Theoretical Values for Numerical Examples

			Measure of Initial Status			
Quantity	A	X	Y(0)	Y(1)	Y(2)	Y(3)
Mean	40	40	35	40	45	50
Variance	123	154	87.6	63.3	48.7	43.8
Difference Between Slopes	.40	.32	-.036	.062	.22	.40
Intersection Point	30	27.5	154	-24.7	26.9	40.7

TABLE 9.2
ATI Analyses of Artificial Data

Sample Quantity	A	X	Initial Status Y[0,2]	Y[1,4]	Y[2,4]	Y[3,5]
Differences Between Slopes	.40 (.079)	.347 (.078)	-.057 (.12)	.071 (.17)	.218 (.19)	.38 (.16)
Intersection Point	30	28.1	104	-29.6	26.7	37.6
95% J-N Simultaneous Region	A<17.8 A>36.1	X<11 X>35	Y(0)<40 Y(0)>23	Y(1)<51 Y(1)>33	Y(2)<57 Y(2)>42	Y(3)<317 Y(3)>46

between the within-group regression slopes may or may not be statistically significant depending on the choice of t_1 and t_2. Moreover, the estimate of the cutting score may be well above or well below the mean of $Y(t_1)$ even though the intersection point for A is approximately one standard deviation below the mean. And the region of significance will indicate very different interpretations depending on the choice of the measure of initial status.

Exponential Growth with Increment to Status

The combination of the exponential growth model for individual maturation and increment to status is given in (8) and depicted in Fig. 9.3. As was done for straight-line growth, results are presented for A, X, or Y_1 as the measure of initial status.

A as Initial Status. With A as the measure of initial status, the difference between the within-group Y_2 on A regression slopes is:

$$(\kappa_1 - \kappa_0)\exp(-\gamma\tau) \tag{23}$$

Thus even with A as initial status, the ATI is diminished by the factor $\exp(-\gamma\tau)$ as a result of the different properties of straight-line and exponential growth. This factor has a stronger influence the longer the interval between the intervention and the posttest. The vertical distance between the within-group regressions as a function of A is:

$$\Delta(A) = [(\eta_1 - \eta_0) + (\kappa_1 - \kappa_0)A]\exp(-\gamma\tau). \tag{24}$$

And the abscissa of the point of intersection of the within-group regressions is:

$$\frac{\eta_0 - \eta_1}{\kappa_1 - \kappa_0} \tag{25}$$

which is identical to (16) for straight-line growth. Thus the population value of the cutting score is not affected by the different model of maturation (i.e., exponential rather than straight-line).

X as Initial Status.   The difference between the within-group Y_2 on X regression slopes is:

$$(\kappa_1 - \kappa_0)\beta_{AX} \exp(-\gamma\tau). \tag{26}$$

The vertical distance between the within-group Y_2 on X regressions is:

$$\Delta(X) = \exp(-\gamma\tau)[\eta_1 - \eta_0 + (\kappa_1 - \kappa_0)\mu_A \\ + (\kappa_1 - \kappa_0)\beta_{AX}(X - \mu_X)]. \tag{27}$$

Thus (26) and (27) differ from (17) and (18) for straight-line growth by this factor $\exp(-\gamma\tau)$. The relation $\Delta(\mu_X) = \Delta(\mu_A)$ also holds for exponential growth with increment to status. The abscissa of the point of intersection of the within-group regressions is:

$$\mu_X - \frac{1}{\beta_{AX}}\left[\mu_A + \frac{\eta_1 - \eta_0}{\kappa_1 - \kappa_0}\right]. \tag{28}$$

Expression (28) is identical to the result in (19) for straight-line growth. Thus the choice of the measure of initial status, but not the form of maturation, influences the intersection point. The comparison of results for A and X following (19) is germane.

Y_1 as Initial Status.   The difference between the within-group Y_2 on Y_1 regression slopes is:

$$(\kappa_1 - \kappa_0)\beta_{AY_1}[\exp(-\gamma\tau)]. \tag{29}$$

The vertical distance between the within-group regressions as a function of initial status on Y_1 is:

$$\Delta(Y_1) = \exp(-\gamma\tau)[\eta_1 - \eta_0 + (\kappa_1 - \kappa_0)\mu_A \\ + (\kappa_1 - \kappa_0)\beta_{AY_1}(Y_1 - \mu_{Y_1})] \tag{30}$$

Expressions (29) and (30) differ from the results for straight-line growth in two respects: (i) the multiplicative factor $\exp(-\gamma\tau)$, and (ii) the somewhat different dependence of β_{AY_1} on the choice of t_1 for asymptotic exponential growth. The factor $\exp(-\gamma\tau)$ causes the difference between the within-group slopes to decrease as τ (the time between the effect of intervention and t_2) increases. The Appendix gives the exact form of the dependence of β_{AY_1} on the time that is chosen to be t_1.

And the abscissa of the point of intersection of the within-group Y_2 on Y_1 within-group regressions is

$$\mu_{Y_1} - \frac{1}{\beta_{AY_1}}\left[\mu_A + \frac{\eta_1 - \eta_0}{\kappa_1 - \kappa_0}\right] \tag{31}$$

Expression (31) has the same form as (22), differing only by different properties of β_{AY_1} for the two types of growth curves.

Exponential Growth with Increment to Asymptote

When the effect of the intervention is an increment to the asymptote as in (9) and Fig. 9.4 instead of an increment to status as in (8) and Fig. 9.3, the results are altered by the replacement of the multiplicative factor $\exp(-\gamma\tau)$ by $[1 - \exp(-\gamma\tau)]$. Thus for incrementation to asymptote the magnitude of the effect increases as the time between the effect of the intervention and t_2 increases. For increment to status in the previous section, the effect decreases as the time between the effect of the intervention and t_2 increases. This difference between the two types of incrementation can be understood by thinking of an increment to status without altering the asymptote (learning potential) as a kind of quick fix whose effects gradually decay, whereas an increment to the asymptote has (increasing) long-term impact.

A as Initial Status.   The difference between the within-group regression slopes is:

$$(\kappa_1 - \kappa_0)[1 - \exp(-\gamma\tau)]. \tag{32}$$

Thus even with A as the initial status, the magnitude of the ATI depends on whether asymptote or status is incremented (compare 32 and 23). Also the ATI is less than that for straight-line growth (compare with 14).

The vertical distance between the within-group regressions is:

$$\Delta(A) = [1 - \exp(-\gamma\tau)][\eta_1 - \eta_0 + (\kappa_1 - \kappa_0)A]. \tag{33}$$

And the abscissa of the point of intersection of the within-group regressions is:

$$\frac{\eta_0 - \eta_1}{\kappa_1 - \kappa_0}. \tag{34}$$

which is identical to (25) and (16). Thus the intersection point is not affected by the different growth model or the form of incrementation.

X as Measure of Initial Status.   The difference between the within-group Y_2 on X regression slopes is:

$$(\kappa_1 - \kappa_0)\beta_{AX}[1 - \exp(-\gamma\tau)]. \tag{35}$$

The vertical distance between the within-group regressions as a function of X is:

$$\Delta(X) = [1 - \exp(-\gamma\tau)][\eta_1 - \eta_0 + (\kappa_1 - \kappa_0)\mu_A \\ + (\kappa_1 - \kappa_0)\beta_{AX}(X - \mu_X)]. \tag{36}$$

And the abscissa of the point of intersection of the within-group regressions is:

$$\mu_X - \frac{1}{\beta_{AX}}\left[\mu_A + \frac{\eta_1 - \eta_0}{\kappa_1 - \kappa_0}\right], \tag{37}$$

which is identical to (28) and (19). Thus with X as the measure of initial status the intersection point is unaffected by the form of the incrementation.

Y_1 *as Measure of Initial Status.*   The difference between the within-group Y_2 and Y_1 regression slopes is:

$$(\kappa_1 - \kappa_0)\beta_{AY_1}[1 - \exp(-\gamma\tau)]. \tag{38}$$

The vertical distance between the within-group regressions as a function of Y_1 is:

$$\Delta(Y_1) = [1 - \exp(-\gamma\tau)][\eta_1 - \eta_0 + (\kappa_1 - \kappa_0)\mu_A \\ + (\kappa_1 - \kappa_0)\beta_{AY_1}(Y_1 - \mu_{Y_1})]. \tag{39}$$

And the abscissa of the point of intersection of the within-group regressions is:

$$\mu_{Y_1} - \frac{1}{\beta_{AY_1}}\left[\mu_A + \frac{\eta_1 - \eta_0}{\kappa_1 - \kappa_0}\right], \tag{40}$$

which is identical to (31). Thus the population value of the cutting score on Y_1 is not affected by the different form of the incrementation.

Results for Exponential Growth with Hybrid Incrementation

In the two previous sections, the intervention was presumed to produce the same type of incrementation (increment to status or increment to asymptote) for both treatment and control groups. In contrast, it can also be specified that in one group, say treatment, the effect of the intervention is to increment the asymptote whereas in the control group the effect of the intervention is to increment status but with no change in the asymptote. That is, δ_p remains defined by (5), but for individuals with $G_p = 1$ incrementation follows (9), whereas for individuals with $G_p = 0$ incrementation follows (8). (Of course, this hybrid construction is simply a special case of a more general model allowing incrementation to both status and asymptote in each group.) In this hybrid construction there appears a kind of *qualitative* difference between the effects in the treatment and control groups in addition to allowing for quantitative differences (represented by the different values of η and κ for the two groups). An informal interpretation of this hybrid incrementation might be that instruction for the treatment group produces long-term effects for achievement (raises learning potential) whereas the instruction for the control group provides a quick fix of increment to status but no change in learning potential.

For A as the measure of initial status, the difference between the within-group Y_2 on A regression slopes is:

$$\kappa_1 - (\kappa_1 + \kappa_0)\exp(-\gamma\tau). \tag{41}$$

Problems with the traditional methods are indicated by (41). Even when measures on A are available, an ATI will be indicated by the conventional regression models even with $\kappa_1 = \kappa_0$ (i.e., no interaction). The vertical distance between the within-group regressions as a function of A is:

$$\Delta(A) = \eta_1 + \kappa_1 A - [\exp(-\gamma\tau)][\eta_1 + \eta_0 + (\kappa_1 + \kappa_0)A] \tag{42}$$

And the abscissa of the point of intersection of the within-group regressions is:

$$\frac{[\exp(-\gamma\tau)](\eta_1 + \eta_0) - \eta_1}{\kappa_1 - [\exp(-\gamma\tau)](\kappa_1 + \kappa_0)}. \tag{43}$$

Only for the fortuitous value of .50 for $\exp(-\gamma\tau)$ will this point of intersection be the same as (16), (25), and (34). This hybrid model, unlike the three matched forms of incrementation in (7), (8), and (9), yields results in which the population value of the cutting score with A as initial status is affected by the form of incrementation or maturation.

With Y_1 as the measure of initial status, the difference between the within-group regression slopes is:

$$\beta_{AY_1}[\kappa_1 - (\kappa_1 + \kappa_0)\exp(-\gamma\tau)], \tag{44}$$

with β_{AY_1} given in the Appendix. Results for the use of X instead of Y_1 differ only by substitution of β_{AX} for β_{AY_1} in (44).

The results obtained from this hybrid incrementation have less benign implications for ATI analyses than earlier results. The results for this hybrid incrementation emphasize that the form of the incrementation resulting from the intervention may have important consequences. Such considerations have not yet received attention in ATI research.

6. Nonrandom Assignment of Individuals

When individuals are assigned to the treatment and control groups by a nonrandom mechanism (haphazard or systematic), the assessment of individual differences in response to the intervention is far more difficult than with random assignment. Even the assessment of mean differences (main effects) using adjustment procedures such as analysis of covariance is nearly impossible without the use of precise information on the mechanism by which individuals are assigned to groups (see, Cronbach, Rogosa, Floden, & Price, 1977; Cronbach, 1983; Weisberg, 1979). The results of this section use the models for individual maturation and response to intervention to indicate some of the consequences of non-random assignment for ATI analyses.

At T^S (time of selection) in Fig. 9.1, individuals are assigned to the treatment and control groups. If assignment is non-random, the two groups can no longer be considered equivalent. In fact, the groups may differ on many attributes. The superscripts (1) and (0) are used to denote within-group moments for treatment and control groups, respectively. In particular, the mean aptitude may differ in the two groups; $\mu_A^{(1)}$ and $\mu_A^{(0)}$ denote the mean aptitudes in the treatment and control groups, respectively. Consequently, for non-random assignment, the average differential between the increments in the two groups is:

$$\beta_{\delta G} = \mu_\delta^{(1)} - \mu_\delta^{(0)} = (\eta_1 - \eta_0) + \kappa_1 \mu_A^{(1)} - \kappa_0 \mu_A^{(0)} \tag{45}$$

Equation 6 is obtained if the mean of A is the same in the two groups.

Group Mean Differences with Straight-line Maturation

For straight-line growth with increment to status, the difference between the group means on Y_2 is:

$$\beta_{Y_2 G} = \beta_{Y_1 G} + \beta_{\delta G} + (t_2 - t_1)\beta_{\pi G} \tag{46}$$

Thus the difference between the group means on Y_2 depends on three terms. For random assignment of individuals both $\beta_{Y_1 G}$ and $\beta_{\pi G}$ are zero because of the equivalence (on the average) between treatment and control groups prior to the intervention.

Of special import is consideration of pretest equivalence. A common strategy in empirical research is to obtain reassurance about the validity of an analysis comparing two nonequivalent groups from a finding that the means on some initial characteristic(s) do not differ (significantly) across the two groups. Pretest-equivalence is not enough for comparability; that is, pretest equivalence is not an adequate justification for the comparison of group means on Y_2. As can be seen from (46), even if pretest equivalence holds, a nonzero value of $\beta_{\pi G}$ will cause the difference of outcome means to be affected by the nonequivalence of the groups.

Slope Differences with A as Initial Status and Straight-line Maturation

For nonequivalent groups the difference between the Y_2 on A within-groups regression slopes can be written:

$$\kappa_1 - \kappa_0 + [\beta_{Y_1A}^{(1)} - \beta_{Y_1A}^{(0)}] + (t_2 - t_1)[\beta_{\pi A}^{(1)} - \beta_{\pi A}^{(0)}]. \quad (47)$$

Thus the difference between the within-group regressions, even with A as the measure of initial status, is greatly affected by characteristics of the nonequivalence between the groups. In particular, (47) differs from $\kappa_1 - \kappa_0$ according to how the regression slopes of Y_1 on A or π on A differ between the groups. Both of these slopes for each group are determined before the initiation of the intervention. Note especially that an equivalence between the groups on μ_A (or any other initial characteristic) does nothing to mitigate the factors causing (47) to differ from $\kappa_1 - \kappa_0$. Thus pretest equivalence should provide no particular solace to ATI researchers forced to work with nonequivalent groups. Moreover, the abscissa of the point of intersection of the within-group regressions is such a complex combination of the characteristics of the nonequivalence between the groups that no useful conclusions about the direction or magnitudes of the effects of the nonequivalence can be drawn even in the case of pretest equivalence.

Slope Differences with Y_1 as Initial Status and Straight-line Maturation

Slightly different results hold for Y_1 as the measure of initial status, but the general conclusions are similar. The difference between the regression slopes of the Y_2 on Y_1 within-group regressions is:

$$\kappa_1\beta_{AY_1}^{(1)} - \kappa_0\beta_{AY_1}^{(0)} + (t_2 - t_1)[\beta_{\pi Y_1}^{(1)} - \beta_{\pi Y_1}^{(0)}] \quad (48)$$

Thus the ATI obtained from the use of Y_1 as initial status also depends on characteristics of the non-equivalence between the groups: namely, the relations among A, Y_1, and π prior to the initiation of the intervention. Results for the use of X as initial status are obtained by substituting X for Y_1 in (48).

7. ATI Analyses for Individuals in Intact Classrooms

In ATI studies of classroom instruction, intact classrooms rather than individuals are assigned to the treatment and control groups. Most importantly, it is not usually appropriate for the ATI analysis to ignore the classroom membership of the individual student, as individuals within a classroom have shared experiences and effects unique to their particular classroom membership (Cronbach, 1976; Cronbach & Snow, 1977; Cronbach & Webb, 1975). Moreover, the hierarchical structure of individuals within classrooms requires a more complex conceptualization of ATI effects than when individuals are considered in isolation. According to Cronbach and Webb (1975):

Aptitude X Treatment interaction effects may arise from the individual's response to the treatment (individual effect); in a laboratory study where persons are treated one at a time, effects are always interpreted in this way. When persons are treated in groups, however, at least two other explanations must be entertained. Some processes may affect the group as a unit. For example, when the mean aptitude of the class is high, the teacher may crowd more material into the course. Consequently, the class as a whole may learn more; or it may, on the average, suffer from the fast pace. The third possibility is comparative effects within a group. Thus, if one method provides special opportunities or rewards for whoever is ablest within the class, the experience of a student with an IQ of 110 depends on whether the mean of his class is 100 or 120.

The comparative effect influences the within-class regression of outcome on aptitude. The class-level process influences the between-class regression. The strictly individual effect influences both regressions. (p. 717)

Data Structure.   An extension of notation is needed to represent membership of individual p in classroom c. Accordingly, X_{cp} indicates the background characteristic X for individual p in classroom c ($p = 1, \ldots, n_c; c = 1, \ldots, C$). Similarly, A_{cp} denotes the aptitude A for individual p in classroom c. The average value of a variable within classroom c is denoted by $\bar{A}_{c.}, \bar{X}_{c.}$ etc. In considering between-class and within-class effects orthogonal decompositions of the form—$A_{cp} = \bar{A}_{c.} + (A_{cp} - \bar{A}_{c.})$—separate the classroom mean ($\bar{A}_{c.}$) and the relative standing within classroom c ($A_{cp} - \bar{A}_{c.}$) for individual p.

Models for Between-Class and Within-Class Effects

The increment to outcome resulting from the intervention depends on both classroom membership and individual characteristics. Following the notions of the *class-level* (between-class) and *comparative* (within-class) effects, increments in response to intervention with a class-level incrementation δ_c^b and a comparative incrementation δ_{cp}^w can be constructed:

Class-level (between-class)

$$\delta_c^b = \begin{array}{ll} \eta_1^b + \kappa_1^b \bar{A}_{c.} & \text{(for } G_p = 1) \\ \eta_0^b + \kappa_0^b \bar{A}_{c.} & \text{(for } G_p = 0) \end{array} \tag{49}$$

Comparative (within-class)

$$\delta_{cp}^w = \begin{array}{ll} \eta_1^w + \kappa_1^w (A_{cp} - \bar{A}_{c.}) & \text{(for } G_p = 1) \\ \eta_0^w + \kappa_0^w (A_{cp} - \bar{A}_{c.}) & \text{(for } G_p = 0) \end{array} \tag{50}$$

Thus, the between-class ATI is represented by $\kappa_1^b - \kappa_0^b$, and the within-class ATI is represented by $\kappa_1^w - \kappa_0^w$. An additive combination of the two effects yields:

$$\delta_{cp} = \delta_c^b + \delta_{cp}^w = \begin{array}{ll} (\eta_1^b + \eta_1^w) + (\kappa_1^b - \kappa_1^w)\bar{A}_{c.} + \kappa_1^w A_{cp} & \text{(for } G_p = 1) \\ (\eta_0^b + \eta_0^w) + (\kappa_0^b - \kappa_0^w)\bar{A}_{c.} + \kappa_0^w A_{cp} & \text{(for } G_p = 0) \end{array} \tag{51}$$

Individual-Level ATI Analyses

Conventional ATI individual-level analyses have ignored the classroom membership of individuals. As Cronbach and Webb (1975) assert, such an analysis will confound the between-class and within-class ATI effects. This confounding can be illustrated using the straight-line growth model for individual maturation in (2) (assuming that the treatment and control groups are formed by random assignment of intact classrooms).

A as Initial Status. For the Y_{2cp} on A_{cp} individual-level regressions, the difference between the slopes is:

$$\phi_A(\kappa_1^b - \kappa_0^b) + (1 - \phi_A)(\kappa_1^w - \kappa_0^w), \tag{52}$$

where

$$\phi_A = \frac{\text{Var}(\bar{A})}{\text{Var}(A)}$$

is between 0 and 1. The variance ratio, ϕ_A, reflects the heterogeneity in the grouping of individual students into classrooms. Expression (52) reveals that the ATI obtained from the individual level analysis with measures of A as initial status is a combination of the class-level and comparative effects which could possibly cancel each other out. Even when measures of A are available for each individual, the hierarchical structure of the data (e.g., individuals within classrooms) cannot be ignored.

The special cases of a "pure between-class" and "pure within-class" effects yield interesting interpretations for (52). If $\kappa_1^w = \kappa_0^w$ (no within-class effect) then (52) reveals that the individual level ATI is the between-class ATI (from 49) diminished by a factor of ϕ_A. (The variance ratio ϕ_A is large when the classes differ greatly on mean aptitude). On the other hand, for $\kappa_1^b = \kappa_0^b$ (no between-class effect) (52) indicates that the within-class effect defined in (50) is diminished by a factor $1 - \phi_A$. Thus with A as initial status the individual level analysis will not recover the class-level or comparative ATI defined in (49) and (50) even when these effects are *pure* and not confounded with each other.

Y_1 as initial status. For an individual-level analysis with Y_1 as the measure of initial status the difference between the within-group regression slopes is

$$\beta_{AY_1}(\kappa_1^w - \kappa_0^w) + \beta_{\bar{A}Y_1}[(\kappa_1^b - \kappa_0^b) - (\kappa_1^w - \kappa_0^w)].$$

Even for the special cases where either class-level or comparative effects are absent, the ATI indicated using Y_1 in an individual level analysis may differ greatly from that specified by (49) and (50).

Hierarchical ATI Analyses

ATI analyses that take into account the hierarchical structure of the data may be stated in a variety of forms. One approach is separate between-class and within-class analyses (Cronbach & Webb, 1975). For measures of initial ability A_{cp}, the separate analyses would consist of both a between-class analysis comparing $\bar{Y}_{2c.}$ on $\bar{A}_{c.}$ regressions in the treatment and control groups and a within class analysis comparing $Y_{2cp} - \bar{Y}_{2c.}$ on $A_{cp} - \bar{A}_{c.}$ regressions in the treatment and control groups. These separate analyses do recover the between-class and within-class ATI built into (49) and (50). An alternative approach is to combine between-class and within-class prediction by a regression of Y_{2cp} on A_{cp} and $\bar{A}_{c.}$ within the treatment and control groups.

With Y_1 as the measure of initial status the separate between-class and within-class regressions can also be compared in the treatment and control groups. However, these analyses will not recover the between-class or within-class ATI. For example, the difference between the treatment and control group regression slopes for the between-class analysis is

$$(\kappa_1^b - \kappa_0^b)\beta_{\bar{A}Y_1}. \tag{54}$$

8.   Summary and Discussion

This chapter promotes the idea that it may be useful to formulate more detailed statistical models than are usually employed in ATI research. Here statistical models for individual maturation are coupled with statistical models for individual differences in response to the intervention. Although the actual implementation of these models is deliberately primitive psychologically, the intent is to follow the recommendations I made in Rogosa (1987) to "model the processes that generate the data" especially at the level of each individual. In their Preface, Cronbach and Snow (1977) state: "What lies before us is the task of accumulating knowledge about how a person's characteristics influence his or her response to the alternatives educators can offer or invent" (p. viii). The statistical models formulated in this chapter can be seen as a first pass at bringing the methodological infrastructure for ATI research more in line with this substantive goal.

Most of the topics in this chapter are linked to the work of Lee J. Cronbach. For the foundations of ATI research there are, for example, Cronbach (1957), Cronbach and Gleser (1957), and Cronbach and Snow (1977). On the topic of the measurement of growth and change there is Cronbach and Furby (1970). On the analysis of nonequivalent group designs there are Cronbach et al. (1977) and Cronbach (1983, Chap. 6). And on issues of aggregation and the analysis of hierarchical data there are Cronbach (1976) and Cronbach and Webb (1975).

It is reasonable to ask, How do the results of this chapter advance ATI research? One response would be that the chapter encourages a rethinking of the research designs and statistical procedures that dominate ATI research. More specifically, the chapter contributes to (i) explanations for past results and controversies in the empirical research and (ii) design and analysis strategies for doing better ATI studies. The formulation in (5) identifies basic parameters of interest for the study of individual differences in response to intervention (i.e. κ_0, κ_1). Moreover, the presentation of a number of issues not previously considered in methodological treatments of ATI research, such as the form of the incrementation resulting from the intervention or the relation between the "aptitude" and the incrementation (given a simple linear form in Equation 5), suggests areas for empirical study. And, of course, the role of models for individual maturation argues for more attention to individual growth and change in ATI research.

Even for similar interventions, aptitudes and individuals, inconsistent results across studies on the existence of ATI abound. What is shown, even for the simplest case of random assignment of individuals, is that the results of standard ATI analyses may depend crucially on the choice of the measure of initial status (aptitude), on the form of individual maturation, on the times at which pre and post measures are obtained, on the duration of the intervention, and on the form of the incrementation resulting from the intervention, and so forth. Insofar as similar studies may differ markedly on one or more of these factors, it is not surprising that results of empirical research appear discordant. Moreover, some of these factors will often serve to attenuate the difference between the within-group regression slopes. As a nonzero difference between the regression slopes is required for the "existence" of ATI, the results of this chapter may require reinterpretations of some of the negative reviews of the empirical ATI research (see also Cronbach & Snow, 1977, Chapter 14).

Although this chapter stops well short of detailing new procedures for the design and analysis of ATI research, some guidance is provided by the results on the properties of conventional ATI analyses. Prominent among the mathematical results based on the coupling of models for maturation and response to intervention in (7), (8), and (9) are those for the abscissa of the point of intersection of the within-group regressions. This quantity (sample estimates of which are central to the Johnson-Neyman region of significance and to the determination of cutting scores) is usually unaffected by the different models for maturation and forms of incrementation—unlike the difference between the within-group regression slopes (the usual criterion for an ATI to exist). Furthermore, the choice of different measures of initial status affects this quantity in relatively simple and understandable ways.

REFERENCES

Bryk, A. S., & Weisberg, H. I. (1976). Value-added analysis: A dynamic approach to the estimation of treatment effects. *Journal of Educational Statistics, 1,* 127–55.

Cronbach, L. J. (1957). The two disciplines of scientific psychology. *American Psychologist, 12,* 671–684.

Cronbach, L. J. (1976). *Research on classrooms and schools: Formulation of questions, design, and analysis.* Stanford University, School of Education, Stanford Evaluation Consortium.

Cronbach, L. J. (1983). *Designing evaluations of educational and social programs.* San Francisco: Jossey-Bass.

Cronbach, L. J., & Furby, L. (1970). How should we measure "change"—or should we? *Psychological Bulletin, 74,* 68–80.

Cronbach, L. J., & Gleser, G. C. (1957). *Psychological tests and personnel decisions.* Urbana: University of Illinois Press.

Cronbach, L. J., & Snow, R. E. (1977). *Aptitudes and instructional methods.* New York: Irvington Publishers.

Cronbach, L. J., Rogosa, D. R., Floden, R. E., & Price, G. G. (1977). *Analysis of covariance in nonrandomized experiments: Parameters affecting bias.* Occasional Paper, Stanford Evaluation Consortium, Stanford University.

Cronbach, L. J., & Webb, N. (1975). Between-Class and Within-Class Effects in a Reported Aptitude x Treatment Interaction: Reanalysis of a Study by G. L. Anderson. *Journal of Educational Psychology, 67,* 717–724.

Glass, G. V., Willson, V. L. & Gottman, J. M. (1975). *Design and analysis of time-series experiments.* Boulder, CO: Colorado Associated University Press.

Hicklin, W. J. (1976). A model for mastery learning based on dynamic equilibrium theory. *Journal of Mathematical Psychology, 13,* 79–88.

Hilgard, E. R. (1951). Methods and procedures in the study of learning. In S. S. Stevens (Ed.), *Handbook of Experimental Psychology.* New York: Wiley.

Rogosa, D. R. (1977). *Some results for the Johnson-Neyman technique.* Doctoral dissertation, Stanford University. (University Microfilms No. 78-02,225).

Rogosa, D. R. (1980). Comparing nonparallel regression lines. *Psychological Bulletin, 88,* 307–321.

Rogosa, D. R. (1987). Casual models do not support scientific conclusions. *Journal of Educational Statistics, 12,* 185–195.

Rogosa, D. R., & Willett, J. B. (1985). Understanding correlates of change by modeling individual differences in growth. *Psychometrika, 50,* 203–228.

Weisberg, H. I. (1979). Statistical Adjustments and Uncontrolled Studies. *Psychological Bulletin, 86,* 1149–1164.

APPENDIX

Properties of $\beta_{AY(t)}$ for Straight-line and Exponential Growth

The dependence of the ATI results on β_{AY_1} is similar for exponential and straight-line growth. The exact form of the dependence of β_{AY_1} on the time that is chosen to be t_1 does differ with the type of growth.

Straight-Line Growth. From the results of Rogosa and Willett (1985) $\beta_{AY(t)}$ is expressed as a function of time:

$$\beta_{AY(t)} = \frac{\sigma_{A\pi}[t - t^1]}{\sigma^2_{Y(t^o)} + \sigma^2_\pi(t - t^o)^2}$$

where the times t^o and t^l are given by,

$$t - t^o = \frac{\sigma_{\pi Y(t)}}{\sigma_\pi^2}$$

and

$$t^l = t^o - (\sigma_{AY(t^o)}/\sigma_{A\pi})$$

The form of $\beta_{AY(t)}$ as a function of t is shown in Figure 5 (assuming $\sigma_{AY(t^o)} > 0$). Depending upon the choice of t_1, β_{AY_1} may be positive ($t_1 > t^l$), negative ($t_1 < t^l$) or even zero ($t_1 = t^l$). The placement of t_1 near t^l is consistent with the results of many research studies which find small negative values for the correlation between change in Y and initial status on Y (see Rogosa & Willett, 1985.) If the Overlap Hypothesis (see Cronbach & Snow, 1977, Ch. 5) were satisfied, then t_1 equals t^o. Also, for t^o midway between t_1 and t_2 the variances of Y at times 1 and 2 will be equal (the condition of dynamic equilibrium).

Exponential Growth.   For asymptotic exponential growth defined in (3),

$$\beta_{AY(t)} = \frac{\sigma_{AY(t^o)} + [\sigma_{A\lambda} - \sigma_{AY(t^o)}](1 - e^{-\gamma(t - t^o)})}{\sigma_{Y(t^o)}^2 + (\sigma_\lambda^2 - \sigma_{Y(t^o)}^2)(1 - e^{-\gamma(t - t^o)})^2}$$

where t^o, the time at which the variance of Y(t) is a minimum, and for which the correlation between change and status at t^o is zero, is defined by:

$$t - t^o = \frac{1}{\gamma} \ln[\sigma_{\lambda[\lambda - Y(t)]}/\sigma_{[\lambda - Y(t)]}^2]$$

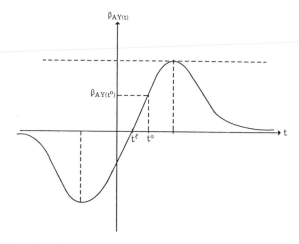

FIG. 9.5.   Functional form of $\beta_{AY(t)}$ for straight-line growth.

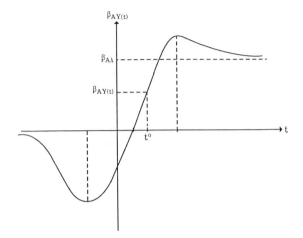

FIG. 9.6.   Functional form of $\beta_{AY(t)}$ for exponential growth.

The form of $\beta_{AY(t)}$ as a function of time shown in Figure 6 is similar to that shown in Figure 5 for straight-line growth. For ATI analyses with Y_1 as the measure of initial status, dependence of the results on the time chosen as t_1 may be severe.

10 The Concept of Aptitude

Richard E. Snow
Stanford University

The term *aptitude* has been used through most of recorded history, and various conceptions about the nature and nurture of aptitude have been carried down through educational and social philosophies to the present century (see, for example, Snow, 1982a). Modern philosophers remain concerned with clarifying these conceptions because they are deemed of central importance in education and in many areas of social policy and planning, as well as in the social sciences in general (see Scheffler, 1985). Indeed, educational, personnel, clinical, and counseling psychologists, both researchers and practitioners alike, grapple with problems of aptitude every day, whether or not these are recognized or labeled as such. Some medical and health scientists have begun to do the same. And experimental psychologists have begun to analyze individual differences in information processing under the heading "aptitude" or "aptitude for learning," as part of the development of cognitive theory. There are also long-standing biological and sociological questions about aptitude that intersect with the psychological, philosophical, and practical ones. In short, aptitude is an old term for an old concept still widely used, but also widely misused and misunderstood, in much scientific, professional, and public parlance today.

But what is aptitude, really? How is the concept used and misused? How might behavioral and social scientists better understand, describe, and use aptitude, and individual differences in aptitude, as a basic property of human functioning? What form might theories of aptitude take? What research methods apply? How might theory and method for research on aptitude be geared to meet the prescriptive, decision-making requirements of educational, clinical, personnel, or other professional practice? These are questions that continue to motivate research today, though on a fractionated and disorganized front; the work goes on under many, superficially unrelated labels.

This chapter attempts to reach a common form for conceptualizations of aptitude across this broad front. It defines a domain called "aptitude theory" within the framework of person-situation interactional psychology. It then exemplifies this form, using selected evidence from aptitude research in several different fields of psychology. The result is to suggest that a radical departure from old styles of theory and research is needed, and may finally be taking shape. Several lines of Lee Cronbach's work over recent decades are shown to be seminal in this development, though no implication should be drawn that he would necessarily endorse any particular statement made here.

TERMS AND CONFUSIONS

Some sense of aptitude is present in virtually all goal-directed human activities, even when other terms are used; whenever people think about the antecedents of observed individual differences in some valued goal attainment, aptitude of some sort is implied. The concept is especially close to the concept of readiness (as in reading readiness), but connects also to concepts such as suitability (for a purpose or position), susceptibility (to treatment or to persuasion), and proneness (as in accident proneness). All these concepts carry the implication of predisposition for differential response by persons to some situation or class of situations. The common thread through these and other related terms seems to be "potential" or "potentiality"—a latent, present, inferred quality or power that makes possible the development, *given specified conditions,* of some further quality or power, positive or negative.

Although all these allied concepts can be misunderstood or misrepresented, and have been at times, *aptitude* as both a term and a concept has been subjected to special wrenching. The distortion seems to have come from a narrowing of meaning in English over several centuries. Specifically in English, aptitude was gradually equated with intelligence, and capacity in the 16th, 17th, and 18th centuries, then misinterpreted and generalized as a single-rank-order of "general intellectual fitness for any situation" in the 19th century, and then captured in this condition by the mental testing movement in the 20th century.

This is not the place for a detailed historical-linguistic analysis of this hypothesis. But it is useful to note briefly some key points of usage in history to contrast the narrow concept of aptitude that has evolved in English-language psychology with the broad, reconstituted concept now recommended here.

Aptitude in English

In its original and broad definition, even in many general English dictionaries, aptitude means aptness, inclination, tendency, propensity, predisposition, fitness, or suitability for performance in some future situation, often involving formal or informal learning. The implication of readiness for some situation, and of mutual person-situation suitability in this condition, seems obvious in these terms even if unspecified. By implication also, such definitions admit many possible personal properties—conative and affective as well as cognitive—as aspects of aptitude. By the 1950s in British and American psychology, however, the concept of readiness had taken on all these implications (which it did not have in English to begin with), whereas the concept of aptitude had lost them: The connection of *aptitude* with *apt* was superseded by the connection with *intelligence* and *capacity;* the latter concepts, of course, have also changed over time.

These four terms all entered English from Latin via French, but *aptitude* came in last. The Oxford Universal Dictionary (1944) gives dates of first known English usage (in parentheses) as follows: *apt* (old English period, 1048), *intelligence* (middle English period, 1150–1450), *capacity* (1480), *aptitude* (1548). It then defines aptitude as:

1. The quality of being fit for a purpose or position, or generally; fitness, suitableness (1643).

2. Natural tendency or propensity (1633).

3. Natural capacity *for any pursuit* (1789); *esp. intelligence, quick-wittedness* (1548); (p. 89, emphasis added).

The definition suggests that *aptitude* was associated with *intelligence* almost immediately upon entry into English in 1548, but not interpreted as "natural capacity for any pursuit" until over 2 centuries later in 1789. Consulting the examples of early usage for *apt* and *aptitude,* the suggestion of subject-situation or subject-subject interaction is clearly evident—"for fat is wondrous apt to burn" and, from Milton, ". . . that sociable and helpful aptitude between man and woman." Even *intelligence* defined as a quality of understanding and a quickness of mental apprehension of something also implied, in early usage (1531), mutual conveyance, communication, or intercourse between mind and thing, mind and knowledge, or mind and mind. There is also the root of current military usage as "information, news, tidings" (1450). *Capacity* was "mental receiving power; ability to take in impressions, ideas, knowledge" (1485), and only later included the implication of "holding" capacity (1702).

In contrast, *readiness* appears in later middle English (1350–1450) to mean "promptness in voluntary action or compliance"; it later meant "state of preparation" (1541) and "quickness or facility in performance" (1585). But its root is "read," deriving from old Teutonic, not Latin, where it first meant "to succeed or accomplish, make out the meaning of, and foresee or predict." With the spread of writing and then printing, it came to mean "ability to understand works written in a language."

By the 1800s, however, *aptitude* and *intelligence,* but not *readiness,* were tightly connected in English with capacity and securely located as a generalized trait, and a fixed entity, within each person's head. The implication of mutual, multivariate, person-situation reciprocity was gone. Though Darwinian theory was clearly interactionist and multivariate at the level of particular individuals and particular environments, the Social Darwinists thought primarily of individuals and environments each rank-ordered on a single scale. In one form of social theory, attributable to Spencer, aptitude (as intelligence) came to mean fitness to survive in any environment. Selection on general merit was the resulting social policy. John Stuart Mill even proposed that mental tests be used to determine how many votes a person should be allotted. Galton connected this generalized aptitude with inheritance and Spearman connected it with a pervasive mental energy that drives all mental engines. Situational variations were largely ignored. In the other form of Social Darwinist theory, attributable to Ward but also to Dewey and James, environments could be ranked from good to bad. The aim was then to find or design the best educational treatments so that aptitude could ultimately be equalized across persons. The first wave sought the best persons, in the general image of the English upper class. The second wave sought the best situations, in the general image of efficient American management. But both images existed on both sides of the Atlantic at the turn of this century (see Cronbach & Snow, 1977, pp. 6–12). And both ignored person-situation reciprocity. On both sides of English-language psychology, also, the measurement of such mental quantities was seen as the best way to build the new science in the image of physics.

Into this Zeitgeist the Binet-Simon scale was imported. Group mental tests soon proliferated, and they seemed to work as predictors. The equating of intelligence and aptitude was thus solidified at the same time that substantial misinterpretation of the evidence set in. The concept of aptitude thus became muddled into—some would say sullied by—the overblown conception of "general" intelligence as fixed capacity and the misconception that one kind of mental test can be titled an "aptitude" or an "intelligence" test whereas another cannot.

The muddling misrepresented both concepts. *Intelligence* as measured came to mean primarily academic intelligence. And, especially in education, *aptitude* came to mean only that which is represented by "scholastic aptitude tests" or "general ability or intelligence tests." Both misrepresentations have severely limited new substantive research in other directions unnecessarily (Cronbach & Snow, 1977; Gardner, 1983; Sternberg, 1985). Both have also prompted substantial controversies throughout this century (see Cronbach, 1975b). As Cronbach (1984) observed:

> It was a great mistake to adopt the words *intelligence* and *capacity* in test titles and in communications with the public. Binet and his fellow clinicians knew full well that they were examining only present performance. Binet wrote eloquently of the hope of finding new methods of cultivation that would 'produce a rich harvest' from children who seemed unpromising.

In British and American discourse, 'intelligence' seemed usually to refer to potentiality as if the test score foretold what level the person would reach if given every educational advantage. The evidence is necessarily one-sided. Good ultimate performance proves capacity, but poor performance does not prove incapacity. (p. 198; emphasis in original)

To make matters worse, both theoretical psychometrics and the several fields of applied measurement gradually specialized over this century, and became isolated from one another. Development of measurement technology outdistanced development of the psychology of measurement, so the meaning of test scores came to be neglected (Anastasi, 1967, Carroll, 1961, McNemar, 1964). Although Cronbach and Meehl (1955) invented construct validity precisely to face the problem of meaning in measurement, applied psychologists could and did avoid the matter. The psychology of the construct intended by the test developer became subordinate either to the logical structure of content specified in test development or to the empirical fact of criterion-related prediction in test use.

Aptitude and Readiness

It is strange that the concept of readiness has taken on the original broad meaning of aptitude as fundamentally a matter of particular person-situation interactions—apparently, as aptitude became intelligence, readiness became aptitude. By the 1950s, English and English (1958) were defining readiness as:

. . . preparedness to respond . . . . a state or condition of the person that makes it possible . . . to engage profitably in a given learning activity . . . . it is a composite of many personal qualities and conditions and differs from one learning task to another. (p. 441)

And, in particular, readiness for reading is:

. . . the *totality of personal factors* conducive to satisfactory progress in learning to read *under given conditions of instruction* . . . the relevant factors may be intellectual, emotional and motivational, or physiological. Both *general maturation* and *effective specific previous experiences* play a part. *A child may be ready for one kind of reading method and not for another.* (p. 441; emphasis added)

These definitions of readiness hark back to Binet. They clearly identify properties, qualities, states, or conditions of persons (as opposed to traits or entities) that enable profitable learning or development under given situational conditions. Different composites are relevant to different learning or developmental situations, and these likely include conative and affective as well as cognitive properties. A complex reciprocity between person and situation is expected wherein a person may be ready to profit from one kind of treatment and not from another aimed at the same goal.

The broad definitions of aptitude include these implications also, even though vaguely. But English and English (1958) define aptitude as:

> . . . the capacity to acquire proficiency with a given amount of training, formal or informal. *Special aptitude* does not necessarily mean very high aptitude, but rather aptitude of a special kind: e.g., *aptitude for mechanics*. *General aptitude* means the capacity to acquire proficiency in many activities. Since all measurement is necessarily of present performance, an *aptitude test* is merely one form of ability test . . . thus an *intelligence test* is a test of fairly general present *ability*, but also of capacity to learn. Hence it is both a *general ability* and a *general aptitude* test. But the distinction remains: *ability* is present and actual, *aptitude* is potential though the same test may measure both. (p. 39; emphasis in original)

Why in 1958 should *aptitude* be defined more narrowly than *reading readiness?* If *reading readiness* is an inferred mixture of cognitive, emotional and motivational, physiological, and experiential properties expected to differ for different instructional methods, should *aptitude for reading* mean something less or something else? Would tests of readiness to learn from phonics reading methods not be aptitude tests? Apparently, English-language psychology at mid-century believed that an aptitude test is "merely an ability test," that one kind of test can be titled an "aptitude test" whereas another cannot, and that the situation for which a test is supposed to indicate aptitude need not be specified, beyond, e.g., "special aptitude for mechanics."

In short, the term *aptitude* has fallen into such frequent misuse that Anastasi (1980) would have it abolished in favor of *developed ability*. In a subset of applications, her proposed substitution might serve well enough. As argued earlier, however, the broad concept of aptitude includes conative and affective states of persons, not just cognitive abilities. And, as argued below, the concept is useful in fields of human science where *aptitude* or some synonym such as *readiness* is a concern, but *developed abilities* are clearly not. Even in education, where *aptitude, ability,* and *achievement* are most easily confused (see Snow, 1980a), the broader definition is to be preferred; it allows new conceptions of aptitude for school learning to draw research attention to other personal properties, such as achievement motivations, interests, and attitudes about self and school, and to the mixtures of these properties that connect individual learners to particular learning tasks in different ways, profitably or unprofitably (Snow, 1986).

Aptitude in Latin, French, and German

If we return to the Latin usage of Quintilian in first century Rome, however, it is clear that the broad definition is intended. He included different abilities as aptitudes, but also other qualities and preferences of students. Moreover, there is the clear implication that aptitudes could be developed and inaptitudes removed by adapting instruction to individual differences, using strengths to work on weaknesses; aptitudes could also be weakened by instruction that ran counter to their "bent." Quintilian used a general intellectual level concept also in that, below a certain level, nothing educational could be done. Above this level, however, aptitude was clearly multivariate. Quintilian also spoke of "natural gifts," but hardly of "fixed capacity." (See the Butler 1954 translation, particularly pp. 265–269; also Snow, 1982a.)

French usage seems to have maintained the broad, composite concept of aptitude and its implication of person-situation reciprocity over this history. At least it is clear in the writings of Binet and Simon (1916, Kite translation; also Wolf, 1973). And modern French dictionaries maintain the broad, situation-connected meaning, associating *aptitude* with *apropos*. Even German dictionaries start their definitions with "apt, appropriate, and suitable" (*Geeignetheit*), working down through several levels of specialization before reaching "ability and talent" (*Befahigung*).

Aptitude in Cronbach's View

Cronbach's usage has been consistently in keeping with the original European continental meaning, not with the narrow misconstrual of modern English-language psychology. After using aptitude in the broad sense in his general proposal to unify correlational and experimental psychology (Cronbach, 1957), he turned his attention to the problem of adapting instruction to individual differences in learning by finding or designing alternative instructional methods to fit different students. This would require:

> . . . a new psychological theory of aptitude. An aptitude, in this context, is *a complex of personal characteristics that accounts for an individual's end state after a particular educational treatment* . . . [It] includes whatever promotes the pupil's survival in a *particular* educational environment, and it may have as much to do with styles of thought and personality variables as with the abilities covered in conventional tests . . . *such a theory deals with aptitude-treatment interactions*. (Cronbach, 1967, p. 23–24; emphasis added)

In the initial search for such interactions, Cronbach and Snow (1977) carried this broad and pragmatic definition further. To keep the research problem as open as possible in this work, *aptitude* was defined as *any characteristic of persons* that forecasts their probability of success under a given treatment. *Treatment* was also broadly defined to cover any manipulable variable the effects of which could be assessed on a common criterion. The bases of such forecasts could then be discovered through more focused analytic studies.

Thus, personality variables, biographical and other nontest measures, and

new kinds of aptitude constructs might predict response to instruction in a particular setting, singly or in combination, and hence might be examined as sources of
aptitude for success in that setting. The possibility of identifying *aptitude complexes* was especially important. After all, other work in differential psychology
had occasionally developed more specialized, multivariate conceptions of aptitude for success in specialized activities, and these often spanned the artificial
distinctions between ability, achievement, personality, etc.: Mechanical knowledge is combined with certain spatial and psychomotor skills to represent aptitude for particular kinds of technical work; esthetic sensitivities, along with
some perceptual skills, help define aptitude for particular artistic activities; a
certain degree of compulsivity may need to be mixed with reasoning ability to
produce aptitude for computer programming, and for learning to program; the
ability to generate and control vivid visual images may combine with motivation
to change as aptitude for certain forms of therapy, such as systematic desensitiza-
tion; even height and weight combine in different ways as aptitude for different
sports. There was thus no a priori reason why aptitude for success in the variety
of instructional situations and activities possible in schools should be less complex, diversified, or specialized, than it is in these other pursuits. The variety of
therapies, occupational classifications, work designs, and organizational climates possible today similarly argues for a broad and diverse view of aptitude.

The aptitude-treatment terminology appears generally applicable to any occupational, educational, or clinical situation. It is thus preferred here and recommended for general use. The broad definition of *aptitude* incorporates the relevant meanings of *potentiality* and *readiness,* and is more flexible than these
terms grammatically. Most importantly, in its original broad usage, *aptitude*
implied not only living organisms functioning in a particular environment but
incorporated the linkage between the two. Although never fully developed, and
indeed lost in English-language psychology, this implication paves the way for a
new kind of aptitude theory—aptitude comes to be viewed not as a characteristic
of persons but as a characteristic of person-situation interactions. This subtle yet
radical shift challenges traditional styles of conceptualization and research in
psychology. It may even require a new relativistic epistemology. The following
sections explore some of the implications, potentials, and problems raised by this
shift. But this chapter cannot do more than open the broad discussion that is
needed.

THE NEED FOR APTITUDE THEORIES

Aptitude Construct Validation

Much of the history of differential psychology has been devoted to the development of potential indicators of aptitude, and to the study of their relationships to
one another, and to various outcome criteria. This was a reasonable endeavor as

far as it went. To establish an individual difference construct, one must demonstrate that its purported measures show convergent and discriminant validity with respect to other constructs and measures (Campbell & Fiske, 1959). To invoke the term aptitude, one must add a demonstration of its promise for prediction of some practically important criterion. But these are only initial, largely empirical, steps. Unfortunately, there has often been vagueness and misunderstanding about the validation of aptitudes as psychological constructs beyond these steps.

Aptitude construct validation cannot be just a raw empirical enterprise. Beyond the measures and data themselves, the construct must also be embedded in an interpretive network (Cronbach, 1971). And one must validate particular practical decision rules to meet a public justification criterion, as well as particular theoretical interpretations to meet a scientific justification criterion (Cronbach, 1980). The particularity of interpretations and decision rules is especially to be emphasized.

First, as argued earlier, because aptitude always implies prediction, it always implies some *particular* job or educational or therapeutic treatment situation wherein persons will function; *describing the situation is thus part of defining the aptitude.* Indeed, the subtle particularities of different situations, even situations that are superficially similar, may demand slightly different mixes of aptitude constructs in a complex, even though these constructs are in abstract terms considered distinguishable. Describing the complex as aptitude for performing mechanical operations in a factory, or for learning from direct instruction in mathematics, or for benefitting from psychotherapy, is a step in the right direction. But situation description will usually need to be carried to much further detail. Deciding on the level of detail needed is a matter for further validation research in each instance.

Second, the term implies that the person characteristics so described are not merely correlated with success in this particular situation but are actually *propaedeutic,* i.e., *needed as a preparation to achieve that success;* a probabilistic determinism is thus claimed that links aptitude, situation, and criterion together. It was reasonable for Cronbach and Snow (1977) to start by defining aptitude as *any* person characteristic that correlated with outcome, but that was only a tactic to avoid premature foreclosure in a new line of inquiry; one cannot leave it at that. Validation research must then bring into focus the mixtures of *needed* preparation, or readiness, that constitute aptitude in each particular situation at hand.

Third, the particularity of such aptitude-situation-criterion links implies *differential validity;* unless the aptitude in question is truly general, there must be situations in which that aptitude is less propaedeutic to success, or not propaedeutic at all. Validity generalization may be demonstrated, for a selection test over a range of jobs, for example, but it should never be assumed (Cronbach, 1982b). Such a substantive generalization must be shown not to depend on the peculiarities of measuring instruments or of the samples of persons and jobs that happen to be studied. Thorough differential validation research is required to set substantive *boundary conditions* on the aptitude construct.

Demonstrating differential validity across situations actually turns out to be a most important aspect of aptitude construct validation because it suggests how the predictor-criterion relations can be *experimentally* manipulated. To the extent that one can manipulate aptitude-outcome relations, one shows to that degree that the *particular* propaedeutic links hypothesized are being validly interpreted. It is also the case that decision rules for the classification of persons among alternative jobs or treatments, as opposed to selection decisions, require just this kind of differential validation. Aptitude measures valid for selection within a job or treatment may well be invalid for classification among jobs or treatments. Classification decisions have long been common in government employment and in the military; they now occur increasingly in private industry. In clinical practice and in education, such decisions underlie many kinds of placement of individuals into alternative available treatments. But it has not generally been recognized that aptitude construct validation for classification decisions requires the demonstration of differential prediction, i.e., aptitude and job or treatment variables must be shown to interact.

Cronbach and Gleser (1965) developed the formal model for the validation of measures used for classification decisions, based on differential prediction. Validation for selection vs. classification could thus be clearly distinguished. Cronbach and Snow (1977) elaborated this view of differential prediction and provided many examples from educational research, where such findings have been called aptitude-treatment interactions, or ATI for short. That work shows that ATI are ubiquitous in education, even though they are not yet well understood, or easily analyzed. Their frequency and variety nonetheless shows why the examination of differential validity, or ATI, must be a part of aptitude construct validation. In short, an aptitude construct must not only describe the situations it incorporates, and explain its propaedeutic claims, it must also demonstrate its boundary conditions, i.e., the range of situations over which it applies, and outside of which it does not.

Beyond the selection and classification functions, however, there is often another function that needs to be served in aptitude construct validation. Sometimes, aptitude-treatment links are assumed or designed to be not only interactive but transactive. Some aptitudes are considered to be modifiable or educable by treatment, and some treatments are considered to be modified, or designed to be modifiable, as a result of aptitude differences or developments therein. Indeed, formal education is increasingly regarded and evaluated as an aptitude development program (Snow, 1982b). Many clinical and occupational treatments claim aptitude development as a primary aim. And many educational and clinical treatments are purposely designed to be adaptive to aptitude differences or to changes in aptitude that emerge during treatment. When an aptitude is defined as capable of modification by treatment, or when a treatment is defined as capable of effecting modification of aptitude, or being adaptable to such changes, validation research should include a demonstration of this capability. The aptitude-treatment reciprocity should be explicated in theory and in evidence.

The educability of aptitude is an empirical and theoretical question addressed only haltingly and sporadically through the history of psychology. But public controversies over past decades (Cronbach, 1975b), as well as the need for improved theory, now demand that the question be systematically addressed. Indeed, the identification, utilization, and *development* of aptitude for success in needed occupations are all vital functions for civilization. Differential psychology entered this century as a part of basic and applied science concerned primarily with all three functions. The earlier quote from Cronbach on Binet is especially to be noted. Now the problem of aptitude *development* has come to center stage. To paraphrase Tyler (1974), successful pursuit of solutions to many of the world's physical and social problems through the close of this century and into the next, especially including the struggle for social equality, depends in significant part not only on understanding human diversity and improving the selection and classification functions, but especially on improving the education functions through which diverse aptitudes can be developed and capitalized upon. Although differential psychology has produced considerable knowledge about individual differences and their measurement, Tyler had to regret how little this knowledge has so far influenced philosophers of the human condition, or educators, or legislators and administrators, or even individuals themselves, in shaping the policies and practices that govern human lives. The problem is no different today than it was when Tyler wrote. The premise of the present argument is that the usefulness of present knowledge is limited by the absence of substantive aptitude theories that can link individual difference constructs with important achievements in the fields of human living, in ways that show how treatments can be designed not only to promote these achievements but also to promote aptitude development through them.

A Framework for Aptitude Theories

By way of summary, a framework of requirements for any aptitude theory can now be stated (see also Snow & Lohman, 1984).

Differential psychology produces individual difference constructs validated by the convergence and divergence of indicators in multitrait–multimethod research. For an individual difference construct then to be interpreted as indicating aptitude, an aptitude theory is needed. Any aptitude theory needs to meet five descriptive goals. These in turn relate to one or more of three prescriptive goals of the theory. The descriptive goals are:

1. To interpret the psychological nature of the individual difference construct as an indicant of aptitude, and the measures considered to reflect this nature.

2. To specify the treatment situations for which the construct serves as aptitude, and the criteria to be used to validate this claim.

3. To demonstrate and explain the predictive, propaedeutic links that connect aptitude, treatment, and criterion constructs and measures.

4. To demonstrate and explain the degree to which differential prediction exists for contrasting treatments and thus the boundary conditions to be placed on the aptitude construct.

5. To demonstrate and explain the degree to which the aptitude can be changed through transactional aptitude-treatment links, and the degree to which treatment also changes in this process.

Such an aptitude theory should also provide decision rules to meet one or more of three prescriptive goals, designed for specific uses of the aptitude construct and its associated measures in a particular situation. If the prescriptive goal is the selection of persons likely to succeed in particular treatments, or the classification of persons into alternative treatments likely to be optimal for each, then the decision rules must specify how the scores indicating aptitude are to be used to accomplish these purposes, following procedures established by Cronbach and Gleser (1965), Cronbach and Snow (1977), Van Der Linden (1981), and other contemporary literature on bias in selection and classification. If the prescriptive goal concerns the direct development of aptitude, then the decision rules must specify procedures to be followed in the design of education, training, or therapy in the particular situation at hand and the criteria to be used in judging its success. The aptitude theory is thus made to support the selection or classification or education functions called for in a particular situation.

The Place of Aptitude Theories in Psychology

Aptitude theory should be thought of as a linking science, aimed at descriptive and explanatory concepts that connect the characteristics and capabilities of persons to features of treatment environments, real or desired, so as to reach goals of field achievement. The place of such theories in psychology can thus be schematized as in Fig. 10.1. The scheme is based in part on Carroll's (1980) discussion of the kinds of theory needed to understand aptitudes in relation to instruction. But the terminology here is intended to be general, applying to clinical, industrial and other settings as well as to education.

At the base are general psychological theories, long and still the aim of most basic research. These are nomothetic theories, or principles and concepts therefrom, developed without reference to individual differences. They may or may not attend to other sorts of boundary conditions on their generalizability. At the top are theories of field achievements, i.e., the societal, institutional, or personal goals. Field achievement here is intended to be close to Anastasi's (1980) meaning, suggesting ". . . a deed in the real world, a contribution one makes to society, such as designing a bridge, composing a symphony, or formulating a theory of learning" (p. 3). These are also theories, however, not just deeds, because they include psychological goal concepts—descriptions of desired psychological states or properties of persons who can perform such deeds. Think of goals such as healthy adjustment to social life, managerial competence or leadership, good citizenship, literacy, or understanding of mathematics. All are constructs that must be interpreted in theory as well as in measures. In education, such theories would likely include statements about the structure of a content domain and value judgments about what ought to be taught and learned, as well as a cognitive psychology of what constitutes expertise or mastery in a field and progress toward it. They would also include a specification of criterion measures for the ultimate goal as well as intermediate indicators or proxies, such as supervisory ratings or achievement tests. At the right of Fig. 10.1 are theories of treatment design. Any purposefully designed organization, instructional or training program, therapy, or person-machine system is implicitly a theory of how a goal can be reached given existing or expected environmental conditions. The usage here is akin to Simon's (1969) vision of design science as a link between abstract principles and the achievement of real world goals.

At times through the history of psychology, general theories have led directly to descriptive or prescriptive theories of field achievements and also of treatment design. At other times, the development of theories of treatment or of field behavior has led back to contribute to general theory. Skinnerian general theory led directly to the educational treatment design of linear programmed instruction,

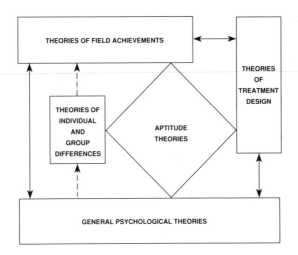

FIG. 10.1.   A schematic representation of the place of aptitude theories in psychological science.

for example (see Glaser, 1978b). Miller's (1957) theory of instructional film design is another example, derived from Hullian learning theory. Discovery-oriented instruction (Shulman & Keislar, 1966) derives, though more loosely and indirectly, from a mixture of cognitive and Piagetian theories of intellectual development, through Bruner's (1966) work. There are now anthologies of instructional treatment design theories derived from different general principles (Gagne & Briggs, 1974; Reigeluth, 1983). Piagetian and cognitive developmental theories are themselves descriptions of when and how levels of thinking about the physical and social world are attained, i.e., they describe the course of field achievement in general terms, and they can be connected directly to principles of instructional design (Case & Bereiter, 1984). Freud also began with a theory of field achievement (or its opposite in the development of nervous disorders and hysteria) and produced a general theory of personality as well as a theory of treatment design (i.e., psychoanalysis). Many other personality theories provide similar links. One can also say that modern cognitive psychology began in part with a theory of field achievement, about expertise in chess (DeGroot, 1965; Simon, 1979). And current cognitive analyses of school learning task designs feed back to enrich general cognitive theory (Greeno, 1980, 1986). Industrial, organizational, and engineering psychology apply general principles to the design of human performance environments but also feed back revised principles or new boundary conditions on them (Dunnette, 1976; McCormick, 1979; Schneider, 1978). A particularly good example of new boundary conditions on old principles comes from Cronbach's (1975a) discussion of the limits of Weber's Law in treatment design and training for World War II sonar operations.

Thus, in the outer ring of Fig. 10.1, strong basic-applied links have developed in one or another decade as manifested in many parts of educational, clinical, industrial-organizational, and engineering psychology. Most of these links, however, were forged on the strong simplifying assumption that individual differences could be ignored. In contrast, differential psychology has been only loosely linked into this picture. The connection of individual difference constructs to constructs of field achievements has been largely empirical and atheoretic. Typically, criterion measures are accepted, as given, to represent field achievements, and a search for predictive correlates in the catalogue of individual difference constructs is undertaken. The relation of such constructs to theories of treatment design has remained largely unexplored, since the treatment environment has also been taken as given. While some individual difference constructs have been fashioned from bases in general theory, these connections have remained vague, unanalyzed, and one directional. Until recently, individual differences were regarded as merely parametric variations within the models of general theorists (Cronbach, 1957) or as a means to test such models (Underwood, 1975).

Aptitude theories would be aimed at welding all this together. It is instructive in explicating this view to examine the traditional form of research on aptitude in somewhat more detail. The traditional approach has been well characterized by Carroll (1974):

> . . . the tasks chosen for aptitude tests were those which were regarded as having *process structures* similar to, or even identical with, the process structures exemplified in actual learning tasks, even though the contents might be different. The tests were therefore measures of the individual's ability to perform the psychological functions embedded in . . . or . . . the information processing . . . characteristic of the criterion learning tasks. The theoretical basis for assuming similarities between aptitude tasks and criterion tasks might be of the vaguest intuitive sort; what mattered was the empirical confirmation of one's intuitions by standard test validation procedures. An important aspect of this vague theory, however, was the assumption that there are stable individual differences in ability to perform specified information processing tasks—an assumption supported, however, by a tradition reaching back many years in the factor-analytic literature. (p. 294)

Hypotheses about cognitive processes involved in task performance certainly did guide much of the work of the major factor theorists (see, e.g., Cattell, 1963; Guilford, 1967; Spearman, 1923; Thurstone, 1938). Even what would now be called "metacognitive" hypotheses appeared in Spearman's concept of "apprehension" and also in Binet's "autocriticism" (see Terman, 1916), for example. As Carroll (1976) has observed, the factor theorists can be regarded as the first *cognitive* psychologists, as that term is used today. Many, furthermore would have subscribed to Thurstone's (1947) view of the role of factor analysis in the building of theory. It was to be a first cut—an initial mapping of the cognitive terrain that ". . . will enable us to proceed beyond the exploratory factorial stage to the more direct forms of psychological experimentation in the laboratory" (p. 56). But the effort to build the differential psychology of cognitive processes envisioned by Thurstone got sidetracked in favor of advancing the development of factor analytic methods. The pursuit of aptitude construct validation, through the identification and interpretation of the *process structures* presumed to underlie aptitude–aptitude and aptitude–achievement relationships, came to a standstill (Snow, 1980b). Correlational methods used alone were inherently limited. The experimental psychology of the time was inhospitable, both to cognitive process hypotheses and to presumed individual differences reflected in them. Cronbach's (1957) call for the unification of theory and method across these domains went largely unheeded.

In the past 2 decades, however, and particularly in the last few years, the pursuit of theoretical interpretations of aptitude constructs has again been taken up. Research on human information processing has shown how theories of complex cognitive processes can be constructed by combining experimental methods with the methods of computer science (Simon, 1979). Individual differences in the information processing parameters of these theories have now been studied directly, using the methods of componential analysis (Sternberg, 1977, 1985).

This work has begun to hook up with the analysis of learning from instruction (Glaser, 1978a, 1982; Snow, Federico, & Montague, 1980a, 1980b). At the same time, research on ATI in educational settings has shown how aptitude differences might be incorporated into the design of instructional theories (Cronbach & Snow, 1977; Snow, 1977b, 1982a; Snow & Lohman, 1984). The development of a cognitive differential psychology of instruction is clearly at hand. Theories of aptitude should be among its primary goals.

The Need for New Language

To meet the descriptive goals of aptitude theory, then, general psychological theories and individual difference theories need to be coordinated with one another and with theories of field achievements under the treatment conditions provided by particular environments. *Coordinated* here means description in a common, or at least conformable, language. Aptitude constructs should be constructions in this language, designed to link into a common system what is known about general and differential psychological phenomena and what is known about field achievements in relation to specified treatment designs. The level of descriptive detail needed in such constructions is a key issue.

This is no small problem. The concepts, and the degree and kind of generalizations they represent, differ substantially at present in different parts of Fig. 10.1. It is not clear what level of descriptive detail is needed or what level is possible. Any construct, indeed any test score, observation, or rating, exists at a certain level of abstraction. A measure is a summary representing a construct which in turn might be interpreted with long or short, or broad or narrow inferences (Cronbach, 1984). The interpretive usefulness of a particular level of summary is a question for validation and, within this, the meaning and usefulness of a more analytic level of representation is a question for experiment.

Unfortunately for the proposed development of aptitude theory, descriptions of field achievements and treatments have traditionally been oversimplified (or "undercomplicated"—Kaplan, 1964), whereas many theories of individual differences have been overcomplicated (or "overdifferentiated"—Humphreys, 1979; McNemar, 1964). For example, single indexes usually represent field achievements to be interpreted as amount learned, work productivity, or recidivation, and simple abstract labels reflect associated treatments interpreted as direct instruction, participative management, or Gestalt therapy, respectively. But the number of separable features of individual differences in ability and personality runs into the hundreds. On the other hand, the kind of information processing analysis now applied in cognitive psychology reaches a much more detailed level of differentiation, while at the same time a higher, more abstract level of generalization, than traditional constructs and measures in all three domains. But cognitive analyses also leave out the conative, motivational, volitional, and affective aspects of performance that must be included in these domains. The theoretical languages available thus exist at different levels of abstraction and remain nonconformable. So the descriptive problem for aptitude theory becomes one of finding a level of abstraction that is "tractable" (Pellegrino & Glaser, 1979)—that allows productive connection between concepts from general and differential theory and the selection, classification, and education functions served by aptitude measures, field achievement measures, and treatment designs. Put another way, we need a language for aptitude constructs that is common to concepts of individual differences, achievements, and treatment designs—that locates aptitude in the nexus between them.

It is noteworthy that general cognitive psychology has recently come to recognize a similar problem. The implication from an increasing number of developmental, cross-cultural, and anthropological studies is that situational specificity is an important feature of cognitive skill (Rogoff & Lave, 1984). In Rogoff's (1984; pages 1, 2, 3) terms:

> . . . cognitive skills seem to fluctuate as a function of the situation, which suggests that skills are limited in their generality.
>
> Increasingly, psychologists emphasize the role of context in cognitive activities . . . (p. 1). Thinking is intricately interwoven with the context of the problem to be solved. The context includes the problem's physical and conceptual structure as well as the purpose of the activity and the social milieu in which it is embedded. One must attend to the content and the context of intellectual activity in order to understand thought processes. This is the case for any situation in which thinking is studied, including the laboratory context, which is not context-free as researchers frequently assume (pp. 2–3).

Thus, in this new view, thinking skills reside in the person-situation interaction, not in the generalized mind of laboratory subjects. General cognitive theory seems to be pushed by these context- and culture-sensitive studies toward the same conception of cognitive skill that comes from the push of ATI research in differential psychology. The aim appears to be the same; create a new conceptual language for theories of person-situation interactions.

TOWARD A RECONSTRUCTION OF APTITUDE CONSTRUCTS

It may be that a new general language for aptitude constructs can be developed, and a new style of inquiry invented, to cover all the needs of basic and applied fields in psychology. Or it may turn out that highly specialized languages and styles will be needed for different kinds of field achievements and treatment designs. But these should then still be recognized as instances of aptitude theory—as attempts to understand and use person-situation interactions.

This section attempts to help development in either direction. It examines three views of the question: How might an interactional reconceptualization of aptitude and research thereon proceed? In one view, aptitude theory development can be considered a design science, because aptitude constructs appear to be "artifacts" in Simon's sense of that term. Much of what Simon (1969) considered as defining a "science of the artificial" may thus apply. In a second view, aptitude theory can be seen as an instance of ecological realism—the approach that has grown from Gibson's theory of direct perception (Gibson, 1966, 1979; Michaels & Carello, 1981). Here, aptitude constructs are understood in the language of "affordances" and "effectivities," which characterize the action of particular persons in particular environments. In still another view, aptitude theory needs to be built on a kind of descriptive, formative evaluation aimed at improving both local understanding and local control of treatments for the benefit of the persons served. Much of what Cronbach (1975a, 1982a, 1982b, 1986) sees as the best style for evaluation studies and for social science generally, also applies. Although these views derive from very different emphases, at base they may not be incompatible.

Aptitude and Design Science

To use Simon's view first, consider the inner system of a person and the outer system of a treatment with respect to some goal. Aptitude constructs arise from the observation of mismatch between the two systems. In Simon's (1969) words:

> An artifact can be thought of as a meeting point—an 'interface' in today's terms— between an 'inner' environment, the substance and organization of the artifact itself, and an 'outer' environment, the surroundings in which it appears. If the inner environment is appropriate to the outer environment, or vice versa, the artifact will serve its intended purpose. (p. 7)

> . . . This way of viewing artifacts applies equally well to many things that are not manmade—to all things, in fact, that can be regarded as 'adapted' to some situation; and, in particular, it applies to the living systems that have evolved through the forces of organic evolution. (p. 7)

> Central to [the nature of artifacts] . . . are the goals that link the inner to the outer system. The inner system is an organization of natural phenomena capable of attaining the goals in some range of environments; but ordinarily there will be many functionally equivalent natural systems capable of doing this. (p. 11).

> The outer environment determines the conditions for goal attainment. If the inner system is properly designed, it will be adapted to the outer environment, so that its behavior will be determined in large part by the behavior of the latter . . . to predict how it will behave, we need only ask 'How would a rationally designed system behave under these circumstances?' The behavior takes on the shape of the task environment. (pp. 11–12)

But matters must be just a little more complicated than this . . . often, we shall have to be satisfied with meeting the design objectives only approximately. Then the properties of the inner system will 'show through'. That is, the behavior of the system will only partly respond to the task environment; partly, it will respond to the limiting properties of the inner system. (p.13)

In a benign environment we would learn from the [inner system] . . . only what it had been called upon to do; in a taxing environment we would learn something about its internal structure—specifically, about those aspects of the internal structure that were chiefly instrumental in limiting performance. (p. 13)

Thus, for a particular person in a particular environment, the empirical evidence of aptitude arises from the inabilities of the behavioral system to adapt perfectly to its environment. Aptitude differences between persons in particular environments "show through" as differences in these "inabilities"—the limiting properties of the inner systems to adapt to the features of taxing environments in order to meet stated goals. For a person who is perfectly suited to a treatment or a treatment that is perfectly suited to a person, the goal is reached successfully; the presence of aptitude is inferred from this fact, but it is attributable to *both* person and environment, that is, to their benign interface. For a person who is not perfectly adapted to a treatment or a treatment that is not perfectly adapted to a person, the goal is not successfully reached; this fact shows that inaptitude of some kind is present. But again, inaptitude is attributable to the interface; either the inner system or the outer system, or both, need redesign to bring them into adaptive harmony.

It seems to follow from Simon's view that research should focus on inaptitudes, not on aptitudes. As there are many functionally equivalent systems that can produce a successful match, the details and idiosyncracies of each can be ignored. Given a mismatch for some person-treatment-goal combination, moreover, research aimed at system redesign need only find and focus on the key inabilities in the interface that constitute the mismatch, and correct them. One does this by abstracting the phenomenon from its details and simulating it. Into a rational system for successful match one builds limitations that reflect the demands of a taxing environment and that thereby reproduce the mismatch. The demand-limitation simulation defines the source of inaptitude for that particular treatment-goal pairing. Simon further assumes that these sources of inaptitude will be relatively simple and relatively few. System redesign can then proceed by reshaping the treatment to eliminate demands, thereby circumventing limitations, or by removing limitations directly by restraining the person.

It is an optimistic view. Again in Simon's (1969) words:

The more we are willing to abstract from the detail of a set of phenomena, the easier it becomes to simulate the phenomena. Moreover, we do not have to know, or guess at, all the internal structure of the system. But only that part of it that is crucial to the abstraction. (p. 16)

It is fortunate that this is so, for if it were not, the top-down strategy that built the natural sciences over the past three centuries would have been infeasible. (p. 17)

This skyhook-skyscraper construction of science from the roof down to the yet unconstructed foundations was possible because the behavior of the system at each level depended on only a very approximate, simplified, abstracted characterization of the system at the level next beneath. (p. 17)

In the best of all possible worlds—at least, for a designer—we might be able to characterize the main properties of the system and its behavior without elaborating the detail of *either* the outer or inner environments. We might look toward a science of the artificial that would depend on the relative simplicity of the interface as its primary source of abstraction and generality. (p. 9)

Certainly the details and idiosyncracies initially left out represent empirical questions. The abstract generalization of Simon's simulation can be tested with other persons, treatments, and goals to locate boundary conditions. And, assuming these boundaries are relatively stable, as they are in the natural sciences, the abstract representation of inabilities and the appropriate redesigns should be made generally servicable.

Even with simple interfaces and stable boundaries, however, an important aspect of individual differences in aptitude seems to be omitted from this formulation. The interface not only displays limitations or weaknesses, it also displays unique strengths. Human performers seek to capitalize on features of the outer environment that match their own strengths—that provide opportunities—and they appear to differ in their ability to do this. This side of the interface seems better illuminated in the view of ecological realism, and particularly in Gibson's concept of affordances.

Aptitude and Ecological Realism

Gibson (1979) addressed the mutuality of person and environment in the control of perception-action sequences as follows:

The *affordances* of the environment are what it *offers* the animal, what it *provides* or *furnishes,* either for good or ill . . . . [the term] implies the complementarity of the animal and the environment [as in an ecological niche]. (p. 127; emphasis in original)

In architecture a niche is a place that is suitable for a piece of statuary, a place into which the object fits. In ecology a niche is a setting of environmental features that are suitable for an animal, into which it fits metaphorically. (p. 129). . . . a niche is a set of affordances. (p. 128)

The concept of affordance is derived from . . . [the Gestalt concept of the valence, invitation, and demand character of objects] but with a crucial difference. The affordance of something does *not change* as the need of the observer changes. The observer may or may not perceive or attend to the affordance, according to his needs, but the affordance, being invariant, is always there to be perceived. (pp. 138–139; emphasis in original)

Thus, for Gibson, affordances are properties of both environment and behavior; they exist in the union of observer and the surfaces—the objects, substances, and other animals and persons—observed. Particular species of organisms, and also particular organisms, are tuned or prepared to perceive particular affordances that invite their particular actions. This usage is at many points close to the old meanings and roots of *aptitude* previously quoted: "fat is apt to burn" equals "fat affords burning", and Milton's "helpful aptitude between man and woman" becomes Gibson's (1979) "what the male affords the female is reciprocal to what the female affords the male" (p. 135).

This implication of aptitude in Gibson's theory has also been elaborated by others.

To say that affordances are perceived means that information specifying the affordances is available in the stimulation and can be detected by a properly attuned perceptual system. To detect affordances is, quite simply, to detect meaning. (Michaels & Carello, 1981, p. 42)

Different animals engage in very different behaviors. The potential purposive behaviors are called its *effectivities* . . . .Whether an animal flies, swims, walks, or slithers; whether it pecks, nibbles, sucks, or licks; whether it smokes, watches television, or mugs old people will 'determine' the affordances it can detect. Because information specifies *behaviors* that are afforded and because different animals have different sets of effectivities, *affordances belong to animal-environment systems and nothing less.* [Thus] . . . information about affordances is 'personal'; it is unique to particular animal-environment units. (Michaels & Carello, 1981; pp. 42–43; emphasis in original)

From the view of ecological realism, research on aptitude requires a detailed analysis of the affordance-effectivity matches of different persons and different treatments. This analysis emphasizes the opportunities offered by a particular treatment to be detected and capitalized upon by a particular person to achieve a goal, not only the mismatches that limit such achievement. It further assumes that the *grain* of this analysis must remain at a level that identifies the unique person-situation synergy in ecological terms. Just as reduction to physical or biological description does not preserve the ecological phenomenon, abstraction to a generalized simulation also does not. Furthermore, ecological information is personal; it is unique to particular person-ecology units. There is therefore no detached or abstracted list of qualities of treatments that will serve all persons equally well, or of persons that will serve all treatments equally well. Aptitude is the unique coalition of affordances and effectivities in particular person-treatment units.

The analysis of affordance-effectivity compatibility can be schematized paraphrasing Shaw, Turvey, and Mace (1981). A treatment T affords action X for person P on occasion O if certain relevant compatibilities between T and P obtain. A person P can effect action X in treatment T if certain relevant mutual compatibilities between P and T obtain. It follows that four compatibility conditions are possible: Case I—T affords actions that P is tuned to effect; Case II—T affords actions that P is not tuned to effect; Case III—T does not afford actions that P is tuned to effect; Case IV—T does not afford actions that P is not tuned to effect. It is then clear that successful performance, e.g. in learning, can occur only in Case I. Case II represents lost opportunity, unless P can somehow become tuned to effect the actions that T affords on future occasions. Case III also represents lost opportunity and perhaps frustration, unless T can somehow be changed to afford actions that P can effect. Case IV is the null set.

In short, the analysis of these compatibility conditions must in the view of ecological realism be conducted for particular persons and particular treatments using coalitional or reciprocal action concepts. No abstract list of P or T characteristics is useful. Unfortunately, examples of this sort of analysis seem to exist only in ecological research on animal behavior or on human perception (see Michaels & Carello, 1981). The complexity of such analyses in educational, psychotherapeutic, or occupational situations would seem to be staggering. Yet, as with the view of Simon's design science, Gibson's ecological realism places the concept of aptitude in the person-situation interface—in its affordance-effectivity structure—not in the head of the person. This is a radical departure from conventional cognitive theory and is therefore controversial. But it seems to provide a new avenue for research on aptitude nonetheless. It also ties in with cognitive psychology's new emphasis on situation specificity.

Aptitude and Formative Evaluation

The third view stems initially from Cronbach's formulation of the ATI problem, as described in a previous section. Aptitude is a multivariate mixture—a complex—of person and treatment characteristics that promotes the person's benefit in that situation. Different treatment situations will involve different mixtures. New aptitude constructs will thus need to be particularized to the local situations of interest.

To this point, the three views interrelate: Simon's concept of inabilities and Gibson's affordances and effectivities fit well within Cronbach's view of aptitude complexes, and all emphasize the interactional interface and its particularity, in one way or another. But Simon counts on finding a simple, short list of abstract features to describe each interface design problem, whereas Gibson expects description to be specific and unique to particular person-ecology units—no abstraction to a general list and also no reduction to physical and physiological description will do. Cronbach's view seems to lie between; he might start with a list of abstract individual difference constructs, though not so short a list as Simon's, but would expect particularized mixtures as emergent constructs in specific person-situation units, as would Gibson. What level of abstraction or specificity one gets in the resulting constructs of course depends on what level one's research style is geared to detect. Thus, Cronbach's recommended research style would leave a place for both other views while departing from both in important respects. In particular, it would go well beyond the other two views in recommending no less than a revolution for research on aptitude, and for psychology generally.

Cronbach's research approach would especially reject the conventions that make up normal psychological science today. His position starts from an examination of the limits of conventional ATI research, but also from his reformulation of the methodology of educational and social program evaluation, of which the ATI problem is but one special part. And it broadens into a general reconstruction of a philosophy of science for social inquiry (see Cronbach, 1975a, 1982a, 1982b, 1986). The general themes of this proposed reconstruction are not reviewed here (see Snow & Wiley, this volume); rather, the present discussion attempts to interpret its implications for aptitude research only.

After careful review of extant work (see Cronbach & Snow, 1977), Cronbach (1975a) recognized that the problem of ATI could not be solved without a radical shift in style of inquiry. Just as ATI findings condition any generalizations about aptitude and treatment main effects, so higher-order ATI condition generalizations about lower-order ATI. And aptitudes and treatments are also multivariate beyond the relations an investigator hypothesizes, or studies. If one attempts to fit multivariate aptitude regression functions to achievement outcome in each treatment in a typical educational experiment, for example, one is forced to obtain a large sample of students in order to ensure a reasonable level of statistical power. A large sample in education means multiple classrooms and teachers, perhaps even multiple schools. This in turn means multiple educational and social contexts within and between treatments, and thus further interactive complexities. Context interactions can be subtle or profound; but their effects usually remain concealed in the typical research design. All this not only poses difficult design, aggregation, and analysis problems for individual studies (see, e.g., Cronbach & Snow, 1977; Cronbach & Webb, 1975). It makes extrapolation beyond the particular context of each such study highly suspect. Replication of study conditions in any strict sense is impossible. In turn, it calls into question the conventional style of research in psychology and social science, which for the most part has remained dedicated to formal testing of simple generalizations stated in advance and attempts at building nomothetic theory atop the network of generalizations thus stated.

This conventional style, borrowed from physics, assumes that natural regularities exist in timeless order waiting to be discovered. If we apply rigorous procedures and decision rules to distinguish empirical truths from falsehoods, and to ensure parsimonious interpretations, we can amass the truths into generalized propositions that can be organized into lawful theories. These will, in turn, support or suggest particular educational policies. Cronbach (1982b) would abandon this style for all but a small portion of the agenda of psychological and social science, and thus all but a fraction of research on aptitude.

The fraction of aptitude research that might retain this style concerns what Cronbach (1986) calls "capacities."

> Capacities are described in propositions about the conductivity of wires of various compositions, for example, and in statements about the number of bits that can be held in short-term memory. A physical law is typically a statement of a capacity, dividing possibility from impossibilities. . . . Capacities are the prime source of the "puzzles" to which Kuhnian normal science attends. (p. 87)

> Scientists often uncover an unrecognized capacity by establishing exceptional conditions . . . massive doses, extensive practice, and the like. Sometimes what has been thought impossible is brought about. . . . (p. 88)

Thus, psychological study of abacus or chess masters or musical, medical, or mathematical experts may suggest how it is that each excels. The work of Ericsson and Chase (1982) explains how the short-term memory of a particular expert can be made to retain some 70 bits beyond the "law" of 7 ± 2, for example. Some capacity puzzles may yield to computer simulation, in the sense that the simulation shows what might be—it demonstrates possible psychological mechanisms. Simon's (1979) researches are a good example. And some capacity puzzles may yield to physiological explanation; the Hendrickson and Hendrickson (1982) theory of cortical evoked potential as an indicant of intelligence might be an example. It would seem that both the limiting inabilities of Simon and the potential effectivities of Gibson are capacity concepts.

But the study of capacities is not the main business of research on aptitude, or of social inquiry generally. For work in this main stream, Cronbach (1982b, 1986) urged that we set aside the conventional hypothesis testing rules and misguided interpretation of parsimony that have confused and stifled research efforts in recent decades. We should reject sheer empirical generalization as a research strategy, and be skeptical of all generalizations that reach beyond time, place, and population. Persons and situations often change rapidly and they cannot be isolated from the many layers of social context in which they are embedded. Therefore, the sorts of stable boundary definitions for phenomena possible in the natural sciences are not available. The simulations and technological redesigns Simon recommends may be useful up to some point, but because of the particularity of context most of that work must involve the designer in on-line, on-site engagement. Even then, the design may have a very short half-life. Gibson's psycho-physical ecological description may also be useful; it captures an important aspect of the interface. But aptitude research will also require a social ecological perspective.

What is needed for most aptitude research is a style akin to formative evaluation. Grounded, rich description of a particular context is the focus and starting point. Any one piece of research on aptitude is a case study: It . . . "reports on events in one or more sites during one slice of time. It can be viewed best as quantitatively assisted history" (Cronbach, 1982b, pp. 73–74). As a case description, locale rather than phenomenal boundary conditions can then be carefully framed to contain the substantive interpretations and conjectures within this context. Clear local boundaries help limit unwarranted generalization, but they also simplify description by bringing higher-order interactions to lower orders, enabling substantive not just empirical description. Predictions are also substantive, not just empirical, and are also local to this locale; they are not generalized as prescriptions even across time in this place without careful monitoring, because conditions change and the changes also need description.

Thus, aptitude theories are not built from generalizations into a network of laws expected to hold unqualifiedly across persons, situations, and times. Rather they are built up within a local context to fit a particular class of persons operating in a particular class of situations over particular periods of time. The researcher becomes a formative evaluator and the aptitude theory evolves in adaptation to local conditions, and changes therein, through continued tinkering, monitoring, and descriptive research.

Generalizations can certainly be imported from elsewhere into this locale, but they are to be regarded as initial questions put to the local design problem for consideration alongside other local questions; they are not prescriptions to be applied and tested blindly there. When viewed from another local context, the produce of this research is not a more refined answer to a fixed and general question, but rather an enriched set of questions and concepts about what may count as aptitude in the new context. Perhaps also the product is a better sense of how to study "what-connects-to-what" in that context. But these are not generalizations.

There are also likely to be emergent properties of aptitude that are uniquely situated in each context studied. The particular demands and affordances of one situation call forth a unique blend of personal strengths and weaknesses—an aptitude complex—that will not be duplicated in the next situation. In significant part, also, the persons studied in any natural context (in schools, clinics, and businesses, but also in laboratories) create their own treatments. They possess inventive individual psychologies. But they are also in communion with others as members of nested social groups (in classrooms, within schools, within communities, for example). As noted, a social ecological perspective has to be added to individual ecological description in aptitude research.

Conceptual productions of these sorts enrich other research on aptitude; they suggest new aptitude concepts that pose questions for research in new locales. Cronbach (1986) sees such products as the main contribution of social science today. Concepts are crystallizations from local historical reports (one or more) and should not be undervalued:

> Investigators attempt to extend historical reports into propositions, and understanding is often identified with the number and power of the propositions. I would stress, however, the benefit that concepts confer when we are not prepared to specify their interconnections or even to define them sharply. A concept captures a line of thought and by its very existence points to an aspect of events that some thinker has considered important. . . . Concepts suggest first-order questions to investigate and aspects of a situation to be observed or put under research control. A concept such as 'electricity' or 'social class' has value even when, in its early days, it is a place marker for a possible building site rather than a keystone of a theoretical arch." (p. 89)

New conceptions of the aptitude complexes important in particular person-situation interfaces have just this character. They are, at least, place markers. Whether a particular aptitude complex then becomes the object for further research investment depends on its perceived importance with respect to the local agenda, and the costs of ignoring it in this regard. As this local research proceeds, evidence will accumulate regarding each of the five descriptive goals listed earlier as characteristic of an aptitude theory. A coherent, integrative story will be formulated about what counts as aptitude in the particular situation at hand, for the particular persons served. The story will interpret how and why person and treatment characteristics match or mismatch as they are observed to do. Local prescriptions may also be formulated, about the further design of adaptive instruction in light of this aptitude concept. Continuing evaluation reports on the prescription then add further to the descriptive story, as well as signal the need for still further revisions.

But does this story count as *theory?* The answer of course depends on what meaning one gives to the term. If the story merely records what happened, as a series of events in some time and place, then most would say there is no theory apparent. But if the story offers a conceptual explanation that is a tenable, responsible interpretation compatible with the observational record, then I would argue that it is a theory just as historical interpretations are theories. It is a local theory, however, not a general theory (Snow, 1977a). Its usefulness as theory rests on the degree to which it sheds new light on local events, problems, and objectives today and tomorrow, raises new questions for further work, and advances audience understanding.

It follows that there will be many different local aptitude theories across a range of situations, and perhaps some will be alternative interpretations for the same situations. This too is useful, if one accepts Cronbach's (1986) pluralistic and fluid style for aptitude research:

> It is reasonable for different persons to accept different interpretations, and unreasonable to hope that empirical research can (or should) resolve all the conflicts among conceptualizations. A conception that some audience finds stimulating ought to be entertained unless and until it is proved untenable. We allow a work of art to throw new light on events without expecting the interpretation to be the whole and only truth; indeed, we value art because its practitioners offer alternative interpretations. . . . [Aptitude] interpretations ought to be afforded the tolerance afforded to art, and fortunately sometimes they are. For example, it was as artistic portrayal that Murray's list of needs and presses made its contribution. Murray offered, not a set of propositions intended to displace all competitors, but an alternative vocabulary for talking about persons, incentives, and gratifications.
>
> Many a realist wants concepts to name entities that exist in nature quite apart from man's construing. [Aptitude research] . . . would be better off without that aspiration. To be sure, interpretations must be compatible with observations. . . . But . . . . Few targets of [aptitude research] . . . function as entities, and such entities as we have are not classifiable into categories as 'real' as those for atoms and plants. There is no reason to think that any one 'structure' for personality . . . is more real than another. Rather, alternative conceptualizations highlight particular aspects of behavior and feeling and so suit particular purposes. (pp. 97–98)

Research on aptitude can be conducted in a manner more detached from any given local context. But it then requires a mixed strategy in which the limits of each method of attack are clearly appreciated and the complementarities among them are used. In particular, the local descriptive character of the aptitude constructs should not be lost from sight. If aptitude patterns in several sites are then seen to be similar, there may be more abstract categories to be formulated that place cases in orderly arrays. But if aptitude theories are eventually to encompass multiple cases, they must first be built from bottom up.

EXAMPLES

The discussion and debate these views open up will and should continue in the years ahead. But the construction of particular aptitude concepts and theories of the form envisioned, and the development of the new research styles needed to do this, will have to proceed by example and be extended by analogy from study to study. In rejecting conventional research styles, each view in its own way implies this as the only avenue of advance.

The extant examples of today are few, and even these are as yet vague and incomplete. But there are a few interesting new starts in educational research, and a few also in research in engineering and industry, and in medicine and psychotherapy. This chapter can conclude with but a taste of examples from each field.

In educational research, Cole (1985) gives several examples of context-sensitive approaches to instruction, which use ecological descriptions of the skills and interests of individual learners when they are not in school to develop teaching methods that afford use of these strengths. In each context, the appropriate aptitude-instruction interface had to be developed and adapted over time. In one instance, highly individualized kinds of out-of-school expertise were discovered among students in a science activity—a student's profound interest in crawfish was one example—that then allowed other instructional activities to connect to each learner's unique prior knowledge. In another, students' home-based Spanish-speaking ability was used to aid discussion of stories read in English, thereby building English reading comprehension. In still others, the particular cultural background of groups of learners could be capitalized upon to design appropriate instructional conditions: Familiarity with the "talk story" format used in Native Hawaiian families suggested a similar format for school lessons; the character of Native American discourse styles yielded a design for similar classroom participation rules. In each case, the particular knowledge, skills, interests and experience patterns of the students are aptitudes for particularly designed instruction; each affords use of the other. But they were discovered and developed through formative evaluation within the boundaries of a particular context. They do not generalize or transfer to other contexts, at least not without new formative evaluation in the new context—and this will inevitably produce variations on each theme. Cole remarks on how seemingly impossible it is to transfer some of the techniques to other teachers from the master teachers who invented them.

A quite different example comes from an evaluation of an innovative medical education program (Snow, 1977b). Conventional ability and personality measures were used in an attempt to trace student trajectories over a series of small-group, problem-centered instructional exercises. The aim was to describe the mixes of aptitude differences characterizing students who did well or poorly in this new situation, which differed markedly from the students' former schooling. These descriptions could then help guide continuing development of the program. In the first month of exercises, students described as highly able and achievement motivated but independent and task oriented did less well than expected, whereas students described as more interpersonally oriented rather than task oriented, and of middle-range ability, did especially well. The interpretation was that the instructional situation suited the latter students but not the former because it demanded a high degree of cooperative interpersonal activity in the learning tasks. By the fifth month of exercises, however, the two aptitude groups had reversed order; the able, motivated, task-oriented students had either adapted to the cooperative environment or found ways to circumvent the group work to learn on their own, whereas the interpersonally oriented students had apparently come to rely unduly on the cooperative process and were ill-prepared as problems became more complex and difficult. Thus the aptitude complex that described performance differences at an early stage of instruction shifted with adaptation to the situation; what at first appeared to be an aptitude for this kind of instruction appeared later to be an inaptitude, and vice versa. Adaptation to this context subtly changed the aptitude construct, for these persons in this time and place. But the continuing improvement of the program and the decreasing novelty of it, for these students and for new waves of students in succeeding years, might well change these patterns of aptitudinal adaptation further. Admission or placement policies based on predictions from this first study would be ill-advised. Indeed, program revision was aimed at eliminating the differential aptitude pattern, not at using it.

Still a third educational example comes from Webb's (1982, 1983) studies of small group interaction in mathematics problem solving. Here the plan was to compare homogenous and heterogeneous ability groups; there were uniform high, middle, and low groups, and groups that mixed two students from each ability level. But the planned comparison led to no generalization. What mattered was the treatment these students created in their interactions. Mixed groups did well if the more able students took on the role of explainer and the less able students asked for and used the help, not otherwise. Uniform high and low groups did poorly, but for reasons that differed according to the interpersonal dynamics the groups adopted. Uniform middle groups did well by avoiding these dynamics. The aptitude complex important in this situation, then, was a wedding of ability and particular interpersonal style adopted in this situation and discovered in observations of the actual sessions. A new aptitude concept emerges from this research, but not a prediction about how other mixed ability groups will necessarily work.

In industrial settings, research on personnel selection has pursued aptitude complexes, usually in the form of studies of configural prediction or moderator effects. These are basically aptitude-aptitude interactions; situation variation has been little studied. Indeed, most work has sought validity generalization, trying to show that situation (and sample) variation can be ignored (see Cronbach, 1982b, on the fallacy in this). Research on organizational structures, climates, and leadership, on the other hand, has produced a few notable examples.

Some old work by Forehand (1968) suggests the possibility that innovative performance in the government organizations studied related positively to cognitive ability in group-centered climates but not in rule-centered climates, whereas personality measures reflecting deference, preference for order, and endurance related negatively in the former but not the latter climate. Also, an aggression score related positively to performance in the latter climate, but not in the former. Quite different aptitude mixtures are thus implied for the two situations. Apparently, however, these implications have not been pursued in related research.

Lines of research summarized by McClelland (1985) and by Miner (1978) suggest that a pattern of leadership motivation based mainly on need for power versus need for affiliation is characteristic of successful managers in nontechnical situations involving social influence, but not in technical managerial situations. Aptitude pattern varies also with level in the organization. And some work has suggested that achievement motivational patterns functional at earlier managerial levels can become dysfunctional at later levels (Heckhausen, 1983). Thus, aptitude complexes can shift significantly between-situation within-person.

Perhaps the most sustained research on person-situation interaction in industry concerns Fiedler's leadership theory (see Fiedler, 1978; Fiedler & Garcia, 1987). The aptitude complex involves several person and situation factors, and curvilinear relations. In brief, individual leaders differ in the degree to which they differentiate among their coworkers, suggesting a distinction between task-oriented and relationship-oriented personalities. But working conditions are more or less favorable to directive versus nondirective leader behavior, as a function of their degree of affective leader-worker relationship, task structure, and the position power of the leader. Task orientation leads to worker effectiveness in situations that are highly favorable or unfavorable; relationship orientation is more effective in intermediate situations. Furthermore, when situations are stressful due to problematic interpersonal relationships, leader cognitive abilities may be negatively related to work group effectiveness, whereas certain leader past experiences may be positively related. Positive ability relations reappear in nonstressful situations. The aptitude complex thus predicts both the leader behavior and situations that make use of cognitive abilities, but also the situations that control the leader behavior. Subtle changes in any of these variables can influence group effectiveness from situation to situation.

Another industrial example begins to suggest how the new kind of aptitude research can influence engineering design of the work place. Egan and Gomez (1985) report a series of studies in which two kinds of computer text editors are compared to show why different abilities account for learning difficulties in each. The research is iterative, gradually homing in on the particular ability-equipment interactions operating in this situation. The result is an analysis of the text editing process that suggests why individual differences in spatial memory influence performance on two of the component steps and why age differences appear on another; two steps in some editors demand storage and retrieval of visual patterns, and another step demands rapid response to complexity. From this, it is possible to identify ways to redesign the interface so that the stimulus processing demands that call these implied inabilities forth are reduced; the authors suggest equipment changes that might do this, but also training designs to avoid the problem without equipment change.

Finally, it is appropriate to turn to research in psychotherapy and medicine, especially since some of Cronbach's ideas about ATI were germinated in that consideration (see Cronbach, 1953; Edwards & Cronbach, 1952). Individual differences are as vast and complex in human biology and biochemistry as they are in human personality, and as they are in human ability. Yet, in contrast to educational or industrial practice, it is striking that medical and also psycho-therapeutic treatment design has rarely included any concept of aptitude or ATI.

One example comes from research on alcoholism. As Cassell (1986) has cogently argued, the disease theory upon which so much of medical research is based has fundamental flaws, especially when it confronts a problem with psycho-social aspects. Disease theory posits a single structural cause for any disease in all human beings; the object is then to find the cause and invent a "magic bullet" to fix it. "Ecological" complexities in the internal or external human environment can be ignored (see Walsh, 1987). In the case of alcoholism, however, despite much work no magic treatment has been found, and the inkling grows that an aptitude theory is needed. Cloninger (1987) has now shown that such a theory might be built on a person typology based on symptoms, inheritance patterning, and personality characteristics. To simplify this continuous multivariate aptitude space, a main distinction types persons who exhibit alcohol-seeking in adolescence and early adulthood, and show characteristics associated with high novelty seeking, low harm avoidance, and low reward dependence, as contrasted with persons who exhibit loss of control in adulthood and show characteristics associated with a passive-dependent or anxious personality (i.e., low novelty seeking, high harm avoidance, and high reward dependence). These subgroups also differ in neurophysiological and biochemical characteristics. Based on these data and other evidence from animal studies, Cloninger has developed a neurobiological learning model in which novelty seeking is associated with a behavioral activation system, harm avoidance with a behavioral inhibition system, and reward dependence with a behavioral maintenance system. Although the model carries implications for differential pharmacological and behavioral therapies based on these distinctions, research has not yet progressed far enough to map the aptitude differences onto clear treatment alternatives. But there is clearly new hope, if the complexity of each person-therapy interface is properly appreciated.

Also, research in psychotherapy is now coming to the recognition that an ATI perspective goes beyond treatment comparisons to describe which treatment may be best for which client. Differential therapeutics based on careful description of each client's characteristics is of growing interest (see Clarkin & Perry, 1987). Some of this literature even uses aptitude constructs to help understand the working mechanisms of particular therapies (see, e.g., Dance & Neufeld, 1988; Shoham-Salomon & Rosenthal, 1987). A final example comes from one of these studies.

Shoham-Salomon, Avner, and Neeman (in press) suggest that paradoxical interventions—that is, therapist directives to engage deliberately in the symptomatic behavior—work in two ways depending on dispositional tendencies of the client. Persons who are reactance-prone try to defy the therapist's directive, to mobilize resistance to it, and thereby regain their freedom not to engage in the symptomatic behavior. Persons who are not reactance-prone exhibit the behavior as directed and thereby gain increased self-efficacy in controlling the symptom. In a series of ATI studies comparing paradoxical with self control therapy in reducing study procrastination among college students, client differences in reactance and perceived self efficacy operated as expected. Reactance was clearly shown to be a mediator of the effectiveness of paradoxical therapy. For the present purpose, it is most important to note that reactance differences were both assessed as a correlational composite and also experimentally induced; it is a person characteristic, but it is also situationally aroused by specific conditions. Together with self-efficacy variations, an important aptitude complex for further research with this particular therapy is thus identified.

CONCLUSION

What constitutes aptitude in these examples differs as a function of person and situation in each instance. Interest in crawfish, ability in Spanish, knowledge of talk-story discourse, orientation toward task completion versus toward interpersonal cooperation, willingness to ask questions or provide explanations to peers, deference, orderliness, endurance, and aggression, need for power versus need for affiliation, directive versus nondirective leadership, spatial memory, adolescent versus adult alcohol seeking, novelty seeking, harm avoidance, reward dependence, reactance-propensity, self-efficacy—these are situated aptitudes (or inaptitudes), not aptitudes in general. In short, aptitude is a person-in-situation concept, as it was for continental Europeans in earlier centuries and as it has been for Cronbach all along in this one. The sooner this concept of aptitude resumes its place in social science, the sooner will social scientists be able to think straight about the importance of individual differences in the study of human affairs.

REFERENCES

Anastasi, A. (1967). Psychology, psychologists, and psychological testing. *American Psychologist, 22*, 297–306.
Anastasi, A. (1980). Abilities and the measurement of achievement. In W. B. Schrader (Ed.), *Measuring achievement: Progress over a decade* (pp. 1–10). San Francisco: Jossey-Bass.
Binet, A., & Simon, T. (1916). (Translation by E. S. Kite). *The development of intelligence in children*. Vineland, NJ: Vineland Training School.
Bruner, J. S. (1966). *Toward a theory of instruction*. Cambridge, MA: Harvard University Press.
Butler, H. E. (1954). (Trans.). *The Institutio Oratoria of Quintilian (Vol. 1)*. Cambridge, MA: Harvard University Press.
Campbell, D. T., & Fiske, D. W. (1959). Convergent and discriminant validation by the multitrait-multimethod matrix. *Psychological Bulletin, 65*, 81–105.
Carroll, J. B. (1961). Neglected areas in educational research. *Phi Delta Kappan, 42*, 339–343.

Carroll, J. B. (1974). Fitting a model of school learning to aptitude and achievement data over grade levels. In D. R. Green (Ed.), *The aptitude–achievement distinction*. Monterey, CA: CTB/ McGraw-Hill.

Carroll, J. B. (1976). Psychometric tests as cognitive tasks: A new 'structure of intellect'. In L. B. Resnick (Ed.), *The nature of intelligence*. Hillsdale, NJ: Lawrence Erlbaum Associates.

Carroll, J. B. (1980). Discussion: Aptitude processes, theory, and the real world. In R. E. Snow, P. A. Federico, & W. E. Montague (Eds.), *Aptitude, learning, and instruction, Vol. 1: Cognitive process analyses of aptitude* (pp. 139–148). Hillsdale, NJ: Lawrence Erlbaum Associates.

Case, R., & Bereiter, C. (1984). From behaviorism to cognitive behaviorism to cognitive development: Steps in the evolution of instructional design. *Instructional Science, 13,* 141–158.

Cassell, E. J. (1986). Ideas in conflict: The rise and fall (and rise and fall) of new views of disease. *Daedalus, 115*(2), 19–41.

Cattell, R. B. (1963). Theory of fluid and crystallized intelligence: A critical experiment. *Journal of Educational Psychology, 54,* 1–22.

Clarkin, J. F., & Perry, S. W. (1987). Differential therapeutics. In R. E. Hales & A. J. Frances (Eds.), *American Psychiatric Association Annual Review* (Vol. 6, pp. 331–335). Washington, DC: American Psychiatric Press, Inc.

Cloninger, C. R. (1987). Neurogenetic adaptive mechanisms in alcoholism. *Science, 236,* 410–416.

Cole, M. (1985). Mind as a cultural achievement: Implications for IQ testing. In E. Eisner (Ed.), *Learning and teaching the ways of knowing* (pp. 218–249). Chicago: National Society for the Study of Education.

Cronbach, L. J. (1953). Correlation between persons as a research tool. In O. H. Mowrer (Ed.), *Psychotherapy: Theory and research* (pp. 376–388). New York: The Ronald Press.

Cronbach, L. J. (1957). The two disciplines of scientific psychology. *American Psychologist, 12,* 671–684.

Cronbach, L. J. (1967). Instructional methods and individual differences. In R. M. Gagne (Ed.), *Learning and individual differences* (pp. 23–39). Columbus, OH: Charles E. Merrill.

Cronbach, L. J. (1971). Test validation. In R. L. Thorndike (Ed.), *Educational measurement* (2nd ed., pp. 443–507). Washington, DC: American Council on Education.

Cronbach, L. J. (1975a). Beyond the two disciplines of scientific psychology. *American Psychologist, 30,* 116–127.

Cronbach, L. J. (1975b). Five decades of public controversy over mental testing. *American Psychologist, 30,* 1–14.

Cronbach, L. J. (1980). Validity on parole: How can we go straight? In W. B. Schrader (Ed.), *Measuring achievement: Progress over a decade. Proceedings of the 1979 ETS Invitational Conference* (pp. 99–108). San Francisco: Jossey-Bass.

Cronbach, L. J. (1982a). *Designing evaluations of educational and social programs.* San Francisco: Jossey-Bass.

Cronbach, L. J. (1982b). Prudent aspirations for social inquiry. In W. H. Kruskal (Ed.), *The social sciences: Their nature and uses* (pp. 61–81). Chicago: University of Chicago Press.

Cronbach, L. J. (1984). *Essentials of psychological testing* (4th ed.). New York: Harper & Row.

Cronbach, L. J. (1986). Social inquiry by and for earthlings. In D. W. Fiske & R. A. Shweder (Eds.), *Metatheory in social science* (pp. 83–107). Chicago: University of Chicago Press.

Cronbach, L. J., & Gleser, G. C. (1965). *Psychological tests and personnel decisions.* Urbana: University of Illinois Press.

Cronbach, L. J., & Meehl, P. E. (1955). Construct validity in psychological tests. *Psychological Bulletin, 52,* 281–301.

Cronbach, L. J., & Snow, R. E. (1977). *Aptitudes and instructional methods: A handbook for research on interactions.* New York: Irvington.

Cronbach, L. J., & Webb, N. (1975). Between-class and within-class effects in a reported aptitude x treatment interaction: Reanalysis of a study by G. L. Anderson. *Journal of Educational Psychology, 67*, 717–724.

Dance, K. A., & Neufeld, R. W. J. (1988). Aptitude-treatment interaction research in the clinical setting: A review of attempts to dispel the "patient uniformity" myth. *Psychological Bulletin, 104*, 192–213.

DeGroot, A. (1965). *Thought and choice in chess*. The Hague: Mouton.

Dunnette, M. D. (Ed.). (1976). *Handbook of industrial and organizational psychology*. Chicago: Rand McNally.

Edwards, A. L., & Cronbach, L. J. (1952). Experimental design for research in psychotherapy. *Journal of Clinical Psychology, 8*, 51–59.

Egan, D. E., & Gomez, L. M. (1985). Assaying, isolating, and accommodating individual differences in learning a complex skill. In R. F. Dillon (Ed.), *Individual differences in cognition, Vol. 2* (pp. 173–217). New York: Academic Press.

English, H. B., & English, A. C. (1958). *A comprehensive dictionary of psychological and psychoanalytical terms*. New York: Longmans Green.

Ericsson, K. A., & Chase, W. G. (1982). Exceptional memory. *American Scientist, 70*, 607–615.

Fiedler, F. (1978). The contingency model and the dynamics of the leadership process. In L. Berkowitz (Ed.), *Advances in experimental social psychology* (pp. 59–112). New York: Academic Press.

Fiedler, F., & Garcia, J. E. (1987). *New approaches to leadership: Cognitive resources and organizational performance*. New York: Wiley.

Forehand, G. A. (1968). On the interaction of persons and organizations. In R. Taguiri & G. H. Litwin (Eds.) *Organizational climate: Explorations of a concept* (pp. 65–82). Boston: Graduate School of Business Administration, Harvard University.

Gagne, R. M., & Briggs, L. J. (1974). *Principles of instructional design*. New York: Holt, Rinehart and Winston.

Gardner, H. (1983). *Frames of mind*. New York: Basic Books.

Gibson, J. J. (1966). *The senses considered as perceptual systems*. Boston: Houghton Mifflin.

Gibson, J. J. (1979). *The ecological approach to visual perception*. Boston: Houghton Mifflin.

Glaser, R. (1978a). (Ed.). *Advances in instructional psychology* (Vol. 1). Hillsdale, NJ: Lawrence Erlbaum Associates.

Glaser, R. (1978b). The contributions of B. F. Skinner to education and some counterinfluences. In P. Suppes (Ed.), *Impact of research on education: Some case studies* (pp. 199–265). Washington, DC: National Academy of Education.

Glaser, R. (1982). (Ed.). *Advances in instructional psychology* (Vol. 2). Hillsdale, NJ: Lawrence Erlbaum Associates.

Greeno, J. G. (1980). Psychology of learning, 1960–1980: One participant's observations. *American Psychologist, 35*, 713–728.

Greeno, J. G. (1986, April). *Mathematical cognition: Accomplishments and challenges in research*. Invited address to the American Educational Research Association, San Francisco.

Guilford, J. P. (1967). *The nature of human intelligence*. New York: McGraw-Hill.

Heckhausen, H. (1983). Concern with one's competence: Developmental shifts in person-environment interaction. In D. Magnusson & V. L. Allen (Eds.), *Human development: An interactional perspective* (pp. 167–185). New York: Academic Press.

Hendrickson, A. E., & Hendrickson, D. E. (1982). The biological basis of intelligence, Part I: Theory, Part II: Measurement. In H. J. Eysenck (Ed.), *A model for intelligence* (pp. 151–228). Berlin: Springer-Verlag.

Humphreys, L. G., (1979). The construct of general intelligence. *Intelligence, 3*, 105–120.

Kaplan, A. (1964). *The conduct of inquiry: Methodology for behavioral science*. San Francisco: Chandler.

McClelland, D. C. (1985). *Human motivation*. Glenview, IL: Scott, Foresman.

McCormick, E. J. (1979). *Job Analysis: Methods and applications.* New York: Amacom.

McNemar, Q. (1964). Lost. Our intelligence. Why? *American Psychologist, 19,* 871–882.

Michaels, C. F., & Carello, C. (1981). *Direct perception.* New York: Appleton-Century-Crofts.

Miller, N. E. (1957). *Graphic communication and the crisis in education.* Washington, DC: National Education Association.

Miner, J. B. (1978). Twenty years of research on role motivation theory of managerial effectiveness. *Personnel Psychology, 31,* 739–760.

Oxford universal dictionary on historical principles. (1944). (3rd ed.). London: Oxford University Press.

Pellegrino, J. W., & Glaser, R. (1979). Cognitive correlates and components in the analysis of individual differences, *Intelligence, 3,* 187–214.

Reigeluth, C. M. (Ed.). (1983). *Instructional design theories and models: An overview of their current status.* Hillsdale, NJ: Lawrence Erlbaum Associates.

Rogoff, B. (1984). Introduction: Thinking and learning in social context. In B. Rogoff & J. Lave (Eds.), *Everyday cognition* (pp. 1–8). Cambridge, MA: Harvard University Press.

Rogoff, B., & Lave, J. (Eds.). (1984). *Everyday cognition: Its development in social context.* Cambridge, MA: Harvard University Press.

Scheffler, I. (1985). *Of human potential.* Boston, MA: Routledge & Kegan Paul.

Schneider, B. (1978). Person-situation selection: A review of some ability-situation interaction research. *Personnel Psychology, 31,* 281–297.

Shaw, R. E., Turvey, M. T., & Mace, W. (1981). Ecological psychology: The consequence of a commitment to realism. In W. Weimer & D. Palermo (Eds.), *Cognition and the symbolic processes* (Vol. 2). Hillsdale, NJ: Lawrence Erlbaum Associates.

Shoham-Salomon, V., Avner, R., & Neeman, R. (in press). You're changed if you do and changed if you don't: Mechanisms underlying paradoxical interventions. *Journal of Consulting and Clinical Psychology.*

Shoham-Salomon, V., & Rosenthal, R. (1987). Paradoxical interventions: A meta-analysis. *Journal of Consulting and Clinical Psychology, 55,* 22–27.

Shulman, L. S., & Keislar, E. (Eds.). (1966). *Learning by discovery.* Chicago, IL: Rand McNally.

Simon, H. A. (1969). *The sciences of the artificial.* Cambridge, MA: MIT Press.

Simon, H. A. (1979). *Models of thought.* New Haven, CT: Yale University Press.

Snow, R. E. (1977a). Individual differences and instructional theory. *Educational Researcher, 6,* 11–15.

Snow, R. E. (1977b). Research on aptitudes: A progress report. In L. S. Shulman (Ed.), *Review of research in education* (Vol. 4, pp. 50–105). Itasca, IL: Peacock.

Snow, R. E. (1980a). Aptitude and achievement. In W. B. Schrader (Ed.), *Measuring achievement: Progress over a decade. Proceedings of the 1979 ETS Invitational Conference* (pp. 39–59). San Francisco: Jossey-Bass.

Snow, R. E. (1980b). Aptitude processes. In R. E. Snow, P. A. Federico, & W. E. Montague (Eds.), *Aptitude, learning and instruction: Vol. 1. Cognitive process analyses of aptitude* (pp. 27–64). Hillsdale, NJ: Lawrence Erlbaum Associates.

Snow, R. E. (1982a). Education and intelligence. In R. J. Sternberg (Ed.), *Handbook of human intelligence* (pp. 493–585). New York: Cambridge University Press.

Snow, R. E. (1982b). The training of intellectual aptitude. In D. K. Detterman & R. J. Sternberg (Eds.), *How and how much can intelligence be increased?* Norwood, NJ: Ablex.

Snow, R. E. (1986). Individual differences and the design of educational programs. *American Psychologist, 41,* 1029–1039.

Snow, R. E. (1987). Aptitude complexes. In R. E. Snow & M. J. Farr (Eds.), *Aptitude, learning, and instruction: Vol. 3. Conative and affective process analyses.* Hillsdale, NJ: Lawrence Erlbaum Associates.

Snow, R. E., Federico, P.-A., & Montague, W. E. (Eds.). (1980a). *Aptitude, learning, and instruc-*

tion: Vol. 1. Cognitive process analyses of aptitude. Hillsdale, NJ: Lawrence Erlbaum Associates.

Snow, R. E., Federico, P.-A., & Montague, W. E. (Eds.). (1980b). *Aptitude, learning, and instruction: Vol. 2. Cognitive process analyses of learning and problem-solving.* Hillsdale, NJ: Lawrence Erlbaum Associates.

Snow, R. E., & Lohman, D. F. (1984). Toward a theory of cognitive aptitude for learning from instruction. *Journal of Educational Psychology, 76,* 347–376.

Spearman, C. (1923). *The nature of intelligence and the principles of cognition.* London: Macmillan.

Sternberg, R. J. (1977). *Intelligence, information processing and analogical reasoning: The componential analysis of human abilities.* Hillsdale, NJ: Lawrence Erlbaum Associates.

Sternberg, R. J. (1985). *Beyond IQ: A triarchic theory of human intelligence.* New York: Cambridge University Press.

Terman, L. M. (1916). *The measurement of intelligence.* Boston: Houghton Mifflin.

Thurstone, L. L. (1938). *Primary mental abilities.* Illinois: University of Chicago Press.

Thurstone, L. L. (1947). *Multiple factor analysis.* Illinois: University of Chicago Press.

Tyler, L. E. (1974). *Individual differences.* New York: Appleton-Century-Crofts.

Underwood, B. J. (1975). Individual differences as a crucible in theory construction. *American Psychologist, 30,* 128–140.

Van Der Linden, W. J. (1981). Using aptitude measurements for the optimal assignment of subjects to treatments with and without mastery scores. *Psychometrika, 46,* 257–274.

Walsh, J. (1987). Is alcoholism treatment effective? *Science, 236,* 20–21.

Webb, N. M. (1982). Student interaction and learning in small groups. *Review of Educational Research, 52,* 421–445.

Webb, N. (1983). Predicting learning from student interaction: Defining the interaction variables. *Educational Psychologist, 18,* 33–41.

Wolf, T. H. (1973). *Alfred Binet.* Illinois: University of Chicago Press.

11 Is There Any Future for Intelligence?

Robert L. Thorndike
Teachers College, Columbia University

It is written in the Book of Job "Your young men shall see visions and your old men shall dream dreams." So being by a fair margin the most venerable of the authors in this book, I shall leave the visions to the others and, exercising the prerogatives of age, dream for a bit.

And as the dreams of the aged tend to return to their childhood, my first dream carries me back some 70 years to an evening when I was taken down sleepy and protesting, to serve as the guinea pig in a demonstration to a group of Teachers College graduate students of the then quite new Stanford-Binet intelligence test. It had been only a year or two before that, in 1916, that Lewis Terman had brought out the Stanford-Binet, his version of the intelligence test that was to be the work-horse of individual ability testing in this country for the next 50 years, though the original publication of Binet's work in Paris had occurred a decade earlier.

Binet's work, and much that followed it, was a response to the problems that the schools had to face for the first time in responding to the then relatively new compulsory education laws that retained all the children of all the people in school. Whereas in earlier times those who did not take kindly to schooling just dropped out and found some sort of a niche in the world of work, the schools were now charged with providing for all children, whatever their adaptability to schooling, and were finding it heavy going. Binet, and his many successors, hoped to help in separating those who could profit from schooling as it was then conceived, but hadn't, from those who simply couldn't. The jury is still out on how well they succeeded.

My next flash-back, some 10 years later in the fall of 1927, is to the rooms of Judd Hall where, during Freshman Orientation Week, Wesleyan's entering class was being exposed to the Otis Self-Administering Test of Mental Ability. Though the College Board Scholastic Aptitude Test had come into being the year before in 1926, when it was administered to a grand total of some 8000 college applicants (compared to current figures of about a million), it was not then required for admission to Wesleyan, so the Otis was administered, presumably for guidance purposes.

I can't say that I saw evidence of it being so used during my college years, but I do know that results for my classmates came in very handy in the analyses of cognitive and personal factors predicting academic achievement that I had undertaken for my Distinction paper. By the time I reached Wesleyan, I had taken, either as a school requirement or as a home pastime, probably half of the ability tests then on the market and had developed a high degree of what has subsequently come to be called "test-wiseness," so it is not too surprising that I was able to knock the top off Mr. Otis' test—and to become, for the rest of my Wesleyan career, an "underachiever." For my college record never quite lived up to that early promise.

By the 1930s both the research and the verbiage addressed to defining the nature of intelligence had become voluminous—and sometimes acrimonious. The statistical techniques for elucidating the nature of ability dimensions were becoming increasingly sophisticated and esoteric, and these became a staple in my graduate school diet. In fact, I spent the whole last summer of that graduate study doing the calculations for a factor analysis of 32 variables that I had derived from observations of a group of white rats—a computational exercise that now, with today's computers, one might reasonably assign as an overnight homework assignment for an undergraduate class.

My first experience with computers, at that point purely as a consumer of their output didn't come until I was 45, and it was only as I reached retirement that I got my first hands-on introduction to FORTRAN. So I am still intimidated by my little APPLE, and struggle over a program that would probably be duck soup to any bright high-school youngster. I am overwhelmed by the exploits of current computer science and by the expertise of those who put into the computer the skills that enable it to play relentless and unforgiving chess and solve all the problems in the ability tests that I generate, to say nothing of making trivial the computational problems over which I sweated in my early professional life.

So it is with a good deal of diffidence that I raise the question: "Is there any future for intelligence?", meaning intelligence as psychology has defined and assessed it over the past 75 years.

The history of ability testing just about spans my lifetime, and during this relatively short history its devotees have divided their interest between strictly practical concerns of placement and guidance of individuals, primarily those at one or the other extreme of the ability spectrum, and the attempt to develop a model and theory of intellectual functioning. Thus, even while Binet in France was pooling a wide diversity of cognitive tasks in an attempt to develop an appraisal procedure that would be useful to the schools, Spearman in England was elaborating the model of a *g,* or general cognitive ability that showed up in all cognitive performances and accounted for the pervasive positive correlations among them. However, during most of the history of intelligence testing both the practical and the theoretical work on intellect have focused on the *products* of intellectual performance, displayed as final answers that can be evaluated, counted, and combined into a test score. Furthermore, both practical and theoretical concerns have focused on *individual differences* in these scores. The concept of general intellectual ability stemmed from the finding that some persons tended to do well and some poorly on a wide range of cognitive tasks.

Over this same period, the experimental psychology of cognition focused its efforts on the attempt to establish a structure of general principles that apply to the cognitive functioning of *all* persons. Traditional topics were perception, memory, concept formation and problem solving. During the past 20 years, the watchword in this camp has been "information processing," and the analogue of the computer as an information processor has become very popular as a model for human cognitive functioning. The literature speaks of sensory buffers, of short-term memory storage and working memory capacity, of executive programs governing the canvassing of long-term memory, and of production programs governing the carrying out of response. Computer modeling has become a powerful tool in the hands of such persons as Herb Simon (1979) at Carnegie-Mellon and his colleagues, in that they have been able to generate computer programs that not only solve the types of cognitive problems that appear on ability tests, but also have the same difficulties and make the same types of mistakes as are made by college sophomores. The research of the cognitive psychologists has focused primarily on the *process* of problem solution rather than on the product. What goes on when a person extrapolates a letter or number series, selects the appropriate alternative to complete an analogy, solves the Tower of Hanoi puzzle, or selects a move in a chess game?

For 30 years now, at least since Lee Cronbach's (1957) presidential address to the American Psychological Association, there have been repeated calls for psychology to integrate these two historically quite separate branches of theory and research—the branch that studies individual differences in test performances and the branch that seeks to understand and model the cognitive functioning of people-in-general. During that time each group does seem to have become more aware of the other. What do the combined efforts offer for the future? On the one hand, what do they offer for a psychological theory of intelligence? On the other, what do they offer for the application of psychological knowledge to assessment of individuals?

A complete psychology of cognition needs to provide insight into the underlying processes through which individuals attack cognitive problems. It needs also to account for the observation that some persons arrive at solutions, whereas others do not. In terms of practical application, we need to know how to modify either the processing that people carry out or the nature of the problem tasks with which they are faced so that persons can cope with their cognitive problems more efficiently. At the same time, it has seemed reasonable to try to match the tasks to the competencies of a particular person to perform those tasks, so that the tasks will be well done and so that the doers will have the satisfaction of success rather than the frustration of failure.

When we ask: "Is there any future for intelligence?" we are really raising two quite distinct, though related questions. On the one hand, we are asking whether there is any role for a construct of general intellectual ability in our theories of human behavior. Does such a construct have any place along with such performance constructs as verbal comprehension, quantitative reasoning, spatial visualizing, or speed of perception, or along with such information processing constructs as encoding information, searching long-term memory or mapping memory images on material encoded in short-term memory? On the other hand, we ask whether one general measure of cognitive functioning can serve as a useful predictor of the individual's responses to educational, vocational, and other life demands. Let us look at each of these issues in turn.

As we have seen, the early rationale for a construct of general intelligence as a dimension with respect to which individuals differ was provided by Charles Spearman in the early years of this century. Impressed by the apparently universal positive correlation among different measures of cognitive functioning, he hypothesized that a universally present g, or general ability factor was responsible for these relationships. The core of g, as Spearman viewed it, was the ability to educe relationships, and to apply the relationship to the eduction of correlates. Some forms of test exercises that have been offered as prototypes of the operation of g are the matrices item, the classification item, the seriation item, and the analogies item, as illustrated in Fig. 11.1.

Other rationales for the pervasive positive correlation among varied cognitive performances were not lacking. In conformity with his general connectionist psychology, Edward L. Thorndike viewed individual differences in general level of cognitive functioning as reflecting differences in the number and richness of connections in the central nervous system. And in somewhat the same vein, Godfrey Thomson in Scotland showed how a general pattern of correlation could arise if each measure sampled more or less randomly from the elemental units of cortical functioning, whatever those might be.

Returning to Spearman and g, it became clear at a fairly early date, and to Spearman as well as to his critics, that the model of individual differences as stemming solely from one general factor and a host of specific factors, each appearing in only a single measure, was inadequate to account for the patterns of relationship that were actually observed in the data that began to be accumulated. Different measures involving words shared, in addition to g, a common verbal factor; different numerical tests shared a common number factor; different tests of spatial visualizing shared a common spatial factor, and so on. The compelling

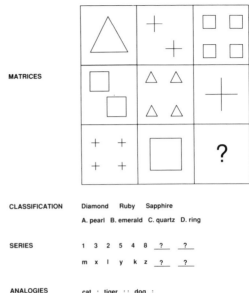

MATRICES

CLASSIFICATION   Diamond   Ruby   Sapphire

A. pearl   B. emerald   C. quartz   D. ring

SERIES   1   3   2   5   4   8   ?   ?

m   x   l   y   k   z   ?   ?

FIG. 11.1. Types of items de-   ANALOGIES   cat : tiger :: dog :
signed to assess *g*.

A. wolf   B. lion   C. puppy   D. terrier

evidence for these group factors of intermediate extent led psychometricians, especially in the United States, to question whether there was any need for a pervasive general factor. In the 1930s L. L. Thurstone at the University of Chicago proposed a multiple factor model to account for the complex pattern of interrelationships among measures of cognitive functioning involving no all-pervasive general ability. In this model, each of the several factors appeared in some but not all of the measures and each of the measures called for only a small fraction of the factors.

For the past 50 years the psychometric literature has been inundated with reports of refinements in the mathematical procedures for carrying out the analyses that generate factor structures and with empirical studies applying these procedures to accumulations of measurement data. A list of more or less cognitive factors that had been identified by 1951 with some degree of confirmation was assembled by French (1951), and is shown in part in Fig. 11.2. The most persistent and ambitious of the programs of factor analytic research, growing out of our experience in the Aviation Psychology Program in the Air Force in World War II, has been that of Guilford and his students at the University of Southern California. Guilford generated, partly on a priori and partly on empirical grounds the so-called Structure of Intellect. This imposing edifice is composed of no less than 120 cells, each representing a particular combination of intellectual content, operation and product, and each presumably corresponding to a distinct measurable and potentially useful psychological construct.

Attention
Deduction
Fluency of Expression
Induction
Ideational Fluency
Integration
Judgment
Associative Memory
Mathematical Background
Mechanical Experience
Number
Perceptual Speed
Planning
Reaction Time
Space
Speed of Association
Spatial Orientation
Span Memory

FIG. 11.2. Replicated factors of cognition reported by French (1951).

Verbal Comprehension
Visualization
Word Fluency

The mathematics of factor analysis has been developed with great sophistication and elegance. But one point on which all devotees are agreed is that no one of the mathematical models is in any sense unique, and that with appropriate numerical transformation one can move from any one model to any other, either accentuating or (in many cases) eliminating a primary general factor running broadly through the complete set of cognitive measures. The number of purely mathematical solutions that equally completely account for the structure of relationships in an extended battery of cognitive measures is unlimited. One must look beyond the mathematical models of individual differences to determine whether our psychological constructs should include or exclude a g, a general factor of cognitive functioning.

A plausible place to look would seem to be at the information processing models that deal with the successive stages of sensing, encoding, storing, and manipulating information, leading to success or failure in coping with cognitive tasks. We turn to the research in cognitive psychology to inquire whether it gives any cues as to where we might find one or more aspects of information processing that would be broadly general in involvement in cognitive tasks, and with respect to which individuals are found to differ. We can follow the processing through from initial encoding of sensory inputs, parking them temporarily in short-term memory, incorporating some of them into a long-term memory network, programming a retrieval search of long-term memory, activating an executive program for manipulating retrieved information in working memory, through to translation of a decision into overt response. We can inquire which processes in this sequence seem as if they ought to be general processes in which excellence would effect performance in a wide range of cognitive tasks. And we can ask which aspects have been found, in research studies, to be correlated with individual differences in the conventional psychometric measures of intelligence.

The first stage in processing is sensing and encoding inputs. Because we have multiple senses and because there are many content domains that are encoded— verbal, quantitative, spatial, interpersonal—much of sensing and encoding seems specific rather than general. But one aspect that could be general is *rate* of perceiving and encoding. At the most elementary level, rate has been thought of as rate of neural conduction. And over the years physiologically oriented psychologists have been fascinated by the possibility that some such simple measure might unlock the door to individual differences in intellect.

At about the time of my graduate studies, a half century ago, Travis and Young (1930) reported a correlation of .85 between speed of Achilles tendon reflex and tested intelligence. This reflex was studied because the neural pathway from the heel to the spinal column and back is 4 or 5 feet in length, so that if individual differences in rate of propagation of the neural impulse were of importance, those differences should have a good chance to show up in this reflex arc. The rationale for expecting a relationship with intelligence was that development of cognitive skills would be favored by establishment of a wealth of connections within the central nervous system, and that rapid peripheral conduction rate would be related to this.

Alas, a further examination of the data from Travis' study led to a retraction of the claimed results, with the interesting explanation that the original correlation had arisen from inaccuracies in reading of the tendon response records. This is the one place that I am aware of where allegedly random measurement error was called upon to account for a dramatic positive result. The scuttlebutt in our graduate lab at the time had it that the real culprit was a misplaced decimal point in the calculation of the correlation coefficient.

But instrumentation for measuring neural functioning was relatively primitive in the 1930s, and direct electrical pick-up of neural and cortical action currents was largely undeveloped. Since the development of instruments and techniques for measuring directly the electrical responses in the brain, attempts to relate one or another indicator of rate or type of neuro-physiological response in the brain to psychometric ability measures has developed a new appeal.

One investigator who reported quite dramatic results for such an indicator in the 1960s was Ertl, working at the University of Ottawa. He studied the latency of the EEG response, and analysed specifically the latency of the third peak of the evoked potential to a brief photic stimulus. That is, the subject was stimulated with a brief flash of light, and the time was measured from the onset of the light to the crest of the third brain wave in response to the stimulus. The average latency over a set of trials was correlated with Bellevue-Wechsler IQ, and the reported correlations were 0.88 and 0.76, respectively, in samples of 22 and 76 university students (Barry & Ertl, 1965). Correlations of this size approach the ceiling set by the reliabilities of the two measures.

These dramatic results led Ertl to carry out a further study based on 573 pupils drawn from the Ottawa public schools, and here the correlation dropped to a more credible, but still quite significant, 0.35 (Ertl & Schafer, 1969). The Ertl Index was not offered as a replacement for psychometric indices of ability, but still appeared to have a genuine relationship to them.

The Index appeared to the Directors of the Educational Records Bureau, a testing agency for a consortium of primarily private schools in the United States, to merit further study in settings outside Ertl's own laboratory. So funds were obtained and arrangements made to test sizeable samples of Black and White pupils in the schools of Mount Vernon, New York. The Index had a good deal of appeal as a culture-free indicator of cognitive abilities, if it worked.

In this study, records were gathered by technicians who had been trained by Ertl, and these were then sent to him to be analysed. However, the precaution was taken of having the records analysed blind, without access to any identifying information about the pupil. The outcome, as reported by Davis (1971), based on a total of almost 800 cases, was a flock of nonsignificant coefficients, with a mid-value for the correlation of Ertl's Index to ability test of 0.01!

I have heard nothing further of Ertl or the Ertl index, but hope springs eternal. The fact that one index fell on its face doesn't deter other enthusiasts from seeking out other brain-wave indicators.

As techniques have improved for both the electrical recording and the computer synthesis of cortical neural activity, quite a large literature has developed on so-called "event related potentials." Most of it is concerned with using these indices as another source of data on specific cognitive processes—such as allocation of attention or subjective probabilities of responses (Donchin & Israel, 1980). However, there has been continued interest in individual differences in evoked potentials as indicators of differences in level of intellectual functioning. The indicators vary from investigator to investigator. One indicator that has been proposed is a "string" measure that sums the up and down deviations of the EEG record over a half-second following a brief sensory stimulus (Blinkhorn & Hendrickson, 1982). Another is a measure of so-called "neural adaptability." This index compares the size of evoked potential to a self-presented (and consequently anticipated) stimulus to one the timing of which cannot be controlled by the subject. The expected stimulus is reported to produce a considerably smaller response than the "surprise" stimulus, and the percentage of reduction is taken as a measure of neural adaptability (Jensen, Schafer, & Crinella, 1981). Each of these indices is reported by its proponent to show a significant relationship to psychometric g. And it is always possible that these relationships will be replicated and sustained by other investigators. If that happens, we shall have to take seriously development of a rationale that would fit them into our concept of intelligence. But so many past neural indicators have fallen by the wayside that I shan't start holding my breath yet.

However, it might well be that the aspect of speed that is important is not the speed of neural conduction but the speed of processing information, of receiving information inputs and responding to them. The rationale would be not that it is the speed of processing any one input that is important per se, but that the fast processor can input more, and in closer conjunction, so that over time a richer store is accumulated in long-term memory.

Measures of reaction time were among the first to be explored as possible indicators of intellectual functioning. James McKeen Cattell studied their relationships in 1890, and his student, Wissler, tried to relate reaction time to academic success in Columbia College freshmen. But when this drew a fairly complete blank, in part because of the inadequacy of the measures, and when Binet's tests involving more complex cognitive activities appeared, interest shifted away from reaction time measures. It is only recently that speed measures of simple information processing have begun to receive renewed attention as important ways of studying the processes of cognition, and perhaps of studying individual differences in cognitive capability.

One of a number of persons active in investigating reaction speed as providing cues to the understanding of cognitive functioning and of individual differences in psychometrically evaluated intelligence is Arthur Jensen. He has provided a recent review of the literature (Jensen, 1980) on relationships between different indices of reaction speed and tested intelligence and has gathered a rather substantial volume of new data on the topic. A summary of his conclusions would go somewhat as follows:

1. There is no question that, at all ages and in all ability ranges, there is a relationship between speed of reaction and tested intelligence.

2. The relationship increases as the complexity of the decision increases. Thus, with choices rather than a simple reaction, and with several choices rather than just two, the correlation is higher.

3. Different reaction time paradigms, involving in differing degrees short-term and long-term memory, are only modestly correlated with one another, and provide supplementary information.

4. Variability of reaction time appears to be as promising or more promising than average time as a predictor.

5. It seems possible that, with allowance for the unreliability of the measures, a suitable composite of several different reaction speed measures could account for substantially all of individual differences in the underlying general ability factor.

The final conclusion constitutes strong medicine. But it does appear that in rate of information processing we have one promising foundation for a general intellective factor.

A next stage in the information processing sequence is holding material in short-term memory so that it can be organized, manipulated, and related to information retrieved from the long-term memory store. Individuals do differ in the amount that can be held in short-term memory, and that capacity increases as individuals mature. One common indicator of the capacity of short-term memory is digit span—the number of digits that can be repeated without error after hearing them read over once. A somewhat different indicator, involving more of coherence and meaning, is sentence span—the length of meaningful sentence that can be repeated precisely as heard and without error of wording or word order. In chidren of any age group from 3 to 10 and above, these two showed a correlation of about 0.50 in some data that I was analyzing recently. And in the manual of the Wechsler Intelligence Scale for Children it is reported that Digit Span correlates, again, about 0.50 with a total score based on the remaining subtests.

One could suggest that the ability to hold more in working memory at any given point in time facilitates current information processing, and at the same time makes possible a more complex associative net as material is stored in long-term memory. Thus, a larger short-term memory capacity might contribute in a general way to the richness of the long-term memory store.

The specific contents of long-term memory would appear to relate more to limited ability factors rather than to a general ability, or g factor. Thus, a child who had had a richer and more extensive exposure to language and who had had the opportunity to store a wealth of semantic associations should excell on a verbal factor, whereas one who had had a wealth of experience with and memory store concerning devices and machines should excell on a measure of mechanical comprehension. These stored contents are sometimes referred to as crystallized, as distinct from fluid intelligence, being viewed as the residue from effective earlier information processing.

Of course, opportunities to store information about the surrounding world can differ in amount as well as in kind. On the negative side, infants raised in very impoverished orphanage environments in which contacts with persons as well as with things were most limited, have been found to display retardation in general indices of mental development. And it may be that, over a considerable range, opportunities to acquire a richer long-term memory store relate to general measures of cognitive functioning—a kind of averaging of experiences over a wide range of contents. Here, we would have the impact of social environment, in contrast to properties of the individual biological organism.

Proceeding further, in the information-processing model of cognitive functioning, reference is usually made to executive programs that direct the processing of information, analogous to the executive programs in a computer that determine what is done with the inputs from various sources. Such programs lie at the heart of computer simulations of human problem solving. In human behavior, they can be viewed as strategies for attacking a given type of problem. For example, in the number series problem 1 2 4 7 11 an executive program might explicitly calculate the difference between each number and the one following it, giving the sequence 1 2 3 4. The program might then, though probably implicitly and automatically, get the differences between the differences, finding that they are all unity. The program would then extrapolate the series of 1's, applying the extrapolation to the first differences to get, as the next members of that series, 5 and 6, and would use these to extend the original series, getting 16 and 22. Often such a program operates almost immediately and without our focal awareness of what has been done.

This example has illustrated a program to deal with a specific problem format. It relates to one limited test performance—to an s factor rather than to g. As such, it can be specifically taught, and with some success, even to persons of limited ability. Campione and Brown (1987) report that mildly mentally retarded children can be taught specific strategies of memorizing, for example, and show considerable temporary improvement on the task for which the strategy was specifically taught. However, it appears that the gain is neither permanent nor transferable. So the ability and/or the propensity to generate effective strategies for learning and for problem solving may be a general capacity entering in an important way into g. We have a good deal to learn about the acquisition and functioning of such strategies, and in the process of doing so we may find out to what extent there is a general capability for acquiring and using them, which may be an important component of intelligence.

I have speculated about some of the aspects of information processing that might be related to g, a general intellective factor. Where there is evidence to support these speculations, it is generally correlational and provides little guidance as to whether the differences in processing among persons should be thought of as signifying causes of or merely concomitants of psychometrically tested intelligence. Clarifying this issue is a worthy research goal for the years and decades ahead. In the meantime it seems to me at least reasonable to retain g, a general intellective ability, as a useful psychological construct.

The second question that we ask is whether an accurate measure of a single general cognitive factor can provide a useful prediction of later academic, vocational, or other life accomplishments. Or to pose a more focused question, we ask how much of the prediction that is possible from a comprehensive battery of more specific ability measures can be provided by a good appraisal of a single general cognitive ability.

When, following the work of Thurstone and his disciples, the work on ability testing focused on the teasing out of a considerable number of more limited ability factors, it was natural to anticipate that different ones of these would prove to be important in different sorts of jobs, and perhaps in different academic endeavors. One might expect that mechanical comprehension would be important for the automotive mechanic, spatial visualizing for the draftsman or architect, rapid and accurate perception for the parts inspector, numerical fluency for the bookkeeper or accountant, and so forth. During and after World War II, placement and guidance batteries were developed in considerable number to supplement or replace the general ability test for educational and vocational guidance and placement. Given these expanded and elaborated batteries, what practical role remains for a general ability measure?

It is of course true that although the tests in these batteries were designed to be measures of separate and distinct ability factors, the tests in them all do (with possible rare exceptions) show positive correlations, and it is possible to derive from any one of the batteries some sort of measure of a general factor that is what the component tests all share in common. We seek to determine what part of the prediction that is possible from the complete set of test scores can in fact be achieved with that single general ability score. In carrying out such analyses, one is limited to test batteries for which reasonably extensive sets of predictive validities are available against job or educational criteria. I shall present three such data sets.

I start with data from the Differential Aptitude Test battery. This set of eight tests, first published in 1947, has been widely used for educational and vocational counseling in secondary schools for the past 30 years. According to their titles, the eight tests measure Verbal Reasoning, Numerical Ability, Abstract Reasoning, Clerical Speed and Accuracy, Mechanical Reasoning, Space Relations, Language Usage—Spelling, and Language Usage—Grammar. However the average of the correlation between any two of the tests is approximately 0.40, so it is possible to extract from the eight a score for a general factor that represents what they all share in common. For one grade group, the correlation of each test with that common factor is shown in the left-hand column of Table 11.1.

It can be seen that all but one of the tests correlates at least 0.60 with the shared common factor. An appropriately weighted composite of the eight tests correlates 0.94 with the common factor, and so provides a quite satisfactory measure of what is common to all the tests. We should hasten to point out that this a strictly ad hoc common factor, that one does not get identical common factor scores from different sets of measures, and so there is not a precise correspondence between an empirically determined common factor score and such a construct as Spearman's g, or any other interpretation of general intelligence. But if the tests in a set are a varied and balanced set of cognitive measures, the first common factor score is at least a working approximation to general intelligence, and common factor scores from different batteries correlate very substantially.

In the manual for the D.A.T. the publishers have reported a fairly voluminous set of correlations of the eight tests with grades in secondary school courses.

TABLE 11.1
Factor Loadings and Validities of Differential Aptitude Tests

Predictor Variable	Correlation with g Factor	Median Validity Coefficient						Correlation 2nd Fact
		English	Mathematics	Science	Social Studies	Language	Commerc.	
Verbal Reasoning	.81	.52	.40	.50	.49	.46	.40	.06
Numerical Ability	.72	.50	.52	.48	.49	.41	.46	-.02
Abstract Reasoning	.72	.42	.41	.40	.37	.25	.32	-.23
Space Relations	.64	.30	.30	.34	.30	.20	.24	-.34
Mechanical Reasoning	.64	.22	.24	.28	.22	.17	.16	-.27
Clerical Speed & Accur.	.24	.28	.20	.24	.26	.16	.26	-.10
Spelling	.60	.46	.30	.38	.42	.42	.40	.53
Sentences (Usage)	.73	.52	.39	.46	.49	.50	.44	.36
First Factor Composite	.94	.59	.51	.56	.56	.49	.48	
Second Factor Composite		.17	.01	.07	.14	.30	.16	.78
Multiple correlation for all 8 variables		.65	.56	.59	.61	.58	.56	

Total Criterion variance accounted for		
Multiple correlations	2.11	
First general factor	1.70	
Second general factor	0.17	

These have been summarized by presenting median values in the middle columns of Table 11.1. The question that we ask is how well a single score representing the general factor common to all eight tests can predict these grades. How does the general factor score compare with the most valid single test among the eight? How does it compare with the very best ad hoc combination of the eight tests— the multiple correlation when they are optimally weighted.

The validity of the first or general factor composite is shown in the row just below the validities of the eight separate tests. Clearly, the general factor composite arrived at purely from the internal relationships among the tests, is a good predictor of academic grades in all six academic areas. In four of the six it clearly is a *better* predictor than any of the tests taken singly; in the other two it closely approximates the best single test.

The third row across the bottom of the table shows the correlations that result when for each subject area in turn the tests are combined in the way that gives the very best possible prediction of that specific subject. Naturally these values are (they must be) somewhat higher than the prediction provided by a score that was developed solely as a representation of what is common to all eight tests. But the difference is not that great! For the six subject areas it ranges from .03 to .09. The best over-all summary is to say that 80% of the criterion variance that can be predicted by individually tailored composites of the eight tests can be predicted by a score representing the one common general ability factor that they share with one another.

One other item of some interest is displayed in Table 11.1. When multiple factor analysis routines are applied to the correlations among a set of tests, factors beyond the first may also be calculated. In the initial mathematical solution, all of these subsequent factors represent differences between what is measured by one subset of the tests and another. Correlations of the eight tests with the second factor are shown at the extreme right or Table 11.1, where one can see that this factor differentiates the measures of verbal achievement— spelling and grammar—from several nonverbal ability measures. We can ask how much validity a second-factor score would have for course grades. The answer is shown in the second row below the body of the table. The contrast between the first general factor and the second differential factor is quite dramatic. The general factor accounts for slightly over *ten times* as much criterion variance as the differential factor. There can be little doubt that in this academic context most of the prediction that is possible from cognitive ability measures is provided by a single general ability factor.

However, the D.A.T. analyses are cast in a strictly school-based setting, with primarily academic subjects. What happens if we go further afield into technical training and actual job performance?

In the years following World War II, all the branches of the military establishment developed differential ability batteries for use in the classification of personnel, and assignment of recruits to different technical schools for specialist training. But Schmidt & Hunter (1977) provided a set of vintage data that has certain special advantages for illuminating the question of the effectiveness of special ability tests, as compared with a uniform general ability measure, for predicting success in specialized technical training. The data consisted of correlations between each of the tests of the Army Classification Battery and end-of-course grades in each of 35 army technical schools. The unique virtue of this data set was that correlations were available for two separate samples of cases from each school. This circumstance made it possible to compare three values for each class in each school: (1) the multiple correlation based on the complete set of tests for the same sample upon which the optimal predictor weights had been determined; (2) the cross-validation of those weights as applied to the sample from the other class in that school; and (3) the correlation from a uniform composite weighted to give the most accurate representation of the first common factor—a type of approximation to g. Samples varied in size, but were typically about 200.

The results are shown in Table 11.2. Most of you won't be interested in the detail of this table, though you may be interested to scan the titles to see what range of specialties was included in the training programs. The crux of the matter, appears, as financial reports put it, in the "bottom line." This shows the average proportion of variance that can be accounted for by, first, the regression-weighted composite as applied to its own sample, second, the weighted composite as applied in cross-validation to the other sample, and, third, the composite, uniform across all schools, that provides the best representation of the first common factor.

As one would expect, there is noticeable shrinkage from the original to the cross-validation sample. The drop is from an average of 54% to 47½% of the variance in the criterion measure of final grades. The cross-validation sample provides an uninflated estimate of how effective a presumably ideally weighted composite of all the tests in the battery will be when it is applied to a new sample of cases. The key comparison, from my point-of-view, is that between the uninflated cross-validation figure and the validity provided by the factor I composite. On the average, across the whole set of 35 training schools, the uniform factor I score accounts for about 43% of the variance in final grades, and this is about 88% as much of the variance as can be accounted for by special composites, individually tailored for each school but applied to a new sample from that school. We lose a little, but not much, by falling back on a single uniform general factor score, applied in the same way to each school.

What if we move to predictions of actual on-the-job performance? Here, data of the scope that we need are extremely hard to come by. There are few instances in which a common test battery had been validated against measures of job success in a range of jobs, and especially in which data are available for two or more distinct samples in each job. The only useable data base of which I am aware is that accumulated over the years by the U. S. Employment Service for

TABLE 11.2
Variance in Final Grades Accounted for in 35 Army Technical Schools

	Predicted Variance*							
	Group A				Group B			
	1	2	3	3/2	1	2	3	3/2
Fixed Sta Radio Repair	707	687	630	918	664	643	570	887
Microwave Mult-Chan Rep	441	318	326	1025	446	316	326	1032
Radar Repair	387	251	304	1210	551	359	350	976
Field Radio Repair	621	555	585	1054	450	403	389	966
Field Wireman	462	415	398	959	659	593	573	966
FC Instrument Repair	514	413	479	1159	627	504	504	1000
Ammunition Supply	479	433	396	914	480	433	358	826
Arty. Mech - Light Weap	753	729	618	847	878	848	701	826
Small Arms - Weapons Mech.	743	724	599	827	759	741	651	879
Turret Arty. Repair	796	753	681	904	733	692	608	879
Welder	593	498	487	978	415	348	345	990
Machinist	618	552	472	855	634	567	540	953
Dental Lab	444	278	364	1308	253	154	099	640
Automotive Mechanic	557	501	373	745	743	667	593	889
Track Vehicle Repair	796	771	643	834	941	912	699	766
Armor Track Veh Maint	601	501	552	1102	646	601	542	897
Fuel & Elect Syst Repair	724	694	612	881	755	724	677	936
Track Veh Chassis Rebuild	667	375	510	1359	527	295	407	1380
Clerk	584	566	419	740	709	661	596	902
Stenographer	348	321	247	769	410	384	212	551
Postal Operations	624	610	506	829	551	536	448	835
Personnel Administration	630	572	448	782	527	480	396	824
Personnel Mgmt (Enlisted)	650	615	472	767	724	686	526	866
Adv. Army Administration	576	493	412	836	605	518	446	861
Machine Accounting	607	555	500	901	546	498	477	959
Ordnance Storage Spec.	815	755	634	839	824	764	738	966
Medical Aidman, Adv.	558	426	515	1210	666	511	432	845
Medical Technician	159	091	113	1241	155	091	138	1513
Dental Assistant	430	392	325	829	579	537	442	824
Cook	244	233	237	1018	174	165	144	871
Military Police, Enl Adv	591	536	457	853	572	520	464	892
Disciplinary Guard, Enl	466	356	415	1165	634	484	520	1074
Criminal Investigation	590	391	466	1193	999	740	581	785
Radio Op, Intermed Speed	131	086	059	687	487	324	269	831
Radio Op, High Speed	321	177	129	728	166	092	067	729
Average Variance (R^2)	549	475	440	925	571	508	452	890
Average Correlation	741	689	663		756	713	672	

Key: 1 = own group, 2 =- other group, 3 = uniform general factor.
*All decimal points omitted.

their General Aptitude Test Battery. The U.S.E.S. reports some data for over 400 different jobs, but I was able to locate results for only 29 jobs in which validity data were reported against a job criterion (as distinct from a training criterion) for two separate samples each composed of at least 50 cases.

The GATB provides eight scores, but three of these are primarily psycho-motor. I have limited my analysis to the five scores that may be considered to be primarily cognitive, scores designated Verbal Aptitude, Numerical Aptitude, Spatial Aptitude, Form Perception, and Clerical Perception. The positive correlations among these five scores range from 0.26 to 0.66, and they yield a first factor score that correlates 0.91 with the hypothetical underlying factor. How does this uniform first factor score compare with individually tailored composites of the five separate measures as a predictor of job performance measures, usually supervisory ratings of effectiveness?

The data are summarized in Table 11.3. Once again, the detail of this table is of limited interest, except as showing the diversity of jobs that were included. The results for specific jobs are quite varied—in part because of the actual diversity of the jobs, but probably even more because of the instability of results from samples of only 50 to 100 cases. But at the heart of the matter are the summary figures at the bottom of the table, showing that on average the first factor score can account for 120% as much criterion variance as the cross-validated regression-weighted composite!

This is a rather startling finding. What it signifies in part is that much larger samples than the 50 to 100 typically involved in U.S.E.S. validation studies are required if score composites individually tailored to specific jobs are to be of value. But it also shows that much of the validity of an aptitude test battery can be provided by the general ability common to all the tests. The common factor score accounts for about 60% as much variance as the clearly inflated self-sample regression weighted composite, but 120% as much when those weights are applied to a new sample. The true index of the common factor's effectiveness lies somewhere between the 60% and 120%. Just where the appropriate percent falls, I am not prepared to say. But these data seem clearly to indicate that for job performance, as for training school performance, much of what is predictable from cognitive measures can be predicted by a uniform measure of a general cognitive factor.

In the decades of the '50s and '60s there were great expectations for comprehensive ability test batteries. And when it is possible to base prediction equations on samples of adequate size—at least several hundred cases—it is likely that a 10 or 15% increase in predicted criterion variance can be achieved. But that still leaves 85 or 90% of the predictable variance that can be accounted for by a single uniform general cognitive ability factor. In the context of practical prediction, g seems to be alive and well.

I have written primarily on what we might call psychometric, or abstract, or academic intelligence. The instruments that we use to assess it build of necessity

TABLE 11.3
Variance in Job Criterion Measure Accounted for in 29 Different Jobs
(GATB Data)

| | Predicted Variance | | | | | | | |
| | Group A | | | | Group B | | | |
Job Category	1	2	3	3/2	1	2	3	3/2
Assembler	166	084	158	1883	194	101	115	1136
Clerk, General	086	071	034	480	200	162	078	483
Counselor	104	043	088	2037	081	033	037	1115
Dental Lab Technician	179	030	021	694	233	039	148	3762
Digital Computer Operator	307	298	176	592	210	204	114	556
Draftsman	246	150	116	768	297	183	268	1465
Electrician	223	200	136	682	136	120	103	855
Flatworks Jobs	108	011	015	1375	170	018	150	8363
Ingot Mold Jobs	194	083	007	081	044	020	021	1042
Manager, Retail Food	343	022	261	11761	212	013	031	2385
Meat Cutter	271	046	055	1195	125	020	086	4277
Module Assembler	129	003	014	5333	104	002	088	39818
Mounter	035	031	001	042	030	028	004	134
Nurse Aid	071	036	051	1460	229	120	111	921
Order Filler	141	014	028	1960	452	047	381	8083
Patrolman	082	001	020	15308	296	006	186	32034
Plumber	205	132	125	940	096	060	046	770
Pressman	129	095	067	707	350	261	288	1105
Programmer, Business	213	104	069	658	188	092	144	1563
Programmer, Eng., Sci.	093	088	067	760	264	247	154	625
Psychiatric Aide	122	120	110	915	174	170	153	901
Radiologic Technician	257	141	059	420	445	242	295	1218
Sewing Machine Operator	460	318	381	1197	472	319	398	1247
Stenographer	230	165	112	681	531	380	214	565
Structural Ship Yard Jobs	282	120	162	1350	092	041	083	2013
Surgical Technician	212	111	170	1531	136	074	062	838
Teller	197	002	011	4613	205	003	073	26036
Tool & Die Maker	575	270	391	1887	359	131	225	1715
Waitress	118	neg	007	--	086	neg	060	--
	1	2	3	3/2				
Average variance (R^2)	.210	.101	.121	1.200				
Average correlation	.485	.318	.348					

1 = own group   2 = other group   3 = uniform general factor.
*All decimal points omitted.

on our shared cultural heritage, and I have made no attempt to explore the extent
to which the substance of a general cognitive factor would be different in other
cultures—for example, in a culture without written language. I have suggested
that there are basic information-processing components in which individuals
differ, and that these may provide the roots for resulting differences in a general
cognitive ability. I have offered some evidence that it is chiefly this general
ability, rather than more limited and specialized abilities, that provides the impor-

tant cognitive basis for effective functioning, always recognizing that cognitive abilities are only a limited part of the totality of what makes a person effective and productive in the world as we know it.

REFERENCES

Barry, W. M., & Ertl, J. P. (1965). Brain waves and human intelligence. In F. B. Davis (Ed.), *Modern educational developments: Another Look* (pp. 191–197). New York: Educational Records Bureau.

Blinkhorn, S. F., & Hendrickson, D. E. (1982). Averaged evoked responses and psychometric intelligence. *Nature, 295,* 596–597.

Campione, J. C., & Brown, A. L. (1987). Linking dynamic assessment with school achievement. In C. S. Lidz (Ed.), *Dynamic assessment* (pp. 82–115). New York: Guilford Press.

Cronbach, L. J. (1957). The two disciplines of scientific psychology. *American Psychologist, 12,* 671–684.

Donchin, E., & Israel, J. B. (1980). Event-related potentials: Approaches to cognitive psychology. In R. E. Snow, P-A Federico, & W. E. Montague (Eds.), *Aptitude, learning and instruction, Vol. 2: Cognitive process analyses of learning and problem solving* (pp. 47–82). Hillsdale, NJ: Lawrence Erlbaum Associates.

Davis, F. B. (1971). The measurement of mental ability through evoked potential recording. *Educational Record Research Bulletin,* No. 1.

Ertl, J. P., & Schafer, E. W. P. (1969). Brain response correlates of psychometric intelligence. *Nature, 223,* 421–422.

French, J. W. (1951). The description of aptitude and achievement tests in terms of rotated factors. *Psychometric Monographs* No. 5.

Jensen, A. R. (1980). Chronometric analysis of mental ability. *Journal of Social and Biological Structures, 3,* 181–224

Jensen, A. R., Schafer, E. W. P., & Crinella, F. M. (1981). Reaction time, evoked brain potentials and psychometric g in the severely retarded. *Intelligence, 5,* 179–197.

Schmidt, F. L., & Hunter, J. E. (1977). Development of a general solution to the problem of validity generalization. *Journal of Applied Psychology, 62,* 529–541.

Simon, H. A. (1979). *Models of thought.* New Haven: Yale University Press.

Travis, L. E., & Young, C. W. (1930). Relations of electromyographically measured reflex times in patellar and Achilles reflexes to certain physical measurements and to intelligence. *Journal of General Psychology, 3,* 374–400.

12

Tyler's Behavioral Objectives: Background Sources, Early Use, and Some Stream-Offs

J. Thomas Hastings
University of Illinois

INTRODUCTION

Lee Cronbach and I, along with many other students, were deeply influenced by Ralph Tyler's approach to educational evaluation. Though Tyler's ideas have been expanded in both his and our usage over the years, Cronbach's writings on evaluation (1982) still best reflect Tyler, both then and now. It thus is appropriate that this chapter examine the development and influence of Tyler's conception of behavioral objectives in educational evaluation, and to contrast this conception with that of others over the years. Cronbach's position with respect to this development will then be clearly seen.

When I was first invited to write this chapter, the tentative title suggested was "The Evolution of Ralph W. Tyler's Behavioral Objectives." Although he was a mentor of mine at the University of Chicago—formal courses and informal conversations—and I have worked with him on several occasions since, extensive reading of articles by Tyler and others, interviews, and behavioral objectives developed in recent literature, led me to believe that "evolution" was not quite the word. That tends, with many people, to be interpreted as survival of the fittest. Tyler's work at the end of the '20s and in the Evaluation of the Eight Year Study of Secondary Education in 1934–42 is probably his most widely known work in behavioral objectives, although he and others have done much more with the processes and definitions since that time. But the new developments were not, in my lexicon, "evolution."

Others have used many of Tyler's ideas. They have, in several instances, applied only parts of them in what I would call *training* as opposed to *education*. They have also left out some of his notions in philosophy of general education—

perhaps correctly for their purposes. Others have even used the term "behavioral objectives" in assessing minimal competencies for promotion or for gaining a diploma. Tyler was not doing that in the Eight Year Study. These various movements are not in my opinion evolution but are better called "stream-offs" of *parts* of Tyler's thinking.

The story line starts with the urge for "scientific management" (industrial settings) and a push for "scientific curriculum" building in the early 1900s and then moves to influences on Tyler from John Dewey's views of general education and Charles H. Judd's emphasis on Transfer of Training and generalization. It then moves to some of Tyler's early work on appraising and clarifying curriculum purposes.

The Evaluation of the Eight Year Study in Secondary Education plays a great part in the story. Tyler's book on curriculum development and a later article that notes changes he might emphasize if he rewrote that book are both mentioned. So is his report on his panel's appraisal of the Florida minimum competencies tests and their uses.

The taxonomies of educational objectives are mentioned as an outgrowth or stream-off of Tyler's evaluation of the Eight Year Study. However, it is pointed out how these miss one of Tyler's main beliefs merely by being published for wide-spread use.

In the last part of this chapter, I demonstrate some of the later work on "educational objectives" and school or student evaluation as a stream-off, which has more to do with training than with education. They are concerned more with "goal attainment" in *specific* performances. Tyler and Cronbach have been more concerned with behavior as *indicators* of progress along certain lines of ongoing education and learning.

SCIENTIFIC MANAGEMENT AND THE CURRICULUM

There are plenty of educational professionals who consider E. L. Thorndike as *the father* of educational (or achievement) measurement. It's true that Rice (1897) did a fairly large study of 8th graders' achievements in spelling using a test he developed. And it proved fruitful in education. As Cronbach (1960) points out, however, the interests of educationists in using tests as Rice did tended to narrow the actual curriculum. Whether or not Thorndike is thought of as the father of achievement testing, there is no denying his profound effects. Again unfortunately, those who used his approaches unwittingly narrowed at least general education. First, they generally obtained their test content from textbooks or a curriculum guide. Second, the overall purposes of the test tended to turn into specific facts and skills to be recalled or recognized. General educational growth and higher mental processes were almost never touched.

In the early 20th century the term "scientific management" became an honored concept in business and industry. Frederick W. Taylor (1978) was one of the leaders in this field. Through time and motion studies of workers engaged in a particular job, Taylor pulled out very specific "behavioral objectives" for efficient execution of the work. These behaviors—or ways of executing particular tasks—were then used for selection and for development of workers and, in many cases, for reorganization of the industry or business.

In the field of Education, besides the work of Thorndike in the measurement area, Franklin Bobbitt (1918, 1924) did something akin to the work of Taylor in developing curriculum. Bobbitt carefully studied what adults actually do and used lists of specific activities as a basis for what should shape the objectives of teaching. Needless to say he ended up with a lengthy list of very specific tasks. He assumed (Bobbitt, 1924) that education was to prepare children and youth for a well-rounded adult life. It was not aimed at "child life."

Another curriculum specialist, Charters (1925), followed some of Bobbitt's procedures. However, there were very significant differences. Charters suggested, for example, that both ideals and activities which are of high value to children should be emphasized. He also brought forward the notion that merely providing information does not fulfill the function of instruction until it can be shown that the new knowledge has actually modified conduct.

The foregoing discussion purposely is not centered on the detail of the various new curriculum developments. Thorndike, Taylor, Bobbitt, and Charters are used as examples of at least two things: a "scientific" approach to management and curriculum and performance or behavioral objectives. For those readers who wish to become more familiar with the detail of the conflicts in "scientific" psychology, the shifts in philosophy in education, and the effects of world views, two readings are especially useful; see Echols and Thurman, 1973, 1982.

RALPH W. TYLER'S BACKGROUND

In order to better understand Tyler's later work in educational objectives, assessments, and curriculum it seems important to know something about his academic background. Tyler went to the University of Chicago to do a Ph.D. in Education in 1926 and finished his degree in 1927. He had come from the University of Nebraska where he supervised student teachers in science education; earlier he had taught high school science.

Both Bobbitt and Charters were on the faculty at Chicago. Tyler knew their work in curriculum construction. He and Charters became quite close as is shown later in the story. Tyler's field at Chicago was educational psychology and C. H. Judd was his main advisor. It must be remembered that Judd was a well known researcher with a strong belief in experimentation. He also espoused the importance of Transfer of Training in educational pursuits. And he felt that acquiring knowledge and the use of "higher mental processes" were qualitatively different. Both needed to be taught.

During his doctoral year Tyler was employed as a research assistant on the Commonwealth Teacher Training Study, headed by Charters. Its title was "Statistical Methods for Utilizing Personal Judgments to Evaluate Teacher Training Curricula." In "An Interview with Tyler" (Nowakowski, 1981), Tyler tells his part in the study. Some two million cards were collected from cooperating teachers across the country. Each card contained a statement about an activity in which the teacher was engaged. Tyler's job was "to classify those two million statements and [find] statistical methods for identifying what were important and crucial or what is often called now the 'critical incidents' for teachers." The outcome was a set called "The Thousand and One Activities of Teachers in America" (p. 2).

In the interview, Nowakowski asked Tyler, "How do we use that information today?" Tyler's response is revealing of a scholar who was very aware of changes, movements, and needs in education over time:

> Well, the Commonwealth Teacher Training Study is a report upon which competency based teacher education in those days was developed. You know about every 20 years or so the uneasy tension between theory and practice in professional education (whether it be doctors or teachers or others), alternates between emphasizing the activities within the profession, or emphasizing the theory that may help to guide the profession. This was one of those times when, as now, the emphasis was on finding the competencies of teachers and trying to focus on them. (p. 2)

Tyler managed to merge both the activities within a profession and the theory to guide the profession in most of his work.

After completing his doctorate, Tyler was employed at the University of North Carolina, working with teachers there to develop more effective curricula and manage the North Carolina State Testing Program. So once again he was working directly with classroom teachers—involved with curriculum development and measurement.

In 1929, Charters, who had left the University of Chicago to direct the Bureau of Educational Research at the Ohio State University, brought Tyler to the Bureau. Tyler's position there was heading the Division of Accomplishment Testing, which involved two separate aspects: (1) About half his time was spent working with schools and teachers in Ohio; (2) A bit more than half-time was spent with various colleges and departments in the Ohio State University, helping to improve teaching and student retention. Again, he was working with teachers in the schools and faculty in the university. Out of those studies with university faculty came a book that was a collection of articles about the work and the indicators of behavior developed. The book, entitled *Constructing Achievement*

Tests (Tyler, 1934a), contains many of Tyler's concepts about measuring the results of college instruction, about formulating objectives—and very helpful examples of measures or indicators developed. It remains important reading for those wishing to understand Tylers' assumptions and philosophy. I will return to this discussion later.

But first, consider another article by Tyler (1934b), describing a "new" program at the Rochester Athenaeum and Mechanics Institute. Tyler was still with the Bureau at OSU, but he was employed by the Rochester Mechanics Institute as the main external consultant. The Mechanics Institute's aims were far more vocationally oriented than are those of a liberal arts school and a secondary school purportedly stressing general education.

In this article Tyler stresses the training as opposed to education function. One finds words such as "mastery" and "performance" more often here than in Tyler's other work. This is amplified in the types of training on which the Institute was focusing. For example, electrical work was a course in which, for one thing, the student was expected to learn how to properly connect a voltmeter into an electrical circuit. Tyler comments, "obviously [the students'] achievement of this objective can best be measured by observing him when he is asked to connect the voltmeter in the circuit." Another example was in the Institute's courses on retail distribution. Specificity is exemplified by the objective of developing skill in approaching a customer. This was "measured" by observation of the student while employed on a cooperative job in retail selling.

The Mechanics Institute example demonstrates that Tyler knows both training and education, respects each in its place, and can work fruitfully in either. However, his total work shows he also knows the difference.

Going back to the aforementioned book (Tyler, 1934a), which grew out of his work at Ohio State, consider the following quotes. They are intended to emphasize a number of his principles and the differences between his tests and those that were currently on the market or being devised locally by others in testing.

> The accepted techniques used by educational testers have been the translation of subject-matter into forms of questions which may be scored objectively, the standardization of the test items in terms of the percentage of pupils who answer items correctly, the computation of the coefficient of correlation between the test results and the teachers' marks, the determination of the relation between the response on an individual item and the total test score, and the computation of the coefficient of correlation between the results obtained from two similar forms of the test. Obviously, then, in the past the desirable training for one engaged in constructing educational measurements was conceived in terms of these techniques.
>
> The extension of the problem of measuring the results of instruction to the college level is changing the conception of the type of training appropriate for educational testers. An analysis of the mental processes characteristic of a given subject assumes an importance heretofore unrecognized. Many college instructors are suspicious of the so-called "objective examinations," and not without reason.

Not only are many objective tests quite different from the examinations to which they are accustomed, but it is also difficult for them to determine whether the tests provide a measure of the objectives of the subject they are teaching. It is, therefore, natural that they should be cautious in relying upon such examinations. Hence, a fundamental task in constructing achievement tests which will be used by college instructors is to make certain that the important objectives of the subject and course are adequately measured. (pp. 3–4)

Note in the above quote the phrase "An analysis of the *mental processes* . . ." (italics added). Mental processes was one root of the Tylerian approach. He wanted indicators of knowing, interpretation, and analysis. This is quite different from some of the later behavioral or performance objectives that have been proposed by Popham (1975), Mager (1973), and Gagne (1965). These later views insist on *overt* acts.

Again from Tyler (1934a) the following quotes note his emphases on mental processes and their lack of relationship to information in a field.

Similarly, in an earlier book, Wood, describing the achievement tests used in Columbia College recognized that the test items were derived directly from an analysis of the informational content of the course only. However, he stated that every experimental study thus far made and reported has shown a very high relationship between measurements of information in a field and intelligence or ability to think in the material of that field. This has not been found true in the elementary biology courses at Ohio State University. We found the correlation with the scores on information tests of tests of application of principles to be only .40; of tests of interpretation of experiments to be only .41; and of tests of the formulation of experiments to test hypotheses to be only .46.

In defense of Mr. Wood's position, it may be pointed out that these correlations are higher in advanced courses. Nevertheless, in elementary courses, the correlations are all too low for one to obtain valid measurements in these classes by use of an information test only. Tests need to be constructed for each of the important objectives in a course. (p. 5)

In his work with various departments at OSU, objectives were classified according to types:

Type A, Information, which includes terminology, specific facts, and general principles;

Type B, Reasoning, or scientific method, which includes induction, testing hypotheses, and deduction;

Type C, Location of Relevant Data, which involves a knowledge of sources of usable data and skill in getting information from appropriate sources;

Type D,   Skills Characteristic of Particular Subjects, which include laboratory
skills in the sciences, language skills, and the like;

Type E,   Standards of Technical Performance, which includes the knowledge
of appropriate standards, ability to evaluate the relative importance
of several standards which apply, and skill or habits in applying
these standards;

Type F,   Reports, which include the necessary skill in reporting projects in
engineering or reporting experiments in science and the like;

Type G,   Consistency in Application of Point of View, which is most apparent
in courses in philosophy;

Type X,   Character, which is perhaps the most inclusive, involving many
specific factors (pp. 6 and 7)

Tyler emphasizes again that these activities—defining objectives and classifying
them into types—must be done by the faculty involved in a given area. He says
that the "technician in test construction can only outline the specifications demanded." Tyler himself was and is a great facilitator of getting others to think
through their problems and come to *their* solutions. He asks proper questions.

The title *Constructing Achievement Tests* may be a slightly misleading name
for some readers. The word "tests" is used broadly. Some of the devices or
procedures developed amount to observation of students in particular settings.
For example in the laboratory skill of using a microscope, Tyler developed—
again with much input from chemistry and biology faculty—a checklist of procedures (both good and bad) used by students. Then, laboratory specialists
observed the students in situations of using the microscope and marked the
checklist with numbers representing the order of actions. They also checked the
time taken. There were other observational procedures used in other areas of
concern.

In straight informational (facts, principles, terms) assessment, he stuck
mostly to ordinary multiple-choice tests. However the alternatives in multiple-
choice tests were usually developed from free responses made by students in
order that reality could be a check on the possibilities of alternative responses.

Another principle that he followed was trying to make sure that the material
used in assessment of types (see quote above) of functioning such as B, C, and E
were done with material new to the student. This attempt to cut down on possible
memory of class or textbook examples was not common at that time in either
commercial or teacher-made tests. For example, sources for situations to test
hypotheses were located in problems suggested for investigation by researchers
in the area but not as yet investigated. In this case the "student cannot depend
upon his memory of the method of attack."

On pages 22 and 23 Tyler (1934a) illustrates the development of objectives and subsequently examinations in foreign language. He ends the discussion with the following:

> These illustrations demonstrate the fact that the first steps in examination building are those involved in determining objectives. It is usually necessary to consider first the major functions or purposes of the course, breaking those up into several more definite major objectives. To make this list of major objectives more nearly complete, the content of the course is then examined, topic by topic, to discover why the topic has been included in the course; that is, to state the things which students are expected to gain from studying the topic. This examination of individual topics usually suggests additions to the list of major objectives. The purpose of these steps is to obtain a relatively complete list of the most important objectives. After the list has been formulated, an analysis is then made of each objective to give it definite meaning by defining it in terms of the behaviour expected of students, and to obtain a comprehensive statement of the specific elements involved in the objective. This analysis provides the basic material from which a complete problem of examinations may be constructed. Finally, a plan of periodic review and revision of these basic materials prevents crystallization of the course and of the examinations. (p. 23)

In his OSU work Tyler (1934a) was concerned with the tendency in then current measurement of limiting the data collection methods.

> Specialization in educational research so confines our thinking that various techniques for accomplishing the same purpose are commonly thought of as belonging to different fields of investigation and are rarely used by the same individual, yet many a problem is most appropriately attacked by several methods rather than by one. Especially is this true in that area called measurement, appraisal, or evaluation. The techniques of objective testing are differentiated from the methods of the psychological laboratory. The observation of child behavior is considered a distinct and separate field from mental testing, the analysis of pupils' written work is contrasted with personal-interview procedures, and the use of interest questionnaires is not identified with the collection of anecdotes.
>
> Essentially, however, these techniques are methods for accomplishing the same purpose; they are all devices for evaluating human behavior. By isolating each device and making it a subject of special study we have probably improved the effectiveness of the device, but we have lost the value which comes from realizing the similarities in all of these procedures. The research worker, teacher, or school administrator confronted with the problem of appraisal is likely to think of one of these devices and fail to recognize that the choice of the particular method of evaluation should depend upon the effectiveness of that method for the particular problem under consideration. A clearer recognition of the common elements in all of these methods of evaluation is needed to provide a basis for choosing the techniques to use in a particular situation.
>
> All methods of evaluating human behavior involve four technical problems: defining the behavior to be evaluated, determining the situations in which it is

expressed, developing a record of the behavior which takes place in these situations, and evaluating the recorded behavior. Regardless of the type of appraisal under consideration, whether it be the observation of children at play, the written examination, the techniques of the psychological laboratory, the questionnaire, or the personal interview, these problems are encountered. The choice of the methods of evaluation rests primarily upon the effectiveness with which the methods solve the particular problems. (pp. 91–92)

TYLER AND THE "EIGHT YEAR STUDY"

In 1932, the Commission on the Relation of School and College of the Progressive Education Association (PEA) started the Eight Year Study. The broad purpose was to arrange for a set of schools to experiment with new curricula. Actually 30 schools, spread across the nation, and better than 200 colleges participated. The colleges agreed to admit or not admit students from the thirty schools on the basis of assessments of the learning of students as opposed to the usual criteria of so many units of specific courses and grade point average.

In 1934, Tyler was asked by the Directing Committee of the Commission to be Director of Research for the evaluation staff in the Eight Year Study. After arranging with OSU to be released half-time from his work in the Bureau of Educational Research he accepted the position. The story of the procedures and products of the evaluation staff is told in Smith, Tyler, and the Evaluation Staff (1942). Smith was Chair of the Committee on Evaluation and Recording. In a Foreword by Wilford M. Aikin, Chair of the Commission on the Relation of School and College of PEA, there is a revealing paragraph that sets the stage for behavioral objectives, comprehensiveness, and teacher involvement.

> The work reported here rests upon three basic convictions: first, that evaluation and recording should always be directly related to each school's purposes; second, that any school's evaluation program should be comprehensive, including appraisal of progress toward *all* the school's major objectives; third, that teachers should participate in the construction of all instruments of evaluation and forms for records and reports. (p. xviii)

The reader will recall that these convictions were a prominent part of Tyler's work with faculty at OSU.

In Chapter I the term "evaluation" is defended as follows:

> The term "evaluation" was used to describe the staff and the project rather than the term "measurement," "test," or "examination" because the term "evaluation" implied a process by which the values of an enterprise are ascertained. To help provide means by which the Thirty Schools could ascertain the values of their new programs was the basic purpose of the evaluation project. (p. 5)

Following this the Chapter includes discussion of five purposes of school and student evaluation. These are best stated in their words.

> One important purpose of evaluation is to make a periodic check on the effectiveness of the educational institution, and thus to indicate the points at which improvements in the program are necessary. In a business enterprise the monthly balance sheet serves to identify those departments in which profits have been low and those products which have not sold well. This serves as a stimulus to a reexamination and a revision of practices in the retail establishment. In a similar fashion, a periodic evaluation of the school or college, if comprehensively undertaken, should reveal points of strength which ought to be continued and points where practices need modification. This is helpful to all schools, not just to schools which are experimenting.
>
> A very important purpose of evaluation which is frequently not recognized is to validate the hypotheses upon which the educational institution operates. A school, whether called "traditional" or "progressive," organizes its curriculum on the basis of a plan which seems to the staff to be satisfactory, but in reality not enough is yet known about curriculum construction to be sure that a given plan will work satisfactorily in a particular community. On that account, the curriculum of every school is based upon hypotheses, that is, the best judgments the staff can make on the basis of available information.
>
> A third important purpose of evaluation is to provide information basic to effective guidance of individual students. Only as we appraise the student's achievement and as we get a comprehensive description of his growth and development are we in a position to give him sound guidance. This implies evaluation sufficiently comprehensive to appraise all significant aspects of the student's accomplishments. (pp. 7 and 8)

The reader should note Tyler's emphasis on a curriculum plan working satisfactorily in a *particular community*. He was never one to make a horse-race out of evaluation in the sense of what is the best plan. Instead the question was "what plan (curriculum) for what purposes and what school seems to succeed?" His third purpose was to come as close as possible to acquiring for the individual as comprehensive a description as possible about *all aspects* of the student's growth and development.

I continue with the five outlined purposes in the evaluation of the PEA Eight Year Study:

> A fourth purpose of evaluation is to provide a certain psychological security to the school staff, to the students, and to the parents. The responsibilities of an educational institution are broad and involve aspects which seem quite intangible to the casual observer. Frequently the staff becomes a bit worried and is in doubt as to whether it is really accomplishing its major objectives. This uncertainty may be a good thing if it leads to a careful appraisal and constructive measures for improvement of the program; but without systematic evaluation the tendency is for the staff

to become less secure and sometimes to retreat to activities which give tangible results although they may be less important. Often we seek security through emphasizing procedures which are extraneous and sometimes harmful to the best educational work of the school. Thus, high school teachers may devote an undue amount of energy to coaching for scholarship tests or college entrance examinations because the success of students on these examinations serves as a tangible evidence that something has been accomplished. However, since these examinations may be appropriate for only a portion of the high school student body, concentration of attention upon them may actually hinder the total educational program of the high school. (p. 9)

In my opinion the emphasis on the potential harmful aspects of schools using "procedures which are extraneous" is applicable in many ways to our schools today: e.g., emphasis on minimum competency tests, on SAT, ACT, and CEEB tests. We have known for years that teachers teach to the tests.

The final purpose stated in Smith, Tyler, and the Evaluation Staff (1942) is stated:

A fifth purpose of evaluation which should be emphasized is to provide a sound basis for public relations. No factor is as important in establishing constructive and cooperative relations with the community as an understanding on the part of the community of the effectiveness of its educational institutions. A careful and comprehensive evaluation should provide evidence that can be widely publicized and used to inform the community about the value of the school or college program. Many of the criticisms expressed by patrons and parents can be met and turned to constructive cooperation if concrete evidence is available regarding the accomplishments of the school. (p. 10)

And it is obvious that the Evaluation Staff did not mean "concrete" evidence presented by scores on a test or a small group of tests.

This is a good place to point out that the term "Tylerian Behavioral Objectives" may be to some extent misleading. Both the processes and the products— as well as purposes and assumptions to be discussed next—were developed by the Evaluation Staff working with teachers, parents, and students. Tyler was Director, but many people such as Louis Raths, Maurice Hartung, Bruno Bettelheim, Hilda Taba, Christine McGuire (to name a few of the outstanding staff) had strong input into "Tylerian Objectives" and purposes of evaluation. This was stressed by Tyler. Note the authorship of *Appraising and Recording Student Progress*—Smith, Tyler, and the Evaluation Staff. Also, chapters in the book are written by a variety of people. This statement is not meant to downgrade Tyler's influence; he put the staff together and managed to get them to use their various skills as a team. Also, his earlier work with school and college faculties amply demonstrates the directions which could have been predicted for evaluation of the PEA Eight Year Study, with him as Director of Research. We all have a tendency to attach a short name to a complex set of constructs and activities. Thus I feel free to use the term "Tylerian Objectives." The use of all the names impinging upon the large idea—including Charters, Judd, and Dewey—would fill a chapter.

Besides enunciating the purposes of the evaluation, as quoted above, the Evaluation Staff had a set of basic assumptions. Eight assumptions are stated; it is necessary to quote at least some from each.

> In developing the program, the Evaluation Staff accepted certain basic assumptions. Eight of them were of particular importance. In the first place, it was assumed that education is a process which seeks to change the behavior patterns of human beings. It is obvious that we expect students to change in some respects as they go through an educational program. An educated man is different from one who has no education, and presumably this difference is due to the educational experience. It is also generally recognized that these changes brought about by education are modifications in the ways in which the educated man reacts, that is, changes in his ways of behaving. Generally, as a result of education we expect students to recall and to use ideas which they did not have before, to develop various skills, as in reading and writing, which they did not previously possess, to improve their ways of thinking, to modify their reactions to esthetic experiences as in the arts, and so on. It seems safe to say on the basis of our present conception of learning, that education, when it is effective, changes the behavior patterns of human beings.
>
> A second basic assumption was that the kinds of changes in behavior patterns in human beings which the school seeks to bring about are its educational objectives. The fundamental purpose of an education is to effect changes in the behavior of the student, that is, in the way he thinks, and feels, and acts. The aims of any educational program cannot well be stated in terms of the content of the program or in terms of the methods and procedures followed by the teachers, for these are only means to other ends. (p. 11)
>
> A third basic assumption was referred to at the opening of the chapter. An educational program is appraised by finding out how far the objectives of the program are actually being realized. Since the program seeks to bring about certain changes in the behavior of students, and since these are the fundamental educational objectives, then it follows that an evaluation of the educational program is a process for finding out to what degree these changes in the students are actually taking place.
>
> The fourth basic assumption was that human behavior is ordinarily so complex that it cannot be adequately described or measured by a single dimension. Several aspects or dimensions are usually necessary to describe or measure a particular phase of human behavior. Hence, we did not conceive that a single score, a single category, or a single grade would serve to summarize the evaluation of any phase of the student's achievement. Rather, it was anticipated that multiple scores, categories, or descriptions would need to be developed.
>
> The fifth assumption was a companion to the fourth. It was assumed that the way in which the student organizes his behavior patterns is an important aspect to

be appraised. There is always the danger that the identification of these various types of objectives will result in their treatment as isolated bits of behavior. Thus, the recognition that an educational program seeks to change the student's information, skills, ways of thinking, attitudes, and interests, may result in an evaluation program which appraises the development of each of these aspects of behavior separately, and makes no effort to relate them. (pp. 12–13)

A sixth basic assumption was that the methods of evaluation are not limited to the giving of paper and pencil tests; any device which provides valid evidence regarding the progress of students toward educational objectives is appropriate. As a matter of practice, most programs of appraisal have been limited to written examinations or paper and pencil tests of some type. Perhaps this has been due to the long tradition associated with written examinations or perhaps to the greater ease with which written examinations may be given and the results summarized. However, a consideration of the kinds of objectives formulated for general education makes clear that written examinations are not likely to provide an adequate appraisal for all of these objectives. (p. 13)

Smith and Tyler and the Evaluation Staff (1942) then go on to provide some examples of which objectives submit to a valid indicator through pencil and paper tests, together with examples of other objectives and the need for other techniques of assessment.

A seventh basic assumption was that the nature of the appraisal influences teaching and learning. If students are periodically examined on certain content, the tendency will be for them to concentrate their study on this material, even though this content is given little or no emphasis in the course of study. Teachers, too, are frequently influenced by their conception of the achievement tests used. If these tests are thought to emphasize certain points, these points will be emphasized in teaching even though they are not included in the plan of the course. This influence of appraisal upon teaching and learning led the Evaluation Staff to try to develop evaluation instruments and methods in harmony with the new curricula and, as far as possible, of a non-restrictive nature.

The eighth basic assumption was that the responsibility for evaluating the school program belonged to the staff and clientele of the school. It was not the duty of the Evaluation Staff to appraise the school but rather to help develop the means of appraisal and the methods of interpretation (p. 14).

On page 15 it is pointed out that other assumptions were made but that these eight were deemed to be of special importance because they guided "the general procedure by which the evaluation program was developed." This illustrates another of the central characteristics of the evaluations which Tyler led, or for which he was a main consultant: There was always an attempt to hold main ideas, big objectives, procedures to a minimum in number so that persons working with them could keep them in mind.

Another good example of this characteristic in the Eight Year Study lies in the general classification of objectives into categories. Tyler and the Evaluation Staff came up with only ten major types of objectives:

Major Types of Objectives

1. The development of effective methods of thinking
2. The cultivation of useful work habits and study skills
3. The inculcation of social attitudes
4. The acquisition of a wide range of significant interests
5. The development of increased appreciation of music, art, literature, and other esthetic experiences
6. The development of social sensitivity
7. The development of better personal-social adjustment
8. The acquisition of important information
9. The development of physical health
10. The development of a consistent philosophy of life. (p. 18)

This is a far different sort of list than the several hundred or even a thousand detailed objectives or outcomes which all of us have seen in some curriculum development or evaluation plans. It also allows the individual teacher (or departmental staff) more leeway in using their own expertise in implementing the detail.

Smith, Tyler, and the Evaluation Staff (1942) then go on to describe the development of situations in which students could display the types of behavior specified. They follow this with a description of how instrumentation for these situations was developed—not always with tests. The tryout and redevelopment of such procedures was given much time with lots of teacher input. They tried to use efficient methods of collecting data, but this was never at the expense of losing track of the "real" behavior.

In discussing clear thinking or critical thinking the following quote is important:

> At the moment, it is necessary to mention only that evaluation of the *disposition* to think critically has not been extensively worked upon and is not discussed in the following pages. In the opinion of the Evaluation Staff, the best available means is some sort of observational record, and this method demands only the simplest of techniques supported by alert sensitivity and perseverance on the part of the observer. Evidence of the disposition to think critically collected by this method would, however, be a valuable addition to other evidence relevant to clear thinking of the sort to be described later. (p. 37)

This is the difference that I like to designate as "can do" versus "does do"—a distinction that most student or program appraisals never seem to worry about. The Eight Year Study (1942) had "does do" as a central focus. Look today at many of our competency testing programs—school or state—and it is difficult to find anything except "can do." Yet many program appraisals speak of "behavioral objectives."

Chapter 11 in *Appraising and Recording Student Progress* (1942) deals with problems of reporting. Again it seems necessary to quote in order to give the actual thinking.

> Many schools were convinced that the single mark in a subject hid the facts instead of showing them clearly. The mark was, in effect, an average of judgments about various elements in a pupil's progress that lost their meaning and their value when thus combined. The schools believed that the value of a judgment concerning the work done by a pupil in any school course or activity depended on the degree to which that judgment was expressed in a form that showed his strengths and his weaknesses and therefore presented an analyzed picture of his achievement that would be a safe basis for guidance.
>
> There was also a feeling that marks had become competitive to a degree that was harmful to both the less able and the more able, and that they were increasingly directing the attention of pupils, parents, and even teachers, away from the real purposes of education toward the symbols that represented success but did not emphasize its elements or its meaning.
>
> The commonest method of replacing marks proved to be that of writing paragraphs analyzing a pupil's growth as seen by each teacher. This method is an excellent one, since good descriptions by a number of teachers combine to give a reasonably complete picture of development in relation to the objectives discussed. On the other hand, a report in this form is very time-consuming for teachers and office, as well as difficult to summarize in form for use in transfer and guidance. The committee decided on a compromise that would make place for giving definite information about important objectives in an abbreviated form and would allow for supplementing this with written material needed to modify or complete the information. (pp. 88–89)

All of the foregoing pages on the Eight Year Study emphasize that merely developing (or talking about) behavioral objectives is *part* and *part only* of a much broader conception. Objectives, types of instrumentation, heavy input from teachers, an attempt at tying evaluation (assessment) close to curriculum development, are all one piece.

As I stated earlier in this Chapter, I have had opportunities over the years of working with Ralph Tyler on evaluation–curriculum projects. The procedures and conceptualizations in the preceeding pages about his work with faculty at Ohio State University and in the Eight Year Study are still typical of his conceptualization of assessment of student progress.

STREAM-OFFS ON EDUCATIONAL OBJECTIVES

Terms such as behavioral objectives (in some cases labeled performance objectives, instructional objectives, or even outcome objectives) became very prominent in the late 1940s and early '50s. Many educators and educationists who were not or had not been very close to program evaluation, nor to student assessment, rather readily equated the resulting discussion to Tyler's work, and many of them did reflect *some* of his ideas.

Perhaps the first items that should be mentioned are the two handbooks on taxonomy of Educational Objectives (Bloom, 1954, and Krathwohl, Bloom, & Masia, 1964). In the interview with Nowakowski (1981) Tyler replied, in part, to a question about keeping in touch with former students by saying, "My two right-hand assistants getting their doctorates in Chicago, in those early days, were Ben Bloom and Lee Cronbach" (p. 18). At the first formal planning session for what turned out to be the two "taxonomies," Ben Bloom was one of the organizers (I was the other), and both Lee Cronbach and Ralph Tyler were present. To suggest that Tyler's influence on those volumes was not immense would be an outright falsehood. They were truly streamoffs of his earlier work.

However, they also notably left out some ideas from Tyler's earlier work with the faculty at OSU in improving courses and programs, and with the schools in the Eight Year Study, and even with Tyler's responses to Nowakowski's interview in 1981. In the first place Tyler always put emphasis upon working closely with teachers, students, and persons in the community, mostly with parents. He saw his evaluation staff in the Eight Year Study as being capable as technical specialists to help with devising and improving instruments for collecting indicators of changes in behavior. But the teachers, students, and community were the real source of what was wanted, useful, and possible. When one looks through the list of names of those involved in the "Taxonomies," they are all technical specialists. Certainly many of them had worked a lot with schools and with college level faculty. And it was evident that they had listened to practitioners' views of purposes. But that, to me, is a different matter than directly involving them in the work.

The very use of the word *Taxonomy* suggests that knowledge (as defined there) comes before comprehension, which comes before analysis, etc. Yet it is certain that Tyler—from classes with him, from his book on *Basic Principles of Curriculum and Instruction* (1950), and from his Eight Year Study work—does not see learning as moving in such a linear fashion. He believes that such things as knowledge and comprehension frequently become internalized through other behavior, for example, application and problem solving.

There is one last reason to suggest that the taxonomies were streamoffs and different from Tyler's work. Whether or not they were intended to be, the two volumes turned out to be "used as Bibles"—not merely suggestive guideline to germinate thought. Tyler's own work in evaluation and assessment always involved the latter. In his *Principles of Curriculum and Instruction* (1950) the last paragraph—after having given the elements involved and their interrelations in a program of instruction—he concludes with: "Another question arising in . . . curriculum revision . . . is whether the sequence of steps to be followed should be the same as the order of presentation in this [book]. The answer is clearly 'No.' " Then he presents his views of how different schools with different staff and in different contexts should start at different places. He had those views in the Eight Year Study. It seems to me that such a view contrasts with the way curriculum developers understand and use the taxonomies.

None of the foregoing is meant to suggest that the "taxonomies" were not of real use to many people. At least they caused many to think about educational objectives and their connection with curriculum or program development and evaluation in a different fashion than they previously had. But in and of themselves they miss many of the principles of operation suggested and used by Tyler in instructional development and evaluation. That is why I prefer the term *streamoff* as opposed to evolution.

Another streamoff from parts of Tyler's work with educational objectives appears in Robert M. Gagne's (1956) highly useful work in instructional development—particularly in his well known *Conditions of Learning*. In the section on "Defining Objectives for Learning" in Chapter 9, Gagne stresses the need for objectives which clearly state observable *overt action*.

> It may be noted that each of the latter kinds of statements of objectives carries the air of objectivity with it. One of the evident reasons for this is the use of certain kinds of verbs, which describes *overt action*. The verbs are *state* (which means make a verbal statement of), *derive* (which means make a sequence of logically consistent statements beginning with certain assumptions), and *identify* (which means simply point out or choose correctly). One has little difficulty in realizing from these statements what it is that can be observed about the student's performance which would lead to the conclusion that the objective had been attained. Quite in contrast are verbs like *understand* or *know*, which simply set the stage for these "objective" objectives and cannot themselves be unambiguously observed.
>
> There are, then, obvious differences between statements of objectives that are ambiguous, and true *definitions* of objectives, which are not. What are the characteristics of a definition of an objective? Such a definition is a verbal statement that communicates reliably to any individual (who knows the words of the statement as concepts) *the set of circumstances that identifies a class of human performances.* There is little room for disagreement about such definitions, excluding semantic ones, which can be made rare. By means of this sort of definition one individual should be able to identify the same human performance as some other individual. In other words, these are "operational definitions." The kind of statement required appears to be one having the following components:
>
> 1. a *verb* denoting observable action (draw, identify, recognize, compute, and many others qualify; know, grasp, see, and others do not).

2. A description of the *class of stimuli* being responded to [for example, "Given the printed statement ab + ac = a(b + c)"].

3. A word or phrase denoting the *object used for action* by the performer, unless this is implied by the verb (for example, if the verb is "draw," this phrase might be "with a ruling pen"; if it is "state," the word might simply be "orally").

4. A description of the *class of correct responses* (for example, "a right triangle," or "the sum," or "the name of the rule." (pp. 242–243)

Thus, where Tyler was working with indicators of "mental processes," Gagne is working with specific overt measures. The former emphasizes transfer more than does the latter. As I read his four statements of the kind of components an objective should have, I get the feeling that Gagne leaned more toward what I would call *training* while Tyler's work dealt more with *education*. In another work by Gagne (1967), he uses the terms "Terminal objectives" and "prerequisite capabilities" several times. These terms suggest to me that he didn't see education as a continuing function as has Tyler. It should be stressed that Gagne was more interested in programmed instruction. His work has been quite useful and exciting (as well as always well written), but it doesn't represent an *evolution* of Tyler's behavioral objectives. It may or may not be a streamoff; that is almost impossible to verify.

Another approach which may be likened to Tyler's work is the one presented in several books by Robert F. Mager (see, e.g., 1973). It seems clear that Mager is proposing the same sort of overt, visible performance that Gagne stresses. Mager writes very clearly and with much more useful humor than one finds in most texts. However, my view is that he tells the reader too emphatically *how to do it*. My inference is that his work conveys this as *the* way to measure instruction intent. As stated previously in this chapter, Tyler worked with teachers on their instructional and educational intents and frequently asked them, for clarification purposes of intent, what behavior they would accept which would satisfy them that the student had changed in the ways they intended. Also, he left the questions open to various answers—but would push for teacher clarification.

In short, Mager seems much more restrictive and mechanical to me. This is not to say Mager's various books are not useful, but they are a streamoff, not an evolution, of Tyler's behavioral objectives. But the reader of this chapter should realize that Mager does not, as nearly as I can find, even mention Tyler.

Although many different authors have written about behavioral objectives (or performance objectives) I discuss only one more: W. James Popham has been very prominent in the field of educational evaluation and especially in our fairly recent splurge of competency testing. But this last example I believe makes my point: Tyler's "behavioral objectives" as seen in all his work have had great influence on evaluation, assessments, and testing, but many of his basic principles have been ignored by others.

In the case of Popham we have much evidence from his own words that Tyler's approach to student and program assessment was influential. For example in the NIE sponsored *Minimum Competency Testing Clarification Hearing* (1981), Popham states in his cross examination of Tyler: ". . . through my own career in education I have used you as sort of a father figure, particularly in the early years, when I borrowed your ideas" (p. 211). Popham should have said "some of your ideas." Popham's work is an excellent example of the "goal attainment" approach; Tyler was and is an excellent example of the "assessment of progress" group. I differentiate clearly between the two groups. The essential difference between the two can be seen in Popham's cross examination of Tyler in the *Minimum Competency Testing Hearing* (1981). But I believe it is best captured in the following quote from Lee J. Cronbach's *Designing Evaluations of Educational and Social Programs* (1982):

> In the educational discourse of the last decade, the meaning of the term *behavioral objectives* has been narrowed; it now looks at instruction through behaviorist spectacles, and that works against full recognition of what instruction based on other views can accomplish. When Tyler (1950) introduced the concept, he did not call for specifying test stimuli and desired responses in advance. Many different school (or life) activities could promote a desired development; the goal was often to prepare the student to cope with situations that cannot be specifically foreseen. For example, if an educator claimed that her program would "build character," Tyler's response would be a disarming invitation to elaborate: "Just so I have that clear, would you give me an example of what a youngster might do that would indicate that she has developed as you would like?" The incidents so elicited provided referential meaning for a vague phrase, and the evaluator was guided to make a relevant observation. But neither the situation the student was being prepared for nor the "correct" response was prespecified.
>
> Those who impose a behaviorist form on instructional objectives—"Students will learn to give response Y to prespecified stimulus X"—restrict the range of outcomes investigated. A few, but only a few, instructional programs set out to train a student to make standard responses to standard tasks. It is difficult, if not impossible, to describe improved judgment, sensitivity, and self-understanding in behaviorist terms. E. L. Thorndike's followers may have gone too far when they told the social scientist, "If anything exists, it can be measured." The neobehaviorist in evaluation certainly goes too far when he suggests that what he does not measure does not exist.
>
> The divergent list of outcomes ought to stretch far into the future, including those observable only after the current evaluation has been completed and reported. As I have already remarked, long-run differences between treatments are unlikely to match those seen on the immediate posttest. (pp. 222–223)

This explains for me the essential difference between Tyler's assessment of progress and the goal attainment approach.

REFERENCES

Bobbitt, F. (1918). *The curriculum.* New York: Houghton Mifflin.

Bobbitt, F. (1924). *How to make a curriculum.* Boston: Houghton Mifflin.

Bloom, B. S. (Ed). (1954). *Taxonomy of educational objectives: Cognitive domain* (Preliminary Edition). New York: Longmans, Green.

Charters, W. W. (1925). *Curriculum construction.* New York: Macmillan.

Cronbach, L. J. (1960). *Essentials of psychological testing* (second edition). New York: Harper & Row.

Cronbach, L. J. (1982). *Designing evaluations of educational and social programs.* San Francisco: Jossey-Bass.

Echols, J. P. (1973). *The rise of the evaluation movement: 1920–42.* Stanford University, Unpublished doctoral dissertation.

Gagne, R. M. (1965). *The conditions of learning.* New York: Holt, Rinehart and Winston.

Gagne, R. M. (1967). "Curriculum Research and the Promotion of Learning" in *AERA Monograph Series on Curriculum Evaluation,* No. 1. Chicago: Rand McNally.

Krathwohl, O. R., Bloom, B. S., & Masia, B. B. (1964). *Taxonomy of educational objectives: Classification of educational goals.* Handbook 2. *Affective domain.* New York: McKay.

Mager, R. F. (1973). *Measuring instructional intent.* Belmont, California: Lear Siegler/Fearon Publishers.

NIE. (1981). *Minimum competency testing clarification hearing.* Washington, D.C.: Anderson Reporting Company.

Nowakowski, J. R. (1981). *An interview with Ralph Tyler.* Kalamazoo, MI: Evaluation Center, Western Michigan University, Paper #13.

Popham, W. J. (1975). *Educational evaluation.* Englewood Cliffs, NJ: Prentice-Hall.

Rice, J. M. (1897). The futility of the spelling grind. *Forum.*

Smith, E. R., Tyler, R. W., and The Evaluation Staff. (1942). *Appraising and recording student progress.* New York: Harpers and Brothers.

Taylor, F. W. (1978). The principles of scientific management. In J. M. Shafritz & P. H. Whitback (Eds.), *Classics of organization theory.* Oak Park, IL: Moore Publishing Co.

Thurman, G. B. (1982). *The evolution of behavioral objectives: 1900–1980.* University of Colorado, Unpublished doctoral Dissertation.

Tyler, R. W. (1934a). *Constructing achievement tests.* Columbus, OH: The Ohio State University.

Tyler, R. W. (1934b). Education and research at a mechanics institute. VII. Measuring individual accomplishments. *The Personnel Journal,* Vol. XII.

Tyler, R. W. (1950). *Basic principles of curriculum and instruction.* Chicago: University of Chicago Press.

13 Developing Tests to Assist in the Improvement of Education

Ralph W. Tyler
System Development Foundation

Until the late 1960s, criticism of educational testing was largely confined to academic debate. Since then, testing has become a center of public controversy. Several major criticisms are now being leveled at current tests and testing procedures. Two of them are the focus of this paper.

The first criticism is that published tests and testing procedures give very little assistance to teachers and often hinder rather than help effective instruction. The other is that the use of published tests by administrators has not helped to focus the efforts of the school system on particular instructional problems and attainable goals.

TO AID THE TEACHER

Background Tests

Most instruction in American elementary and secondary schools is organized into a series of topics. These may be relatively short, for example, a lesson on *the sound of short e* in reading, or on *carrying in adding,* or they may be quite long as in a unit on the *westward migration* in American history, or on *photosynthesis* in science. Typically, the teacher introduces a new topic to the entire class.

The purpose is threefold: (1) to explain the subject, or describe the skill in a way that relates it to the students' experience; (2) to arouse the students' interest in learning about the subject or in developing the skill; (3) to explain the subsequent activities that are to be carried on by the students (seat work, homework, lesson assignments) to help them develop a fuller understanding of the subject or gain competence in the skill.

Although some computer programs have been devised to enable students to obtain an elaborated explanation of the topic, I do not think that this kind of assistance is desired by the teacher. Teachers generally believe that they make their most significant professional contribution in explaining topics so that they become clear to their students and in arousing student interest and encouraging students to undertake the learning activities (seat work, homework, lesson assignments). They perceive this kind of computer assistance as taking away the teacher's role. However, they generally want textbooks, references, and supplementary materials that they can use to help explain or illustrate or make the topic interesting to students. But, teachers want such materials to be under their control so they can be selected and employed in situations which they consider appropriate.

Tests are not generally employed nor desired for this phase of classroom instruction. However, I have talked with a number of teachers who think that a background test could be very useful to them in planning, either a whole course or a smaller unit, or both. They would like to know for each student and a summary for the entire class: What experiences the student has had that are relevant to the topic and on which explanations could be based? What interests he has that could help to furnish motives for studying the unit or the course? What concepts or skills he has developed which would be an asset in learning this unit or course?

Some teachers use published achievement tests as pretests, but they are so focused on specifics to be learned in the course or unit that they give little help in informing the teacher about the assets on which relevant teaching could be based.

I know of no testing group that is working on such tests, yet I think some can be developed that could give the teacher concrete and appreciated assistance. The Student Profile of ACT illustrates some of the possibilities, but at the college level. The initial effort might be to prepare a series of background tests for several age groups in the elementary and secondary schools.

Tests for Mastery and Diagnosis

An increasing number of schools, particularly elementary schools, are organizing instruction in terms of the concepts of *mastery* and *continuous progress*. Originally proposed by Henry Morrison in 1922, the basic ideas have been more fully developed and adopted in recent times. The curriculum is constructed in the form of sequential units, each instructional unit emphasizing concepts or skills that are essential to the work of subsequent units. The goal is to enable each student to master the essential elements of each unit before proceeding to the next one. Because time requirements to master the elements of a unit differ, provision is made for students to continue their progress through the sequentially organized units until they have completed the course or the cycle of instruction. Hence, the guiding principles are different from those of courses not so organized. In the latter case, all students are expected to move on to the next topic whether or not they have mastered the essential elements of the topic on which they have been working. Teachers are asking for systems of testing and management for subjects organized in sequential units, where mastery is the goal. This includes not only mastery tests but diagnostic tests, to help the student and the teacher identify the particular elements to be learned which the student has not mastered in his initial efforts at work on the unit.

A difficulty likely to be encountered in developing such tests is that there is no single sequence found among the courses that are organized for mastery and continuous progress. There are a number of defensible sequences in each of the subjects, and it is not likely that one sequence will become universal. However, the essential elements identified in subjects like arithmetic and reading are largely identical although developed in different order. An effort could be made to design tests that appraise the student's mastery of each of the common essential elements and then devise a system for using these tests in courses that represent a variety of sequences.

Periodic Appraisals of Student Achievements

Teachers are asking for tests or other devices to help them appraise the achievement of their students over a longer time span than the typical unit. They feel that they could helpfully use a more comprehensive survey not less often than once a year nor more often than the times at which reports are given parents. They are somewhat doubtful about depending on the unit mastery test results as the sole evidence of the student's attainments because they believe that the internalization and use of concepts and skills involves an integration of what is learned in several units and experience with applying what is learned to situations outside the classroom.

They are generally skeptical or opposed to the use of the usual published achievement tests because these tests do not sample reliably what the students in the classes are being taught and because they furnish only relative scores. The teachers want tests that assess what they have been teaching and report, with examples, what the student has learned. This can be made intelligible to parents and the public whereas the present achievement test reports are not understood by most parents and laymen.

In developing such tests, it would be easiest to begin with one that assesses what children have learned by the end of the primary school period (end of 3rd grade, or other recognized milestone). At this time, for example, an appropriate reading test could sample simple stories, rules for children's games, simple news items, and the 2000 most commonly used words, and report to parents that their child can comprehend the main ideas of stories like these, news items like these, and recognize X percent of the most widely used words in American print, such as, (several words given as examples). The purpose of reporting one or more examples for each achievement is to give the parent a sense of what the child has learned rather than how he compares with other children.

I suggest developing such tests initially for the primary grades because there is greater commonality among the diverse American schools in what is to be learned in the primary grades than there is in the order of the instruction or the particular approaches used.

Before the development of standardized tests, teachers in the *better schools* reported concrete items and put together booklets of things done by children, but this became unpopular because of the general belief that the samples were special and not representative of the students' work. Tests of this sort carefully constructed by testing specialists would have greater weight both with teachers and parents.

TESTS TO AID THE PRINCIPAL AND/OR THE INSTRUCTIONAL COMMITTEES IN THE LOCAL SCHOOL

The principal's role as instructional leader can be aided by obtaining information useful in establishing attainable goals for the school and in monitoring the progress being made in reaching these goals. In schools where instructional committees are responsible for or play a part in establishing goals and monitoring progress, these committees can be aided in similar fashion.

Establishing Instructional Goals

In establishing goals, information is needed regarding:

1. the progress students are making in the instructional program in terms that will identify the number and proportion of students making little or no progress in each subject as well as the distribution of students by amount of progress made,

2. profile of all the students showing distribution of interests, previous experiences, and activities and thus to indicate assets on which programs can be built as well as suggestions for further educational experiences,

3. distribution of attendance data which may be indicative of a school problem,

4. extent of vandalism both in terms of monetary costs and frequency,

5. other indices of educational attainments and needs such as teacher and student morale,

6. what parents expect of the school and their attitudes toward it.

Information about the progress of students in the instructional program could be obtained by the principal or instructional committees from the records kept by each teacher. If the program is one of continuous progress to mastery the teachers could report the distribution of each class by number of units completed by the end of the year or at other convenient times. For all kinds of instructional programs the class distributions on appropriate survey tests could be reported.

To provide information about student profiles, a summary could be obtained from the interest and activities questionnaires used in each class. This summary need not reproduce all of the information but focus on the data of school-wide significance. Almost all schools keep attendance records so that it is only necessary to devise a practicable plan for summarizing or sampling the data to furnish this information which is useful in setting goals. The vandalism data may require a new form to obtain and summarize the data. Other useful information that could be obtained may require new instruments for its collection. This is almost certainly necessary to obtain useful data from parents about their expectations because most currently used questionnaires to parents regarding student needs do not explain the special role of the school in educating children but tend to raise false expectations as to what the school can and should undertake.

I believe that we need to develop materials that could substantially aid a local school at the building level to establish appropriate educational goals. The tests and questionnaires useful to the classroom teacher can furnish some of the necessary information. New instruments could be developed and marketed to obtain data on attendance, vandalism, morale of students and teachers and parents' expectations. A very important contribution could be made be developing and publishing a guide for school staffs in setting goals and monitoring progress. Furthermore, we need to develop the software for processing the variety of information suggested into a comprehensible summary which could provide the basis for discussion and decisions by staff and parents.

Monitoring Progress

I do not believe that it is necessary to develop additional instruments for monitoring the progress the school is making toward the achievement of its goals; rather the guide would suggest the data collection schedule that would enable the principal and staff to review the progress perhaps once a term or once a year, and to compare progress with the previous year's achievements.

Helping Teachers

In addition to establishing goals and monitoring progress toward them, the principal and/or other school personnel bear the responsibility of helping teachers who encounter problems in instruction. To meet this responsibility there should be a means by which problems of each classroom can be identified and some methods of diagnosis provided. To furnish the information about problems of each classroom, a summary distribution of the student's achievements could be prepared periodically, probably as often as parents are informed of their children's progress. Some schools will prefer to make an independent check of progress by using a matrix sampling survey test rather than depending on the teacher's records.

Reporting to Parents

Many principals conduct parent interviews about the progress and problems of the children. In most schools, however, these interviews are conducted by the child's teacher unless an interview with the principal is requested. Hence, the data useful to teachers in reporting to parents which was mentioned earlier, seems to me to be helpful whether or not the interview is conducted by the teacher or the principal.

A CAVEAT

I need hardly point out that the effective efforts of the school staff to improve learning in the school requires a great degree of mutual trust. Problems will not be brought out and discussed by the teachers involved if they believe that any negative experience will be used as an indication of their competence. So it is with test results at the classroom level. Distrust can be replaced by trust largely on the basis of positive experiences. The guides for the use of tests, questionnaires, and other instruments should strongly emphasize the positive purposes and the steps to be followed in order to replace fear and suspicion with trust and commitment to improvement.

TESTS TO AID THE SUPERINTENDENT AND OTHER PERSONNEL IN THE DISTRICT OFFICE IN GUIDING AND SUPPORTING THE INSTRUCTIONAL PROGRAM

A constructive role for the central administration of a school system is to see that an appropriate planning process is carried on in each local building, to review proposed goals and strategies for achieving them, to monitor the progress toward the goals and to provide assistance when problems are encountered which the building staff find insoluble. To perform this role, tests can help in furnishing needed information.

Oversight of the School Planning Process

A profile of each school should be in the central office, a profile which includes relevant information about socio-economic characteristics and occupations of the families in the school community, summaries of indices of school problems such as attendance, vandalism, drop-outs at each grade level, and educational progress of the students. Summaries of pupils' assets, and community resources that could aid student learning are also useful parts of a school profile. Most of these data are helpful to local school staffs in their planning and when routinely collected at the local level, copies could be provided to the central administration. Most schools need help in devising computer programs to process this large amount of information in terms and forms that the central staff could interpret and use. They also need forms for collecting these data, as suggested in the section relating to the local school's needs. These forms will include tests, questionnaires, blanks for abstracting other records, like census data, and the like. A useful brochure would be a simple manual describing and explaining a planning process that can be used by local schools together with the procedures that can be used by the central office in guiding and monitoring the planning process.

A chief weakness of most schools and colleges is the failure to establish annually definable and defensible goals that focus on attacking identified problems and recognized opportunities for improving the curriculum and instruction. Schools can be helped by simple explanations of the planning process and its usefulness and by providing forms (tests, questionnaires, etc.) that can help the school staff to identify problems and assets upon which better programs can be built. Stimulation from the central office can furnish the impetus to establish such a program and the central office can also provide help to the school in setting goals, and being guided by them.

Monitoring School Progress

As plans are formulated at the local school level, the central office needs to monitor the progress the school is making in achieving its goals. Interim reports can be submitted by the local school, not more often than reports are provided parents nor less often than semiannually. Periodically, the central office will find it helpful to institute independent checks, both in verifying local school reports and in indicating to the local community that the central office really cares about the progress of the instructional program and thus, like the reports of the local school staff, the central office staff shows its accountability.

This periodic check on school progress need not be, and probably should not be, a repetition of the testing done by the local school. It can be a more comprehensive check on the attainment of major goals. Since the central administration seeks information about the school as a whole and not about individual students, matrix sampling can be used to obtain more comprehensive data without requiring more than one class period of time from each student. Probably, most central administrators would want to limit this comprehensive check on school achievement to no more than two or three subject areas each year. This would be frequent enough to furnish checks on local school assessments and frequent enough to help schools establish long-term goals where serious problems are identified or unusual opportunities for educational improvement are found.

Reporting to the Community

The central office also has the responsibility of reporting to the Board of Education and the larger community about the progress, problems, plans, and achievements of the school system. To avoid the superficial reactions the public often makes when it obtains a scrap of data, the central office reports would do well to include background information, a kind of charting of the schools' tasks as the district has developed and changed and the needs and opportunities for educated persons have grown. Against this background, the central office can report, in concrete terms, a summary of the goals, progress, problems, and attacks on the problems. Clearly such reports can go a long way in demonstrating the school district's serious efforts and in satisfying the demand for accountability. But it does require tests that furnish information about what students have learned and are learning, rather than an abstract number which is intended to show where individual students are on an assumed continuum of largely undefined educational progress.

IN SUMMARY

In our preoccupation with the development and use of tests for other purposes we have neglected to focus our attention on developing tests that can assist teachers in improving instruction and aid school administrators to help schools improve their educational efforts. This neglect can be remedied and this chapter suggests a number of possibilities for exploration and development.

14

An Intelligent Tutoring System for Exploring Principles of Economics

Valerie Shute
Air Force Human Resources Laboratory

Robert Glaser
Learning Research and Development Center

INTRODUCTION

> *I am impressed by the possibility that some experience in discovering principles in a field of knowledge will radically alter the relation the learner perceives between himself and the knowledge, and his way of behaving when he forgets a solution or encounters an unprecedented problem.*
>
> —(Cronbach, 1966, p. 86)

The intelligent tutoring system we discuss in this chapter provides an environment for discovering principles in a field of knowledge. It was designed to achieve this by enhancing students' inductive inquiry skills using the specific subject-matter knowledge of elementary economics for exploring the laws of supply and demand. *Inductive inquiry skills* in this context refers to the students' effectiveness in collecting, organizing, and understanding data, concepts, and relationships in a new domain. This environment uses both discovery learning and more directive approaches: when appropriate, the students are free to explore the domain under study, extracting facts, and organizing principles as they work. When needed, the system can take charge and direct the student in the activities that are most likely to explicate the topic under study.

The implementation of this approach has been developed on a Xerox 1108/1186 Lisp machine, a powerful stand-alone computer that allows self-paced, individualized, and interactive instruction in a rich data source. The plea for such a system can be witnessed as far back as 28 years ago when Suchman (1961) wrote,

The need for improvement is great. Current educational practice tends to make children less autonomous and less empirical in their search for understanding. . . . The schools must have a new pedagogy with a new set of goals which subordinate retention to thinking. It is clear that such a program should offer large amounts of practice in exploring, manipulating and searching. The children should be given a maximum of opportunity to experience autonomous discovery. (cited in Wittrock, 1966, pp. 37–38).

We hypothesize that discovery learning can contribute to a rich understanding of domain information by increasing students' ability to access and organize information. Knowledge can be viewed as being structured in a network composed of units of "nodes" (concepts) and "links" (relations) (Anderson & Bower, 1973; Collins & Quillian, 1969; Norman & Rumelhart, 1975). Various cognitive processes can create or operate on these structures and activation may spread through the declarative network arousing associated concepts (e.g., Collins & Loftus, 1975). Active exploration should lead to more interconnected links being established between 'nodes' during acquisition, as compared to more passive knowledge acquisition about the same concepts.

We also believe that effective interrogative skills are instructable if the particular skills involved can be articulated and practiced under circumstances which require them to be used. Cronbach (1966) called for assessing the relative effectiveness of learning by discovery versus more didactic approaches by focusing on a narrow problem under limited circumstances. Today, such a circumscribed learning arena is typically called a *microworld environment*. This type of instructional setting can be designed so that students can engage in discovery through determining what data are gathered, making observations, formulating explanatory generalizations, and making experimental predictions. Moreover, a system could be designed so that students could learn from and reflect upon their own knowledge-acquiring activities.

More recently, Sleeman and Brown have commented on the benefits of learning-by-doing where factual knowledge is transformed into experiential knowledge. Tutorial intelligence (i.e., knowing *what* to say, *how* best to say it, and *when* to interrupt the student's problem-solving activity), in conjunction with a microworld environment, can potentially "transform a student's conceptual flounderings and misconceptions into profound and efficient learning experiences, ones rooted in an individual's own actions and hypotheses" (Sleeman & Brown, 1982, p. 2). In experiential learning, as students interact with new subject-matter situations, they compare their observations with their current beliefs and theories. Consequently, these beliefs may be temporarily rejected, accepted, modified, or replaced (see Glaser, 1984). In the course of this developing knowledge, students ask questions, make predictions, make inferences, and generate hypotheses about why certain events occur with systematic regularity.

Such knowledge interrogation is made possible in the present system by having an underlying architecture of knowledge hierarchially organized according to a pedagogical sequence of prerequisite knowledge. This knowledge base can be interactively accessed in various ways by the student. Students can explore the microworld, *Smithtown*, by way of menu-driven options that allow them to: Change the population, change the weather conditions, see sales market information, and so on. Additionally, there are online tools available to help students organize and systematize their information. These tools include: a Notebook to collect data, A Table to sort data, a Graphing package to plot data, as well as a Hypotheses menu to state different variable relationships and conditions under which they hold. There is also an ongoing record maintained of the students' actions (i.e., their menu selections and experiments) which is accessible to both the system and the student. Market simulations that students run comprise "experiments" that allow them to generate and test hypotheses, as well as form generalizations about economic phenomena.

The remainder of this chapter, which is an initial report of this work, is organized as follows.

1. Purpose of this research
2. Parts of the system
     The Simulation: *Smithtown*
     Tools for interrogating the system
     The Knowledge base
     The Diagnostician
     The Student Model
     The Coach
3. Individual differences in interrogative strategies
     Protocol analysis: Effective interrogative behavior
     Protocol analysis: Less effective interrogative behavior
4. Evaluation issues relating to the effectiveness of the tutor
5. Summary and future directions

PURPOSE

Students are provided with a microworld environment that they can actively explore. The main purposes of this system are: (a) to investigate individual differences in inductive reasoning and hypothesis generation of the kind involved in scientific inquiry; (b) to study how students' general inquiry skills might be enhanced; and (c) to teach elementary concepts and relationships in microeconomics. The domain of economics is used as an exemplary vehicle to this end. The unique feature of our system, called *Smithtown*,[1] is that in addition to providing a microworld environment for exploring and discovering, it has been designed to be an intelligent, interrogatable microworld where the intelligence is incorporated into the "Diagnostician" and the "Coach" components. These components serve to assist students in becoming more effective interrogators rather than explicitly instructing the domain knowledge.

Smithtown contains a range of levels-of-guidance that can be gradually increased or decreased, depending on the characteristics of the learner at any point in time. The lower end of the range is the more guided environment and this explicitly teaches the interrogative skills that we have determined to be most effective in extracting information from a body of knowledge.[2] The less structured end of the range, or discovery environment, allows the learner to exercise those skills without tutorial intervention.

Students start out in the discovery mode of the tutor; however, it is believed that individuals will show different patterns of exploratory behavior and will differentially benefit from such an unstructured environment. Those individuals who do not do well in the discovery mode are provided with supplemental tutoring in effective interrogation skills. That is, students are placed in the discovery environment until they are unequivocally unsuccessful, at which point the system automatically places them into progressively more structured modes of inquiry.

PARTS OF THE SYSTEM

The system is composed of four main components: (1) the Knowledge Base, (2) the Diagnostician, (3) the Student Model, and (4) the Coach. The knowledge base includes the targeted elements to be learned, such as the *law of demand,* which is an example of economics domain knowledge and *generalization of a concept,* which is an example of inquiry skill knowledge. The Diagnostician is a set of software "critics" that monitor the student's success in applying the inquiry behaviors and learning the domain concepts. The student model is the updated representation of the student's evolving knowledge base, both in terms of economics knowledge and inquiry skills. Finally, the Coach instructs the student based on information provided to it by the student model regarding unsystematic or ineffectual skills. Before discussing each of these components, we provide an

---

[1]The system is named for Adam Smith who observed in *The Wealth of Nations,* 1776, that the forces of the market are guided as if by an invisible hand.

[2]These interrogative skills were derived from protocol analyses of individuals interacting with the system and are summarized in the section outlining the Diagnostician.

overview of the simulation, and how it appears to the student. This is followed by a description of the inquiry tools.

The Simulation: *Smithtown*

The microworld is a simulated town, *Smithtown,* where the student can participate in various markets and manipulate economic conditions. Student interrogation of the microworld is through certain allowable actions in a scenario which take place in some market where a particular good is bought and sold. Students can select any good or service from a menu and run a market simulation on it; for example, adjusting the market price and observing the repercussions in the market (e.g., changes in quantity supplied or demanded, and in surplus or shortage, etc.) or allow the computer to make a price adjustment. In addition, town or global conditions may be altered, such as per capita income, or the town's population, as well as specific conditions per good, such as the number of current suppliers in town.

To begin an experiment or query, the following flow of menus occurs (see Fig. 14.1): First, a student selects an item from the "Goods and Services" menu. Second, a "Planning menu" pops up containing all possible variables that either may be changed by the student, or that change as a function of one of the independent variables. The student must state the variables they are interested in investigating; that is she must make a statement of intention. This assists the system in understanding and classifying student activities. Third, a menu with relevant economic indicators for *Smithtown* appears. These variables include average income, population, weather, consumer preference index, number of suppliers, and labor costs. Each of these variables has a system supplied default value (e.g., population = 10,000), and the current value for each of these indicators is shown on the screen (see Fig. 14.2: the gauges on the left side of the figure).

After the student examines and/or modifies the indicators, she may see the "Prediction" menu. The student is asked if she would like to make a prediction regarding the outcome of the current investigation. Making a prediction is optional. After observing events and effects in the microworld for some time, the student should be ready to predict outcomes. When the student does make a prediction, the system classifies the student as conducting an experiment rather than just exploring the world. For example, suppose a student was interested in looking at how changing the price of donuts affected the market for donuts in *Smithtown*. The student could collect data on what happened in the market after increasing and decreasing the price of donuts. This would be classified as 'exploratory behavior' by the system. Over time, the student would be in a position to correctly predict that, when the price of donuts increased: (a) the quantity demanded would decrease while (b) the quantity supplied would increase.

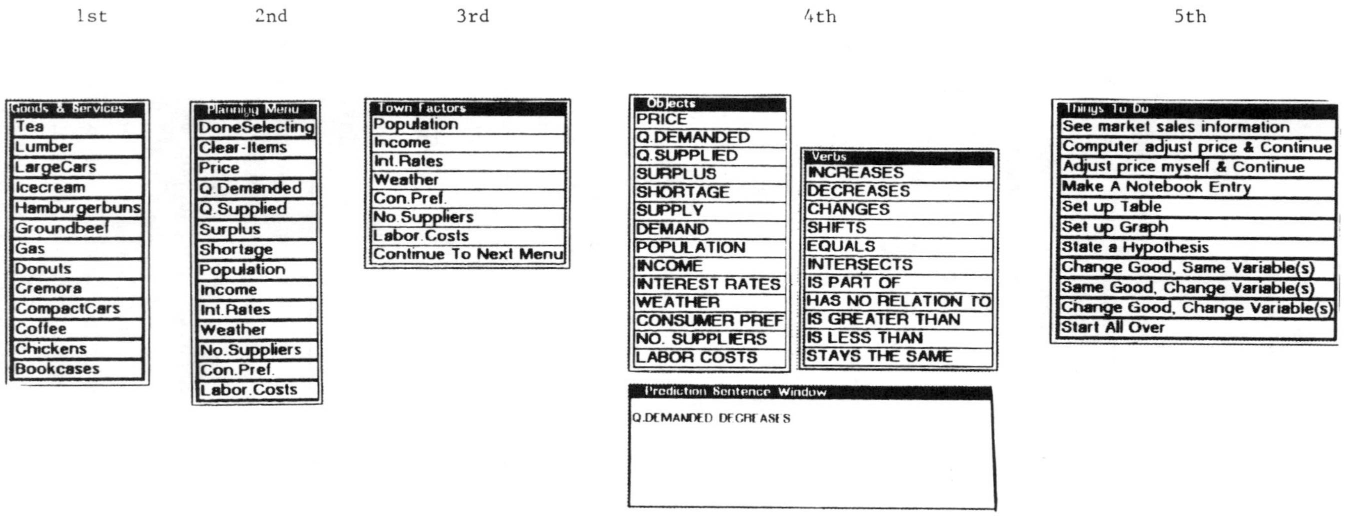

1st

Goods & Services
- Tea
- Lumber
- LargeCars
- Icecream
- Hamburgerbuns
- Groundbeef
- Gas
- Donuts
- Cremora
- CompactCars
- Coffee
- Chickens
- Bookcases

2nd

Planning Menu
- DoneSelecting
- Clear-Items
- Price
- Q Demanded
- Q Supplied
- Surplus
- Shortage
- Population
- Income
- Int.Rates
- Weather
- No.Suppliers
- Con.Pref.
- Labor Costs

3rd

Town Factors
- Population
- Income
- Int.Rates
- Weather
- Con.Pref.
- No.Suppliers
- Labor Costs
- Continue To Next Menu

4th

Objects
- PRICE
- Q DEMANDED
- Q SUPPLIED
- SURPLUS
- SHORTAGE
- SUPPLY
- DEMAND
- POPULATION
- INCOME
- INTEREST RATES
- WEATHER
- CONSUMER PREF
- NO. SUPPLIERS
- LABOR COSTS

Verbs
- INCREASES
- DECREASES
- CHANGES
- SHIFTS
- EQUALS
- INTERSECTS
- IS PART OF
- HAS NO RELATION TO
- IS GREATER THAN
- IS LESS THAN
- STAYS THE SAME

Prediction Sentence Window

Q DEMANDED DECREASES

5th

Things To Do
- See market sales information
- Computer adjust price & Continue
- Adjust price myself & Continue
- Make A Notebook Entry
- Set up Table
- Set up Graph
- State a Hypothesis
- Change Good, Same Variable(s)
- Same Good, Change Variable(s)
- Change Good, Change Variable(s)
- Start All Over

FIG. 14.1. Flow of menus in *Smithtown*.

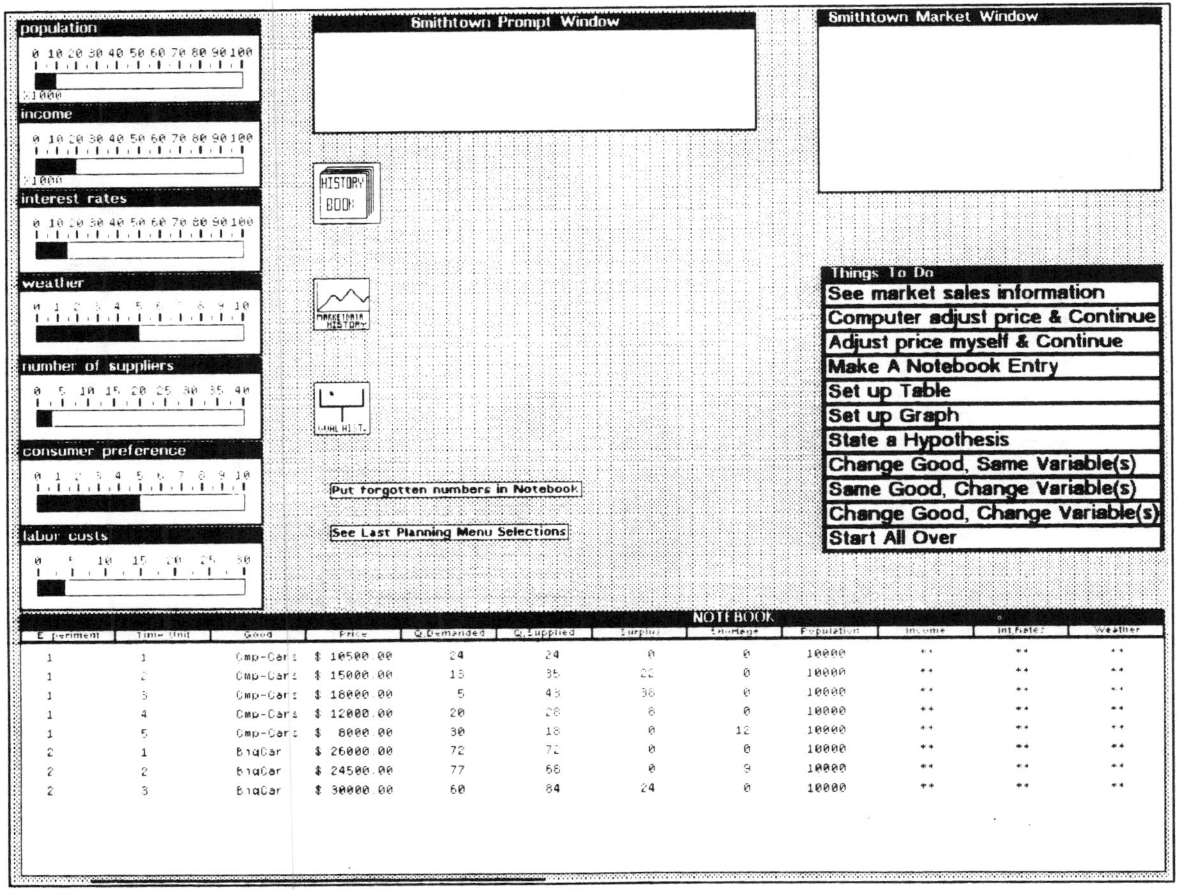

FIG. 14.2. Screen interface in *Smithtown*.

Finally, the student is presented with a "Things to Do" menu where she can see the effect of market manipulations on price, quantity demanded, quantity supplied, surplus, or shortage. At this point, the student may do one of three global actions: (1) Adjust the market price or have the computer make a price adjustment, (2) Use the inquiry tools to assist in the investigation (e.g., graph two variables), or (3) Select an experimental framework. The experimental frameworks let the student manipulate the market in various systematic ways and observe the effects. The three global actions increase in terms of complexity, and we expect to see individual differences in applying them in the microworld, starting off more tentatively changing the price of goods around and gradually learning to employ the various tools and the experimental frameworks for more formal and sophisticated experiments.

An experiment is defined as a series of student actions or tests carried out to see how variables relate to each other in *Smithtown,* or to find out what happens as a result of some specific parameter change. More sophisticated actions are made possible via three experimental frames available to the student:

1. Change Good, Same Independent Variable(s)
2. Same Good, Change Independent Variable(s)
3. Change Good, Change Independent Variable(s)

The first frame can either be a continuing experiment or a new experiment, depending on the intentions of the student. That is, if the student elects to change a good (e.g., coffee) to either a substitute (e.g., tea) or complement (Cremora) while holding the independent variables constant then this is classified as a continuing experiment; otherwise, changing the good to something else, (e.g., large cars), would constitute a new experiment. Changing the good while holding the independent variables constant is an experiment in the generalization of a concept as it holds across various goods. The second frame defines a new experiment where the effects of different independent variables are investigated within a common market (e.g., donuts). Finally, the third frame is a new experiment with different independent variable(s) and different goods. For any experiment, in this sense, the dependent variables in the marketplace that may change are the: market price, quantity demanded, demand, quantity supplied, supply, surplus and shortage.

The demarcation into either *continuing* or *new* experiments presumes that the student attempts to explore the *Smithtown* microworld in a systematic manner. However, often in initial explorations, individuals have no such systematic plan in mind; rather, they randomly change variables and observe the effects. The system recognizes several types of systematic investigations. These include *explorations:* observing and obtaining information from the microworld in order to generate and refine hypotheses about the microeconomic concepts and laws;

experiments: a series of student actions conducted to confirm or differentiate hypotheses; and *exercises:* tests on a previously confirmed hypothesis, perhaps to see the extent or limitations of its application (see Shrager, 1985, for a similar demarcation). Experiments carry a specific prediction from the "Prediction" menu while explorations do not.

Given this framework for collecting student actions, we are interested in monitoring changes in these experiments over time. To do so, we employ the Diagnostician component, described in a later section. Now we discuss the inquiry tools that the system makes available to the student to assist in his or her investigations.

Tools for Interrogating the System

As indicated, we have included several "online tools" for the students to use in their explorations of this microworld. These include: a Notebook for collecting data and observations, a Table to organize data from the notebook, a Graph Utility to plot data, a Hypothesis Menu to state relationships among variables, and three History Windows that allow the students to see a chronological listing of behaviors, data, and concepts learned so far. Each of these tools is now discussed in turn.

The students can keep a Notebook of data about their explorations of *Smithtown.* For the user, this is optional, but the computer always keeps a history of all data that have been collected. An example of the online Notebook is seen at the bottom of Fig. 14.2. The students can select which variables they want recorded, and the values are automatically put into the notebook.

Once students have collected data in the Notebook, they can elect to isolate some of the data and put them into a special Table where various sorting tools for reordering the entries are available (see Fig. 14.3). When students want to separate out some variables for more intensive study, they choose the option of setting up a Table from the "Things to Do" menu. The screen is cleared, and they can specify which variables they would like to put together (e.g., market price and quantity supplied). This is an important tool for reducing and making sense of raw data. For instance, after collecting and recording data on the good, compact cars, a student may begin to sense the relation between the price of compact cars and the quantity supplied (i.e., as the market price increases, the quantity supplied increases). To test this developing idea, he or she can have the system isolate these two variables in the Table and sort one of the variables by ascending (or descending) order. Once this is done, the function relating the two variables should be clearer. This table reveals suppliers' behavior and allows for a possible hypothesis of an economic principle to emerge; that is, the law of supply.

The Graph utility allows the student to plot data, either from the notebook or from the table that has been constructed. This is included as an alternative way of

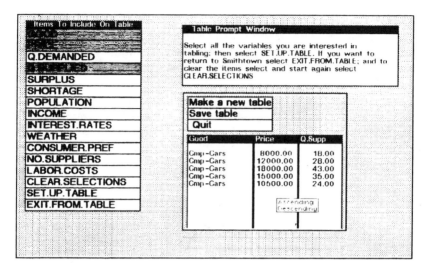

FIG. 14.3.   Table package.

viewing relations between variables. Some individuals can better understand information when it is depicted in a graph than in tabular form. To apply this utility, students must select the menu option: "Set up a Graph" from the "Things to Do" menu, informing the system of the variables they wish to plot. An example of a graph with two variables plotted together can be seen in Fig. 14.4. The system has two other options in the Graph utility: (1) Save a Graph, and (2) Superimpose Graphs. The first option saves a particular graph by shrinking it down to a small window, preserving the graph functions on the outside of the window. The shrunken window can be moved and placed anywhere on the screen by the student, and enlarged again by just buttoning within its region.[3] The second option lets the student plot two or more graphs together, providing they share a common independent variable on one of the axes. This allows students to see curve shifts, interactions, and so on.

A framework is provided for the students to make inductions or generalizations of relationships from the data in the form of a Hypothesis menu (see Fig. 14.5). When a student believes she is ready to state a hypothesis, she can choose this option from the "Things to Do" menu. As with the Table and Graph options, the screen clears and the instructions to the student appear, prompting on how to select words from the following four interconnected menus to construct a statement about some variable relationships. One menu consists of *connectors* such

---

[3]'Buttoning' refers to the action taken with the 'mouse', the device which lets students make menu selections by pressing one button on its top.

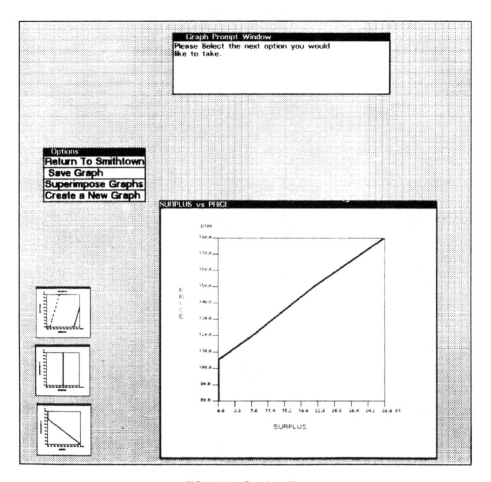

FIG. 14.4.   Graph utility.

as: if, then, as, when, and, the. Another menu consists of *market variables* such
as: income, population, quantity demanded, demand, quantity supplied, supply,
market price, surplus, shortage, and so on. A third menu consists of *direct
objects* including: over time, down/right, up/right, down/left, up/left, along the
demand curve, along the supply curve, zero, left, right, price changes, changes
other than price, and changes to. Finally, the last menu includes *verbs* describing
the change: decreases, increases, equals, intersects, is part of, has no relation to,
is greater than, is less than, slopes, moves, shifts as a result of, changes as a
result of. As students choose words from these menus, the emerging statement
appears in the Hypothesis Statement Window. For the example given above in
the market for compact cars, a student could state, "As price increases, quantity

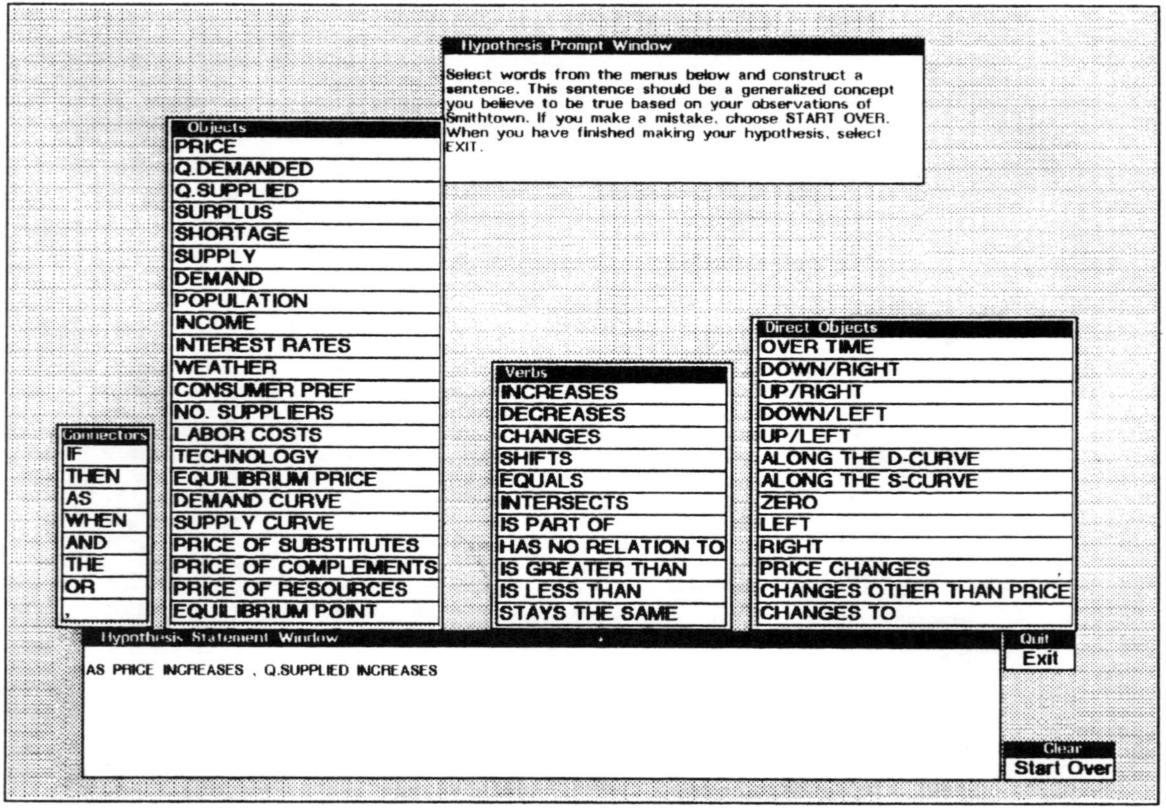

FIG. 14.5. Hypothesis menu.

344

supplied increases".[4] A pattern matcher analyzes key words from the input and checks to see if this matches any stored relationships for each targeted concept. If so, the system flags that concept as having been conditionally learned. Otherwise, the student is informed that the statement is not understood.

Three history windows are included in the system. As students continue to interact with the microworld, histories accumulate summarizing the various student actions resulting from different explorations and experiments. This summary is maintained in the *Student History Window* and is accessible to both the student and the system. The grain size for this summary is at a small enough level to give a detailed chronological accounting of all menu items chosen, predictions and hypotheses made, and how the tools were employed (e.g., STUDENT SET UP A GRAPH PLOTTING QUANTITY DEMANDED ON THE X AXIS AND PRICE ON THE Y AXIS). The *Market Data Window* keeps a record of all variables and associated values that have been manipulated. If a student forgot to enter some values in the notebook, she may go to this window and retrieve the necessary values for any given experiment or time unit within an experiment. Finally, there is the *Goal History Window*. This provides a representation of what the student has successfully learned in terms of concepts targeted by the system. Moreover, there is a listing of the concepts not yet learned. The student can see this list at any time by enlarging this window. The concepts already learned are shaded while those concepts remaining to be learned are left untouched. This provides a means for the student to gauge progress in the acquisition of relevant concepts.

Given these tools, the system can judge how effectively the student applies them in the interrogation of the microworld. Since coaching assistance is embedded in the domain knowledge, we now present the organization of the domain knowledge.

The Knowledge Base

The tutor has a well-defined instructional domain which is broken down into key concepts that are organized in a bottom-up manner (i.e., from simpler to more complex ideas). An understanding of these concepts should result from the students' experiments in the microworld.

The hierarchy of domain knowledge was developed by first reviewing six introductory microeconomics textbooks and determining the presentation order of information, and second, discussing the optimal ordering of these concepts for student learning in the classroom with a college instructor of economics. Although a student is not required to learn the concepts in any prescribed order, the hierarchy shown in Figure 6 provides the system with information about where

---

[4]This is equivalent to expressing the relation as, "Quantity supplied increases as the market price increases".

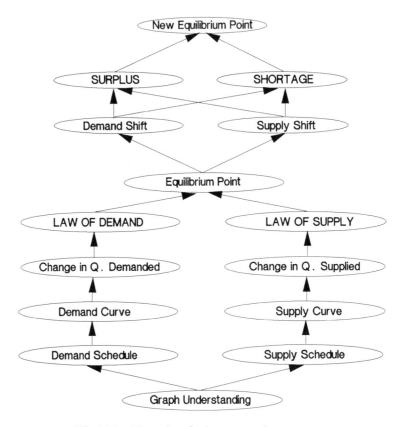

FIG. 14.6.   Hierarchy of microeconomic concepts.

the student is likely to be with regard to his or her knowledge acquisition. That is, the concept of "equilibrium point" can be more readily understood after the individual concepts of supply and demand have been learned, both of which have their own prerequisite knowledge. Appendix I contains a summary of the content, concepts, and model underlying *Smithtown*. The knowledge base for the inquiry skills is delineated in the following section.

The Diagnostician

Smithtown was designed to provide a range of guidance that can be increased or decreased, depending on the characteristics of the learner's performance. At one end of the range is the discovery environment. As long as the student is progressing, the microworld will remain in a discovery mode. "Progress" is defined as (a) demonstrating appropriate investigative behaviors, and (b) learning the domain concepts in a reasonable amount of time. At the other end of the range is the directive environment that explicitly assists the student in using an interrogative skill that is deemed problematic for him/her. For example, the system might instruct a student to enter data in the notebook from the market before altering any variables.

The Diagnostician evaluates how a student interrogates the system, ascertaining whether he or she is proceeding in a systematic, efficient manner. The Diagnostician works in conjunction with the Student Model and Coach. The Coach intervenes when necessary. We characterized students' effectiveness in interrogative strategies over the course of their experiments by analyzing the protocols of effective and less effective behaviors (see section on Protocol Analysis). To do this, an explication of effective inquiry behaviors is required, as well as a definition of a test, which specifies the students' experiments within the microworld and determines their systematicity or buggy version of a test. We call these tests "critics." With this information, the Diagnostician can monitor how the student performs in the microworld. Using the inquiry tools provided, there are various dimensions on which student investigative performance can be evaluated. Following is a listing of inquiry behaviors:

Exploratory Data Collection

Baseline Data Collection: For an initial exploration, were data collected from the market in equilibrium, before any variables were altered?

Baseline Data Entry: For an initial exploration, were data entered into the notebook from the market equilibrium, before any variables were altered?

Monitoring the Market—Computer Price Change: Did the student allow the computer to make adjustments to the market price of a good (to see ensuing repercussions)?

Planning for an Experiment

Entry of Planning Menu Items: Did the student enter data into the notebook for those variables she expressed an interest in investigating from the planning menu?

Systematic Notebook Entries

Independent Variable Data Entry: Did the student make a notebook entry every time she changed a variable or variables?

Dependent Variable Data Entry: Did the student enter those variables that changed as a result of a manipulation?

Data Organization

Table Usage: Did the student use the table package to organize data that were entered in the notebook?

Isolating Variables in the Table: Did the student put only a few variables into the table to reduce and make sense of the data?

Sorting on Relevant Variables: Was the sorting option used on relevant variables in the table? For example, if the price was systematically varied, then it should have been sorted instead of something not varied, like income.

Graph Package Usage: Was the graph package used by the student to plot data?

Plotting Variables: Did the student select variables to plot that had been manipulated, or that changed as a result of a manipulation?

Saving Graphs: Did the student save a graph after plotting variables that had been changed?

Superimposing Graphs: Was there an attempt made to superimpose two graphs to see relationships between functions, like supply and demand, or two curves in parallel?

Systematic Experimental Behaviors

Manipulating the Market Price/User Price Change: Did the student make adjustments to the market price of a good to see the market changes? For experiments, manipulating the price oneself is probably more effective than observing the computer adjust the price.

Sufficiently Large Change to Variables: Were initial changes made to variable(s) sufficiently large enough to detect any market effects?

Sufficiently Small Change to Variables: Were later changes made to variable(s) sufficiently small enough to discriminate and refine patterns in the data?

Number of Variables Changed: Did the student change only one variable at a time for comparison and/or recording? This is related to what a student already knows; over time, a student can progressively handle more variables.

Inductive/Generalization Strategies

Replicating an Experiment: Did the student attempt to redo an experiment upon getting confirming or negating results for a given prediction?

Generalize a Concept Across All Goods: Did the student try to generalize an economics principle as it holds for all goods? For example, having learned the law of demand operating in the donut market, did the student attempt to generalize the principle for *all* goods?

Generalize a Concept Across Related Goods: Did the student try to generalize an economics principle across specifically related goods, like between tea, coffee, and Cremora, or between lumber and wooden bookcases?

Hypothesis Specification: Were any hypotheses stated as a result of observed systematicities in the data from the Notebook, Table, or Graph?

Complexity of Hypotheses: Was there an increase over time in the chaining of variables when the student generated hypotheses? As knowledge increases, the number of variables strung together should go from two or more, in progressively more complex relationships.

Strategies Used With Negating Evidence

Failure-Driven Behaviors: If an experiment was conducted testing some specified belief or prediction, and the results of the experiment were not supported, did the student: (a) Redo the experiment with parameter changes, attempting to get the data to fit the existing theory, or (b) Generate a new hypothesis that fit the observed data?

Each of these specific actions has been translated into a critic which is a test of sequences of student actions. In addition, there are points in each critic where the student might go astray constituting unsystematic behaviors, or buggy versions of the critics (see asterisk in example, below). For instance, the critic for the first inquiry behavior would look like the following (paraphrased):

> BASELINE DATA COLLECTION: CRITIC 1

If:	It is an exploration or experiment, AND
	It is the first action in this investigation, AND
	A good or service was selected, AND
	From the Planning menu there is a list of variables interested in, AND
*	From the Economic indicators menu there are no variables changed

Then: BASELINE DATA COLLECTION: CRITIC 1 has been demonstrated.

Otherwise: Alert the Coach for possibly helping the student, depending on the value of the Critic-counter which tallies the number of times the student erred on this skill (applied a buggy version of it) or failed to apply it when it was relevant. The Coach then may help the student according to the appropriate level of explicitness required.

The Diagnostician evaluates an experiment in terms of the values assigned to each specific critic and indicates to the Coach whether or not a given sequence of student actions has reached some predetermined level of adequate performance.

Because the system knows when each concept has been learned (i.e., when the student specifies a correct economic principle), and there is a fixed set of concepts, the system can ascertain relationships between specific inquiry behaviors and the accuracy and quantity of concepts being learned. That is, some skills may be more powerful and necessary than others in the extraction of domain information. So, the Diagnostician characterizes students in terms of their declarative and procedural knowledge at any point in time. For *declarative knowledge,* the system knows when concepts the student currently understands, as evidenced by a successful statement about variable relations and conditions under which they hold. For *procedural knowledge,* the system knows which and how the student applies the various tools to extract information, and how she creates tests for conducting different experiments on the data. Specifically, the Diagnostician determines how a student is: collecting data and observations from experiments (Notebook entries); isolating out specific variables for study of relationships (Table or Graph); testing the emerging hypotheses by way of different experiments; and specifying variable relationships (Hypothesis menu).

The Student Model

The hierarchy of concept elements provides the basis for a model of student knowledge. Each concept is associated with a rule or relationship among economic variables. For example, the law of demand relates price and quantity demanded in an inverse relationship. When a student uses the hypothesis menu and generates a valid statement about the underlying variable relationships for a particular concept, the system flags that concept or relationship as having been learned. This appears in the Goal History Window, checked off from the curriculum list of domain elements to be learned.

Similarly, a student model is constructed for effective usage of the inquiry tools. Actual student performance is compared to optimal performance in an overlay sense (Carr & Goldstein, 1977). The effectiveness of performance is determined by two statistics maintained for each student as he or she interacts with the microworld: (a) Demonstrating an inquiry behavior when it was appropriate; or (b) Applying a buggy version of that behavior. A "batting average" is computed for each behavior consisting of the number of times the skill was used, divided by the number of times it *should* have been used. If that number is less than some threshold (e.g., <50%), the Coach would be prompted to intervene. Also, if several inefficient behaviors were demonstrated, the Coach can address each one in turn based on a hierarchy of coaching where, for instance, the behavior for *Baseline Data Collection* takes precedence over *Save a Graph,* and so on. The way the Coach actually operates is described next.

The Coach

The purpose of the Coach is to take the information provided by the Student Model, and if there is evidence of student floundering, to act appropriately. An example of less effective interrogative behavior would be if the student consistently made only slight changes to variables being investigated during preliminary experiments (i.e., not employing the critic: *Sufficiently Large Change to Variables*). Such manipulations, as changing the population from 12,000 to 12,500, or the number of suppliers of a particular good from 10 to 11, are typically too small to result in any real changes in the marketplace. The Coach's intervention would consist of a suggestion to try to make the changes larger, and hence, more observable.

For each student experiment, the Diagnostician assesses the specific inquiry actions, then updates information in the Student Model. Those actions failing to reach the predetermined level of success or criterion performance would thereby become candidates for possible assistance. Because our Coach is relatively unobtrusive, it requires several corroborations of failure (i.e., ineffective behaviors across successive experiments) before actively intervening. In other words, it maintains an ongoing list of student problems and, when the evidence for floundering is unequivocal, it intervenes. In the event that there are several ineffective behaviors, the Coach makes a decision as to which one needs addressing first. Again, it addresses the students' interrogative behaviors and not the domain knowledge, *per se.* Assistance is provided in the context of the student's current investigation.

In order to encourage an independence of thinking, tutorial guidance progresses in terms of explicitness. For the initial intervention, the Coach provides a subtle hint. The next time it is called for the same behavior, the intervention is clearer, providing analogies to the student to map onto the current situation. Finally, the third intervention provides explicit instructions for conducting a particular experiment. For example, if the student continued to alter variables before recording the results of the market prior to the changes, the Coach would intervene with the following, varying levels of explicitness:

Explanation 1 (vague): You changed ⟨variable = X⟩. If you are interested in seeing how the change affects the market, what do you need to do before you begin making changes?

Explanation 2 (analog mapping): You changed ⟨variable = X⟩. If you wanted to measure the affects of some drug on performance, first you would have to find out what the performance level of the subject was *before* the drug was given. Apply the same logic here.

Explanation 3 (explicit): You changed ⟨variable = X⟩ without recording its value before the change. You should choose the 'Continue To Next Menu' option from the Town Factors menu and then make a notebook entry of the current market information before changing the variable's value. This gives you baseline data to make comparisons against later on.

When a student has conducted several experiments and discovered an economic principle, she may use the hypothesis menu to generate a statement about the underlying variable relationships for that concept. If the student is successful, she is provided with a congratulatory statement by the Coach, including the proper label for the concept. For instance, the system may respond to a student having just specified the law of demand (i.e., As price increases, quantity demanded decreases), with: "*Congratulations! You have just discovered what economists refer to as the Law of Demand. Please note that the converse is also true. As price decreases, quantity demanded increases.* Can you conduct an experiment that illustrates the Law of Demand?" The request for an experiment guarantees that the student possesses not only declarative knowledge about the concept in question, but also procedural knowledge about how to construct an exemplary experiment. When the student has successfully stated the concept in the hypothesis menu and has generated an experiment typifying this regularity or law, the concept is checked off as "learned" in the Goal History Window.

In summary, the Coach attends to three preliminary principles for interrupting a student's activity:

1. The student's particular problematic behavior must be apparent. An "apparent" level of ineffective behavior was initially an arbitrary threshold ratio, later refined after experimentation.

2. Feedback should not be always critical, but also appreciative of any good aspect of a student's behavior.

3. Any instruction or guidance should be spaced. At least a gap of two events should occur between interruptions.

INDIVIDUAL DIFFERENCES: INTERROGATIVE STRATEGIES

Over the course of system development, we collected protocol data on effective and less effective interrogative strategies from individuals interacting with *Smithtown*. The pilot data we collected have been used in building the Diagnostician, discussed earlier. This information focuses the Diagnostician on particular issues in the developing student model. We anticipated that the better students would attempt to derive and test generalizations about their experiences whereas the less successful students would work longer at the more concrete level of manipulating variables, changing parameters, and observing specific effects. In addition to knowledge-level differences, we also expected that the histories of students' interrogations would give evidence of differences in self-regulatory behavior. We anticipated that successful learners would show more activities summarizing and organizing information, more frequent testing of their current knowledge, and systematic predictions to check the limitations of the hypothesis being considered.

There were, as expected, large individual differences in the strategies used to interrogate a new domain where the purpose was to extract the underlying principles and systematicities. None of the subjects had any formal economics training and all were volunteers.

Protocol Analysis: Effective Interrogative Behavior

To illustrate a contrast in interrogative behaviors, two extractions from protocols follow. The first is an effective methodology and the second is a less effective one. To maintain subject confidentiality, we use the generic pronoun "he" to describe our two subjects.

The first subject clearly shows how someone can optimally extract information from an unfamiliar domain. This individual had no formal economics training. He spent one and a half hours interacting with the system and verbalized his actions, the justifications for them, current hypotheses of variable relationships, and predictions of different events. He completed a total of six distinct experiments within the system and showed a marked learning of the domain knowledge from the beginning to the end of the session.

Our subject used the same good, ice cream, for the six experiments and changed only one variable per trial (e.g., increasing overall population from 10,000 to 20,000). This subject was aware of his systematicity. When he was asked about his strategy, he replied,

> I'm trying to hold everything the same, then change one variable at a time, one of the ones I've identified as being independent for some reason, and keep running the simulation through the time units until there's 0 shortage and 0 surplus. The market would be stable.

Initially he used the option of letting the computer adjust the market price of a selected good. Our subject only began adjusting the price himself in the 4th of the total six experiments that he conducted. This was in accord with our belief that a more efficient interrogator would initially observe a phenomenon before becoming an active experimenter within the system. For instance, he observed how the computer made changes in the market price and the resulting changes that occurred to such variables as quantity demanded, quantity supplied, and so on. This served as a model for future explorations by the subject.

Our subject also demonstrated increasing selectivity in the variables he chose to record. Initially, he recorded all of the variables in the notebook.

> So, now I'm sort of regretting having used all these fields since I'm only experimenting with the suppliers. So I'm going to throw out the rest, other than the basic variables: quantity demanded, quantity supplied, surplus, shortage, market price and suppliers. I don't want to fill out the rest since I've decided that these are more critical, like they are independent variables and I'm only looking for variation within suppliers.

As his domain knowledge increased, this was clearly reflected in the content of hypotheses generated at the beginning of each experiment. For instance, after checking out and recording the market sales information for ice cream, he wanted to change the population of the town to see the effect on quantity demanded, quantity supplied, and other variables. When asked for specific hypotheses, he had none. In experiment #3, when he increased the number of suppliers, his hypothesis was a little more substantive,

If there are more suppliers, the going price will be lower than it was because competition will be more intense.

Contrast that with a hypothesis generated during the final experiment. He doubled the population of Smithtown, had previously cut everyone's income by half, and had 10 ice cream shops in town. He hypothesized,

Since the population is up, and even at their newly poor state, quantity demanded ought to go up. In fact, it ought to double. So, suppliers can raise their prices since there are going to be shortages. The new equilibrium price is going to be higher, and the route to this end is that there's going to be big shortages, and the price will move up until it reaches equilibrium.

Another strategy that changed was the *type* of experiments he created. His experiments became increasingly more controlled and precise. He began his explorations with a vague experiment, saying, "I'd sort of like to see what's gonna happen, like if I changed the population to see what happens to quantity demanded, and stuff." By contrast, at the end of his interaction with *Smithtown* he stated,

You know what I'd like to do now? A whole series of experiments using 10, 11, 12, 13, and 14 suppliers, and look at what the market price is for each one of those and actually get curves . . . jump up a level of detail and look just at the equilibrium price and ignore the other variables.

The effective behavior of questioning the meaning of variable relationships is illustrated when our subject reflected on the repercussions of his cutting the average per capita income by half.

So, what's the basic mechanism? Why is it that when income goes down, and people have less money to spend . . . they're less likely to buy ice cream? So they don't have money to blow on frivolties like ice cream. Hmmm, they're just gonna stay away from ice cream stores in droves. So, in order to encourage people to go to their stores, the shopkeepers lower their prices. As the price goes down, the people are more likely to go into the stores. If the shopkeepers drop their price way too far, people will clean them out and the shopkeepers will think, "We can do better than that", so they will up the price to readjust itself. Hey, they makes sense!

Finally, our subject's initial experimentations dealt with factors he was familiar with. When asked why he chose the number of suppliers as one of the first variables he manipulated, he responded that it was something he knew about and that he also knew, theoretically, the effects it would have in the marketplace.

Protocol Analysis: Less Effective
Interrogative Behavior

The second subject illustrates how someone can extract minimal domain knowledge with ineffective inquiry skills. This individual also had no formal economics training and spent 1½ hours interacting with *Smithtown*, verbalizing all actions, predictions, and hypotheses. He completed a total of three experiments and gave evidence of learning only one elementary principle of supply and demand.[5]

For experiment #1, the market selected was compact cars, and the variable manipulated was income, which was increased from $8,000.00 to $10,000.00 in order to make it more "reasonable." This strategy of selecting values for variables that were more "normal" persisted throughout the entire session. There was no attempt to conduct scientific investigations of causal relationships. Instead, all attempts and changes centered around "making the town more normal." At the end of experiment #2, when the subject had decreased the price of compact cars and was asked why, he responded, "Because I wanted people to be able to afford to buy a car, really. I was putting myself in their place." In addition, the changes that *were* made were often inadequate. For instance, in one experiment, the price of chicken was changed by the subject from $1.33/lb. to $1.29/lb. This action reduced the price by only 4 cents to make it conform to what the subject believed was a "reasonable" and observed sales price. The action was not carried out as an experiment on the potential affects of changing price on the other variables.

Notebook entries continued to be incomplete, and contained unnecessary information. In his final experiment, the subject selected the market for chickens and made no changes to any variables. After seeing "Sales Market Information," he made a notebook entry of the variables: market price, quantity supplied, surplus, suppliers and consumer preference. The other essential variables, good, quantity demanded, and shortage, were missing. The inclusion of suppliers and consumer preference was unnecessary, as they had nothing to do with the subsequent manipulation, which dealt with price changes in the market.

Hypotheses regarding relationships between variables were based on surface structure characteristics of the simulations. When the subject was asked at the end of experiment #1 (market for compact cars, income changed) about any hypotheses for resulting variable relations, he responded,

> It just seems to me that there doesn't really seem much to do in this town for these people to need cars, you know what I mean? Not a whole lot, except to get back

---

[5]The law of demand was understood, illustrated by the statement: "*If I decreased the market price to something like $6,500.00, then more people are going to want to come out and buy the cars.*"

and forth to work. Most of them just can't afford a car. You make $10,000.00 and you're gonna take $7,000.00 and buy a car?!

Similarly, the subject understood causal relations among variables from an ethical perspective; if suppliers reduced the price of chickens, for instance, then they "should have" supplied a sufficient quantity of chickens for all who wanted them. The basic mechanism underlying the supply and demand model eluded the subject, as seen in the following statement, when the subject was astounded to find out that when the price of chickens was reduced, the amount of chickens supplied actually *decreased*.

Why did they go down on the supply then? I mean, if they [the suppliers] knew it was going to go down, that they were going to have this sale for $1.29/lb., they should have . . . [put more chickens out]. Why did they do that? The shortage of chickens equals 65 pounds, I want to know why they did that. Now, wouldn't *you* provide more chickens?

When the price of chickens was increased from $1.29/lb. to $1.43/lb., the response was again incredulous,

They gave *more* chickens! When they knew it was going to go up [the price], and they knew people wouldn't buy it at that rate . . . that *really* doesn't make sense! If this is really true, somebody should put a stop to it!!

Finally, when asked at the end of the experiment if he had applied any strategies to the explorations, he responded, "No, not really. I was just going by what I know from day to day experience."

The contrast between these two interrogative styles is clear. In terms of the inquiry behaviors listed earlier, our more effective subject demonstrated a systematicity in the varying of variables, a concern with making changes to variables sufficiently large, a selective recording of notebook entries, a progression from 'computer' to 'self' price adjustments,[6] as well as a tendency to start with more familiar knowledge, and increase the complexity of his hypotheses as his domain knowledge increased. The relationship between his behaviors and his growing comprehension of the domain knowledge was also apparent. The less effective subject's behavior showed an absence of most of these skills. In addition, he attended more to the surface structure characteristics of events at the expense of the more principled relationships describing the laws of supply and demand and their interaction.

---

[6]Alternatively, this strategy could be characterized as progressing from *observing* the microworld to more actively *experimenting* within the microworld.

EVALUATION

In order to determine what the experience with the microworld actually taught, we investigated student knowledge and skill acquisition in a controlled design (see Shute, Glaser, & Raghavan, 1989 for a complete discussion of these results). Pretest and posttest batteries covering economic principles dealing with the laws of supply and demand were developed in conjunction with an economics expert working on the project. There were three tests per battery: alternative/matched forms of a multiple choice test, a short answer test, and complex scenarios test requiring subjects to solve "What would happen if . . ." type of problems. The complex scenarios test was designed to externalize an individual's problem representation by having the subject identify the relevant variables in the problem, chart which variables were related, and indicate the nature of the relationships.

These test batteries were administered to 30 subjects divided equally into three groups: a control group receiving no intervention, a group from an introductory microeconomics classroom, and a group interacting with *Smithtown*. Relative performance on these tests showed that *Smithtown* was effective in imparting domain knowledge. Subjects in the economics classroom and those working only with *Smithtown* demonstrated very similar gain scores (from pretests to posttests) even though the classroom group spent more than twice as much time on the same curriculum material than the *Smithtown* group. Moreover, *Smithtown* did not directly instruct economics; rather, the instruction was specific for inquiry skills.

Two data sources were used in the analysis of experimental subjects interacting with the microworld. First, there were verbal protocols consisting of the verbalizations from the subject. Second, there were the computer-recorded student histories of all actions in the microworld. A rational categorization of behaviors was made based on the verbal protocols, dividing the learning behaviors into three global categories: (a) gross activities, (b) data management behaviors, and (c) scientific actions. These were further subdivided into more refined categories, each containing individual learning indicators or critics (see Shute & Glaser, 1990, for more information on the validity of these categories).

A large-scale study (N = 530) was conducted using *Smithtown* to investigate individual differences in learning behaviors within this type of environment (see Shute & Glaser, 1990). This study showed that a factor indicating the degree to which a person engaged in hypothesis-generating and testing was the most predictive of successful learning in *Smithtown*, accounting for considerably more of the variance in our learning criterion (i.e., total number of concepts acquired) than a measure of general intelligence. The individual learning indicators comprising this factor consisted of: total number of hypotheses made, number of times findings from one experiment were generalized across related and unrelated markets, and having sufficient data collected prior to making a hypothesis.

SUMMARY AND FUTURE DIRECTIONS

The economics microworld discussed in this chapter was designed as an instructional system using a laboratory environment for studying inquiry and inferencing behaviors. If a student is not progressing in that environment, there is a mechanism to provide tutorial assistance. Such discovery microworlds provide excellent opportunities for observing and reacting to individual differences in learning styles, creating a more active and adaptive curriculum than is currently possible in many traditional classroom or computer settings. The system can react to individual differences by exemplifying effective interrogative strategies that can be emulated by individuals, or by providing explicit instruction on interrogation strategies to uncover consistencies and regularities in a body of knowledge.

In summary, *Smithtown* is based on a set of general instructional design principles:

• The instructional situation provides the learner with opportunities to interrogate the microworld and to formulate and test hypotheses through questions and simulated experiments.

• The instructional environment permits actions at different levels. The student is able to conduct experiments, record the results, and select and analyze subsets of that database. For example, the student can tabulate variables and see the results, make a statement of a hypothesized relationship, and obtain further information about its adequacy or limitations.

• The computer screen serves as a memory aid for students, allowing them to see the results of explorations to date. The information is displayed in various forms (e.g., graphical or tabular) or in terms of verbal statements of relationships.

• There is hierarchy of domain knowledge available in the microworld, and the system has the information about what subset of it has been learned by the student and what subset of it is still available for learning. This information is accessible to the student.

• A history of the student's actions, in selecting information and formulating and testing hypotheses, are sequenced and stored in a way that permits student performance to be displayed and evaluated in a structured manner.

• As the student explores *Smithtown,* the Diagnostician accesses prerequisite skills necessary for activity in the microworld, knowledge components that the student has discovered and acquired, and strategic issues like the moves of the student with respect to interrogation and hypothesis formation.

• The Diagnostician passes a list of problem behaviors on the Student Model which uses this information, when necessary, to recommend situations to the

Coach for possible student assistance. This guidance should enable the student to demonstrate more effective interrogative procedures.

Because an individual's learning style (e.g., passive vs. active) is believed to interact with the instructional environment (e.g., discovery vs. didactic), as well as the domain (i.e., microeconomics), this raises several questions regarding *Smithtown* that have not yet been tested: (1) How much flexibility of behaviors should be allowed before the Coach intervenes? Because there is not just one way to use the tools optimally to conduct experiments to induce regularities, what should the criteria be for saying that a given student is floundering or behaving unsystematically? In a primarily discovery environment such as *Smithtown,* how do we disambiguate the passive learners who are not active because of cognitive deficits rather than because of an acquired learning style? (2) Because the Diagnostician monitors students' experiments in terms of the systematicity of their actions, how should it identify those interrogative skills that have not been demonstrated? Some effective interrogative behaviors are not demonstrated because they are not understood, or they have yet to be applied but are understood, or they are simply not preferred (e.g., the student chose not to graph data). (3) What are the trends of the learning indicators over time? How does increasing domain knowledge relate to inquiry behaviors? For example, as an individual learns more about economics, can he or she manipulate progressively more independent variables simultaneously? (4) How generalizable are these findings regarding the delineated "effective" and "less effective" inquiry skills? Does training on these skills transfer to successful performance in a different domain? These issues should be sorted out as more data accumulate.

To test the effectiveness of the acquisition of inquiry skills, we have planned a series of transfer studies where students interacting with one system will subsequently learn a new body of knowledge from another inquiry system. There are several microworlds now developed that are similar in system architecture to *Smithtown,* but differ in the domain knowledge contained: (a) light refraction and reflection, (b) orbital mechanics, and (c) basic principles of electricity.

In conclusion, we have been obtaining rich information on how students collect and organize information, how they use evidence to generate a test hypotheses, and form generalizations in the course of scientific inquiry with computer-based laboratories.

ACKNOWLEDGMENTS

The authors gratefully acknowledge the many persons whose contributions are invaluable to this project: Jeff Blais, Jeff Bonar, Alan Lesgold, Kalyani Raghavan, Peter Reimann, and Paul Resnick. Last but hardly least, we offer a special thanks to Jamie Schultz for his contribution of ideas and code, making this project an online reality.

The research reported herein was supported by the Learning Research and Development Center, supported in part as a research center by funds from the Office of Educational Research and Improvement (OERI) of the U.S. Department of Education. The opinions expressed do not necessarily reflect the position or policy of OERI and no official endorsement should be inferred.

REFERENCES

Anderson, J. R. (1983). *The architecture of cognition.* Cambridge, MA: Harvard University Press.

Anderson, J. R., & Bower, G. H. (1973). *Human associative memory.* Washington: Winston and Sons.

Carr, B., & Goldstein, I. P. (1977). Overlays: A theory of model for computer-aided instruction (*AI Memo 406*), MIT A.I. Lab.

Collins, A. M., & Loftus, E. F. (1975). A spreading activation theory of semantic processing. *Psychological Review, 82*, 407–428.

Collins, A. M., & Quillian, M. R. (1969). Retrieval time from semantic memory. *Journal of Verbal Learning and Verbal Behavior, 8*, 240–247.

Cronbach, L. J. (1966). The logic of experiments on discovery. In L. S. Shulman & E. R. Keisler (Eds.), *Learning by discovery.* Chicago: Rand McNally.

Glaser, R. (1984). Education and thinking: The role of knowledge. *American Psychologist, 39*, 93–104.

Norman, D. A., & Rumelhart, D. E. (1975). *Explorations in cognition.* San Francisco: Freeman.

Pitt, R. B. (1983). Development of a general problem-solving schema in adolescence and early adulthood. *Journal of Experimental Psychology: General, 112*(4), 547–584.

Shrager, J. C. (1985). *Instructionless learning: Discovery of the mental model of a complex device.* Unpublished doctoral dissertation, Carnegie-Mellon University.

Shute, V. J., Glaser, R., & Raghavan, K. (1989). Inference and discovery in an exploratory laboratory. In P. L. Ackerman, R. J. Sternberg, & R. Glaser (Eds.), *Learning and individual differences.* New York: W. H. Freeman.

Shute, V. J., & Glaser, R. (1990). A large-scale evaluation of an intelligent discovery world: *Smithtown. Interactive Learning Environments*, Vol 1.

Sleeman, D., & Brown, J. S. (1982). *Intelligent tutoring systems.* New York: Academic Press.

Wittrock, M. C. (1966). The learning by discovery hypothesis. In L. S. Shulman & E. R. Keisler (Eds.), *Learning by discovery.* Chicago: Rand McNally.

APPENDIX I

Smithtown: The Content, Concepts and Model

This appendix overviews the content and concepts that are included in the system, representing the central economic principles that we want students to learn. We discuss how these concepts are implemented in our system, detailing the underlying model which drives the simulation. The principles, thus, will be discussed as they exist and function in *Smithtown*.

Microeconomic Principles

One of the central concepts in economics is the concept of a market. In the economic sense, a market is the interaction between buyers and sellers. Their interaction determines the quantities of various goods and services (products and resources) which will be bought and sold during some period of time, as well as the prices at which these exchanges take place. Thus, through markets, we make most of our basic decisions about how resources in our society will be used: What will be produced, how will it be produced, and who will get it once it is produced. In a market, buyers and sellers independently consider the price of the product in determining the quantities they want to buy and sell; however, price affects buyers and sellers differently.

Supply and Demand.   The buyers' side of the market is called *demand*. The law of demand states that the quantity of a product which consumers would be willing and able to purchase during some period of time is negatively related to the price of the product. If the price of gasoline goes up, we will demand a smaller quantity of gasoline; if the price goes down, we will demand a larger quantity. The same is true for most products. If we draw a graph of the combinations of price and the resulting quantities demanded, we get what is called a *demand curve.*

The sellers' side of the market is called *supply*. The law of supply is that the quantity of a product which producers would be willing and able to produce and sell during some period of time is positively related to the price of the product. If the price of color television sets goes up, producers will be willing and able to offer more television sets for sale. If the price of color television sets goes down, producers will reduce the number of television sets they put on the market. If we draw a graph of the combinations of price and the resulting quantities supplied, we get what is called a *supply curve.*

The Equilibrium Point.   Both buyers and sellers consider the market price in making decisions, but price affects buyers and sellers differently. If the price rises, sellers will make larger quantities available for sale, but buyers will demand smaller quantities. If the price falls, buyers will demand larger quantities, but sellers will make smaller quantities available for sale. It is because of these opposite reactions to price changes that buyers and sellers can reach an agreement. When a price is reached where the quantity that sellers want to sell is equal to the quantity that buyers want to buy, we say that the market is at a point of *equilibrium.*

Competitive markets always tend toward points of equilibrium. If the market is higher than the equilibrium price, buyers will demand smaller quantities than sellers are supplying. *Surpluses* of unsold goods will convince sellers to lower their price down toward the equilibrium level. If, for some reason, the market price is lower than the equilibrium price, buyers will demand larger quantities than sellers are supplying. *Shortages* will lead to price increases, and the price will rise toward the equilibrium level.

Changes in Demand and Supply.   The equilibrium point in the market can change if either demand or supply change. Price determines the quantity demanded. Other factors also play a role in determining demand. Some of these other determinants are: 1) consumers' income—normally, if income increases, demand will increase; 2) consumers' tastes—if tastes shift in favor of a product, the demand will increase; 3) the price of substitute products—the demand for a product will increase if the price of a substitute increases; and 4) the price of complementary products—the demand for a product will decrease if the price of a complement increases. Other factors such as interest rates, the weather, population, and expectations about the future can also affect the demand for some products.

Graphically, a change in one of these other determinants results in a shift in the demand curve. This is called a *change in demand*. A shift to the right represents an increase in demand where a larger quantity will be demanded at each price. A shift to the left represents a decrease in demand where a smaller quantity will be demanded at each price.

In addition to price, other factors play a role in determining supply, including: 1) the cost of resources—if the cost of resources rises, the supply will decrease; 2) technology—if technology improves, supply will increase; 3) profits available in other lines of production—the supply of a product will decrease if other lines of production available to the seller become more profitable; and 4) the number of sellers—if the number of sellers increases, supply will increase.

Graphically, a change in one of these other determinants results in a shift to the supply curve. This is called a *change in supply*. A shift to the right represents an increase in supply—a larger quantity will be supplied at each price. A shift to the left represents a decrease in supply where smaller quantity will be supplied at each price.

Establishing a New Equilibrium.   Competitive markets tend to converge toward equilibrium points. Equilibrium, once established, can be disturbed by changes in demand and/or supply. If demand and/or supply change, a surplus or shortage will result at the original price, and price will move toward a new equilibrium. A shortage at the original price will cause price to rise to the new level and cause changes in the quantities supplied and demanded. A new equilibrium will be established at the second price and the second quantity.

Economic Misconceptions.   There are certain beliefs about the market that students typically have as they begin an introductory economics course. Three fairly ubiquitous misconceptions are outlined below.

1) Students often have difficulty distinguishing between a change in the quantity demanded (i.e., a movement along the curve) and a change in demand (i.e., a shift of the curve). They often believe that the curves shift in response to price changes, but in reality, curves shift as a function of factors *other* than price, like population changes or interest rate changes.

2) In order to understand how markets work, supply and demand must be seen as independent of each other—linked only by a common determinant (i.e., price). Students often think that changes in demand cause changes in supply instead of just changes in the quantity supplied, which is the true state.

3) Students often think of the demand curve as having a positive slope: "The price of a product will be high if people are demanding a large quantity of it." They also see the supply curve as having a negative slope: "Sellers lower the price when they want to supply a large quantity." These errors result from a misunderstanding of the demand and supply functions. It is price which determines the quantities demanded and supplied and not vice versa.

Student Actions in *Smithtown*

On their initial encounter with the system, students are instructed to experiment within the microworld, make changes to different variables, and see the results. Depending on the efficiency of their inquiry behaviors (e.g., systematicity of experiments), students can extract differing amounts of information regarding how supply and demand interact in a competitive market. For example, students starting out with no previous economic knowledge may design the following simple experiment: select a familiar good (e.g., donuts), not make any changes to the global variables (income, population, etc.), then collect information about the markets as it stands (baseline data).

To learn an elementary concept like the law of demand (i.e., the inverse relationship between price and quantity demanded), students can alter the price of donuts and see sales market information. Sales market information includes: quantity demanded, quantity supplied, surplus, and shortage. After collecting several instances of price changes and affects, the student can use some of the available tools included in the program to sort and order the data. One observation which should become apparent, then, is that as price goes up, quantity demanded goes down.

As discussed earlier, for both demand and supply, we have included in the model the factors that shift the respective curves. For each good represented in the system, coefficients are assigned to these variables indicating strength or relative importance. For instance, interest rates will have a larger coefficient for large and compact car markets, yet only minimal or no influence on the market for donuts. On the other hand, weather conditions will have a significant impact on the demand curve for ice cream, but less influence on the market for chicken.

Following are the variables the student may manipulate, affecting the demand and supply curves.

Demand Shifters

Population: For most goods, as population increases, the demand curve shifts to the right, the magnitude of shift determined by the strength of the coefficient.

Income: As income increases, the demand curve generally shifts to the right. Again, each good has its own coefficient indicating how far to shift the curve, the amount of shift dependent on the particular good. Some goods or services may have 0 as coefficients (e.g., water) or even negative coefficients (e.g., inferior goods).

Weather Conditions: For some goods, better weather may cause the demand curve to shift, either left or right. We have represented differential weather conditions in the system on a scale of 1 (cloudy, cold day) to 10 (beautiful, sunny day).

Interest Rates: As interest rates increase for some goods, the demand curve shifts to the left (e.g., cars). Again, the degree of shift is dependent on the underlying coefficient per market.

Consumer Preferences: A number, from 1 (low) to 10 (high) may be assigned to represent the consumer taste or preference for that good. This variable is unrelated to price, and can be affected by things like advertising, word of mouth, and so on.

Price of Substitute Goods: As this price goes up, there is a shift to the right of the good in question since more people will demand the alternative good (e.g., the price of butter increases, resulting in a shift to the right for the demand curve for margarine). Coefficients for this variable are positive.

Price of Complementary Goods: Complementary goods, those associated with the selected good, have negative coefficients, therefore as the price of complementary goods go up, the demand curve for the current good shifts left since they are typically purchased in conjunction with each other.

Preference Changes to Substitute and Complementary Goods: In addition to reactions through price, the demand for certain goods will react to tastes/preferences (scaled 1 to 10) for certain other goods.

Supply Shifters

Number of Suppliers: A change in the number of suppliers of a good will shift the supply curve for that good. Each good has a coefficient indicating how far to shift the supply curve. The coefficient is positive where, more suppliers of a good results in more of the good being supplied (i.e., a shift to the right of the supply curve). The converse is also true.

Cost of Resources: As this variable increases, there is an inverse effect on the supply curve for the good that uses the resource, thus it is a negative coefficient. For instance, if the cost of sugar increased, this would shift the supply curves for donuts and ice cream to the left.

Technology: If there are technological advances impacting a particular market, then this will have a positive effect on the supply curve for that market. To illustrate, suppose a new technology was developed for increasing the production of compact cars (robots in the factory). The supply curve for small cars would subsequently shift right reflecting the increased output.

Labor/Wage Costs: If the labor cost increases, this will have an inverse effect on the supply curve for the good that requires this service, so it has a negative coefficient.

Computer Calculations and Representations

Currently, we have a total of 13 goods in the system for students to manipulate. These are: coffee, tea, Cremora, donuts, ice cream, compact cars, large cars, gasoline, chicken, ground beef, hamburger buns, lumber, and wooden bookcases. For each one of these there is a list of variables containing default values: that is, the variables set in *Smithtown* when the student begins his or her investigations. Some of the more important ones include: equilibrium price, equilibrium quantity, intercept for supply curve, slope of supply curve, intercept for demand curve, slope of demand curve, list of substitute goods, list of complementary goods, current price, time frame,[7] as well as the coefficients for each of the shifter variables listed above.

Once a student has selected a good from the menu, the default values are initialized and a new menu appears. This menu contains a list of variables the student may choose to alter current default values (e.g., population is initially set at 10,000 Smithtonians). If an item from this menu is selected and changed, the action causes the demand or supply curve to shift from its default situation. Since both the intercept and the slope values are stored per good, and each good knows the relative influence of a particular variable on it, then the curve shifts by an amount indicated by the coefficients. To illustrate, suppose a student was investigating the effects of a changing population on the market for donuts, increasing the population from 10,000 to 20,000 residents. The demand curve will shift since population it is known to be a demand shifter, and the magnitude of the shift will be:

$$(0.1)(10,000) = 1000 \text{ scaled units}$$

where the 0.1 is the coefficient attached to population for donuts, and 10,000 it the amount of change (i.e., $20,000 - 10,000 = 10,000$). The coefficients vary

---

[7]This represents the time period during which the market is monitored.

according to their relative influence on the shifters in a particular market.[8] The slope remains constant, so the shift is a uniform 1000 units to the right. Now, an updated equilibrium price can be calculated from the new point of intersection between the shifted demand curve and the unchanged supply curve.

In the demand and supply curves, the intercept and slope values for each good have been initially set at reasonable market values. For example, the equilibrium price for donuts is set at $0.50 per donut (i.e., the price at which quantity demanded equals quantity supplied), the quantity demanded intercept is set at 100 (i.e., the maximum number of donuts demanded in a given period of time such as one week), and the demand slope is set at -2, thus the initial demand curve is fully specified. Similarly, the supply curve for donuts has the same equilibrium price of $0.50, a supply intercept of -3, and a supply slope of 2.

---

[8]That is, the size of the shift is determined by the size of the coefficient. The coefficients for each good were based on observations about how much the different variables affected the different markets. For instance, interest rates strongly affect the market for large cars, but do not affect the market for donuts, thus, the interest rate coefficient for large cars is larger than for donuts.

15

In Illinois and in Japan: Lee Cronbach as a Mentor

Hiroshi Azuma
University of Tokyo

I worked under Lee Cronbach from 1956 to 1962, sometimes as one of more than ten and sometimes as the only one. It was his last period in Illinois which covered the period from the time he was elected President of APA to the time he decided to move to Stanford. In retrospect, it was one of his "Strum und Drang" periods both academically and personally, and I wonder how he found the time to work so closely and patiently with us students and assistants who started as novices in the psychometric problem field he was struggling to explore. Later he even agreed to spend a year in Japan which was at that time virgin territory as far as his major interests were concerned.

At the request to write about Lee Cronbach as a mentor, I would like to recall a few episodes typical of those periods. He was not "soft" with students, but he was always nice, was friendly in its true meaning of the word. It was a rare good fortune for me to have had a mentor like Lee Cronbach, and I feel a deep gratitude to him and to our science for that good fortune. It was one of Cronbach's weaknesses that he could not dismiss even a weak student as long as the student was striving for something.

THE START

In 1956 when I was awarded a Fulbright grant to study at the University of Illinois, E. G. Williamson of the University of Minnesota was conducting a summer workshop at the University of Tokyo. I took that opportunity to experience for myself the counseling of that famous counseling psychologist known for his "directive" approach. He listened carefully to my desire to pioneer an experimental psychology oriented educational psychology in Japan. He then looked through the catalog of the University of Illinois and said, without any explanation, "You should study under Cronbach". I did not like the idea at first because at that time I knew Cronbach only as a test expert. I took another hour to explain that my training and my interests both lay in the experimental study of perception and learning, that I had not taken any interest previously in tests and so-called educational psychology and that I would rather study under one of a number of famous experimental psychologists in Illinois who were conducting studies potentially relevant to education. Williamson listened silently and then said, "The more I hear you, the more I believe that you should work under Cronbach." I gave up. After all, I was under no obligation to follow the advice. I thanked Williamson for his time and was about to leave when Williamson said: "Well, write a letter asking Cronbach to take you as his student and bring it to me tomorrow morning. I will correct your English and send it to Cronbach together with my letter." It started like that, and that is the reason I still favor a "directive" approach to counseling with certain kinds of problems and persons.

In early September of 1956 I flew from Tokyo to Chicago to attend the APA Convention being held there. I was in the audience at a symposium in which Cronbach participated as the new President of the Association. As a new foreign student, I was not able to follow much of the discussion, but I watched Lee with curiosity and a certain ambivalence. As the meeting ended, Lee suddenly walked down to me and said: "You must be Azuma. I will expect you in my office at the Bureau of Educational Research in Champaign in the morning of next Friday."

YOU CAN GET TRUE TRAINING

Williamson was right. Lee Cronbach had a quiet zeal for opening up educational research as a disciplined study. He held joint appointments in psychology and education and the majority of his students were in psychology. Nevertheless, his self-identity was always that of an educational researcher and he was proud of it.

During my first year as a graduate student in education at Illinois, I worked closely with Charles Eriksen in the Psychology Department whose works were in line with the research I had conducted in Japan, and completed a couple of studies with him. He suggested to me, for quite practical reasons, to switch to psychology as a major. The fellowship I had was the kind that could be carried over to any major. I could remain a student of Cronbach because he was also a psychology professor, and most of the courses I was taking were in psychology. I did not need to change any of my plans or any course work, as I had completed all courses required for the first year graduate student in psychology. Besides, I would then be exempted from introductory level education courses required of all education students. They rather bored me. "And," he added, "honestly in the U.S., psychology degrees are more prestigeous than education degrees".

It was clear that Eriksen made this suggest for my benefit, and it sounded like a good one. I then consulted with Lee about the possibility. He was understanding and he did not object, but he was not happy about it. He asked: "Do you think that you will work with people in education in the future?" When I answered I did, he said: "Then stay with education. The difference in the prestige, which undoubtedly exists, can be overcome by what you do and under whom you study." Then he picked up the telephone in front of me, called the Office of the College of Education and negotiated that some of the education courses required of me could be substituted by more demanding courses of similar content which I had already taken. A few weeks later he came up with another proposal. To give up my fellowship and take an assistantship in his project. He was quite clear that it would leave me less freedom, the number of credits I could take in one semester would be restricted, and it would take one or two years longer if I wanted to get a degree. "But," he said, "you can get a true training." Having learned by that time that he was a "terrific" teacher, the offer was too challenging to reject.

Incidentally, at the end of the semester which followed, Cronbach posted on a bulletin board his comments on the term papers of his class. At the end he added: "Another thing which I noted was that there was no difference between education and psychology students. The top scorer was an education student."

YOU DIDN'T MAKE ANY PROGRESS
IN SO MUCH AS 24 HOURS

It was not easy to live up to his expectations as his assistant. The work load in an ordinary sense was not heavy. He declared that he did not hire assistants to do petty jobs which a professor could do. One day, for example, he found that the light on my desk was not adequate. He said he would take care of it and brought back a new one within a couple of hours himself. For a student reared in oriental traditions, to have the professor do that kind of job was unimaginable. Throughout the years I worked for him, he never asked me or his other assistants to run errands, to score papers, or to perform clerical chores.

Instead Cronbach wanted us to use our minds. That was "training"! He would casually drop in to the office I occupied with Nageswari Rajaratnam and Milton Meux, and ask a question like: "Why do we call the mean the best estimate? Why don't we use other variables to regress from?" Each one of us would mumble something, to which he listened silently. Next day in his office, he would ask the same question again. I would give the same answer as the day before. Then he would shout: "Now, do you mean that you didn't make any progress in so much as 24 hours?" He would then lay down on his couch, start reading, and completely ignore me.

On another occasion he asked me to review a few papers that criticized his concept of construct validity. My paper, I thought, was able to point out over-sights, inconsistencies and misunderstandings of those critics, and to support Cronbach's position. Contrary to my expectation, he seemed displeased to the point of contempt. "You are making a straw man", he said, "and beating it up. Perhaps they made some mistakes, but you have been picking up mistakes without trying to understand them. Don't be run by the party-mind. Although I don't agree with them, I know that they are good thinkers".

OF COURSE!

Sometimes, perhaps quite often, Cronbach made mistakes. He liked to have his mistakes pointed out. After lecturing, he would lie on a couch exhausted and refused to see people. but if a student knocked at his office door claiming that he found what Lee said in his lecture of that day wrong, Lee would spring up, let the student in, and pose to listen.

In 1958, he directed me to compare several correction formulas for coefficient alpha applied to tests composed of dichotomous items of varying difficulty. The strategy Cronbach used was a rudimentary form of a computerized simulation study, a very fresh idea for that time. Pools of items were hypothesized to be characterized by different inter-item tetrachoric correlations and distributions of item difficulties. Formulas were applied to fictitious tests generated by sampling items from a pool under given constraints. The task would have been simple at today's level of technology, but it was a time when only a limited number of researchers in the social sciences had access to high-speed computers and before efficient compiler languages for programming were available.

Lee apparently knew computers well in their functions and potentialities, but had only limited experience actually programming. He taught me how to pro-gram simple arithmetic routines and then I was left to tackle the actual problem. He could have hired someone with more experience, but he said that I would profit from some experience working with this new machine which was destined to become very important. And he was right. But, as a student without any experience, working with a gigantic ILLIAC assisted only by a thick assembler handbook was not easy.

After many weeks of trial and error, I somehow got the job done and came up with a result that showed clearly that Cronbach's stratified alpha behaved better than any correction formula, just as Lee had predicted. Instead of being easily satisfied with this "positive" result, he scrutinized the data, and finally said that I must have made some programming error. The behavior of the formulas deviated from what he would predict based on the response of phi coefficient for dif-ferences in item difficulties.

There followed a few more weeks reexamining every step, but I found no errors. Lee maintained that I must have made an error. To convince him I needed something more than a printout. Finally, I was able to demonstrate that the phi coefficient and phi covariance behave differently in relation to the difference in item difficulties and that Lee was led to an incorrect prediction because he neglected the fact that it was the phi covariance, not the phi coefficient, that was part of the alpha formula.

Lee listened to my explanation carefully and at the end said in an amused voice: "Of course!" No apology, no excuse and no appreciation of effort. But that jolly "Of course" sufficed to relieve the fatigue of weeks' of frustrating toil.

I DON'T KNOW NOTHING, SIR!

Cronbach hated studies that were superficially neat but did not penetrate into honest truth.

My dissertation was on concept learning. The "concept" was the position of an imaginary point in a space. This position could be determined by combining two cue values with differential weights buried in the stimulus figure, and ignoring other cues.

I obtained a nice smooth curve which apparently represented the process by which subjects attained the correct solution. After I received my doctorate with this study, however, Cronbach insisted that a nice curve and "significant" differences were not enough. We should go back to individual data and find out how each individual solved the problem. At first I thought that this was a cruel demand. After all, everybody else gets away with nice curves and significant results; others are not required to explain deviations of individuals from the mode, to explain "errors."

The task, which I did rather reluctantly, turned out to be revealing. Very few subjects proceeded in the manner represented by the group curve. A typical subject would start out from one of a fantastic variety of hypotheses, would keep adding smaller hypotheses to deal with the type of items which did not fit the original hypothesis, and would arrive at either a complicated system of procedures or a set of type specific hypotheses. This was my first exposure to the strength of a process-oriented approach to cognition.

There still remained a number of mysterious cases out of which we were not able to make sense. Cronbach was determined to squeeze out everything in the data. So, one year after we had collected the data, he decided to interview these mysterious cases. The students were duly tracked down and each one was told to come to the office of Dr. Cronbach. One student was very tense when he appeared. He must have thought that he had done something wrong, and was to be interrogated as in a criminal court. Lee placed our stimulus sheet in front of him and asked: "Do you remember taking this test last year?" The poor student hardly looked at the sheet. He screamed: "No sir, I don't know nothing, sir!" After dismissing him, Lee was muttering: "He didn't know nothing."

IN JAPAN

After returning to Japan to begin university teaching, I appreciated how much I had learned from Cronbach and thought my students also deserved a good mentor, one better than me. I wanted to share my good fortune of studying under Lee Cronbach with my colleagues and students. Finally Cronbach agreed to spend a year at the University of Tokyo and came to Japan in 1967 as a Fulbright Professor. The timing was not optimal, however. As elsewhere in the world, campus unrest was gradually coming into view at the University of Tokyo. The campus atmosphere was uneasy. The Faculty of Education building was under construction. The winter was cold, and Lee and his family suffered flue for several months. Our students' ability to communicate in English was not adequate at that time to exchange ideas freely with him. In spite of those adverse conditions, he worked hard and achieved a great deal. The draft of many chapters of "The Dependability of Behavioral Measurements" and a couple of papers on validity, plus many other papers and reports, were written with my old fashioned semiautomatic portable Smith-Corona.

He also used his full power in teaching. He prepared lectures carefully, using many slides so that students with difficulty in English could keep up. He frequently asked students to write reports and commented on each with highly encouraging tone. His efforts bore fruit. The strongest core of our educational research grew out of some 20 regular participants of his classes. Yoshio Takane, who was introduced to psychometrics in Cronbach's class, is now at McGill University and has been President of the Psychometric Society. Tadashi Hidano, who subsequently went to Stanford to spend a year under Cronbach, led the Japanese Association of Educational Psychology for three terms and now heads the research division of the University Entrance Examination Center, the Japanese equivalent to ETS. Sukeyori Shiba, one of the founders of Japanese Behaviometric Society, is the present President of JAEP. To conclude and also to represent the many other fine participants, I cite here from a letter by Giyoo Hatano of Dokkyo University. (I took, with his permission, the liberty of substantially abridging his text.)

> Dr. Cronbach's stay in Japan was the most impressive and most influential event in my early career. I still remember very vividly his lectures and comments to each of the presenters at *Evenings with Professor Cronbach*. At that time I was just promoted to an associate professor at Dokkyo University, and thought innocently that I was approaching the very top of psychological and educational science. Dr. Cronbach clearly showed me that the top was still very far and I had so many things to learn. Since we were not able to communicate effectively in English, interactions in the first evening were mostly "mediated" by Dr. Azuma, the organizer of *Evenings*. However, by the end of the evening, we felt as if we had interacted directly—in spite of the language barrier, his ideas reached the participants without losing their brilliance, and his replies always revealed that he had grasped the

intended meanings of the questions exactly. This experience of acquiring knowledge through subjectively direct communication motivated many young educational psychologists, including myself, to learn to speak English and also to write papers in English. I think Dr. Cronbach's contribution to the internationalization of Japanese educational psychology was, though he never intended it, as great as that of the International Congress of Psychology in Tokyo in 1972.

Dr. Cronbach showed us, among other things, the pleasures to be had from thinking deeply. In his case, this was inseparable from analyzing and checking the given data in a variety of ways. His style tended to be "bottom-up". He seemed to love observing and interpreting data more than building and developing conceptual models without empirical data. What distinguished him from others was his ability to think of alternative interpretations and also his capacity to devise procedures for checking each interpretation against the data.

Professor Hatano is now perhaps the Japanese developmental psychologist best known internationally.

16

"I'm Sorry But . . . "; Our Intellectual Heritage From LJC

Leigh Burstein
University of California, Los Angeles

Michael M. Ravitch
Northwestern University

Richard J. Shavelson
University of California, Santa Barbara

Noreen M. Webb
University of California, Los Angeles

INTRODUCTION

When Lee exclaimed, "I'm sorry but . . . ," you knew you'd said, or written, something that had failed his *test* of logic/coherence/accuracy. After thinking about your position, he was unconvinced; *skeptical* charitably describes his state of mind. With considerable trepidation, you then considered reframing your argument or, more likely, thinking about its logic/coherence/accuracy and delaying, until after due consideration, your next attempt at running it by "The *Perfesser.*"

In this manner, Lee took everything we said and did seriously. The notion that, on the one hand, someone so famous and brilliant should take us—mere grad students—seriously, and, on the other, that we should be held accountable for our thoughts, scared the daylights out of us and most of our contemporaries. Although we certainly agreed on the importance of accepting personal and professional responsibility for our words and deeds, little in the past could have led us to anticipate the constant pressure for intellectual growth, a process, hopefully, from which we have not, hopefully, and will never emerge.

Work with Lee, then, was a "stretching experience," to say the least. We felt the attention of that enormous intellect focused sharply on our fuzzy ideas and inadequate words. High demands were implicit; discussions were seldom routine. The amount of feedback was prodigious. We'd often wonder how he found the time to provide such extensive written comment ("what did I do to warrant so much attention?"), but then we'd realize that we weren't special; others received equal treatment. How he managed to keep tabs on all of us, and find time to publish so much, given his penchant for continual reediting, is truly remarkable. That Lee Cronbach influenced our intellectual development and careers tremendously falls short of an understatement. His impact permeates both the manner in which we go about our professional work and the topics we choose to work on.

In what follows we have tried to recapture what it was like to work as a graduate student, yet always a colleague, with Lee during our Stanford era. Although we recognize that he taught us by setting high expectations and by reviewing, criticizing, and liberal editing of our ideas and papers, no elaboration of his teaching methods and principles could possibly capture The Perfesser as teacher. Rather his methods and influence are best inferred from events. Accordingly, we sample anecdotal snapshots from our experiences. They are presented as a set of educational and professional *passages*—as those stages of graduate-student development that each and everyone of us has passed through, albeit at a somewhat different time and in a somewhat different way.

To set the stage, our collective student careers at Stanford spanned the period 1968 through 1977. During this time Cronbach's activities covered a vast array of intellectual turf including *Research for Tomorrow's Schools* with Patrick Suppes (Cronbach & Suppes, 1969), the measurement of change paper with Lita Furby (*Psychological Bulletin*, 1970), his comments on Arthur Jensen's reawakening of the nature-nurture controversy (*Harvard Education Review*, 1970), the third edition of *Essentials of Psychological Testing* (Lee's own "red book", 1970), the validity chapter in Robert Thorndike's *Educational Measurement* (1971), the completion of the generalizability monograph (*Dependability of Behavioral Measurements*, with Goldine Gleser, Harinder Nanda, and Nageswari Rajaratnam, 1972), "Beyond Two Disciplines of Scientific Psychology" (*American Psychologist*, 1975), *Research on Classrooms and Schools* (1976), *Aptitudes and Instructional Methods* with Richard Snow (1977), and "Analysis of Covariance in Nonrandomized Experiments: Parameters Affecting Bias" (with David Rogosa, Bob Floden, and Gary Price, 1977). Also the seeds were already sown for what evolved into the Evaluation Consortium and two major books on evaluation and social policy (Cronbach, 1982; Cronbach et al., 1980).

CLASSES: "THE HURDLES"

During our Stanford years, Lee taught three courses on a regular basis: Introduction to Test Theory, Advanced Measurement, and Curriculum Evaluation. Each course was an experience.

In Test Theory, students from the Mathematical Methods, Psychological Studies, and Mathematics Education programs studied the development of a theory of measurement against the backdrop of real-world problems in research and practice. The inductive development of classical theory through a mixture of measured doses of mathematical proof and practical "thought" exercises stretched even the most sophisticated and experienced student—with the one exception noted below.

Advanced Measurement, on the other hand, drew a more specialized audience. Only those students whose programs warranted the most sophisticated, state-of-the-art thinking about psychometrics ventured into the course. During the year when *Dependability of Behavioral Measurements* was being completed, Lee and Goldine Gleser devoted most of the course to Generalizability Theory but there was still time for student-led presentations on the most recent work on item-response theory, multitrait multimethod validation, decision theory, and the like.

The Curriculum Evaluation course was an altogether different kind of experience. During the late '60s and the '70s, this was the only evaluation course taught at Stanford. Lee managed to make it an invigorating experience. Students chose a program to evaluate and then "conducted" the evaluation in a paper exercise with multiple cycles of feedback from Cronbach. At each review cycle, Cronbach's written commentary was as extensive as the student's draft for that cycle. The course's challenge was clear: keep ahead of Lee.

Where many experts are poor teachers because they don't remember how they gained their knowledge, this does not describe Lee. He was superb at listening to students explain their work so that he could identify their errors in thinking. He explained verbally, algebraically, geometrically—in one way or another—to achieve his goal as a teacher.

Occasionally, however, Lee's best intentions failed. The final exam for Test Theory in 1969 was one such instance. The exam was intended to be a 2-hour open book exercise. After 2 hours, Lee saw that more time was needed. After 3 hours, some students were still not finished.

At a post mortem review (a common event following a Cronbach course), Lee told us that 2 hours should have been plenty of time. Why just the day before he had given the exam *orally* to a blind student who had finished it in less than an hour. We all laughed. No wonder; that student was a brilliant psychology major (he later switched to statistics), who, throughout the course, asked penetrating questions that pushed Lee to think carefully before responding. Most of us, however, struggled through the course. We were pleased that Lee considered us in the same league but that was preposterous.

RESEARCH TRAINING: TRIAL BY FIRE

Lee took every aspect of our research training seriously. Everything—research collaboration, teaching assistantships, manuscript reviews for journals, and, of course, the dissertation—was to be experienced, not merely tasted. This meant "trial-by-fire."

He continually assessed our strengths and weaknesses, and concerned himself with how to round out our training. Rounding out did not mean doing everything with him. He was always on the lookout for experiences elsewhere in the department, in the university, and in the community that would fill in gaps and expand our horizons. While he was honest about your needs—"You just don't understand American education"—he made sure you knew how to fill them.

Being Lee's research assistant (paid or otherwise), for instance, was an intensive, collaborative experience. He showed, by example, the importance of fully participating in all aspects of a research project. He stayed very close to the data in any analysis, doing runs on the computer himself to test hunches. (Indeed, bumping into him at the computer center at odd hours was not uncommon.) Moreover, he didn't let our vacations stand in the way of progress either. He simply picked up the data analysis where you left off and provided a 5-page written commentary when you returned.

Right from the beginning, then, Lee expected professional contributions from us. We were not mere students. We were professionals who happened to be at an earlier point in our careers than he was in his. At one point during a lengthy exchange of memorandum regarding one of the myriad of generalizability-analysis examples, he made clear his beliefs about the student/assistant's responsibilities:

> Any collaboration works back and forth across the terrain, with the person holding the ball at any moment moving what he thinks is downfield. They can't move always in step like a three-legged race. Takes much too much time—even if I weren't in collaboration with Snow, Gleser, and some others at the same time.

Collaborating with Lee on a research paper was the trial-by-fire experience par excellence; it also created the most work for him. Although we sometimes wrote the first draft, not many of those first words appeared in the final version. It would have been much easier for Lee to junk that first attempt and start over himself. Instead, he worked with it, salvaged what he could, and encouraged a collaborative writing and editing process. He shared the responsibility for responding to reviewers' comments and communicating with the journal, even leaving us in charge when he went out of town—quite a thrill for a neophyte graduate student.

We also learned that Lee, for all his prodigious intellect, was quite human. This last observation came from a session on NAEP when Lee was wrong in some calculation, estimation or choice of methods, and our faces must have displayed mixed astonishment and amusement that The Perfesser could make a mistake. "Well, I'm sorry, but I'm allowed to make mistakes, too," he grumbled—obviously not unhappy with his error, but rather with our reaction. This reaction certainly had been observed in others many times before (and since), and has been one that conveyed our belief that he was different from us. We were correct in believing that he was and still is faster, deeper, and broader in his thinking than we, but were wrong in ascribing other attributes. Great intelligence does not protect against mistakes, nor does it necessitate interests, tastes, emotions, and needs different from others.

Our "trips to the woodshed" during our research apprenticeships often laced chiding and humor. As part of the work on *Dependability of Behavioral Measurements,* for example, we spent months developing exercises that illustrated applications of components of variance and components of covariance. The Jackknife study, an attempt to set confidence bands for estimated variance components, was particularly trying. Lee had provided references on jackknifing from the statistical literature, references that seemed to have more Greek than English characters. Nevertheless, the numerical example that emerged seemed to provide a nice example for the book.

However, this proved not to be the case. When Goldine Gleser arrived at Stanford some months later, on leave from Cincinnati to work with Lee in polishing and proofreading the manuscript, she recalculated the statistics and got different results. Turns out our nice example had a transposition error.

LJC, with all that those initials embody for a graduate student, reacted with a whimsical pained expression:

> I can only tell you what Ralph Tyler told me once, 'I am quite able to make my own mistakes; that wasn't what I wanted *you* to do for me.'

TEACHING ASSISTANT

Working as Lee's teaching assistant revealed many of the same characteristics as other students encounter—intense, educative experiences. A teaching assistantship, in educational psychology at least, meant working in a team with three other teaching assistants. Each of us wrote exam questions, graded exams, led a weekly discussion section, and gave a lecture in the course.

These responsibilities did not, however, relieve any of Lee's burden in the course. Rather, they created even more work for him because he monitored and evaluated our every activity. He critiqued every exam question and every exam we graded, visited and evaluated our discussion sections, and gave us extensive feedback about our course lectures. "Performing" in front of Lee wasn't easy and it wasn't much fun either, but we did learn what teaching a course was about. And, unlikely as it would have seemed at the time, the tools we acquired endured.

PRELIMINARY (QUALIFYING) EXAMS

During our Stanford "tenure," the qualifying exam for admission to doctoral candidacy took a variety of forms, all difficult. The Holy Grail would have been easier to pursue. As always, Lee took the exercise very seriously. The following experience is illustrative:

As prelims approached, one student balked at the idea of sitting down for 2 days for a closed book exam, and he suggested to the Psych Studies faculty that they let the qualifying examination consist of work samples that provide a realistic measure of professional maturity. At first opposed to the idea, Lee shifted his opinion and agreed that the idea was worth trying.

One of the tougher questions on the exam was a test analysis/grading problem. "Suppose an instructor lets students circle exam items the students think are ambiguous or are otherwise bad, and the instructor agrees to omit from scoring any items circled by 10% of the students. Using the data in the table below, evaluate this approach to testing."

The appearance of this question on this student's exam wasn't chance. Lee had used precisely that method in his test theory course and in the individual differences course he taught during Spring 1970. In the latter course, many students circled their full quota of items, more because the items were difficult than because they were "bad"—this was a large class, the Cambodian bombing was front page news (Vietnam war era), and students were not behaving in the spirit of the course. Lee was upset that students had abused his test method, and so he was not pleased when this student asked whether the exam was even valid with so many items deleted.

The student regretted the comment instantly, recalling the admonition from a colleague that Lee was loyal and honest to colleagues and students, strongly principled, and unforgiving of those who did not behave with decency and respect. (Certain of imminent doom following this intemperate question about the validity of the examination, this student desperately considered finding another advisor, another university, or possibly another planet.) And so it was that an interesting problem on testing appeared on the student's doctoral qualifying examination.

DISSERTATION: "THE BATTLE"

The dissertation was, perhaps, the ultimate educational experience for Lee. It provided the connective tissue for the myriad of "first-hand experiences" Lee had arranged for us. It was a rite of passage in every respect. It was, in no uncertain terms, the final intellectual battleground, you and the Perfesser, one on one, as Lee made quite clear:

In some ways I'm the ideal reader for you and in some ways the worst possible. Assuming that I try hard to follow what you are saying, the fact that I am totally lacking in background regarding most of the literature you are reviewing and the theoretical position you are taking makes a good test. If I know what you are saying, anybody will. On the other hand, the fact that I have never absorbed this literature implies a considerable lack of enthusiasm for it, and maybe means that I am blocking where I shouldn't.

Working on a dissertation with Lee was never smooth sailing, at least for us. If we hadn't learned something well enough before, Lee made sure we learned it before the dissertation was finished. If our thinking had been fuzzy, or our analyses haphazard and poorly explained, or our writing sloppy and unclear before, Lee had no intention of letting these bad habits survive the dissertation experience. No more kid gloves; you had to be ready to defend your ideas.

Some of us were more stubborn and slower to learn than others. Sometimes we resisted Cronbach's attempts to reach agreement on the substantive findings of the dissertation (some of those disagreements still persist today). Other times we simply couldn't write clearly about our ideas and findings (as Lee helped us learn). Drafts, some of them the tenth revision, were covered, front and back, with Lee's scribbled green-red-purple-blue-black, typically penetrating comments.

Sometimes the *battle* turned on the fact that we spoke different mathematical languages. Often our native tongue was algebra; Lee has a penchant for geometry. (Virtually every student has seen Lee at one time or other juggle six pens, and maybe an upturned chair, to depict variables in a factor space.) At several points during arguments over algebraic derivations, Lee would shift to geometry, trigonometry, polar coordinates, etc., to try to show why our interpretations seemed illogical. Babel was a piece of cake.

Regardless of whether the exchange was over mathematical or verbal language, communication was the heart of the matter: "I don't think your writing meets adequate standards of lucidity. Too much attempt to communicate by allusion and abstract words instead of a reasonable concrete and operational description." "You have to see the reader of a research paper as a student being led along; not a dull student or a slow student, but one who is not able to supply the argument for himself."

To Lee, written language was a window into our minds. If the language wasn't clear, neither were our thoughts and logic. One student recounts Cronbach's sage advice to him on this score: Reading sections of the student's dissertation-in-progress, the student's wife offered advice on clarity as well as checking spelling and punctuation. She expressed some difficulty in understanding the dissertation chapter on components of variance. Her husband let her know that he was dealing with some very advanced statistics that he couldn't expect her to understand, but that scholars in this area would follow well enough. The chapter came back from LJC with a brief marginal note:

> I find this presentation hard to follow and I wrote the book on this analysis. Imagine how hard it would be for others to understand this analysis. I suggest that you give each chapter to your wife to read; when it is clear enough for her to understand, send it on to me.

The battles were always objective and intellectually honest. They were the source of learning, not only about scholarship, but also about one's self. Each of us, for example, experienced the anxiety that comes from wondering if we'd ever finish. Lee's position was clear on this issue:

> As of now, I think it would be pointless to try to meet the July 20 deadline. I don't object to signing a draft the moment it is right . . . I know all about wanting to get a job over with. Learning to fight that impatience is also a part of the game.

At these times of intense personal trauma, Lee's humanity showed most. We wondered when the Dissertation would come to an end. Battles sometimes waxed and waned for years when it became clear that a month of blitzkreig writing at Stanford wouldn't polish off the dissertation. Indeed, even during such months, new problems sometimes surfaced. In a letter following one such unfortunate turn of events, Lee recounted a story about his mind set and changing position during the preceding months. The letter described how his thinking had evolved and changed, leading to a version of what became *Beyond Two Disciplines of Scientific Psychology.*

> You feel bad because we found an error. I kept telling you to be glad we found it "in time." Now I'll tell you an autobiographical story, at least down to this moment.
>
> I developed a notion, in the course of putting the last chapter of ATI together, that interactions were almost infinitely complex. . . . Then I found Gene Glass' 1972 paper that argues forcefully that generalizations are impossible in educational research. All this locked into a gross line of argument that I decided to work up into my address for APA in August. . . .
>
> So in June I sent off [a] revised . . . manuscript to a dozen people with please comment. . . . Phillips pinpointed a confusion that came in just because I found some attractive rhetoric and wrote some sweeping statements. When he showed that that could mean five things—and what was really in my mind?—it turned out pretty hard to pin down, but I still knew, down to this week, what I was saying. . . .
>
> I was going to do the next to final draft this weekend, still on the theme, essentially, social science is probably an unrealizable dream. Maybe I still think that, but it is going to come out differently. Shulman and I went to lunch and he started chatting about Merton and asked if I'd thought of Merton's theories of the middle range in this connection. No, so I looked up Merton whom I respect greatly,

and found that particular line wasn't useful but that he had quite explicitly addressed those who conclude that social science is impossible. While his was not quite a refutation of my position, it forced me to decide if I really wanted to say I knew more about social science than Merton.

O.k., so I went to bed last night thinking I had better state my argument more gently. I work up this morning with a new argument in place. It has to be written, and it will change. It will reconcile the interaction notion with the construct validation notion, which conflict had been giving me trouble before. It won't change my final recommendations, but it will develop a case that most social scientists can accept, and will save me from having to defend the paper against (or having it rejected by) persons who are committed to the search for theory. We shall see.

What do we see. (1) The strategy of going through drafts and expecting to change. (2) The strategy of looking for criticism instead of fighting it. (3) Luck. I could easily have had this insight after I was committed to the thing in print. That is what I mean by negative contribution!

For each of us the dissertation, and the battle, came to an end. The specifics might have differed, but the occasion upon which each of us was notified that the dissertation had been completed had striking similarities. It was without ceremony. As The Perfesser scurried down the hall past the Dean's office on a day in late July, you might hear mumbled, ever so faintly, those sweet words: "Well . . . I guess we're done."

THE FUTURE

It's not hard to detect the depth of our admiration and affection for Lee nor the lasting debt. Upon learning that Lee was retiring a year early, even as Stanford raised the retirement age to 70, a former student wrote Lee that it was a great loss to future generations of graduate students that they would never know the stilletto sharpness of his multicolored felt-tipped pens. These thoughts speak for us all.

Fortunately, his colleagues continue to correspond and collaborate, and his brilliant marginal strokes continue to provoke us to deeper thought, broader perspective and clearer statements that we might otherwise achieve.

Such is our legacy from Lee.

17 Methodological Studies—A Personal Retrospective

Lee J. Cronbach

My most sustained line of investigation, with publications extending over more than 40 years, has had to do with methods for appraising the accuracy of psychological or educational measurements and of inferences from them. Goldine Gleser's collaboration made possible an intellectual climb to a level I would never have achieved unaided. This essay[1] is centered on events that culminated in our *Psychological tests and personnel decisions* (utility theory, 1957; 2d ed., 1965) and *Dependability of behavioral measurements* (generalizability theory, 1972). It mentions some motivational influences, some stimuli that moved thoughts into one channel rather than another, some false starts and misjudgments, and some of the work left undone. This display of hindsight is neither modest nor penitent; rather, I hope to offer to persons entering mathematical psychometrics a realistic perspective on a career.

Theory of error down to about 1945 considered one variable at a time or, at most, a difference between two scores. Measurement error, moreover, was treated as a variable not subject to dissection. In my work I tried instead to frame appropriate questions about multivariate measurement and to disentangle types of error. The classical theory had its origin in Spearman's quest for an idealized central dimension of mind. After mass standardized testing of achievement began, the theory was restated in terms of equivalent test forms. Spearman's algebraic formulation was useful even for the prominent practical tests that had

[1] A broader personal history appears in Lindzey (1989). I have taken the present editors' invitation as an opportunity to discuss some studies of measurement in more detail than would have been suitable for Lindzey's audience.

mixed content because every test in a "parallel" set reflects the same composite factor and hence is a near fit to the classical model.

By 1945, testing *practice* had moved on to multiscore tests: batteries for vocational guidance, measures of Thurstone's primary abilities, and the profile-oriented Wechsler-Bellevue and Strong interest blank. The tests of Ralph Tyler's Eight-Year Study (in which I served as assistant in 1939) subdivided mathematical reasoning, sensitivity to social issues, and other kinds of educational outcome, reporting a separate score for each aspect. Multiscore tests—the MMPI, Rorschach, and Wechsler in particular—had become mainstays of clinical testing. Trying to evaluate those tests intensified my interest in psychometric theory for profiles and my interest in distinguishing among errors associated with test forms, occasions, and testers or interpreters.

My conviction that meanings and performances are complex had grown out of my interest as educational psychologist in identifying just where and how a learner is having difficulty. One of my few efforts at test development illustrates this thinking. E. L. Thorndike had inspired among educational psychologists an interest in measuring size of general vocabulary, and Sidney Pressey had gone on to assess command of technical terms (in algebra, for example, *exponent* and *coefficient*). I encountered this work when I entered the field, but thought that a numerical summary of competence says much less to the teacher than a report on how the pupil or class interprets each key concept in turn. For my 1936 masters thesis at Berkeley I developed 35 miniature tests, on as many concepts. Thus there were five *yes–no* items for *coefficient,* essentially of the form "In the expression $(a + 2)x$, is 2 the coefficient of x?"

A second recurrent methodological theme is my resistance to abstract ideals of test purity. Many models for test development, past and present, reflect the idea that items contributing to a score should all "measure the same thing." Spearman could not observe pure g but he did hope to isolate its effects by a statistical adjustment for impurities as well as for error of measurement. Thurstone and his followers sought "factorially pure" tests. My sympathies were with Binet's view: Problem-solving is an intricate and ever–shifting combination of processes. Influenced by Dewey and Judd, I looked for similar multiple processes in educational development. For me, then, test tasks ought to represent a somewhat heterogeneous but still coherent domain of performances.

HOW EVALUATE HOMOGENEITY?

A test score is *unreliable* if scores are likely to vary from one measurement to another. Testers who have applied a test just once often examine the consistency between scores on halves of the test. Because a test can be split in many ways, many split-half coefficients are possible. Formula 20 of Kuder and Richardson (1937) reached a unique internal-consistency coefficient by examining consistency across items instead of half-tests. It applied to items scored 1 or 0, and the derivation assumed strict homogeneity, all intercorrelation among items arising from a single pervasive factor. In the Eight-Year Study, one of my tasks was to apply the formula to various attitude and ability scores. The results were often sensible even when items entering the score were heterogeneous; but the results sometimes were senseless, as when reliability coefficients had negative signs. I stored up a puzzlement.

In 1941 Louis Guttman asserted that the ideal attitude scale is homogeneous: Whoever endorses a favorable statement should endorse every weaker favorable statement in the set. In an ideal ability scale, by analogy, passing one item would imply ability to pass all easier items. To approach that ideal, Jane Loevinger (1947) proposed selecting items so as to maximize the ratio between the KR20 coefficient and the theoretical value of KR20 for an ideal scale with the same item difficulties.

For most kinds of testing, extreme homogeneity has seemed to me neither realistic nor advisable. Applying standards of the Guttman-Loevinger type could whittle test content down to a splinter of the relevant domain. Any affective reaction or intellectual performance is likely to be multiply determined, and a test whose items incorporate subordinate factors can give a reproducible measure of the overarching construct. With good reason, the Thurstone-Chave (1929) scale on attitude toward the Church touched on varied aspects of the response: aesthetic, philosophical, and social. Studying vocabulary, I had found several dimensions in so narrow a domain as knowledge of a single technical term, because separating instances of a concept from noninstances requires multiple discriminations. Mathematics teachers did not agree at all closely in interpreting the crucial concept of *function;* a dozen dimensions were required to characterize their divergent interpretations (Cronbach, 1943).

The coherence of items in a test is not well indexed by Loevinger's formula. Philip DuBois was present at the 1949 meeting where I presented that contention, along with an index of homogeneity I favored (an adaptation of KR20). Because he, Loevinger, and Gleser were under contract to develop homogeneous measures for the Air Force, DuBois invited me to St. Louis as consultant. Goldine mediated the divergence of views so astutely that the project could gracefully abandon the Loevinger index *and* reject my proposed index, yet settle on an alternative responsive to the issues I had raised (Loevinger, Gleser, & DuBois, 1953). I promptly recruited Goldine as consultant to my project of the time, and before long she was co-investigator.

α and Stratified α

Among citations to my writings, an absurdly large fraction are to the "Coefficient Alpha" paper covering these issues (Cronbach, 1951). The convenience of the label "Cronbach's alpha" brought me a laughable status as eponym; the formula was not my creation (and I had duly cited the priority of Cyril Hoyt). My first reason for introducing the label α was to distinguish the general formula from the KR20 version limited to pass-fail items. Second, Cattell's "data box" array, of scores of many persons responding on many occasions to many items, led me to see that α addresses one of six analogous questions (Cronbach, 1984). I promised later papers on coefficients β, γ, ...

Whereas the α formula was not new, some of my interpretation was. I had discovered by brute calculation that interclass correlation coefficients obtained by splitting a test in many ways and applying the Spearman-Brown formula average out close to α. Given that hint, I managed to prove that the stepped-up *intra*class correlations from all possible half-splits average out exactly to α, and inferred that α estimates the correlation between tests whose items are drawn randomly from the same universe. Stepping down α in the Spearman-Brown manner, from the coefficient for a *k*-item test to that for a single item, estimates the typical interitem correlation. As *this* index of homogeneity renders a favorable verdict on tests with somewhat mixed content, it does not foster narrow specification of variables. Moreover, the Jackson-Ferguson (1941) "battery reliability" formula could then be reinterpreted as a stratified α, suitable for tests constructed by random sampling within specified subuniverses of content. Stratifying is a basis for planned heterogeneity.

Distance Measures

Formulas analogous to α did not work out. The analogue β was to be an index of the similarity among profiles in a group of persons. The calculation of the coefficient was only a step or two removed from William Stephenson's "*Q* correlation" between profiles of two persons. Fred Fiedler, who had studied with Stephenson, in 1951 became my colleague in a study of leadership. Initially, we were using Q to test the hypothesis that successful leaders perceive teammates as having personality profiles similar to their own. (The first findings, which pointed in almost the opposite direction, became the basis for Fiedler's prominent theory of leadership.) Discrepancies between β and *Q* set a puzzle for Goldine and me. After tracing how each formula weighted various aspects of a score profile, we rejected the β and *Q* approaches in favor of "distance measures" of similarity which encompassed more information (Cronbach & Gleser, 1953; see also Cronbach, 1955).

As my students and colleagues applied distance measures, I came to see that they compressed information severely. My last paper on the subject (Cronbach, 1958) recommended against any summary index of similarity because it must ignore the nature and direction of differences. Perhaps because that paper appeared in a symposium volume rather than a mainstream journal, almost nobody reacted to it or used it. The papers of 1953 and 1955 are cited nowadays three times as often as the 1958 paper that withdrew their advice.

UTILITY THEORY

I backtrack to a 1949 visit to a Navy laboratory. There I heard J. C. R. Licklider lecture on Shannon's new information theory, as it might apply to the psychology of signal detection. When Licklider talked of "signal" and "noise," provocative parallels to the true score and error of psychometrics ran through my mind; over the next year, I drew out a long string of implications.

Information theory recognized the tension between the desire to obtain many facts and the desire for accuracy. A noisy system can deliver a message with high fidelity *if* the transmission is redundant enough; then the receiver can be nearly certain as to the message sent. A less redundant transmission puts more information into the channel, but noise then creates great uncertainty at the receiving end. In Shannon's terms, to gain "fidelity" one must give up some "bandwidth," and vice versa. So also in testing. The limited time available for testing a person may be used to measure a few characteristics (no report being made on the remaining ones), *or* used to cover many characteristics, leaving any one report less dependable. The former strategy accepts absence of information regarding many variables, for the sake of sharper estimates of the chosen few. Procedures such as profiling of abilities and interviewing sacrifice precision for the sake of greater comprehensiveness.

My manuscript built upon Shannon's definition of information as $-\Sigma P_i log P_i$, where P_i is the prior or posterior probability of message i (in test theory, the probability of having score or score-pattern i). Upon reading the draft, Goldine and Fred Lord both pressed me to justify the definition. This was a bit of a shock, because by that time the definition was widely used in engineering, applied mathematics, and sensory psychology. A close look showed that Shannon's definition fits the requirements of the field where it originated, cryptography. In an efficient code, each string of signals is a distinct message. The *sequence* of scores in an array, however, has no significance for psychologists (Cronbach, 1956). For a time, I considered a variance model of George Ferguson in which sequence is ignored; but that model was like Shannon's in treating all errors as equally serious (again, sensible enough for coded transmissions). A model for test information had to recognize the costs of various errors, so I made a start on one.

A report on all this went to the source of my research funds, the psychology branch of the Office of Naval Research. A routing slip carried it to the mathematics branch, where someone saw that I was laboriously constructing an amateur version of the statistical decision theory Abraham Wald had developed during the war. The mathematicians urged me to rely on Wald, and with that resource Goldine and I went on to derive answers to the questions Shannon had inspired, and several others (Cronbach & Gleser, 1957). The bandwidth-fidelity metaphor held up in the new formulation. Traditional theory implicitly favored concentrating effort so as to maximize accuracy. It is generally better to distribute effort over plural dimensions, we showed, but the appropriate distribution depends on the specifics of the decisions the information will be applied to.

Our model stressed not error of measurement or prediction as such but the cost of errors in decisions. Mainstream theory had taken a dim view of the usefulness of aptitude testing. When the test-criterion correlation is .40—a typical value— the standard error of a prediction is "only 8% better than chance." Clark Hull, having focused on this percentage when writing his 1928 book *Aptitude testing*, was left so discouraged that he abandoned the measurement field (Hull, 1952, p. 151). Taylor and Russell, however, pointed out in 1939 that tests with modest validity are valuable under many circumstances, and in 1946 Brogden added as a key consideration the importance of the decision being made. Our utility theory extended this insight and gave a structure for considering a number of problems of test construction and use. The utility concept is now playing a significant part in evaluating employment testing and other personnel practices. The original models took the perspective of the employing firm or military service; Hunter and Schmidt (1982) have made a start toward examining payoffs to the society as a whole. And, in a qualitative extension, information and utility theories provided metaphors to guide program evaluations (Cronbach, with Shapiro, 1982).

Testing for Educational Placement

Looking seriatim into the kinds of decisions based on tests, Gleser and I came to placement. Placement of pupils in special education was a major function of testing from the days of Binet, yet measurement theory ignored those decisions. Psychometrics asked a "placement" test to meet only the standard pertinent to a *selection* test: an appreciable statistical relationship between the test score and some later attainment. Predicting how well entrants will do in the "regular" program is insufficient. Utility for placement requires that the regression of outcome onto test have a different slope in each instructional program (or each clinical treatment) for which the examinee is eligible. Indeed, it can be all to the good if some regressions have negative slopes.[2] Contrasts between slopes are difficult to investigate and even harder to pin down. The widely used College Board placement test in English seems to fall short; in most colleges, outcomes from regular and remedial writing courses fail to show the nonparallel regression lines that would empirically justify assigning low scorers to remedial groups (Cronbach, 1985).

If this point of view ever captures full attention, the switch from seeking a test that predicts outcome to seeking one that predicts *differentially* as a function of

---

[2]Brogden (1951) developed this reasoning in a model for multidimensional measures used to assign military personnel to specialties. He thus formalized the common sense of the guidance movement and the famous Air Force system of World War II. Remarkably, the complex case (classification) was understood before the one-dimensional case (placement) received psychometric attention.

treatment will constitute a Kuhnian "paradigm shift." Concern for aptitude-treatment interactions (ATI) in instructional research (Cronbach & Snow, 1977) was a direct outgrowth of the formal model for placement.

Sequential Testing

Wald had demonstrated the advantages, in hypothesis testing, of collecting on any one case or hypothesis only enough data to permit a decision (as contrasted with fixing a uniform sample size in advance). In making decisions about persons, would it not be profitable to test those close to a critical borderline more thoroughly than others? Two-stage or multistage testing did increase efficiency in accept/reject decisions. After confirming that, Gleser and I rejected multistage testing for obtaining scores *on a continuum*. The strategy would be to choose easier test questions for a next stage of testing for persons who have been doing poorly, and harder questions for those doing well. Our mathematics indicated that tailored testing offers negligible benefit when the biserial correlations of the underlying variable with the test items are at the levels reached in well-constructed tests; Lord's (1970) extended trial of tailored testing supported this view. Today, however, the "tailored" or "adaptive" testing we dismissed is seen as promising, particularly for testing by computer. Were we wrong? We had in fact noted, as did Lord, that the sequential strategy would reduce testing time if the biserial correlations reached remarkable levels. As Green (1983) explains, biserial correlations *are* high in some current testing—because the persons examined have an unusually wide range or because a narrow variable is measured. So tailored testing fills two specialized niches.

Almost certainly, my prejudice against tightly homogeneous domains lies behind our failure to develop the case for tailored testing. Another story testifies to the same resistance to narrow variables. I was engaged in 1955 to travel in Europe and search out psychological research Americans should know of. In Copenhagen, Gunnar Rasch proudly showed me his now-famous rationale for scaling test items. I saw no merit in the scheme and neglected it in my reports. Rasch's ideal for scales was perfectionist beyond Guttman's; Rasch called not only for rank correlation of 1.00 between item true scores but also for a latent variable with uniform intervals and a "true zero." Though I had good reason to consider this unrealistic, time would show that (as with Spearman or KR20) an idealization can generate an analytic method having considerable value for ordinary messy data.

GENERALIZABILITY THEORY

In 1957 I obtained funds from the National Institute of Mental Health to produce, with Gleser's collaboration, a kind of handbook of measurement theory. It would explain how the purposes of measurement and one's substantive hypotheses should govern choice of mathematical model, design of instruments, and choice of analytic technique. The book would discuss types versus traits, the evolutionary construction of variables, interval scales versus ordinal scales, analysis of profiles, and much else. "Since reliability has been studied thoroughly and is now understood," I suggested to the team, "let us devote our first few weeks to outlining that section of the handbook, to get a feel for the undertaking." We learned humility the hard way—the enterprise never got past that topic. Not until 1972 did the book appear (Cronbach, Gleser, Nanda, & Rajaratnam) that exhausted our findings on reliability reinterpreted as generalizability. Even then, we did not exhaust the topic.

When we tried initially to summarize prominent, seemingly transparent, convincingly argued papers on test reliability, the messages conflicted. Papers on ratings and observations entailed much the same conflict in other forms. Let me illustrate:

1. If pass-fail items are regarded as a random sample of the relevant content, the binomial theorem gives the standard error of the person's percentage-correct score (that is, his standard error of measurement) as $[\pi(1-\pi)k]^{1/2}$, where π is that person's probability of success over the pool of items and k is the number of items in the sample (Lord, 1955). Averaging over persons before taking the square root gives a standard error for persons in general.

2. If two test forms are regarded as equivalent measures of the same variable, the standard error of measurement for persons in general equals $\sigma_x(1 - \rho^2)^{1/2}$, where ρ is the correlation between test forms (Gulliksen, 1950).

When estimation procedures based on these formulas are applied to the same data, the results almost always disagree.

One of Gulliksen's stated assumptions—that equivalent tests have the same mean in the population of persons—cannot be true of tests formed by sampling items randomly from a pool in which difficulty varies. Did that difference in postulates explain the difference in conclusions? No; the assumption about means did not enter Gulliksen's derivation (his p. 34). After some time, team member Nageswari Rajaratnam[3] zeroed in on the "constant error" associated with the difficulty of a particular test form or the leniency of a rater. Paragraph 2 above leaves constant errors out of consideration, since they do not affect the product-moment correlation. In Paragraph 1, however, they are added into the standard error.

Here as with information theory, we reached closure by specifying formally

---

[3]I note with pleasure how international the team was. Nages was Tamil (Ceylonese). (She died in 1963 after holding University posts in British Columbia and Minnesota.) Our other associates over the years included at least one person from each of the following countries: Canada, Germany, India, Japan, the Netherlands, South Africa, and Switzerland.

the use of the instrument in making decisions. Decisions based directly on raw scores ("criterion referenced," in the current jargon) are always affected by constant errors. Where decisions are based on ranks, the constant error matters only if the persons compared were assessed with different instruments.

Facet Designs for G and D Studies

To express this and other key points, we distinguished a generalizability (G) study from a decision (D) study; the former serves to check out the measuring procedure, whereas the latter affects the subject's life. A G-study starts with scores of many persons measured under two or more "conditions" (combinations of item-sets, occasions, raters, etc.). Error of measurement is reinterpreted as variation associated with some of the conditions and their interactions.

Two-way analysis of variance evaluates components of variance for persons (true scores), conditions, and residual. For some decisions, the residual alone constitutes the error variance; then Gulliksen's estimate very nearly agrees with that from analysis of variance of two randomly parallel test forms, whereas Lord's is too large. For other decisions, all within-persons variance (condition and residual components together) counts as error; then Lord's statement fits, and Gulliksen's estimate is too small. Neither had made an error of mathematical reasoning. Rather, a significant aspect of the world being modeled had been left unmentioned.

After R. A. Fisher introduced factorial design—simultaneous variation of several features of an experimental treatment—Cyril Burt and E. F. Lindquist had initiated its application to collection and analysis of reliability data. Their ideas (published in 1955[4] and 1953, respectively) were extended by us with the aid of a newly developed statistical theory for "random model" analysis of variance components. Occasions, test forms, etc. become facets in a design for collecting multiple measures of the same kind, from which one can assess how much variance arises from each source. Julian Stanley had developed a correlational analysis for such multifacet data; variance-component analysis agreed with his results, and added others. As in a one-facet study, proposed interpretations define what is to count as error. Certain investigators, for example, are primarily interested in a subject's state or action at specified times; then observers and test stimuli are sources of error whereas the occasion helps specify the variable under study.

Once we had captured in mathematics the options available, we went on to demonstrate how a G study can help in designing a measuring procedure. Doubling the measurement effort reduces error. But is it better to double the number of observers, or the number of occasions observed? or to strike some compromise?

---

[4]Burt had priority. His prewar lectures influenced several analyses of data published long before the theoretical writings.

A multifacet G study helps the investigator distribute effort in a D study so as to obtain maximum accuracy for its particular purposes.

Univariate G theory is a tapestry that interweaves ideas from at least two dozen authors, giving the contributions a more significant pattern. All the prominent reliability formulas, including α, could be cast in terms of variance components. A statistical rationale from Cornfield and Tukey (1956) enabled us to base the formulas in sampling theory. Their expected-value argument escapes from restrictions such as equal variances, intercorrelations, and single-factoredness that were present in nearly all earlier derivations for either reliability or anova. In consequence, our model can represent ratings and behavioral observations, which almost never are classically equivalent. (Incidentally, the old puzzle about negative values of KR20 reduces, in most cases, to merely a variant of finding an F-ratio less than 1.00 in an analysis of variance—a matter of sampling error.)

Guttman once made the provocative remark that a test belongs to several sets, and therefore has several reliabilities. "List as many 4-letter words that begin with t as you can." That word-fluency task fits into at least three families: 4-letter words beginning with a specified letter, t words of a specified length, and 4-letter words with t in a specified position. The investigator's theory, rather than an abstract concept of truth and error, determines which family contains tests that "measure the same variable." Analyzing generalizability becomes a part of validating the construct represented in the chosen universe, hence studies of "error" have substantive importance.

Once our technical reports of 1960 and 1961 were revised for publication (Cronbach, Rajaratnam, & Gleser, 1963; Rajaratnam, Cronbach, & Gleser, 1965; Gleser, Cronbach, & Rajaratnam, 1965), we thought the work finished. After moving to Stanford in 1964, I encouraged use of the methods in research going on there, and was pained to find our recommendations inadequate. Prospective users evidently needed many concrete examples of the protean computations and interpretations for multifacet designs. Moreover, many of the measurement procedures were complex, so estimating and interpreting the variance components required considerable judgment and sometimes required extension of the techniques. Harinder Nanda analyzed diverse batches of data my colleagues were using, and a 1966 report compiled those examples.

Multivariate Theory

Despite the long-standing interest Gleser and I had in profiles, all of G theory down to 1966 considered one score at a time. The impetus for multivariate G theory came mostly from papers on multivariate psychometrics by Ledyard Tucker and Darrell Bock. My students analyzed profile data with some of the new procedures, and Kenneth Travers, a postdoc, converted the equations of single-score G theory to a vector form. Multivariate G theory required fresh distinctions such as a scheme to keep track of the correlated errors that enter when, for example, a teacher is observed on two variables during the *same* class period.

After Nanda returned to India, Gleser and I undertook to assemble in one volume all of G theory—point of view, mathematical rationale, and numerical methods, plus illustrative calculations substantively interpreted. We tried to set down all we had learned, and probably succeeded. That aspiration, however, made for poor pedagogy and the book proved indigestible. Fortunately, a few enthusiasts are spreading the ideas through simpler presentations, and these may yet bring G theory into the mainstream of psychometric practice. The book fell short in another way. As Gleser in Ohio and I in California were far apart and had other projects, we contented ourselves with a succinct outline of the multivariate theory. A decade of work was required to expose the twists and turns of the simpler univariate multifacet theory, so surely much multivariate theory remains to be developed.

It was not because we set out to answer particular questions that we arrived at G theory. Rather, the theory forced itself upon us, revealing questions that measurers should be asking. We started complacently, because a mountainous, generally self-satisfied literature on reliability seemed to need only a bit of collation, plus conversion to uniform symbols. The problem turned out to be almost the opposite; papers using the same words and symbols were unwittingly addressing different questions. The language of variance components, forcing us to state questions about error more clearly, gave not only a superior rationale for the simple formulas but an endlessly adaptable multifacet system. The system was so logical that it seemed self-explanatory, until attempts to apply it disclosed that we had been stringing notes together and not making music. Trial of the scheme on data is what made G analyses functional. The multivariate scheme was not put through similar trials. It will surely be adapted and extended when some methodologist seeks opportunities to apply it and collates his experiences.

ANALYSIS OF DATA FROM COLLECTIVES

Now and then I have discovered, in a commonplace, long-accepted research method, flaws sufficient to discredit many substantive findings. But such discoveries have come slowly, as this final story illustrates.

In 1940 I completed my doctorate at Chicago and took a position on the West Coast. The American Educational Research Association was to meet in San Francisco in 1941 and my thesis adviser, to help my career along, programmed me as a discussant. The report I was to discuss covered the Minnesota dissertation of G. L. Anderson, done under the estimable guidance of T. R. McConnell and Palmer Johnson. Teachers had been asked to use one of two styles of teaching arithmetic in their classes. The experiment was not randomized, but the data analysis had the unusual feature of taking aptitude into account by means of the then-new Johnson-Neyman method. Akin to analysis of covariance, the method identified the region (if any) in the pretest space where meaningful instruction was significantly superior, the region in which rote instruction was advantageous, and an intermediate zone of uncertainty. I responded warmly to this pioneer ATI study, and it remained important in my thinking about instruction and about research method.

Three decades later, my students and I were evaluating a new curriculum at Stanford. Students in the courses had rated them, and we wished to know whether engineers, for example, had more favorable opinions than liberal-arts majors. We knew only the proportion of engineers in each class and could not correlate individual attitude with individual major. I asked Leigh Burstein to check into the possibility of drawing conclusions from class means on attitude, and the proportions in various majors. Burstein came back with a discouraging answer, bringing citations to a large sociological literature including Robinson's (1950) warning about the pitfalls of "ecological" (group-level) correlation. I "knew" that paper, even owning a reprint; but only in talking with Burstein did I perceive that improper handling of data from groups was prevalent in instructional research (and, I came to think, in sociology).

As we studied the matter—first in Burstein's dissertation, then with a grant from the Spencer Foundation—three kinds of regression had to be distinguished: that for class means (say, of $\bar{Y}$ on $\bar{X}$), that within classes ($Y - \bar{Y}$ on $X - \bar{X}$), and a regression of Y on X calculated from individuals' scores without regard to class membership. (Further complications enter when schools or communities are considered as well as classes.) Ordinarily only the third regression has been used to analyze educational data. Being a weighted average of the first two, however, it has no general meaning of its own. Sociologists frequently have considered the first and third regressions together, interpreting any disparity as a causal "contextual effect."

I concluded that the first two are the most interpretable. In a path analysis, an analysis of covariance, an ATI study, etc., a between-groups regression coefficient is almost sure to differ from the corresponding pooled-within-groups coefficient. Two influences are responsible: the composition of the groups (which has consequences comparable to those of restriction of range), and causal processes operating on or through groups. Substantive explanations in terms of the behavior of collectives are suggested by a two-level analysis. Unresolved, however, is the problem of distinguishing causal influences from mere compositional effects. My best efforts to trace compositional effects appear in Cronbach and Schaeffer (1981) and Cronbach (with Shapiro, 1982, Chap. 6). There I was able to handle only restricted cases, and in an abstract rather than a practical manner.

Noreen Webb and I reworked the Anderson data from 1941. Anderson, analyzing without regard to class membership, had concluded that arithmetic taught meaningfully is best suited to pupils whose general mental ability is strong and whose initial computational skill is weak (contrariwise, when the emphasis is on drill). Reanalysis reduced the findings to rubble (Cronbach & Webb, 1976). The within-class regressions differed negligibly across treatments. Anderson's effect seen in an overall regression could be traced back to between-class regressions that meant nothing. At best, a regression coefficient calculated from eight data points is tossing on a tidal wave of sampling error. Worse, in this instance a near-perfect correlation of class means on two aptitude variables, arising from unlucky sampling, had removed all warrant for fitting a two-predictor between-groups regression. Many other data sets, including massive files from Head Start and Follow Through evaluations, proved to be equally problematic. Even investigators aware of the multilevel problem seem to have preferred the conventional individual-level analysis because its spuriously numerous degrees of freedom tend to make relationships look "significant." Multilevel reanalysis typically invalidates such conclusions.

In social, educational, or policy research, concern with "the unit of analysis" ought to begin as the investigation is first formulated. Sampling and assignment plans ought to reflect the place of collectives in the substantive hypothesis. Analysis and interpretation, in turn, are strongly constrained by the design. This was the thesis of the technical report (Cronbach, with Deken and Webb, 1976). Examples from experiments and quasiexperiments, structural regressions, reliability studies, and factor analysis all demonstrated the prevalent confusion. The material was not carried to publication because some important analytic problems still puzzled me. I was unable to give them attention while completing other projects, and young scholars, who took up the problem about when I did, have now developed techniques far more elegant and subtle than those we reached.[5] The technical findings did become the basis for some crucial last-minute modifications in *Aptitudes and instructional methods* (Cronbach & Snow, 1977). The nonmathematical insights (especially, regarding the statistical indeterminacy endemic in psychological studies of collectives) strongly influenced my later writings on evaluation and on strategy for social inquiry.

HOW METHODOLOGY PAYS OFF

My story has included some hints about a methodologist's sources of gratification: intellectual puzzles, the force of a completed mathematical argument, vigorous interaction with peers (the oneupmanship looming less large than the satisfaction of cooperative trail-blazing), and esthetic pleasure from having joined bits and pieces into an intellectual structure.

Methodological work is far from systematic. Psychometric specialists capitalize on advances in statistics and other disciplines, but not by reading each new article to see what they can use. Most of us go a long way with ad hoc and partly

---

[5]For the state of the art as of a recent date, see Bock (1989).

intuitive constructions before we are able to see the relevance of a development in statistics, or to ask statisticians a question sufficiently pointed to elicit the right piece of their knowledge. After ONR told me to attend to Wald, I recalled that a colleague had actually talked with me a year earlier about applying a Wald formula to a test of his. Only after independently recasting my problem in terms of costs and benefits could I see that Wald was addressing my concerns. Our field was similarly imperceptive about the connection of internal-consistency reliability formulas to Fisher's well-known intraclass correlations, and about ecological correlation.

One need not be a skilled mathematician to advance methodology; you call upon an expert once you know what to call for. The crucial contribution—which mathematicians cannot be expected to make—is an adequate formal description of an interesting set of social or psychological events. If you start with a mathematician's model not tailor-made for you, something in it probably distorts your real concern (as in my attempt to piggy-back on Shannon). And when you construct your own model, as the classical reliability or prediction theorist did, you are likely to leave out something that deserves attention. There is no sure procedure for deliberately locating the blind spots in a mathematical formulation; one must simply be on the alert for oversimplifications and trace their consequences.

Because a methodological insight bears on a wide variety of investigations, a small investment can have large consequences. For our work on collectives the direct cost was roughly $10,000 (for student assistants and computer time). Our improved analysis called into question findings purchased with hundreds of thousands of research dollars—on, for example, science curricula and compensatory education. Our successors, after no great further expenditure, have now proposed even better analyses. If these ideas reach a wide audience, the first consequence will be a warning that society should distrust the published findings of the studies reviewed and all like them. A second potential consequence will be better use of educational research budgets, far into the future.

Before psychologists in our sense existed, Robert Browning invented one, and wrote an ironic "autobiography." During my years as methodologist and reviewer of research, my thoughts have often turned to Cleon's words about his achievements:

I have written three books on the soul,
Proving absurd all written hitherto
And putting us to ignorance again.

REFERENCES

Bock, R. D. (Ed.). (1989). *Multilevel analysis of educational data*. Hillsdale, NJ: Lawrence Erlbaum Associates.

Brogden, H. E. (1951). Increased efficiency of selection resulting from replacement of a single predictor with several differential predictors. *Educational and Psychological Measurement, 11*, 173–196.

Cornfield, J., & Tukey, J. W. (1956). Average values of mean squares in factorials. *Annals of Mathematical Statistics, 27*, 907–949.

Cronbach, L. J. (1943). What the word "function" means to algebra teachers. *Mathematics Teacher, 36*, 212–218.

Cronbach, L. J. (1951). Coefficient Alpha and the internal structure of tests. *Psychometrika, 16*, 297–334.

Cronbach, L. J. (1955). Processes affecting scores on "understanding of others" and "assumed similarity". *Psychological Bulletin, 52*, 177–194.

Cronbach, L. J. (1956). On the non-rational application of information theory in psychology. In H. Quastler (Ed.), *Information theory in biology*. Glencoe, IL: Free Press.

Cronbach, L. J. (1958). Proposals leading to analytic treatment of social perception scores. In R. Tagiuri & L. Petrullo (Eds.), *Person perception and interpersonal behavior*. Stanford: Stanford University Press.

Cronbach, L. J. (1984). A research worker's treasure chest. *Multivariate Behavioral Research, 19*, 223–240.

Cronbach, L. J. (1985). College Board Scholastic Aptitude Test and Test of Standard Written English. In J. V. Mitchell, Jr. (Ed.), *The ninth mental measurements yearbook* (Vol. I, pp. 363–364). Lincoln: University of Nebraska.

Cronbach, L. J., with the assistance of Joseph Deken and Noreen Webb. (1976). *Research on classrooms and schools: Formulation of questions, design, and analysis*. Stanford University School of Education, unpublished. ERIC Document 135 801.

Cronbach, L. J., with the assistance of Karen Shapiro. (1982). *Designing evaluations of educational and social programs*. San Francisco: Jossey-Bass.

Cronbach, L. J., & Gleser, G. C. (1953). Assessing similarity between profiles. *Psychological Bulletin, 50*, 456–473.

Cronbach, L. J. & Gleser, G. C. (1957). *Psychological tests and personnel decisions*. Urbana: University of Illinois Press.

Cronbach, L. J., Gleser, G. C., Nanda, H., & Rajaratnam, N. (1972). *The dependability of behavioral measurements: Theory of generalizability for scores and profiles*. New York: Wiley.

Cronbach, L. J., Rajaratnam, N., & Gleser, G. C. (1963). Theory of generalizability: A liberalization of reliability theory. *British Journal of Statistical Psychology, 16*, 137–163.

Cronbach, L. J., & Schaeffer, G. (1981). *Extensions of personnel selection theory to aspects of minority hiring* (Project Report 81-2). Stanford University: Institute on Educational Finance and Governance.

Cronbach, L. J., & Snow, R. E. (1977). *Aptitudes and instructional methods: A handbook for research on aptitude-treatment interactions*. New York: Irvington.

Cronbach, L. J., & Webb, N. (1976). Between-class and within-class effects in a reported Aptitude × Treatment interaction: Reanalysis of a study by G. L. Anderson. *Journal of Educational Psychology, 67*, 717–727.

Gleser, G. C., Cronbach, L. J., & Rajaratnam, N. (1965). Generalizability of scores influenced by multiple sources of variance. *Psychometrika, 30*, 395–418.

Green, B. F. (1983). Comments on tailored testing. In H. H. Wainer & S. Messick (Eds.), *Principals [sic] of modern psychological measurement* (pp. 184–197), Hillsdale, NJ: Lawrence Erlbaum Associates.

Gulliksen, H. (1950). *Theory of mental tests*. New York: Wiley.

Hull, C. L. (1952). [Autobiography]. In E. G. Boring, H. S. Langfeld, H. Werner, & R. M. Yerkes (Eds.), *History of psychology in autobiography* (Vol. 4). Worcester, MA: Clark University Press.

Hunter, J. E., & Schmidt, F. L. (1982). Fitting people to jobs: The impact of personnel selection to national productivity. In M. D. Dunnette & E. A. Fleishman (Eds.), *Human capability assessment*. Hillsdale, NJ: Lawrence Erlbaum Associates.

Jackson, R. W. B., & Ferguson, G. A. (1941). *Studies on the reliability of tests*. Toronto: University of Toronto.

Kuder, G. F., & Richardson, M. W. (1937). The theory of the estimation of test reliability. *Psychometrika, 2,* 151–160.

Lindzey, G. (Ed.). (1989). *History of psychology in autobiography* (vol. 8). Stanford, CA: Stanford University Press.

Loevinger, J. (1947). A systematic approach to the construction and evaluation of tests of ability. *Psychometric Monographs, 61,* No. 4.

Loevinger, J., Gleser, G. C., & DuBois, P. H. (1953). Maximizing the discriminating power of a multiple-score test. *Psychometrika, 18,* 309–317.

Lord, F. M. (1955). Estimating test reliability. *Educational and Psychological Measurement, 15,* 324–336.

Lord, F. M. (1970). Some test theory for tailored testing. In W. H. Holtzman (Ed.), *Computer-assisted instruction, testing and guidance* (pp. 139–183). New York: Harper and Row.

Rajaratnam, N., Cronbach, L. J., & Gleser, G. C. (1965). Generalizability of stratified-parallel tests. *Psychometrika, 30,* 39–56.

Robinson, W. S. (1950). Ecological correlations and the behavior of individuals. *American Sociological Review, 15,* 351–357.

Thurstone, L. L., & Chave, E. J. (1929). *The measurement of attitude*. Chicago: University of Chicago Press.

Curriculum Vitae and Bibliography

Lee J. Cronbach

Born Fresno, California, April 22, 1916
Fresno State College, A.B., 1934
University of California, Berkeley, M.A., 1937
University of Chicago, Ph.D. (educational psychology) 1940
Degrees hon. c.:
             Yeshiva University, L.H.D., 1967
             University of Gothenburg, Ph.D., 1977
             University of Chicago, L.H.D., 1979
             University of Illinois, Urbana, L.H.D., 1982
             University autónoma, Madrid (L.H.D.), 1985
Medal of honor, Teachers College, Columbia University, 1975

Professional Employment

Fresno public schools; High school teacher, 1936–1938
Evaluation staff, Eight-Year-Study, Progressive Education Association; Research assistant, 1939–1940
State College of Washington; Instructor to Assistant Professor of Psychology, 1940–1946
University of California Division of War Research, San Diego; Research psychologist, 1944–1945
University of Chicago; Assistant Professor of Education, 1946–1948
University of Illinois, Urbana; Associate Professor to Professor of Educational Psychology, 1948–1964; Professor of Psychology, 1958–1964
Office of Naval Research, London; Scientific Liaison Officer, 1955–1956
Stanford University; Professor of Education, 1964–1966; Vida Jacks Professor of Education, 1966– (Emeritus, 1980–); Fellow, Stanford Center for Youth Development, 1980–
University of Tokyo, Faculty of Education; Fulbright Lecturer, 1968–1969

Awards and Honors

Member, Institute for Advanced Study, 1960–1961
Fellow, Center for Advanced Study in the Behavioral Sciences, 1963–1964; Visiting Scholar, 1971–1972
Fellow, John Simon Guggenheim Memorial Foundation, 1971–1972
Fellow, Jerusalem Van Leer Foundation, 1976
Visiting Scholar, London School of Economics, Department of Social Psychology, 1977–1978
Award for contributions to educational measurement, Educational Testing Service, 1971
Distinguished Scientific Contribution award, American Psychological Association, 1974
Award for contributions to research in education, American Educational Research Association, 1977
Alva and Gunnar Myrdal Prize for contributions to evaluation methodology, Evaluation Research Society, 1978
Stanford University School of Education, Distinguished Teaching Award, 1971
Member, National Academy of Education
Member, American Philosophical Society
Member, American Academy of Arts and Sciences
Member, National Academy of Sciences
Miembro de Honor, Sociedad Española de Psicologia, 1978
Fellow, Division on Evaluation and Measurement, American Psychological Association
Sometime Fellow, Division of Educational Psychology, Division of Personality and Social Psychology, American Psychological Association
Sometime Fellow, American Statistical Association
Sometime Fellow, American Association for the Advancement of Science
Member: Sigma Xi, Phi Delta Kappa, Kappa Delta Pi

Responsibilities in Professional Organizations

American Educational Research Association, President, 1963–1964
American Psychological Association; Committee on Test Standards, Chairman, 1950–1953; Committee on Psychological Tests, 1962–1966; Publications Board, 1951–1953, and Chairman, 1952–1953; Committee on International Relations in psychology, 1957–1960; Division on Evaluation and Measurement, President, 1954–1955; Board of Directors, 1952–1958; President, 1956–1957.
American Psychological Foundation; Board of Trustees, 1957–1964; President, 1961–1963
Midwestern Psychological Association: Secretary-Treasurer, 1952–1955
National Academy of Education: Chairman, Section on Psychology, 1965–1967; Second Vice-President, 1969–1971; Chairman, Committee on Educational Research, 1966–1969
National Academy of Sciences: Committee on Science and Public Policy, 1978–1981
Psychometric Society President; 1953–1954
Social Science Research Council; Committee on Learning and the Educational Process, Chairman, 1960–1966; Board of Directors, 1964–1971
Unesco Institute for Education, Hamburg; Governing Board, 1968–1972

Consultancies and Committees

Annual Review of Psychology, Editorial Board, 1962–1966
California State Legislature, Committee on Education; Committee on the Statewide Testing Program, Chairman, 1971–1972; Consultant to California Assessment Program, 1972–1976
Carnegie Commission on the Education of Educators, 1960
Educational Testing Service; Research Committee, 1950–1954, 1957–1970
Exploratory Committee on Assessing the Progress of Education; Technical Advisory Committee, 1968–1972
Federal Judicial Center, Committee on Continuing Education, 1968–69.
Guggenheim Memorial Foundation; Member, Educational Advisory Board, 1966–1981
Johnson Foundation, Infant Health and Development Program, Research Advisory Committee, Chairman, 1983–1984
National Institute of Mental Health: Mental Health Study Section, 1952–1955; Behavioral Sciences Study Section, Chairman, 1956–1958
National Longitudinal Study of Mathematical Abilities; Technical Advisory Committee, 1963–1966.
National Research Council; Committee on Undersea Warfare, 1946–1949; Committee on International Directory in Psychology, 1956; Steering Committee, Woods Hole Conference on Psychology and Education, 1960; Board on Fellowships and Assistantships, 1976–1977; Committee on Ability Testing, 1978–1982; Panel on Outcomes in Early Childhood Education, 1980–1982
National Science Foundation: Director, Conference on Evaluation for Science Curriculum Projects, 1963
NATO Conference on Crosscultural Influences on Mental Tests, Director, Istanbul, 1971
Research Conferences on Learning and the Educational Process, Co-Director, Stanford, 1964, 1965, Bangkok, 1972; Organizing Committee, Shepparholmen, 1966
Terman Study of Children of High Ability, Co-Investigator, 1963–
U.S. Office of Education, Curriculum Improvement Panel, Chairman, 1963–1965
U.S. War Department, SCAP Civil Information and Education Division, Tokyo, 1947
University of Michigan project on assessment of clinical psychologists, 1948–1950

PUBLICATIONS*

Books and Monographs

Exploring the wartime morale of high school youth. *Applied Psychology Monographs,* 1943, No. 1.
Essentials of psychological testing. New York: Harper and Row, 1949. Revised editions 1960, 1970, 1984, 1990.
Educational psychology. New York: Harcourt Brace & World, 1954, Revised editions 1963, 1977.

---

*Asterisk indicates LJC is a junior author.

With Foster McMurray, Wilbur Schramm, Robert Bierstedt, and Willard B. Spalding. *Text materials in modern education.* Urbana: University of Illinois Press, 1955.

With others. Technical recommendations for psychological tests and diagnostic techniques. *Psychological Bulletin,* 1954, *51* (2, Part 2, Supplement). Revised edition*, 1966.

With others*. *Technical recommendations for achievement tests.* Washington, D.C.: American Educational Research Association, 1955.

With Goldine C. Gleser. *Psychological tests and personnel decisions.* Urbana: University of Illinois Press, 1957. Second edition, 1965.

Edited, with Patrick C. Suppes. *Research for tomorrow's schools: Disciplined inquiry in education.* New York: Macmillan, 1969.

With Goldine C. Gleser, Harinder Nanda, and Nageswari Rajaratnam. *The dependability of behavioral measurements: Theory of generalizability for scores and profiles.* New York: Wiley, 1972.

Edited, with Pieter J. D. Drenth. *Mental tests and cultural adaptation.* The Hague: Mouton, 1972.

With Richard E. Snow. *Aptitudes and instructional methods: A handbook for research on interactions.* New York: Irvington, 1977.

With others. *Toward reform in program evaluation.* San Francisco: Jossey-Bass, 1980.

With the assistance of Karen Shapiro. *Designing evaluations of educational and social programs.* San Francisco: Jossey-Bass, 1982.

Social inquiry in the public interest. Vernon-Wall Lecture, Education Section of the British Psychological Society, London, 1984.

Chapters in Books

The meanings of problems. In G. T. Buswell (Ed.), *Arithmetic, 1947. Supplementary Educational Monographs,* 1947, 66.

With T. G. Andrews.* Transfer of training. In W. S. Monroe (Ed.), *Encyclopaedia of educational research.* New York: Macmillan, 1949.

With W. D. Neff. Selection and training. In F. W. Irwin (Ed.), *Human factors in undersea warfare.* Washington, D.C.: National Research Council, 1949.

Educational psychology. In C. P. Stone (Ed.), *Annual review of psychology,* vol. 1. Palo Alto: Annual Reviews, Inc., 1950.

Correlation between persons as a research tool. In O. H. Mowrer (Ed.), *Psychotherapy: Theory and research.* New York: Ronald, 1953.

The counselor's problems from the perspective of communication theory. In V. H. Hewer (Ed.), *New perspectives in counseling.* Minneapolis: University of Minnesota Press, 1954.

New light on test strategy from decision theory. In *Proceedings, 1954 Invitational Conference on Testing Problems.* Princeton, N.J.: Educational Testing Service, 1955.

On the non-rational application of information theory in psychology. In H. Quastler (Ed.), *Information theory in psychology.* Glencoe, Ill.: Free Press, 1955.

Assessment of individual differences. In P. R. Farnsworth (Ed.), *Annual review of psychology,* vol. 7. Palo Alto: Annual Reviews, Inc., 1956.

Proposals leading to analytic treatment of social perception scores. In R. Tagiuri & L.

Petrullo (Eds.), *Person perception and interpersonal behavior.* Stanford: Stanford University Press, 1958.

Psychological issues pertinent to recent American curriculum developments. In G. S. Nielsen (Ed.), *Child and education.* Copenhagen: Munksgaard, 1962.

Evaluation for course improvement. In R. W. Heath (Ed.), *New curricula.* New York: Harper & Row, 1964.

Psychological background for curriculum experimentation. In P. C. Rosenbloom (Ed.), *Modern viewpoints in the curriculum.* New York: McGraw-Hill, 1964.

Issues current in educational psychology. In L. N. Morrisett & J. Vinsonhaler (Eds.). *Mathematical learning. Monographs of the Society for Research in Child Development,* 1965, 30(1).

The logic of experiments on discovery. In L. S. Shulman & E. R. Kieslar (Eds.), *Learning by discovery.* Chicago: Rand-McNally, 1966.

Mental test theory and decision theory. In *Psychological measurement theory. Proceedings of the NUFFIC International Summer Session in Science.* The Hague: NUFFIC, 1966.

With H. Azuma. Concept attainment with probabilistic feedback. In K. R. Hammond (Ed.), *The psychology of Egon Brunswik.* New York: Holt, Rinehart & Winston, 1966.

How can instruction be adapted to individual differences? In R. M. Gagne (Ed.), *Learning and individual differences.* Columbus, O.: Charles E. Merrill, 1967.

Validation of educational measures. In *Proceedings, 1969 Invitational Conference on Testing Problems.* Princeton, N.J.: Educational Testing Service, 1970.

Test validation. In R. L. Thorndike (Ed.). *Educational measurement.* Washington, D.C.: American Council on Education, 1971.

Judging how well a test measures. In L. J. Cronbach & P. J. D. Drenth (Eds.), *Mental tests and cultural adaptation.* The Hague: Mouton, 1972.

Measured mental abilities: Lingering questions and loose ends. In B. D. Davis & P. Flaherty (Eds.), *Human diversity: Its causes and social significance.* Cambridge, Mass.: Ballinger Publishing Co. 1976.

On the design of educational measures. In D. N. M. de Gruijter and L. J. Th. van der Kamp (Eds.) *Advances in psychological and educational measurement.* London: Wiley, 1976.

Validity on parole: How can we go straight? In *New Directions in Tests and Measurements.* No. 5. San Francisco: Jossey-Bass, 1980.

In praise of uncertainty. In P. H. Rossi (Ed.), *New directions in program evaluation,* 1982, No. 15.

Prudent aspirations for social science. In W. W. Kruskal (Ed.), *The social sciences: Their nature and uses.* Chicago: University of Chicago Press, 1982.

Social inquiry by and for Earthlings. In D. W. Fiske and R. A. Shweder (Eds.), *Metatheory in social science: Pluralities and subjectivities.* Chicago: University of Chicago Press, 1986.

Five perspectives on validity argument. In H. Wainer & H. I. Braun (Eds.) *Test validity.* Hillsdale, NJ: Lawrence Erlbaum Associates, 1988.

Construct validation after thirty years. In R. E. Linn (Eds.), *Intelligence: Measurement, theory, and public policy.* Urbana: University of Illinois Press, 1989.

Lee J. Cronbach. In G. Lindzey (Ed.), *A history of psychology in autobiography* (Vol. VIII). Stanford, CA: Stanford University Press, 1989.

Emerging views on methodology. In T. D. Wachs & R. Plomin (Eds.), *Conceptualization and measurement of organism-environment interaction*. Newbury Park, CA: Sage Publications, 1990 in press.

Published Papers

Individual differences in learning to reproduce forms: A study in attention. *American Journal of Psychology*, 1941, *54*, 197–222.

Measuring students' thinking about a presidential election. *The School Review*, 1941, *49*, 679–692.

An experimental comparison of the multiple true-false and multiple multiple-choice tests. *Journal of Educational Psychology*, 1941, *32*, 533–543.

The reliability of ratio scores. *Educational and Psychological Measurement*, 1941, *1*, 269–278.

An analysis of techniques for diagnostic vocabulary testing. *Journal of Educational Research*, 1942, *36*, 206–217.

Studies of acquiescence as a factor in the true-false test. *Journal of Educational Psychology*, 1942, *33*, 401–415.

What the word "function" means to algebra teachers. *Mathematics Teacher*, 1943, *36*, 212–218.

A practical procedure for the rigorous interpretation of test-retest scores in terms of pupil growth. *Journal of Educational Research*, 1943, *36*, 481–488.

Measuring knowledge of precise word meaning. *Journal of Educational Research*, 1943, *36*, 528–534.

On estimates of test reliability. *Journal of Educational Psychology*, 1943, *34*, 485–494.

With Betty Mae Davis. Belief and desire in wartime. *Journal of Abnormal and Social Psychology*, 1944, 39, 446–458.

A case study of the split-half reliability coefficient. *Journal of Educational Psychology*, 1946, *37*, 473–480.

Response sets and test validity. *Educational and Psychological Measurement*, 1946, *6*, 475–494.

Test "reliability": Its meaning and determination. *Psychometrika*, 1947, *12*, 1–16.

A validation design for qualitative studies of personality. *Journal of Consulting Psychology*, 1948, *12*, 365–374.

Statistical methods applied to Rorschach scores: A review. *Psychological Bulletin*, 1949, *46*, 393–429.

"Pattern tabulation:" A statistical method for analysis of limited patterns of scores, with particular reference to the Rorschach test. *Educational and Psychological Measurement*, 1949, *9*, 149–171.

Further evidence on response sets and test design. *Educational and Psychological Measurement*, 1950, *10*, 3–31.

The group Rorschach in relation to success at the University of Chicago. *Journal of Educational Psychology*, 1950, *41*, 65–82.

Statistical methods for multi-score tests. *Journal of Clinical Psychology*, 1950, *6*, 21–26.

Coefficient alpha and the internal structure of tests. *Psychometrika*, 1951, *16*, 297–334.

With W. G. Warrington. Time-limit tests: Estimating their reliability and degree of speeding. *Psychometrika*, 1951, *16*, 167–188.

With W. G. Warrington. Efficiency of multiple-choice tests as a function of spread of item difficulties. *Psychometrika*, 1952, *17*, 127–147.

With A. L. Edwards.* Experimental design for research in psychotherapy. *Journal of Clinical Psychology*, 1952, *8*, 51–59.

With Goldine C. Gleser. Assessing similarity between profiles. *Psychological Bulletin*, 1953, *50*, 456–473.

Report on a psychometric mission to Clinicia. *Psychometrika*, 1954, *19*, 263–270.

With David R. Krathwohl. Suggestions regarding a possible measure of personality: The squares tests. *Educational and Psychological Measurement*, 1954, *16*, 305–316.

Processes affecting scores on "understanding of others" and "assumed similarity." *Psychological Bulletin*, 1955, *52*, 177–194.

Les exigences de la validation des techniques projectives. *Revue de Psychologie Appliquée*, 1955, *5*, 245–253.

With N. L. Gage. Conceptual and methodological problems in interpersonal perception. *Psychological Review*, 1955, *62*, 411–422.

With Jack C. Merwin. A model for studying the validity of multiple-choice items. *Educational and Psychological Measurement*, 1955, *15*, 337–352.

With Paul E. Meehl. Construct validity in psychological tests. *Psychological Bulletin*, 1955, *52*, 281–303.

The two disciplines of scientific psychology. *American Psychologist*, 1957, *12*, 671–684.

With Goldine C. Gleser. Interpretation of reliability and validity coefficients: Remarks on a paper by Lord. *Journal of Educational Psychology*, 1959, *50*, 230–237.

With Hiroshi Azuma. Internal-consistency reliability formulas applied to randomly sampled single-factor tests: An empirical comparison. *Educational and Psychological Measurement*, 1962, *22*, 645–666.

With Goldine C. Gleser and N. Rajaratnam. Theory of generalizability: A liberalization of reliability theory. *British Journal of Statistical Psychology*, 1963, *16*, 137–163.

With Hiroshi Ikeda and R. A. Avner. Intraclass correlation as an approximation to the coefficient of generalizability. *Psychological Reports*, 1964, *15*, 727–736.

With Peter Schönemann and Douglas McKie. Alpha coefficients for stratified-parallel tests. *Educational and Psychological Measurement*, 1965, *25*, 291–312.

With N. Rajaratnam* and G. C. Gleser. Generalizability of stratified-parallel tests. *Psychometrika*, 1965, *30*, 39–56.

With G. C. Gleser* and N. Rajaratnam. Generalizability of scores influenced by multiple sources of variance. *Psychometrika*, 1965, *30*, 395–418.

With H. Azuma.* Cue-response correlations in the attainment of a scalar concept. *American Journal of Psychology*, 1966, *89*, 38–49.

Year-to-year correlations of mental tests: A review of the Hofstaetter analysis. *Child Development*, 1967, *38*, 284–289.

Current ideas on educational evaluation. *The National Educational Council Journal* (Bangkok), 1968, *2*(12), 1–37.

Intelligence? Creativity? A parsimonious reinterpretation of the Wallach-Kogan data. *American Educational Research Journal*, 1968, *5*, 491–511.

Heredity, environment, and educational policy. *Harvard Educational Review*, 1969, *39*, 338–347.

Mental tests and the creation of opportunity. *Proceedings, American Philosophical Society*, 1970, *114*, 480–487.

With Lita Furby. How we should measure "change"—or should we? *Psychological Bulletin*, 1970, *74*, 68–80. Errata, *ibid.*, *74*, 218.

With Walter Zwirner* and others. Pupil perceptions of teachers: A factor analysis of "About My Teacher." *Western Psychologist*, 1972, *3*, 78–98.

Five decades of public controversy over mental testing. *American Psychologist*, 1975, *30*, 1–14.

Beyond the two disciplines of scientific psychology. *American Psychologist*, 1975, *30*, 116–127.

With Noreen Webb. Between-class and within-class effects in a reported Aptitude × Treatment interaction: Reanalysis of a study by G. L. Anderson. *Journal of Educational Psychology*, 1975, *67*, 717–724.

Equity in selection—Where psychometrics and political philosophy meet. *Journal of Education Measurement*, 1976, *13*, 1, 31–41.

The Armed Services Vocational Aptitude Battery—A test battery in transition. *Personnel and Guidance Journal*, 1979, *57*, 232–237.

Selection theory for a political world. *Public Personnel Management*, Jan–Feb. 1980, *9*(1), 37–50.

With E. Yalow and G. A. Schaeffer. A mathematical structure for analyzing fairness in selection. *Personnel Psychology*, 1980, *33*, 693–704.

What price simplicity? *Educational Measurement: Issues and Practice*, 1983, 2, No. 2, 11–12.

A research worker's treasure chest. *Multivariate Behavioral Research*, 1984, *19*, 223–240.

Abilities and ability testing: Recent lines of thought. *Evaluación Psicológica*, 1985, *1*, No. 1–2, 79–97.

Balancing the qualitative and the quantitative in psychological research. *Evaluación Psicológica*, 1986, 2, No. 3, 3–12.

Tyler's contribution to measurement and evaluation. *Journal of Thought*, 1986, *21*(1), 47–52.

Statistical tests for moderator variables: Flaws in analyses recently proposed. *Psychological Bulletin*, 1987, *102*, 414–417.

Internal consistency of tests: Analyses old and new. *Psychometrika*, 1988, *53*, 63–70.

Other Notes and Short Articles

The true-false test: a reply to Count Etoxinod. *Education*, 1941, *62*, 59–61.

A mathematics class takes music lessons. *Mathematics Teacher*, 1943, *36*, 34–35.

Pupil morale after one year of war. *School and Society*, 1943, *57*, 416–420.

Note on the reliability of ratio scores. *Educational and Psychological Measurement*, 1943, *3*, 67–70.

Stereotypes and college sororities. *Journal of Higher Education*, 1944, *14*, 214–216.

Educational reform in Japan. *School Review*, 1948, *56*, 183–200.

Norms and the individual pupil. *Proceedings, 1948 Invitational Conference on Testing Problems*. Princeton, N.J.: Educational Testing Service, 1949.

A note on negative reliabilities. *Educational and Psychological Measurement*, 1954, *14*, 342–346.

Education approaches period of constructive change. *Nation's Schools*, 1959, *63*, 72–75.

With Goldine C. Gleser. Quantal and graded analysis of dosage-effect relations. *Science*, 1961, *133*, 1924–1925.

Guidance and counseling. In H. Chauncey (Ed.), *Talks on American education*. New York: Bureau of Publications, Teachers College, Columbia University 1962.

Learning research and curriculum development. *Journal of Research in Science Teaching*, 1964, *2*, 204–207.

The role of the university in improving education. *Phi Delta Kappan*, 1966, *47*, 539–545.

Can a machine fit an applicant to continuing education? *Measurement and Evaluation in Guidance*, 1969, *2*, 88–90.

With Thomas J. Quirk. Test validity. In *Encyclopedia of education*. New York: Macmillan, 1971.

With Evalore Parey. Bibliographie Curriculum Evaluation. In K. Wulf (Ed.), *Evaluation*. Munich: Piper, 1972.

A Long-Term Project in Psychology. *Science*, 1972, *176*, 785–786.

Evaluation in a context of accommodation. In R. M. Bossone (Ed.), *Proceedings, the Second National Conference on Testing: Major Issues*. Center for Advanced Study in Education, City University of New York, 1978.

Validity of inference in applied social research. In H. Dahl et al. (Eds.), *A spotlight on educational problems*. Oslo: Universitetsforlaget, 1979.

Selected Unpublished Papers

Psychological aspects of the technical vocabulary of elementary algebra. Unpublished masters thesis, University of California, Berkeley, 1936.

A generalized psychometric theory based on information measure. Bureau of Research and Services, University of Illinois, Urbana, 1952.

With J. W. Deken and N. Webb. Research on classrooms and schools: Formulation of questions, design, and analysis. School of Education, Stanford University, 1976.

With D. R. Rogosa, R. E. Floden, & G. G. Price. Analysis of covariance in nonrandomized experiments: Parameters affecting bias. School of Education, Stanford University, 1977.

With Gary Schaeffer. Extensions of personnel selection theory to aspects of minority hiring. Institute on Educational Finance and Governance, Stanford University, 1981.

With Gary Schaeffer. Tables relating quality of persons hired to selection rate for minority applicants. Institute on Educational Finance and Governance, Stanford University, 1981.

Selected Book and Test Reviews

With Goldine Gleser. W. Stephenson, *The study of behavior: Q-technique and its methodology. Psychometrika*, 1954, *19*, 327–330.

F. N. Freeman. *Mental Tests. The School Review*, 1967, *75*, 67–75.

J. R. Bormuth. *On the theory of achievement test items. Psychometrika*, 1970, *35*, 509–511.

J. H. Block (Ed.). *Mastery learning: Theory and practice. International Review of Education*, 1972, *18*, 250–252.

J. Block. *Lives through time. Science*, 1972, *178*, 785–786.

Analysis of Learning Potential. In *Seventh Mental Measurements Yearbook*. Highland Park, N.J.: Gryphon, 1972.

With Jillian M. Keepes. P. W. Musgrave (Ed.), *Contemporary studies in the curriculum. American Educational Research Journal*, 1975, *12*, 211–220.

J. C. Loehlin et al. *Race differences in intelligence. Contemporary Psychology*, 1976, *21*, 389–390.

With Lee Ross and others. M. Guttentag and E. Streuning (Eds.). *Handbook of evaluation research. Proceedings of the National Academy of Education*, 1976, *3*, 81–107.

Safran Culture Reduced Intelligence Test. In *Seventh Mental Measurements Yearbook*. Highland Park, N.J.: Gryphon, 1978.

The BITCH Test (Black Intelligence Test of Cultural Homogeneity). In *Eighth Mental Measurements Yearbook*. Highland Park, N.J.: Gryphon, 1978.

USES Basic Occupational Literacy Test. In *Eighth Mental Measurements Yearbook*. Highland Park, N.J.: Gryphon, 1978.

L. S. Hearnshaw. *Cyril Burt, psychologist. Science*, 1979, *206*, 1392–1394.

R. J. Sternberg (Ed.). *Handbook of human intelligence. American Journal of Psychology*, 1984, *97*, 455–459.

College Board Scholastic Aptitude Test and Test of Standard Written English. In *Ninth Mental Measurement Yearbook* Vol. 1. Lincoln: University of Nebraska, 1985.

J. Gleick. *Chaos. Educational Researcher*, 1988, *17*(6), 46–49.

R. L. Linn (Ed.). *Educational measurement*, Third Edition. *Educational Measurement: Issues and Practice*, 1989, 8(4), 22–25.

Author Index

Subject Index